Gerry Frank's

Where to
Find It,
Buy It,
Eat It
in
New York

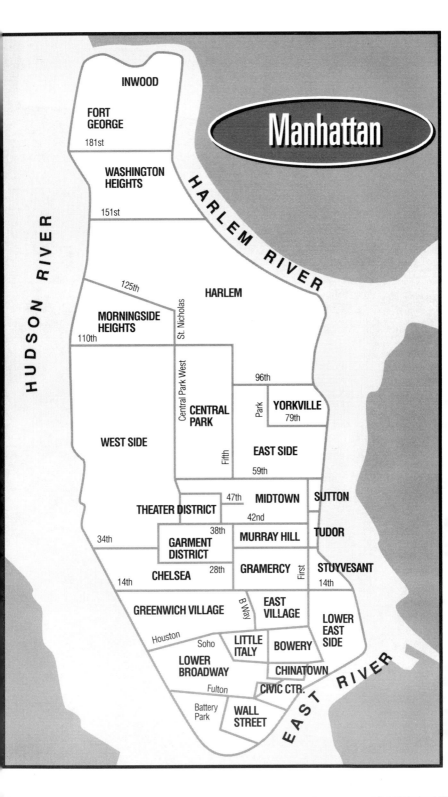

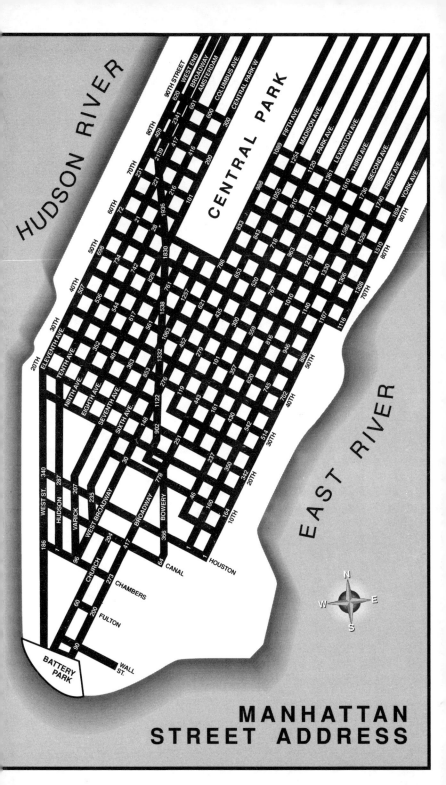

MANHATTAN
STREET ADDRESS

MY SPECIAL PLACES

Gerry Frank's

Where to
Find It,
Buy It,
Eat It
in
New York

For additional copies (special quantity prices available),
write or call:

Gerry's Frankly Speaking

P.O. Box 2225
Salem, Oregon 97308
503 585-8411
FAX: 503 585-1076

Gerry Frank's
Where to Find It, Buy It, Eat It in New York
Copyright © 1980, 1981, 1983, 1985, 1987, 1989, 1991, 1993
by Gerald W. Frank.

Printed in the United States of America
Library of Congress Catalog Card Number 80-7802
ISBN: 1-879333-03-1
First Edition 1980
 Second Printing 1980
Second Edition 1981
 Second Printing 1981
 Third Printing 1982
Third Edition 1983
 Second Printing 1984
 Third Printing 1984
Fourth Edition 1985
 Second Printing 1986
 Third Printing 1986
 Fourth Printing 1987
Fifth Edition 1987
 Second Printing 1988
Sixth Edition 1989
Seventh Edition 1991
 Second Printing 1991
Eighth Edition 1993

Preface

If someone had told me 15 years ago that I would be sitting down to write a preface for a book on New York that would sell over a half million copies, I would have told them they were crazy! But it is the truth. This is the eighth edition of a volume that has become Manhattan's best-selling complete guide, a book that New Yorkers and visitors alike live by. I am deeply grateful to you, my faithful readers, for the confidence you have placed in me and the support that you have shown over the years. Then, too, a host of New York eating establishments, food shops, services, stores, hotels, museums, attractions, and all the rest have cooperated to such a degree that I am able to present to you what I think is the best of this great city.

The question I am asked most often is, "How did a fellow from Salem, Oregon, come to write the most popular guide to New York?" My answer makes sense, I believe. I was born into an Oregon department-store family, spending 17 years in the retail business plus numerous short stints during school vacation. I often traveled to New York—where we had our own buying office—with our store buyers, spending time in the various markets and generally becoming entranced with the excitement and energy of this great city. I *love* New York!

After the family business was sold, I joined forces with U. S. Senator Mark Hatfield from Oregon. I served as his assistant and chief-of-staff in Washington, D.C., for 26 years and left that position in the spring of 1992. During that period, I spent two weekends a month in New York, walking the neighborhoods, inspecting the stores, dining in the restaurants, sampling the food shops, trying out the services, and just generally exploring. I continue to do so. What I've found I now share with you.

My qualifications? As a former retailer I think I have an eye for the values and service that are essential for a successful operation. I have had the privilege of traveling to over 130 nations, so I am able to identify good food, good accommodations and good value. As the proprietor of a restaurant and specialty-food operation in Oregon. I have developed an eye for what customers are looking for in the ever-changing food world. I have eaten in more than 1,800 restaurants of all descriptions in Manhattan. All the walking around has allowed me to keep a moderate waistline, but that is becoming increasingly difficult! I have learned many of the fine points of reviewing from Bryan Miller, a good friend who writes for the *New York Times*.

I like to point out what makes this book a bit different than the dozens of other guides to this city. First and foremost, this one is complete. You need nothing else. There are excellent specialty volumes available on various aspects of life in this bewildering and sometimes overpowering city, but this one alone combines all the ingredients that residents and visitors are interested in. Where many books of this nature are the combined product of a number of people who write different sections, this book is almost exclusively my evaluation only. (I have had specialized advice on some sections where I do not feel qualified, like beauty shops.) You may not agree with all of my comments, but rest assured that I am being honest and forthright. Remember, also, that no one pays to get in this book, and no one tells me what should or should not be included. Believe me, many have tried!

You are obviously aware that a city as dynamic as this one changes almost overnight. This is a great plus for you, because I am able to bring you new and exciting places in each edition. This one has over 500 new places, and nearly 80% of the write-ups have some new information. But this reality also has a downside. It is impossible to keep a book like this one absolutely up-to-date. The day it is printed, a store or restaurant might close. However, because I self-publish, my deadline is much closer than that of major publishers, so you can be assured that what you are reading is the most current information possible. Every entry is checked and updated with each new edition.

The story of the book has become a legend in the publishing business. I had no idea that I would write a book. My only previous experience in journalism had been publishing a newspaper when I was a youngster. I presently write a weekly column for *The Oregonian,* a major newspaper in the Pacific Northwest, and I am a special correspondent for "Northwest Reports," a weekly prime-time television news magazine on KPTV-12 in Portland. People who knew I spent a great deal of time in New York would ask about where to eat, stay, shop, and so on. I collected and assembled all the data I'd compiled from 25 years of exploration and took it to the New York book publishers.

Their reaction could not have been more negative. The attitude was, "What is some hick from Oregon doing writing a book on New York?" They wouldn't give me the time of day. I am not the sort of person who likes to be told "no," so I decided to publish and distribute the volume myself. It was a lot of work, and the enterprise had its share of problems and discouragements, but the end product has been worth it. Not only are we Number One in this highly competitive market, but some of the same publishers who originally turned me down now want to publish the book. One of my very greatest joys is to be able to say, "Thanks, but no thanks. Where the dickens were you when I needed you?"

This book is also published in a convenient pocket-sized abridged edition (for $7.95) that deals mainly with the food and restaurant scene. It is used a great deal by groups visiting Manhattan. Special prices on quantity lots of all editions (limited, regular, abridged) are available.

Please contact me by phone (503 585-8411), FAX (503 585-1076), or by mail (P.O. Box 2225, Salem, Oregon 97308).

The consistent input from you, my readers, has been invaluable. Hardly a day goes by that someone does not tell me about some special find. (Sometimes they don't want me to mention them!) If you have questions or disagree with my evaluations, I want to hear about it. I take each comment very seriously and often reevaluate their inclusion in the book.

A book like this would not be possible without the administrative help of a number of people. I am particularly indebted to my very talented researcher, Carrie McMillan Klein; to my editor, Parke Puterbaugh; to my office assistant, Cheryl Johnson; to my inspiration, Esther Benovitz; and to my support personnel, Jeryme English, Linda Wooters, and LaVelle Blum. Tim Prock, a talented young artist, did the cover.

This volume is *not* the Yellow Pages. It is, however, the best and most interesting guidebook about what is out there in the most fascinating city in the world. Enjoy!

Contents

III. WHERE TO FIND IT: SPECIAL ACTIVITIES, TOURS, AND OTHER EXPERIENCES

IV. WHERE TO EAT IT: NEW YORK'S BEST FOOD SHOPS

V. WHERE TO FIND IT: NEW YORK'S BEST SERVICES

VI. WHERE TO BUY IT: NEW YORK'S BEST STORES

xiii

VII. WHERE TO "EXTRAS"

I. The World's Greatest City

GETTING THERE

So you're headed for New York! Whether you're a frequent visitor, a foreign tourist, or an American citizen taking the family for a once-in-a-lifetime visit, you're in for a real treat. But first you need to get here.

AIRPORTS – New York City is served by three major airports, La Guardia Airport is most frequently used for domestic flights, while John F. Kennedy International Airport has flights going to and from just about every country on earth. Both are in the borough of Queens. Newark International Airport, across the Hudson River in New Jersey, handles a large volume of both domestic and international flights. The three most common ways of getting into Manhattan from any of these airports are by taxicab, shuttle bus, and private car or limousine.

Taxicab lines form in front of most terminals at all three airports, and the exits to them are usually well marked. These lines are legitimate and usually move quickly. Under *no* circumstances should you go with someone who comes up to you either inside or outside the terminal and asks if you want a cab – it may seem tempting if the airport is crowded, but you'll end up paying far more than you should, and you'll have no recourse. Assuming you don't run into bad traffic, cab fare to midtown Manhattan will run between $20 and $25 from La Guardia and between $30 and $35 from either Kennedy (also called JFK) or Newark, plus the bridge or tunnel toll and tip. (For more information about taxicabs in New York, see the "Transportation" section in this chapter.)

If those prices seem a little steep to you, several companies run shuttle buses and vans between Manhattan and the airports. You can really save money by taking a shuttle bus – but it may not be worth it if there are three or four people in your party or if you're headed for a friend's apartment or an out-of-the-way hotel. Shuttle bus tickets and schedules are available at the ground transportation desks at all three airports. The two largest shuttle companies are Carey and Gray Line. Carey has frequent scheduled bus service between La Guardia and Kennedy and to and from Grand Central Station, Pennsylvania Station, and several other midtown locations. Tickets cost between $8.50 and $10 to or from La Guardia and between $11 and $12.50 to or from Kennedy per person (call 718 632-0500 for more information). Gray Line operates a share-ride van and bus service from all three airports to major hotels and other midtown locations. Tickets cost $12 to or from La Guardia, $15 to or from Kennedy, and $17 to or from Newark per person (call 212 757-6840 in Manhattan or 800 451-0455 for more information). You can also take New Jersey Transit bus 300 between the Port Authority Bus Terminal's special airport bus center (on the ground floor near the Eighth Avenue and West 42nd Street entrance) and any airline terminal at Newark. You can purchase a one-way ticket for $7 or a round trip ticket for $12 per person (call 201 762-5100 for more information). Like everything else, these prices are subject to change. These companies are by no means the only airport shuttle services. For a more complete list of options, call the Port Authority's Air-Ride recording (800 247-7433).

A third option is calling ahead for a private car or limousine service and having a driver meet you at the gate or in the baggage claim area. The driver holds up a sign with your last name on it—which, depending on your personality, can make you feel important, embarrassed, or a little bit of both. Be forewarned that this can be pretty pricey, particularly if the driver has to wait because your flight is delayed. (They charge for waiting time.) Costs run anywhere from around $40 plus tip if you just want a sedan and everything goes smoothly to well over $100 if there are delays or you request a limousine. Carey operates a sedan service from La Guardia and Kennedy (call 718 632-0500 for more information or to make reservations). You can also go to the ground transportation desks at any of the three airports to get a sedan or limousine after you've arrived. (For the names and phone numbers of other reputable companies, see the "Transportation" section in this chapter.)

TRAINS—Dozens of Amtrak trains come in and out of New York City every day. The service is concentrated in what's called the Northeast Corridor (between Washington, D.C., and Boston), but you can catch a train between New York and Florida, Chicago or even Seattle and many cities in Canada. The trains arrive and depart from Pennsylvania Station (usually called Penn Station), underneath Madison Square Garden between West 31st and West 33rd streets and Seventh and Eighth avenues. Penn Station is a major subway hub, but you also can find a legitimate and well-organized taxicab line outside. (Under *no* circumstances should you go with someone who comes up to you either inside or outside Penn Station asking if you need a cab.) You can choose between the Metroliner, sleeping cars, and other kinds of service, and multi-day excursion passes are also available. (Call Amtrak at 800 872-7245 for fare and schedule information and at 800 523-8720 for Metroliner information.)

DRIVING—If you can avoid driving to or in New York, by all means do. You will end up paying exorbitant prices for tolls and parking (and your mental health will inevitably suffer, too). The fact that most New Yorkers don't own cars ought to tell you something! Once you're in New York, the only time you would possibly need a car is if you want to leave for a day or two—and then you can rent a car, as a lot of New Yorkers do. The public transportation system in New York is excellent and is used frequently by just about everyone.

If you still aren't convinced or have no alternative, get a map before setting out and study it carefully. The three major approaches to the city are the New England Thruway (I-95), the New York State Thruway (I-87), and the New Jersey Turnpike (I-95). The toll for most bridges and tunnels is $3 (you pay only when entering Manhattan), and there are often long waits during rush hour. Tune in AM radio stations 770, 880, or 1010 for area traffic reports if you're trying to decide which approach to take (you can also call 201 939-6688 for information).

GETTING AROUND

In case you don't already know, I'll let you in on a secret: this book isn't really about New York. It isn't even about New York City. It's about Manhattan. Most people (including me throughout this book) use New York, New York City, "the city," and Manhattan synonymously. But New York is one of the Northeast's largest states, and New York City actually includes five separate boroughs: Manhattan, Staten Island, the Bronx, Queens, and Brooklyn. Of those five boroughs, only the Bronx is attached to the mainland; Manhattan and the other three are islands.

A LITTLE HISTORY — Now that you know we're talking only about the island of Manhattan, a little history may help you make sense of how the city is laid out. Algonquin Indians and members of other tribes were the first known residents of this area. Italian explorer Giovanni da Verrazano (for whom the Verrazano Narrows Bridge, between Brooklyn and Staten Island, is named) sailed into New York Harbor in 1524 and "discovered" Manhattan for his French patron, King Francis I. In 1609, Dutch East India Company trader Henry Hudson sailed into the harbor and up the river that now bears his name. The first permanent European settlement in Manhattan, a Dutch trading post called Nieuw Amsterdam, was established in 1625 at the very southern tip of the island, where Battery Park is today. The story you've probably already heard is true: the island was "bought" by the Dutch West India Company a year later from local Indians with beads, cloth, and other goods worth roughly $24. It was renamed New York in 1664 after the British gained control of the still tiny settlement.

It's hard to imagine today, but such areas as midtown and even Greenwich Village were way out in the country for another 150 years. Indeed, Wall Street is so named because a wall of logs was erected there in the middle of the 17th century to protect the farms in lower Manhattan from the wilderness beyond. New York's population—only 60,000 as late as 1800—remained concentrated on the southern tip of the island, while most of Manhattan was used for country estates and farmland or just left as forests and wilderness. When a commission headed by engineer John Randall, Jr., laid out a grid system for the largely undeveloped area from Houston Street north to 155th Street in 1807, the city's tiny population laughed at the thought that it would ever be necessary.

THE RANDALL PLAN — For those of us trying to find our way around Manhattan, the so-called Randall Plan is a godsend. The streets below Houston (pronounced *House*-ton), particularly those below Canal Street, are laid out like the Dutch farm trails they once were. Even those that are relatively straight were not built for 20th-century traffic: the world-famous Wall Street, for example, is more narrow than the typical suburban driveway. Truth be told, not much about the layout scheme makes sense south of 14th Street.

Thanks to the Randall Plan, everything north of 14th Street is about as simple as a major city can be. Other than Broadway, originally an Indian path and now one of the country's longest roads (it goes all the way from the southern tip of Manhattan to Albany), and some of the streets in northern Manhattan, the streets and avenues are laid out in a north-south, east-west grid. All of the east-west streets are numbered, as are many of the north-south avenues. (See the "Key to Addresses" section immediately following this one if you need to find a specific address.)

EAST SIDE, WEST SIDE — The city is divided into east and west sides by Fifth Avenue. It starts just north of Washington Square Park at about 8th Street in Greenwich Village. Broadway acts as the dividing line south of the park, although down there it's a little east of where Fifth Avenue would be. That east-west distinction is all-important, as most addresses in New York have two identically numbered versions — 125 East 52nd Street and 125 West 52nd Street, for example, are two distinct locations several blocks apart.

Let's start with the east side of the city. Moving east from Fifth Avenue toward the East River, you'll find Madison Avenue, Park Avenue (called Park Avenue South below East 34th Street and Fourth Avenue below that), Lexington Avenue, Third Avenue, Second Avenue, and First Avenue. Madison Avenue doesn't start, however, until East 23rd Street. Sutton Place starts at about East 51st Street between First Avenue and the river, turns into York Avenue at East 60th Street and then stops again at East 92nd Street. East End Avenue runs between York Avenue and the river from East 79th Street to East 90th Street. All of these avenues run north-south, parallel to Fifth Avenue, and FDR Drive runs between the easternmost avenue and the river, all along the east side of the island.

The west side of Manhattan is a little more confusing. Moving west from Fifth Avenue toward the Hudson River, you'll find Avenue of the Americas (or Sixth Avenue, as everyone except map makers still calls it, despite the name change in the 1950s), Seventh Avenue, Eighth Avenue (Central Park West north of West 59th Street), Ninth Avenue (Columbus Avenue north of West 59th Street), Tenth Avenue (Amsterdam Avenue north of West 59th Street), and Eleventh Avenue (West End Avenue north of West 59th Street until it ends at West 107th Street). You'll also find Broadway on the west side above West 23rd Street. Avenue of the Americas and Seventh Avenue both end at the bottom of Central Park. Riverside Drive runs between West End Avenue and the river, beginning at West 72nd Street. All of these avenues run north-south (except Broadway, which meanders from time to time before more or less straightening out around West 79th Street) parallel to Fifth Avenue. The Henry Hudson Parkway (also known as the West Side Highway and sometimes called Twelfth Avenue around midtown) runs between the westernmost avenue and the river all along the entire west side of the city.

Central Park lies between 59th and 110th streets, further dividing Manhattan's east and west sides. Fifth Avenue runs along the east side of the park, and everything east of it is known as the Upper East Side. Central Park West runs along the west side of the park. Everything west of it is known as the Upper West Side. Both the Upper East Side and the Upper West Side are largely residential, although most of the north-south avenues (as opposed to the east-west numbered streets) have plenty of shops and stores.

NORTHERN MANHATTAN—The avenues on the east side remain pretty consistent as they move north of Central Park into the area known as East Harlem. West of Fifth Avenue and north of the park in Harlem itself, Lenox Avenue (which soon becomes Malcolm X Boulevard) picks up where Avenue of the Americas left off below the park, Adam Clayton Powell, Jr. Boulevard resumes where Seventh Avenue left off, and Central Park West becomes Frederick Douglass Boulevard. Amsterdam Avenue, Broadway, and Riverside Drive all remain relatively consistent as they move north, but such new roads as Convent Avenue, Saint Nicholas Avenue, Edgecombe Avenue, and Fort Washington Avenue also appear in Harlem and in the northern tip of Manhattan.

KEY TO ADDRESSES

So how do you find an address in Manhattan? I'm not sure who came up with the following systems, but I do know they work, and I promise they aren't as complicated as they look.

AVENUES—If you know the address of someplace on one of the north-south avenues, you can determine the approximate cross street by canceling the last number of the address, dividing the remainder by two, and adding or subtracting the relevant number listed below.

First Avenue	Add 3
Second Avenue	Add 3
Third Avenue	Add 10
Lexington Avenue	Add 22
Park Avenue South	Add 8
Park Avenue	Add 35
Madison Avenue	Add 26
Fifth Avenue	
Address up to 200	Add 13

Between 201 and 400	Add 16
Between 401 and 600	Add 18
Between 601 and 774	Add 20
Between 775 and 1286	Subtract 18
Between 1289 and 1500	Add 45
Above 2000	Add 24
Avenue of the Americas	Subtract 12
Lenox Avenue (Malcolm X Boulevard)	Add 110
Seventh Avenue	Add 12
Adam Clayton Powell, Jr. Boulevard	Add 20
Broadway	
Up to 750 is below 8th Street	
756 to 846	Subtract 29
847 to 953	Subtract 25
Above 953	Subtract 31
Eighth Avenue	Add 10
Ninth Avenue	Add 13
Columbus Avenue	Add 60
Tenth Avenue	Add 14
Amsterdam Avenue	Add 60
Eleventh Avenue	Add 15
West End Avenue	Add 60

The two avenues that don't fit into this formula but have one of their own are Central Park West and Riverside Drive. To find the cross street for a building on Central Park West, divide the address by 10 and add 60. To find the cross street for a building on Riverside Drive, divide the address by 10 and add 72.

A word of caution: because certain addresses, particularly those on Fifth, Madison, and Park avenues, are thought to be prestigious, many buildings use them even though their entrance is on a side street. If you can't find a building with such an address (this is most common in midtown and on Fifth Avenue along the Upper East Side), look around the corner.

CROSS STREETS—The numbered cross streets run east-west. Addresses on them are easy to find. Allow for a little variation below East 23rd Street (because Madison, Eleventh, and Twelfth avenues have yet to begin) and throughout the city whenever Broadway is involved.

EAST SIDE

1 to 49	Between Fifth Avenue and Madison Avenue
50 to 99	Between Madison Avenue and Park Avenue
100 to 149	Between Park Avenue and Lexington Avenue
150 to 199	Between Lexington Avenue and Third Avenue
200 to 299	Between Third Avenue and Second Avenue
300 to 399	Between Second Avenue and First Avenue
400 to 499	Between First Avenue and York Avenue

WEST SIDE BELOW 59th STREET

1 to 99	Between Fifth Avenue and Avenue of the Americas
100 to 199	Between Avenue of the Americas and Seventh Avenue
200 to 299	Between Seventh Avenue and Eighth Avenue
300 to 399	Between Eighth Avenue and Ninth Avenue
400 to 499	Between Ninth Avenue and Tenth Avenue
500 to 599	Between Tenth Avenue and Eleventh Avenue
600 and up	Between Eleventh Avenue and Twelfth Avenue

WEST SIDE ABOVE 59th STREET

1 to 99	Between Central Park West and Columbus Avenue
100 to 199	Between Columbus Avenue and Amsterdam Avenue
200 to 299	Between Amsterdam Avenue and West End Avenue
Above 300	Between West End Avenue and Riverside Drive

Odd-numbered addresses on east-west streets are on the north (or uptown) side of the street, while even-numbered ones are on the south (or downtown) side.

If the above formula is too confusing, try this chart guide, which roughly covers the area between Union Square and Times Square.

CROSSTOWN GUIDE

Fifth Avenue	
Sixth Avenue	100W
Seventh Avenue	200W
Eighth Avenue	300W

STREET GUIDE

Street	Madison Avenue	Fifth Avenue	Sixth Avenue	Seventh Avenue	Broadway
18		130	615	135	875
20		150	655	170	900
22		170	695	210	935
24	20		730	245	1100
26	45	210	770	285	1135
28	80	250	810	320	1180
30	120	275	855	365	1215
32	155	320	885	405	1255
34	185	350		440	1315
36	215	390	980	480	1350
38	250	420	1020	525	1400
40	280	450	1065	560	1430
42	300	500	1100	600	1470

NEIGHBORHOODS

It may be hard for visitors to think of it this way, but New York is really a collection of small neighborhoods. Some are more famous than others, but each one has a history and flavor all its own. To get a full sense of this wonderful city, I encourage you to visit as many of these neighborhoods as possible.

WASHINGTON HEIGHTS – Home to General George Washington's forces during the Revolutionary War, this neighborhood covers all of Manhattan north of about West 151st Street. (The area at the very tip of Manhattan across the Harlem River from the Riverdale section of the Bronx is known as Inwood.) Racially and ethnically mixed, this neighborhood includes both middle-class and quite poor areas. The Cloisters, Fort Tryon, Inwood Hill and Highbridge parks, Yeshiva University, Dyckman House, Columbia-Presbyterian Hospital, the Hispanic Society of America, and the Museum of the American Indian are all in Washington Heights, as is the entrance to the George Washington Bridge.

HARLEM – There are actually two Harlems: East Harlem (also called Spanish Harlem) and Harlem proper. East Harlem begins at about East 96th Street and runs to the northern tip of the island's east side. The population of this area is almost entirely Latino, and Spanish is spoken more frequently than English here. El Museo del Barrio is on the southwestern edge of East Harlem, while La Marqueta, one of the best places in the city to buy fresh fruit and vegetables, is a little further north. Harlem itself begins as a small corridor in the middle of the island at the top of Central Park (at West 110th Street) and then extends both north and west at the famous and always busy 125th Street. The population of Harlem is almost entirely African-American, and the historic neighborhood is known around the world as a center of African-American music, politics, and culture. As does Washington Heights, Harlem includes both middle-class and very poor areas. You'll find the Schomburg Center for Research in Black Culture, Abyssinian Baptist Church, and the Studio Museum of Harlem here.

MORNINGSIDE HEIGHTS – This relatively small but vibrant area runs between Morningside Drive and the Hudson River from West 110th Street north to West 124th Street. The area is dominated by three large and well-known institutions: Columbia University, Riverside Church, and the Cathedral Church of St. John the Divine. Grant's Tomb is also here, in Riverside Park directly across the street from Riverside Church at West 122nd Street. The neighborhood is full of students and professors from all over the country and, indeed, the world.

UPPER WEST SIDE – A primarily residential area extending west of Central Park to the Hudson River from West 59th Street all the way north to West 110th Street, the Upper West Side is home to such famous apartment buildings as the Dakota and the Ansonia. The neighborhood is racially and ethnically mixed, and its residents pride themselves on their reputation for being politically progressive and tending toward the Bohemian (although by SoHo or East Village standards, Upper West Siders are decidedly conventional). Lincoln Center dominates cultural life in the southern part of the neighborhood. The fabulous food store Zabar's and the American Museum of Natural History are the landmark institutions farther north. Columbus Avenue, Amsterdam Avenue, and Broadway are lined with shops, while Central Park West, West End Avenue, and Riverside Drive are almost exclusively residential. The most elegant living sections of the Upper West Side are on Central Park West and the cross streets in the high 60s, the 70s, and the low 80s; on the other hand, you definitely don't want to spend time wandering around Columbus and Amsterdam avenues above West 96th Street.

UPPER EAST SIDE – Although it's best known for its art museums, galleries and upscale boutiques, the Upper East Side is also a prestigious residential neighborhood. It covers the area east of Central Park from Fifth Avenue to the East River between East 59th Street and East 96th Street. Fifth Avenue (also known as Museum Mile) is dominated by such famous institutions as the Metropolitan, Guggenheim and Cooper-Hewitt museums. It is also home to a large number of expensive apartment buildings, former mansions, and foreign consulates. You'll find the Whitney Museum and lots of galleries and upscale boutiques on Madison Avenue. Park Avenue and most of the cross streets are home to residential buildings and such institutions as the Asia Society. From Lexington Avenue east to the river above East 75th Street (an area sometimes called Yorkville), rents go down a bit. You'll find Gracie Mansion, the mayor's residence, in Carl Schurz Park overlooking the river at about East 88th Street; Bloomingdale's is a major retail force in the southern end of the Upper East Side.

MIDTOWN – Squarely in the middle of the island south of Central Park, midtown is one of the busiest places on earth on a weekday and almost deserted on Sunday (except during the Christmas season). The area extends from 59th Street to 42nd Street between Seventh Avenue and Third Avenue. Fifth Avenue is the heart of midtown and one of the world's most famous shopping areas. Tiffany's, F.A.O. Schwarz, Lord & Taylor, Saks Fifth Avenue, Bergdorf Goodman, and all sorts of other upscale stores are located here, as are a number of bookstores. St. Patrick's Cathedral and several other churches are also on Fifth Avenue, St. Bartholomew's is on Park Avenue, and the stately Central Synagogue is on Lexington Avenue. Landmark buildings like the Citicorp Center, Trump Tower, Rockefeller Center, and the Chrysler Building dominate the skyline here. Carnegie Hall and Radio City Music Hall reside on the western edge of midtown, and Grand Central Station and the New York Public Library are located on its southern end.

CLINTON – This is the area once known as Hell's Kitchen. It stretches south from West 59th Street to West 34th Street between Eighth Avenue and the Hudson River, but there just isn't much to see or do here except catch a bus at the Port Authority Bus Terminal or visit the Jacob Javits Convention Center and the piers along the river. Eighth Avenue is pretty X-rated around the bus station and West 42nd Street but gets much better as you move north toward Central Park.

MURRAY HILL – Covering the area between East 42nd Street south to East 34th Street, Murray Hill begins at Park Avenue and runs to the East River. This area is almost entirely residential; you'll find the nicest part around Park Avenue in the upper 30s. The only real attraction for a visitor here is the Pierpont Morgan Library.

CHELSEA – Another largely residential neighborhood, Chelsea extends from West 34th Street down to West 14th Street from Sixth Avenue west to the Hudson River. Madison Square Garden, Penn Station, and the city's main post office can all be found in the northeast corner of Chelsea. It's surprisingly quiet and relatively clean in the southwestern part of this neighborhood, and southern Chelsea is known for its interesting and increasingly upscale shops. Barney's, a clothing store that both men and women in New York swear by, is probably the best known.

FLATIRON DISTRICT – Named for the historic Flatiron Building at the intersection of Broadway and Fifth Avenue at 23rd Street, this area was known in the late 19th century as Ladies' Mile for its elegant department stores. (They've all long since moved or gone out of business.) It runs between Park Avenue South and Sixth Avenue from 23rd Street south to 14th Street. This part of Fifth Avenue has undergone a bit of a resurgence lately (which is not to say it's particularly elegant), and is now home to some good stores and small shops. The Church of the Transfiguration (affectionately known as "the Little Church Around the Corner"), the Marble Collegiate Church, and the Empire State Building are all just north of here.

GRAMERCY PARK – This aging but still pleasant neighborhood was once the city's most elegant residential area. It covers the area between Park Avenue South to Second Avenue from East 34th Street south to East 14th Street. The small area east of Gramercy Park is known as Stuyvesant. The Flatiron district and the Gramercy Park area meet at Union Square, a lively area that serves as the dividing line between them and Greenwich Village. Theodore Roosevelt's birthplace is on the western edge of this neighborhood, and Stuyvesant Park occupies both sides of Second Avenue between East 15th and East 17th streets.

EAST VILLAGE – Probably the city's funkiest neighborhood, the East Village lies roughly between Avenue B and Broadway from East 14th Street south to East Houston Street. Stay away from Alphabet City (the avenues that begin in the eastern part of the East Village with lettered names) and Tompkins Square, but a walk along the main streets in the western part of the East Village can be lots of fun. The Ukrainian Museum, St. Mark's in the Bowery, and Grace Church are all in the northern part of the East Village.

GREENWICH VILLAGE – Long known for its artists, writers, and well-heeled eccentrics, this remains one of the city's most vibrant centers of culture and an extremely nice neighborhood as well. It covers the area from Broadway west to the Hudson River from West 14th Street south to West Houston Street. The section from Seventh Avenue west to the river is sometimes called the West Village. The beautiful Jefferson Market Library, the Forbes Magazine Galleries, New York University, and lots of interesting shops and clubs are located here, as is the always lively (and usually dirty) Washington Square Park, with its famed arch.

SOHO – Short for SOuth of HOuston, SoHo is a very trendy neighborhood known for its galleries, lofts, and hip café. It begins on West Houston and runs south to Canal Street between Broadway and Sixth Avenue. The neighborhood is most alive on weekends and in the evening. Almost everything down here stays open later than similar establishments in the rest of the city. You'll find the Alternative Museum, the Museum for African Art, the New Museum of Contemporary Art, and the Guggenheim SoHo on the same block of Broadway between Houston and Prince streets. The commercial galleries are concentrated on and around West Broadway (a separate street four blocks east of Broadway) between Houston and Broome streets.

TRIBECA – An acronym that is shorthand for TRIangle BElow CAnal, TriBeCa used to be a rather dull and dirty commercial district but lately is becoming both residential and every bit as chic as SoHo. It covers the area from Canal Street south to Chambers Street from Broadway west to the Hudson River. Although it doesn't look as upscale as you might expect, look for emerging (and emerged) artists, commercial galleries, converted loft apartments, a couple of movie stars (Robert DeNiro has built a film production studio here), and some good restaurants.

CHINATOWN – Home to the largest Chinese-American community in the United States, this is one of those neighborhoods with boundaries nobody can agree how to define. I'll use the Chinatown Tourism Council's definition: from Grand Street south to Worth Street between Broadway and Allen Street. Its busiest streets are Mott and Pell. Chinatown's population of well over 100,000 includes immigrants from all over the world, but its character is most definitely Chinese.

LITTLE ITALY – No longer home to many Italian immigrants, this area is nonetheless the emotional heart of the entire region's Italian-American population, and many return for weddings, funerals, holidays, and other special occasions. Mulberry Street (also called Via San Gennaro) between Canal and Prince streets is the center of Little Italy and is known for its restaurants and frequent festivals.

LOWER EAST SIDE — Many people use the Lower East Side as a geographic umbrella for Chinatown, Little Italy, and the Bowery, but I know it as a distinct neighborhood where generations of Eastern European and other immigrants first settled in overcrowded tenements and worked in sweatshops so their children could have better lives. (Many newer immigrants still live here.) I also know it as one of the city's most amazing discount shopping districts, particularly on Sunday. Because many of the area's businesses are run by observant Jews, Friday afternoon and Saturday are not the times to shop here. Canal and Orchard streets are the area's heart, but it extends broadly from East Houston south to Canal and from the Sara D. Roosevelt Parkway east to Ludlow Street. The area is pretty run-down, but it's still well worth a visit. (Make sure to stop by the Lower East Side Tenement Museum on Orchard Street while you're here.) The even more run-down area known as the Bowery is just west of here.

DOWNTOWN — This area is a little hard to define except to say its centered around City Hall. Very roughly speaking, it runs between Chambers Street south to Fulton Street and from West Broadway east to Pearl Street. Lots of mom and pop stores as well as major chains are sited here, and its streets are always busy, but the beautiful St. Paul's Chapel, the Woolworth Building, the entrance to the Brooklyn Bridge's pedestrian walkway, and City Hall are about the only reasons for a tourist to come down here. It's not a dangerous area, but it always seems dirtier than the rest of the city.

LOWER MANHATTAN — This is the southern tip of the city, extending from Battery Park in the south through Wall Street and other older parts of the Financial District in the north. Things are very compact and tall down here. The streets are narrow and the buildings tower. The boat to the Statue of Liberty and Ellis Island leaves from near Castle Clinton National Monument in Battery Park, and the Staten Island Ferry's terminal sits nearby at the foot of Whitehall Street. Look for Trinity Church, the Federal Hall National Monument, Fraunces Tavern Museum, and the New York Stock Exchange down here.

BATTERY PARK CITY — A relatively new residential area built entirely on landfill, this collection of high-rise apartment buildings is on the western side of Manhattan's southern tip, starting a little bit north of Battery Park itself. The neighborhood lies adjacent to the World Financial Center (and the World Financial Center is itself adjacent to the World Trade Center), where a lot of its residents work.

SHOPPING DISTRICTS

If you were going to open a specialty store, would you choose a location right between two existing stores that specialize in exactly the same thing? No? Then you're not a real New Yorker. Unlike other cities where the whole idea is to move into a neighborhood that doesn't have whatever you're selling, New York has districts for everything from diamonds to flowers to beads and trimming. The merchants seem to thrive on the competition.

Two basic rules govern shopping in New York: you should never need to pay retail, and the best deals are often in "the districts." While there are not as many cohesive districts as there once were in New York, the ones that remain are all well worth a visit.

ANTIQUES – Because rents are so expensive and the antique market has gone soft, many dealers have moved in together. If you're looking for really elegant pieces and money is not an option, try some of the galleries in the two-story underground Place des Antiquaires (135 East 57th Street, between Park and Lexington avenues). The Manhattan Art and Antiques Center at 1050 Second Avenue and East 56th Street is another shared space that may be worth a visit. You'll also find individual stores of varying quality along the stretch of Broadway just south of Union Square, in Greenwich Village, and sprinkled throughout the Upper East Side.

DIAMONDS – This is the epitome of the New York shopping district and one of those places you have to see to believe. Located on West 47th Street between Fifth and Sixth avenues, the diamond district glitters with great deals on diamonds and other jewelry. Be careful, however. I've recommended a couple of places in the "Jewelry" section of Chapter 6, and I urge you to stick with them. Whatever you do, insist on seeing the Gemological Institute of America's report on any stone you're thinking about buying. (All diamonds have one.) Many of the businesses in the diamond district are run by observant Jews, which means that you should visit sometime other than Friday afternoon or Saturday.

FABRIC, BEADS, AND TRIMMING – Part of the spillover from the garment district, this area is in the upper West 30s and lower West 40s between Sixth and Seventh avenues. A lot of stores are located up a flight or two of stairs, where the rents are cheaper. In addition to every imaginable kind of fabric, beads, and trmming, you'll find hats, feathers, buckles, and bangles in this area. You can also find a couple of good fabric stores in the Lower East Side and on Broadway between Leonard and Broome streets. Look in the "Fabrics, Trimming" section of Chapter 6 for particularly good ones.

FISH – There's only one place to go in New York if you want fresh fish: the Fulton Fish Market, next to South Street Seaport at South Street and the eastern end of Fulton Street (just above the Financial District). They do sell to individuals, and the prices are great, but six in the morning is considered late for a shopping expedition. (It's open from midnight until about nine in the morning.)

FLOWERS – Roses are now sold at deep discounts in specialty stores all over the city, and some flower wholesalers are moving out to the

South Bronx because of escalating rents. Still, the area between West 26th and West 30th streets and Sixth and Seventh avenues is *the* place to get the best prices on flowers and plants. Planters, soil, and other supplies also are sold in this area.

FUR – Visit the wholesale fur district between West 27th and 30th streets on and around Seventh Avenue if you want some great buys. As with diamonds and oriental rugs, be careful. (I've listed some particularly good stores under "Furs" in the "Clothing and Accessories" section in Chapter 6.) While animal rights advocates have made significant inroads into this market, I'm always surprised by how many men and women still wear furs in New York in the winter. If you have questions, call the American Fur Industry at 212 564-5133.

FURNITURE – The wholesale furniture warehouses and showrooms are on Lexington Avenue between East 29th and East 33rd streets (the actual construction is done in the Carolinas), but the public is not welcome at most of them. It's worth going down there, however, as some showrooms have special sales when they change their displays and a few will let you come in. Another good bet is the North Carolina Furniture Showroom on Fifth Avenue at 21st Street. The public *is* welcome here.

HANDBAGS – For reasons nobody seems to know, the area in the high 20s and 30s off Fifth Avenue has all sorts of good handbag stores. Look up, as most of them occupy upper floors. The Lower East Side also has a couple of stores with good discounts on fine leather and other handbags. (I've listed some of the best stores in both areas under "Women's Accessories" in the "Clothing and Accessories" section of Chapter 6.)

JUNK – I'm really talking junk here, although one man's treasure. . . . You can find the strangest assortment of gadgets and pieces of I-don't-know-what inside and outside stores along the western part of Canal Street. This area is the dividing line between SoHo and TriBeCa.

KITCHENWARE, LIGHTING, AND RESTAURANT SUPPLIES – The only reason you would ever want to go down to the area known as the Bowery is to shop in this district. It's fairly safe but dirty, decidedly downscale, and otherwise quite dull. "Restaurant Row" runs on and around Bowery Avenue (an extension of Third Avenue) from Canal Street north to Cooper Square (East 7th Street). Whether you're in the market for a butcher block, odd lighting fixtures, or 100 matching glasses, this is the place to go. Lately, I've also noticed a lot of discount lighting stores clustered around First and Second avenues in the high East 50s and low East 60s.

MEN'S DISCOUNT CLOTHING – Look in the Flatiron district on and around Fifth Avenue between 18th and 21st streets for some really good deals on men's clothing. This is another neighborhood where you need to look up to find most stores, although the people handing out flyers for the stores will be more than happy to give you directions. (I've listed some of the best stores under "Men's, General" in the "Clothing and Accessories" section of Chapter 6.)

MUSICAL EQUIPMENT — Classical sheet music and pianos are sold in the immediate neighborhood of Carnegie Hall (Seventh Avenue at West 57th Street). Other musical equipment, especially electric guitars, is sold on West 48th Street between Sixth and Seventh avenues.

ORIENTAL AND AREA RUGS — If you'll excuse the pun, I urge you to tread lightly here: unless you really know what you're doing, you could get badly burned. To be safe, shop in the excellent but decidedly retail-priced home-furnishings department of Bloomingdale's or in one of the stores listed in the "Floor Coverings" section of Chapter 6. But if you're up for the challenge, look in the warehouse area around West 12th Street and the Hudson River. High rents have pushed many retailers out of their traditional area in the high 20s and low 30s between Fifth Avenue and Park Avenue South, but you might look around there, too. Finally, make sure to check the *New York Times* for auctions or close-out sales (although be a bit careful about the latter).

THRIFT SHOPS — You can find some offbeat thrift shops in the East Village, but the more upscale ones are on Madison Avenue in the East 80s and in the Yorkville section of the Upper East Side (First, Second, Third, and Lexington avenues in the upper East 70s, 80s, and lower 90s). We aren't talking Salvation Army here, but, as a general rule, the quality goes down the further north and east you go. (I've included a couple of particularly good thrift shops under "Thrift Shops" in the "Clothing and Accessories" section of Chapter 6.)

WOMEN'S DISCOUNT CLOTHING — Probably the highest concentration of nice discount women's clothing stores (and shoe stores) is along Orchard Street on the Lower East Side, from East Houston south to Grand Street. (Look under "Women's — General" and "Shoes" in the "Clothing and Accessories" section of Chapter 6 for some of my favorite places here.) Because many of these stores are run by observant Jews, don't plan a trip on Friday afternoon or Saturday. Sunday is definitely *the* shopping day in this area.

There are a couple of districts I didn't include in the list because they are not so easily defined and because I've covered them extensively in other parts of the book. If you're interested in art, look in the "Auctions" and "Galleries" sections of Chapter 3. Bookstores are listed in Chapter 6 under "Books." Fifth Avenue in midtown is a good place to start. If you're interested in electronics or cameras, look for advertisements in the Sunday *New York Times* or try 47th Street Photo. If you want a more personal touch along with good discounts, try Kaufman's Electronics on the Lower East Side. Finally, whatever you're looking for, make sure to check my exclusive list at the beginning of Chapter 6.

OTHER DISTRICTS

FINANCIAL DISTRICT – Probably better known as Wall Street, the financial district does include Wall Street but covers lots of other streets, too. The older part of the district sits between Broadway and Water Street from Maiden Lane south to Exchange Place. The New York Stock Exchange, the Federal Reserve Bank of New York, the Fraunces Tavern Museum, Trinity Church, Federal Hall National Memorial, and all sorts of financial institutions are located here. The newer part of the financial district is adjacent to the northwest corner of the original district, including both the World Trade Center and the World Financial Center. It extends from Church Street east to the Hudson River between Vesey and Albany streets.

GARMENT DISTRICT – This district, also known as Seventh Avenue or Fashion Avenue, is dedicated to just one thing: the wholesale dressing of American women. It's located between Broadway and Seventh Avenue from West 39th south to West 35th Street. Fashion models, clothing racks, and trucks filled with fabric jam the streets, especially in the summer. Make sure to look (up) for stores selling such garment district overflow as fabrics, beads, and trimmings throughout this area and a bit north of it as well.

MUSEUM MILE – Beginning at East 70th Street and running north for almost 40 blocks along Fifth Avenue, Museum Mile is actually closer to two miles. Whatever you call it, it's the most stunning concentration of museums anywhere in the world. The highlights, from south to north, are the Frick, the Metropolitan, the Guggenheim, the National Academy of Design, the Cooper-Hewitt, the Jewish Museum, the International Center for Photography, the Museum of the City of New York, and El Museo del Barrio. In warm weather you'll find all sorts of outdoor vendors selling books, crafts, T-shirts and other items on the west side of Fifth Avenue, immediately south of the Metropolitan in the high and mid 70s.

THEATER DISTRICT – Broadway is on Broadway. Right? Wrong, at least for the most part, and it's not on 42nd Street, either. The theater district is just west of Broadway between West 44th and West 51st streets. Sadly, the area (particularly around Times Square) is full of X-rated theaters and the like. I don't recommend wandering around here during the day with the family. If you're going to see a play or musical, however, the area is full of theatergoers at night (although I recommend taking a taxicab to and from the area).

TRANSPORTATION

New York is really very compact and easier to navigate than many other large cities I've visited. You have a whole range of choices for how to get around. I've listed them here in order of my own preferences.

WALKING — Without question, this is my favorite way to get around New York. It may seem a little overwhelming at first (particularly in midtown at rush hour), and you'll stick out like a sore thumb if you wait on the curb for the "walk" signs, but it's definitely the best way to see the city and get a sense of its different neighborhoods. If you're walking north-south (uptown or downtown) in midtown, the Upper East Side or the Upper West Side, 20 blocks are equivalent to a mile. Most east-west (crosstown) blocks, particularly those between Fifth and Sixth avenues and Sixth and Seventh avenues, are much longer. Unless you have small children who tire easily or are going from Columbia University (at West 116th Street) to New York University (at West 4th Street), walking is the least expensive and most interesting way to travel. Be sure to bring comfortable walking shoes.

SUBWAY — Some visitors and New Yorkers alike love to ride the subway, while others will do anything and everything to avoid it. For the several million people who take the subway to and from work or school on weekdays, however, it's the most efficient way to travel. Whatever else you think of the subway system, there's no arguing the fact that it's the fastest way to get around Manhattan.

The subway system is the result of a merger of private lines like the BMT and the IRT, which sprang up at the turn of the century. (Most of the stations and some of the cars are old, so don't expect the relative luxury of BART in San Francisco or the Metro in Washington, D.C.) Its 714 miles of track and 469 stations connect every borough except Staten Island. The system is primarily concentrated in Manhattan south of 110th Street and particularly south of 59th Street. Maps of the entire system are available at token booths inside the stations and are posted in most cars and most stations. (If you need to spend time studying a map, I suggest you do so in your hotel room or some other private place.) You'll also find a detailed map of the entire subway system in the front section of the Manhattan Yellow Pages.

Subway stations are marked by globes and signs with route numbers or letters. A red globe means that the entrance is restricted or closed and no tokens are sold there. A green globe means that both the entrance and a token booth are open. In most of Manhattan, subway stations are underground. You'll find the token booths at the bottom of the stairs. Inside the station, signs point to the appropriate platform for the uptown or downtown (sometimes "Brooklyn-bound") train you want. Keep an eye out for "express" trains — they're great timesavers if you want to go where they're going, but they make a limited number of stops. The line number or letter, along with information about whether it's a local or an express and the name of the last stop, are written on the side of each subway car.

As many as three children under 44 inches tall can ride free if they're accompanied by an adult, but a subway ride costs $1.25 for adults, and you must use a token to get through the turnstiles. (A fare increase to

$1.50 and an automated card system are being debated as this is being written.) Tokens can be purchased individually or in packets of 10 at any token booth. The attendant will not take anything but cash and cannot accept bills larger than $20. Once you've gone through the turnstile and are inside the station, you can transfer between lines or ride as long as you like. Stops usually are announced inside the cars over a public address system, but the announcements are often garbled. Look at the signs posted in the station as you pull in if you need to know where you are. Some lines stop running for a couple hours in the early morning, and many have less frequent or different service at night and on weekends, but the system itself runs 24 hours a day, 7 days a week. If you have questions about routes or a problem, call the Metropolitan Transit Authority any day between 6 a.m. and 9 p.m. at 718 330-1234. (Non-English speakers can call 718 330-4847 between 7 a.m. and 7 p.m.)

Finally, a word about safety. The subway stations and the cars themselves are often dirty and all sorts of strange people wander through them, but statistically the system is really no more dangerous than any other mode of transportation. But do use common sense. *Don't* ride late at night or very early in the morning, particularly if you're alone. *Don't* enter deserted stations. *Don't* ride in an otherwise empty car. *Don't* wear flashy jewelry. *Don't* wander around aimlessly. *Don't* stand too close to the tracks. *Don't* use the bathroom inside any station. (Most of them are closed now anyway.) And whatever else you do, watch your wallet or purse, particularly if you are riding a crowded car.

TAXIS – All of the officially licensed medallion taxicabs in New York are yellow, have the words "NYC Taxi" and fare information written on their side doors, and have their medallion number in a box on the roof. Inside, you'll see a meter and the driver's license (with his or her picture) and medallion number displayed on the dashboard, usually on the passenger's side. The city, particularly outside midtown, is full of "cars for hire" (a.k.a. "gypsy cabs") that are not legally allowed to pick up people hailing a cab south of 96th Street. Still, they sometimes try to do just that. I strongly encourage you to stick with the medallion cabs.

The cost of a ride in a medallion cab is calculated per trip rather than per person, which means that a short trip for four adults in a cab can actually be cheaper than a bus or subway ride. That said, however, the fare can add up quickly, particularly if you're stuck in heavy traffic. The charge begins at $1.50 the moment you get in and is 25 cents for every fifth of a mile traveled or 75 seconds stopped or slowed in traffic. You pay for any tolls, and there's a 50 cent surcharge for rides between eight at night and six in the morning. The meter in the front keeps a running total of your fare, and the driver is required to give you a receipt if you request one. A tip of between 15 and 20 percent of your fare is expected, and you probably will need to pay in cash. (A few cabs now take American Express and other credit cards.)

Drivers are required to take you anywhere you request within the five boroughs of New York City, to Westchester and Nassau counties, and to Newark Airport. That's the law, but the reality is that some cab drivers will make a fuss if you ask to go to one of the airports or to one of those suburban counties. If you have that or any other problem, I strongly encourage you to jot down the driver's name and medallion number and write the New York City Taxi and Limousine Commission (221 West 41st Street, New York, NY 10036) or call them (212 221-8294) to complain. These folks take their oversight responsibilities pretty seriously. New York's reputation depends on it!

So how do you go about getting a cab? Stand on the curb or in the street just off it and hold your arm up and out. If the number (but not the "off duty" sign) is lit in the rectangular box on a cab's roof, it's empty and on duty. Finding a cab in midtown on a rainy Friday afternoon is not always easy, but you won't have any trouble finding one in most parts of the city at most times of day. If you do have trouble, go to a major hotel or join the cab line at Penn Station, Grand Central Station, or the Port Authority Bus Terminal. If you want the driver to take a particular route (it's a good idea to know exactly where you're going), tell him when you get in. Passengers ride in the back seat, although the driver will usually let one person ride in the front seat if there are four.

BUSES — In the last edition of this book, I wrote that the only reason to take a city bus is if you have a lot of time and are afraid of the alternatives. A friend who lives in New York and rides the bus every day objected strongly. First of all, she pointed out, most buses are wheelchair-accessible (which the subway decidedly is not) and "elderly-friendly" in that the driver can lower the stairs at the entrance for anyone who has trouble climbing high steps. Probably precisely because the people who ride the bus aren't in a hurry, they tend to be friendlier than the people who ride the subway and often will get up to give an older person or a hassled-looking parent their seat. The buses are very safe and usually don't attract the same strange people who habituate subway cars and stations. Because there is a driver, you can ask questions or get directions. Finally, the bus stops frequently and you can always see where you're going — a good and relatively cheap way to get a flavor of the city. I still find the bus system slow and sometimes incomprehensible, but I was a little harsh in the last edition and will admit that some New Yorkers wouldn't think of traveling around the city any other way.

Buses run up and down most avenues and on most major cross streets. Uptown buses stop at designated stops every two or three blocks and crosstown buses stop on every block, assuming someone is waiting at a bus stop or someone on the bus has pushed the tape or pulled the cord that alerts the driver that a stop is requested. (Many buses have a limited express version that only stops every ten blocks or so — an orange "limited" sign is clearly visible in their front windshields.) Many bus stops have covered waiting areas and route maps, and all of them have blue signs with route numbers on them. Some stops are for more than one route. Check the screen on the front or side of each bus for its route number, or simply ask the driver. Your fare entitles you to one transfer, and you should request the transfer ticket from the driver when you board the bus. You are supposed to use the transfer only for a continuous trip, but you actually have a couple hours to continue your trip without a problem. (You cannot, however, get off and then reboard another bus on the same route.)

The bus costs $1.25 for adults and you must use change or the same tokens you would use for the subway (a fare increase to $1.50 is being debated as this is being written). The fare box, located directly in front of you when you board, will not take pennies or bills, and the driver cannot make change. You can buy tokens at any subway station token booth and at some McDonald's and Love's drug stores. If you're going to ride the bus with any frequency, I suggest you buy several tokens at one time or a packet of ten so you don't use up all your quarters or need to keep going back to subway stations. Small children can ride the bus for free. Many buses run all night, although service is less frequent on weekends, late at night, and early in the morning.

You can get a map of bus routes in Manhattan on most buses (ask the driver or look for boxes by the front and back doors), at most subway token booths, and from the New York Convention and Visitors Bureau (2 Columbus Circle, across from the southwest corner of Central Park at West 59th Street). You can also find a detailed map of the entire bus system at the front of the Manhattan Yellow Pages. The map will tell you where the buses run and the frequency of service at different times and on different days. If you have questions about how to get from one place to another on the bus, call the Metropolitan Transit Authority between 6 a.m. and 9 p.m. at 718 330-1234. (Non-English speakers can call 718 330-4847 between 7 a.m. and 7 p.m.)

CAR SERVICES – If you notice a particularly large number of Lincoln Town Cars and other black sedans in midtown and the financial district, the reason is car services. Unlike taxicabs that cruise the streets looking for business, car services are available only by reservation and often exclusively for corporate clients. If you're in New York on business, your company may arrange to have you picked up from the airport and shuttled around town by one of these services. Chances are you will be given an account number and pay with a voucher provided either by your company or the driver. The most common way that clients find the correct car (half a dozen or more will be lined up outside major office buildings at the end of the day) is a name and car number posted in the window of the car. You'll be told in advance what to look for.

Some car services (and limousine companies, too) take reservations from individuals. They include Alpine (212 744-8360), Excel (718 265-5200), Bell Taxi (212 206-1700) and Olympic (800 872-0044). You can have a car meet you at the airport, be shuttled around town for a day, or simply arrive and depart from the opera in style. The cost is calculated by the hour or by the trip rather than by mileage, and there usually is a minimum charge. Reservations are required. I would make them a day in advance and then call to confirm several hours before you expect to leave. If you want a specific kind of car (or limousine), say so when you're making your reservations. These car services are on the high end of the business. You'll find lots of gypsy cabs and low-end car services in the outer boroughs and outside midtown, but I suggest avoiding them.

DRIVING — If you read my comments about driving in New York earlier in this chapter, you already know that I strongly recommend against it. Leave the hassles and headaches to the cab and bus drivers. The parking regulations alone ought to discourage you. There are alternate-side rules (call 212 566-4121 for specific information about these and other parking regulations), special rules for several dozen official holidays, and weekend rules. And that's if you find a space. The fines for illegal parking start at $30 and go up quickly — the penalty for parking in some zones is a $185 fine, plus having your car towed! If you can't find a space on the street or want the security of a garage, expect to pay big bucks. (Call 718 786-6621 for a list of municipal lots. I once was charged $18 per half hour at a garage in midtown, and then they cheated on the clock! If that's not bad enough, car thieves are not unusual even in the nicest parts of the city and carjackings at stoplights have become a problem. If you must drive, I *highly* recommend becoming a member of AAA or some other major automobile club and obtaining all the information they have about traffic laws and driving in the city. Whatever else you do, make sure you know where you're going and be prepared for a lot of honking. Drivers in New York are not very patient people.

WHAT TO EXPECT

According to the 1990 Census, 1.5 million of the 7.3 million people who live in the five boroughs of New York City live in Manhattan. New York City is easily the largest city in the United States. Manhattan alone roughly has the combined population of Alaska, Vermont, and Wyoming — on an island 12 miles long and only 2.5 miles across at its widest point.

Its detractors argue that Manhattan is the most crowded, dirtiest, and rudest place in the world. To some extent, they're right on all three points. It *is* crowded. More people live in a residential city block in Manhattan than in many small towns. On any given weekday, there are enough people in the World Trade Center to make it the fourth largest city in my home state of Oregon! And Manhattan *is* dirty. During one recent wind storm, several people were injured by flying debris (a polite way to say trash). The trash that isn't lying around loose is put out on the streets in bags for collection — heaven help you if you happen to be in New York during a sanitation strike in the summer! And who would argue that New Yorkers aren't rude — at least some of them, some of the time (although what they mostly are is blunt)? Everyone seems to be in a hurry, and chances are that anybody who smiles at you on the street isn't just being friendly.

So why visit? Because crowds, dirt, and rudeness aside, New York is the most interesting, exciting, and diverse city in the world. Although they sometimes don't act like it, most of the people who live here are very proud of their city and can't imagine why anyone would want to live anywhere else. At the very least, anyone who lives in the United States or who visits this country ought to spend a week or two getting to know this incredible city.

There is something for everyone in New York. Whether you love the opera, jazz, or tribal drums; whether you're interested in history, architecture, or modern art; whether you like to shop, jog, or go to lectures; whether you live for Italian, Ethiopian, or Chinese food . . . you get the idea. This book is all about finding *your* New York—the little slice of this magnificent apple just right for your tastes and appetite.

TIPPING AND OTHER EXPENSES

Be forewarned: New York is expensive. Really expensive. Most nice hotel rooms in midtown run about $200 a night—and that's before room taxes (almost 20%, plus $2 a night for rooms costing over $100) are added on! The average meal can easily run upwards of $50 per person, and most theater and opera tickets are just plain outrageous. Everybody expects a tip. It's up to you, of course, but a minimum of $1 per bag to the bellman, between 15% and 20% of your fare to the cab driver, and between 15% and 20% of your pre-tax restaurant bill (just double the tax —its 8.25 percent on just about everything) to your waiter are expected. Most people also tip wine stewards (10% of the wine bill), parking valets ($2), private tour guides (at least $5 a day), and doormen who hail cabs ($1), among others.

You can find cheaper hotels, less expensive restaurants, and some events and activities that are actually free. (Make sure to check the "Manhattan for Free" section in Chapter 7 if you want to plan a money-saving itinerary, and look in the "Tickets" section of Chapter 3 for information about how to get half-price tickets to the theater and other performances.) But in general, my advice is to be prepared to spend money and lots of it if you're here for a special visit. Don't nickel and dime yourself out of enjoying what could be a once-in-a-lifetime treat!

SAFETY

It makes sense that there are more crimes committed in New York than in any other city, because there are more people living in New York than in any other city in the United States. But New York is not as dangerous as you might think. In fact, there are fewer crimes committed per capita in New York than in at least a dozen other U.S. cities and the violent crime rate actually has been going down for several years. The percentages definitely are with you, especially if you observe some common-sense "don'ts." *Don't* display big wads of money or flashy watches and jewelry. *Don't* open your wallet in public. *Don't* keep your wallet in your back pocket, unless it's buttoned. *Don't* wear your purse slung over one shoulder—put the strap over your head and keep the purse in front of you or to the side. *Don't* take the subway late at night or very early in the morning. *Don't* walk down empty streets or into empty subway stations. *Don't* go jogging in Central Park or anywhere else when it's dark. *Don't* let yourself believe that staying in "good" neighborhoods protects you from crime—the only time I was ever mugged was on Park Avenue at East 62nd Street. (You can't find a better neighborhood than that!) *Don't* let anybody in your hotel room, even if they say they work for the hotel, unless you've specifically asked them to come or you've checked with the front desk. *Don't* talk to strangers who try to strike up a conversation unless you're very sure of their motivations. *Don't* leave bags unattended. *Don't* put your purse or anything else on the floor or on the back of the door in a public bathroom stall. *Don't* walk around with your mouth open, your camera slung over your shoulder, and your map out while saying things like, "Gee, honey, they sure don't have buildings like that back home." And *don't* ever be afraid to cross the street or shout for help if somebody is bothering you.

You should also be on the lookout for a few common scams. One is for people to knock on your hotel door or even call in advance claiming they are from the hotel's maintenance staff and want to check something. The simple solution is not to open the door until you've called the front desk and made sure that the maintenance staff has indeed sent someone up. Another common scam is for people to call rooms on some pretense designed to find out whether you're alone. If you're a woman, mention "my husband and I" or "we" and you won't be bothered. All the same, call the front desk *immediately* to report such a phone call or anything else suspicious. Another common scam is for people to bump into you in a crowd, drop something that breaks, and then demand to be paid for its cost. The obvious solution is to walk away (don't be intimidated if the person yells obscenities at you). And then there are always pickpockets and purse snatchers, so be on the lookout and guard your belongings tightly.

Finally, it's impossible to walk for more than a block or two in New York without seeing a homeless person. Outside banks and grocery stores are particularly common places to find people with paper cups asking for change. These sad people exist in other cities, too. It's just that in New York you see them more often because you're walking rather than driving. Be cautious but don't be scared of these people. The vast majority are completely harmless and few of them will say anything at all if you just walk right by them. Many people simply refuse to make eye contact with them and ignore their pleas. Others keep spare change in their pocket to give out. Still others won't give money but offer to buy food. It's up to you to decide how to respond.

WHERE TO AND WHERE NOT TO

Like any great city, New York not only has a host of wonderful things to do and see, but it has its share of unpleasant things. The following list is certainly not complete, but it will give you an idea of what to expect.

On the plus side, try:

Taking in an afternoon game at Yankee or Shea Stadium on a warm summer day.

Visiting the Statue of Liberty.

Walking with friends in Central Park in the spring or fall.

Looking out over the East River at the Manhattan skyline from Lighthouse Park on Roosevelt Island.

Browsing through the 2.5 million volumes in the New York Public Library (Fifth Ave at 42nd St).

Viewing one of the more than 50 parades that excite the city each year.

Buying a classy new suit without breaking the budget at Gorsart (9 Murray St, 10 E 44th St).

Getting in touch with your own history while visiting the Museum of Immigration on Ellis Island.

Taking a six-year-old to F.A.O. Schwarz (767 Fifth Ave).

Taking a ride on one of the 388 elevators in Rockefeller Center (preferably to the top).

Sitting on one of the 7,674 benches in Central Park on a glorious spring day.

Wandering through the grandeur of the Frick Collection (1 E 70th St).

Looking down one of the open grates that expose 238 miles of subway tracks below the city streets.

Watching the magazine mogels lunch at 44 (44 W 44th St).

Visiting the Romanesque/Byzantine-style St. Bartholomew's Church (built in 1919) on Park Avenue between 50th and 51st Sts.

Ogling the authentic American Indian crafts at Saity Jewelry (Trump Tower, 5th level, 725 Fifth Ave, at 57th St).

Reliving your first date at Sonia Rose Restaurant (132 Lexington Ave).

Enjoying a musical performance at Lincoln Center for the Performing Arts (Broadway at 64th St).

Spending a day at the Metropolitan Museum of Art (Fifth Ave at 82nd St).

Gawking at the Fabergé eggs at the Forbes Magazine Galleries (62 Fifth Ave).

Sampling Martine's chocolates at Bloomingdale's (1000 Third Ave, 6th floor).

Enjoying a leisurely and luxurious weekend at the new Four Seasons Hotel (57 E 57th St).

Taking in the farmer's market on Wednesdays, Fridays, and Saturdays at Union Square (14th St and Broadway).

Tuning in to Joan Hamburg for great consumer advice (WOR—710 AM radio—weekdays from 10 a.m. to noon).

Sipping a cup of espresso or cappuccino in Little Italy.

Visiting 75½ Bedford St (in Greenwich Village), site of the city's narrowest house.

Scooping up bargains by the cartful at Bed, Bath and Beyond (620 Sixth Ave).

Having a romantic dinner at "One If by Land, Two If by Sea," Aaron Burr's former carriage house (17 Barrow St).

Watching a favorite episode of a favorite television show at the Museum of Television and Radio (25 W 52nd St).

Getting up as early as 4 a.m. to witness the activity at the Fulton Fish Market (South Street Seaport).

Losing yourself in a frozen hot chocolate at Serendipity 3 (225 E 60th St).

Visiting the Federal Hall National Memorial (26 Wall St), where George Washington took oath as the first U.S. President.

Relaxing in the Ford Foundation's garden atrium (E 43rd St off Second Ave).

Taking the kids to see the medieval collection at the Cloisters (Fort Tryon Park, 193rd St and Fort Washington Ave).

Finding a small restaurant in TriBeCa that isn't trendy or even recommended but where you feel at home.

Taking a Circle Line cruise around Manhattan's 31 miles of shoreline (call 212 269-5755).

Visiting the United Nations.

Answering the question "Who is buried in Grant's Tomb?" (Riverside Drive at 122nd St).

Taking a boat trip on the lake in Central Park on a summer day (Loeb Boathouse).

Ice skating at Wollman Rink in Central Park at Rockefeller Center.

Touring backstage at the Metropolitan Opera.

Taking a bargain ride on the Staten Island Ferry.

Shopping Orchard Street on Sunday.

Feasting your eyes on the marble and glitter of Trump Tower (Fifth Ave at 57th St).

Having an evening meal in the Crystal Room at Tavern on the Green in Central Park.

Learning about early 19th-century New York at the Abigail Adams Smith Museum (421 E 61st St).

Riding through Central Park in a hansom cab.

Buying a hot bagel from H&H Bagels (80th St and Broadway or 1551 Second Ave).

Gallery hopping in SoHo on a Saturday afternoon.

Dancing at the Rainbow Room, atop Rockefeller Center.

Attending the flea market and antiques sale on Sunday at Sixth Avenue and 26th Street.

Having tea or Sunday brunch in the Palm Court at the Plaza Hotel (Fifth Ave and Central Park S).

Enjoying the awe-inspiring view from atop the World Trade Center.

Listening to real gospel singing during services at the Abyssinian Baptist Church (132 W 138th St).

Sampling dim sum in Chinatown.

Exploring the towering beauty of the Cathedral Church of St. John the Divine (Amsterdam Ave at W 112th St).

Watching the lights on the Statue of Liberty while walking along the promenade at Battery Park.

Viewing the model furniture rooms at Bloomingdale's (Third Ave and 59th St).

Enjoying happy hour at Molly Bloom's (150 W 47th St).

Getting a loaf of Eli's sourdough bread at almost any gourmet shop.

Enjoying the New York skyline from the River Cafe in Brooklyn (1 Water St).

Buying fresh coffee at Zabar's (80th St and Broadway).

Getting the early edition of the Sunday *New York Times* to read in bed on Saturday night.

Catching the Knicks and the Rangers at Madison Square Garden (Seventh Ave and W 33rd St).

Getting lost in the downstairs stacks at the Strand Book Store (12th St and Broadway).

Enjoying the open-air entertainment at the South Street Seaport.

Running in Central Park before heading to the office.

Getting stuffed at the Carnegie Deli (Seventh Ave and 55th St).

Enjoying the Easter flower show at Macy's (Herald Square).

Gawking at the dinosaurs in the American Museum of Natural History (79th St and Central Park W).

Securing a bargain ticket for a Broadway matinee at the TKTS booth in Times Square.

Watching the Rockettes at Radio City Music Hall (50th St and Sixth Ave).

Getting into a political discussion with a cab driver.

Taking the kids for an after-dinner treat at Peppermint Park (1225 First Ave).

Browsing the "New York Is Book Country" book fair on Fifth Avenue in September.

Eating until you burst at the Polish Veselka Coffee Shop (Second Ave and 9th St).

Spending an afternoon at the Museum of Modern Art (11 W 53rd St).

Spending the day getting pampered at Elizabeth Arden (691 Fifth Ave).

Having one of the finest French dinners anywhere at La Reserve (4 W 49th St).

Visiting Theodore Roosevelt's birthplace (28 E 20th St) and George Washington's headquarters (1785 Jumal Terrace).

Taking advantage of any rest room you come across, especially those in hotels. (Others may not be so handy or clean.)

Having a mountainous burger at Jackson Hole Wyoming Burgers (232 E 64th St).

Taking home fresh fruit and vegetables from Grace's Marketplace (1237 Third Ave).

Getting a glass of fresh-squeezed orange juice at 1428 Sixth Avenue (just off 58th St).

Visiting the Winter Garden atrium at the World Financial Center.

Then there are the negatives:

Midtown on St. Patrick's Day.

Walking around alphabet land (Avenues A, B, C, and D).

Buying knockoff Hard Rock Cafe sweat shirts from street vendors.

Establishing eye contact on the subway.

Trying to find buildings with addresses on Fifth and Park Avenues and entrances on side streets.

Restaurant maitre d's who seat you in the bar when the dining room is not filled.

Subway stations on muggy summer days.

Cab drivers who take the Triboro Bridge rather than the 59th Street Bridge to get to La Guardia Airport.

Watching the numbers go up and up on the National Debt Clock (Sixth Ave and 43rd St).

Upper East Side singles bars.

New York in August.

Dogs whose manners are unacceptable to everyone but their owners.

Buying an overpriced pretzel on Fifth Avenue near Central Park.

Garbage bags rotting in the hot summer sun.

Trying to find a bargain apartment in the Real Estate section of the Sunday *New York Times*.

"Happy Birthday" being sung off-key by waiters at quality restaurants.

Street phones that don't work.

Cabs that take short corner turns, moving the puddle from the gutter to your new suit.

Using a Manhattan garage.

The drug scene in Union Square Park.

Restaurants that include tax in the check total so the tip will be larger.

The person who knows so much about New York that no one can tell him or her anything ("I've lived here all my life").

Seeing rats scurrying off the subway track when a train is coming.

Getting ripped off by an electronics store on Fifth Ave.

Department store clerks who remind the customer, "That isn't my section."

Cab drivers who refuse to take people to the airports.

People who need to draw attention to themselves by having the largest and loudest portable radio on the street.

The VIP (in his or her mind only) who instructs a secretary not only to ask who is calling, but also to inquire about the subject matter.

Wearing a gold necklace! You're bound to attract ripoff artists.

Trying to get a cab at 5 p.m. on a wet Friday afternoon.

Watching an unsuspecting person buy a fake Rolex watch from a street
   vendor.
Restaurants that automatically add a 15% to 20% service charge to the
   check.

CHECKLISTS

If you're planning a trip to New York a couple of months in advance,
I suggest you think about what you want to do and read through the relevant sections of this book carefully. (Pay special attention to the "Tours"
and "Tickets" sections of Chapter 3 and the "Annual Events" and
"Newspapers, Magazines, and Other Resources" sections of Chapter 7.)
Some items—tickets to certain events, television show tapings, and tours,
for example—require advance planning. Other things—special sales or
events, for example—require that you visit at certain times of the year.
Whenever you come and whatever you plan to do, however, I recommend packing a couple of key items:

- Student ID card (Most museums offer discounts for students, but
  only with identification.)
- Comfortable walking shoes (Nobody in New York cares what your
  feet look like.)
- An umbrella and raincoat (There's nothing worse than being un-
  prepared for rain.)
- A jacket and tie or a nice dress (in case you want to go to the opera
  or a fancy restaurant)
- Opera glasses (You'll be glad you have them if you go to the opera
  or the theater.)
- An address book and postcard stamps (so you don't need to hunt for
  a post office)
- Prescriptions (in case your luggage is lost or your purse is stolen) and
  an extra pair of glasses
- Traveler's checks
- A camera
- Tickets (airplane and otherwise)

All the little things you may want in your hotel room during your stay
cost a lot less at home than they do in New York. Most hotels supply
small sewing kits and night lights, and some will let you borrow an umbrella or hair dryer for free. But think of packing things like tissues,
film, aspirin, instant coffee, snacks, and gum.

Once you're in New York, I suggest you plan what you're going to
need for the day before leaving your hotel room. A lot of people just
put a couple of credit cards, their driver's license, and some money in
a secure pocket or money belt and everything else in a shoulder bag so
there's no worrying about a stolen purse or wallet. You might want to
leave your key at the front desk. Depending on the time of year, here
are the things I would take with me for a day of exploring:

- The addresses and phone numbers of places you plan to visit and details about how to get there
- The address and phone number of your hotel
- A bus and subway map
- Tissues
- A list of public bathrooms in the areas you'll be going (see Chapter 7)
- An umbrella
- A coat or sweater
- Subway tokens (They work on the bus, too.)
- Some loose change and small bills

Finally, don't forget this book!

II. Where to Eat It: Manhattan à la Carte

There is no shortage of guides to eating in Manhattan, because this city remains one of the great places in the world to dine out . . . and also because more and more of us are abandoning the home dining-room table. We are enjoying the pleasures of a vast selection of eating establishments that range from simple diners and coffee shops and cafes to colorful bistros, specialty houses that feature exotic foreign flavors, and grand rooms that are reserved for very special occasions.

I have tried to uncomplicate the Manhattan restaurant scene and provide you with useful information so that you can enjoy your experiences and get the most for your dollar. I have eaten in over 1,800 establishments of every kind and description in Manhattan and have investigated just about every food shop worth its salt. No other city in the world has the diversity or the quality that this one does . . . not even Paris. The problem is that so many choices can be intimidating and bewildering.

Let me set the guidelines. I make no pretense of being a professional food critic. I am presenting information from my own perspective: that of an average person who has spent over a quarter of a century in the field, who owns and operates his own restaurant and cake shop in Oregon, and who has had the opportunity to make judgments based on dining experiences in over 130 nations.

The New York restaurant scene is in constant change. No longer is it "in" to be extravagant; this is reflected in the prices at most Manhattan eating establishments. Price-fixed meals have become very popular, and even the fanciest places have taken a second look at their out-of-sight tabs.

Expense accounts are being carefully monitored. Food has become simpler and healthier. Casual attire is now taken for granted; it is the rare establishment that sticks to a serious dress code. Trendiness rules; the mob hops from one new hot spot to another. In the restaurant biz, it is truly the survival of the fittest. An interesting anomaly in all of this: never have fancier and richer desserts been more popular! (Le Cirque keeps five dessert chefs busy.)

Many restaurant guides give stars or ratings. I have chosen not to go that route. Only those establishments that I feel are especially commendable (for food, ambience, service, price) are included herein. The also-rans are not included, except in the "Don't bother" section, where I think you should know my feelings about some of the better-known places.

There are a number of things I look for. Good food, of course. A clean and inviting establishment. Value for money. Spotless kitchens and rest rooms. A tolerable noise level. Reservations that are efficiently honored. Uncrowded conditions.

I also have some personal peeves. Paper tablecloths. Polyester napkins. Imperious maitre d's. Tiny plates overflowing with food. Items piled in an unappetizing manner. Dirty, greasy menus. Chatty servers. Lengthy recitations of "specials" by waiters. Bills with taxes added into the total, thereby inflating tip calculations. Cold bread. Tepid soups. Overseasoned entrees. Hyper-sophisticated food combinations. Day-old desserts. Ice cream and sherbets that have been re-frozen. Being seated by the rest-room door. Haughty attitudes. You get the picture!

The first section of "Manhattan à la Carte" lists the outstanding places I have found, including address, neighborhood location, type of cuisine, and whether the establishment is open on Sunday. The next section features listings for different kinds of meals and occasions, such as breakfast, brunch, late evening, outdoor cafes, bistros, places for kids, coffeehouses, personal favorites. burgers, seafood, ethnic specialties, and more. In the following section, I have compiled a listing of major food items and dishes, telling where the best can be found. Rest assured, this is the cream of the crop, and the prices are right! Finally, I list and describe several hundred places that deserve special attention. These reviews include the important features of the establishment (location, phone, pricing, meals served) and a general feel for the ambience. In most cases I have purposely not been too specific on menu items, as they tend to change almost overnight. I have eliminated trendy establishments that will not survive, in my opinion, in this fast-changing environment.

A few housekeeping details. "Inexpensive," to me, means under $15 for a meal, per person, without drinks. "Moderate" is roughly $16–$34; "moderately expensive," $35 – $45; "expensive," $46 and up. Most establishments take all major credit cards, although a few will accept American Express only. Sometimes the owners will take only cash. When applicable, information is mentioned in the listings. These establishments will usually take a check, if proper identification is presented. I am not a wine expert, therefore commentary on wine lists is not included. If you have a question about dress codes, call the establishment. If a gentleman forgets his jacket and the dress code requires one, most places will provide a loaner. Specify "no smoking" if you so desire.

In many cases, reservations are essential. An increasingly annoying habit is for the establishment to ask for a telephone contact or a reconfirmation. I strongly object to the latter. If you arrive on time, you should be seated immediately and not be shoved off to the bar so that your drink tab will grow heftier. You have every right to talk to the person in charge if the food, seating, or service is not to your liking. Do not make a scene, however. Check your bill carefully. Mistakes can happen. Figure your tip (a chart is included in this volume) on the total amount of food and drink. An additional gratuity to the maitre d' or captain is necessary only

when a special service has been offered. A money-saving tip: more and
more restaurants are offering off-menu daily specials. Be careful, because
the pricing is usually considerably higher than printed menu items. Don't
be afraid to ask for prices.

Again I must mention how volatile the eating scene is in Manhattan.
Chefs and owners come and go. Restaurants change their format overnight. What is great one day can be not-so-great the next day. Because
I self-publish, my information is more current than that provided by large
publishers, but still some things may become out-of-date. If this happens, please accept my apologies. If you disagree with an evaluation,
please remember that this is an informed but *personal* opinion. I would
like to hear from you if you have had a particularly good or bad
experience.

Bon appetit!

Quick Reference Guide

Over 500 Best Taste Treats (Eat In and Takeout)—An Exclusive List:

Antipasti, hot: Pasta Roma (315 W 57th St)
Antipasto bar: Trattoria dell'Arte (900 Seventh Ave) and Da Umberto (107 W 17th St)
Appetizers, gourmet: Russ & Daughters (179 E Houston St)
Apple pandowdy: An American Place (2 Park Ave)
Babka: Babka Bakery Cafe (2372 Broadway) and Gertel's (53 Hester St)
Bagels: Bagel City (720 W 181st St), H&H Bagels East (1551 Second Ave), and Mom's Bagels (15 W 45th St)
Baked Alaska: Rainbow Room (30 Rockefeller Plaza)
Baked Alaska (by order): G&M Pastries (1006 Madison Ave)
Baklava: Alleva Dairy (188 Grand St)
Barbecue items, Chinese: Quon Jan Meat Products (79 Christie St)
Baskets, corporate: Basketfull (1133 Broadway) and Manhattan Fruitier (210 E 6th St)
Baskets, picnic: In a Basket (226 E 83rd St)
Bass, striped: Scarlatti (34 E 52nd St)
Bean curd, stuffed: Golden Unicorn (18 E Broadway)
Beef, boiled: North Garden Restaurant (24 Pell St)
Beef bourguignonne: Philippe (1202 Lexington Ave)
Beef stroganoff: Pie Restaurant (340 E 86th St)
Beef Wellington: One If by Land, Two If by Sea (17 Barrow St)
Bialys: Kossar's (367 Grand Ave)
Bigoli (Venetian pasta): Remi (145 W 53rd St)
Biscuits, blueberry-peach: Taylor's Prepared Foods (523 Hudson St)
Biscuits, pepper: Vesuvio Bakery (160 Prince St)
Blini: The Pie (340 E 86th St)
Blintzes: Mama Leah's (429 Amsterdam Ave), Kiev Restaurant (117 Second Ave), and Ludlow Cafe (85 Ludlow St)
Bouillabaisse: Gotham Bar and Grill (12 E 12th St)
Bratwurst: Schaller & Weber (1654 Second Ave)
Bread, Afghan: 764 Ninth Ave
Bread, basil with mozzarella: Pâtisserie Encore (141 Second Ave)

Bread, chocolate: Ecce Panis (1120 Third Ave)

Bread, corn: Moishe's Bakery (181 E Houston St, 115 Second Ave) and 107 West (2787 Broadway)

Bread, Eli's: E.A.T. (1064 Madison Ave) and other gourmet shops

Bread, general: Hot & Crusty (various locations, including Third Ave at 17th St, Second Ave at 44th St, Second Ave at 63rd St, and Broadway at 87th St)

Bread, Indian: Akbar (475 Park Ave) and Dawat (210 E 58th St)

Bread, Italian whole wheat; D&G Bakery (45 Spring St)

Bread, raisin-nut: E.A.T. (1064 Madison Ave)

Bread, Swiss health: Thorough Bread (450 Park Ave)

Bread, whole wheat: The Bread Shop Café (3139 Broadway)

Bread, whole wheat French: Dean & Deluca (560 Broadway)

Brie, baked: Carnegie Hill Cafe (1308 Madison Ave)

Brioche: Lipstick Café (885 Third Ave) and Café Europa (347 E 54th St)

Brownies: Karen's (187 Columbus Ave)

Buns, sticky: William Greenberg (1377 Third Ave) and Pâtisserie Les Friandises (972 Lexington Ave and 665 Amsterdam Ave)

Burritos: Chelsea Kitchen (218 Eighth Ave)

Burritos (to go): Benny's Burritos (113 Greenwich Ave)

Cake, apple: The Cream Puff (1388 Second Ave)

Cake, Black Forest: Éclair (141 W 72nd St)

Cake, blackout: Gertel's (53 Hester St) and Serendipity 3 (225 E 60th St)

Cake, butter cream and chocolate: Moishe's Bakery (181 E Houston St)

Cake, carrot: Carrot Top Pastries (5025 Broadway)

Cake, chocolate: Hard Rock Cafe (221 W 57th St) and Jo-Jo (160 E 64th St)

Cake, chocolate meringue with chocolate mousse: Bakery Soutine (106 W 70th St)

Cake, chocolate mousse: Parioli Romanissimo (24 E 81st St)

Cake, chocolate mousse, individual: City Bakery (22 E 17th St)

Cake, chocolate raspberry: Caffe Roma (385 Broome St)

Cake, chocolate trianon: Colette French Pastry (1136 Third Ave)

Cake, coconut brandy: Metropolis Cafe (31 Union Sq)

Cake, fudge layer: Caffe Bianco (1486 Second Ave)

Cake, fruit, Milanese Italian: Bleecker Street Pastry (245 Bleecker St)

Cake, gourmet: Les Délices Guy Pascal (1231 Madison Ave, 2241 Broadway, and 939 First Ave)

Calamari: Extra! Extra! (767 Second Ave)

Cal-Mex offerings: Bertha's (2160 Broadway)

Calzone: Little Italy Gourmet Pizza (65 Vanderbilt Ave and other locations) and Piatti Pronti (34 W 56th St)

Cannelloni: Piemonte Ravioli Company (190 Grand St) and Giambelli (46 E 50th St)

Cannoli: Caffe Vivaldi (32 Jones St) and De Roberti's Pastry Shop (176 First Ave)

Cassoulet: La Côte Basque (5 E 55th St), La Colombe d'Or (134 E 26th St), Les Halles (411 Park Ave), Les Pyrénées (251 W 51st St), and Quatorze (240 W 14th St)

Caviar: Petrossian (182 W 58th St)

Caviar, Beluga: Iron Gate (424 W 54th St)

Ceviche (marinated seafood): Albuquerque Eats (375 Third Ave) and Rosa Mexicano (1063 First Ave)

Champagne: Garnet Wines and Liquor (929 Lexington Ave) and Gotham Liquors (1543 Third Ave)

Cheese cart: Parioli Romanissimo (24 E 81st St)

Cheese selection: Grace's Marketplace (1237 Third Ave) and Murray's Cheese Shop (257 Bleecker St)

Cheesecake, combination fruit: Eileen's Cheese Cake (17 Cleveland Pl)

Cheese sticks and cheese rolls, gourmet: Cheesestick Factory (410 E 13th St)

Chicken, baked: Harper (1303 Third Ave, at 74th St)

Chicken, beggar's: Shun Lee Palace (155 E 55th St)

Chicken, Cajun: Susan Simon (32 E Second Ave)

Chicken, Dijon: Zabar's (2245 Broadway)

Chicken dishes: International Poultry (432 Sixth Ave)

Chicken, free-range: Amazing Foods (807 Washington St)

Chicken, fried: Yellow Rose Cafe (450 Amsterdam Ave) and Lola (30 W 22nd St)

Chicken, grilled: Rainbow Chicken (2801 Broadway, at 108th St)

Chicken-in-the-pot: Fine & Schapiro (138 W 72nd St) and Golden's Restaurant Deli (148 W 51st St)

Chicken liver with truffle mousse paté: Main Course (1608 Third Ave)

Chicken pot pie: Cafe at Between the Bread (141 E 56th St) and Jim McMullen's (1341 Third Ave)

Chicken salad: China Grill (52 W 53rd St) and Michael's (24 W 55th St)

Chicken salad, coriander: Petak's (1244 Madison Ave)

Chicken salad, sesame: Indiana (80 Second Ave)

Chicken salad, smoked: Madeline's (177 Prince St)

Chicken, skinless and marinated: Koo Koo Roo (792 Lexington Ave)

Chicken soup: Second Avenue Kosher Delicatessen and Restaurant (156 Second Ave)

Chicken, Southern-fried: Memphis (329 Columbus Ave)

Chili: Manhattan Chili Company (302 Bleecker St)

Chili, Texas: As You Like It (120 Hudson St)

Chinese vegetables: Kam Man (200 Canal St)
Chocolate desserts: Baratti & Milano (697 Madison Ave)
Chocolate ovation dessert: Josephina (1900 Broadway)
Chocolate plate: Arizona 206 (206 E 60th St)
Cholent: Second Avenue Kosher Delicatessen and Restaurant (156 Second Ave)
Chops, mutton: Keens Chop House (72 W 36th St)
Chorizo (Spanish sausage): La Ideal (166 Eighth Ave)
Cioppino: Coastal (300 Amsterdam Ave)
Clams, baked: Frank's Trattoria (371 First Ave)
Coffee beans: Porto Rico Importing Company (201 Bleecker St) and Zabar's (80th St and Broadway)
Coffee, iced: Oren's Daily Roast (Third Ave and 30th St)
Coffee, morning: Caffe Dante (81 MacDougal St)
Cookies, almond: Fung Wong Bakery (30 Mott St)
Cookies, butter: CBK of New York (226 E 83rd St)
Cookies, chocolate chubbie: Sarabeth's Kitchen (423 Amsterdam Ave)
Cookies, fortune (wholesale): Key Lee Fortune Cookies (178 Lafayette St)
Cookies, oatmeal: Cafe 1112 (2885 Broadway)
Corned beef hash: Broadway Diner (1726 Broadway) and Carnegie Deli (854 Seventh Ave)
Couscous: Provence (38 MacDougal St, on Sunday), Cafe Crocodile (354 E 74th St) and La Kasbah (70 W 71st St)
Crab: Pisacane Midtown Corp. (940 First Ave)
Crab cakes: Acme Bar and Grill (9 Great Jones St) and Metropolis Cafe (31 Union Square W)
Crabmeat salad in dill sauce: Fledermaus (1 Seaport Pl)
Crabs, Maryland spiced: Sidewalkers (12 W 72nd St)
Crème brûleé: Le Cirque (58 E 65th St), Tribeca Grill (375 Greenwich), and La Métairie (189 W 10th St)
Crème caramel: Barbetta (321 W 46th St) and Man Ray (169 Eighth Ave)
Crêpes: Crêpes & Co (30 Carmine St)
Croissants: Paris Croissant (609 Madison Ave, 1776 Broadway, and other locations)
Danish, cheese: Budapest Pastries (207 E 84th St)
Deli items, Italian: Lisa's (901 Park Ave)
Delicatessen assortment: Dean & Deluca (560 Broadway)
Doughnuts: Fisher & Levy (875 Third Ave)
Doughnuts, jelly: Gertel's Bake Shop (53 Hester St)
Doughnuts, whole wheat: Cupcake Cafe (522 Ninth Ave)
Duck: Apple Restaurant (17 Waverly Pl)
Duck, Peking: Peking Duck House Restaurant (22 Mott St) and Shun Lee Palace (155 E 55th St)

Duck, roasted: La Bohême (24 Minetta Lane) and Four Seasons (99 E 52nd St)

Dumplings: Chin Chin (216 E 49th St) and Dumpling House (111 Lafayette St)

Dumplings, Chinese: Excellent Dumplings (111 Lafayette St), Pig Heaven (1540 Second Ave), and Great Shanghai (27 Division St)

Egg cream: Carnegie Deli (854 Seventh Ave), EJ's Luncheonette (433 Amsterdam Ave), Mill Luncheonette (2895 Broadway), and Moisha's Luncheonette (239 Grand St)

Eggplant salad: Juliana (891 Eighth Ave)

Eggs, fresh Jersey: (72 E 7th St, Thurs only: 7 a.m. - 5:30 p.m.)

Eggs, Jersey (extra large): 1750 Second Ave

Eggs, Scotch: Myers of Keswick (634 Hudson St)

Empanadas: Ruben's (64 Fulton St)

Enchiladas: Lucy's Restaurant (503 Columbus Ave)

Espresso: Caffe Dante (79-81 MacDougal St)

Fajitas: Zarela (953 Second Ave)

Falafel: Lox Around the Clock (676 Sixth Ave) and Pita Cuisine of SoHo (65 Spring St)

Fish, fresh: Citarella (2135 Broadway) and Central Fish Company (527 Ninth Ave)

Fish, smoked: Russ & Daughters (179 E Houston St), Barney Greengrass (541 Amsterdam Ave), and M. Schacht Company (99 Second Ave)

Fish, smoked, with toasted French bread: Délices de France (289 Madison Ave)

Flapjacks, walnut apple: West Side Storey (700 Columbus Ave)

Foie gras: La Caravelle (38 W 55th St)

Food and kitchen extravaganza (best all-around in the world): Zabar's (2245 Broadway)

Frankfurters: Leo's Famous (861 Sixth Ave)

French fries: Café de Paris (924 Second Ave), Tout Va Bien (311 W 51st St), Café de Bruxelles (118 Greenwich Ave), Steak Frites (9 E 16th St), and Michael's (24 W 55th St)

French toast: Lox Around the Clock (676 Sixth Ave, 1700 Second Ave)

Frozen dessert, low calorie: Tasti D-Lite (Lexington Ave at 86th St)

Fruit tarts: Bett's Best (203 Eighth Ave)

Fruits and vegetables, fresh: Fairway (2127 Broadway) and Balducci's (424 Sixth Ave)

Fruit dessert plate, fresh: Primavera (1578 First Ave)

Game, fresh: Ottomanelli's Meat Market (285 Bleecker St)

Gâteau Charlene Blanche: Lanciani (275 W 4th St)

Gelati: Caffe Dante (81 MacDougal St) and Gelateria Siracusa (65 Fourth Ave)

Goose, barbecued: Oriental Pearl (103 Mott St)

Grill, mixed: Delmonico's (56 Beaver St)
Groceries, discount: Gourmet Garage (47 Wooster)
Guacamole: Manhattan Chili Company (302 Bleecker St) and Rosa
   Mexicano (1063 First Ave)
Gumbo: Century Cafe (132 W 43rd St)
Ham, apricot-glazed: Word of Mouth (1012 Lexington Ave)
Ham (Westphalian) and brie: Food Store (58 Greenwich Ave)
Hen, roasted Guinea: 44 (44 W 44th St)
Hens, Cornish: Lorenzo and Maria's Kitchen (1418 Third Ave)
Herbs, Chinese: Hang Fung Tai (78 Mulberry St)
Hamburgers: Jackson Hole Wyoming Burgers (232 E 64th and
   other locations), Corner Bistro (331 W 4th St), Hamburger
   Harry's (157 Chambers and 145 W 45th St), and Taste of the
   Apple (1016 Second Ave)
Heros: Italian Food Center (186 Grand St) and Hero Boy (492
   Ninth Ave)
Hotcakes: Royal Canadian Pancake House (145 Hudson St)
Hot dogs: Gray's Papaya (8th St and Sixth Ave)
Hotpot, Japanese: Seryna (11 E 53rd St)
Ice cream: Serendipity 3 (225 E 60th St)
Jambalaya: 107 West (2787 Broadway)
Jambon: Raoul's Boucherie (180 Prince St)
Jerk pork: Vernon's Jerk Paradise (252 W 29th St)
Kale, deep-fried: New Haven Pizza Co. (140 W 13th St)
Kebabs: Afghan Tea Room (631 Ninth Ave) and Turkish Kitchen
   (386 Third Ave)
Kielbasa: First Avenue Meat Products (140 First Ave)
Kosher corned beef: Bernstein-on-Essex (135 Essex St)
Lamb, rack of: Alcala (349 Amsterdam Ave) and La Côte Basque
   (5 E 55th St)
Lamb stew: Pamir (1437 Second Ave)
Lamb sandwich, baked: Arizona 206 (206 E 60th St)
Lasagna: Green Noodle (313 Columbus Ave)
Linzer torte: T.A.S.T.E. Sensations (412 E 9th St)
Liver, chopped: Mama Leah's to Go (429 Amsterdam Ave) and
   Second Avenue Kosher Delicatessen (156 Second Ave)
Lobster: Shell Lobster & Seafood (412 W 13th St), Docks
   (2427 Broadway, 633 Third Ave), and Wilkinson's
   (1573 York Ave)
Lobster bisque: Neuman and Bogdonoff (1385 Third Ave)
Lobster, poached: La Petite Ferme (973 Lexington Ave)
Lobster thermidor: Rainbow Room (30 Rockefeller Plaza)
Marzipan: Cream Puff (1388 Second Ave) and Elk Candy
   Company (240 E 86th St)
Meat, kosher, grilled: Cafe Masada (1239 First Ave)
Meat loaf: Cafe Mortimer (155 E 75th St)
Meat, wholesale: Old Bohemian Meat (452 W 13th St)

Meats and poultry (reasonably priced): Empire Purveyors (901 First Ave)

Meats, prime: Jefferson Market (455 Sixth Ave) and City Wholesale Meats (305 E 85th St)

Meringue, chocolate hazelnut: De Roberti's (176 1st St)

Morels: Amazing Foods (807 Washington St)

Moussaka: Periyali (35 W 20th St)

Mousse, white chocolate, in a bittersweet chocolate basket: Manhattan Ocean Club (East River at 30th St)

Mozzarella: Alleva Dairy (188 Grand Ave) and Melampo (105 Sullivan St)

Mozzarella and ricotta, homemade: Russo and Son Dairy Products (334 E 11th St)

Muffins: Between the Bread (141 E 56th St), Michael's Muffins (158 Seventh Ave), My Favorite Muffins (2330 Broadway), Petak's (1244 Madison Ave), Lee & Elle (336 Madison Ave), and Connecticut Muffin (206 Elizabeth St)

Muffin tops: Bloomingdale's Bakery (1000 Third Ave)

Mushrooms, wild: Grace's Marketplace (1237 Third Ave)

Nachos: Benny's Burritos (93 Ave A)

Napoléon: Ecco (124 Chambers St)

Natural foods: Whole Foods in SoHo (117 Prince St)

Noodles: Marnie's Noodle Shop (466 Hudson St)

Noodles, buckwheat: Honmura An (170 Mercer St)

Noodles, Chinese: Yat Gaw Min Company (100 Reade St)

Noodles, cold with hot sesame sauce: Sung Chu Mei (1367 First Ave)

Nuts: A. L. Bazzini Co. (339 Greenwich St)

Nuts and packaged dried fruits (great prices): J. Wolsk and Company (81 and 87 Ludlow St)

Oatmeal: What's Cookin' (18 E 41st St) and Sarabeth's Kitchen (1295 Madison Ave)

Olives: International Grocery Store (529 Ninth Ave)

Omelets: Romaine De Lyon (29 E 61st St) and Potbelly (92 Christopher St)

Onion rings: Palm (837 Second Ave) and Lola (30 W 22nd St)

Orange juice, fresh-squeezed: hole-in-the-wall stand at 1428 Sixth Ave

Organic foods: Angelica's (147 First Ave)

Organic produce: Bink & Bink (117 Perry St)

Oysters, Long Island: Café des Artistes (1 W 67th St)

Oyster stew: Grand Central Oyster Bar Restaurant (Grand Central Station)

Paella: Sevilla (62 Charles St)

Pancakes: Friend of a Farmer (77 Irving Pl) and Royal Canadian Pancake House (145 Hudson St and 1004 Second Ave)

Pancakes, blue corn: Mesa Grill (102 Fifth Ave)

Pancakes, potato: Rolf's (281 Third Ave)
Pasta: Arqua (281 Church St), Gabriel's (11 W 60th St), and
   Todaro Bros. (555 Second Ave)
Pasta, angel hair: Contrapunto (1009 Third Ave), Piemonte
   Homemade Ravioli Company (190 Grand St), Nanni's (146 E
   46th St), and Remi (145 W 53rd St)
Pasta, handmade egg: Balducci's (424 Sixth Ave)
Pasta (inexpensive): La Marca (282 Third Ave)
Pasta (to go): Primo Piatto (1498-B First Ave)
Pasta, Venetian: Remi (145 W 53rd St)
Pastrami: Bernstein-on-Essex (135 Essex St) and Carnegie
   Delicatessen and Restaurant (854 Seventh Ave)
Pastries, Hungarian: Budapest Pastries (207 E 84th St) and
   Hungarian Pastry Shop (1030 Amsterdam Ave)
Paté: Les Trois Petite Cochons (453 Greenwich St)
Paté, chicken liver: Café de la Gare (143 Perry St)
Peanut butter: Country Life (48 Trinity Pl)
Peanuts, candied: A. L. Bazzini Co. (339 Greenwich St)
Pecan squares: Slice of Orange (987 Lexington Ave)
Penne with Prosciutto: Petak's (1244 Madison Ave)
Peppers, roasted: Rao's (455 E 114th St)
Peppers, stuffed: Bo Ky (80 Bayard St)
Petit fours: Colette (1136 Third Ave)
Pheasant: An American Place (2 Park Ave)
Pickles: Guss Pickles (35 Essex St)
Pie, apple: William Greenberg Jr. Desserts (912 Seventh Ave)
Pie, caramel-nut crunch: Houlihan's (729 Seventh Ave)
Pie, cheddar-crust apple: Little Pie Company of the Big Apple
   (424 W 43rd St)
Pie, chocolate pecan: Gindi Desserts (935 Broadway)
Pie, deep-dish apple: One Hudson Cafe (1 Hudson St)
Pie, Key lime: Little Pie Company (424 W 43rd St)
Pie, rum pecan: A Sweet Place (301 E 91st St)
Pie, shepherd's: Landmark Tavern (626 11th Ave)
Pie, sour-cream apple: Gindi Desserts (935 Broadway)
Pie, walnut sour-cream apple: Little Pie Company (424 W 43rd
   St)
Pies, pot: Alain's Cheese Please Deli (158 E 39th St)
Pig sandwich (pulled pork): Hard Rock Cafe (221 W 57th St)
Pig, suckling: Sabor (20 Cornelia St)
Pig's feet: Brasserie des Théatres (243 W 46th St)
Pizza: John's Pizzeria (278 Bleecker St), Yellowfingers di Nuovo
   (200 E 60th St), Famous Ray's (465 Sixth Ave), and Fisher &
   Levy (875 Third Ave)
Pizza, deep-dish: PIZZAPIAZZA (785 Broadway)
Pizza, Sicilian: Sal's and Carmine Pizza (2533 Broadway)
Pizzas, designer: Paper Moon Milano (39 E 58th St)

Poor-boy sandwiches: Two Boots (37 Ave A)
Popcorn: Creative Corn Co. (1275 Lexington Ave)
Popovers: Popover Cafe (551 Amsterdam Ave)
Pork: Faicco's Pork Store (260 Bleecker St)
Pork, European-style cured: Salumeria Biellese (376 Eighth Ave)
Pork loin: Sabor (20 Cornelia St)
Potato chips, homemade: Amsterdam's Bar and Rotisserie (454 Broadway)
Potato pancakes: Ideal Lunch and Bar (238 E 86th St)
Potatoes, home-fried: Ideal Lunch and Bar (238 E 86th St)
Pot-au-feu: La Grenouille (3 E 52nd St)
Pot roast: Café des Artistes (1 W 67th St)
Pretzels: Pennsylvania Pretzel Company (295 Greenwich St)
Pretzels and cookies, hand-dipped chocolate: Evelyn's Chocolates (4 John St, 9-A Beaver St)
Prime rib: Smith & Wollensky (201 E 49th St)
Profiteroles: Chez Ma Tante (189 W 10th St)
Pudding, bread: Mark's (25 E 77th St)
Pudding, bread (whiskey-flavored): Washington Market (162 Duane St)
Pudding, chocolate: Jim McMullen (1341 Third Ave)
Pudding, Japanese bread: The City Bakery (22 E 17th St)
Pudding, rice: Marti Kebab (228 E 24th St) and Chelsea Central (227 Tenth Ave)
Quiche: Chez Laurence (245 Madison Ave)
Quiche Lorraine: René Pujol (321 W 51st St)
Raspberry Charlotte: Dolci on Park Caffe (12 Park Ave)
Ravioli: The Ravioli Store (75 Sullivan St), Piemonte Homemade Ravioli Company (190 Grand St), and Di Palo Dairy Store (206 Grand St)
Ravioli, steamed Vietnamese: Indochine (430 Lafayette St)
Raw bar: Citarella Fish Company (2135 Broadway)
Relish, cranberry: Artichoke (968 Second Ave)
Ribs: Bistro 95 (718 Amsterdam Ave), Sylvia's Restaurant (328 Lenox Ave), Tony Roma's (400 E 57th St and other locations), Wylie's Ribs and Company (891 First Ave), and Brother Jimmy's Bar-B-Q (1461 First Ave)
Ribs, barbecued: Mesa Grill (102 Fifth Ave)
Ribs, short, braised: Lespinasse (St Regis Hotel, 2 E 55th St)
Ring, apple: Lafayette (298 Bleecker St)
Risotto: Il Nostro (520 Columbus Ave)
Rugelbach: Royale Pastry Shop (237 W 72nd St)
Salad: Blazing Salads (228 W 4th St and 1135 First Ave), Cafe Melville (110 Barrow St), The French Bakery (54 W 55th St), Courtyard Cafe (130 E 39th St), and The Salad Bowl (566 Seventh Ave)
Salad, Caesar: The Post House (28 E 53rd St)

Salad, cucumber: Neuman and Bogdonoff (1385 Third Ave)

Salad, potato, Nicoise: Manny Wolf's (145 E 49th St)

Salad, seafood: Gotham Bar and Grill (12 E 12th St)

Salad, tuna: Todaro Bros. (555 Second Ave)

Salad, vegetable: Michelle's Kitchen (1392 Madison Ave)

Salmon, marinated: La Réserve (4 W 49th St)

Salmon mousse: Silver Palate (274 Columbus Ave)

Salmon, sandwich, smoked Norwegian: Peter Dent (120 Hudson St)

Salmon, smoked: Starfish Enterprises (233 Ninth Ave)

Salta in Bocca: Salta in Bocca (179 Madison Ave)

Sandwiches: Cucina & Company (200 Park Ave), La Boulangère (49 E 21st St), Cooper's Coffee (2151 Broadway), Jerry's (103 Second Ave), Olive's (120 Prince St), and Donald Sacks (3 World Financial Ctr)

Sandwich, brisket: Second Avenue Kosher Delicatessen (156 Second Ave)

Sandwich, focaccia: Yellowfingers di Nuovo (200 E 60th St)

Sandwich, Italian: Panini (365 E 62nd St)

Sandwich, puff-pastry: Dufour Pastry Kitchens (808 Washington St)

Sandwich, tea: Mortimer's (1057 Lexington Ave)

Sandwich, turkey: Viand Coffee Shop (673 Madison Ave)

Sandwich, vegetable paté: Lamston's (205 E 42nd St) and Fisher & Levy (1026 Second Ave)

Sauerkraut: Katz's Delicatessen (205 E Houston St)

Sausage: Kurowycky Meat Products (124 First Ave)

Sausage, French: P. Carnevale and Son (631 Ninth Ave)

Sausage, Hungarian: Tibor Meat Specialties (1508 Second Ave)

Scallops: Bouley (165 Duane St) and Le Bernardin (155 W 51st St)

Schnecken: William Greenberg Jr. (1377 Third Ave, 1000 Madison Ave and 912 Seventh Ave)

Schnitzel: Eva's (1589 First Ave)

Scones: the Water Club (East River at 30th St), the Muffin Shop (Columbus Ave and 70th St), and Mangia (54 W 56th St)

Seafood dinners: Wilkinson's (1573 York Ave), Le Bernardin (155 W 51st St), and Le Pescadou (18 King St)

Seafood platter: Mezzogiorno (195 Spring St)

Shrimp, blackened Louisiana: Four Seasons (99 E 52nd St)

Shrimp creole: Jezebel (630 Ninth Ave)

Shrimp, fresh: Sun Golden Island (1-3 Elizabeth St)

Shrimp, frozen: Hyfund Company (75 Mulberry St)

Smorgasbord plate: Aquavit (13 W 54th St)

Snacks, soups, sandwiches: Serendipity 3 (225 E 60th St)

Snails: Lutèce (249 E 50th St)

Sole, Dover: Le Régence (37 E 64th St) and La Côte Basque (5 E 55th St)

Sorbet: La Boîte En Bois (75 W 68th St)

Soufflé, chocolate cappuccino: Trumpets (Grand Hyatt Hotel, 109 E 42nd St)

Soufflés: Capsouto Frères (451 Washington St) and La Côte Basque (5 E 55th St)

Soup, black bean: Union Square Cafe (21 E 16th St)

Soup, Chinese: Chao Chow (111 Mott St)

Soup, French onion: La Bonne Soupe (48 W 55th St)

Soup, Mandalay fish: Road to Mandalay (380 Broome St)

Soup, minestrone: Genoa (271 Amsterdam Ave) and Il Vagabondo (351 E 62nd St)

Soup, sorrel: The Box Tree (250 E 49th St)

Soup, tomato: Sarabeth's Kitchen (423 Amsterdam Ave and 1295 Madison Ave)

Soup, vegetable: Country Host (1435 Lexington Ave)

Soups, homemade: Kiev Restaurant (Second Ave at 7th St)

Southern-style food: Memphis (329 Columbus Ave)

Spareribs, Chinese: Fu's (1395 Second Ave)

Spices: Aphrodisia (282 Bleecker St)

Spices, Indian: Spice and Sweet Mahal (135 Lexington Ave)

Spinach pies, Greek: Poseidon Bakery (629 Ninth Ave)

Spring rolls, crab: Vong (200 E 54th St)

Steak: Sparks (210 E 46th St)

Steak, Black Angus, and French fries: Steak Frites (9 E 16th St)

Steak, Cajun rib: The Post House (28 E 63rd St)

Steak, pepper: Chez Josephine (414 W 42nd St)

Steak, Porterhouse: Manhattan Cafe (1161 First Ave)

Steak tartare: Voulez-Vous (1462 First Ave)

Strawberry shortcake: An American Place (2 Park Ave)

Strudel: The Cream Puff (1388 Second Ave) and Mocca Hungarian (1588 Second Ave)

Sushi: Iso (175 Second Ave), TakeSushi (71 Vanderbilt Ave), Ten Kai (920 W 56th St), Hatsuhana (17 E 48th St), Nippon (155 E 52nd St), and Akemi (1128 Third Ave)

Sweetbreads: Orso (322 W 46th St)

Swordfish, grilled: Chez Ma Tante (189 W 10th St)

Tabbouleh: Benny's (321½ Amsterdam Ave and 37 Seventh Ave) and La Kasbah (70 W 71st St)

Tacos: Rosa Mexicano (1063 First Ave)

Tapas, Spanish: Alcala (349 Amsterdam Ave), El Cid (322 W 15th St), and Pamplona (4 W 22nd St)

Tart, apple: Quatorze (240 W 14th St and 323 E 79th St)

Tarts and logs, stuffed puff pastry: Dufour Pastry Kitchen (808 Washington St)

Tarts, coconut: Saint Honoré Bakery (28 Bowery)

Tartufo: Erminia (250 E 83rd St), Il Corallo (176 Prince St), and Tartufo Gelato (37-22 13th St)

Tea and coffee, iced: Henri's (357 Bleecker St)

Tempura: Mitsukoshi (461 Park Ave) and Inagiku (Waldorf-Astoria, 111 E 49th St)

Tirami su ("lift me up") dessert: Mezzogiorno (195 Spring St), Caffe Dante (79 McDougal St), and Biricchino (260 W 29th St)

Tofu: Little Mushroom Café (1439 Second Ave)

Torte, chocolate mocha: Ecce Panis (1120 Third Ave)

Torte, delizia: Sant Ambroeus (1000 Madison Ave)

Torte, Viennese chocolate: Peacock Caffe (24 Greenwich Ave)

Truffles: Black Hound (149 First Ave), La Maison du Chocolat (25 E 73rd St), and Gindi Desserts (935 Broadway)

Truffles, champagne: Teuscher (25 E 61st St)

Truffles, chocolate: Rich Treats (18 W 55th St)

Truffles, Grand Marnier: Normandie Chocolat (338 E 116th St)

Truffle tart: Encore (141 Second Ave)

Turnover, apple: La Boulangère (49 E 21st St)

Veal: Pierre au Tunnel (250 W 47th St)

Veal chops: Aperitivo (29 W 56th St)

Veal cutlet: Trastevere (309 E 83rd St)

Veal scaloppini: Zinno's (126 W 13th St)

Veal stew: Pierre au Tunnel (250 W 47th St)

Vegan baking: Whole Earth Bakery & Kitchen (70 Spring St)

Vegetables, Chinese: Sun Kwong Lee (85 Mulberry St)

Vegetable terrine: Tropica (200 Park Ave) and Montrachet (239 W Broadway)

Vegetarian items: Vegetarian's Paradise (144 W 4th St)

Vegetarian meals: Natural Gourmet Cookery School (48 W 21st St)

Venison: Chanterelle (2 Harrison St)

Vinegars: Marketplace (54 W 74th St)

Waffles: Berry's (180 Spring St)

Waffles, Belgian: Cafe Bruxelles (118 Greenwich Ave)

Waffles, pumpkin: Sarabeth's Kitchen (1295 Madison Ave)

Whiskeys, malt: SoHo Wines and Spirits (461 W Broadway)

Wines, European: Quality House (2 Park Ave)

Wursts: Wurst (2832 Broadway)

Yogurt, frozen: Yogen Fruz (2151 Broadway)

Yogurt shake: TCBY (1452 Second Ave)

Zabaglione: Il Monello (1460 Second Ave) and Parioli Romanissimo (24 E 81st St)

Egg cream is a New York specialty drink. Here is the formula: combine and shake one quart of milk, a bottle of seltzer water, and two scoops of Fox syrup. Actually, there is no egg and no cream in the drink!

Barbecues

Great barbecue spots are not generally a Manhattan specialty, but here are some of the better ones:

Big Wong (67 Mott St): Chinese style.
Brother's Bar-B-Q (228 W Houston St): Smoked ribs.
Buckaroo's (1431 First Ave): Let them buck!
Copeland's (547 W 145th St): Harlem setting.
Dallas BBQ (1265 Third Ave, 27 W 72nd St, 21 University Place, 132 Second Ave, 315 Sixth Ave): Big and busy, but only fair in quality.
Rusty's (1271 Third Ave): All-American tasty baby back ribs.
Shun Lee Cafe (43 W Fifth St): Classy Chinese.
Sylvia's (328 Lenox Ave): Reputation better than the food.
Wylie's Ribs (891 First Ave): Consistently good.

Before Theater

It is best to let your waiter know when you sit down that you are planning to go to theater so that service can be properly adjusted. Also, if it is raining, be sure to allow extra time for getting a taxi. Some restaurants have specially priced pre-theater dinners.

Alo Alo (1030 Third Ave)
American Festival Cafe (Rockefeller Center)
Andiamo (1991 Broadway)
Antolotti's (337 E 49th)
Aquavit (13 W 54th St)
Arqua (281 Church St)
Barbetta (321 W 46th St)
Brasserie des Théatres (245 W 48th St)
Cafe Botanica (Essex House, 160 Central Park S)
Cafe de Bruxelles (118 Greenwich Ave)
Café Greco (1390 Second Ave)
Café Un Deux Trois (123 W 44th St)
Century Cafe (132 W 43rd St)
Charlotte (Macklowe Hotel, 145 W 44th St)
Chez Josephine (414 W 42nd St)
Cité (120 W 51st St)
Darbar (44 W 56th St)
Dawat (210 E 58th St)
Edwardian Room (Plaza Hotel, Fifth Ave at 59th St)
"44" (Royalton Hotel, 44 W 44th St)
Four Seasons (99 E 52nd St)
Gino (780 Lexington Ave)
JW (Marriott Marquis Hotel, 1535 Broadway, at Times Sq)
La Boîte en Bois (75 W 68th St)
La Caravelle (33 W 55th St)

La Réserve (4 W 49th St)
Le Chantilly (106 E 57th)
Marchi's (251 E 31st St)
Olde Garden and Winery (15 W 29th St)
Orso (322 W 46th St)
Rainbow Room (Rockefeller Center, 65th floor)
Sam's (152 W 52nd St)
Symphony Cafe (950 Eighth Ave)
Tavern on the Green (Central Park W at 67th St)
Trionfo (224 W 51st St)
Tropica (Met Life building, 200 Park Ave)
Voulez-Vous (1462 First Ave)

Bistros

What is a bistro? It is a small restaurant with food based on the hearty cuisine of Lyons, which is designed to go with wine. (This is by contrast with a brasserie, which is beer-oriented.) A bistro serves lunch and dinner, is usually owned by a family, and has a *prix fixe* menu (as well as simple à la carte selections).

Bistro du Nord (1312 Madison Ave)
Bistro 790 (Sheraton Manhattan Hotel, 790 Seventh Ave)
Bistrovia (1278 Third Ave)
Brasserie des Théatres (Paramount Hotel, 245 W 46th St; a
    brasserie, not a bistro)
Cafe (210 Spring St)
Cafe des Sports (329 W 51st St)
Cafe Europa (347 E 54th St)
Café Loup (105 W 13th St)
Capsouto Frères (451 Washington St)
Chez Jacqueline (72 MacDougal St)
Chez Josephine (414 W 42nd St)
Chez Ma Tante (189 W 10th St)
Corner Bistro (331 W 4th St)
Ferrier (29 E 65th St)
Florent (69 Gansevoort St)
Gascogne (158 Eighth Ave)
Jean Lafitte (68 W 58th St)
Jo-Jo (160 E 64th St)
Jour Et Nuit (337 W Broadway)
La Bohême (24 Minetta Lane)
La Boîte En Bois (75 W 68th St)
La Lunchonette (130 Tenth Ave)
La Métairie (189 W 10th St)
La Petite Auberge (116 Lexington Ave)
La Petite Ferme (973 Lexington Ave)

La Ripaille (605 Hudson St)
L'Auberge Du Midi (310 W 4th St)
Le Bilboquet (25 E 63rd St)
Le Relais (712 Madison Ave)
Les Halles (411 Park Ave S)
Paris Commune (411 Bleecker St)
Park Bistro (414 Park Ave S)
Pierre Au Tunnel (250 W 47th St)

Breakfast

Doesn't anyone eat breakfast at home anymore? In Manhattan, the "power breakfast" has become a big thing. Even if you're not consummating a deal to take over General Motors, it's fun to watch the major players (and some minor leaguers who think they are) emptying briefcases and making calls from portable telephones.

The action these days is centered around the Plaza Hotel's **Edwardian Room** (Fifth Ave at 59th St), the **Paramount Hotel** (235 W 46th St), the **Regency Hotel** (540 Park Ave), **"21"** (21 W 52nd St), the **Peninsula Hotel** (700 Fifth Ave), the **Carlyle Hotel** (35 E 76th St), **Café Pierre** at the Pierre Hotel (Fifth Ave and 61st St), the New York Palace's **Trianon Room** (455 Madison Ave), and the **Grand Hyatt Hotel** (at Grand Central Station).

If people-watching is secondary to solid fare to start the day, try **Chelsea Square Restaurant** (369 W 23rd St), **American Festival Cafe** (20 W 50th St), **Courtyard Cafe** (130 E 39th St), the **Empire Diner** (210 10th Ave), or **Sarabeth's Kitchen** (1295 Madison Ave or 423 Amsterdam Ave). The **Cottonwood Cafe** (415 Bleecker St) features Grandma Bronson's buttermilk biscuits on weekends, while the **Cupping Room Café** (359 Broadway) is the place to go for French toast. You might also try the **Pink Tea Cup** (42 Grove St), **Viand Coffee Shop** (300 E 86th St), the **Paris Commune** (411 Bleecker St), **Delmonico's** (way downtown at 56 Beaver St), **Aggie's** in SoHo (146 W Houston St), **Carnegie Deli** in midtown (854 Seventh Ave), or **West Side Storey** (700 Columbus Ave) on the Upper West Side. Also, don't miss the blintzes at **B&H Dairy** (127 Second Ave, at St Mark's Pl) and the freshest orange juice in town at the tiny hole-in-the-wall stand at 1428 Sixth Ave.

If money is no object, the breads and other temptations at Eli Zabar's **E.A.T.** (1064 Madison Ave) are as delicious as they are outlandishly priced. The bakery section at **Bloomingdale's** opens early; go at the start of the day for a large selection. Another good bet is the **Royal Canadian Pancake House and Restaurant** (145 Hudson St), where you can fill up on your choice of 53 varieties of pancakes. **EJ's Luncheonette** (433 Amsterdam Ave) serves challah, and **Friend of a Farmer** (77 Irving Pl) is great for a late pancake feast. The **City Bakery** (22 E 17th St) offers whole-wheat turnovers with raspberry preserves and local farmstead yogurts.

Other good choices for breakfast include:

Bubby's (120 Hudson St)
Cafe Word of Mouth (1012 Lexington Ave)
Emily's (1325 Fifth Ave)
Good Enough To Eat (483 Amsterdam Ave)
Lipstick Cafe (885 Third Ave)

Brunch

Personally, I don't care for the usual eggs-and-sausage brunch. I look for restaurants with broader and more appealing menus. The classiest Sunday brunch is offered at the **Palm Court** at the Plaza Hotel (Fifth Ave and 59th St). The entire Palm Court is opened up to showcase a dazzling array of hot and cold dishes, seafood, salads, and fresh fruit, along with a dessert selection that can only be equaled at Gerry Frank's Konditorei in Salem, Oregon! **Cafe Botanica** at the Essex House is excellent. A special brunch treat, along with a delicious assortment of dairy, butcher's market, seafood, pastry, and produce dishes, is the view from the 54th-floor setting atop the **Rihga Royal Hotel** (151 W 54th St). Also consider **Café des Artistes** (1 W 67th St), where both the ambience and the food are classy; **Berry's** (180 Spring St) for Nova Scotia salmon; **Barclay Restaurant** (111 E 48th St) at the Hotel Intercontinental; **Capsouto Frères** (451 Washington St); the Waldorf-Astoria's **Peacock Alley**; **Sarabeth's Kitchen** (423 Amsterdam Ave, 1295 Madison Ave, 945 Madison Ave at the Whitney Museum); **Provence** (38 MacDougal St); **(Gospel) Lola** (30 W 22nd Ave); **Miracle Grill** (112 First Ave); **Mortimer's** (1057 Lexington Ave) for people-watching; or **Voulez-Vous** (1462 First Ave) for marvelous steak tartare. Other possibilities include the **Rainbow Room** (Rockefeller Center) for nostalgia; **Tavern on the Green** (Central Park at W 67th) for entertaining your out-of-town guests; **Friend of a Farmer** (77 Irving Pl); the **Russian Tea Room** (150 W 57th St), which is better than anything in Moscow; **Tartine** (253 W 11th St); the **Water Club** (500 E 30th St); the classy **Mark's Restaurant** (25 E 77th St); and **Good Enough to Eat** (483 Madison Ave).

Burgers

Everyone has a nominee for best burger in town. I vote for **Jackson Hole Wyoming Burgers** (232 E 64th St, Third Ave at 35th St, and Second Ave at 84th St). These burgers are seven juicy ounces of sheer goodness. Runners-up include **Corner Bistro** (331 W 4th St), **Hamburger Harry's** (157 Chambers St and 145 W 45th St), **Hard Rock Cafe** (221 W 57th St), where the action is as tasty as the burgers, **Penguin Cafe** (581 Hudson St), **Taste of the Apple** (1016 Second Ave), **Diane's** (249 Columbus Ave), **Billy's** (948 First Ave), **Harper** (1303 Third Ave), **P. J. Clarke's** (915 Third Ave), and **Planet Hollywood** (140 W 57th St).

Cheap Eats

Today it is fashionable to seek out inexpensive places where you can get good food and good value. Here are some of the better deals in town!

Bella Donna (307 E 77th St)
Bendix Diner (219 Eighth Ave)
Bernstein-on-Essex (135 Essex St)
Book-Friends Cafe (16 W 18th St)
Buckaroo's Bar & Rotisserie (1431 First Ave)
Cafe Lalo (201 W 83rd St)
Caffe Vivaldi (32 Jones St)
Carmine's (2450 Broadway)
Chez Brigette (77 Greenwich Ave)
Christine's (438 Second Ave and 208 First Ave)
Coffee Shop (29 Union Sq W)
Corner Bistro (331 W 4th St)
Cottonwood Cafe (415 Bleecker St)
Crêpes & Co (30 Carmine St)
Cucina de Pesce (87 E 4th St)
Cucina Stagionale (275 Bleecker St)
Cupcake Cafe (522 Ninth Ave)
Dallas BBQ (1265 Third Ave, 27 W 72nd St, and
   21 University Pl)
**Dining Commons, City University of New York
   Graduate Center** (33 W 42nd St, 18th floor)
Eighteenth & Eighth (159 Eighth Ave)
Film Center Cafe (635 Ninth Ave)
Frank's (431 W 14th St)
Golden Unicorn (18 E Broadway)
Good Enough to Eat (483 Amsterdam Ave)
Gray's Papaya (2090 Broadway)
Hamburger Harry's (157 Chambers St)
John's Pizza (278 Bleecker St)
Katz's Delicatessen (205 E Houston St)
La Bonne Soupe (48 W 55th St)
Lulu (430 Broome St)
McDonald's (160 Broadway)
Mee Noodle Soup (795 Ninth Ave)
Moondance Diner (Sixth Ave at Grand St)
Ollie's Noodle Shop and Grille (190 W 44th St)
Papaya King (179 E 86th St and 201 E 59th St)
The Pie (340 E 86th St)
PIZZAPIAZZA (785 Broadway)
Rao's (455 E 114th St)
Ray's Pizza (465 Sixth Ave)

Royal Canadian Pancake House (145 Hudson St)
Second Avenue Kosher Delicatessen and Restaurant
  (156 Second Ave)
7th Regiment Mess (643 Park Ave)
Sevilla (62 Charles St)
Siu Lam Kung (18 Elizabeth St)
SoHo Kitchen and Bar (103 Greene St)
Spring Street Natural Restaurant (62 Spring St)
Sylvia's (328 Lenox Ave)
Teresa's (1O3 First Ave)
Thai Express (1750 First Ave)
Veronica (240 W 38th St)
Veselka (144 Second Ave)
Viand (1011 Madison Ave, 673 Madison Ave, and 300 E 86th St)
Wong Kee (113 Mott St)

Coffeehouses

No city in the world has as many colorful and comfortable coffeehouses as New York. You can relax, enjoy good company, and drink at the following:

Aupetit Beurre (2737 Broadway)
Cafe La Fortuna (69 W 71st St)
Cafe Lalo (201 W 83rd St)
Cafe Orlin (41 St. Mark's Pl)
Caffe Biondo (141 Mulberry St)
Caffe Dante (79 MacDougal St)
Caffe Reggio (119 MacDougal St)
Caffe Roma (385 Broome St)
Caffe Vivaldi (32 Jones St)
Cooper's Coffee and Espresso Bar (2151 Broadway)
Cupcake Cafe (522 Ninth Ave)
Cupping Room Cafe (359 W Broadway)
Daily Caffe (Rockefeller Center)
Dean & Deluca (560 Broadway)
Dolci on Park (12 Park Ave)
Ferrara's (195 Grand St)
Hungarian Pastry Shop (1030 Amsterdam Ave)
Lipstick Cafe (885 Third Ave)
Pane & Cioccolato (10 Waverly Pl)
Peacock (24 Greenwich Ave)
Sant Ambroeus (1000 Madison Ave)
Sarabeth's Kitchen (1295 Madison Ave)
Veniero Pasticceria (342 E 11th St)
Veselka Coffee Shop (144 Second Ave)

Cosseting

You'll be treated in a gentle and efficient manner at all of the following:

Adrienne (Peninsula Hotel, 700 Fifth Ave)
Bouley (165 Duane St)
Café des Artistes (1 W 67th St)
Chanterelle (2 Harrison St)
Chin Chin (216 E 49th St)
Daniel (20 E 76th St)
Dawat (210 E 58th St)
Hudson River Club (4 World Financial Center)
La Caravelle (33 W 55th St)
La Côte Basque (5 E 55th St)
La Grenouille (3 E 52nd St)
La Métairie (189 W 10th St)
La Réserve (4 W 49th St)
Le Bernardin (155 W 51st St)
Le Périgord (405 E 52nd St)
Les Célébrités (Essex House, 160 Central Park S)
Lespinasse (St Regis Hotel, 2 E 55th St)
Mark's (Mark Hotel, 25 E 77th St)
Rainbow Room (30 Rockefeller Plaza, 65th floor)
Restaurant Raphael (33 W 54th St)
River Cafe (1 Water St)
Shun Lee West (43 W 65th St)
Sign of the Dove (1110 Third Ave)
Terrace (400 W 119th St)

Delis

Barney Greengrass (541 Amsterdam Ave)
Bernstein-on-Essex (135 Essex St)
Carnegie Delicatessen and Restaurant (854 Seventh Ave)
Fine & Schapiro (138 W 72nd St)
Katz's Delicatessen (205 E Houston St)
Second Avenue Kosher Delicatessen and Restaurant (156 Second Ave)
Stage Deli (834 Seventh Ave)

Desserts

Want to give yourself a treat? New York combines the best of London, Paris, Rome, and all points in between! To really splurge, these are must-trys. Note: Most also serve fine coffee, espresso, and cappuccino.

Café Lalo (201 W 83rd St): The best European-style cafe!
Caffè Biondo (141 Mulberry St): Little Italy's star

Caffè Bondi (7 W 20th St): Italian tortes
Caffè Pertutti (2862 Broadway): A waist-expanding experience
Carnegie Delicatessen and Restaurant (854 Seventh Ave):
  Everything here is big
Délices de France (289 Madison Ave): The name says it all
Dolci on Park Caffè (12 Park Ave): Undiscovered gem
Éclair Pastry Shops (Grand Central Terminal, Herald Square, 54th
  St at First Ave and 141 W 72nd St): Good selection
Ferrara (195 Mulberry St): Italian gelati
Gindi (935 Broadway): Great pastries
Halcyon (151 W 54th St): Spectacular!
Hard Rock Cafe (221 W 57th St): All-American treats
Le Cirque (58 E 65th St): World famous!
Les Délices West (370 Columbus Ave): Fine French pastries
Les Friandises (972 Lexington Ave): Fabulous chocolate mousse
  cake
Luxe (24 E 21st St): Elegant
Madeline's (117 Prince St): End of a great meal
One Fifth Avenue (1 Fifth Ave): Follow your seafood dinner with
  a sweet
One Hudson Cafe (1 Hudson St): Sinful
Palm Court (Plaza Hotel, 59th St at Fifth Ave): Vintage New York
Pappa's Place (510 Sixth Ave): Ice cream plus
Pâtisserie J. Lanciani (271 W 4th St): Pastries plus
Peppermint Park (1225 First Ave): Outrageous offerings
Sant Ambroeus (1000 Madison Ave): Rich and classy
Serendipity 3 (225 E 60th St): An institution for the young-at-heart
Succès la Côte Basque (Henri Bendel, 1032 Lexington Ave): Suc-
  cessful for curing hunger pangs!
Tavern on the Green (Central Park W at 67th St): There's nothing
  like it back home!
Zabar's Cafe (80th St at Broadway): Big treats, low prices

Dim Sum

"Dim sum" translates as tidbits or snacks, Chinese-style, served mid-morning until late afternoon. People eat it on a daily basis in Chinatown and Hong Kong. In Southern China, for instance, dim sum is eaten while having tea. Dim sum includes all kinds of dumplings, a variety of noo-dle and rice dishes, and desserts. Some of the best are stuffed bean curds, Peking spareribs, shredded chicken rolls, egg custards, sesame shrimp toast, fried wontons, curry beef dumplings, beef balls, braised duck feet, and crab claws. Dim sum items are often wheeled to your table on carts, offering the diner an amazing array of choices. For the most authentic and delicious dim sum in New York, I recommend:

China Royal (17 Division St)
Golden Unicorn (18 E. Broadway) Serves an especially appetizing
  presentation

H.S.F. (46 Bowery and 578 Second Ave)
King Fung (20 Elizabeth St)
Mandarin Court (61 Mott St)
Nice Restaurant (35 E Broadway)
Oriental Pearl (103 Mott St)
Shun Lee Cafe (43 W 65th St)
Sun Hop Shing Tea House (21 Mott St)
Tai-Hong-Lau (70 Mott St)

Diners

There are not many classic diners left in Manhattan, but the best survivors are:

EJ's Luncheonette (433 Amsterdam Ave and 1271 Third Ave)
Empire Diner (210 Tenth Ave)
Moondance Diner (Sixth Ave at Grand St)
Market Diner (Eleventh Ave at 43rd St)

Dining and Dancing

Le Bar Bat (311 W 57th St)
Rainbow Room (30 Rockefeller Plaza, 65th floor)
Tavern on the Green (Central Park W at 67th St)
World Yacht Cruises (Pier 81, W 41st St at the Hudson River)

Dining Solo

Arizona 206 (206 E 60th St)
The Ballroom (253 W 28th St)
Brasserie (100 E 53rd St)
Broadway Diner (590 Lexington Ave and 1726 Broadway)
Café des Sports (329 W 51st St)
Carnegie Delicatessen and Restaurant (854 Seventh Ave)
Chez Napoleon (365 W 50th St)
Coffee Shop (29 Union Sq W, at 16th St)
Elephant & Castle (68 Greenwich St, Seventh Ave at 11th St)
Grand Central Oyster Bar Restaurant (Grand Central Station)
Hosteria Fiorella (1081 Third Ave)
Jackson Hole Wyoming Burgers (232 E 64th St, Third Ave at
   35th St, and Second Ave at 84th St)
Jour et Nuit (337 W Broadway)
La Bonne Soupe (48 W 55th St)
May We (1022 Lexington Ave)
Mme Romaine de Lyon (29 E 61st St)
Raoul's (180 Prince St)

Sarabeth's Kitchen (1295 Madison Ave, 423 Amsterdam Ave, and 945 Madison Ave at Whitney Museum)
Second Avenue Kosher Delicatessen and Restaurant (156 Second Ave)
Stage Deli (834 Seventh Ave)
Trattoria dell'Arte (900 Seventh Ave)
Tropica (Met Life Bldg, 200 Park Ave)
Union Square Cafe (21 E 16th St)
Viand Coffee Shop (300 E 86th St, 1011 Madison Ave, and 637 Madison Ave)
Yellowfingers di Nuovo (200 E 60th St)
Zoë (90 Prince St)

Don't Bothers

Too many restaurants spoil the real reason for coming: to get a good meal in a comfortable setting at a decent price. With so many great restaurant choices in Manhattan, why waste time and money on poor or mediocre ones? Many on the following list are well known and popular, but I feel you can get better value elsewhere.

Angelo of Mulberry St: The portrait of former prez Reagan is their only claim to fame.
Bice: Very "in," very noisy, very unimpressive
Black Sheep: Once was fun, but that's history
Brasserie Pascal: Void of people, atmosphere, and value for the buck
Cafe Crocodile: Too bad Andree took her name off
Café de la Paix: Only things worth watching are the other customers
Camelback and Central: The street-sign décor is the most appealing aspect
Charley O's: The Benetton of the food scene
Chiam: Charming in every way except the most important: the food
Christ Cella: Forget about what you may have heard
Country Club: Big, empty, mediocre
Démarchelier: Overhyped, ordinary
Elaine's: You gotta be kidding
Eli Zabar's Cafe: Fantastic food, exorbitant prices
El Teddy's: Only the desserts are worth the effort
Ernie's: The pickup scene must be awfully good, though
Italica: The atmosphere is not appetizing
Jockey Club: Way behind in the stretch
Lello: A few smiles would help
Le Veau d'Or: Heaven help the stranger
Lexington Avenue Grill: Poor service
Mamma Leone's: Tourissimo!

Memphis: I'd rather go South
Mortimer's: For the eyes only
New York Deli: It was better as an Automat
Nusantara: Indonesia is a long way from here
Old Homestead: "Old" is the best description
Ottomanelli Cafe: Haven't they heard what happens
  to conglomerates?
Positano: Positively not up to the billing
Ratner's: Why pay to get insulted?
Rosolio: Plain Jane ambience and Plain Jane plates
Rumpelmayer's: Badly faded
San Domenico: Overpriced, inconsistent
Sardi's: Once great; twice bad; thrice, coming back slowly
Savoy: Uncomfortably "cute," unappealing plates
Sfuzzi: What's all the "sfuss" about?
Sloppy Louie's: Lives up to the name
Taste of Hong Kong: It was left behind
Tennessee Mountain: Not much at the top
Two Eleven: Disinterested help, serving interesting food

Family Style Dining

Carmine's (2450 Broadway)
Coco Pazzo (23 E 74th St; Fri, Sat, and Sun)

Foreign Flavors

In response to suggestions from readers, I have tried to make this edition more convenient for those looking for restaurants in a specific part of town that serve a given foreign cuisine, and are, perhaps, open on Sundays. This listing combines information on the several hundred restaurants reviewed herein. You can easily scan the list and pick out an establishment that suits your taste. However, there are some unusual foreign flavors featured that do *not* have full write-ups in this book. For those who may be interested, here are the best of the more exotic cuisines.

Afghan: Afghanistan Kebab House (764 Ninth Ave)
Belgian: Café de Bruxelles (118 Greenwich Ave)
Brazilian: Banana Café (111 E 22nd St)
British: Tea & Sympathy (108 Greenwich Ave), Telephone
  Bar/Grill (149 Second Ave)
Burmese: Road to Mandalay (380 Broome St)
Caribbean: Caribe (117 Perry St), Tropica (200 Park Ave)
Chinese: Sun Golden Island (1–3 Elizabeth St), Sunny East (21 W
  39th St), Fu's (1395 Second Ave), Au Mandarin (200–250 Vesey

---

Ordering a Chinese Meal

Get together a large party in order to sample a wide variety of dishes. While everyone's taste should be taken into account, it is advisable to let one person organize the order. A well-balanced meal comprises the five basic tastes of Chinese cuisine: acid, hot, bitter, sweet, and salty. Texture should vary between dry and sauced, crisp and tender. A good rule of thumb is to order one dish per diner, plus one soup. Your utensils will be chopsticks, which are ideal for the small pieces of food commonly found in Chinese cooking, but most restaurants will gladly supply chopstick novices with knives, forks, and spoons.

A Chinese meal usually starts with a cold meat dish and is then followed by fish or seafood, red or white meat, vegetables, and soup. Steamed white rice is a usual accompaniment, but you can also order a fried noodle or rice dish to be served at the end of the meal. In northern Chinese-style restaurants, bread or noodles often replace rice.

St), Shun Lee West (43 W 65th St), Golden Unicorn (18 E Broadway), and H.S.F. (46 Bowery)

Cuban: Victor's (240 Columbus Ave)

Czech: Vasata (339 E 75th St), Mingala West (325 Amsterdam Ave)

Dominican: La Sarten (564 Amsterdam Ave)

Ethiopian: Zula (1260 Amsterdam Ave)

German: Kleine Konditorei (234 E 86th St) and Rolf's (281 Third Ave)

Greek: Periyali (35 W 20th St)

Hungarian: Red Tulip (439 E 75th St) and Mocca Hungarian Restaurant (1588 Second Ave)

Indian: Darbar (44 W 56th St), Akbar (475 Park Ave), and Dawat (210 E 58th St)

Irish: Neary's (358 E 57th St)

Japanese: Chikubu (12 E 44th St), Iso (175 Second Ave), Shinwa (645 Fifth Ave), The Gibbon (24 E 80th St), Omen (113 Thompson St), Umeda (102 E 22nd St), Itcho (402 E 78th St), Mitsukoshi (461 Park Ave), Japonica (100 University Pl), Honmura An (170 Mercer St), Hatsuhana (17 E 48th St), Benihana (120 E 56th St), and Nishi NoHo (380 Lafayette St)

Lebanese: Yaldzlar (566 Third Ave)

Malaysian: Chiew's Garden (22 E Broadway) and Malaysia Restaurant (48 Bowery)

Mediterranean: Gus' Place (149 Waverly Pl) and Provence (38 MacDougal St)

Mexican: La Frontera (430 Broome St), El Parador (325 E 34th St), Miracle Grill (112 First Ave), and Tortilla Flats (767 Washington St)

Middle Eastern: Café Greco (1390 Second Ave) and Cleopatra's Needle (2485 Broadway)

Milanese: Biricchino (260 W 29th St)

Peruvian: Peruvian Restaurant (688 Tenth Ave)

Polish: Christine's (438 Second Ave and 208 First Ave)

Russian: Russian Samovar (256 W 52nd St) and Cafe Andrusha (1742 Second Ave)

Spanish: Ballroom (253 W 28th St), Solera (216 E 53rd St), and El Parador (325 E 34th St)

Swedish: Snaps (230 Park Ave) and Aquavit (13 W 54th St)

Thai: Thai House (151 Hudson St), Tommy Tang's (323 Greenwich St), and Vong (200 E 54th St)

Tibetan: Tibetan Kitchen (444 Third Ave)

Ukrainian: Veselka (144 Second Ave)

Vietnamese: Le Bar Bat (311 W 57th St)

Game in Season

Aquavit (13 W 54th St)
Barbetta (321 W 46th St)
Chanterelle (2 Harrison St)
Hudson River Club (4 World Financial Ctr)
Jo-Jo (160 E 64th St)
La Réserve (4 W 44th St)
Le Cirque (58 E 65th St)
Mesa Grill (102 Fifth Ave)
Park Bistro (414 Park Ave)
Primavera (1578 First Ave)
"21" Club (21 W 52nd St)
Union Square Cafe (21 E 16th St)

Healthy Fare

Menu alert from the Mayo Clinic: If you are watching your diet, be cautious about menu items described as *au jus, in broth, cocktail sauce, tomato base, pickled,* or *smoked.* The experts also tell you to avoid *au gratin, basted, braised, buttered, buttery, casserole, creamed, crispy, fried, hash, hollandaise, butter sauce, cheese sauce, cream sauce, prime, sauteed, scalloped,* and *stewed.* My goodness, what's left to enjoy? More than you might think! You can find healthy fare at the following restaurants, some of which have special menus.

Akbar (475 Park Ave): Indian
Angelica Kitchen (300 E 12th St)

Bernard & Steve's (277 Church St)
Bouley (165 Duane St)
Buckwheat and Alfalfa (182 Eighth Ave)
Four Seasons (99 E 49th St): Expensive
Fraunces Tavern Restaurant (54 Pearl St): Historic
Great American Health Bar (several locations)
Health Pub (371 Second Ave)
Healthy Candle (Lexington Ave at 71st St)
Luma (200 Ninth Ave)
Madras Woodlands (308 E 49th St)
Nosmo King (54 Varick St)
Orfeo (18 Second Ave)
Quantum Leap Natural Food (88 W 3rd St)
Salad Bowl (721 Lexington Ave)
Scarlatti (34 E 52nd St)
Spring Street Natural Restaurant (62 Spring St): Your best bet
Time Cafe (380 Lafayette St)
"21" Club (21 W 52nd St): For the health- and status-conscious
Whole Wheat 'n Wild Berrys (57 W 10th St)
Zen Palate (663 Ninth Ave)

Hotel Dining

One of the biggest changes on the restaurant circuit in Manhattan is the resurgence of hotel dining. No longer are these on-premises eateries just for the convenience of guests. Now they are, indeed, destinations for those who desire a bit more atmosphere and a less trendy scene. Following are some of the best:

Algonquin (59 W 44th St): Rose Room, Oak Room (evening cabaret)
Carlyle (35 E 76th St): Carlyle Restaurant (features Bobby Short, very expensive)
Doral Court (130 E 39th St): Courtyard Café (outdoors in summer)
Doral Park Avenue (70 Park Ave): Park Avenue Grill (American cuisine)
Doral Tuscany (116 E 39th St): Time & Again (cozy, comfortable)
Drake Swissotel (440 Park Ave): Café Suisse (casual)
Essex House (160 Central Park S): Les Célébrités (very classy) and Café Botanica (more casual)
Four Seasons (57 E 57th St): 57-57 (superb dining)
Grand Hyatt (Grand Central Station and Park Ave): Sun Garden (nice setting), Trumpets (dressier)
Holiday Inn Crowne Plaza (1605 Broadway): Broadway Grill (pre- or after-theater)

Inter-Continental (111 E 48th St): Barclay (American cuisine)
Kitano (66 Park Ave): Hakubai (Japanese)
Lowell (28 E 63rd St): Post House (very good meat and potatoes), and Pembroke Room (Continentl)
The Mark (25 E 77th St): Mark's Restaurant (one of the very best)
Macklowe (145 W 44th St): Classy
Marriott Marquis (1535 Broadway): four restaurants, including The View (top floor, revolving)
Mayfair Regent (610 Park Ave): Le Cirque (society plus, see and be seen)
New York Hilton (1335 Sixth Ave): Grill 53 (steaks, chops) and Cafe New York (snacks)
New York Palace (455 Madison Ave): Le Trianon, Harry's New York Bar (for fun), Gold Room (for tea)
Omni Berkshire (21 E 52nd St): La Galerie (country French)
Paramount Hotel (245 W 46th St): Brasserie des Théatres (attractive bistro)
Peninsula (700 Fifth Ave): Adrienne (overlooks Fifth Avenue, outstanding)
Pierre (61st St at Fifth Ave): Café Pierre (stately and beautiful)
Plaza (768 Fifth Ave): Edwardian Room (overlooks Central Park), Palm Court (vintage New York), Oak Room (serious), Oyster Bar (seafood)
Plaza Athénée (37 E 64th St): Le Régence (elegant)
Regency (540 Park Ave): 540 Park Ave Restaurant (power scene)
Rihga Royal (151 W 54th St): Halcyon (beautiful appointments and fine food)
Royalton (44 W 44th St): 44 (chic, favorite of publishing moguls)
Sheraton Manhattan (790 Seventh Ave): Bistro 790 (very good midtown value)
Sheraton New York (811 Seventh Ave): Streeter's (first class) and Hudson's Bar and Grill (casual dining)
Sheraton Park Avenue (45 Park Ave): Russell's American Grill (solid and dependable)
St. Regis (Fifth Ave at 55th St): Lespinasse (you can't do better)
Stanhope (995 Fifth Ave): The Dining Room (French)
United Nations Plaza (44th St at First Ave): Ambassador Grill (sophisticated)
Vista International (3 World Trade Center): Greenhouse (casual) and American Harvest (Yankee food)
Waldorf-Astoria (301 Park Ave): four restaurants, including Bull & Bear (British atmosphere), Inagiku (Japanese), and Peacock Alley (it has come back to life)
Wales (1295 Madison Ave): Sarabeth's Kitchen (delightful)
Warwick (65 W 54th St): La Locanda (quiet and refined)
Westbury (840 Madison Ave): Polo (gracious)

Kosher

There will never be a shortage of pastrami or chicken soup in New York, but nowadays the kosher diner can sample a wider variety of flavors, from Afghan to Indian. Here's a partial list:

Bernstein-on-Essex (135 Essex St): Quintessential kosher deli (Hint: If you want to be "in," refer to Bernstein-on-Essex as "Shmulk's."

Boychik's (19 W 45th St): Pasta, salads, and quick takeouts

Café Masada (First Ave at 67th St): Israeli grill

Cheers (120 W 41st St): The accent is Italian, the menu meaty

Dairy Planet (182 Broadway): Health food, vegetarian

Deli Kasbah (251 W 85th St): Grill, deli, and salad house

Eden Terrace (475 Park Ave S): Elegant deli and restaurant

Galil (1252 Lexington Ave): Middle Eastern grill

Goldie's (211 E 46th St): Crowded noontime deli

Great American Health Bar (all over town): Vegetarian and dairy menu

Jerusalem II (1375 Broadway): Pizza and falafel

Kosher Delight (1365 Broadway): Kosher burger joint

La Kasbah (70 W 71st St): Moroccan

Levana (141 W 69th St): Outstanding European cuisine

Lou G. Siegel (209 W 38th St): Businessman's delight

Maccabeem (147 W 47th St): Chicken soup and more, served cafeteria-style

Madras Place (104 Lexington Ave): Vegetarian South Indian

Madras Woodlands (308 E 49th St): Indian vegetarian

Mosha Peking (40 W 37th St): Elegant Chinese

Naftali's (77 Fulton St): Continental meat and seafood

Ratner's (138 Delancey St): For nostalgia alone

Verve Naturelle (157 W 57th St): California-style health food

Late Hours (See also "Manhattan at Night")

The city that never sleeps . . .

Never closes:
Brasserie (100 E 53rd St)
Coffee Shop (29 Union Sq W; closed between 6 and 7 a.m.)
Empire Diner (210 Tenth Ave)
Florent (69 Gansevoort St)
Gray's Papaya (2090 Broadway)
Veselka (144 Second Ave)
Viand (1011 Madison Ave, 673 Madison Ave, and 300 E 86th St)

Open until about 3 a.m.:
Carnegie Delicatessen and Restaurant (857 Seventh Ave)
Corner Bistro (331 W 4th St)

Fisher & Levy (875 Third Ave)
Lolabelle (206 E 63rd St)
Lucky Strike (59 Grand St)
Mr. Fuji's Tropicana (61 Fifth Ave)
P.J. Clarke's (915 Third Ave)

Open until about 2 a.m.:
Chefs and Cuisiniers Club (36 E 22nd St)
Elaine's (1703 Second Ave)
Hard Rock Cafe (221 W 57th St): Open later on weekends
Odeon (145 W Broadway)
Telephone Bar and Grill (149 Second Ave)
Wollensky's Grill (205 E 49th St)

Open until about 1 a.m.:
Amsterdam's (454 Broadway)
Ballroom (253 W 28th St)
Broome Street Bar (363 W Broadway)
Halcyon (Rihga Royal Hotel, 151 W 54th St)
I Tre Merli (463 W Broadway)
Jackson Hole Wyoming Burgers (232 E 64th St, Third Ave at
    35th St, and Second Ave at 84th St)
J.G. Melon (340 Amsterdam Ave and 1291 Third Ave)
La Métairie (184 W 10th St)
Mezzaluna (1295 Third Ave)
Neary's (358 E 57th St)
Odeon (145 W Broadway)
Papaya King (179 E 86th St and 201 E 59th St)
Planet Hollywood (140 W 57th St)
Stage Deli (834 Seventh Ave)
Trattoria dell'Arte (900 Seventh Ave)
Walker's (16 N Moore St, at Varick St)

Until midnight:
Algonquin Hotel (59 W 44th St)
Alo Alo (1030 Third Ave)
Bellevues (496 Ninth Ave)
Bice (7 E 54th St)
Broadway Diner (590 Lexington Ave and 1726 Broadway)
Café des Artistes (1 W 67th St)
Cameos (169 Columbus Ave)
Chelsea Commons (242 Tenth Ave)
Chez Josephine (414 W 42nd St)
Contrapunto (200 E 60th St)
Docks (2427 Broadway and 633 Third Ave)
Fu's (1395 Second Ave)
Girasole (151 E 82nd St)
Golden Unicorn (18 E Broadway)

La Bonne Soupe (48 W 55th)
La Cité (120 W 51st St)
La Focaccia (51 Bank St)
Le Comptoir (227 E 67th St)
Le Madri (168 W 18th St)
Madeline's (177 Prince St)
Manhattan Chili Company (302 Bleecker St)
Manhattan Ocean Club (57 W 58th St)
Marylou's (21 W 9th St)
Metropolis Cafe (31 Union Sq W)
Mickey Mantle's (42 Central Park S)
Nicola's (146 E 84th St)
Orso (322 W 46th St)
Paper Moon Milano (39 E 58th St)
Plaza Hotel Oyster Bar (58th St bet Fifth and Sixth Ave)
Post House (28 E 63rd St)
Primavera (1578 First Ave)
Provence (38 MacDougal St)
Rose Cafe (24 Fifth Ave)
Royal Canadian Pancake House (145 Hudson St)
Serendipity 3 (225 E 60th St)
Sfuzzi (58 W 65th St)
SoHo Kitchen and Bar (103 Greene St)
Sylvia's (328 Lenox Ave)
Tavern on the Green (Central Park W at 67th St)
"21" Club (21 W 52nd St)
Vince and Eddie's (70 W 68th St)
Voulez-Vous (1462 First Ave)
Yellowfingers di Nuovo (200 E 60th St)
Zarela (953 Second Ave)

Munching at the Museums

Tasty possibilities while you get some culture:

American Museum of Natural History (Central Park W
   at 79th St)
Guggenheim Museum (1071 Fifth Ave)
Metropolitan Museum (Fifth Ave at 82nd St)
Museum of Modern Art (11 W 53rd St)
Whitney Museum (945 Madison Ave)

Neighborhood

Anglers and Writers (420 Hudson St)
Beinvenue Restaurant (21 E 36th St)
Billy's (948 First Ave)
Café (210 Spring St)

Caffè Pertutti (2862 Broadway)
Donahue's (845 Lexington Ave)
Fanelli's Cafe (94 Prince St)
Gene's (73 W 11th St)
Meridiana (2756 Broadway)
Peter McManus Cafe (152 Seventh Ave)
Tartine's (253 W 11th St)

Offbeat

Looking for someplace just a bit different? Here are some ideas:

Acme Bar & Grill (9 Great Jones St): Swinging
Afghan Kebab House (764 Ninth Ave and 1345 Second Ave):
   Kebab
Barney Greengrass (541 Amsterdam Ave): You're in the 1940's
Becco (355 W 46th St): Family dining
Bellevues (496 Ninth Ave): Bistro
Boathouse Cafe (Central Park Lake): Overlooks water
Brother Jimmy's Bar-B-Q (1461 First Ave): Great ribs
Buckaroo's (1431 First Ave: Bar and rotisserie
Coco Pazzo (23 E 74th St): Crazy chef!
Frank's (431 W 14th St): Meat and potatoes
Great Jones Cafe (54 Great Jones St): Eclectic
Khyber Pass (34 St Mark's Pl): Afghan
Landmark Tavern (626 Eleventh Ave): Historic
NoHo Star (330 Lafayette St): Diner
Nosmo King (54 Varick St): Organic
Rao's (455 E 114th St): Way uptown
Red Tulip (439 E 75th St): Hungarian
Ruby's River Road Cafe (1754 Second Ave): Cajun
Sabor (20 Cornelia St): Cuban
Sammy's Roumanian (157 Chrystie St): Lower East Side
Seventh Regiment Mess (643 Park Ave): Unusual setting
Sugar Reef (93 Second Ave): Caribbean
Sylvia's (328 Lenox Ave): Soul food
Vasata (339 E 75th St): Czech
Veselka Coffee Shop (144 Second Ave): Polish-Ukrainian

Old-timers

How far back do you want to go?

1763: Fraunces Tavern Restaurant (54 Pearl St)
1836: Delmonico's (56 Beaver St)
1842: Sweet's (2 Fulton St)
1854: McSorley's Old Ale House (15 E 7th Ave)
1864: Pete's Tavern (129 E 18th St)
1865: Landmark Tavern (626 Eleventh Ave)

1868: Old Homestead (56 Ninth Ave)
1879: Gage & Tollner (372 Fulton St, Brooklyn)
1885: Keens Chop House (72 W 36th St)
1887: Peter Luger (178 Broadway, Brooklyn)
1890: P.J. Clarke's (915 Third Ave)
1905: Ratner's (138 Delancey St)
1906: Barbetta (321 W 46th St)
1912: Frank's (431 W 14th St)
  Olde Garden Cafe (15 W 29th St)
1913: Grand Central Oyster Bar Restaurant
  (Grand Central Station)
1914: Café des Artistes (1 W 67th St)
1920: Ye Waverly Inn (16 Bank St)
1922: "21" Club (21 W 52nd St)
1926: Palm (837 Second Ave)
  Russian Tea Room (150 W 57th St)
1927: Minetta Tavern (113 MacDougal St)

Outdoor Dining

A taste of the outdoors in a garden or patio or on the sidewalk.

American Festival Cafe (Rockefeller Center)
Aureole (34 E 61 St)
Barbetta (321 W 46th St)
Barolo (398 W Broadway)
Boathouse Cafe (Central Park Lake, Fifth Ave at 72nd St)
Buckaroo's (1431 First Ave)
Caffè Bondi (7 W 20th St)
Caffè Bianco (1486 Second Ave)
Caffè Dante (79 MacDougal St)
Chelsea Commons (242 Tenth Ave)
Chez Ma Tante (189 W 10th St)
Coastal (300 Amsterdam Ave)
Courtyard Cafe (130 E 39th St)
Da Silvano (260 Sixth Ave)
Empire Diner (210 Tenth Ave)
Gascogne (158 Eighth Ave)
Giordano (409 W 39th St)
Hatsuhana (17 E 48th St)
Il Monello (1460 Second Ave)
Jackson Hole Wyoming Burgers (232 E 64th St)
La Bohême (24 Minetta Lane)
La Petite Ferme (973 Lexington Ave)
Le Madri (168 W 18th St)
Le Relais (712 Madison Ave)
Lox Around the Clock (676 Sixth Ave)
Manhattan Chili Co (302 Bleecker St)

March (405 E 58th St)
Mezzogiorno (195 Spring)
Miracle Grill (112 First Ave)
Mortimer's (1057 Lexington Ave)
Museum of Modern Art (11 W 53rd St)
Nick & Eddie (203 Spring St)
One If by Land, Two If by Sea (17 Barrow St)
Orson's (175 Second Ave)
Pete's Tavern (129 E 18th St)
Pierre's (170 Waverly Pl)
Pigalle (111 E 29th St)
Provence (38 MacDougal St)
River Cafe (1 Water St, Brooklyn)
The Saloon (1920 Broadway)
San Pietro (18 E 54th St)
Sign of the Dove (1110 Third Ave)
Spring Street Natural Restaurant (62 Spring St)
Stanhope Hotel (995 Fifth Ave)
Summerhouse (50 E 86th St)
Sumptuary (400 Third Ave)
Tavern on the Green (Central Park W at 67th St)
Trattoria dell'Arte (900 Seventh Ave)
Vince & Eddie's (70 W 68th St)
Voulez-Vous (1462 First Ave)
White Horse Tavern (567 Hudson St)

Party Rooms

Most major hotels have private function rooms. (See also the special section on unusual party places in Chapter VII in the regular edition.)

Akbar (475 Park Ave)
An American Place (2 Park Ave)
Barbetta (321 W 46th St)
Bouley (165 Duane St, bet Greenwich and Hudson St)
Brasserie (100 E 53rd St)
Café Botanica (Essex House, 160 Central Park S)
Cameos (169 Columbus Ave)
Capsouto Frères (451 Washington St)
Chez Josephine (414 W 42nd St)
Darbar (44 W 56th St)
Delmonico's (56 Beaver St, at William St)
Ernie's (2150 Broadway)
Four Seasons (99 E 52nd St)
Frank's (431 W 14th St)
Fraunces Tavern Restaurant (54 Pearl St)

Gabriel's (11 W 60th St)
Golden Unicorn (18 E Broadway)
Hard Rock Cafe (221 W 57th St)
Hatsuhana (17 E 48th St)
Hudson River Club (World Financial Center)
Il Vagabondo (351 E 62nd St)
Indochine (430 Lafayette St)
Jim McMullen (1341 Third Ave)
Keens Chop House (72 W 36th St)
La Caravelle (33 W 55th St)
La Grenouille (3 E 52nd St)
La Réserve (4 W 49th St)
Le Bar Bat (311 W 57th St)
Le Bernardin (155 W 51st St)
Le Cirque (58 E 65th St)
Le Madri (168 W 18th St)
Le Périgord (405 E 52nd St)
Lutèce (249 E 50th St)
Luxe (24 E 21st St)
Manhattan Ocean Club (57 W 58th St)
Montrachet (239 Broadway)
One Hudson Cafe (1 Hudson St)
One If by Land, Two If by Sea (17 Barrow St)
Palio (151 W 51st St)
Palm (837 Second Ave)
Park Bistro (414 Park Ave)
Periyali (35 W 20th St)
Peter Luger (178 Broadway, Brooklyn)
Planet Hollywood (140 W 57th St)
Primavera (1578 First Ave)
Provence (38 MacDougal St)
Rainbow Room (Rockefeller Center, 65th fl)
Russian Tea Room (150 W 57th St)
Sea Grill (19 W 49th St)
Serendipity 3 (225 E 60th St)
Sign of the Dove (1110 Third Ave)
Smith & Wollensky (201 E 49th St)
Sonia Rose (132 Lexington Ave)
Sparks (210 E 46th St)
Tavern on the Green (Central Park W at 67th St)
TriBeCa Grill (375 Greenwich St, at Franklin St)
Tropica (200 Park Ave)
West Broadway (349 W Broadway)
World Yacht Cruises (Pier 81, W 41st St at Hudson River)
Zarela (953 Second Ave)
Zip City Brewing (3 W 18th St)

Pasta

Arqua (281 Church St)
Artepasta (81 Greenwich Ave)
Baci (412 Amsterdam Ave)
Caffè Pertutti (2862 Broadway)
Contrapunto (200 E 60th St)
Figaro (42 W 56th St)
Parkside (107-01 Corona Ave, Queens)
Remi (145 W 53rd St)
Trattoria dell'Arte (900 Seventh Ave)

People Watching

Aureole (34 E 61st St)
Banana Café (111 E 22nd St)
Bellini (777 Seventh Ave)
Bice (7 E 54th St)
Bouley (165 Duane St)
Chanterelle (2 Harrison St)
Chefs & Cuisiniers Club (36 E 22nd St)
Daniel (20 E 76th St)
Duane Park Cafe (157 Duane St)
Ecco (124 Chambers St, bet W Broadway and Church St)
Elaine's (1703 Second Ave)
"44" (44 W 44th St)
Four Seasons (99 E 52nd St)
Gotham Bar & Grill (12 E 12th St)
Harry Cipriani (Fifth Ave at E 59th St)
Jim McMullen (1341 Third Ave)
Jo-Jo (160 E 64th St)
La Côte Basque (5 E 55th St)
La Grenouille (3 E 52nd St)
La Réserve (4 W 49th St)
La Cirque (Mayfair Regent Hotel, 58 E 65th St)
Le Madri (168 W 18th St)
Le Périgord (405 E 52nd St)
Mickey Mantle's (42 Central Park S)
Mortimer's (1057 Lexington Ave)
P.J. Clarke's (915 Third Ave)
Palio (151 W 51st St)
Palm (837 Second Ave)
Palm Court (Plaza Hotel, Fifth Ave at Central Park S)
Paper Moon Milano (39 E 58th St)
Planet Hollywood (140 W 57th St)
Provence (38 MacDougal St)
Rainbow Room (Rockefeller Center, 65th fl)

Remi (145 W 53rd St)
Russian Tea Room (150 W 57th St)
San Domenico (240 Central Park S)
Sette Mezzo (969 Lexington Ave)
Tavern on the Green (Central Park W at 67th St)
Trattoria dell'Arte (900 Seventh Ave)
TriBeCa Grill (375 Greenwich St, at Franklin St)
"21" Club (21 W 52nd St)
Union Square Cafe (21 E 16th St)
Vong (200 E 54th St)
Zoë (90 Prince St)

Personal Favorites

Everybody has a list of favorite places, and I am happy to share mine:

Adrienne (Peninsula Hotel, 700 Fifth Ave): Elegance
Andiamo (1991 Broadway): Italian
Bouley (165 Duane St): Class plus
Café des Artistes (1 W 67th St): Restful
Café des Sports (329 W 51st St): Homey French
Edwardian Room (Plaza Hotel, 59th and Central Park S): Right on the park
Gabriel's (11 W 60th St): Sophisticated
Gotham Bar & Grill (12 E 12th St): Darn good food
Il Mulino (86 W 3rd St): Italian heaven
Jackson Hole Wyoming Burgers (various locations): Simply the best
La Bohême (24 Minetta Ln): Unpretentious
La Grenouille (3 E 52nd St): Beautiful
La Métairie (189 W 10th St): Cozy
La Réserve (4 W 49th St): Perfection!
Le Chantilly (106 E 57th St): Civilized
Le Périgord (405 E 52nd St): Impeccable
Lespinasse (St Regis Hotel, 2 E 55th St): Grand
March (405 E 58th St): Imaginative
Mark's (Mark Hotel, 25 E 77th St): As hotel dining should be
Nick and Eddie's (203 Spring St): Lively
One If by Land, Two If by Sea (17 Barrow St): Romantic
Parkside (107-01 Corona Ave, Queens): Come here to *eat*!
Primavera (1578 First Ave): Superb service
River Café (1 Water St, East River, Brooklyn): Oh, that view!
Rosemarie's (145 Duane St): Intimate
Sonia Rose (132 Lexington Ave): The place to propose!
Terrace (Columbia University, 400 W 119th St): Great outlook
Wong Kee (113 Mott St): Basic Chinatown

Pizza

Everyone has a favorite pizza place. You can't go wrong with any of these:

Allegria (66 W 55th St)
Arturo's Pizzeria (106 Houston St)
Barocco (297 Church St)
Broadway Grill (Holiday Inn Crowne Plaza, 1605 Broadway)
Figaro (42 W 56th St)
Fisher & Levy (875 Third Ave)
Hosteria Fiorella Seafood Grill (1081 Third Ave)
Il Corallo (176 Prince St)
John's (278 Bleecker St and 408 E 64th St)
La Bohême (24 Minetta Lane)
Le Madri (168 W 8th St)
Mezzogiorno (195 Spring St)
New Haven Pizza Co. (140 W 13th St)
Orso (322 W 46th St)
Patsy's Pizza (2287–91 First Ave)
PIZZAPIAZZA (785 Broadway)
Sal's & Carmine's Pizza (2533 Broadway)
Trattoria dell'Arte (900 Seventh Ave)
Vinnie's Pizza (285 Amsterdam Ave)

Pubs

To feel the real flavor of New York, visit a pub on St. Patrick's Day. However, these spots feature good brew, good times, and good company every day of the year.

Billy's (948 First Ave)
Great Jones Street Cafe (54 Great Jones St)
Jimmy Day's (186 W 4th St)
Landmark Tavern (626 Eleventh Ave)
McSorley's Old Ale House (15 E 7th St)
Peculier Pub (145 Bleecker St)
Pete's Tavern (66 Irving Pl): New York's oldest continuously
  operating pub
P.J. Clarke's (915 Third Ave)
SoHo Kitchen and Bar (103 Greene St)
Telephone Bar & Grill (149 Second Ave)
White Horse Tavern (567 Hudson St)
Zip City Brewing (3 W 18th St)

Romantic

Some great places for hand-holding (or whatever):

Alison on Dominick Street (38 Dominick St)
Barbetta (321 W 46th St)

Bouley (165 Duane St)
Café des Artistes (1 W 67th St)
Café Pierre (Pierre Hotel, 61st St at Fifth Ave)
Café Trevi (1570 First Ave)
Caffè Vivaldi (32 Jones St)
Chanterelle (2 Harrison St)
Chez Josephine (414 W 42nd St)
Four Seasons (99 E 52nd St)
Hudson River Club (World Financial Center)
La Bohème (24 Minetta Ln)
La Caravelle (33 W 55th St)
La Côte Basque (5 E 55th St)
La Grenouille (3 E 52nd St)
La Métairie (189 W 10th St)
La Petite Ferme (973 Lexington Ave)
La Réserve (4 W 49th St)
Le Chantilly (106 E 57th St)
Le Cirque (Mayfair Regent Hotel, 58 E 65th St)
Le Périgord (405 E 62nd St)
Les Célébrités (160 Central Park S)
Le Train Bleu (Bloomingdale's, 1000 Third Ave)
Mark's (Mark Hotel, 25 E 77th St)
One If by Land, Two If by Sea (17 Barrow St)
Palm Court and Edwardian Room (Plaza Hotel, Fifth Ave and Central Park S)
Paola's (347 E 85th St)
Parioli Romanissimo (24 E 81st St)
Pete's Tavern (129 E 18th St)
Provence (38 MacDougal St)
Rainbow Room (Rockefeller Center, 65th fl)
River Cafe (1 Water St, East River, Brooklyn)
Russian Tea Room (150 W 57th St)
Sign of the Dove (1110 Third Ave)
Sonia Rose (132 Lexington Ave)
Tavern on the Green, Crystal Room (Central Park W and 67th St)
Terrace (Columbia University, 400 W 119th St)
Time & Again (Doral Tuscany Hotel, 116 E 39th St)
Trastevere (155 E 84th St)
World Yacht Cruises (Pier 81, W 41st St at Hudson River)
Zoë (90 Prince St)

Sandwiches

There are thousands (yes, thousands) of places that serve sandwiches in Manhattan, and most of them are pretty ordinary. But the following turn out exceptionally good combinations for eating in or taking out.

America (9–13 E 18th St)
Brasserie (100 E 53rd St)

Burke and Burke (2 E 23rd St)
Carnegie Delicatessen and Restaurant (854 Seventh Ave)
Casanas & Sons (461 Columbus Ave)
Cleaver Company (229 W Broadway)
Délices de France (289 Madison Ave)
Donald Sacks (World Financial Center)
Jerry's (101 Prince St)
Manganaro's Hero Boy (492 Ninth Ave)
Olive's (120 Prince St)
Peter Dent (120 Hudson St)
Small Feast (1173 Second Ave)
Telephone Bar and Grill (149 Second Ave)
Thorough Bread (450 Park Ave S)
Union Square Cafe (21 E 16th St)
Yellowfingers di Nuovo (200 E 60th St)

Seafood

Captain's Table (860 Second Ave)
Coastal (300 Amsterdam Ave)
Docks (2427 Broadway and 633 Third Ave)
Fishin Eddie (73 W 71st St)
Grand Central Oyster Bar Restaurant (Grand Central Station, E 42nd St)
Jane Street Seafood Cafe (31 Eighth Ave)
King Crab (871 Eighth Ave)
Le Bernardin (155 W 51st St)
Le Cirque (Mayfair Regent Hotel, 58 E 65th St)
Manhattan Ocean Club (57 W 58th St)
Maryland Crab House (237 Third Ave)
Marylou's (21 W 9th St)
Oceana (55 E 54th St)
Oriental Town Seafood (14 Elizabeth St)
Primola (1226 Second Ave)
Remi (145 W 53rd St)
Sea Grill (19 W 49th St)
Tropica (Met Life Building, 200 Park Ave)
Trumpets (Grand Hyatt Hotel, 109 E 42nd St)
Wilkinson's (1573 York Ave)

Shopping Breaks

To replenish your energy, here are some good places to eat in the major Manhattan department stores:

Café L'Etoile (balcony), the **Fountain** (5th floor), and the **Patio Restaurant** (8th floor) at Macy's (151 W 34th St)
Cafe SFA (8th floor) at Saks Fifth Avenue (Fifth Ave at 50th St)

Cafe Vienna (7th floor) and **Pasta and Cheese** (5th floor) at Bergdorf-Goodman (754 Fifth Ave)

40 Carrots (lower level), **Le Train Bleu** (6th floor), **Showtime Cafe** (7th floor), and **Pasta and Expresso Bar** at Bloomingdale's (Third Ave at 60th St)

Le Petit Cafe and **Le Salon de Thé** (2nd floor) at Henri Bendel (712 Fifth Ave): Be sure to notice the magnificent Lalique windows.

Red Rose (6th floor) and **Soup Bar** (10th floor) at Lord & Taylor (424 Fifth Ave)

745 Cafe at Bergdorf-Goodman for Men (745 Fifth Ave)

Sports Bars

Park Avenue Country Club (381 Park Ave S)
Play-by-Play (4 Penn Plaza)
Polo Grounds (1472 Third Ave)
Runyon's (932 Second Ave)
Rusty's on 5th (575 Fifth Ave)
Sporting Club (99 Hudson St)
Sports on Broadway (2182 Broadway)

Steaks

Even though most of us have cut down on red meat, there's always a time when a really good steak hits the spot. For meat-and-potato lovers, here are the best steaks in town:

Ben Benson's (123 W 52nd St)
Frank's (431 W 14th St)
Gage & Tollner (372 Fulton St, Brooklyn)
Gotham Bar & Grill (12 E 12th St)
Keens Chop House (72 W 36th St)
Le Steak (1089 Second Ave)
Manhattan Cafe (1161 First Ave)
Palm and Palm Too (837 Second Ave and 840 Second Ave)
Pen and Pencil (205 E 45th St)
Peter Luger (178 Broadway, Brooklyn)
Pietro's (232 E 43rd St)
Post House (28 E 63rd St)
Smith & Wollensky (201 E 49th St)
Sparks (210 E 46th St)
Steak Frites (9 E 16th St)

Swingers and Sayers

Acme Bar & Grill (9 Great Jones St)
America (9–13 E 18th St)
Amsterdam's (454 Broadway)

Arizona 206 (206 E 60th St)
Banana Cafe (111 E 22nd St)
Benny's Burritos (93 Avenue A)
Brasserie des Théatres (100 E 53rd St)
Café Lalo (201 W 83rd St)
Carmine's (2450 Broadway)
Carnegie Delicatessen and Restaurant (854 Seventh Ave)
Corner Bistro (331 W 4th St)
Dallas BBQ (1265 Third Ave, 27 W 72nd St, 21 University Pl,
    132 Second Ave, and 315 Sixth Ave)
Docks (2427 Broadway and 633 Third Ave)
EJ's Luncheonette (433 Amsterdam Ave and 1271 Third Ave)
Ernie's (2150 Broadway)
Gotham Bar & Grill (12 E 12th St)
Gray's Papaya (2090 Broadway)
Hard Rock Café (221 W 57th St)
Houlihan's (729 Seventh Ave)
Hows Bayou (355 Greenwich St)
Jackson Hole Wyoming Burgers (232 E 64th St)
Jim McMullen (1341 Third Ave)
John's Pizzeria (278 Bleecker St and 408 E 64th St)
Mickey Mantle's (42 Central Park S)
Peter Luger (178 Broadway, Brooklyn)
Planet Hollywood (140 W 57th St)
Sarabeth's Kitchen (1295 Madison Ave, 423 Amsterdam Ave,
    and 945 Madison Ave)
Serendipity 3 (225 E 60th St)
Smith & Wollensky (201 E 49th St)
Steak Frites (9 E 16th St)
Tavern on the Green (Central Park W at 67th St)
TGIFriday's (many locations)
Union Square Café (21 E 16th St)
Zarela (953 Second Ave)
Zip City Brewing Co. (3 W 18th St)

Takeout

This volume features several sections on take-home possibilities. First,
study the list of "Best Taste Treats" at the start of this set of listings;
practically every item mentioned is available for take-home purchase.
Then, look at the food section under "Delis, Catering, Food to Go" (not
available in the pocket edition) for a complete listing of the best takeout
places in town. The four major gourmet stores all have outstanding selections of dishes to go.

Balducci's (424 Sixth Ave)
Dean and Deluca (560 Broadway)
Grace's Marketplace (1237 Third Ave)
Zabar's (2245 Broadway)

Teatime

The age-old custom of afternoon tea has returned with class to a number of Manhattan spots. Besides cream and sugar, proper accessories include a pitcher of hot water and a small silver strainer to catch the tea leaves. Most of these places have delicious accompaniments for your cup of tea:

Anglers and Writers (420 Hudson St)
Baratti & Milano (697 Madison Ave)
Barclay Restaurant at the Hotel Inter-Continental (111 E 48th St)
Cafe SFA at Saks Fifth Avenue (611 Fifth Ave)
Carlyle Hotel Gallery (35 E 76th St)
Cocktail Terrace at the Waldorf-Astoria (301 Park Ave)
Danal (90 E 10th St): Different!
57-57 (Four Seasons Hotel, 57 E 57th St)
Gold Room at the New York Palace (455 Madison Ave)
Gotham Lounge at the Peninsula Hotel (700 Fifth Ave)
Le Cafe at Barney's (Seventh Ave at 17th St)
Le Salon at the Stanhope (995 Fifth Ave)
Le Salon de Thé at Henri Bendel (712 Fifth Ave)
Le Train Bleu at Bloomingdale's (Third Ave at 59th St)
Les Délices Guy Pascal (939 First Ave and 1231 Madison Ave)
Little Nell's Tea Room (343 E 85th St)
Mayfair Regent Hotel (610 Park Ave)
Oak Room at the Algonquin Hotel (59 W 44th St)
Palm Court at the Plaza Hotel (Fifth Ave at 59th St)
Pembroke Room at the Lowell Hotel (28 E 63rd St)
Polo Lounge at the Westbury Hotel (Madison Ave at 69th St)
Regency Hotel (540 Park Ave)
Rotunda at the Hotel Pierre (2 E 61st St)
Sant Ambroeus (1000 Madison Ave)
Serendipity 3 (225 E 60th St)
Stone Room at the National Academy of Design (1083 Fifth Ave)
"21" Club (21 W 52nd St)

View

Contrary to the axiom that good food does not come with a good view, the food at all of these "rooms with a view" is terrific.

American Festival Cafe (Rockefeller Plaza) From the sidelines of the skating rink, the art deco monuments of Rockefeller Plaza tower above you.
Boathouse Cafe (Central Park, East Side entrance) From lakeside, you get a perfect view of Central Park, and the city skyline looms above the treetops.
Delegate's Dining Room (United Nations, First Ave at 42nd St, visitor's entrance)
Hudson River Club (World Financial Center, 250 Vesey St)

Le Pactole (2 World Financial Center) Hudson River views

Rainbow Room (30 Rockefeller Center, 65th fl) This elegant and romantic perch provides a panoramic midtown view.

River Cafe (1 Water St, Brooklyn) A window seat gives you that famous view of the downtown skyline you've seen on postcards and in movies.

Tavern on the Green (Central Park W at 67th St) Magical!

Terrace (400 W 119th St) The windows here show you what the city looks like from uptown.

Top of the Tower (3 Mitchell Pl)

The View (Marriott Marquis Hotel) You're high above Times Square – and revolving.

The Water Club (East River at E 30th St) Try the view with Sunday brunch.

World Yacht Cruises (Pier 81, W 41st St at Hudson River) Manhattan from the water.

Western

These places are a good distance from the Wild West, but they do their best to deliver a taste of cattle country!

Arizona 206 (206 E 60th St)
Border Cafe (2637 Broadway)
El Rio Grande (Third Ave bet 37th and 38th St)
Mesa Grill (102 Fifth Ave)
Yellow Rose Cafe (450 Amsterdam Ave)

Wine Bars

Manhattan's better-known wine bars include:

Café Europa and **La Brioche** (347 E 54th St)
I Tre Merli (463 W Broadway)
SoHo Kitchen and Bar (103 Greene St)

Young People's Choices

Many time the older folks have just as much fun as the kids at some of the trendier places in town. Here is a sample of places where children of all ages will have a ball:

America (9 E 18th St): Big place, big menu

American Festival Cafe (20 W 50th St): Skating at Rockefeller Center

Arizona 206 (206 E 60th St): A taste of the Southwest

Banana Cafe (111 E 22nd St): The only thing missing is monkeys.

Bellevues (496 Ninth Av): Funky

Boathouse Cafe (Central Park, E Park Dr at 72nd St): Overlooks Central Park lake

Brother Jimmy's Bar-B-Q (1461 First Ave): Great ribs

Carnegie Delicatessen and Restaurant (854 Seventh Ave): For big appetites

Corner Bistro (331 W 4th St): Burgers deluxe

Dallas BBQ (1265 Third Ave, 27 W 72nd St, 21 University Pl, 132 Second Ave, and 315 Sixth Ave): Texas-style

Food Fairs: Pier 17 (South Street Seaport) and A&S Plaza (Herald Sq)

Gray's Papaya (2090 Broadway): Hot dogs and all the trimmings

Hamburger Harry's (157 Chambers St, 156 Seventh Ave, and 145 W 45th St): The name says it all

Hard Rock Cafe (221 W 57th St): It's worth the battle

Jackson Hole Wyoming Burgers (232 E 64th St, Third Ave at 35th St, and Second Ave at 84th St): The best

John's Pizzeria (408 E 64th St and 278 Bleecker St): Crispy and delicious

Landmark Tavern (626 Eleventh Ave): Historic

Lox Around the Clock (676 Sixth Ave): Action

McDonald's (160 Broadway): A classy one

Mickey Mantle's (42 Central Park S): Jock hangout

Nice Restaurant (35 E Broadway and 64 Fulton St): It is nice

Papaya King (179 E 86th St and 201 E 59th St): Stand-up dogs and drinks

Pappa's Place (510 Sixth Ave): Treasure house for kids

Peppermint Park Cafe (1225 First Ave): Waffles, candies, ice cream, sandwiches, pastries, calories

Pig Heaven (1540 Second Ave): Chinese heaven

Planet Hollywood (140 W 57th St): New York Disneyland

Seventh Regiment Mess (643 Park Ave): A secret military winner!

Serendipity 3 (225 E 60th St): Very "in."

Tavern on the Green (Central Park W at 67th St): Magical

Tony Roma's (several locations): Great ribs and onion loaf

Yellowfingers di Nuovo (200 E 60th St): Pizzalike breads

Yellow Rose Cafe (450 Amsterdam Ave): Southern-fried goodies

Zarela (953 Second Ave): South of the border

New York Restaurants: Best of the Lot

ADRIENNE
The Peninsula Hotel
700 Fifth Ave (at 55th St)   212 247-2200
Breakfast: Daily; Lunch: Mon-Fri; Dinner: Tues-Sat;
Brunch: Sun
Moderately expensive

In keeping with the current New York trend of a rebirth of fine dining in a number of the better hotels, the Peninsula offers delicious food and professional service in a luxurious setting at their Adrienne restaurant. This is a dress-up type of room, whether you come for breakfast, lunch, dinner, Sunday brunch (which is very special), or afternoon tea. A business lunch is offered, if you want to impress an important client with a pheasant and wild mushroom dish, for example. Other possibilites: classy sandwiches (like smoked salmon on sourdough), pastas, and grilled seafood dishes. Afternoon tea includes finger sandwiches, wonderful hot scones with Devonshire cream, and sinful cakes and tarts. All of this reminds one of the namesake hotel in Hong Kong! A pre-theater dinner menu is available, as well as a full dinner selection of seafood, poultry, and meat specialties. Don't rush, but when you are ready ask to be surprised with a special dessert. They all taste just as good as they look!

AKBAR
475 Park Ave (bet 57th and 58th St)   212 838-1717
Lunch: Mon-Fri; Dinner: Daily
Moderate

If you are interested in north Indian cuisine, you can't do better than Akbar. You'll get a real taste of the region in a distinguished atmosphere, where muglai cooking at its very best is featured. The nice part of the food here is that it is not hot or oily. Wonderful tandoori breads, baked in a traditional clay oven, are special treats. There are other tandoori specials: several chicken dishes, minced lamb, cubes of fish, or large

---

Want to know where to go when you just don't know where you want to go? I have just the right place. It is cozy, homey, comfortable, plenty of T.L.C., good food and very efficient personnel. The menu is basic French. The name is Café du Soir, 322 E 86th St (212 988-4991). This end of E 86th Street reminds one of the ugly business strip areas in most American cities, but this tiny restaurant is a real find. It is open for lunch on week-ends in the summer, but daily in the winter, and welcomes you seven nights a week for dinner.

prawns. You can have a taste of them all in a mixed grill plate. At noontime there are set menus. In the evening, you can choose from delicious vegetarian dishes (very reasonably priced), traditional lamb entrees, or mildly spiced seafood specialties. Try some lassi with your meal; it is a drink made from yogurt, salted or sweet. Although most folks don't come to an Indian restaurant for desserts, the cottage cheese and milk flavored with rose water is surely different!

AMERICA
9–3 E 18th St   212 505-2110
Lunch, Dinner: Daily; Brunch: Sat, Sun
Inexpensive to moderate

Only in New York could you find a place like this. It's big, big, big! The building is enormous—it used to be a carpet showroom. The bar is enormous—when it's full, it looks like a yuppie convention. The menu is enormous—not dozens, but hundreds of items. The portions are enormous. And the noise level is enormous when all 350 to 400 seats are filled. But the good news is that the tab is small. Well, where do you start? They have a dozen or so egg dishes and just as many omelets. There are delicious griddle cakes, including sweet-potato pancakes. Excellent side dishes range from "hashslinger" potatoes to white-corn hush puppies to Boston brown bread and even "Cincinnatis" (shoestring French fries drenched in gravy). Appetizers run the gamut from New Orleans Cajun popcorn (deep-fried crawfish tails) to Buffalo chicken wings (deep fried and marinated) to New Mexican black-bean cakes to Oregon mushroom cakes—to which, as you'd expect, I am partial. There are several dozen main-course entrees, from American chop suey to New England roast turkey to shrimp jambalaya to South Carolina crab cakes and everything in between. Oh, and add hamburgers, chili, pasta, pizza, and absolutely the best sandwiches you can imagine. Then there are the desserts: Tennessee Black Bottom pie, Tollhouse cookies, Death by Chocolate, Key lime mousse, New Orleans pralines. . . . You name it, they've got it. Come on down, especially if you're escorting a group of youngsters.

AMERICAN FESTIVAL CAFE
20 W 50th St   212 246-6699
Lunch: Mon-Fri; Dinner: Daily; Brunch: Sat, Sun
Moderate

The big attraction here is the location. The ice-skating rink at Rockefeller Center is glamorous in summer or winter. There's always a lot going on at Rockefeller Center: entertainment, shopping, eating, and people watching. I'd say it's a must for any visitor to the city. The cafe serves good salads, sandwiches, and items from the charcoal grill. The chef's salad (greens, veal bacon, corncob ham, smoked turkey, peppered beef, and cheese) is delightful, as are the grilled lamb chops. For kids, the hamburgers are just right, and the desserts are unusually appetizing. Try the Key lime pie, bread pudding with sour-mash whiskey sauce, or strawberry shortcake. A large selection of domestic and imported beers is also available.

AN AMERICAN PLACE
2 Park Ave (at 32nd St)   212 684-2122
Lunch: Mon-Fri; Dinner: Mon-Sat
Moderately expensive to expensive

If there ever was a restaurant that reflected the personality of its owner, this is the place! An American Place is the dream of Larry Forgione, a well-known and well-respected chef who has created a winning establishment that features classic regional-style American dishes, using only fresh American products. The ambience can best be described as adequate . . . it is the food and the service that excel. Be prepared for large portions of such delicious dishes as warm potato crisp Napoleon with Hudson Valley foie gras and forest mushrooms; terrine of three smoked fish with their respective caviars and champagne dressing; or cedar-planked Atlantic salmon with toasted corn sauce, winter squash, and an apple cider vinegar with toasted pumpkin seeds. Of course, the menu will vary with the seasonal specialties. Being a red, white, and blue flag-waver myself, I almost want to sing "God Bless America" after a meal here; I think you will, too. Oh yes, the desserts are pure Yankee, like the fabulous strawberry shortcake (in season), banana betty, or your choice of bread or double chocolate pudding.

ANGELS
1135 First Ave (bet 62nd and 63rd St)   212 980-3131
Daily: 11:30-11:30
Inexpensive

Wouldn't you expect two people named Angela and Angelo to open a place called Angels? Well they did, and it has heavenly food at heavenly prices. Angels is a non-fancy pastaria, with angels all over the place—on the plain tables and on the plain walls. The food is contemporary Italian, with a heavy emphasis on delicious pastas, salads, and chicken. You are treated here as a member of the family, with informal service and loving care. It is no wonder that the place is busy all day and evening. Desserts include gelati, Oreo cheesecake, and a wonderfully rich Mississippi (in an Italian restaurant?) mud cake. The goodies don't stop here. Make sure you go around the corner to their takeout at 365 E 62nd St (212 371-8484), where you will find an absolutely fantastic assortment of bakery and prepared foods, pastas, sandwiches, and salads all made in the Angels kitchen. The prices are extremely reasonable, the quality exceptional. Catering services are available, and so is delivery.

ANTOLOTTI'S
337 E 49th St   212 688-6767
Lunch: Mon-Fri; Dinner: Daily
Moderate

When you've been successful in the same business for nearly four decades, you must be doing something right. And Antolotti's surely is. You can tell from the moment you enter: the greeting is pleasant and the seating prompt and efficient. No sooner have you taken your place in the pleasant, compact room – decorated with an eclectic mix of pictures and memorabilia – than one of the crisply professional staff places excellent bread, healthy nibbles, and cole slaw in front of you. Then you're presented with a huge menu of Italian and continental choices. It seems impossible for a kitchen to do a dozen veal dishes so well, but they do. In addition, there are wonderful seafood items, from sole to lobster, chicken any way you want it, pork and lamb chops, steaks, and a wide choice of typical Italian dishes. The homemade manicotti, cannelloni, and lasagna can't be beaten. Nothing is cooked ahead of time. If you can muster up the appetite for spumoni or rum cake, more power to you. I chose the big iced dish of fresh fruit to finish the meal. Two generations of the Antolotti family are on the job. Dad is seated at a booth, keeping an eye on his success story, while his son tends bar and greets a host of regular customers who have been coming here for years. An attractive party room is also available.

AQUAVIT
13 W 54th St   212 307-7311
Lunch: Mon-Fri; Dinner: Mon-Sat
Café: Moderately expensive; Dining Room: Expensive

Just as you would expect from the organized and hospitable Scandinavians, Aquavit presents an attractive, wholesome background for some very tasty – and expensive – meals. The setting is also a feast for the eyes: you have a choice of eating upstairs in the moderately priced café, or in several areas downstairs, including an attractive covered patio with a waterfall. Here the diner looks eight stories skyward at an unusually attractive atrium. The meal starts with a healthy breadbasket, including delicious seven-grain bread. Upstairs, the café offers appetizers heavy on the fish side: a herring plate, Scandinavian shrimp soup, and smoked Swedish salmon. Main course specialties include delicious Swedish meatballs, whole cold poached lobster, a typical smorgasbord plate, and Kaldolmar (Savoy cabbage rolls with lingonberry). Downstairs, hold on to your wallet for the three-course, price-fixed dinner. The first course features a choice of ten items, including blinis, traditional gravlax, and marinated arctic venison. Then on to such second-course entrees as poached halibut, turbot, or salmon; fillet of veal and sweetbreads; and snow grouse (a real delight!). No ordinary dessert menu here. Choices include Swedish pancakes, Swedish blueberry pie, and a fabulous chocolate cake with burned almond crust. You will be impressed with the very polite and attractive ladies and gentlemen who guide you through this sumptuous banquet. They are as low-key as the prices are high.

ARIZONA 206
206 E 60th St   212 838-0440
Lunch: Mon-Sat; Dinner: Daily
Moderate

The American Southwest never jumped like this place! Always popular, a new chef has brought renewed vigor to this claustrophobic spot that serves probably the best Arizona/New Mexico-type food in town. Forget about a pleasant greeting; many times there is no one there to assist with reservations and coats. And you have to fight your way through one of the busiest and noisiest bar scenes in town. Then on into a room that does little for the visual senses but much for tummy satisfaction. Great tequila-cured salmon and red chili duck ham to start. On to anchovy-glazed poussin with buckwheat sourdough pancakes, cinnamon-rubbed pork loin, or grilled Maine lobster with stuffed squid and clams in a red chili shellfish broth. Hey, partner, don't forget the desserts: pumpkin whiskey bread (with mascarpone pumpkin mousse), a *cajeta* banana sundae (with cinnamon ice cream), and best of all . . . the Arizona chocolate plate, with a taste of everything chocolate one could dream of!

ARQUA
281 Church St   212 334-1888
Lunch: Mon-Fri; Dinner: Mon-Sat
Moderate

There are Italian restaurants of every size, price range, and specialty in almost every neighborhood of Manhattan. I sometimes wonder if there aren't more Italian restaurants in Manhattan than in all of Italy. To be outstanding in New York, an Italian restaurant must have something special going for it. Arqua is really special because the staff does things so plainly and simply. This is not a fancy, pricey restaurant of the moment. Arqua (named for a small city near Venice) is situated in an old warehouse with high ceilings, which adds to the noisy atmosphere. The folks who run this place are not fancy, either. It shows in the TLC they give all the patrons, and the food is exceptional. You can have your choice of homemade pastas, Venetian dishes, marinated salmon, and ravioli with butternut squash. Squab and duck are specialties. There are also excellent veal dishes. The flourless espresso chocolate cake is exceptional.

AU TROQUET
328 W 12th St   212 924-3413
Dinner: Daily
Moderate

This is one of those difficult-to-find places in the Village. Allow extra time if you're arriving by taxi since most drivers will have trouble delivering you to the front door. And be sure you call for reservations; the place is small, and it is very popular with neighbors as well as knowledgeable people who have previously enjoyed Au Troquet's dining delights. This is a no-nonsense French country restaurant, where professional people prepare food professionally. Your plate looks like a colorful magazine ad—flamboyant in presentation—and it's especially good in the taste category. Au Troquet deserves special mention for its seasonings alone; they know how it's done. The soups are all delicious, as is the pâté de foie de canard. You can go on to fillet of sole, grilled salmon, lobster, or a fabulous rabbit dish. There is almost always a fine selection of lamb dishes available. Homemade desserts include a great mousse and sorbets. This is the kind of place you want to go to when you feel like having a relaxed, cozy dinner for two. It will surely help cement that business relationship—or maybe a more personal one!

AZZURRO
245 E 84th St (bet Second and Third Ave)   212 517-7068
Dinner: Daily
Moderate

This is a must for Southern Italian cuisine. I'd give Azzurro an A-plus for their polite and well-informed help. What a joy it is to find a restaurant that has no affectations, no unnecessary waiting, and no maitre d' with permanently outstretched palm. Instead, you find really nice folks who want to make your dining experience a pleasant one. There is a wholesome, informal atmosphere in this recently expanded spot. Neither the waiters nor the customers are dressed up, but the food is! An absolutely marvelous fresh minestrone soup is great to start with, as is the mixed eggplant, Sicilian style. The linguini with tuna fish and the *maccaruna chi sarde* (*bucatini* with fresh sardines, raisins, pinoli nuts, and wild fennel) are outstanding. For heartier appetites, there are grilled items every day. The folks in the kitchen are evidently as talented as the ones out front. You'll have a great time and a great meal. Be sure to call for reservations; they are very busy.

BANANA CAFE
111 E 22nd St   212 995-8500
Lunch, Dinner: Daily; Brunch: Sun
Moderate

This place is an experience! A few words of warning: if you like noise and crowds and confusion, sit on the main floor, but if conversation is a part of the evening, opt for balcony seating. At first blush you might think this is some kind of yuppie club, but the truth is the open kitchen features some of the tastiest food in town! The décor is what you might expect—monkeys and bananas and all that kind of stuff—but the real decor is in the outstanding presentation of the food. The menu is mainly pure Americana, with a hint of Brazilian touches. You can choose from pasta, risottos, and great pizzas. Saturday lunches feature *feidoada*—specialty cuts of beef and pork with black beans. The Sunday brunch offers whole-wheat pancakes, brioche French toast, plus many of the items from the daily menus. Fabulous desserts: frozen banana praline parfait, hazelnut tartufo, carrot cake trifle and, of course, America's favorite banana split! For late-evening diners (until 3 a.m.), there is a lot going on underground in the Banana Down Gallery. Deejay music every night (except Sunday and Monday) is an added feature.

BARBETTA
321 W 46th St (bet Eighth and Ninth Ave)   212 246-9171
Lunch, Dinner: Mon-Sat
Moderate to expensive

This is an elegant restaurant with Piemontese cuisine. Piemonte is located in the northern part of Italy, and the cuisine reflects that charming part of the country. You can dine here in European elegance. It is one of New York's oldest restaurants that is still owned by the family that founded it; the family has been here for nearly eight decades. One of the special attractions about Barbetta is dining alfresco in the garden during the summer. There is an à la carte luncheon menu, as well as a six-course before-theater dinner menu, which offers a fish specialty, baby salmon, and a number of other selections served expeditiously so that you can make the opening curtain. If you have more time and can enjoy a leisurely dinner, think about the minestrone soup (which is almost a meal in itself), ravioli that is made by hand, or the fabulous mushroom salad. Barbetta specializes in fish and game dishes that vary daily. If you're lucky enough to find squab on the menu, by all means try it. Other selections include veal kidneys, beef braised in red wine with polenta, or a delicious sirloin of beef. Desserts include several chocolate offerings and an assortment of cooked fruits, as well as one of the best crème caramels in the city. An added attraction: ballroom dancing after 8 p.m.

on Thursday, Friday and Saturday evenings. To be in business in the highly competitive restaurant field for such a long time, Barbetta has to be doing something right—and they are.

BARCLAY RESTAURANT
Hotel Intercontinental (111 E 48th St)   212 421-0836
Breakfast, Lunch, Dinner: Daily (except Sat lunch);
Brunch: Sun
Moderate

The grande dame of New York Sunday brunches is at the Palm Court in the Plaza Hotel; the setting there is without equal in the city. But if a little less class and a little less of a tab is in your program for a Sunday, I'd strongly suggest a visit to the Barclay Restaurant (so named after the forerunner to the Intercontinental). Everything that makes for a great Sunday festive occasion is here: extremely polite personnel, grand buffet tables of seafood, salads, roasts, cheeses, glorious desserts, champagne, and live music. And the tab is quite reasonable, by New York standards. There are special prices for the kids, and your waiter seems to have a champagne bottle ready whenever you are. The room is open for meals during the entire week, but the Sunday show is the winner.

BAROCCO
301 Church St   212 431-1445
Lunch: Mon-Fri; Dinner: Daily
Moderate

If you are looking for simple and well-prepared food in the TriBeCa area, this *trattoria* with a Tuscan flavor is your best bet. Barocco has a special way with seasonings that make their dishes light and easy to digest. This style of dining attracts many of the celebrities, who are so mindful of their figures! Specialties include wonderful homemade grilled bread with garlic and olive oil (*fettunta*), lasagna, spinach ravioli, grilled Norwegian salmon, grilled lamb chops, roast chicken, and prime New York strip steak. Top it all off with Tuscan almond cookies. Many of the items served in the restaurant are available for takeout next door Monday through Friday from 8 a.m. to 6:30 p.m.

BILLY'S
948 First Ave   212 355-8920, 212 753-1870
Lunch, Dinner: Daily
Moderate

For those who like old-fashioned setups, complete with white tiled floors, checkered tablecloths, and a busy bar right in the center of the dining area, Billy's is your kind of place. Established in 1870, this bustling pub/restaurant is a First Avenue institution, where the food is just as inviting as the atmosphere. It's been in the same family since opening day! No menus, just a blackboard listing steaks, scallops, chops, hamburgers, and the like. All are well prepared, with large portions accompanied by fair French fries or baked potatoes. Cole slaw is served when you are seated. Oh, yes. The waiters are vintage New York. For example, when a party of four arrives, they'll ask, "Do you wish to sit together?" But they are efficient, pleasant guys. A word about the bread. The ethnic mix of the Big Apple makes for exceptional talent in baking, and you can take advantage of these fine breads at many restaurants like Billy's. Desserts include delicious ice cream, cheesecake, pies, and homemade rice pudding. Try the Irish coffee with real whipped cream to top it all off. There are now *prix fixe* menus at lunch and early evening.

BOATHOUSE CAFE
Central Park   212 517-CAFE
Lunch: Daily (Mar 15–Nov 28);
Lunch and Dinner: Daily (May 1–Nov 28)
Moderate

Central Park has come back to life, and the Boathouse Cafe is one of its best attractions. It's situated in a charming spot on the east side of the park, between the 72nd Street and 79th Street entrances. A free trolley brings patrons from the 72nd Street and Fifth Avenue park entrance beginning at 7 p.m. The dockside has been partially tented and an authentic Venetian gondola is available (by reservation) for rent, as are rowboats. The view is great, the setting couldn't be more romantic, and the food is tasty and well presented. The menu is Northern Italian, with a variety of pasta. There is a great private party area located in a landscaped English garden. What a spot to launch your hot new product!

BOULEY
165 Duane St   212 608-3852
Lunch: Mon-Fri; Dinner: Mon-Sat
Moderately expensive

This is probably the most talked-about restaurant in Manhattan, and rightfully so. David Bouley is a genius in a business that is short in that category. He has created a charming, gracious, and warm atmosphere in which to serve some of the most attractive and tastiest dishes in the country. You will begin a meal of wonderment from the time you enter the marvelously ornate doors to the placing of beautiful Limoge china in front of you. Reasons for this success include the use of wonderfully fresh regional ingredients and painstaking time in the preparation of every dish. So be warned: if you are in a hurry, this is not the place to go. Dining at Bouley is for the relaxed, unhurried guest. The menu is involved; best to get advice from your very well-schooled waiter. The dessert selection is fabulous; the chocolate soufflé with hot chocolate sauce is an experience. But the same can be said for the entire meal!

BRASSERIE DES THEATRES
243 W 46th St   212 719-5588
Lunch, Dinner: Daily
Moderate to moderately expensive

The theater district has long needed some attractive dining spots, and now it has one. The creators of Park Bistro and Les Halles, both successful Park Avenue operations, have made their new property a very satisfying (and overpriced) place to dine before and after the performance. If only the service, which is shaky, could equal the excellent quality of the food, this would be one of the top new houses in midtown. One has a choice of soups, egg dishes, salads, pâtés, fish, meat and chicken dishes, with a nice selection of typical French offerings (grilled pig's-feet, *pot-au-feu,* and *choucroute royale*). For those who are really hungry, there are several fish platters with a large variety of delicacies. Oysters are another specialty. Homemade sherbets, ice creams, crêpes, and tarts will round off a very pleasant meal.

BRAVO GIANNI
230 E 63rd St   212 752-7272
Lunch: Mon-Fri; Dinner: Mon-Sun
Moderately expensive

Fans of Bravo Gianni—and there are many—may be upset that I'm mentioning it in this book. They want to keep it a secret. It's so nice and comfortable and the food is so good that they don't want it to become overcrowded and spoiled. But it doesn't look like there's any real danger of that happening, as long as Gianni himself is on the job. The not-too-large room is pleasantly appointed, with beautiful plants on every table. The intimate atmosphere makes it seem as though you're in your own private dining room. And what tastes await you there! You can't go wrong with any of the antipasto selections or soups. But do save room for the *tortellini alla panna* or the *fettuccine con ricotta*; no one does them better. I can recommend every dish on the menu, with top billing going to the fish dishes and the rack of lamb. Marvelous desserts, many of them made in-house, will surely tempt you. Legions of loyal customers come back again and again; it's easy to see why. But please, keep all of this to yourself!

CAFÉ
210 Spring St (at Sixth Ave)   212 274-0505
Lunch, Tea (4–6), Dinner: Daily; Brunch: Sat, Sun
Moderate

When knowledgeable New Yorkers say, "Let's go to the Café," they don't mean just any café. They mean *the* Café. This is a Parisian French bistro with a medieval twist. In cold weather, the place is warm and inviting, with soft lighting and music from time to time. In the summer, the porch is an attractive outdoor café that takes care of about 45 people. There are standard bistro dishes like steak au poivre, prime rib, grilled tuna, and rack of lamb. But there are also great pâtés, salads, pastas, and seafood dishes, all served with tender loving care by Richard Widmaier-Picasso (yes, grandson of the great one) and his friendly associates. The crème brûlée is about the best in town.

CAFE BOTANICA
Essex House
160 Central Park S   212 247-0300, 212 484-5120 (direct)
Breakfast, Lunch, Dinner: Daily (Brunch on Sunday)
Moderate

Chalk up another winner for the increasing number of good dining spots in Manhattan hotels. The recently renovated Essex House features two excellent top-quality restaurants, very much in keeping with the fine ambience of this Nikko property. Cafe Botanica overlooks Central Park, with the added pleasure of magnificent table settings to go along with the tasty fare. Villeroy and Bosch's "Botanica" pattern is the theme for the serving pieces: along with the colorfully backed chairs and the light and airy feel of the room, the china makes the terrace area of the restaurant one of Manhattan's most attractive dining rooms. Spicy crab cakes or a selection of cold appetizers will get you started well. There are great pizzas and pastas, and excellent grilled tuna and swordfish steaks. It's a wonderful spot for a very special occasion lunch—the closest thing possible to a private dining room in the park!

The best way to find out all about New York restaurants is to use the book you are now reading. However, a new twist is available from some enterprising entrepreneurs: FOODPHONE (777-FOOD) covers over 40 different types of cuisine, at the touch of a dial. The cost is only that of a local call. You will receive informative descriptions of restaurants, including food type, location, and price range. Special attractions—such as desserts, hotel restaurants, and places for kids—are also available from this service.

CAFE DE BRUXELLES
118 Greenwich Ave   212 206-1830
Lunch, Dinner: Tues-Sun
Moderate

One of the treats at a county fair is the Belgian waffles booth. There always seems to be a queue at that concession, and for good reason. In New York, you don't have to go to the county fair. Just make your way to the Village, where Thierry, the chef, and his wife, Patricia, set an informal table brimming with specialities from Belgium. The waffles are served with whipped cream and chocolate and strawberry sauce; they are a meal in themselves. But here I go talking about desserts before we've even started our meal. Hot chicken-liver custard in port-wine sauce, homemade country pâté, and stuffed mussels with garlic (yes, heavy on the garlic) are some of the house hors d'oeuvres. Entree choices range from medallions of monkfish to dark Belgian beer stew, a house specialty, to several steak dishes. On certain nights, Belgian dishes like chicken *waterzooi,* Bruxelle bouillabaisse, and a very tasty *choucroute* (sauerkraut) dish are offered. They're also available anytime, if you give them adequate notice. But back to those desserts. If you don't try the waffles, at least sink your teeth into the tasty apple or apricot tarts made in Thierry's own kitchen.

CAFE DES ARTISTES
1 W 67th St   212 877-3500
Lunch: Mon-Fri; Dinner: Daily; Brunch: Sat, Sun
Moderate

George Lang has created an absolute masterpiece on the west side, just off Central Park. It's truly a landmark. There are several dining levels and some hidden tables, giving each diner the impression of being in a small, cozy establishment. Beautiful murals by Christy complement the charming décor, the personnel are wonderfully accommodating, and the food is absolutely delicious. Try the unusual Sunday brunch. Some of the mouth-watering selections include smoked salmon Benedict, asparagus omelet, spicy Virginia crab cakes, and delicious stuffed French toast. Dinner appetizers include dill-marinated fish, duck or chicken liver, and a number of seafood items. For the main course, there is sea bass; grilled Coho salmon; broiled veal chops; pork, lamb, and beef dishes; and a pasta. By all means, don't overlook the desserts: such dandies as Key lime pie, toasted almond cake, chestnut cream torte, and a great dessert platter that features a sample of each. Three-course price-fixed lunches and dinners are offered. This is a lovely, romantic place at any time, but I especially recommend it for an after-theater supper.

CAFÉ DES SPORTS
329 W 51st St   212 581-1283, 212 974-9052
Lunch: Mon-Fri; Dinner: Daily
Inexpensive

This is a cozy spot with an intensely loyal following developed over 35 years of serving good, wholesome food in generous amounts at reasonable prices. The selections change daily, depending on what is available from the marketplaces. I have found the homemade sausage and the London broil to be exceptionally good values. Blue jeans and your most comfortable housedress are perfectly acceptable here. You'll smile along with the hospitable personnel, especially when they hand you a very realistic tab for a most satisfying meal.

CAFE EUROPA and LA BRIOCHE
347 E 54th St   212 755-0160
Lunch: Mon-Fri; Dinner: Mon-Sat
Moderate

This is simply described as a charming café. It gives you the feeling of walking in from the streets of Paris or Munich. I recommend it for either lunch or dinner. For lunch, you might be interested in the imperial sandwich (steak tartare with caviar, icy vodka, and beer), but my choice is chicken brioche with fresh tarragon, celery, carrots, and mushrooms. It's a hefty portion that's just right for a delightful lunch. The brioche offerings change from time to time, variously featuring curried beef, veal marengo, or shrimp and mushroom. The dinner menu is also varied, with entree selections ranging from chicken breast to beef stroganoff. There is a large selection of desserts, from strawberries Romanoff to Mississippi mud cake. Another dessert alternative is the French, English, or Italian cheese selection, served with fruit or nuts. There is an interesting combination of European and Oriental personnel in the kitchen and out front. It all adds up to a most pleasant dining experience.

CAFÉ UN DEUX TROIS
123 W 44th St   212 354-4148
Lunch: Mon-Fri; Dinner: Daily; Brunch: Sat, Sun
Moderate

Want to see one of your favorite actors? This café could be his or her hangout! Paper tablecloths seem like a stingy way to dress a restaurant table, but at this bustling café, there's a reason. Two reasons, in fact. One is that it helps keep the tab down. The other is to provide drawing paper; crayons are furnished on every table. Doodling helps pass the time, and isn't it something you've always wanted to do since you were a kid? The surroundings (an old hotel lobby) are plain, but the location is handy if you're going to the theater. Service is very prompt and cordial, and prices are moderate. Though the menu is limited, each item is handled with obvious attention to quality and taste. Begin with a hearty onion soup, salade nicoise, or pâté de canard. Seafood *en papillote* is an excellent selection. The steak tartare is the best in the city. This spot is also popular with the recording industry and young people. Maybe aspiring singers will be able to make the deal of their lives over a cup of cappuccino.

CAFFE BONDI
7 W 20th St (nr Fifth Ave)   212 691-8136
Lunch, Dinner: Mon-Sat; Brunch: Sun
Moderate

In the mood for a high start and a heavy finish? Well, this is the place. The lunches and dinners are excellent, with an emphasis on the Italian look, but the desserts are superb. You can sit indoors or on the outside patio and savor every one of those delicious calories in the shape of marvelous tortes and cakes. It's a convenient place for meeting friends if you are working Broadway or Fifth Avenue in the twenties. Great Danish and coffee are available for breakfast carryout.

CAL'S
55 W 21st St   212 929-0740
Lunch: Mon-Fri; Dinner: Daily
Moderate

Lower Fifth Avenue is blossoming with renewed vigor. New stores and restaurants have brought life and color to an area that was pretty drab for a number of years. One of the most popular bistros is Cal's, a high-ceilinged, spacious, and noisy spot that sports a huge old-fashioned bar lined with a large selection of wines. Casual dress is the order of the day, but service is anything but casual! Young, well-trained personnel offer a selection of a dozen or so salads and seafood items as starters. Entrees are international in scope, with a number of Italian, French, and German specialities (like linguini, wienerschnitzel, and *pot-au-feu*) and some old Yankee fare (like steak tartare) as well. Crepes stuffed with lingonberries, walnuts, and bananas, topped with chocolate sauce and whipped cream, will insure the "diet days" start tomorrow!

CAN
482 W Broadway (at Houston St)   212 533-6333
Lunch, Dinner: Daily
Moderate

In the days when Phnom Penh was the Paris of the Orient, there was no better place to feast upon French-Vietnamese cuisine. Now New Yorkers have the opportunity to try such unusual dishes as barbecued beef wrapped in vine leaves, barbecued Gulf shrimp on sugar cane (you don't eat the cane), wok-fried bass, or grilled young stuffed squid. The setting is attractive and clean, and the personnel seem happy to guide you through some of the hot dishes. But don't worry about that spicy taste lasting too long. The profiteroles with caramel ice cream, the "symphony of chocolate" (an eye-popping collection), or homemade ice creams and sorbets will happily cool off any fire in the belly.

CANTON
45 Division St   212 226-4441, 212 966-7492
Lunch, Dinner: Wed-Sun (closed one month during summer)
No credit cards
Moderate

For those in the know, Canton has been a favorite spot for some time. Why? The place is clean, and the personnel are friendly and very polite. But most of all, unlike so many Chinese restaurants, the cooking is done on an individual basis. It's almost like stepping into the kitchen of a Chinese family. Tell your waiter the kind of Cantonese delicacies you wish to have. You will be delighted with the results! I would suggest butterfly shrimp, diced chicken with Chinese vegetables and mushrooms, or fried young squab, Chinese style. All the seafood is fresh and tasty. So gather up a group of friends for a special Chinese treat. You'll be pleased with the quality of your food *and* the moderate bill.

CAPSOUTO FRÈRES
451 Washington St (one block S of Canal St)   212 966-4900
Lunch: Tues-Fri; Dinner: Daily; Brunch: Sat, Sun
Moderate

In 1891, when the building where Capsouto Frères is located was built, this might have been the "in" area. But, alas, times (and neighborhoods) have changed. The Landmark Building is still a beauty; however, the rest of the surroundings are pretty sad. Inside, it's another story. Three brothers and their mother team up to operate a classic establishment, complete with ceiling fans, wooden tables, good cheer, and tasty plates. At noon a special *prix fixe* lunch is offered, or you can order from an à la carte menu laden with salads, fish and meat dishes, or pasta. In the evening, they offer more of the same, along with quail, duckling, or first-rate sirloin steak. This bistro is a great setting for a casual, let-your-hair-down evening with good friends who like to live it up!

CAPTAIN'S TABLE
860 Second Ave (at 46th St)   212 697-9538
Lunch: Mon-Fri; Dinner: Mon-Sat
Moderate

For fresh seafood at moderate prices, it is difficult to beat the recently re-energized Captain's Table, located on a dreary midtown block along Second Avenue. Once inside, the clean, comfortable surroundings will add to a very pleasant meal. There are dozens of hot and cold seafood appetizers, soups, salads, special daily pastas, fresh vegetables, and a vast selection of mussel, crab, scallop, shrimp, lobster, and fish dishes. A takeout section from the fish market at the entrance is available from noon until 10 p.m. Service is congenial and helpful. Stock up on your seafood selection, as the dessert menu is not worth considering.

CARMINE'S
2450 Broadway (bet 90th and 91st St)   212 362-2200
Dinner: Daily

200 W 44th (bet Seventh and Eighth Ave)   212 221-3800
Lunch, Dinner: Daily

American Express
Moderate

Are you thinking *big* and *Italian*? The first thing you want to do is round up at least six of your heavy-eating friends, call Carmine's for reservations, and show up famished and wearing loose clothing. You won't be disappointed! Carmine's presents Southern Italian family dining fare, with *huge* portions and zesty seasonings that come with the territory. Not only are the platters full, they are delicious. If you go with fewer than a half-dozen friends, my advice is to go early – the wait can be as long as an hour, as they will not reserve tables for smaller parties. The menu choices run the gamut of pizzas, pastas, chicken, veal, seafood, and some very tasty Italian appetizers, such as calamari. Oh, yes, there is no printed menu. Wall signs explain the offerings.

CARNEGIE DELICATESSEN AND RESTAURANT
854 Seventh Ave (at 55th St)   212 757-2245
Breakfast, Lunch, Dinner: Daily (6:40 a.m.-4 a.m.)
No credit cards
Moderate

There's no city on earth with delis like New York's, and the Carnegie is one of the best. Its location in the middle of the hotel district makes it perfect for midnight snacks. Everything is made on the premises, and Carnegie offers free delivery between 7 a.m. and 3 a.m., if you're within a five-block radius. Where to start? Your favorite Jewish mother didn't make chicken soup better than the Carnegie's homemade variety. It's practically worth getting sick for! It comes with matzo balls, garden noodles, and fresh rice, fresh homemade kreplach, or real homemade kasha. There's more: Great blintzes. Open sandwiches, hot and delicious. Ten different deli and egg sandwiches. A very juicy burger with all the trimmings. Lots of fish dishes. Corned beef, pastrami, and rare roast beef. A choice of egg dishes unequaled in New York. Salads. Side orders of everything from hot baked potatoes to potato pancakes. Outrageous cheesecake topped with strawberries, blueberries, pineapple, or cherries (or just served plain). Desserts from A to Z – even Jell-O.

CHANTERELLE

2 Harrison St (at Hudson St)   212 966-6960
Lunch, Dinner: Tues-Sat
Expensive

Mention Chanterelle to New Yorkers with well-honed taste buds, and a smile occurs immediately! It was only a matter of time before Karen and David Waltuck would have to move from their tiny SoHo restaurant on Grand Street. The place simply wasn't big enough to handle the legion of loyal customers who feel that Chanterelle is one of New York's better restaurants. Well, the Waltucks moved to a space with a larger dining room (seats about 60), a bigger kitchen, and a cute after-dinner area. The setting is formal and attractive, with interesting high, stamped-tin ceilings in the historic Mercantile Exchange Building in TriBeCa. The menu changes periodically, but that really isn't important since every dish is a masterful creation. With David in the kitchen, making use of his marine biology background preparing great fish and lobster dishes, and Karen out front pampering her guests, it is a good bet you won't even notice the size of the tab for the *prix fixe* dinner or tasting menu.

CHELSEA CENTRAL

227 Tenth Ave (bet 23rd and 24th St)   212 620-0230
Lunch: Mon-Fri; Brunch: Sun; Dinner: Daily
Moderate

Officially, this is what is known as an American bistro. But it really is much more than that. The turn-of-the-century atmosphere is unimposing, the tile floors not fancy, the tablecloths paper rather than linen, but the food is great. Eating in the Chelsea district can be dicey, so this spot is a sure bet for hungry shoppers or visitors to the area. Luncheon specialities are heavy on salads and chicken dishes. But there are also omelets, burgers, and crisp tasty homemade potato fries. For dinner there are more choices: sea scallops, pork chops, pastas, duck, steak, and seafood. The Sunday brunch has a few unusual items, like corn pancakes with cinnamon, raisin, and walnut polenta, or poached eggs with crisp crab cakes. In keeping with the current interest in desserts, Chelsea Central continues to shine in the caloric goodies department. (Try the chocolate flourless cake.)

CHELSEA TRATTORIA ITALIANA

108 Eighth Ave   212 924-7786
Lunch: Mon-Fri; Dinner: Mon-Sun
Moderate

The Bitici brothers, owners of the Chelsea Trattoria, are hard-working Italian boys who know how to make a restaurant tick. The brother who personally takes care of it is a jewel. Working in the kitchen and out front, he runs a good show. The restaurant, complete with a tile floor and brick walls decked out with wine bottles, looks like the local trattoria in an Italian village. The whole place is friendly, unimposing, and bustling; it's definitely not a trendy, pricey Italian novelty. You come here for good, hearty Italian food, beautifully presented by professional waiters. The menu runs the gamut from great soups and pasta to veal scaloppini; boneless breast of chicken sauteed in white wine, sausage, mushrooms, and garlic; bay scallops; scampi; and many daily specials. The dessert cart is gorgeous and loaded with goodies made in-house, including an incredible white and dark chocolate cake. The folks here couldn't be more accommodating. They will even do their best for the drop-in diner—but I strongly suggest making early reservations.

CHEZ JACQUELINE
72 MacDougal St   212 505-0727
Dinner: Daily
Moderate

This modest French bistro in the Village is one of the undiscovered pleasures of Manhattan. The atmosphere is very relaxed. You'll see cozy couples eating at the bar or serene seniors holding hands at one of the small number of tables in this popular neighborhood restaurant. Fresh, large salads are a specialty, as well as country pâté, duck liver mousse, and mussels with garlic. Among the dozen items regularly available as entrees, house favorites include the broiled rack of lamb, chicken casserole, veal kidneys, veal sweetbreads, and a hearty beef stew in a red wine, tomato, and carrot sauce. The portions are very generous and the prices fair. If you can manage a dessert, the crème brûlée or the white and dark chocolate mousse cake will convince you the kitchen knows what it's doing.

CHEZ JOSEPHINE
414 W 42nd St   212 594-1925
Dinner: Mon-Sat
Moderate

Those who follow the entertainment business will remember the late Josephine Baker, who was the toast of Paris in the first quarter of this century. Well, one of her adopted children, Jean-Claude, has kept the showbiz interest and added the food business to his accomplishments. He has created a first-class atmosphere with sexy and attractive décor, a background of live jazz music, and delicious food to match. Chez Josephine is a haven for those who have made it and those who wish they had—it is dining with theatrics, plus. This is a great place for a late-night, after-theater rendezvous. If Jean-Claude settled down for a minute, you would find him fascinating company. The menu has French tones; however, it is really in the dessert category that the place shines. The warm apple and rhubarb cake is very special, as is the *bombe pralinee*. A private party room is available upstairs. The bistro is a charmer, and so is Jean-Claude!

CHEZ MA TANTE
189 W 10th St   212 620-0223
Dinner: Daily; Brunch: Sun
Moderate

This Village café is small and unassuming, and you've probably never heard of it. Its main claim to fame is that it's associated with Ferrier, one of uptown's most expensive dining spots. The difference between the two restaurants is the price. Chez Ma Tante does an excellent job at a very reasonable tab. Friendly and cozy in the winter, this bistro opens onto the sidewalk in summer. Manager Andres Calro and chef Francis Cheru handle the duties up front and in the kitchen, and they do a consistently good job, since the place is filled with regular patrons. Hors d'oeuvres include homemade duck pâté, *romate au Montrachet,* and seafood in puff pastry. Outstanding entrees are grilled Norwegian salmon with mustard sauce, and "French's favorite dish" (steak, French fries, and green salad). Grilled swordfish or tuna are also specialties of the house. The profiteroles topped with white and dark chocolate sauce (and served hot) is a delicious variation on this popular dish.

CHEZ MICHALLET
90 Bedford St (at Grove St)   212 242-8309
Dinner: Daily; Brunch: Sun
Moderate

Imagine you are sitting in the window of a quaint little French restuarant in a picturesque village in the French countryside. The place has about a dozen tables, the décor is eclectic, the kitchen tiny . . . but the food and the service are wonderful. All this is true, except you are looking out on the corner of Bedford and Grove Streets in Greenwich Village! But what a charming place this is. The friendly waiters couldn't be more helpful in explaining the varied menu: steak, salmon, duck, lamb, veal, chicken, or fish . . . anything your heart desires. The desserts are good as well. Choose from tarts, a great chocolate truffle cake, crème caramel, profiteroles, or fresh berries. For a perfectly satisfying and relaxing evening, this spot is hard to beat. There is also a special pre-theater menu.

CHEZ NAPOLÉON
365 W 50th St   212 265-6980
Lunch: Mon-Fri; Dinner: Mon-Sat
Inexpensive to moderate

With all the problems of daily life, it's fun to go to a place where the atmosphere is cheerful. Chez Napoleon is that kind of place. The lady who owns it greets you like a long-lost friend and seats you in a small, clean dining area. It's an old house—warm, cozy, and obviously a neighborhood favorite for many years. The cooking is dependable and hearty. My top recommendations from the large menu are coquille St. Jacques, bouillabaisse (served only on weekends), rabbit with mustard sauce, and sweetbreads. Many of the desserts are homemade. But the big plus here is the freshness of the dishes and the gracious feeling that they're truly glad to have you.

CHIN CHIN
216 E 49th St (bet Second and Third Ave)   212 888-4555
Lunch: Mon-Fri; Dinner: Daily
Moderate to moderately expensive

Chin Chin is a very classy Chinese restaurant, and the ambience and price reflect the superior style of Chinese cooking. There are two rooms, including a garden in back. The soups and barbecued spareribs are wonderful for starters. The Szechuan jumbo prawns are sensational. As a matter of fact, I'd concentrate on the seafood dishes. But you might also try the wonderful Peking duck dinner, with choice of soup, crispy duck skin with pancakes, fried rice, poached spinach, and homemade sorbet or ice cream. The menu is much the same for lunch or dinner. This is an excellent choice for a business lunch with a client who has a hankering for improving East-West relations.

CITY CAFE
1481 York Ave (bet 78th and 79th St)   212 570-9810
Lunch: Mon-Fri; Brunch: Sun; Dinner: Mon-Sun
Moderate

Cathy and Eric Miller have created a pleasant and comfortable oasis for a leisurely lunch or dinner on the Upper East Side. In nice weather an outside patio is available for those who would like a little sun with their sandwich or salad. Nothing fancy, just good wholesome food served with a smile and at a sensible price. I'd recommend any of the sandwiches (all served on country bread with crispy French fries): grilled chicken, shrimp BLT, grilled filet mignon, or grilled burger. At dinner, there are great pastas, fresh seafood, duckling, or herbed roast chicken.

CLAIRE
156 Seventh Ave (at 19th St)   212 255-1955
Lunch: Mon-Fri; Brunch: Sat-Sun; Dinner: Mon-Sun
Moderate

Key West may be a long way from Chelsea, but the owner of this bustling seafood emporium decided he wanted to make that move. Neighborhood regulars are glad he did! Don't come here unless you are in the mood for fish, although burgers and steaks are also on the menu. Appetizers include gravlax (fresh cured salmon), mussels, oysters, smoked trout, and fresh tuna. Hungry diners will enjoy the Fisherman's Harvest, which includes shrimp, mussels, scallops, and red snapper. Other entrees that are usually available include broiled fillet of flounder, tilefish, grouper, monkfish, or salmon. If you are a crawfish lover (like your author), the bayou crawfish patties are outstanding. Many other

Southern-style fish dishes are featured as specials. The establishment has a professional air, with prompt and efficient service. As you might expect, Key lime pie and Mississippi mud cake head up the dessert menu.

COASTAL
300 Amsterdam Ave (at 74th St)   212 769-3988
Dinner: Daily
Moderate

Coastal went through an early-life crisis. At the start, it was a noisy, very "in" place where the circus atmosphere was secondary to the food. Well, that kind of restaurant does not last long in today's environment. Coastal has now settled down to what it should be — an excellent neighborhood seafood house. Soundproofed ceiling tiles have been added, and the waiters now act like normal human beings. Coastal does well with their sauces. In the spring, cioppino conjures up images of Fisherman's Wharf in San Francisco. It's a great stew with jumbo shrimp, scallops, mussels, clams, and assorted fish served with buttered pasta. Fresh American regional pastas are offered every day. An extensive gourmet home-delivery menu is available. And in keeping with the times, a Coastal Café is open at 1359 First Avenue (near 73rd St), with an eye to moderate prices.

COLORS
237 Park Ave (enter on 46th St)   212 661-2000
Lunch: Mon-Fri; Dinner: Mon-Sat
Moderate to moderately expensive

A totally new "color" has been applied to this rather hard-to-find hideaway in the Park Atrium Building. But don't get discouraged, for the journey is worth the effort. Erik Blauberg, an enterprising young chef who was well-trained by David Bouley, has brought French modern cooking to an essentially American restaurant. This bistro has two dining areas: the main room, which features pastel coloring and attractive modern art, and an adjacent open atrium. Dishes here are light and healthy, but still very tasty . . . especially the lobster halibut and other seafood presentations. Pasta dishes are exceptional, as is the roast loin of lamb. A big plus here is the tender loving care given the operation by genial general manager Phil Hughes, who made many friends when he was the top man at the Plaza Hotel.

CONTRAPUNTO
200 E 60th St (at Third Ave)   212 751-8616
Lunch, Dinner: Daily
Moderate

Contrapunto is ideal for pooped-out shoppers! The thing that struck me first about Contrapunto was the airiness and lightness of the dining room. It's located on the second floor of a busy corner building across the street from Bloomingdale's, with full-length windows allowing a view of the activity on Third Avenue. It's a delightful place for a delicious and different Italian lunch. The pastas are unique! All portions are good-sized, and you will be impressed with the quality. If there is one drawback, it's that service is very slow; don't come here if you have an appointment within the hour. This place advertises itself as a pasta, wine, and gelati house, and it is just that. Be sure to save room for dessert; the chocolate cake is absolutely sinful. I also recommend that you try the chocolate, praline, or strawberry gelati.

CORRADO
1373 Sixth Ave (at 55th St)   212 333-3133
Lunch: Mon-Fri; Dinner: Daily
Moderate

Young men who are looking, and older men who are wishing, take note. The attraction here is not just the tasty food, but also the stunning and shapely show that goes along with it! For years this was a rather humdrum midtown location. Then some wise operators put the personnel in the front of the house in eye-catching outfits, and the clientele followed suit. Now Corrado jumps with some of the most attractive young people in town. They come to look at each other and, incidentally, eat some of the best Italian fare in midtown. There is gnocchi, ravioli, clam linguine, grilled dishes of fish, chicken, or chops, and excellent rare paillard of beef. If they have strawberry pizza for dessert when you're there, be sure to try it. A nice touch: special wines are suggested for each dessert item. The location is handy to midtown hotels.

CUCINA STAGIONALE
275 Bleecker St   212 924-2707
Lunch, Dinner: Daily
No credit cards
Inexpensive

When you serve good food at a small price, word gets around. So it's no wonder there's a line in front of this small Village café almost any time of the day. Its name translates as "seasonal kitchen," and the seasonal specialties are real values, indeed. It's a bare-bones setup, with seating for only several dozen hungry folks. Service is impersonal and nonprofessional, but who cares at these prices. Innovative Italian cuisine is served here – tasty, attractive, and filling – and you can do very well on a slim budget. Recommended appetizers include smoked salmon with endive and radiccio, and sauteed wild mushrooms. For a few pennies more, you can get a large dish of vegetarian lasagna, linguini, or ravioli. I'm constantly asked about inexpensive places that serve quality food, and I have no hesitation in recommending this spot. One word of warning: don't go if it's raining, because you'll probably have to wait to get seated, and the wait is outside.

DARBAR
44 W 56th St   212 432-7227
Lunch, Dinner: Daily
Moderate

It's a joy to walk into an appealing and well-designed restaurant where the tables are separated by partitions and one can really have a private conversation. Darbar is such a spot, and all of the staff wait on you in a quick and respectful manner while providing informed, efficient service and presenting fresh, attractive Indian dishes. A wonderful start for your meal would be the murgh pakoras (tender pieces of chicken sauteed in yogurt and Indian spices and batter-fried). Specialties from the charcoal clay oven are sizable in selection: chicken, prawns, and lamb. The tandoori prawns are my favorite. By all means, try some of the Indian breads. A real taste treat is the vegetarian paratha – unleavened whole wheat bread filled with vegetables and baked in the tandoor with butter. Rice dishes are excellent, and the desserts are exceptional. The chocolate cinnamon ice cream is worth the visit in itself. There is a buffet lunch daily.

DA SILVANO
260 Sixth Ave (bet Houston and Bleecker St)   212 982-2343
Lunch: Mon-Fri; Dinner: Daily
Moderate

Long a favorite for those who like food inspired by the chefs of Florence, this small northern Italian restaurant, housed in a Village storefront, presents dishes that are handled with taste and talent. The pasta and antipasto, like the grilled shrimp with vegetables, are superb. Try *tortellini alla panna* (tortellini with heavy cream, parmesan cheese, and butter) or *spaghettini puttanesca* (chunks of tomato, garlic, black olives, capers, and anchovies). In the seafood column, the roasted pompano filled with fresh herbs and lemon is a house favorite. There are nearly 30 specials every day. For dessert, try the *pannacotta* (baked cream topped with hot melted chocolate). Casual service, cozy brickwall ambience, and outside dining in nice weather all add up to make this a very pleasant place to dine.

DA UMBERTO
107 W 17th St (off Sixth Ave)   212 989-0303
Lunch: Mon-Fri; Dinner: Mon-Sat
Moderate to moderately expensive

Da Umberto is for serious Italian diners! This Florentine bistro is a feast for the eyes as well as the palate. A groaning table of inviting antipasto dishes greets the guests; one could easily make an entire meal just from this selection. The appealing part of the presentation is that all of the platters look so fresh and healthy. Umberto Assante himself is around much of the time, insuring that the service is as good as the food. One can look into the glass-framed kitchen at the rear to see how real professionals work. What to have? Lasagne. Gnocchi. Linguine. Risotto. The three-color salad is a house specialty. On to well-prepared fish or veal or chicken. Your waiter will have many specials to detail. If you have room, the chocolate *bombe* is the best of the dessert selection.

DAWAT
210 E 58th St   212 355-7555
Lunch: Mon-Sat; Dinner: Daily
Moderate

Dawat is a quality operation. It serves tasty, reasonably priced Indian food in a refined atmosphere with superior service. There are a number of wonderful seafood choices, including a sensational shrimp entree cooked with herbs and spices. You'll also find chicken dishes, goat and lamb offerings, and such vegetarian selections as homemade cheese cubes with delicious vegetables, eggplant with sweet-and-sour tamarind sauce, and stir-fried cauliflower with ginger and cumin seeds. One of the trademarks of an Indian restaurant is its bread, and at Dawat they do it to perfection. Different varieties are offered, and no meal is complete without trying a couple of them. But forget about the desserts here; they're nothing special.

DELMONICO'S
56 Beaver St   212 422-4747
Breakfast, Lunch, Dinner: Mon-Fri
Moderate to expensive

Some folks think there are no good eating places in the financial district. Not true. Those who are familiar with the Wall Street area know about Delmonico's. It has been a tradition for decades, and it is still a class act, resplendent with elegant furnishings and polite service well-honed from years of experience. Whether you're here for a business lunch or a social dinner, I heartily recommend this consistent, established institution. It's hard to pick out only a few specialties, but I would suggest the swordfish; the marvelous fillet of sole glazed with white wine, mushrooms, and tomatoes; the boneless breast of chicken in brandy mustard sauce; or the mixed grill, comprising lamb chop, filet mignon, liver, and bacon. Bitter chocolate with vanilla sauce is the Delmonico dessert showpiece.

DINING COMMONS
City University of New York Graduate Center
33 W 42nd St (18th floor)   212 642-2013
Mon-Fri: 8-8
Inexpensive

This is definitely a find for those who don't mind cafeteria dining. Right in the center of town, on the top floor of City University Graduate Center, is a first-class cafeteria that offers excellent food all day long in nice surroundings at very reasonable prices. Continental breakfasts, featuring muffins, danishes, croissants, bagels, and fruit, are available from 8 a.m. to 11:30 a.m. Lunch and dinner—deli sandwiches, salads, hot entrees with vegetables and potatoes, desserts and beverages—are available until 8 p.m. You can eat heartily for under $10; if a sandwich is all you want, the tab will be half that. Seating is available, but all items may be taken out. A full-service bar is adjacent to the Commons, which offers a special catering menu with rock-bottom prices. The cafeteria is open to faculty, students, and the general public, with students getting a special discount upon presentation of CUNY identification cards. This is not your run-of-the-mill fast-food operation. Restaurant Associates does a particularly good job of offering tasty and adequate portions, without the fancy touches that cost extra bucks. A great midtown spot for groups, young people, singles, and folks in a hurry.

DIVINO
1556 Second Ave (at 81st St)   212 861-1096
Dinner: Daily
Moderate

It's always a thrill to watch a well-trained team in action, and Divino has one of the best in town. The owner is on the job, and this Northern Italian house is orchestrated with the baton of a master. The moment you enter (better make reservations), you notice an attractive and unusual bowl of relishes on the bar. Every sight and sense is a happy one, and there's plenty of good, hot, fresh Italian bread. To start, try the seafood salad or, if it's a cold evening, the *tortellini in brodo* (meat-filled pasta in broth). What a selection of pasta! Pasta stuffed with meat, spinach, and cheese; Genovese-style pasta in garlic and basil sauce; and pasta and seafood. Steamed clams, Italian-style bouillabaisse, and scampi with tarragon are featured, but my prime choices are the veal chop Primavera or swordfish Divino. All entrees are served with fresh vegetables. Desserts are baked daily on the premises.

DOCKS
2427 Broadway (bet 89th and 90th St)   212 724-5588
Lunch: Mon-Sat; Dinner: Daily; Brunch: Sat, Sun
633 Third Ave (at 40th St)   212 986-8080
Lunch: Mon-Fri; Dinner: Daily; Brunch: Sun
Moderate

For those who appreciate a great raw bar, Docks is the place to anchor! Sail right up Broadway or to Docks' larger and newer location on Third Avenue. At both lunch and dinner, you can find fresh swordfish, lobster, tuna, Norwegian salmon, red snapper, and other seafood specials of the day. The crab cakes are outstanding. In the evening, you can enjoy a raw bar with four oyster varieties and three different selections of clams. All this comes with Docks' cole slaw and potatoes or vegetables. For a lighter meal, try the steamers in beer broth or the mussels in tomato and garlic. Delicious smoked fish, like sturgeon and whitefish, is available. Docks has a special New England clambake on Sunday and Monday nights. For dessert, the chocolate mud fudge is a fitting way to finish your culinary cruise. The atmosphere is congenial, and so are the professional waiters.

DUANE PARK CAFE
157 Duane St   212 732-5555
Lunch: Mon-Fri; Dinner: Mon-Sat
Moderate

If you find yourself in TriBeCa, take advantage of some interesting places to eat in the area. Many are located on or near Duane Street. Some have revamped already existing operations that couldn't make the grade; Duane Park Cafe is one of them. This nondescript room serves much better food than the décor would suggest. The menu is eclectic. There is a touch of Italian, a heavy emphasis on seafood, and a nod to Cajun and Japanese influences. The dishes sparkle, especially because of the tasty manner in which herbs are used. Even some of the delicious homemade breads have herbal flavors. A selection of pasta is offered at all times. The desserts are also done on the premises, showing off the vivid imagination of pastry chef John Dudek.

EDWARDIAN ROOM
Plaza Hotel (Fifth Ave and Central Park S)   212 759-3000
Breakfast, Lunch: Daily; Dinner: Tues-Sat
Expensive

There are some New York experiences that one never forgets. I remember a magical evening in the Edwardian Room at the Plaza Hotel, overlooking the heart of New York at Fifth Avenue and Central Park. Outside, the streets and sidewalks were being dusted by a snowfall; inside, the tables sparkled with the finest silver, china, and glassware. The candles flickered, and the piano music provided the final romantic ingredient. This was years ago. Alas, the room has undergone many changes over a long period of time by a series of uncaring owners. In keeping with the current popularity of hotel dining, this distinguished room once again glows. There just isn't another spot like it anywhere in New York. Hansom cabs sit outside your window, and the kitchen is once again turning out superb cuisine, in keeping with the room's history. This is the place to take your guests to celebrate an engagement or important occasion. With gorgeous flowers and old-time waiters, along with an extensive menu of continental favorites, who could ask for anything more?

EL PARADOR
325 E 34th St (nr First Ave)   212 679-6812
Lunch, Dinner: Daily
Moderate

When you have been in the restaurant business for over three decades in New York, you are obviously doing something customers like. El Parador is doing just that: serving delicious Mexican food in a fun atmosphere at down-to-earth prices. Besides all that, they are some of the nicest folks in the city. Warm nachos are put on the table the minute you arrive; from here you have a choice of specialties. There are tortillas, Spanish sausages, and pinto bean soup to start. Delicious shrimp and chicken dishes follow. (The chicken wings are great.) You can create your own tacos and tostaditas if you like. How about stuffed jalapenos? You'll probably want some tequila to make the evening complete. How do you drink it? Hold a wedge of lime or lemon in your left hand, then place a little salt in the well at the base of the thumb and index finger. Lick the salt, swallow some tequila, then suck the lemon or lime. Caramba!

ERMINIA
250 E 83rd St   212 879-4284
Dinner: Mon-Sat
American Express
Moderate

The Trastevere operation now has five branches, and Erminia, the smallest, is the jewel in the crown. It has about a dozen tables in a pleasant and rustic atmosphere just right for a leisurely, intimate dinner. I've found it an absolutely charming spot with helpful personnel and outstanding food. To start, try the artichokes cooked in olive oil. In the pasta category, you can't go wrong with tender dumplings with potatoes and tomatoes or large noodles with ricotta cheese. The number of entrees is limited. Some are grilled and served with delicious vegetables. There is grilled chicken, seafood items on skewers, a special fish dish, and lamb or veal chops. Dessert selections vary daily. Jackets are required!

FELIX

340 W. Broadway   212 431-0021
Lunch: Tues-Sun; Dinner: Daily
Cash Only
Moderate

A taste of France has been transplanted to SoHo, where a noisy and trendy clientele can enjoy delicious continental delicacies like roast rabbit, fricasseed chicken, or hanger steak. I particularly enjoyed the twice-baked potatoes; not too many places do this item properly. The setting is bistro-like; the ceilings are high, with old-fashioned fans operating; and the waiters are informal and helpful. Note: They do not take plastic, so bring cash.

FERRIER

29 E 65th St   212 772-9000
Daily: 11 a.m.–1 a.m.
Moderate

Convenient location. Great people-gazing, especially for the gentlemen. Cozy atmosphere. Pleasant personnel. Moderate prices. Oh yes, good food, too! This is exactly what Alain Chevreux has put together at his busy bistro. He got his start with Chez Ma Tante in the Village and brought the best aspects of that operation to the Upper East Side. There is a wide choice of hot and cold hors d'oeuvres, pastas, chicken dishes, seafood, salads, pâtés, and goodies that you can munch on at any time of the day (or evening). Homemade sorbets, caramelized apple tarts, and sinful profiteroles look good by sunlight or starlight. A good place to remember when hunger pangs strike at inconvenient hours!

57-57

57 E 57th St (Four Seasons Hotel, 2nd level)   212 758-5700
Breakfast, Lunch, Dinner: Daily; Brunch: Sun
Moderate to moderately expensive

One can always be assured when the name Four Seasons is on the door that the service on the inside is going to be something special. And so it is at 57-57, Manhattan's newest star in the continuing trend towards excellence in hotel dining rooms. The room is highlighted by handsome cherry floors with mahogany inlays, Danish beechwood paneling, and bronze chandeliers. The table tops match the floor in both material and design. In an informal yet elegant atmosphere, the food presentation has the authority of classic American cooking. The menu changes by season, featuring big-time flavors, such as some exceptionally well-thought out pasta entrees. This is a room where taste and personal attention, not the ego of a famous chef, is the name of the game. A thoughtful touch is the offer of rapid service for breakfast guests.

FISHIN EDDIE
73 W 71st St   212 874-3474
Dinner: Daily; Brunch: Sat, Sun
Moderate

This popular Upper West Side establishment serves some of the best seafood in the area. The setting is casual and attractive, employing colors and material that blend with the nautical theme. Many of the dishes are well presented, but some (like the house specialty, cioppino) look better than they taste. Generally speaking, however, you can do well with any number of grilled specialties (like shrimp, scallops, trout, or swordfish), or rely on some very good pasta dishes, like linguine with mixed seafood. Lots of eager young folks are around to make you feel at home. I was impressed by the fact that they feature Dungeness crab from the West Coast. Their homemade fries have to be some of the best around town.

44
Royalton Hotel
44 W 44th St (bet Fifth and Sixth Ave)   212 944-8844
Breakfast, Lunch, Dinner: Daily; Brunch: Sat, Sun
Moderately expensive

Forget about the fact there's no name on the door (it is the Royalton Hotel), the stark lobby (filled with noisy yuppies), the outrageously uncomfortable seating, the ugly black uniforms of the servers, and concentrate solely on the food. You will not be disappointed. The food is as magnificent as the ambience is unappealing. Every dish is a work of art, from the spit-roasted sweetbreads and *duck l'orange* appetizers to the dozen fish, poultry, and meat entrees. The roasted guinea hen comes in two courses (one would be plenty for anyone), the grilled ribeye steak melts in your mouth, and the whole Maine lobster is a picture. Those crisp *roesti* potatoes with bacon and shallots are addictive. To top it off: profiteroles (with three ice creams and two chocolate sauces), black pepper canoli (with caramel mascarpone and fresh berries), or chocolate crêpes with roasted bananas and milk-chocolate malt ice cream.

FOUR SEASONS
99 E 52nd St (bet Park and Lexington Ave)   212 754-9494
Lunch: Mon-Fri; Dinner: Mon-Sat
Expensive

For anyone who appreciates fine dining, likes to see and be seen, and doesn't have to worry about the size of their credit-card balance, there is no place like this institution. I say "institution," because that is exactly what this superb continental restaurant really is. There are two areas:

the Grill Room, outside the main dining hall, inhabited at noon by the power elite of the city (especially those in the publishing business), and the Pool Room, a magnificent setting complete with a marble pool for those very special dining moments. The huge menu changes almost every day, but the accommodating staff will fix just about anything you want. Each entree is a masterpiece of presentation. The dessert selection can only be described as obscene, with the individual soufflés in coffee cups a splendid treat. Both rooms are popular at noon and in the evening. In between the serving of the superior (and very pricey) dishes, watch how a really well-trained restaurant operates. An attractive feature in the Grill Room at night is a complete dinner with a tab ranging from about $27 to under $40.

FRANK'S
431 W 14th St   212 243-1349
Lunch: Mon-Fri; Dinner: Mon-Sat
Moderate

At lunch, this old-time spot is crowded with nearby butchers, sporting blood on their aprons and large stomachs to fill. If that kind of clientele doesn't bother you, come on down early. But dinner is really the best at Frank's, which is operated by five members of the Molinari family, the third generation in a business started in 1912. Reservations are difficult, especially on weekends (a week in advance is necessary), since they can take care of only 65 people. When cloths come out on the tables for dinner, the family chef will offer you superb prime ribs of beef, fresh fish, veal, lamb, great steaks, and pasta. The neighborhood is seamy, the desserts are ho-hum, and the ambience is Pittsburgh diner, but the food is absolutely top-drawer.

FRANK'S TRATTORIA
371 First Ave (at 22nd St)   212 677-2991
Lunch, Dinner: Daily
Inexpensive

It's true in New York, just as it is anywhere else in the country: No one knows the best inexpensive places to eat better than the boys in blue. Manhattan's finest are some of the best customers of this modest trattoria, and it is easy to see why. The menu runs the gamut of Florentine dishes, each one prepared to order and each served piping hot. And so is the bread, which is always a good sign. There is a large seafood selection, and all the fish are first quality and very fresh. You can choose from over 20 different pizzas, served whole or in individual pieces. Everyone here is very informal and friendly, and Frank, the boss, is delighted that the good word about his place has spread beyond the neighborhood regulars.

FRAUNCES TAVERN RESTAURANT
54 Pearl St   212 269-0144
Breakfast, Lunch, Dinner: Mon-Fri
Moderate

General George Washington is supposed to have said goodbye to his officers at a reception at Fraunces Tavern in 1783. George obviously had good taste, if the tavern was as top-notch then as it is now. It's an inviting, historic spot serving authentic American fare in a charming part of lower Manhattan. The dining areas are spacious and comfortable, the service is very professional, the prices are reasonable, and the menu is sizable. One of the outstanding appetizers is the seafood sampler, consisting of fresh lump crab and Maine lobster meat, shrimp, oysters, and clams—a feast in itself. A specialty of the house is the baked chicken à la Washington (cubes of tender chicken and mushrooms baked *en casserole* au gratin). Absolutely delicious! I'd suggest making a beeline here on Wednesdays for the Yankee pot roast with red cabbage and potato pancakes. On Tuesdays you can sample ales from around the world. And don't overlook dessert! The cheesecake, Georgia pecan pie, and chocolate mousse are well worth investigating. After your meal, go upstairs and visit the Fraunces Tavern Museum, one of the oldest museums in the city and a historic landmark. There you'll find exhibits focusing on 18th- and 19th-century life in America. The "long room" is especially well done. By the way, the breakfast menu offers a fine selection of omelets, eggs, fruit, and muffins. It's one of the best buys in New York.

GABRIEL'S BAR & RESTAURANT
11 W 60th St (bet Broadway and Ninth Ave)   212 956-4600
Lunch: Mon-Fri; Dinner: Mon-Sat
Moderate

There is something special when you walk into a restaurant, are greeted by an extremely friendly host (who happens to be Gabriel, a co-owner with chef Ralph Perroti) and the background music is "Gabriel . . . Gabriel"! But there is much more. Wonderful homemade pepper biscuits and delicious bread. Fresh melon and blood orange juice. A bowl of fresh fruit on the bar. A fine assortment of Italian appetizers. Then on to really first-class pastas (like *tagliatelle* with pesto), chicken, steaks, and grilled seafood dishes. The in-house gelati creations are among New York's best, as is the chocolate expresso torte. To cap it all off, Gabriel offers a selection of nine different unusual teas (like peach melba, raspberry, French vanilla). Gabriel doesn't have to blow his own horn here; the satisfied customers will do it for him!

GINO

780 Lexington Ave (at 61st St)   212 758-4466
Lunch, Dinner: Daily
Cash only
Moderate

As you look around the crowded dining room of this famous New York institution, you can tell immediately that the food is great. Why? Because this Italian restaurant is filled with native New Yorkers. You'll see no tourist buses stopping out front. The menu has been the same for years: a large selection of popular dishes (over 30 entrees), from antipasto to soup, pasta to fish. There are daily specials, of course, but you only have to taste such regulars as the chicken à la Capri, the Italian sausages with peppers, or scampis à la Gino, and you are hooked. Gino's staff has been there forever, taking care of patrons in an informed, fatherly manner. The best part comes when the tab is presented. East Side rents, as you know, are always climbing, but Gino has resisted the price bulges by taking cash only and serving delicious food that keeps the tables full. No reservations, so come early.

GIORDANO

409 W 39th St   212 947-9811
Lunch, Dinner: Mon-Sat
Moderate

When a restaurant has been in the same family for three decades, it should be a fine-tuned establishment. And indeed, the Creglia family runs a first-rate operation at Giordano. An attractive bar greets you with trays of appetizers during the cocktail hour. There are several pleasant dining areas, including an outdoor patio. The cuisine is Northern Italian, highlighted by such delicious pastas as *fettuccine al fungetto, tortellini alla panna, fettuccine alfredo,* or *linguini al sugo.* For entrees, I'd suggest the *langostine alla mugnaia,* an excellent seafood dish, or the calf's liver *alla veneziana.* A side order of fried zucchini or eggplant parmigiana tops off a superb meal. Although the food is excellent, I was also impressed with how well the old-time waiters take care of you; they sure know what they're doing. For no-nonsense Italian food at reasonable prices, you can't beat Giordano. A banquet room has been added.

GOLDEN UNICORN

18 E Broadway (at Catherine St)   212 941-0911
Lunch, Dinner, Dim Sum: Daily
Inexpensive

Spencer P.S. Chan presides over this bustling Hong Kong-style two-floor Chinese restaurant that serves delicious dim sum every day of the week. He personally is the best person to ask about your dinner order. Besides the delicacies from the rolling carts, diners may choose from a wide variety of Cantonese dishes from the regular menu. Pan-fried noodle dishes, rice noodles, and noodles in soup are house specialties. Despite the size of the establishment (they can take care of over 400 diners at one time), you will be amazed at the fast service, the cleanliness, and (most of all) the price tag. This has to be one of the best values in Chinatown.

GOTHAM BAR & GRILL
12 E 12th St   212 620-4020
Lunch: Mon-Fri; Dinner: Daily
Moderately expensive

It is rewarding to see how the Gotham has painstakingly worked itself up the ladder to become one of Manhattan's outstanding restaurants. It is now well worth the sizable price tag. In a cavernous setting that is anything but intimate, the high-ceilinged coldness is broken by direct lighting spots on each table. Fresh plants give a bit of color, but the real treat here is the carefully prepared food. Several wonderful salads, including a seafood presentation of squid, scallops, Japanese octopus, mussels, and lobster in lemon and olive oil, will get you off to a good start. Each entree is well seasoned, attractively presented, and uniformly tasty. The rack of lamb is one of the finest served in the city. Desserts are all made in-house; try the espresso crème brûlée or the Gotham chocolate cake! Dining here can best be summed up in one word: exciting. So can the talented chef, Alfred Portale.

GRAND CENTRAL OYSTER BAR RESTAURANT
Grand Central Station (lower level)   212 490-6650
Mon-Fri: 11:30-9:30
Moderate

If you are a native New Yorker, you know about the 80-year-old institution that is the Oyster Bar at Grand Central. It was once popular with commuters and residents. A midtown institution that was neglected for years, it has been restored, and is doing nicely, thank you. (They serve over 2,000 folks a day!) Located in the caverns of Grand Central, it is attractive, the young help most accommodating, and the drain on the pocketbook minimal. The menu boasts more than 90 seafood items (new, fresh entrees daily), a dozen different kinds of oysters, super oyster stew, clam chowder (Manhattan and New England), oyster pan roast, bouillabaisse, coquille St. Jacques, Maryland crab cakes, broiled Maine lobster, and marvelous homemade desserts.

GUIDO'S
511 Ninth Ave (at 39th St)   212 502-4842
Lunch: Mon-Fri; Dinner: Mon-Sat
No credit cards
Inexpensive

You might ask yourself what a nice person would be doing in the middle of Ninth Avenue, having lunch in the back room of a macaroni factory? Well, this is no usual back room and no usual macaroni factory! Up front, as you walk in, you'll see a display of 23 brands of macaroni. That was the original business, but now it's just a sideline. The real draw is the smallish restaurant in the back, which is as busy as Times Square. Tom Scarola is the third-generation family member who runs this unusual operation. Whether you're coming for lunch or dinner, make sure you have a reservation. You might rub shoulders with some celebrities. Even if they're not there in person, their pictures (along with the blue checkered tablecloths and wine bottles on the ceiling) help create a special atmosphere at Guido's. You don't want to miss the lobster, rigatoni with vodka sauce, shrimp *francese,* the veal sorrentino, or the house specialty, chicken alla Guido. The pasta is freshly made, authentic, inexpensive, and delicious. Finish with an assortment of mixed pastries and fresh cakes along with a special espresso, and you will have had a marvelous meal. Lunch specials include four different chicken, veal, and shrimp entrees, as well as linguini or spaghetti with all the trimmings.

HALCYON
Rihga Royal Hotel (151 W 54th St)   212 468-8888
Breakfast, Lunch, Dinner: Daily
Moderately expensive

This is an oasis of civility for dining. The Halcyon has a duel life: It is a free-standing room of its own, and it also serves as the dining area for the adjoining hotel. The room is spacious and elegant, quiet and calming. Table settings are enhanced by beautiful Villeroy and Boch French Garden place plates, and fresh flowers adorn each table. The menu is continental: salads, soups, pastas, seafoods, and grilled items. There is a pre-theater dinner, a popular late light supper (10:30 p.m.– 1 a.m.), and on Sunday a brunch is served in a 54th-floor top-of-the-hotel room with a fabulous view of Manhattan. The kitchen will accommodate deviations from the set menu—a nice touch in these days of restricted ordering. It is in the dessert area, however, that the operation really shines. Each plate is an absolute work of art, with the signature name drizzled on the presentation dish. Ask to see the daily selection, as well as the set dessert menu, which changes by season. Nightly entertainment is an additional feature.

HARD ROCK CAFE
221 W 57th St   212 459-9320
Sun-Thurs: 11:30 a.m.–2 a.m.;
Fri, Sat: 11:30 a.m.–4 a.m.
Inexpensive

This New York offshoot of the original (and very successful) Hard Rock, which opened in London in 1971, is a noisy, swinging hangout for the younger generation. Stop at the small counter as you enter and buy one of the Hard Rock Cafe sweat shirts for your son or daughter, and your popularity rating at home will soar. The food, incidentally, is really good here. Specialties of the house include the pig sandwich (hickory-smoked pulled pork, served with cole slaw and French fries); barbecued chicken and pork ribs; a great BLT sandwich; and marvelous burgers and salads. But the real treats are from the fountain and dessert menu: homemade apple pie, hot-fudge brownies, shortcakes, and absolutely outrageous sundaes and shakes. The multi-level cafe is decorated with artifacts of rock and roll culture (such as gold records and musical instruments once owned by famous stars), and the background music is just what you'd expect: loud rock and roll. So come on in, let your hair down, and see how the other half rocks.

HARRY'S
The Woolworth Building
233 Broadway   212 513-0455
Lunch, Dinner: Mon-Fri
Moderate

Never mind that you're not a member of the Harvard or Yale Club or that you don't have a gold pass to the private dining room of Citicorp or Chase Manhattan. Just head for the lower level of the Woolworth Building, and you'll find a remarkable eating spot called Harry's. You would probably never know about it unless you worked in a nearby office – or read this book! What with all the wood and leather (a very masculine atmosphere), good food, and reasonable prices, it's a real find. Although dinner is served until 10:30, this is basically a luncheon spot. Ladies are certainly welcome, but the clientele is predominantly male (the important-looking, three-piece-suit variety). While big deals are being made at the tables around you, you can feast on clams, smoked trout, marinated herring, and smoked sturgeon. Omelets and homemade pastas are available, as well as selections from the cold buffet, including chicken salad, sliced turkey, and tuna salad platters. There are also grilled items, cold sandwiches, seafood, and several specials each day. If you drop by on Tuesday, try the braised sauerbrauten, and if you visit on Friday, the boiled brisket of beef is outstanding. This is an ideal place to take business associates; they will, no doubt, be pleasantly surprised to learn about it. Harry's is open on weekends only for private events.

HATSUHANA
17 E 48th St   212 355-3345
Lunch: Mon-Fri; Dinner: Mon-Sat
Moderate

Hatsuhana has deservedly become known as the best sushi house in Manhattan. One can sit at a table or at the bar and get equal attention from the informed help. There are several dozen choices of appetizers, including broiled eel in cucumber wrap; steamed egg custard with shrimp, fish, and vegetables; squid mixed with Japanese apricots; and chopped fatty tuna with aged soybeans. Next, try the salmon teriyaki (fresh salmon grilled with teriyaki sauce) or any number of tuna or sushi dishes best described by the personnel. Forget about the desserts, and concentrate on the exotic offerings for your meal.

HOSTERIA FIORELLA
1081 Third Ave (at 64th St)   212 838-7570
Daily: 11 a.m.–11:30 p.m.
Moderate

This Italian seafood grill is operated by the same folks that run Trattoria dell'Arte, so you know that it is first-rate. If romance is not to follow the meal, start with the house special – garlic bread alla Hosteria, with goat cheese and tomato. Other choices include appetizers from the antipasto bar, fresh shrimp and oysters from the seafood bar, and all sorts of seafood pastas. Next, it's on to grilled seafood dishes, a good selection of sensibly priced lobster specialties, grilled meats, or pizzas and sandwiches. They will adjust any recipe for those with allergies. The place is huge, so don't worry about reservations. They can take care of *hundreds* for private parties, so just bring your appetite.

HUDSON RIVER CLUB
4 World Financial Center, lobby level   212 786-1500
Lunch: Mon-Fri; Dinner: Mon-Sat
Moderate to moderately expensive

How often can you dine in sight of the Statue of Liberty? The setting for the Hudson River Club is magnificent: spacious, with high ceilings and a view of the river and yacht harbor. Nothing has been spared to make the destination (as difficult as it is to find) worth the trouble. Don't be put off by the word *Club*; the house is open to everyone, but it serves as a special place for residents of Battery Park City. The menu is strictly American, with an emphasis on food from the Hudson Valley. A five-course dinner offers specialties from the area for every course. Luncheons feature excellent soups, several salads (like corn-crusted scallop or Maine lobster), and such marvelous lighter dishes as Hudson Canyon omelet or herbed, free-range chicken. In the evening they serve a large selection of seafood and house specialties like brandy-braised rabbit, roast squab, shank of veal, and Hudson Valley venison chop and loin. Desserts are a feast for the eye and the palate. The warm sack of baked bananas or five-layer chocolate-chip sundae will knock your eyes out. This is a delightful place to entertain someone who thinks he or she has been "everywhere" in the Big Apple.

IL GIGLIO
81 Warren St (bet W Broadway and Greenwich St)
212 571-5555
Lunch, Dinner: Mon-Fri
Moderate

Il Mulino's "little brother" is doing well. So well, in fact, he might be even more handsome than his father! If you can find the place (the neighborhood is drab and dull, to say the least), you will be delighted to find a bright, clean, classy operation that serves absolutely great Northern Italian food. Smallness is a virtue here, as the two dozen tables are looked after by a crew of highly trained, tuxedo-clad waiters, most of whom have been on the premises since its opening. The specials are almost as numerous as the menu items (be sure to ask for prices), and by all means look over the display of fresh fruits, desserts, and other goodies by the entrance. The scampi and veal dishes are superb, and few places in TriBeCa (or elsewhere in Manhattan) do pasta any better. Moreover, all desserts are made in-house.

Il MULINO
86 W 3rd St (bet Sullivan and Thompson St)   212 673-3783
Lunch: Mon-Fri; Dinner: Mon-Sat
American Express
Moderately expensive

Those who live to eat will want to pay attention to this entry. Never mind that reservations usually must be made a week or so in advance. Never mind that it's always crowded, the noise level is intolerable, and the waiters nearly knock you down as you stand waiting to be seated. It's all part of the ambience at Il Mulino, one of New York's best Italian restaurants. Your greeting is usually "hi, boss," which gives you the distinct impression that the staff is accustomed to catering to members of the, uh, "family." When your waiter finally comes around, he reels off a lengthy list of evening specials with glazed-over eyes. On the other hand, a beautiful, mouth-watering display of the daily specials is arrayed on a huge table at the entrance. Once you're seated, the waiter delivers one antipasto after another while he talks you into ordering one of the fabulous veal dishes with portions bountiful enough to feed King Kong. *Osso buco* is a favorite dish. By the time you finish one of the luscious desserts, you'll know why every seat in the small, simple dining room is kept warm all evening.

IL VAGABONDO
351 E 62nd St   212 832-9221
Lunch: Mon-Fri; Dinner: Daily
Inexpensive

This bustling restaurant has been a favorite with knowledgeable New Yorkers for more than two decades. The atmosphere is strictly old-time, complete with checkered tablecloths, four busy rooms, and an èven busier bar. No menus are offered; the pleasant but harried waiters reel off the regular items and daily specials. You may have spaghetti or ravioli, an absolutely marvelous minestrone, chicken parmesan, or sliced beef. I can also heartily recommend the Friday scampi or lobster special. There is no pretense in this place. It is a great spot for office parties and for folks with slim pocketbooks. You won't see Jackie O. here, but you will see happy faces, compliments of a delicious meal and the extremely reasonable bill. Save room for the great bocce-ball dessert (*tartufo*). Il Vagabondo, you see, is the only restaurant in New York with an indoor bocce court!

INDOCHINE
430 Lafayette St   212 505-5111
Dinner: Daily
Moderate

All over America, Indochinese cuisine has become very popular because of the craze for healthy meals at reasonable prices. Then, too, a number of our military personnel were exposed to this kind of cooking during their service abroad. Indochine is undoubtedly the best restaurant of its type in New York. If you are nervous about ordering, the staff is very helpful in explaining the exotic tastes. Specialties of the house include an unusual fish soup, steamed Vietnamese ravioli, crispy frog legs, spicy salad of fillet of beef with shallots and lemon grass, crispy whole fish with pimento sauce, and boned roast duck with ginger. An early *prix fixe* menu is available for those who want to go to the nearby theaters. The negatives here include a disinterested service staff and very ordinary desserts.

JACKSON HOLE WYOMING BURGERS

232 E 64th St	Third Ave at 35th St	Second Ave at 84th St
212 311-7187	212 679-3264	212 737-8788
Mon-Sat:	Mon-Sat:	Mon-Thurs:
10:30–1 a.m.;	10:30–1 a.m.;	10:30–1 a.m.;
Sun: 12–12	Sun: 12–12	Fri, Sat: 10:30–4 a.m.;
		Sun: 11 a.m.–midnight

No credit cards
Inexpensive

You might think that a burger is a burger is a burger. But having done burger taste tests all over the city, I've chosen Jackson's as the best. Each one weighs in at seven juicy, delicious ounces. All ingredients are fresh, and the taste tells the story. You can get all types of hamburgers, along with great coffee and French fries. You can have a pizza burger, an alpine burger, an English burger, or a Baldouney burger (mushrooms, fried onions, and American cheese). Or try an omelet, if you prefer. A Mexican menu has been added. The atmosphere isn't fancy, but once you sink your teeth into a Jackson Hole burger, accompanied by great onion rings and one of the homemade desserts, you'll see why I'm so enthusiastic.

JIM McMULLEN'S
1341 Third Ave (at 77th St)   212 861-4700
Lunch, Dinner: Daily
American Express
Moderate

I'm always a bit suspicious of a restaurant where the waiting line moves irregularly, and this is one spot where that happens. If the maitre d' or Jim McMullen knows you, or if your name is well known, the wait is short. Otherwise, it's ridiculous. But people do wait, I guess, not only because it is chic to see and be seen here, but because the food is good and the prices are certainly right. Jim was a model, and the place is a favorite hangout for the famous and nearly so. The menu is unimaginative, featuring the usual appetizers. But the chicken pot pie is worth a visit in itself. There is a good selection of fish dishes, and several steak offerings. The chocolate brownie pie is an A-1 dessert, and the hot fudge sundae is not the usual ice-cream store variety. There is also a private dining room (seating up to 100) which is available for lunch or dinner. Now a wine and spirit store at 1381 Third Avenue (212 288-2211) also bears the McMullen name.

JOE'S
79 MacDougal St   212 473-8834
Dinner: Wed-Mon
Moderate

Joe's belongs in the "very good" Italian category, not only for the quality of the food but also for the value you get for your dining dollar. Joe himself is on the job, as he has been for several decades, imparting Old World charm to this small Village establishment. His staff is made up of similarly experienced, efficient, no-nonsense old-timers. Spaghetti (fixed six different ways), baked ziti, linguini, and homemade egg noodles are all excellent starters. I'd stick to the veal scaloppini (fixed five different ways), veal chops, or veal cutlets for entrees. Shrimp and clams are featured, and the breast of chicken *alla parmigiana* is a winner. My favorite meal here is cannelloni served with great Italian bread and a very fresh salad "alla Joe's." A perfect meal at a modest price.

JOHN'S PIZZERIA
278 Bleecker St   212 243-1680
408 E 64th St (bet First and York Ave)   212 935-2895
48-50 W 65th St (bet Broadway and Central Park)   212 721-7001
Daily: Noon–11:30 p.m. (Fri, Sat until 12:30 a.m.)
Moderate

Pete Castelotti (there is no John) is known as the "Baron of Bleecker Street." However, he has expanded to the Upper West Side and the Upper East Side, so most New Yorkers can taste some of the best brick-oven pizza in the city. Pete offers 55 — count 'em — varieties, from cheese and tomatoes to a gourmet extravaganza of cheese, tomatoes, anchovies, sausage, peppers, meatballs, onions, and mushrooms. If homemade spaghetti, cheese ravioli, or manicotti is your preference, this is also the place for you. The surroundings on Bleecker Street are a bit shabby, but things are higher class uptown.

JO-JO
160 E 64th St   212 223-5656
Lunch, Dinner: Daily
Moderate to moderately expensive

It is satisfying and fun to share in a real American success story. For years Jean-Georges Vongeerichten presided over the outstanding kitchen at Lafayette, a grand four-star French dining establishment. Although only in his mid-30s, he decided that if he were going to work so hard, he'd rather do so for himself. Jo-Jo is the result. It is a happy, classy establishment, with those extra touches that make dining a memorable experience: Unusual napkin rings. Wonderful warm bread. Pleasant and helpful waiters. A very classy lady maitre d'. There are only a half-dozen appetizers, entrees, and desserts; every one is unique, tasty, and beautifully presented. Rabbit, soup, or salad are among the choices to start; then move on to fish, lobster, chicken, lamb, or duck. Superb warm chocolate cake or brioche with caramelized apple is the way to finish. Upstairs is a charming room with fireplace for private entertaining or after-dinner drinks and conversation. Don't miss Jo-Jo! (Now he has another winner: Vong, with a Thai accent.)

KATZ'S DELICATESSEN
205 E Houston St (at Ludlow St)   212 254-2246
Sun-Wed: 8 a.m.–9 p.m.; Thurs: 8 a.m.–10 p.m.;
Fri, Sat: 8 a.m.–11 p.m.
No credit cards
Inexpensive

Lower East Side hunger pangs? Try Katz's Delicatessen. It is a super place with some of the biggest and best sandwiches in town, hand-carved and overstuffed. The atmosphere goes along with the great food, and the prices are reasonable. You can go right up to the counter and order (it is fun watching the no-nonsense operators slicing and fixing) or sit at a table where a seasoned waiter will take care of you. Try dill pickles and sauerkraut with your sandwich. Incidentally, Katz's is a perfect way to sample the unique "charm" of the Lower East Side. When you wait at a table for an hour or discover that the salt and pepper containers are empty and the ketchup is missing, you'll know what I mean.

KEENS CHOP HOUSE
72 W 36th St   212 947-3636
Lunch: Mon-Fri; Dinner: Mon-Sat
Moderate

Some of the best old restaurants in New York tend to get lost in the shuffle. With glamorous new places opening every week and people always wanting to know which places are "in," we sometimes forget about the dependable restaurants that consistently do a good job. One of them is Keens Chop House, a unique New York institution. I can remember going there decades ago when those in the garment trade made Keens their lunch headquarters. This has not changed. Keens still has the same attractions: the bar reeks of atmosphere, and there are great party facilities and fine food to match. Keens opened in 1885, and it has been a fixture in the Herald Square area ever since. For some time it was a "gentlemen only" place, and although it still has a masculine atmosphere, ladies now feel comfortable and welcome. The famous mutton chop with mint is the house specialty, but other delicious dishes include veal, steaks, lamb, and fish, and a special omelet of the day. For the light eater, especially at lunch, there are some great salads. There's a hearty, robust atmosphere about the place, and the waiters are the no-nonsense type. If you have a meat-and-potatoes lover in your party, this is the place to take him. Make sure you save a little room for the deep-dish apple pie.

KLEINE KONDITOREI
234 E 86th St   212 737-7130
Sun-Thurs: 11 a.m.–11 p.m.; Fri, Sat: 11 a.m –midnight
Moderate

If you're in the mood for sauerbraten, potato dumplings, red cabbage, wiener schnitzel, goose, venison, steak tartare, or an outrageously calorie-laden linzer torte, try Kleine Konditorei. It is one of the very few German restaurants worth visiting in New York. The cakes and pastries stack up against the fine little pastry shops you'd find in Munich. East 86th Street is one of New York's most colorful areas, and a walk around the neighborhood (which you'll need after a stop here) is interesting. I recommend Kleine Konditorei for an after-show visit or a special lunch when a golden-brown German pancake sounds just right. There is also a bakery section for takeout orders.

LA BOHÊME
24 Minetta Lane (Sixth Ave bet W 3rd and Bleecker St)
212 473-6447
Dinner: Tues-Sun; Brunch (and full menu): Sun
Moderate

Pari Dulac likes people and food, and it shows. The part-Iranian, part-French hostess is right on the job in her cozy, informal Bohemian bistro, dispensing delicious edibles at moderate prices. The setting is a quiet, charming street in the Village. When the front doors are open in the nice weather, you get the impression of being in a quaint European town. Inside, soothing music puts you in the mood to enjoy some of the best pizza you have ever tasted. In the back, an open kitchen puts out pasta, salads, and French dishes done to perfection. On Sundays, you can't beat the Country French brunch or the unique omelet selection. Dessert specialties include tarts made in-house, as well as first-class chocolate mousse cake and lemon soufflé with raspberry sauce. Pari has been wise in using only the best ingredients in her dishes, and she has resisted the temptation to raise prices to a point where value is questionable. Pari is part of a restaurant family; her husband runs the reincarnated Le Chantilly, on East 57th Street.

LA BOÎTE EN BOIS
75 W 68th St   212 874-2705
Dinner: Daily
No credit cards
Moderate

This restaurant is packing them in every evening for obvious reasons. The owner, an ex-chef, has hit upon that winning combination: delicious food, personal service, and moderate prices. The salads are unusual; the *escargots aux champignons des bois* is a great beginner. For an entree, I recommend the fillet of snapper, roast chicken with herbs, or the escalope loin of veal. The atmosphere is intimate, and all the niceties of service are operative from start to finish. The desserts are made in-house; I suggest one of their sorbets. By all means call for reservations, since La Boite en Bois is very small and very popular.

LA CARAVELLE
33 W 55th St (at Fifth Ave)   212 586-4252
Lunch: Mon-Fri; Dinner: Mon-Sat
Expensive

Yes, a great restaurant can have a second life! For years La Caravelle was a truly classic restaurant in food, service, and ambience. For a while, though, I felt it was going downhill, relying on past glories instead of keeping up with the times. True, if they knew you, the attention would be superb. But if you were a stranger, it was another story altogether. Now La Caravelle seems to have undergone a revival, and even the old décor and beautiful murals have taken on a new life. The classic menu is still there, but now it de-emphasizes the heavier dishes of the past. As with so many new restaurants, concern for health is evident in a number of menu selections. There is even a hint of Oriental influence in some of the preparations. If you are looking for an absolutely superb meal, order the tournedos of Black Angus or the lobster medallions and finish off with one of La Caravelle's great soufflés.

LA COLOMBE D'OR
134 E 26th St   212 689-0666
Lunch: Mon-Fri; Dinner: Daily
Moderate

La Colombe d'Or is always busy, and it is because they provide well-prepared meals at a reasonable price. The place has an intimate French *provençal* atmosphere; the service is prompt and efficient. Take note of this spot, since there are not too many good eateries in this part of town. I'd suggest the *bouillabaisse maison* for a very good lunch dish. I also recommend the pasta. For dinner, you might try the cassoulet (in winter), duck, or beef stew. Gateau Victoire, their chocolate cake, is first-rate. One of the nicest features is the number of specialty coffees flavored with cognac, Triple Sec, Calvados, or Cafe Morello topped off with whipped cream, chocolate shavings, orange rindlets. . . . Let's start with coffee and dessert for a change!

LA CÔTE BASQUE
5 E 55th St   212 688-6525
Lunch, Dinner: Mon-Sat
Expensive

My uncle started taking me here over 30 years ago. I remember thinking even then that it was a fantastic place to see, to be seen, and to enjoy. It still is. The "beautiful people" flock to this restaurant for fine French food, and if you're a gourmet, this is a spot you won't want to miss. The food is as tasty as the people watching is enthralling. And the elegant Basque murals and flowers are matched by the elegant guests. Once in a while, we are all tempted to try some spectacular dish that we can't make at home. This is the place to go (with a very full wallet or the company credit card) when you have that desire. Specialties of the house include pepper steak, roast duck, sweetbreads, quail, cassoulet, and lobster dishes, all served in hefty portions. Save room for raspberry soufflé or the out-of-this-world *dacquoise*. (Note: La Côte Basque regulars get distinctly preferential treatment over newcomers.)

LA FONDUE
43 W 55th St   212 581-0820
Lunch, Dinner: Daily
No credit cards
Inexpensive

This business is an outgrowth of a cheese store that was founded in Greenwich Village over 25 years ago. La Fondue is always busy. It's a great spot for a quick snack, a good lunch, a no-frills dinner, or an after-theater repast. Because of its popularity, they have added more than 100 seats. My favorite starters include onion, cheddar-cheese, or Swedish green-pea soup—all very well made and filling. The specialty of the house for light snacks is a cheese and sausage board, featuring a great variety of imported cheeses and sausages from all over the world. This attractive offering includes salad, bread, and relishes. You can also have fun with a prime filet mignon fondue or a genuine imported Swiss cheese fondue. There's even a Continental Cheese Tour, which comprises a fine selection of international cheeses, plus bread, fresh fruit, and crackers. Pasta dishes have been added to the menu. Dessert choices include the famous Swiss chocolate fondue, with fruit and fruit bread; the banana fruit bread; and rum raisin ice cream. This is a top-flight spot, where your stomach will be satisfied and your pocketbook treated kindly.

LA GAULOISE
502 Sixth Ave (at 13th St)   212 691-1363
Lunch: Tues-Fri; Dinner: Tues-Sun; Brunch: Sat, Sun
Moderate

La Gauloise was on its death bed. Alas, they have breathed new life into it! This long-time favorite of Village diners has new folks in charge, and the menu shows a positive change. A classic French room featuring food from southern France, it looks very much like turn-of-the-century San Francisco. It sounds like Manhattan, however, i.e.—loud! There is wonderful smoked salmon, tasty chicken dishes, a real cassoulet, and gourmet saddle of rabbit, all done with class by a chef who had five years experience at the classy Le Regence. Crème brûlée and rice pudding head the dessert list. *Prix fixe* and à la carte menus are available at lunch.

LA GRENOUILLE
3 E 52nd St (at Fifth Ave)   212 752-1495
Lunch, Dinner: Tues-Sat
Expensive

Giselle Masson and her son, Charles, have set their establishment apart. La Grenouille is one of those special places that one really has to see to believe. It's impossible to describe. The beautiful fresh flowers are but a clue to a unique, not-to-be-forgotten dining experience. The food is as great as the atmosphere, and although the prices are high, it's worth every penny. Celebrity-watching adds to the fun. You'll see most of the famous faces in the front of the room; also-rans are delegated to rear tables. The French menu is complete, the staff professional. Be sure to try their cold hors d'oeuvres; they're a specialty of the house, as are the lobster dishes and the sweetbreads. Nowhere in New York are sauces any better. Don't miss the superb dessert soufflés. The tables are very close together, but what difference does it make when the people at your elbows are so interesting?

LA LUNCHONETTE
130 Tenth Ave (at 18th St)   212 675-0342
Lunch: Mon-Fri; Dinner: Mon-Sat
Moderate

Readers who think that only fancy restaurants are included in this book are wrong. Many establishments listed in this section are quite plain and inexpensive, but they serve good food at an attractive price. La Lunchonette definitely falls into the "unfancy" category. It's located in a rather run-down neighborhood of the city, and since it lacks an eye-catching sign out front, you're likely to pass La Lunchonette without a second look. But some distinctive and delicious things happen inside. In a space that looks as though it were decorated with objects that didn't sell at last year's church bazaar, Zoe Porte serves up some of the tastiest dishes around. The selection is sophisticated: you could have sweetbreads vinaigrette or lobster bisque to start, then go on to swordfish with capers and lemon butter or a delicious gratinee of lobster, crab, and scallops. Part of the kitchen area is curtained off, but one can still see that really primitive equipment is capable of turning out some of the best food when the user is talented.

LA MÉTAIRIE
189 W 10th St (bet W 4th and Bleecker St)   212 989-0343
Lunch, Dinner: Daily
Moderate

Once just a tiny hole in the wall, La Métairie ("a small communal farm") has expanded into a delightful place to dine in the Village. The atmosphere is still cozy, the food still exceptional, the service still prompt and accommodating—and the price is still right! The kitchen, under the supervision of chef Philipp Roussel, offers a wide choice of French dishes. Specialties of the house include couscous, wild boar stew with fresh noodles, bouillabaisse, and rack of lamb.

LANDMARK TAVERN
626 11th Ave (at 46th St)   212 757-8595
Daily: 11:45 a.m.–midnight; Brunch: Sun
Inexpensive

How about a cozy meal by a fireplace or potbellied stove? Landmark Tavern is open friendly hours for sandwich platters, a variety of salads, fresh seafood, steaks, and roast prime rib of beef. Blue-plate specials have been added to the dinner menu. But the real treat here is Sunday brunch. A tradition in the city since 1868, the Landmark is not content to be a carbon copy of everyone else's fare. Indeed, the normal brunch items are available, but so is shepherd's pie (ground lamb sauteed with herbs), delicious lamb steaks, and English-style fish and chips. There is the added pleasure of sampling their famous soda bread, made fresh every hour and served with imported jams and marmalade. Corned beef hash is a favorite. And those great homemade desserts will make you want to come back every Sunday: spiced apple cake, chocolate truffle pie, Landmark "little" cake, and cranberry almond torte. The bar is friendly, the help is harried, and the atmosphere reeks of nostalgia. More important, the food is delicious, and the prices are a bargain.

LA PETITE FERME
973 Lexington Ave (at 70th St)   212 249-3272
Lunch, Dinner: Mon-Sat
Moderate

La Petite Ferme was a very small spot down in the Village the first time I visited it. It has since grown to be a larger, fancier place on Lexington Avenue. The atmosphere is still intimate, and the same sort of blackboard menu is available to a large group of faithful customers. As the seating is quite limited, calling for reservations is a good idea. Without them, it is easier to get in during the early part of the dinner hour. The cuisine is French country, and the featured entree selections (which change nightly) are all tastefully prepared, whether it's poached bass, veal, sole, or whatever. I give high marks to their vegetables, because they don't overcook them. There is an attractive garden downstairs, and although the service is a little confusing (the kitchen is upstairs), the staff manages to do a very satisfactory job.

LA RÉSERVE
4 W 49th St   212 247-2993
Lunch, Dinner: Mon-Sat
Expensive

The first question that is always asked of anyone who writes restaurant reviews is their personal favorites. When I am faced with this inquiry my answer is always "La Réserve." Why? First, because the host and owner, Jean-Louis Missud, is one of the most charming, talented and accommodating gentlemen in the business. But that is only the start. In a city of great restaurants, this one has a special luster. The seductive ambience, the beautifully prepared dishes, the gracious and informed service, and the feeling that you are a very special guest combine to make a meal here an experience you will never forget. It would be impossible to list the best items on the menu. I would suggest letting Jean-Louis or one of his talented captains order for you. Then sit back and relax on your way to culinary heaven. A pre-theater dinner is available, and private party facilities are yours for the asking.

LA RIPAILLE
605 Hudson St (at W 12th St)   212 255-4406
Dinner: Mon-Sat
Moderate

There's a new menu every night at this small and romantic Parisian-style café, so call ahead to see what's available. I find it to be a cozy spot for an informal dinner. The tables are rickety, but the chef puts his heart into every dish. Most entrees are done to perfection, the seafood is always fresh (seafood in puff pastry is a specialty), and they do an excellent job with sweetbreads and rabbit. White chocolate is a house favorite; at least half of the dessert offerings use it as an ingredient. Proudly displayed at the front of the room are rave notices from a number of New York gourmets. They can add mine, too!

LATTANZI RISTORANTE
361 W 46th St   212 315-0980
Lunch: Mon-Fri; Dinner: Mon-Sat
American Express
Moderate

The so-called restaurant row on West 46th Street has always been an unappetizing neighborhood to me. First, there are too many eating establishments. Second, they are consistently going in and out of business. And third, the ones that do stay around are not of star quality – that is, with two exceptions: Orso and Lattanzi. The latter is a very busy place, particularly before theater. However, the quarters have been expanded, and things are not quite so hectic. In fair weather, the rustic outdoor garden is inviting. The menu features Northern Italian cuisine, with some Roman-Jewish specials that you will not find elsewhere. The homemade pastas are delicious. I'd suggest coming here for a late-evening meal.

LE BERNARDIN
155 W 51st St   212 489-1515
Lunch, Dinner: Mon-Sat
Very expensive

Le Bernardin is a magnificent restaurant, no *ifs, ands,* or *buts* about it. Well, there is one *but,* which I'll get to later. The room itself is tasteful and classy, with colorful fishing scenes adorning the walls. The service is friendly, unobtrusive, and highly professional, just as you'd expect from Maguy and Gilbert LeCoze. The seafood dishes are marvelously fresh, tasty, and superbly seasoned with just the right sauces. The bass, sea scallops, and warm lobster salad are terrific appetizers. Then you may feast upon sea scallops, halibut, snapper, salmon done several different ways, and at least four different lobster dishes. The dessert selection includes warm mousse of passion fruit with raspberry and caramel (this takes first place) and a variety of ice creams and sorbets, my favorite being the bitter chocolate. Now for the *but* — and it is a big one. The prices are simply outrageous. The same quality dishes, served perhaps in a less impressive atmosphere, are available in several other Manhattan seafood houses at half the price. But there are always those who equate high prices with "the place to go," and as long as that is the case, establishments like Le Bernardin will prosper.

LE BIARRITZ
325 W 57th St (bet Eighth and Ninth Ave)   212 757-2390
Lunch: Mon-Fri; Dinner: Mon-Sat
Moderate

New York is full of "neighborhood" restaurants, and Le Biarritz is one of the best. It seems like home every evening as the regulars claim most of the seats in this warm, smallish eatery. The place has been in the same location and in the same hands for three decades. Gleaming copper makes any eating establishment look inviting, and here you can see a first-rate collection of beautiful French copper cooking and serving pieces. If you're in the mood for *escargots* to start, the chef knows how to prepare them well. You might also try the real French onion soup or crêpes à la Biarritz (stuffed with crab meat). You can't go wrong with either. Entrees include frog's legs *provençale*, duck in cherry sauce with wild rice, and roast goose with chestnuts. The menu includes all kinds of chicken, lamb, beef, veal, and fish dishes, each served with fresh vegetables. Although there are no unusual desserts, all are homemade and very good. The reasonably priced dinners include soup, salad, and a choice of dessert. I recommend Le Biarritz if you are going to a Broadway show or an event in the Lincoln Center area.

LE BILBOQUET
25 E 63rd St   212 751-3036
Lunch, Dinner: Daily
American Express
Moderate

Philippe presides over this cozy Upper East Side Parisian sidewalk café as if it were his own backyard. He seems to know everyone; indeed, most of the loyal clientele live in the neighborhood. Nonetheless, hungry visitors looking for good, informal dining all day long will feel just as welcome. It's amazing that so tiny a kitchen can turn out such good food. The pâté and the *terrine de saumon* are both delicious appetizers. Le Bilbouquet is best known for its salads; the nicoise and duck salad with mangoes are the best bets. All of the assorted tarts are excellent, but my favorite is lemon. The chocolate *gâteau* is definitely waist-expanding! Philippe's constant presence is surely the secret of Le Bilboquet's success.

LE CHANTILLY
106 E 57th St (near Park Ave)   212 751-2931
Lunch: Mon-Sat; Dinner: Daily
Expensive

It is sad to see an old friend fade, but when that friend comes back better than before, it is especially heartening. This is exactly what has happened at Le Chantilly. It's always been a gracious and romantic dining spot, but things got a bit ragged at the edges for a time. With an outstanding new, young chef in the kitchen and charming Camille Dulac (the owner) out front, they once again have a winning team at this classic beauty. One thing is for sure: you can't beat the professional service. What to recommend? Salmon and lobster are outstanding. Many of the items have a Mediterranean accent, thanks to the chef's background. For an exotic taste, how about seared squab? A reasonably priced pre-theater dinner (three courses for $29) is first-rate. By the way, this is a great room for a special-occasion lunch, if you are not battling the time clock. Don't leave without trying the Cognac crème brûlée or the Grand Marnier soufflé.

LE CIRQUE
Mayfair Hotel (58 E 65th St)   212 794-9292
Lunch, Dinner: Mon-Sat
Expensive

Le Cirque is like no place else in New York. Owner Sirio Maccioni is a legend in the restaurant world of New York, and well he should be. While many of the grand, old-time restaurants rest on their laurels, Sirio is innovative and ingenious. Above all, he's a showman. His magnificent restaurant is crowded with famous folks and those who would like to be. Elegant food draws an elegant clientele. It is a pleasure to watch the superbly orchestrated staff make sure every person in the room feels that he or she is someone very special. Each dish, whether it's game, fish, or meat, comes with superb sauces and is served in satisfying portions. The must-try dishes are the sea scallops fantasy, the fettucine with truffles, and the crème brûlée. Take along your goldest credit card, and be prepared for an institution that could restore anyone's faith in the concept of the United Nations—i.e., a great American restaurant serving superb French food, orchestrated by an Italian.

L'ÉCOLE

462 Broadway (at Grand St)   212 219-3300
Lunch: Mon-Fri; Dinner: Mon-Sat
Moderate

Class is in session at the kitchen of L'École, the dining room of the French Culinary Institute. The students, eager and excited, are preparing daily meals under the watchful eyes of the dean of culinary studies, their head chef, and his team. They are learning their lessons well. Out front, the neighborhood is hardly inviting, and the maitre d' adds little to the effort inside. The room itself is attractive enough, if you can keep your eyes at table height and forget about the tall, unbecoming ceiling. But the meals here are a real bargain! Dinner consists of a *prix fixe* three- or five-course gourmet presentation. It is obvious that the instructors are watching very carefully, for each dish is presented beautifully and is uniformly delicious. Because there is a limited menu, the would-be chefs are able to concentrate on a few dishes. Semiprofessional waiters serve at a leisurely pace; don't come if you are in a hurry. But the price is right, and the school cafeteria you remember from years back was never this good! P.S. an ala carte menu has now been added.

LE MADRI

168 W 18th St (at Seventh Ave)   212 727-8022
Lunch: Mon-Fri; Dinner: Daily
Moderate

Pino Luongo's mother would be very proud. With Le Madri ("the mother"), he has created a great restaurant that is as busy and exciting as it should be, because he is serving first-class fare. The fact that he is personally on the job adds to what is surely one of the more pleasant newer places in Manhattan. The site used to be the stables for Macy's and, later, a warehouse of Barney's. Today it is a charming establishment, with a delightful garden patio for warm evenings and an appetizing interior, including a fabulous fresh vegetable and cheese display as you enter. The staff fits right into the ambience, many of them bearing authentic Italian accents and native words of advice on the varied menu. Wonderful Italian bread gets you started. You can have a Tuscan bread salad, if you desire. On to pastas, pizzas, or grilled and marinated vegetables. The place is spotless, noisy, colorful, and fun: although the youngish clientele is enough to keep you amused and intrigued, food is the big draw here. Pino's dream of an Italian renaissance will continue to be a winner . . . that is, as long as he remembers the special lessons his mother taught him in the kitchen at home!

LE PÉRIGORD

405 E 52nd St   212 755-6244
Lunch: Mon-Fri; Dinner: Mon-Sat
Expensive

Style and then some! Le Périgord should be reserved for special occasions, because this is, indeed, a very special restaurant. Right from the start, when you are cordially greeted at the door by the charming owner, Swiss-born Georges Briguet, to the time you reluctantly leave the warm, cozy premises completely satisfied, the experience is a brief interlude with a level of class that is rapidly disappearing from our world. The French menu features a *prix fixe* tab ($29 at lunch, $49 at dinner), with certain specialty items a slight bit more. But it is worth the cost in every way. The room is appealing, the service highly professional, the quality of the food unbeatable. This is one of the few places in Manhattan that adheres strictly to a proper dress code: jackets and ties are a must. (And why not, once in awhile, when you want to do something special?) What to eat? Whatever you have always longed for at a superb French restaurant. Don't overlook the soufflés!

LE PISTOU

134 E 61st St (bet Lexington and Park Ave)   212 838-7987
Lunch and Dinner: Mon-Sat
Moderate

The accent is unmistakably French — and the prices unmistakably a bargain — at this East Side bistro. Conceived by the folks at La Côte Basque, Le Pistou is an ideal feasting place for those who are starting or finishing their shopping expeditions and have a lighter wallet. Loud French music pervades the atmosphere; this is probably all for the best, as many tables are too close together for intimate conversation. The place is spotlessly clean, the décor features dozens of beautiful French puppets, and the personnel are gracious in the extreme. What's more, the food matches the surroundings. Baby artichokes in olive oil or *potage Saint-Germain* are excellent starters. Main-course favorites include breast of capon, veal scallopine, and a wonderful lamb stew with vegetables. The desserts are also first-class. From the time the wonderful warm bread arrives at your table to the final cup of delicious cappuccino, you're going to have a very pleasant French outing.

LE RÉFUGE

166 E 82nd St (bet Third and Lexington Ave)   212 861-4505
Lunch, Dinner: Daily
No credit cards
Moderate

In any city other than New York this would be one of the hottest restaurants in town. But aside from the folks in the neighborhood, nobody seems to have heard of Le Réfuge, a charming, three-room French country inn that offers excellent food, professional service, and delightful surroundings. The front room (for nonsmokers) is cozy and comfortable, and the back two sections provide nice views and pleasant accommodations. This is another house where the owner is the chef, and as usual, it shows in the professionalism of the presentations. Specialties of the house: duck with fresh fruit, *bouillabaisse de crustaces,* and couscous Mediterranean with shrimp. Finish off the meal with the flourless *gâteau soufflé au chocolate!* A delightful *prix fixe* brunch is served on weekends.

LE RÉGENCE
Hotel Plaza Athenee (37 E 64th St)   212 734-9100
Lunch, Dinner: Daily; Brunch: Sun
Expensive

This is a very classy restaurant. The setting is understated and immensely attractive, and the tables are far enough apart to allow private conversation. The presentation is outstanding, and the food is superb! One impressive point is that the personnel are not smitten with self-importance. The waiters and maitre d' are pleasantly accommodating, hard working, and well informed. You can't go wrong with any of the selections, but a few favorites stand out. Since it's mainly a seafood house, I strongly recommend the Dover sole fillets in champagne sauce, the lobster ravioli, and the braised striped bass in a marvelous wine sauce. The luncheon salads are magnificent; a real treat is the sliced chicken breast salad with hazelnuts. It's so inviting to look at, you hate to eat it! Even something as mundane as French-fried potatoes are done to perfection. And don't overlook the meat entrees, like the veal chops and delicious steaks. The Rostangs, a famous French family of restaurateurs, supervise this fine operation.

LES CÉLÉBRITÉS
Essex House (160 Central Park S)   212 247-0300
Dinner: Tues-Sat
Expensive

Close your eyes for a moment and forget you are in a hotel dining room on Central Park in the midst of teeming Manhattan. You can imagine you are in the grand dining room of a luxurious estate in the early part of the century. This is as fine and magnificent a room as there is in New York. Decorated in superb taste, it is small enough to be intimate and large enough to give the feeling that dining here is a grand occasion. The name comes from the selection of artwork that adorns the walls, all paintings created by American celebrities, including Phyllis Diller, Van Johnson, Peggy Lee, and Elke Sommer. The works are for sale; proceeds go to local charities. The menu matches the décor in splendor. A six-course menu degustation is available, as well as seasonal specialty *prix fixe* dinners. The à la carte menu changes but usually offers the kind of dishes you wouldn't prepare at home: burger of duck foie gras; squab with cabbage in a white truffle oil; lobster with asparagus, snow peas, and grated truffles. What else but a Grand Marnier (with vanilla ice cream and orange sorbet) or chocolate (with praline ice cream) soufflé for dessert? Or the candied orange-peel tart with bitter chocolate sorbet? You won't want to wake up after this sumptuous culinary dream.

LES HALLES
411 Park Ave S (bet 28th and 29th St)   212 679-4111
Daily: Noon to midnight
Moderate

Les Halles has struck a responsive note on the New York restaurant stage. Perhaps it is because France remains the romantic scene to many gourmets or that bistros have become the "in" thing in Manhattan. But most probably it is because this establishment provides most of the necessary ingredients in today's restaurant sweepstakes: tasty food in an appealing atmosphere at reasonable prices. Les Halles is no place for those who want a quiet, leisurely meal. Specialties like blood sausage with apples, lamb stew, or fillet of beef are served in hefty portions, with a fresh salad and delicious French fries on the side. Harried waiters try their best to be polite and helpful, but they are not always successful, as tables turn over more rapidly than at most fast-food outlets. As a matter of fact, most of the personnel here could profit from a course in customer satisfaction! If a week in Paris is more of a dream than a reality, you might settle for snails, onion soup, and classic cassoulet at this busy establishment. Unless you are big in the tart department, the dessert selection is a disappointment. (P.S. An attractive butcher shop is at your service right by the front door!)

LESPINASSE
St. Regis Hotel (Fifth Ave at E 55th St)   212 753-4500
Breakfast, Lunch, Dinner: Daily
Expensive

To dine here is an event and an experience. In a setting that befits the magnificent $100 million renovation of this historic hotel property, Lespinasse is a crown jewel in hotel dining in Manhattan. The room, with high ceilings and magnificent floral arrangements, is comfortable and sophisticated. The tables are far enough apart to allow for the kind of intimate conversation one feels is in keeping with the atmosphere. (What a place to propose!) Waiters are there when you need them, but disappear into the background while you enjoy your food and drink. And what food! The marinated beef short ribs are the best I have ever tasted. There are seafood selections, venison, duckling, and everything else you would expect from a classy establishment. Desserts? To die for. The classics (crème brûlée, honey-apple strudel, chocolate mousse), plus three other chocolate choices and more. Of course, you pay the price, but it is worth it. The crowning touch of class: the coat-check lady doesn't even give you a check. She remembers everyone's garment! *You'll* remember Lespinasse.

LE TRAIN BLEU
1000 Third Ave (Bloomingdale's, 6th floor)   212 705-2100
Lunch, Brunch: Mon-Sat; Afternoon tea (3–5): Mon-Fri;
Dinner: Thurs
Moderate

All aboard! Those who are old enough to remember when eating on a train was elegant and fun can relive a bit of that experience on the sixth floor of Bloomie's, at the end of the "Main Course" housewares area. You are seated in a mock dining car, with authentic atmosphere and accessories. (The view through the windows, however, does not change.) The menu is unusual and well done. You can dine lightly or with gusto on salads (there's one with goat cheese), pasta, or omelets. An especially tasty dish is onion soup with croutons. Very rich desserts will fortify you for additional use of your plastic card: crème brûlée, pecan tarts, and chocolate ganache cake are just a few examples. Afternoon tea is very elegant. Le Train Bleu is available for private receptions and dinners, and it features one of the most extensive wine lists of any department-store restaurant. But what else would you expect from the ever-innovative folks at Bloomingdale's?

LION'S ROCK
316 E 77th St   212 988-3610
Dinner: Daily; Brunch: Sun
Moderate

New York history buffs will know that Jones Wood was a favorite picnic spot in the last century. The area was famous for its outcroppings of red granite—a real attraction in those days. Of all things, the land was part of an estate owned by a bishop (Samuel Provost) that was popular as a location for romantic trysts. Now the Lion's Rock restaurant serves very tasty food in the same spot, with chef Dan Rogers substituting for the bishop! It's a particularly cozy spot for a snowy winter evening, with two fireplaces at work. In the summer you can still see some of that granite in the backyard dining area. The menu is "wholesome American," specializing in wonderful salads, pastas, roasted chicken breast, broiled fish dishes, and grilled items (like swordfish, veal chops, and ribeye steaks). The brunch menu has the usual Sunday items but an unusually attractive price!

LITTLE NELL'S TEA ROOM
343 E 85th St (bet First and Second Ave)   212 772-2046
Lunch: Tues-Fri; Dinner: Tues-Sun; Tea: Daily;
Brunch: Sat, Sun
Moderate

Little Nell is really Judy Nell Pickens, whose mother is also Nell. So it is only natural that she should be intrigued with Nell, of Charles Dickens' Old Curiosity Shop fame. Nell's cozy restaurant features Dickens on the wall, eclectic English memorabilia throughout, and especially friendly people who seem to have a wonderful time serving you. There are two small rooms, with a kitchen in between. Ask to be seated in the room to your left as you enter; it is brighter and more attractive. The food, like the surroundings, is hearty but not fancy, served with tender loving care, and sure to satisfy. For lunch there are salads, pasta, and light entrees. Afternoon teas are very popular, with plenty of homemade goodies as accompaniment. Dinners feature grilled Cornish hen and grilled marinated swordfish, along with a wonderful chicken breast sauteed with apple Calvados sauce. The brunches are a neighborhood favorite, offering melt-in-your-mouth buttermilk waffles topped with fresh fruit, and potato pancakes with scallions and sauteed mushrooms. Nell and her associates make Dickens come to life with fond memories of friends, food, and fun.

LORA
104 W 13th St (at Sixth Ave)   212 675-5655
Dinner: Daily
Moderate

This is one of those unpretentious places that someone who has always wanted to own a restaurant dreams about. Obviously, Lora, the owner and the chef, did just that. You might never find it if you didn't know the address; it is hidden away on quiet West 13th Street. There is a small bar and eating area at the entrance and a more charming room in the back. A rather limited menu features Italian appetizers, but the entrees from the wood-fired grill are hearty American: grilled salmon, tuna, ribeye steak, and leg of lamb. Try one of the delicious tarts for dessert. The portions are hearty, the service unsophisticated, the atmosphere jolly, and you can always tell your friends that you found a charming little place in Manhattan.

LOU G. SIEGEL
209 W 38th St   212 921-4433
Sun-Thurs: 11:30–10; Fri: 11:30–3
Moderate

Lou G. Siegel has been around longer than most New Yorkers can remember. It opened its doors in 1917, and customers have been pushing through them ever since. Its reputation, of which it is well aware ("The best-known kosher restaurant in the world," says Siegel's Eddie Share), is based mostly on their cold cuts, especially the pastrami. Workers in the garment district fill the place during lunch and dinner hours. Remember that, and schedule your visit for an early lunch or a "white tablecloth" dinner.

LOUISIANA COMMUNITY BAR & GRILL
622 Broadway (bet Bleecker St and Broadway) 212 460-9633
Dinner: Daily
Moderate

This is the place for you if you are under 40 and love Cajun food! Noisy, informal, friendly, and fun best describe the ambience, and "hot" best describes some of the dishes! You can go South with totally hot Cajun jambalaya or smoked tuna cakes with jalapeno hollandaise. (Watch out for that jalapeno bread . . . wow!) There is music to keep the taste buds stirred up, and wonderful po' boy sandwiches (bronzed chicken, fried oyster, or fried catfish) for those who can't finish the huge entree platters. What would a Cajun watering hole be without sweet potato pecan pie? Yes, but the fresh coconut cake takes the prize, in my estimation.

LUTÈCE
249 E 50th St (bet Second and Third Ave)   212 752-2225
Lunch: Tues-Fri; Dinner: Mon-Sat
Expensive

Lutece is an institution that never changes! The standard by which so many restaurants in Manhattan are judged is Lutece. It's so high-toned that they don't even list prices on the menu. Almost every restaurant guide rates it number one. I'm not sure it's that good, but certainly the chefs are masters and the service is impeccable. The owner, Andre Soltner, has received many awards, and they're well deserved. Lutece is housed in a former brownstone that's tastefully decorated with handsome furnishings and shimmering tableware. An indoor garden at the back adds to the charm. The restaurant features three great s's — soups, snails, and sauces. All are about the best in New York. Try the caviar over sour cream, the game and fowl dishes, braised baby lamb, and the soufflés. But be prepared for less-than-great service if they don't know you. Still, you can't beat Lutece.

MANHATTAN CAFE
1161 First Ave (at 64th St)   212 888-6556
Lunch: Mon-Fri; Dinner: Daily; Brunch: Sun
Moderate to expensive

New York does not have all that many classy continental steakhouses, although several have opened in recent years. Manhattan Café is one of them, and it is indeed an attractive, pleasant place to dine. But it is more than that! The steaks are large and delicious, as are the lamb chops and prime rib. Even the seafood, especially the fillet of sole, is worth trying. A number of veal dishes are available, with the veal piccata being particularly good. Accompany your choice with the excellent cottage-fried potatoes. For dessert, the *tartufo* equals any I've tasted in Italy (except for Tre Scalini's in Rome), and the cheesecake melts in your mouth. A pre-theater menu is available daily before 6:30 p.m. This polished establishment is an excellent place for an expense-account outing.

MARCH
405 E 58th St (bet First Ave and Sutton Place)   212 838-9393
Dinner: Mon-Sat
Expensive

If you want to be spoiled, you might start here. For in this attractive townhouse, with high ceilings and teak floors, you will dine in one of three rooms in absolutely regal style. Executive chef Wayne Nish and partner Joseph Scalice (who oversees the front house) have raised the art of dining to perfection. I would like to come back here eight nights, for only in that way could one try all eight of the unusual appetizers, eight of the fabulous entrees, and eight of the gourmet desserts. The *prix fixe* menu ($50) is well worth the tab, for the sky is the limit when it comes to service and quality. This is one of the few Manhattan restaurants that has not downsized in the wake of tough times in the industry. The fact that it continues to be busy is a tribute to the format. An attractive, glass-enclosed back porch looks over a small garden in this Sutton Place neighborhood.

MARCHI'S
251 E 31st St   212 679-2494
Dinner: Mon-Sat
Moderate

This must be one of the best-kept secrets in New York. Indeed, there's no sign out front, but Marchi's has been a New York fixture since 1930, when it was established by the Marchi family in an attractive brown-stone townhouse. The Marchis, joined by their three sons, are still on hand, giving a homey flavor to the restaurant's three dining rooms and garden patio (a great spot for a private dinner). It's almost like going to dinner at your favorite Italian family's house, especially since there are no menus. Be sure to bring a hearty appetite so you can take full advantage of a superb feast. The first course is a platter of antipasto, including radishes, finocchio, and Genoa salami, plus a salad of tuna fish, olives, and red cabbage. The second is an absolutely delicious homemade lasagna. The third is either crispy deep-fried fish or sauteed chicken livers; the side orders of cold beets and string beans are light and tempting. The entree is delicious roast chicken and roast veal served with fresh mushrooms and a tossed salad. For dessert, there is a healthy bowl of fresh fruit, cheese, a lemon fritter, and sensational *crostoli* (crisp fried twists sprinkled with powdered sugar). The price tag is decidedly underwhelming. Come to Marchi's for a unique, leisurely meal and an evening you will long remember.

MARK'S RESTAURANT
Mark Hotel (25 E 77th St)   212 879-1864
Breakfast, Lunch, Dinner: Daily; Brunch, Sun
Moderately expensive

In a setting reminiscent of an English club, one can enjoy a delicious dinner with refined service and no distractions from a very pleasant meal. The appetizers are heavy in the seafood area. Oysters, scallops, red snapper, salmon, and prawns are all uniquely presented. Main-course possibilities run the gamut from staples like filet mignon and roast rack of lamb to more exotic fare, such as lobster baked potato or red snapper on eggplant cavier. Desserts are all made in-house and feature great possibilities like profiteroles with three different kinds of ice cream. Beautiful flowers, nice wood tables, gorgeous china, and informed servers complete what is one of the best dining experiences on the Upper East Side.

MARYLOU'S
21 W 9th St   212 533-0012
Dinner: Daily; Brunch: Sun
Moderate

Marylou used to operate a fish market as well as a restaurant, but now she has directed her ample talents in just one direction: providing an A-1 dining room. The menu is so complete and varied that even the pickiest eater will find something to like. The Village setting is spacious, with four areas (including a most attractive garden room in the rear) and a busy bar in the front. The appetizers are heavy, with an Italian accent, but there are also good salads and homemade soups and chowders. Pasta lovers will find an interesting selection, and in keeping with Marylou's background, there are all kinds of seafood entrees, including hefty platters. Marylou's bouillabaisse is exceptional. The chicken and meat entrees are served with potatoes and rice, and the folks here are good about accommodating special orders. (Nothing great for dessert, though.) Omelet lovers will be in their glory at the Sunday brunch.

MAY WE
1022 Lexington Ave (at 73rd St)   212 249-0200
Dinner: Tues-Sun; Brunch: Sun
Moderate

Small and classy . . . that's May We in a nutshell. Nini and Mark May (she is the hostess, he the French-trained chef) have created a wonderful spot in what used to be Jack's, then 1022. But now May We (get it?), with tables up a spiral staircase and outside, features great food in a cozy atmosphere with personnel who couldn't be more accommodating. The glassware shines brightly, the fish dishes are superb, and the desserts are somewhat overwhelming. You can go all-out for appetizers like grilled quail or ragout of pig's feet, or you can have something simpler. The entrees are uniformly delicious, whether seafood, steak, lamb or chicken. And the desserts are splendid! How does warm chocolate fondant with homemade vanilla ice cream sound? Or upside-down apple tart with cinnamon ice cream? Or chocolate and banana mousses with almond crisps?

McSORLEY'S OLD ALE HOUSE
15 E 7th St (at Third Ave)   212 473-8800
Mon-Fri: 11–midnight; Sat: noon–midnight; Sun: 1–midnight
No credit cards
Inexpensive

If it's local color you want, you've got to visit McSorley's Old Ale House. Established in 1854, it's one of the original New York pubs. Abe Lincoln, the Roosevelts, and John Kennedy have all guzzled here. It's certainly not on the beaten track, but the atmosphere is terrific and the ale is great. One can conjure up visions of the good times spent in this old watering hole. It completely lacks the pretentiousness of so many New York eating places. The sawdust on the floor completes the picture of the classic spot to take your drinking buddy. And now, after all these years, women are welcome. The menu is limited and secondary to the ales, but hearty sandwiches, cheese platters, and burgers are available. Put on your jeans, take a stroll down to old New York, and listen while you sip. Everyone in the place is a character.

MESA GRILL
102 Fifth Ave (near 15th St)   212 807-7400
Lunch: Mon-Fri; Dinner: Daily; Brunch: Sat, Sun
Moderate

The Tex-Mex dishes here are among the best in Manhattan. This is surely the main reason for dining here, as the atmosphere and the décor are unappealing. The person responsible for the excellent fare is Bobby Flay, and he could make his mark anyplace in the Southwest! He serves wonderful appetizers like barbecued ribs, grilled tuna tostada, and grilled rabbit and goat cheese enchiladas. For your entree try a grilled dish like swordfish steak, whole red snapper, or pork chops adobo. Sound hot? They are. And there is cilantro risotto cake, roasted garlic mashed potatoes, or sweet potato tamales to go along! To take care of the heartburn, relax with an apple-Mexican cinnamon tart or a mint white-chocolate ice cream sandwich for dessert.

MEZZOGIORNO
195 Spring St   212 334-2112
Lunch, Dinner: Daily
Moderate

One of the most charming cities in the world is Florence, Italy, not only for its abundance of great art but for the wonderful small restaurants on every street corner. At Mezzogiorno, a Florence-style trattoria in New York, the food is just as good, though some of the art is questionable. The restaurant certainly adds a tasty new dimension to the SoHo area. The place is busy and noisy, and tables are so close together that secrets are impossible. The décor is best described as "modern Florence"; check out the unusual writing on the ceiling. Better yet, keep your eyes on the food. The salad selection is outstanding, as are all the meat *carpaccios*. If you like lasagna, theirs is one of the best. Mezzogiorno is also famous for the pizzas it serves. You'll find all the ingredients for a wonderful make-believe evening in Florence.

MINETTA TAVERN
113 MacDougal St   212 475-3850
Lunch, Dinner: Daily
Moderate

Do you want to take your guests to a Village restaurant where the coat-and-tie, meat-and-potatoes set will feel comfortable? Well, Minetta Tavern—established in 1937 and serving excellent food for generations—is the place to go. Located on the spot where Minetta Brook wandered through Manhattan in the early days, this Tavern was made famous by Eddie "Minetta" Sieveri, a friend of many sports and stage stars of yesteryear. Dozens of old pictures adorn the walls of this intimate, scrupulously clean tavern, where professional personnel serve no-nonsense Italian food at attractive prices. Grilled mushrooms, baked clams, or the traditional spinach and egg soup are good ways to get the juices flowing. Follow that up with pasta with red lettuce and shrimp or *branzino*—a great combination of sea bass, onions, vinegar, tomato cubes, and white wine. If you'd like something a bit heftier, grilled Cornish game hen and steaks are also available. The almond cake would make a wonderful cap to a satisfying meal. By the way, if you have to wait, the bar stools are among the most comfortable in New York.

MME. ROMAINE DE LYON
29 E 61st St (at Madison Ave)   212 758-2422
Lunch: Daily; Dinner: Mon-Fri
Moderate

The best omelets in New York are served at Mme. Romaine's. If you can't find what you want from their 545 varieties, it probably doesn't exist. How about a lobster, spinach, or chicken omelet? They will make any combination you want. When you're in the mood for a light lunch or dinner, this is the place to go. If omelets are not your preference, you might try the chef salad or the smoked salmon. At dinnertime, a full menu of continental cuisine is available.

MONTRACHET
239 W Broadway   212 219-2777
Lunch: Fri; Dinner: Mon-Sat
American Express
Moderately expensive

TriBeCa is not picturesque, but thriving and exciting places like Montrachet make the area a very appealing place to visit. Once inside Montrachet, the feeling of drabness dissipates. You can concentrate, undistracted, on a fine array of seafood, game, and meat prepared to perfection by the restaurant's latest super chef, Debra Ponzek. One of her predecessors, David Bouley, was so good that he has gone on to open his own successful restaurant. The menu changes regularly, with exciting things done with fresh produce. If you are lucky enough to find a bouillabaisse dish on the menu, go for it. Roast pheasant, roast chicken, and roast duck are outstanding choices, and lobster dishes are done to perfection. The three simply decorated rooms do not detract from the main reason you are there: good eating. The desserts have finally come up to par with the rest of the menu, with soufflés at the top of the list. Having tasted many crème brûlées, I can say with authority that Montrachet's is top-notch.

MOONDANCE DINER
Sixth Ave at Grand St   212 226-1191
Sun-Thurs: 8:30 a.m.–midnight; Fri, Sat: 24 hours
No credit cards
Moderate

Remember that old song: "Dinner in the diner, nothing could be finer?" Well, it *could* be finer than the Moondance, but it would surely cost you a heck of a lot more. Larry Panish, a graduate of the Culinary Institute of America, turned an old greasy spoon into a spotless, efficient operation that serves absolutely first-class "simple" food at a price anyone can afford. There is the usual counter and about a dozen tables; what isn't usual is the great taste of wholesome salads and sandwiches for lunch and the gourmet-style chicken, steak, veal, and what-have-you for dinner. The help is extra polite; the plates are balanced and attractive. Specialties include great onion rings, outstanding chili, pastas, and homemade apple pie. Daily specials are listed on the blackboard, and takeout orders are available. Drop by for breakfast, and you'll be starting the day out right! Larry's Lox Around the Clock (676 Sixth Ave) is equally well operated. Note the extended weekend hours!

NICK AND EDDIE

203 Spring St (at Sullivan St)   212 219-9090
Lunch, Dinner: Daily
Moderate

This place is so popular it looks like the only ones missing are Nick and Eddie themselves. It turns out that the place was named for two kids in the neighborhood. It is easy to understand the popularity: good food in a hearty atmosphere at reasonable prices. If there is one word to describe the plates, it is *wholesome*. There are no affectations with the menu or the service; everything is just what you would want to be served at home. Potato pancakes and apple compote or an ice-cold salad make fine starters. The salads are tasty and filling. Main courses include burgers, grilled fish dishes (salmon, catfish, red trout, shrimp), and tender steaks with real mashed potatoes and well-cooked veggies. Banana bread with ice cream and hot fudge is the best dessert. Better call ahead for reservations, for at these prices word is sure to get around!

NICOLA'S

146 E 84th St (bet Lexington and Third Ave)   212 249-9850
Dinner: Daily
Moderately expensive

This is *the* place for upper-crust New Yorkers who like a clubby atmosphere and good food (which are not too often found together). In a setting of rich wood and familiar faces on the walls, and a noise level that sometimes can reach that of a Broadway opening, the no-nonsense waiters serve delicious platters of pasta, veal, chicken, and steak dishes. There are daily specials in every category, and each is uniformly inviting. It is difficult to come up with really good home fries in a busy restaurant, but Nicola's has the secret . . . theirs are sensational. Concentrate on the early part of your meal; the desserts show little imagination.

OCEANA

55 E 54th St (bet Park and Madison Ave)   212 759-5941
Lunch: Mon-Fri; Dinner: Mon-Sat
Moderately expensive

In one of the warmer and more inviting rooms in Manhattan (it used to house Le Cygne), Oceana is carving a special niche for delicious seafood presentations. The three-course *prix fixe* dinner includes a selection of delicious appetizers, all with a flavor of the lake or ocean. You can feast upon oysters, lobster salad, lump crab parfait, or South American prawns. Depending upon what is fresh, entrees might include pan-seared salmon, sea bass, or yellowfin tuna with foie gras. The desserts are just as good: bittersweet chocolate torte, apple tart with caramel mousse (a winner), or warm caramelized bananas with coconut ice cream. Oceana is very civilized and charming, and well worth a visit.

OLD DENMARK

133 E 65th St (at Lexington Ave)   212 744-2533
Mon-Sat: 9-5:30
No credit cards
Inexpensive to moderate

Old Denmark is really a gourmet food shop, but it is also a good spot to go for a light, quick, different kind of lunch. If you are keen on Scandinavian food items, you can stock up here. There is no menu, but you have your choice of assorted salads and appetizers, tasty breads, and cakes. Old Denmark is very handy when you are out shopping and don't want something too heavy. The personnel are particularly helpful.

OLDE GARDEN CAFE & WINERY

15 W 29th St   212 532-8323
Lunch: Mon-Fri; Dinner: Mon-Sat
Inexpensive to moderate

So you're all worn out after pushing through the crowds at Macy's or shopping the discount photo stores. Or maybe you just got off the train at Penn Station. Whatever the case, it's an easy walk to the Olde Garden Cafe & Winery on W 29th Street, an enchanting place established in 1912. It was originally an antiques shop that offered tea and sandwiches to its customers. Folks liked the eats so well that the owners decided to give up the antiques and concentrate on the treats. An open garden in the back has now been covered. The restaurant encompasses several warm and attractive rooms with wooden floors and partial brick walls. A smattering of antiques are still around, and the comfortable captain's chairs and wooden tables add to the inviting ambience. This is a great place for lunch. All kinds of salads are offered: diced chicken platter, Olde Garden Club salad, and the "executive salad bowl," with Swiss cheese, ham, shrimp, and anchovy and herb dressing. Entree selections include ocean sole, sea scallops, wiener schnitzel, Western prime rib of beef, eggs Benedict, and several omelets. All entrees are served with potato and garden vegetables. Reasonably priced desserts include a wonderful apple strudel and freshly baked pies.

ONE HUDSON CAFE

1 Hudson St (at Chambers St and W Broadway)   212 608-5835
Lunch: Mon-Fri; Dinner: Mon-Sat
Moderate

It is reassuring to know there still are restaurants in Manhattan that are not trendy, big, or expensive, but just do things really nicely. One Hudson is one of the those places. The crystal and silverware gleam; the servers are neat, efficient, and informed; the bread basket is served warm and tempting; the tablecloths are immaculately white and clean; the flowers on each table are fresh. And the food is great. You can feast upon seafood, steak, lamb, veal, or chicken in a serene atmosphere and not feel the slightest bit rushed. Especially at the noon hour, in a neighborhood that is decidedly not classly, this place stands out. Oh, that homemade deepdish apple pie. Who could ask for anything more?

ONE IF BY LAND, TWO IF BY SEA
17 Barrow St (bet Seventh Ave and W 4th St)   212 228-0822
Dinner: Daily
Expensive

Finding this place is a bit of a challenge, but what a reward when you do! The building that was once Aaron Burr's old carriage house is truly unique, and the atmosphere is warm (with working fireplaces) and friendly. One If by Land is especially popular with young people, who appreciate the romantic ambience and the extraordinary food. Make reservations before coming and allow yourself time to find Barrow Street (one of the Village's most charming yet hard-to-find side streets) and the restaurant (there's no sign out front). Be sure to spend a few minutes enjoying a drink at the spacious bar by the fireplace. Try to get a table on the balcony level; it's especially romantic. As for dinner, the roast rack of lamb, Norwegian salmon, grilled filet mignon, and beef Wellington are all excellent. Dessert is an ever-changing selection of delicious homemade goodies.

ORSO
322 W 46th St   212 489-7212
Mon, Tues, Thurs, Fri, Sun: noon-11:45;
Wed, Sat: 11:30 a.m.–11:45 p.m.
Moderate

This restaurant features the same menu all day, which is great for those with unusual dining hours and handy for those going to the theater. Orso is one of the most popular places on midtown's "restaurant row," so if you're thinking about a six o'clock dinner, be sure to make reservations. The smallish room is cozy and comfortable and watched over by a portrait of Orso, a Venetian dog who is the mascot for this Italian bistro. The kitchen is open in the back and visible to diners; you can see for yourself just how experienced the staff is. The changing menu includes many good appetizers, like cold roast veal and fried artichokes. A variety of pizzas and some excellent pasta dishes are also offered. For an entree, you can't go wrong with the lamb sausage or the veal shank. The truffle gelati, one of many homemade desserts, will finish a great meal.

ORSON'S
175 Second Ave (bet 11th and 12th St)   212 475-1530
Dinner: Daily (until 2 a.m.)
Moderate

You have just come out of a movie and the hunger pangs are at work. The dress is casual and so is the mood. This tiny East Village hotspot is just the place for a late evening meal, as they serve food until 2 a.m. and the bar stays wet until 4 a.m. There are just a handful of noisy tables, the service is pleasant and informal, and the food is surprisingly good. There are clam fritters, warm seafood and chicken salads, great burgers, fresh fish, pasta, chili, and gnocchi. Two unusual and delicious desserts: molasses bread pudding and warm chocolate cake with roasted banana sauce. (It tastes far better than it sounds.) While a model train steams around the ceiling area, savvy New Yorkers let off steam at the bar and partake of some of the best food buys in Manhattan.

PALM   PALM TOO
837 Second Ave (at 44th St)   840 Second Ave (at 44th St)
212 687-2953   212 697-5198
          Lunch: Mon-Fri; Dinner: Mon-Sat
          Expensive

Steak and lobster lovers in Manhattan have a special place in their hearts for the Palm and Palm Too. These restaurants are located across the street from each other, and both have much the same atmosphere. The waiters will tell you what's available—there is no printed menu. They're noted for huge, delicious steaks, chops, and lobsters, but don't miss the Palm fries—homemade potato chips—which are the best. Or try a combination order of fries and onion rings. It's an earthy spot, so don't get too dressed up. There is sawdust on the floor, thick tobacco and grease smoke in the air, and outrageous caricatures on the dirty walls. You are only part of the passing scene to the indolent waiters, but come early (it's usually crowded) and enjoy the good bread, excellent salad, and expensive entrees. You won't forget it.

PAMIR
1437 Second Ave (bet 74th and 75th St)   212 734-3791
Dinner: Tues-Sun
Inexpensive

You probably don't have Afghanistan at the top of your list of countries to visit, but this small Afghan restaurant definitely should be. Turnovers are an Afghan specialty, and Pamir offers several. If you like extraspicy food (like that served in the native country), they will gladly oblige. The Afghan bread is great, and you get some with each entree. Lamb is the order of the day: seasoned lamb with rice, almonds, and pistachios; chunks of lamb in an onion-and-garlic-flavored spinach sauce; lamb and eggplant cooked with tomatoes, onions, and spices; lamb on a skewer, marinated in spices; lamb chops broiled on a skewer . . . all are worth a try. Several vegetarian dishes are also available. Eat heartily from the start, because the desserts are zilch. The folks here are so unpretentious, the desire to please so sincere, and the prices so modest that this ranks as one of the best ethnic restaurant choices.

PAOLA'S
347 E 85th St　　　212 794-1890
Dinner: Daily
American Express
Moderate

One of the pleasures of writing a book like this is hearing from readers who have a special question or an unusual need. Several times young ladies have called, asking me to suggest a place to take their boyfriends for a cozy and romantic evening. One young lady even called the next day to tell me it had worked: the young man proposed! Paola's, a tiny hole-in-the-wall, is a prime spot for such an evening. The only problem might be that you'll have an audience for the proposal, since the room has just ten tables, and it gets crowded. But no matter. The Italian home cooking is first-class. Paola is in the kitchen taking care of the food. Great homemade pasta, superb veal dishes, and tasty, hot vegetables (like grilled radicchio) are house specialties. Take along a Velamint if romance is in the air, because they don't spare on the garlic. Mirrors reflect the warmth and flicker of the candles, and the lady of the house will charm any guest. To top off the reasonably priced dinner, try a dish of rich, creamy espresso ice cream.

PAPER MOON MILANO
39 E 58th St　　　212 758-8600
Lunch: Mon-Sat; Dinner: Mon-Sat
Moderate

This offshoot of the well-known Milan House bills itself as a "restaurant-pizzeria." It does a good job in both departments. In a high-rent area, the atmosphere is friendly and casual; patrons in jeans and sportswear will feel perfectly comfortable. Décor is simple and appealing. The harried help tries its best to be accommodating. A fine selection of salads and pastas is offered, each presented with a finesse that comes from years of experience in Italy. The full menu includes fish, meat, and poultry dishes, as well as several *carpaccio* dishes (thin slices of raw beef with various toppings). But you will be missing something special if you don't try the pizzas. A talented young Italian pizza chef turns out some of the lightest, tastiest combinations you have ever savored. Each is a meal in itself. A refreshing dish of gelati will top off a wonderful lunch or dinner.

PAPPA'S PLACE
510 Sixth Ave (at 13th St)   212 924-3799
Breakfast, Lunch, Dinner: Daily
Moderate

Not only do Pappa and Mamma like this place, so do the kids. What an assortment of goodies! There are low-fat chicken burgers, seafood à la Pappa's (shrimp and mussels over linguini), grilled eggplant, big pastas, great sandwiches, chicken Rossini, quiches, and much more. Breakfast items like blintzes, pancakes, omelets, and waffles are served all day. Kids will go wild over the dessert and candy selections. Prices are moderate. Some low-calorie items are available, and there are lots of international cappuccinos and coffees to choose from. The ultimate is the Jennie Roll: a huge, fresh pancake stuffed with bananas, vanilla ice cream, chocolate syrup, and topped with oodles of whip cream. What a way to go!

PARIS COMMUNE
411 Bleecker St   212 929-0509
Lunch: Mon-Fri; Dinner: Daily; Brunch: Sat, Sun
Moderate

Tony and Ari operate this small, charming Greenwich Village bistro, complete with fireplace. It is a neighborhood gathering place, and each evening the rooms fill up quickly with regulars. The food is absolutely first-rate, with prices no one could complain about. There are just a dozen tables, each one promptly served by attentive, friendly waiters. Even the owners take orders, bus dishes, and help with all those little things that make dining a pleasure. At noon on Saturday and Sunday, a super brunch features the best French toast anywhere, along with cereals, eggs, omelets, English muffins, and *pomme frits*. The delicious omelets include cheddar cheese and bacon, apples and Jarlsberg cheese, and marinated artichoke hearts and mozzarella. On the regular dining menu, which changes seasonally, there is always a good selection of soups, salads, and poultry, meat, and fish entrees. The mustard-grilled chicken is a house favorite. If you are there on a Tuesday night, try the couscous special. The dessert course is a must; their chocolate mousse cake with espresso whipped cream is sensational.

PARK AVENUE CAFE
100 E 63rd St (at Park Ave)   212 644-1900
Lunch: Mon-Fri; Dinner: Mon-Sat; Brunch: Sun
Moderately expensive

In a setting that once was Le Périgord Park and later Hubert's, restaurant maestro Alan Stillman (Post House, Manhattan Ocean Club, Smith & Wollensky) has created a crisp, sparkling setting for a neighborhood that loves new and "in" places to dine. Professional waiters in green-and-white shirts and suspenders, walls filled with novel pieces of American folk art, and a breadbasket that looks much better than it tastes had food faddists on the Upper East Side scrambling for reservations for months. There is no question that chef David Burke is very talented; perhaps it is another case of instant success that makes the anticipation here more satisfying than the experience. In any case the American menu presentations are terrific to look at. Some, like a delicious asparagus risotto served in a ceramic asparagus mug, taste great, too. If you want to listen in on some big operators, come on down. A large party area is available.

PARK BISTRO
414 Park Ave S (bet 28th and 29th St)   212 689-1360
Lunch: Mon-Fri; Dinner: Mon-Sun
Moderate

These days it is special fun to go to a place with smiles, and the Park Bistro is it! This is a small, homey dining room that specializes in cuisine from the Provence region of France. It's a jewel. From the start, when warm and tasty bread is placed before you, to the finishing touch of rich and luscious homemade desserts (like crème brûlée, tortes, and a sinful chocolate gâteau), you are surrounded by attentive service and magnificent food. Don't miss the hanger steak or the braised lamb shank. A professional team runs this place, and it shows.

PARKSIDE
107-01 Corona Ave (at 51st Ave and 108th St, Corona, Queens)
718 271-9274
Lunch, Dinner: Daily
Moderate

Do you want to show that person who "knows everything about New York" something he or she doesn't know? Do you want to eat on your way to or from La Guardia or Kennedy airport? Do you want a special meal in an unusual setting? Well, all of the above are excellent reasons to visit Parkside, in Queens. I make an exception in including a restaurant not in Manhattan because it *is* exceptional. Richard D'Angelo runs a first-class, spotlessly clean restaurant that serves beautiful and wonderful Italian food at prices that make most New York restaurateurs look like highway robbers. Start with garlic bread and then choose from two dozen kinds of pasta and an opulent array of fish, steak, veal, and poultry dishes. The meat is all prime cut — nothing frozen here. You'll also find polite, knowledgeable waiters in an informal atmosphere. Get a table in the garden room or the new Marilyn Monroe room upstairs (entertainment on weekends). Eat until your heart's content, and be amazed at the tab.

PATSY'S
236 W 56th St (bet Broadway and Eighth Ave)   212 247-3491
Lunch, Dinner: Daily
Moderate

For half a century, the Scognamillo family has operated this popular eatery, specializing in Neapolitan cuisine. At the moment the son is taking care of the front of the house, while the grandson is following the family tradition in the kitchen. "Patsy" was an immigrant gentleman chef whose nickname was soon attached to a New York tradition that has now grown into a two-level restaurant. Each floor has its own cozy atmosphere and convenient kitchen. The family makes sure that every guest is treated as if they were in a private home; courtesy and concern are the name. of the game. A full Italian menu is available, with numerous specials that include a different soup and seafood entree each day. If you can't find what you like among the two dozen pasta choices, you are in deep trouble!

PEPPERMINT PARK CAFE & BAKERY
1225 First Ave (bet 66th and 67th St)
212 288-5054 (cafe); 212 288-5415 (bakery)
Breakfast, Lunch, Dinner: Daily (open late)
Moderate

There are five excellent reasons to visit Peppermint Park: if you want a light meal, if you're a dessert lover, if you want to eat after a show, if you've got kids with you, or if you simply prefer informal restaurants with a carnival-like atmosphere. For sustenance, there are fantastic crêpes, like the Crêpe Train Robbery (creamed spinach with your choice of sharp cheddar or Roquefort cheese) or Crêpe Canaveral—they say it blasts your spirits into orbit. Another good combination: fresh mushrooms, sauteed onions, melted Gruyere, and blended herbs. Several dessert crêpes are also available, such as one with maple syrup, melted butter, and powdered sugar. There are all kinds of Belgian waffle concoctions and a few quiches. The big news, though, is the fantastic selection of homemade ice creams (from mocha chip—number one for me—to rum raisin and black raspberry), several sherbets and sorbets, big banana splits, really thick shakes, yogurts, a selection of ten toppings (among them walnuts in syrup, crushed cherries, and hot butterscotch), and an array of pastries, cakes, and cookies you won't believe.

PIERRE'S
170 Waverly Pl   212 929-7194
Lunch: Mon-Fri; Brunch: Sat, Sun; Dinner: Daily
No credit cards
Moderate

For over a decade Pierre's has been providing "Café Theatre" to happy diners in the Village. Owners Pierre Bezai and George Lefevre have hit upon a distinctive formula: crowded tables, great music, lots of fun, and very good food, all at a modest price. In the evening there is light entertainment, aided by personable waiters, most of whom are comedians in their own right. The bistro food is very French, with a good selection of salads, seafood items, and delicious quiches. All of the entrees, including an outstanding sirloin steak and beef stew in wine sauce, are served with fresh vegetables cooked to perfection. Don't dress up, don't expect fancy digs, be prepared for an impromptu show, and you won't be disappointed.

PIETRO'S
232 E 43rd St   212 682-9760
Lunch: Mon-Fri; Dinner: Mon-Sat
Expensive

Pietro's is a steakhouse with Northern Italian cuisine; everything is cooked to order. The menu features great salads, steaks and chops, seafood, chicken, and an enormous selection of veal. Tell your companion not to bother getting dressed up. Bring your appetite, though, because the portions are huge. Although steaks are the best known of Pietro's dishes, you will also find eight chicken dishes and ten veal selections (marsala, cacciatore, scallopine, piccata, francaise, etc.). And for meat-and-potato lovers, there are eight different potato dishes. Prices border on expensive, and the service is boisterous, but you'll certainly get your money's worth. By the way, Pietro's is very child-friendly.

PIGALLE
111 E 29th St (bet Park and Lexington Ave)   212 779-7830
Lunch: Sun-Fri; Dinner: Daily
Moderate

This is one of the nicest bistros in Manhattan, appealing in every way. The attractive room is inviting and comfortable, the food is prepared and presented in a most appetizing manner, the service is prompt and professional, and the price is certainly reasonable. There are pâtés and pastas, first-class homemade soups, especially good salads, and a selection of fish, poultry, and meat dishes for your main course. Unusual tarts are the dessert feature. Banquet and reception facilities are available, and in good weather you can sit outside and watch the passing parade.

PIG HEAVEN
1540 Second Ave (bet 80th and 81st St)   212 744-4333
Lunch, Dinner: Daily
Moderate

There is no other place quite like Pig Heaven west of the Great Wall! The look is French country, the food is Chinese, and pigs are everywhere. You'd never know you were in a Chinese restaurant, judging from the wood-covered walls and the fresh flowers. This is one of David Keh's operations; he owns and operates several Chinese eating spots in Manhattan. The menu offers many hot and cold pork dishes, the best of which are spring rolls and steamed dumplings in a basket. The barbecued spareribs are super. Other winners include beef with snow peas and flattened shrimp in shells with hot pepper sauce. A number of dishes are spicy, so be forewarned. You can look through a glass window at the kitchen and see the various items being prepared for both house consumption and to go. Finally, someone got smart about desserts in a Chinese restaurant. Instead of the limited selection offered in most, here you can enjoy American apple pie, Peking snow balls, and a sensational frozen praline mousse.

PINOCCHIO
170 E 81st St   212 650-1513, 212 879-0752
Lunch: Tues-Sat; Dinner: Daily
American Express
Moderate

I'm happy once again to include this unusually good restaurant in my new edition. Pinocchio is off the beaten path: a small and inexpensive restaurant that serves the kind of Italian food Geppetto's grandmother used to make. You won't find the menu limited to spaghetti and pizza. Pinocchio specializes in regional Italian cooking, and if you're puzzled about what to order, the friendly waiters are happy to advise. Unlike too many restaurants, families are welcome here, perhaps because it's a family-run place. Sal Petrillo and his four children do the honors. Small parties are also treated well. What a difference a little personal attention can make!

PIZZAPIAZZA
785 Broadway (at 10th St)   212 505-0977
Lunch, Dinner: Daily
Inexpensive

Does deep-dish pizza sound good to you? Go to PIZZAPIAZZA in a hurry. Their pizza comes in three sizes, all made to order and chockablock full of cheeses, vegetables, and meats. All are prepared without preservatives. If you're a crust lover, like I am, you'll definitely like these. The pizzas are served piping hot, and they taste as good as they look. There are over a dozen possibilities, from chicken Mexicana to Piazza pepperoni, Cajun pizza, the "all-American," or the "ultimate Piazza special," which includes bacon, sweet sausage, sliced mushrooms, broccoli, pepperoni, onions, artichoke hearts, roasted garlic, tomato sauce, and three cheeses. Get the picture? Forget about the burgers and chili; concentrate on the absolutely super specialty of the house. If you have any room left for dessert, ask for the Bailey's Bombe: coffee ice cream with Irish cream liqueur and chocolate coffee beans. Takeout and delivery are also available.

PLANET HOLLYWOOD
140 W 57th St (bet Sixth and Seventh Ave)   212 333-7827
Daily: 11 a.m.–1 a.m.
Inexpensive to moderate

Don't come here for the food. This is purely entertainment, Hollywood-style. The place is outrageously decorated with submarines and rockets, the noise level is intolerable, the waiting lines are long (no reservations), but it sure is fun. The kids will love Planet Hollywood, and you'll find it easy on the pocketbook. When you do get down to eating, the menu is mainly sandwiches, pizzas, salads, pastas, and a good selection of appetizers. Sizzling fajitas are served piping hot, accompanied by goodies like sauteed onions, guacamole, whole-wheat tortillas, and much more. As you might expect, the dessert course is the best: bread pudding, apple strudel, brownies, Snickers pie, yogurts, malts, shakes, and ice cream.

PLAZA HOTEL PALM COURT
Plaza Hotel (59th St at Fifth Ave)   212 759-3000
Breakfast, Lunch: Mon-Sat; Tea, Supper: Daily; Brunch: Sun
Moderate

Some rooms, like some people, just get better with age, and happily this is one of them. If just one place in the city could be singled out as the embodiment of all that folks dream of as the New York of yesteryear—romantic and carefree, delicious and proper—it would have to be the Palm Court at the Plaza Hotel. The great and near-great have laughed and loved here with the likes of Eloise and Auntie and Uncle, creating thousands of memories of special times. You can enjoy breakfast, luncheon quiches, salads, wonderful teas with tea sandwiches, and caloric goodies, all to the accompaniment of classic piano and violin music. There are also supper snacks, seafood salads, assorted smoked fish, and some unusual sandwiches and pastries. The fabulous Sunday buffet—the largest and most glamorous in the city—is a popular New York tradition. Many three-generation families show the young ones where they used to go in the "good old days." A real treat, day or night, and a must for the New York visitor.

POLO
Westbury Hotel (Madison Ave at 69th St)   212 439-4835
Breakfast, Lunch, Dinner: Daily; Tea: Sat, Sun
Moderately expensive

The Polo Restaurant, located just three blocks down the street from Ralph Lauren's magnificent Rhinelander Mansion store, captures the cache of the Polo name, although there is no connection. In an intimate hotel dining room, with tables far enough apart to make a visit comfortable and personal, you can enjoy a power breakfast, a pricey but delicious lunch, or a dinner in just the right setting for the fortieth wedding anniversary of your in-laws. The guests and staff are on their best behavior, the room is bathed in piano melodies, and the dishes are served in a flurry of polished silver covers. Under them you'll find delicacies such as seared Atlantic salmon (the special house dish) and wonderful veal dishes. Save some room for the creamy and delicious chocolate ice-cream sandwich! Doesn't sound fancy enough for this place, does it? But it is fancy and rich. This restaurant, like the stock market, has its ups and downs, but the current outlook is bullish.

POST HOUSE
28 E 63rd St   212 935-2888
Lunch: Mon-Fri; Dinner: Daily
Moderate to expensive

The best way to describe the Post House would be as an "in" social and political hangout on East 63rd Street that serves excellent food in comfortable surroundings. The guest list usually includes many well-known names and easily recognizable faces. They are attracted, of course, by the fact that this spot has been written up favorably in the gossip columns. Hors d'oeuvres like crabmeat cocktail, lobster cocktail, and stone crabs are available in season, but the major draws are steak and lobster. Prices for the latter two entrees are definitely not in the moderate category; ditto for lamb chops. However, the quality is excellent, and the cottage fries, fried zucchini, hash browns, and onion rings are superb. Save room for the Post House chocolate box (white and dark chocolate mousse with raspberry sauce). If you can walk out under your own steam after all this, you're doing well! The Post House is not as earthy as the Palm or as macho as Christ Cella. It is, however, a fitting spot to take your favorite lady for a hearty dining experience or a client when you want to close an important deal.

PRIMAVERA
1578 First Ave (at 82nd St)   212 861-8608
Dinner: Daily
Expensive

There are hundreds of Italian restaurants in Manhattan. When I'm asked which is the greatest, my answer is always Primavera. So many times an establishment reflects a proprietor's personality and talent; nowhere is this more apparent than at Primavera. Nicola Civetta, the owner, is the epitome of class. He knows how to make you feel at home and how to present a superb Italian meal. Don't go if you're in a hurry, though. This place is for relaxed dining. I could wax eloquently with descriptions of the dishes, but enough said: you can't go wrong, no matter what you order. Let Nicola choose for you, as there are specials every day. To top it all off, they have one of the most beautiful desserts anywhere: a gorgeous platter of seasonal fruit that looks too good to eat. Primavera is always busy, so reservations are a must.

PRIX FIXE
18 W 18th St   212 675-6777
Lunch: Mon-Fri; Dinner: Mon-Sat
Moderate

Prix Fixe has succeeded in an area that has not been a fortuitous one for many restaurants. Their varied and attractive lunch and dinner menus provide enough reasonably priced alternatives for most hungry diners. The setting is a cold, cavernous room that has been inhospitable to a number of former occupants. Happily, you will find several *prix fixe* luncheon and dinner suggestions that include appetizer and main course or main course and dessert. Grilled breast of chicken and a great sirloin burger sandwich on homemade roll are suggested for lunch. At dinner time, the seafood items are top-notch as appetizers and for the main course. A number of homemade desserts (like warm chocolate-banana burst with candied pecan ice cream) will complete a memorable meal. By the way, all items on the menus are available à la carte. Even though the restaurant is anything but cozy and friendly, the personnel make up for this shortcoming with prompt and attentive service.

PROVENCE
38 MacDougal St (at Prince and Houston St)   212 475-7500
Lunch, Dinner: Daily
American Express
Moderate

You won't quickly forget a visit to Provence! This bustling region of France has been transported, in a charming manner, to Greenwich Village, where tasty and wholesome food is professionally served at sensible prices. Garlic is another reason you won't forget this bistro. If you like this taste, you'll love Provence! The French country menu is served in several spaces: one noisy room by the bar, overlooking the Village streets; another more romantic area in the back; and a comfortable outside patio. You'll find dishes typical of the region (fish and steamed vegetables) on the menu. If you like some of the signature dishes (*pot-au-feu,* cassoulet, bouillabaisse, couscous), I'd suggest calling to find out what item is being featured that evening. Wonderful French fries come with some dishes. Top it all off with a Provence tart.

QUATORZE (Now FO URTEEN)   QUATORZE BIS
240 W 14th St   323 E 79th St
212 206-7006   212 535-1414
       Lunch: Tues-Sun; Dinner: Daily
       Moderate

The genius of the two Quatorze restaurants is their simplicity. They have a limited menu, with quality food and professional service. The portions are enormous; for friends with large appetites, this is a safe bet. Lunch features a great offering of soups and sandwiches. For dinner, the *choucroute garnie* is a specialty. Other choices include grilled Black Angus sirloin, roast chicken, braised duck, fresh oysters, grilled salmon, cassoulet, bouillabaisse, and sauteed brook trout. Their specialty dessert, the chocolate regal, is superb. Both outlets serve an indentical menu, and both houses are attractive and comfortable.

RAINBOW ROOM
30 Rockefeller Plaza (GE Bldg, 65th floor)   212 632-5000
Dinner: Tues-Sun
Expensive

On October 3rd, 1934, the Rainbow Room opened atop Rockefeller Center, giving New Yorkers and visitors a thrill found nowhere else. The lights of the city below were vibrant and visible from the opulent room, where celebrated chefs and famous bands worked to make the evening a special event. On December 29th, 1987, that scene was re-created when a spectacular two-floor facility, redone by the Rockefellers at a cost of $20 million, opened on the same site. Joe Baum has turned the 64th and 65th floors into a magnificent private club during the day and a great dining and dancing spot in the evening. The Rainbow Room, a two-story, glass-enclosed jewel, is the showpiece of the new layout. Smartly uniformed personnel serve gourmet food to the accompaniment of a 12-piece dance band. The Rainbow Promenade is a smaller room, with cozy tables and light meals. Rainbow and Stars is the dining and supper club, which features live cabaret entertainment. Views from all rooms are spectacular, but the one facing directly north to Central Park is breathtaking. The sights inside the rooms aren't so bad either; a million-dollar collection of 40 pieces of modern American art adorn the walls. An evening of being pampered and spoiled by Joe Baum and his professional crew is certain to be quite an occasion for even the most jaded diner. The Rainbow also offers party and banquet facilities.

RAO'S
455 E 114th St   212 534-9625
Dinner: Mon-Fri
No credit cards
Inexpensive

If you want to go to Rao's, an intimate old-time (1896) Italian restaurant run by an aunt and an uncle in the kitchen and a nephew named Frank out front, you should plan a bit in advance. The place is crowded all the time for two good reasons: the food is great, and the prices are ridiculously low. Don't walk or take a car; hail a taxi and get out in front of the restaurant. When you're ready to leave, have Frank call a local taxi service to pick you up. Frank is a gregarious and charming host who makes you feel right at home; he'll even sit at your table while you order. Be prepared for leisurely dining. While you're waiting, enjoy the excellent bread and warm atmosphere. Among the offerings that are especially tasty, I enjoyed the pasta and piselli. Veal marsala and veal piccata are excellent choices, as are any number of shrimp dishes. Believe it or not, the Southern fried chicken is absolutely superb; it would be my number-one choice. Don't miss this spot in Spanish Harlem. Hint: Try appearing unannounced at the door or call the same day. Tables are often available on the spur of the moment.

RAOUL'S
180 Prince St   212 966-3518
Dinner: Daily
Moderate

There are dozens of good places to eat in SoHo, and Raoul's is one of the best. The long, narrow restaurant used to be an old saloon. There are paper tablecloths and funky walls covered with a mishmash of posters, pictures, and calendars of every description. The bistro atmosphere is neighborly, friendly, and intimate, the prices moderate, and the service attentive. The trendy clientele runs the gamut from jeans to mink. The house specialties are the broiled salmon and the rack of lamb. Raoul's is a natural for those whose days begin when the rest of us want to hit the sack.

RAYMOND'S CAFE
88 Seventh Ave (bet 15th and 16th St)   212 929-1778
Lunch, Dinner: Daily; Brunch: Sat, Sun
Moderate

If some of the old haunts in the Chelsea area have lost their appeal, here is a new one with a lot going for it. Chef Raymond himself is in the kitchen, and he is obviously a perfectionist. The place is spotlessly clean, the food well presented and very tasty. The choices run the gamut from pastas and sandwiches at noon to delicious hot and cold appetizers and fresh seafood items at dinner. The weekend brunch features omelets, various linguini dishes, and warm chicken salad. A private dining room is available, and there is free delivery within eight blocks. The early-bird dinner is a real three-course bargain!

(THE FAMOUS) RAY'S PIZZA OF GREENWICH VILLAGE
465 Sixth Ave (at 11th St)   212 243-2253
Sun-Thurs: 11 a.m.–2 a.m.; Fri, Sat: 11 a.m.–3 a.m.
No credit cards
Inexpensive

You must be named "Ray" to be in the pizza biz in Manhattan—or so it seems. None of the pizzerias in the Big Apple are any better than this one, supposedly featuring the *real* Ray. The pizza is gourmet at its best, and you can create your own from the many toppings offered. You can have a fresh slice, a whole pizza, or a Sicilian square, all fresh.

Kids love the baby pizzas. What do you feel like today: cheese, pepperoni, sausage, onions, peppers, or mushrooms? You won't leave hungry, as all pizzas are a generous 18 inches. Free delivery is available.

REMI
145 W 53rd St (bet Sixth and Seventh Ave)   212 581-4242
Lunch: Mon-Fri; Dinner: Daily
Moderate

When Remi closed on the Upper East Side, many loyal fans felt they had lost a real friend. Not to worry. Remi has reopened in a spectacular space in midtown, handy to hotels and theaters. In an unsually long room dominated by a dramatic 120-foot Venetian wall painting by Paulin Paris, the food soars as high as the setting. In nice weather, doors open up and diners can enjoy tables in the adjoining passageway. Waiters, chairs, and wall fabrics all match in attractive stripes. The menu is much the same as the original house's. Antipasto like smoked goose prosciutto or roasted quail wrapped in bacon will get you off to a delicious start. Main dishes are not the usual variety; the spaghetti, linguine, and ravioli can match any house in Venice. Of course, there are fish and meat dishes for the more mainstream appetites. The caramelized banana tart, served with toasted almond ice cream and caramel sauce, is enough to make anyone feel guilty. Being a gelati lover myself, I found the homemade cappuccino flavor sensational. Paddle on down (Remi means "oar") for a first-class experience!

RENÉ PUJOL
321 W 51st St   212 246-3023
Lunch: Mon-Fri; Dinner: Mon-Sat
Moderate

This very attractive French restaurant is an ideal spot for a pre-theater dinner. It's always busy, and it's obvious that a large number of customers are regular patrons, which always speaks well of a restaurant. One reason Rene Pujol is so successful is that it's a family enterprise. The owner is on the job, and the waiters are superb. Housed in an old brownstone, the restaurant has two warmly decorated, cozy, and comfortable dining rooms, complete with a working fireplace in winter. There are private party rooms upstairs, and they are attractive, too. The menu is vintage French, with broiled sardines, lamb shank, filet mignon, and tasty tarts being the specialties of the house.

RESTAURANT RAPHAEL
33 W 54th St   212 582-8993
Lunch: Mon-Fri; Dinner: Mon-Sat
Expensive

You don't have to worry about quality when you take guests here. It is expensive, but worth it! This classy, intimate French restaurant, which does a few things very well, is for the serious diner. Tasty smoked salmon, gnocchi, or onion tart get you off to a great start. Main courses of lamb, veal, duck, and house smoked red snapper are served imaginatively, with superb seasonings and sauces. There is no on-the-job training for the servers; they all know what is expected in a first-class operation. Take your time, savor the taste of classic French cooking, and finish with a warm, crusty chocolate cake that is as rich and delicious as any you have tasted.

RIVER CAFE
One Water St, Brooklyn   718 522-5200
Lunch, Dinner: Daily
Moderately expensive

The River Cafe isn't in Manhattan, but it *overlooks* Manhattan. And that's the main reason to come here. The view from the window tables is fantastic, awesome, romantic—you name it. There's no other skyline like it in the world. And so, just across the East River, in the shadow of the Brooklyn Bridge, the River Cafe remains an extremely popular place. Call at least a week in advance to make reservations, and be sure to ask for a window table. This is a true Yankee, flag-waving restaurant, proud of its American cuisine. There's no point in describing the dishes in detail, since you'll be looking out the window more than down at your plate. The seafood, lamb, and game entrees are particularly good. The desserts are uniformly rich and fresh.

ROLF'S
281 Third Ave (at 22nd St)   212 477-4750
Lunch, Dinner: Daily; Brunch: Sun
Moderate

For years I have been looking for a German restaurant in Manhattan worth recommending. At last I have found one. Rolf's is a colorful spot, with several dozen tables and wooden benches that fit in perfectly with the eclectic décor. Fake Tiffany lampshades, old pictures, tiny lights, strings of beads, and what-have-you add up to a charming and cozy spot for some tasty German dishes. The schnitzels, goulash, sauerbraten, boiled beef, and bratwurst are served in ample portions with delicious potato pancakes and sauerkraut. For pancake lovers there are German, apple, and potato varieties available, with apple sauce on the side. For dessert, save room for the French opera chocolate ganache with edible 22K gold and coffee buttercream filling, or the black and white chocolate mousse biscuit wrapped in dark and light chocolate. Oh, yes, what would a German restaurant be without apple strudel? Rolf's is plenty good.

ROSA MEXICANO
1063 First Ave (at 58th St)   212 753-7407
Dinner: Daily
Moderate to moderately expensive

No touristy Mexican dive, this is the real thing. If you are lusting for classic Mexican cuisine, an evening here will be something special. Start with the guacamole *en molcajete;* prepared fresh at the table, it is the best around. There are also great appetizers like small tortillas filled with sauteed shredded pork, small shrimp marinated in a mustard and chili vinaigrette, and raviolis filled with sauteed chicken and served with tomato and onion. Main course entrees include tasty (and huge) crepes filled with shrimp and a multi-layered tortilla pie with all manner of goodies. Grilled specialties like beef short ribs and whole red snapper are tempting possibilities. Even the desserts are first-class. Choose from a traditional flan, cornmeal custard smothered with chocolate sauce, or a layered chocolate mousse cake with a taste of chili and placed in a coffee sauce. The atmosphere is friendly, the energy level high, and the dining satisfaction top-drawer.

ROSEMARIE'S
145 Duane St (bet W Broadway and Church St)   212 285-2610
Lunch: Mon-Fri; Dinner: Mon-Sat
Moderate

This is one of those hidden treasures that regulars don't talk about. Rosemarie's is indeed hidden in the junky atmosphere of a TriBeCa street. Leaving the real world behind, you enter a smallish establishment that seems more like a private dining room than a restaurant. Both the luncheon and dinner menus provide an excellent choice of Italian dishes, all done with the tender care of a loving kitchen. The risotto with wild mushrooms is first-class; so are the seared salmon and grilled red snapper. A *prix fixe* menu is offered at noon. Indulge yourself with homemade gelati for dessert.

RUSSIAN TEA ROOM
150 W 57th St (at Seventh Ave)   212 265-0947
Lunch, Dinner: Daily; Brunch: Sat, Sun
Moderate

Standing aloof on a block surrounded by skyscrapers, the scrappy little Russian Tea Room continues to be a popular hangout for celebrities and socialites. I would be less than honest if I didn't report that the ambience draws more folks than the food, although the latter is a far cry from what you might be served in Moscow! Specialties of the house include chicken Kiev, mushrooms à la Russe, *blinchiki,* and *karsky shashlik* supreme (grilled-marinated loin of lamb). Of course, there is wonderful caviar (sevruga, osetra, or beluga) and delicious smoked salmon. (Red salmon caviar, too.) Popular new features are the *prix fixe* menus at lunch, brunch, dinner, supper, and pre-theater hours. There is much to attract here: glitzy customers, an expanded cabaret program, plus 29 varieties of vodka to wash away all your worldly troubles!

RUSTY STAUB'S ON 5TH
575 Fifth Ave (at 47th St)   212 682-1000
Lunch: Mon-Sat; Dinner: Daily
Moderate

For all-Americans everywhere, on or off the playing field, Rusty Staub's is as red, white, and blue as motherhood, baby back ribs, mashed potatoes, and deep-dish apple pie. The place is divided into a sports bar upstairs, several dining areas downstairs, and tables in the atrium of the building. There are *prix fixe* three-course dinners offered each evening. It's a hefty meal at a non-hefty price. The entrees, which change every night, include ribs, duck, trout, salmon, veal, or beef. You'll find both the surroundings and the help informal, the location handy (especially at noon), and the portions just right for an all-American appetite.

SAN PIETRO
18 E 54th St   212 753-9015
Daily: 11:30 a.m.–midnight
Moderate

In a convenient location in the heart of the Fifth Avenue shopping area, San Pietro is an ideal stop for an excellent Italian lunch or dinner. Southern Italian cooking is featured at this sister establishment of Sistina, an Upper East Side favorite for years. Naturally, seafood is featured; snapper is one of the best items on the menu. Lobster medallions make an excellent first course, and the pastas are unusual and varied. There is spinach ravioli, buckwheat-flour pasta with cabbage, or chickpea-flour pasta with pesto. The desserts are all homemade and uniformly good. Bowls of fresh fruit add to the cozy, friendly ambience in the two rooms. Call early, especially at lunch, as tables fill up quickly.

SARABETH'S KITCHEN
423 Amsterdam Ave (at 80th St)   212 496-6280
Breakfast, Lunch, Dinner: Daily

1295 Madison Ave (at 92nd St)   212 410-7335
Breakfast, Lunch, Dinner: Daily

SARABETH'S AT THE WHITNEY
(in the Whitney Museum of American Art)
945 Madison Ave (bet 74th and 75th St)   212 570-3670
Lunch: Tues-Fri; Brunch: Sat, Sun

We can now partake of outstanding visual and culinary art at the same time! Swinging, it is not. Reliable, it is. One is reminded of the better English tearooms when visiting one of Sarabeth's locations. The big draw is the homemade quality of all the dishes, including the baked items and the excellent desserts. They also make gourmet preserves and sell them nationally. Menu choices include excellent omelets for breakfast, a fine assortment of light items for lunch, and fish, game, or meat dishes for dinner. The chocolate truffle cake, lemon soufflé, and cinnamon apple ice cream with macadamia nuts are outrageous desserts. Service is rapid and courteous. This would be an ideal place to take your mother-in-law.

SCARLATTI
34 E 52nd St   212 753-2444
Dinner: Daily
Moderately expensive

The ambience of this refurbished house is totally top-drawer. Tables are far enough apart to allow for pleasant, private dining. The waiters act like prime candidates for a stress clinic, so service can be hectic. But the food is excellent. One of the nicest ways to start your meal is to order a selection of antipasto, a small portion of a number of delicious dishes. The menu is focused on pastas, salads, and vegetables. The servings are just right, and the presentation is superb. A low-cholesterol menu is also available.

SECOND AVENUE KOSHER DELICATESSEN AND RESTAURANT
156 Second Ave (at 10th St)   212 677-0606
Daily: 5:30 a.m.–midnight (Fri, Sat till 2 a.m.)
American Express
Inexpensive

You've heard all about the great New York delicatessens; now try one of the really authentic ones, located in the historic East Village. From the traditional *k*'s—knishes, kasha varnishkes (buckwheat groats with pasta), and kugel—to boiled beef or chicken in the pot (with noodles, carrots, and matzo balls), no one does it quite like the Lebewohl family. Portions are enormous. Homemade soups, three-decker sandwiches (the tongue and the hot corned beef are sensational), deli platters, complete dinners—you name it, they've got it. The smell is overwhelmingly appetizing, the atmosphere is "caring Jewish mother," and they don't mind if you take out your meal instead of dining in the colorful back room. Don't leave without trying the chopped liver or warm apple strudel.

SERENDIPITY 3
225 E 60th St   212 838-3531
Sun-Thurs: 11:30 a.m. – 12:30 a.m.;
Fri: 11:30 a.m.–1 a.m.; Sat: 11:30 a.m.–2 a.m.
Moderate

The young and young-at-heart count this place as *numero uno* on their list of "in" places. In an atmosphere of nostalgia set in a quaint, two-floor brownstone, this full-service restaurant offers a complete selection of delicious entrees, sandwiches, salads, and pastas. The real treats are the fabulous desserts, including favorites like hot fudge sundaes and frozen hot chocolate. An added pleasure is the opportunity to browse a shop loaded with gifts, books, clothing, and accessories, all very trendy. If you are planning a special gathering for the teen members of your clan, this should be the destination!

SETTE MEZZO

969 Lexington Ave (at 70th St) 212 472-0400
Lunch, Dinner: Daily
Cash only
Moderate

It's small, professional, and very busy. There are no affectations at Sette Mezzo in décor, service, or food preparation. This is strictly a business operation, with the emphasis where it should be: on serving good food at a reasonable price. Don't worry about wearing your best gown or a suit and tie; many diners are informally dressed, enjoying a variety of Italian dishes done to perfection. At noon the menu is tilted toward lighter pastas and salads. In the evening, all of the grilled items are excellent. Fresh seafood is a specialty. Ask about the special pasta dishes; some of the combinations are marvelous. For more traditional Italian plates, try the breaded rack of veal, stuffed baked chicken, grilled boneless quail, or fried calamari and shrimp. All of the desserts are made in-house. They include several caloric cakes, tasty lemon tarts, sherbet and ice cream, and (take it from an expert) one of the best *tartufos* you've ever sinned over.

SHELBY

967 Lexington Ave (bet 70th and 71st St) 212 988-4624
Lunch: Mon-Fri; Dinner: Daily; Brunch: Sat, Sun
Moderate

A little bit of Tennessee has been moved to Manhattan's Upper East Side! The owner of Shelby hails from the Memphis area, which happens to be in Shelby County, Tennessee. (Thus the name.) The Southern influence is obvious in much of the cooking. Shelby has become a very popular business restaurant for lunch and a neighborhood watering hole and eating spot for dinner. Friendly, intimate, and professional would best describe this establishment. With Chip (the owner) overseeing his crew, it is obvious that these folks deserve the success they are having. A bit of Italy creeps into the menu with the delicious pastas, while the Southern accent is apparent in the roast pecan-smoked pork chops. The roast baby lamb chops are superb. An attractive and refreshing dessert, fresh fruit in a nut-lace cookie, deserves special mention.

SHINWA
Olympic Tower (645 Fifth Ave)   212 644-7400
Lunch, Dinner: Mon-Sat
Moderate to moderately expensive

If you're looking for a classy, authentic Japanese restaurant, look no further. Shinwa, in the midtown high-rent district, offers a full menu of traditional Japanese dishes, served beautifully in an understated atmosphere that puts the emphasis on food. Each course is brought to your table on a tray; the presentation is a feast of color and flavor. There are literally dozens of appetizers, from sushi and tempura to more exotic dishes like eel and cucumber with vinegared rice or preserved squid. Entrees include tempura zen with seasonal appetizers; sashimi zen, with appetizers, vegetable soup, and ice cream; *unagi* zen, with a choice of *kabayaki* and rice; and *una jue,* with eel. My favorite is Shabu Shabu—sliced prime rib of beef, which you dip and cook to your liking in a boiling broth. There are two kinds of noodle dishes, one made from wheat flour and one from buckwheat flour. If you can find room at the end of the meal, you might try seaweed, codfish, or cooked squid in a dish called *chazuke,* which is served with green tea and white rice. The green-tea ice cream is also fabulous. This is one of the best places to sample and savor the flavors of Japan.

SHUN LEE CAFE/SHUN LEE WEST
43 W 65th St   212 769-3888
Lunch: Sat, Sun; Dinner: Daily
Moderate

Dim sum and street-food combinations are served in an informal setting adjoining Shun Lee West, an excellent old West Side Chinese restaurant. A large selection of special items is offered by a waiter who comes to your table with a rolling cart and describes the various goodies. The offerings are different from time to time, but don't miss the stuffed crab claws, if they are available. Go on to the street-food items: delicious roast pork, barbecued spareribs, a large selection of soups and noodle and rice dishes, and a menu full of both mild and hot, spicy entrees. Sauteed prawns with ginger and boneless duckling with walnut sauce are great choices. A vegetarian dish of shredded Chinese vegetables is cooked with rice noodles and served with a pancake (like Moo Shu pork but without the meat). It's a fun place where you can try some unusual and delicious Chinese dishes. For the heartier appetites, the adjoining Shun Lee West restaurant is equally good. Some of the best Chinese food in Manhattan is served here. If you come with a crowd, family-style dining is available. Prices are a bit higher in the restaurant than in the café.

SIGN OF THE DOVE
1110 Third Ave (at 65th St)   212 861-8080
Lunch: Tues-Fri; Dinner: Daily; Brunch: Sat, Sun
Moderately expensive

There has never been any question that Sign of the Dove is one of the most beautiful restaurants in New York. But there has been a lingering question about the quality of the food and service in this up-and-down favorite of Big Apple romantics. Currently the Santos family (who also operate Yellowfingers di Nuovo, Contrapunto, and Arizona 206) has brought "Mrs. New York" back so that the eating is as good as the looking. First, their bakery (Ecce Panis, next door at 1120 Third Ave) supplies the house with a great breadbasket full of goodies. Then on to a fabulous oyster selection or wonderful treats like casserole of lobster and marinated soft-shell crabs. For entrees, you have your choice of fresh fish (like salmon, sea bass, or yellowfin tuna), chicken, veal, duck, or lamb, each presented as magnificently as the décor. The chocolate and banana mousse gâteau dessert is sensational, as is the rhubarb tart and homemade ice creams.

SISTINA
1555 Second Ave (at 80th St)   212 861-7660
Dinner: Daily
Moderate

Don't come here expecting beautiful decorations and extravagant surroundings. One comes to Sistina for the food, and it can't be beat. Four brothers run this outstanding Italian restaurant; one is in the kitchen, the others are out front. The only decoration is a picture of its namesake, the Sistine Chapel, on the wall. The specialty of the house is seafood; both the Mediterranean red snapper and the salmon are excellent dishes. There are also the usual choices of pasta, veal, and chicken, as well as daily specials. The philosophy of this family operation is that the joy is in the eating, not the surroundings, and for that they get top marks.

SMITH AND WOLLENSKY
797 Third Avenue (at 49th St)   212 753-1530
Lunch: Mon-Fri; Dinner: Daily
Moderate to moderately expensive

This is a big place for big appetites. If you have teenagers or some college friends you want to treat to a special meal, I can't think of a better place. Fancy and elite, it is not. Hearty, fun, and satisfying, it is, with two floors of facilities that give off a comfortable and rather masculine atmosphere. There is no shortage of help; lots of bright, young men are eager to help you. The bread is varied, tasty, and warm. The lobster cocktail, though expensive, is the best in New York. The big sellers among the entrees are the steaks, prime ribs of beef, lamb chops, and lobster. On the side, you won't want to miss the cottage fries, onion rings, and fried zucchini. A word about the baked potatoes: they don't use foil — *three cheers*! And a couple of words about the desserts: the white chocolate mousse with raspberry sauce is super, and the hot deep-dish apple pie with vanilla sauce will top off a great dinner.

SOHO KITCHEN & BAR
103 Greene St   212 925-1866
Lunch, Dinner: Daily
Inexpensive to moderate

With over 100 wines by the glass and 14 different cold draft beers, this is one of the busiest bar and restaurant scenes in the lower canyons of Manhattan. They offer wine "flights," which are servings of from four to eight glasses of wine from a particular group (French, Spanish, chardonnays, and the like). Beer tastings are offered, too. But it is not only in the liquid department that the SoHo Kitchen shines. Besides soups, salads, and pastas, there are great hamburgers and omelets. A delicious fruit and cheese plate is a welcome change from heavy eating. The real treat here is the pizza, made with homemade pizza dough. You can choose from wild mushroom, pesto, vegetarian, or a fantastic Italian combination of sausage, roasted peppers, grilled eggplant, mozzarella, and provolone. Prices are very reasonable. A good place for a casual encounter.

SOLERA
216 E 53rd St (at Third Ave)   212 644-1166
Lunch: Mon-Fri; Dinner: Mon-Sat
Moderately expensive

If visions of romantic Spain are dancing around in your head (and your stomach) I'd suggest trying Solera, a charming and romantic east side Spanish restaurant. Start off with *tapas* at the bar, then head for the back rooms, where classy, authentic fare is served from a *prix fixe* menu. A great variety of appetizers is available: garlic shrimp, roasted red peppers stuffed with duck confit, Catalin-style mussels, boneless quail on red cabbage with chestnuts. How about shellfish or vegetable paella for the main course? There is much more, like cod dishes or pine nut-crusted lamb chops. The anise praline parfait with coffee sauce is a winner at dessert time. Health-food addicts will be pleased to know that no butter or cream is used. The friendly staff complements an outstanding meal.

SONIA ROSE RESTAURANT
132 Lexington Ave (bet 28th and 29th St)   212 545-1777
Lunch: Tues-Fri; Dinner: Mon-Sat
Moderate

Tucked away in the middle of the Indian section of Manhattan, with a locked door that opens only after you are buzzed in, is one of the most charming and delicious restaurants in the city. There are only about a dozen tables, each with a single rose and a flickering candle. The menu is *prix fixe* for both lunch and dinner, with supplemental charges for several special items. Sonia is in the front, charming and helpful; her partner is in the kitchen, dishing up some of the most attractive and delectable continental-style dishes you could imagine. The charm is in the exceptional attention to detail in both service and food. There is plenty of well-trained help. And the food plates are a sight for the eyes, as if an artist had arranged each bite. From the time you start with a refreshing hot towel to the ending selection of a half-dozen dessert samples, this is perfection.

SPARKS STEAK HOUSE
210 E 46th St   212 687-4855
Lunch: Mon-Fri; Dinner: Mon-Sat
Moderately expensive

You come here to eat, period. This is a well-seasoned and popular beef restaurant with little ambience. For years, businessmen have made an evening at Sparks a must, and the house has not let time erode its reputation. In the meat category, you can choose from veal and lamb chops, beef scaloppine, and medallions of beef, as well as a half-dozen steak items, like steak *fromage* (with Roquefort cheese), prime sirloin, sliced steak with sauteed onions and peppers, and top-of-the-line filet mignon. Seafood dishes are another specialty; the rainbow trout, fillet of tuna, and halibut steak are as good as you'll find in most seafood houses. The lobsters are enormous, delicious, and expensive. Skip the appetizers and dessert, and concentrate on the main dish.

SPRING STREET NATURAL RESTAURANT
62 Spring St (corner Lafayette St)   212 966-0290
Daily; 11:30 a.m.–midnight; Fri-Sat until 1 a.m.
Inexpensive

Even before eating "naturally" was a big thing, the Spring Street Natural Restaurant was a leader in the field. That tradition continues today. In attractive surroundings, their kitchen provides meals prepared with fresh, unprocessed foods, with everything cooked to order. Neighborhood residents are regular customers here, so you know the the food is top-quality. Blackboard specials are offered every day, with a wide variety of salads, pastas, vegetarian meals, poultry, and seafood. Brown rice and steamed veggies have been served here since 1973. The best is saved for last: Spring Street believes in great desserts, like chocolate walnut pie, honey raspberry blueberry pie, and honey pear pie. The latter two have no sugar and no dairy products.

STEAK FRITES
9 E 16th St (bet Fifth Ave and Union Sq)   212 463-7101
Lunch, Dinner: Daily
Moderate

The Black Angus steak and accompanying French fries, the house signature, are fabulous. All the rest is for the birds! The room is crowded and noisy, the waiters are poorly trained and disorganized, the appetizers and the desserts are mediocre, and the place reeks of unprofessionalism. But outside of the steaks that you grill on your own patio barbecue, these have to be the best in town. (Don't say I didn't warn you about the rest.)

STEPHANIE'S
994 First Ave (bet 54th and 55th St)   212 753-0520
Lunch: Mon-Fri; Dinner: Daily; Brunch: Sat, Sun
Moderate

Stephanie's is a casually elegant but simple and spotless neighborhood establishment that turns out excellent food at modest prices. To add to the pleasant atmosphere there is live piano music on Friday and Saturday nights. Stephanie's is owned by three partners, including the daughter of actress Joan Bennett, so the place has a theatrical clientele. The menu changes daily, but it usually includes such popular dishes as grilled Atlantic salmon and Gulf prawns, rack of lamb, fresh roasted duck, and sauteed soft-shell crabs. Sunday brunch favorites are challah bread French toast, Irish soda bread French toast, toasted wild-mushroom sandwiches, crab cakes, and homemade biscuits and muffins.

STREETER'S NEW YORK CAFE
Sheraton New York Hotel (811 Seventh Ave at 52nd St)
212 581-1000
Breakfast, Lunch, Dinner; Daily; Brunch: Sun
Moderate

There is no scene quite like the passing parade on a busy New York avenue. Streeter's provides a dramatic street-level view of the color and diversity of bustling Seventh Avenue. The room is new, as is the rest of the recently renovated Sheraton New York. Breakfast is a winner. Besides the regular (and extensive) à la carte menu, one can choose from an attractive and delicious early-morning express buffet (both hot and cold items) every day of the week, with additional dishes available for Sunday brunch. Streeter's is especially convenient for those who are on the run for an early-morning meeting or plane. Lunch and dinner menus are easy on the pocketbook, with salad, pasta, sandwich, seafood, and grilled items featured.

TALIESIN

Hotel Millenium, (55 Church St, 3rd floor)   212 312-2000
Breakfast, Lunch, Dinner: 6:30 a.m.–10:30 p.m.;
Brunch: Sat, Sun
Moderate

Hotel dining is no longer the wasteland it used to be. In keeping with this welcome change, the sparkling new Millenium Hotel in the World Trade Center area offers an intimate room with first-class food and highly personalized service. It would be difficult to find better seared Atlantic salmon or tastier veal and lamb chops than those offered here. A "health first" selection features ingredients low in fat, cholesterol, and sodium. Dessert freaks will be right at home: wonderful homemade ice creams and sorbets, a wicked bittersweet chocolate mousse with caramelized bananas and crème Anglaise, or an oatmeal Napoleon with apples and cinnamon ice cream. See what I mean? Wall Street visitors need no longer travel uptown for a memorable meal!

TAVERN ON THE GREEN

Central Park W (at 67th St)   212 873-3200
Lunch, Dinner: Daily
Moderate to moderately expensive

Isn't it time to escape from the ordinary? The setting here is absolutely magical. In the evening, when the trees are aglow with small lights, it is New York at its very best! Be sure to ask for seating in the Crystal Room; it is a wonderful place for a party for your kids or a special evening with the folks from out-of-town. The cuisine is continental. Translated, that means good, solid food—what you would expect from a place as large and busy as this one. The service can be a bit distracted, but don't let that keep you from a visit to one of New York's "musts." The pre-theater and after-theater menus are bargains!

THE TERRACE

400 W 119th St   212 666-9490
Lunch: Tues-Fri; Dinner: Tues-Sat
Moderate to moderately expensive

You'll have to go a bit out of the way to visit the Terrace restaurant, but it's well worth the time. The Terrace is located on the roof of a Columbia University building, providing a superb view of Manhattan. A table by the window is absolutely enchanting. You'll be impressed by the classy atmosphere, the beautiful table settings (attractive china, candlelight, and a single red rose), and the soft dinner music. The tables are spaced nicely apart, giving one a chance to talk confidentially. Indeed, if there's one word that describes this operation, it's *style*. The food is as good as the atmosphere. The menu is classical French with some touches of Mediterranean cuisine. Special services include free valet parking.

TRASTEVERE
309 E 83rd St   212 734-6343
Dinner: Daily
Moderate

Tradition is important here! But so is good food. The room is very small (about a dozen tables) and the décor is far from glamorous. But the food preparation is very professional. Brochette of cheese and prosciutto with anchovy sauce, mussels in light tomato sauce, pasta à la spaghettini and vegetables, and the fettucine with peas, prosciutto, mushroom, and cream are all sensational! Also first-rate are sizable offerings of various chicken dishes, rack of veal breaded with tomato salad on top, and fillet of sole with mushrooms, scallions, and wine. Be sure to save room for the Napoleon dessert or the chocolate *cartufel*. You can tell a lot about a restaurant by the little things, and these people obviously know what they are doing. The glassware literally gleams, and the waiters are well-informed and friendly. The bread is warm and delicious, the vegetables are fresh, and the seasonings have just the right amount of garlic to be tasty without being offensive. It's a good idea to call early for reservations, since the place is always busy.

TRATTORIA DELL'ARTE
900 Seventh Ave (at 57th St)   212 245-9800
Lunch: Mon-Fri; Dinner: Daily; Brunch: Sat, Sun
Moderate

Just because you don't hear a lot about a restaurant doesn't mean that it isn't of star quality. This is the case with Trattoria dell'Arte, a bustling spot across the street from Carnegie Hall. The natives surely know about it, as the place is bursting at the seams every evening. A casual café is at the front, seats are available at the antipasto bar in the center, and the dining room is in the rear. One would be hard-pressed to name a place at any price with tastier Italian food than is served here. The antipasto selection is large, fresh, and inviting; you can choose a platter with various accompaniments. There are daily specials, superb pasta dishes, grilled fish and meats, *focaccia* sandwiches, and salads. Wonderful pizzas are available every day but Monday, the *pizzaiolo's* rest day. Chocolate macadamia torte or raspberry zabaglione Napoleon will finish off a very special meal. The atmosphere and personnel are warm and pleasant. I recommend this place without reservation—although you'd better have one if you want to sit in the dining room.

TRIBECA GRILL
375 Greenwich St (at Franklin St)   212 941-3900
Lunch: Mon-Fri; Dinner: Daily; Brunch: Sun
Moderate

First, please note the address is Greenwich *Street,* not Avenue! The setting is a TriBeCa warehouse. The inspiration is Robert De Niro. The bar comes from the old Maxwell's Plum restaurant. The kitchen is first-class. The genius is Drew Nieporent (of Montrachet fame). Put it all together, and you have a winner. A huge old coffee-roasting house in a decidedly unglamorous neighborhood now plays host to a very glamorous clientele, who enjoy a spacious bar and dining area, a fabulous private movie-screening room upstairs, paintings by Robert De Niro, Sr., and banquet facilities for private parties. The food is stylish and wholesome. Excellent salads, seafood, veal, steak, and first-rate pastas are house favorites. So are the potato pancakes! I was critical of the desserts in previous visits, but now the tarts, tortes, mousses, and ice cream rate with the best.

TROPICA
200 Park Ave (Met Life Building)   212 876-6767
Lunch, Dinner: Mon-Fri
Moderate

Hidden away on the concourse of the Met Life building is this bright, charming, tropical seafood house, which serves as drinking and eating headquarters for the hordes who work in this edifice. But others are finding their way to this excellent relative newcomer on the Manhattan horizon. You won't find the usual seafood appetizers here. Instead, you can experiment a bit with a delicious black bean and sausage soup or seared octopus. Daily grilled fish specials are fresh and tasty. You can choose from salmon, swordfish, frog's legs, and such oddities as doctor fish and John Dory! For an absolutely delicious entree, try the Tamarind barbecue shrimp. Other main plates and specialties include crab cakes, roasted monkfish, and Caribbean bouillabaisse. Non-seafood lovers will find chicken and steak. The Valencia orange flan wins the dessert sweepstakes. If a busy bar is your bag, you might want to arrive early and join the throng there.

TURKISH KITCHEN
386 Third Ave (at 28th St)   212 679-1810
Lunch: Mon-Fri; Dinner: Daily
Moderate

For those fond of Turkish food, this is probably the best destination in Manhattan. Immediately one is struck by the cleanliness of the establishment and with the almost overbearing TLC of the staff. Every day there are tasty specialties, like Turkish-style potato pancakes, roasted baby lamb with pine nuts and currant pilaf, and grape leaves stuffed with rice and herbs. If hot yogurt soup is offered, give it a try. The regular menu features just about anything you could find in a romantic dining spot in Istanbul: hummus (mashed chick peas and tahini seasoned with lemon and garlic sauce), *zeytinyagli enginar* (fresh artichoke with vegetables marinated in lemon and olive oil), moussaka (layers of eggplant and ground meat), and a number of fresh fish dishes, mostly baked

or grilled. And how about fermented turnip juice to wash it all down?
I'll take vanilla.

238 MADISON BISTRO
238 Madison Ave (bet 37th and 38th Ave)   212 447-1919
Lunch: Mon-Fri; Dinner: Mon-Sat
Moderate

This is a happy stop for a pleasant luncheon interlude while you are
in midtown. Neighbors have discovered the excellent food and prompt
service; the place is crowded for lunch but also provides unhurried dinners. Many of the salads are full meals in themselves. Assorted pastas
are presented in a most appealing manner. Entrees include mixed grilled
seafood, marinated grilled leg of lamb, grilled veal chop, and roast herb
chicken with the most delicious mashed potatoes I have tasted in a long
time. Homemade ice cream and sorbet provide a nice finish.

TWO TWO TWO
222 W 79th St   212 799-0400
Dinner: Daily
Moderate

This one is a surprise for several reasons. First, the location, which
is hardly the center of great Manhattan dining. Second, the size: a smallish
townhouse, with one crowded and very noisy room and several dozen
tables. Oh yes, there is also a miniature cubicle (if you really want
togetherness) that takes care of four persons . . . just. But put all that
aside. The dinners are great, and the service is of the same caliber. Grilled
dishes are featured: tuna steak, sirloin steak, breast of chicken. By now
you might have guessed that rack of lamb is one of my favorite dishes,
and they do it very well at Two Two Two. The crème brûlée is superb.
There is an early-bird *prix fixe* dinner that is a good value. For heavy
eaters (and heavy spenders) a five-course tasting menu is obscene (the
amount of food, that is!). All in all, this is a good choice if you want
to rub shoulders with Manhattan's "dining out" crowd and leave the
tourists behind.

UNION SQUARE CAFE
21 E 16th St   212 243-4020
Lunch: Mon-Sat; Dinner: Mon-Sun
Moderate

The Stars and Stripes fly high here; Union Square Cafe is very much
an American restaurant. The clientele is as varied as the food, with the
coversations often oriented toward the publishing world, and well-known
authors and editors in attendance at lunch. The menu is uniformly
creative, the staff unusually down-to-earth, and the prices are very much
within reason. Owner Danny Meyer offers such specialties as oysters

Union Square, hot garlic potato chips, and wonderful black bean soup. For lunch, try the tuna club or the burger, served on a homemade poppy seed roll. Dinner entrees from the grill are always delicious (tuna, shell steak, or veal). I go here just for the homemade caramel and mocha ice cream tartufo, or the warm banana tart with honey-vanilla ice cream and macadamia-nut brittle. A Yankee winner!

UNITED NATIONS DELEGATES' DINING ROOM
United Nations Headquarters
First Ave and 46th St   212 963-7626, 212 963-7099 (banquets)
Lunch: Mon-Fri (open nights and weekends for special functions)
Moderate

Don't let the name put you off! The public can eat here and enjoy the special international atmosphere, with conversations at adjoining tables conducted in almost every conceivable language. The setting is charming, overlooking a patio and the river. The room is large and airy, the service polite and informed. Although there is a large selection of appetizers, soups, salads, entrees, and desserts on the regular menu, by far the best deal is the Delegates' Buffet. A huge table of salads, baked specialties, seafoods, roasts, vegetables, cheeses, desserts, and fruits await the hungry noontime diner. (The room is used for private gatherings in the evening.) There isn't a more appetizing complete daily buffet available in New York than this one, and all the dishes are attractively presented and very tasty. After a tour of the United Nations building, this is a great place to relax, dine, and discuss world affairs!

VERONICA RISTORANTE
240 W 38th St   212 764-4770
Breakfast, Lunch: Mon-Fri
Inexpensive to moderate

A friend who works in the garment district told me about a fantastic Italian restaurant in the area, but he wouldn't give me the exact location or the name because he was afraid I'd spoil his secret by putting it in my book. As you can imagine, this was enough to pique my interest, so I did some investigating. The restaurant turned out to be Veronica, a tiny place in the heart of the garment district, and it's only open for breakfast and lunch. This marvelous cafeteria-style restaurant serves sensational home-cooked food and is run by Andrew Frisari and his wife, Ceil Hermes. What wonders they serve up! There is veal piccata, mouthwatering homemade lasagna, delicious tortellini, and chicken salad. Other favorites are pasta primavera and chicken florentina (breast of chicken with creamed spinach, prosciutto, mozzarella, and mushrooms in cream sauce). Low-fat and cholesterol-free items are featured. The clientele is sophisticated, the atmosphere informal and homey. Don't forget to try the homemade cheesecakes. Most food items are available for takeout, for individual orders, or for parties and special occasions.

VESPA
1625 Second Ave (bet 84th and 85th St)   212 472-2050
Dinner: Daily
Moderate
No credit cards

This was once the tiny space that made Azzurro famous. (They have since moved nearby to larger quarters.) Now the same ownership has created another jewel. The diners at the dozen or so tables are treated to truly loving Italian fare in an informal atmosphere with boss Marlo Gitto right there to insure your dinner is something very special. The regular dinner menu includes several different kinds of *carpaccio* (paper-thin slices of beef), mussels, cold cuts, and salads as starters. Then a great array of Italian treats: linguine, spaghetti, risotto, *farfalle*, and much more. Daily specials in the seafood category taste like they just came out of the water. For dessert, there are wonderful profiteroles, baked apples or poached pears, sorbets, tartufo, and tirami su. Top rating.

THE VIEW
Marriott Marquis Hotel
1535 Broadway (Times Square)   212 704-8900
Dinner: Daily; Brunch: Sun
Moderate to moderately expensive

Restaurants that are sky-high rarely excel at sky-high quality dining, but The View is a happy exception. The big attraction at The View is the fact that this is Manhattan's only revolving-rooftop eating spot. The outlook is indeed spectacular; come early if you want a window table, as it is first-come, first-seated. There is a special three-course pre-theater menu, inexpensive "all you can eat" appetizer and dessert buffets, and live entertainment and dancing five nights a week. You have your choice of American, French, or Italian cuisines. This is a good bet from any point of view!

VILLAGE ATELIER
436 Hudson St (corner of Morton St)   212 989-1363
Lunch: Mon-Fri; Dinner: Mon-Sat
American Express
Moderate

We all know of friends whose cooking is so good that we are excited when a dinner invitation arrives. The Village Atelier is like a good neighbor whose kitchen produces some of the best dishes around! Just 12 eclectic tables make up this establishment, many showing off handsome wooden tops. Take a look at the cozy bar at the back of the room; it is just like one you would like to have in your own home! Each dish tastes like it was cooked just for you—fresh and cool when it should be, well seasoned and warm when called for. Each day a special soup is offered, along with a wide selection of salads, fish, and unusual appetizers. The roast stuffed *poussin* (baby chicken) is the best I have ever tasted. It is smothered with Montmorency cherry and maple glaze. Feast well on your main course, though; the dessert selection hardly befits this fine establishment.

VINCE & EDDIE'S
70 W 68th St   212 721-0068
Lunch: Mon-Sat; Dinner: Daily; Brunch: Sun
Moderate

The name "Eddie" is almost as popular as "Joe" when it comes to naming Manhattan eateries. Eddie and Vince have taken rooms that housed several now-defunct operations and have created in the small quarters a homey, well-priced bistro that is at once charming and professional. I have a problem with the long, narrow quarters, as you must pass by the rest rooms and the kitchen to reach the rear dining room and garden. But never mind. The cozy fireplace near the entrance will make you feel wanted, even if the help seem a little overpowered by their attentive customers. The menu selections will please most any taste; nothing fancy, just good home cooking. Let's hope that 70 W 68th does not go through any more reincarnations. I like this one just the way it is!

VIVOLO
140 E 74th St   212 737-3533
Lunch: Mon-Fri; Dinner: Mon-Sat
Moderate

Angelo Vivolo has created a neighborhood classic in an old townhouse that has been converted into charming two-story restaurant with cozy fireplaces and professional service. Now he has expanded his empire to include a specialty food shop (Cucina Vivolo) next door at 138 E 74th St. There are great things to eat in both places. You can sit down and be pampered or have your goodies ready for takeout or delivered to your front door free of charge (from 69th to 80th streets). The Cucina menu offers wonderful Italian specialty sandwiches, made with all kinds of breads, as well as soups, cheeses, sweets, espresso, and cappuccino. In the restaurant proper there are daily specials, wonderful pastas, stuffed veal chops, and much more. The capellini primavera pasta is the house favorite. At Vivolo there are over 60 different scaloppine preparations. Their secret is simple: they use vegetable oil when sauteeing the scaloppine and add butter later when finishing the sauce. (Butter alone burns at the high temperatures required.) To romance your taste buds, this is a great choice. Save room for the cannoli alla Vivolo, a pastry filled with ricotta cream. There is a special *prix fixe* menu after 9 p.m.

VONG

200 E 54th St (bet Second and Third Ave)   212 486-9592
Lunch: Mon-Fri; Dinner: Mon-Sat
Moderate to moderately expensive

Good taste describes Vong, both in the unusual and appealing ambience, and in the high quality of the Thai dishes served. There is no shortage of Thai restaurants in Manhattan, but most are hardly world-class. This one is. Jean-Georges Vongerichten, the chef and owner, has had a distinguished career for his young age . . . top marks at both the highly rated Lafayette and Jo-Jo. A romantic and almost authentic Thai atmosphere is created by the use of burnt orange coloring, sexy lighting, and unusual seating areas in the back room. The only drawback can be the intense noise level. Wonderful crab spring rolls and great lobster and turnip salad will please any adventurous diner. Entrees range from spiced codfish to steamed squab to grilled beef in ginger broth. The roasted poussin is magnificent. Imagine a chocolate freak like your author not recommending the bitter chocolate tart. The banana and passion fruit salad with white pepper ice cream is better than any you'll get at Bangkok's Oriental Hotel! Just one problem here: to create an ambience of great demand, reservations can be hard to come by. However, in several cases I've noted any number of empty tables at peak dining hours.

VOULEZ-VOUS

1462 First Ave (at 76th St)   212 249-1776
Lunch: Mon-Sat; Dinner: Mon-Sun; Brunch: Sun
Moderate

You can't help but enjoy this friendly bistro, no matter what day of the week you come to savor their special dishes. A rotating menu features a different region of France every Tuesday evening. Other times you can enjoy French specialties like *choucroute* Alsacienne, cassoulet Toulousain, *pot-au-feu,* bouillabaisse, and *coq au vin.* Jacques Rameckers makes sure that his guests are well-taken care of from the time they enter

One of the hottest new restaurants in town is **Daniel,** located at 20 E 76th St (212 288-0033). Lunch is served Monday through Friday, and dinner Monday through Saturday. Daniel is Daniel Boulud, who, until he opened his own place, was chef at Le Cirque. In a plush setting (reportedly done at a cost of $2 million), Daniel is serving top-drawer French cuisine at top-drawer prices. The dessert creations (by former Le Bernardin pastry master Francois Payard) are fantastic. There are plans to also serve breakfast (check for details). A major problem: They will try to give you the "no reservations for two weeks" routine. Bargain a bit, or drop by, as some folks may not show up.

until they leave, stuffed and satisfied. A special pre-theater *prix fixe* dinner is offered. The Sunday brunch menu is outstanding, as is the dessert selection. The cappuccino frozen soufflé is sensational.

WATER CLUB
East River at 30th St   212 683-3333
Lunch: Mon-Sat; Dinner: Daily; Buffet Brunch: Sun
Moderately expensive

Warning: Do not fill yourselves with the marvelous small scones that are made fresh in the Water Club's kitchen and served warm! They are absolutely the best things you have ever tasted, but they can be devastating to your appetite for what will be an excellent meal to follow. The Water Club presents a magnificent setting right on the river; when making reservations, be sure to ask for a table by the window. The place is large and noisy but has a fun atmosphere that is ideal for special occasions. (They also have excellent private party facilities.) A large selection of seafood appetizers is available, including a great seafood gumbo served in a cast-iron crock. Entrees include numerous fish dishes, but you can also find meat and poultry items, as well as a special pasta dish. Homemade ice cream and sorbet, along with dessert soufflés and fresh-baked apple tarts, will round off a special meal. The Water Club flourless chocolate cake, served with devil's-food ice cream and mango sauce, competes favorably with the famous one originally served at the Coach House. On the down side, getting here from the north can be a problem and the serving staff is nice but inexperienced.

WEST SIDE STOREY
700 Columbus Ave (at 95th St)   212 749-1900
Daily: 8 a.m.–11 p.m.
Moderate

This is not a fancy place, but if you're looking for a wholesome, delicious, and inexpensive meal, you'll find it here. The breakfast plates include French toast and flapjacks with delicious whipped butter and Vermont maple syrup. In fact, walnut apple flapjacks are the specialty of the house. You also have your choice of omelets: Vermont cheddar cheese; country cream cheese and parsley; herb; ham, green pepper, and onion; or nova and cream cheese. All eggs and omelets are served with home fries and toast. You can also order sweet breakfast pastries. (If you're not an early riser, you'll be happy to note that breakfast is served late.) The salads are equally great. The West Side salad Nicoise is a delicious combination made with fresh tuna or salmon, new potatoes, green beans, and a Dijon vinaigrette. You won't believe the moderate prices. All the salad bowls are served with fresh bread and whipped butter. And what a selection of sandwiches! You name it, they'll make it. You also have your choice of breads. Hot dishes include quiche, pastas, pizza, vegetarian plates, meat, fish, grilled hamburgers, chili, and turkey.

The small fry can dine for pennies (almost!) on frankfurters and beans or spaghetti and meatballs. It's easy to see why this is such a popular spot for quick dining.

WILKINSON'S SEAFOOD CAFE
1573 York Ave (bet 83rd and 84th St)   212 535-5454
Dinner: Daily
Moderate to expensive

Everything looks good at Wilkinson's! The people look good because the lighting is flattering. The pink tones make the diners look as though they've just returned from a holiday in the sun. The food looks good, because it really is. This is a delightful, intimate seafood cafe; it does not pretend to be everything to everybody but does particularly well with a somewhat limited menu. The appetizers are unique. My favorite is the cured Norwegian salmon. For an entree, don't miss fresh lump crab cakes with wild rice. Other possibilities are broiled swordfish and tuna with tomato sauce. You can also enjoy such delicious desserts as chocolate mousse cake or the caramelized apple tart. As a thoughtful gesture, no cigars or pipes are allowed in the main dining area.

WINDOWS ON THE WORLD
1 World Trade Center

As of publication date, the future of this magnificent location for a restaurant is still uncertain. Since the bombing episode in the spring of 1993, the room has been closed. Hopefully, new operators will give Windows a much-needed facelift, both physically and food-wise. In recent years, the operation had sadly gone downhill. Stay tuned.

WOO CHON
8 W 36th St (off Fifth Ave)   212 695-0676
Daily: 24 hours
Moderate

Sparkling clean, friendly, and inviting describe this Korean restaurant, which has thrown away the keys to its front door. For a group dinner, order a variety of beef, pork, or shrimp dishes and have fun broiling them right at your table. All of the accompanied dishes add a special touch to your meal. Besides the marinated barbecue items, there are such tasty delights as oriental noodles and veggies, Chinese herbs and rice served in beef broth, a variety of noodle dishes, and dozens of other Far East treats. If you are unfamiliar with Korean food, the helpful personnel will do their best to explain what you are eating and how to eat it! Woo Chon is a fun experience for a different style of dining.

WOO LAE OAK OF SEOUL
77 W 46th St   212 869-9958
Lunch, Dinner: Daily
Moderate

If you've had the opportunity to visit Korea, you've undoubtedly enjoyed Korean barbecue, certainly one of that country's tastier delights. In New York, there's an outstanding version of the real thing, courtesy of an establishment that's been in business for nearly a half century. One word of warning: many items at Woo Lae Oak are very hot and spicy, so order carefully. A delicious appetizer is *sewu tuigim* (deep-fried shrimp and vegetables). Of course, the big attraction is the authentic Korean barbecue. The meat, broiled right at your table, is marinated in a special sauce and served with rice, soup, and vegetables. Choice of meat includes sliced beef, short rib cubes, sliced chicken, beef tongue, beef liver, beef heart, beef tripe, and sliced pork. Hot-pot casserole is also cooked at your table and served with rice and vegetables, as well as your choice of sliced beef, shrimp, fish, or chicken. Rice dishes, porridge, and noodles are available. Reservations are a necessity for large groups; be prepared to wait if you arrive with a small party at regular dining hours. Service is rapid, but don't rush your meal. Savor that barbecue!

WYLIE'S RIBS & COMPANY
891 First Ave (at 50th St)   212 751-0700
Daily: 11:30 a.m.–midnight
Moderate

Finding a convenient, pleasant, not-too-crowded rib joint in Manhattan that serves great food at reasonable prices is not always easy. If you like Texas-style barbecued chicken and ribs, Wylie's is the best in this department, offering ample platters of the tastiest, crispiest back ribs you have ever gotten all over your fingers—and some of the tenderest Northern fried chicken available. I suggest the combination dish served with excellent steak fries and cole slaw. You can also order half-pound burgers, barbecued-beef sandwiches, salads, chili, and a special onion loaf. The dinner menu leans more toward steak and fish, in addition to their famous ribs. The atmosphere is informal, the service efficient. Early evening hours are the least hectic.

YELLOWFINGERS DI NUOVO
200 E 60th St   212 751-8615
Lunch, Dinner: Daily
Moderate

Yellowfingers was conceived with a wonderful idea called *fa vecchia*. The name comes from *faccia vecchia,* which was used in the past for pizzalike breads baked without a topping. Yellowfingers has put together absolutely delicious *fa vecchia* combinations. One is baked with fresh tomato and mozzarella; another with potatoes, pancetta, and rosemary (my favorite). You can also order them garnished with such items as prosciutto, braised onion, and parsley. They are crusty, but not too filling — just right for a unique lunchtime meal. If this kind of pizza is not to your liking, there are plenty of excellent salads, the best being the rosemary-roasted chicken salad with sweet peppers, pine nuts, and greens. The *focaccia farcita* sandwich (grilled eggplant, mozzarella, roasted peppers, basil, capers, and *gremolata*) is worth a try. For more substantial appetites, there's a house-ground hamburger on grilled *focaccia*. Various homemade desserts are available. This place is noisy, fun, handy, and moderately priced — a great addition to New York's Upper East Side lunch scene.

YELLOW ROSE CAFE
450 Amsterdam Ave (at 82nd St)   212 595-8760
Lunch, Dinner: Daily; Brunch: Sat, Sun
Inexpensive

Barbara Clifford of Fort Worth, Texas, has transplanted Texas-style chicken-fried steak, Southern fried chicken, smothered pork chops, and El Paso cheese enchiladas to her friendly and hospitable 12-table Upper West Side café. Accompanied by buttermilk biscuits, red chili, real mashed potatoes, and home-grown vegetables from her father's garden in Texas, Barbara's portions are huge, delicious, and incredibly inexpensive. The café is cactus filled, homey, and very busy. Strawberry rhubarb pie, pecan pie, or sweet potato pie will top off a great meal during the week or a hearty country brunch on weekends. Look for the unique Western bar next door.

YE WAVERLY INN
16 Bank St   212 929-4378
Dinner: Daily; Brunch: Sat, Sun
Moderate

English food is not very fancy, but English pubs do have atmosphere, and they do some things quite well. In the Village there's Ye Waverly Inn, a picturesque pub in confined quarters, which dates from the early part of the century. There are four rooms and an outside eating area with adequate though uncomfortable furnishings, but the atmosphere is truly delightful. One is certain the food is good, because the place is always crowded and there are a number of famous folk who often dine here. If all this is not reason enough to go to the Inn, their chicken pot pie should be. It is absolutely one of the best I have ever tasted. Other possibilities would be the sauteed calf's liver, barbecued rack of ribs, boiled beef and horseradish sauce, or the boneless chicken breast. Before the main course, try the fresh fruit and cheese, French-fried eggplant, or a delicious fresh vegetable marinade. The dessert selection is excellent, especially the tasty pecan pie. I can see why legions of Village regulars flock here, and you will, too.

ZARELA
953 Second Ave (bet 50th and 51st St)   212 644-6740
Lunch: Mon-Fri; Dinner: Daily
Moderate

If you want the very best Mexican meal in New York, get yourself invited to the home of Zarela Martinez. Failing that, head for her charming and busy restaurant, a two-story building on Second Avenue. Don't let them seat you downstairs, because the second-floor dining room, complete with fireplace, is much more quaint and colorful. You'll understand how Zarela has earned her reputation for some of the best south-of-the-border cuisine when you taste her *antojitos*, which include a wonderful poblano chile stuffed with chicken and dried fruit, rolled fried-chicken tacos, and fried calamari in a spicy sauce. And there is much more: such seafood dishes as shrimp sauteed in a spicy jalapeno sauce; grill-smoked salmon; several chicken dishes; grilled duck breast with peanut and pumpkin-seed sauce; delicious meat entrees, like the *jalisco*-style pork and hominy stew; and a great selection of Mexican side dishes like refried black beans, golden-fried cauliflower, and fried plantain slices with mole sauce. Even the desserts are special. The chocolate crêpes are heaven-sent. But if you're going Mexican all the way, try the Mexican fruit-bread pudding with applejack brandy butter sauce or the banana, pineapple, and peach-jam cake.

ZIP CITY BREWING CO
3 W 18th St (bet Fifth and Sixth Ave)   212 366-6333
Lunch: Mon-Fri; Dinner: Daily; Brunch: Sat, Sun
Moderate

A brewery located in the former digs of the National Temperance Society? Yes. Zip City is the only operating brewery in New York City, with a copper brewhouse visible to all customers in the three-level facility. On any given day they feature two of their five house-brewed beers, along with a comprehensive menu featuring appetizers, light plates, more filling entrees, and rich desserts. I'd recommend this unique spot for a light lunch (salad, sandwiches) or a late-evening meal (steak, chops, pot roast) for those who like a congenial and informal atmosphere. The weekend brunch menu is intriguing: eggs with Scottish oatcakes, ginger-bread waffles, and Irish oatmeal with brown sugar and berries.

ZOË
90 Prince St   212 966-6722
Lunch: Tues-Fri; Dinner: Tues-Sun; Brunch: Sat, Sun
Moderate

The setting is an old building, with the original tiles and columns still in view. But something new and inviting has been added: a wood-burning grill, a wood-fueled pizza oven, and a rotisserie all in open view. You can even sit at the bar-like counter and watch all the kitchen action. The menu is described as contemporary American, with items like swordfish with barbecue sauce, spit-roasted baby lamb, hanger steak, and braised baby chicken in a clay pot. Some Italian dishes sneak their way in also. If the dessert menu offers poppyseed shortcake with mixed berries, jump at the chance to try one of the most delicious dishes in town. The area around Zoë might be pretty sad, but the atmosphere inside is very much upbeat.

JAMES BEARD HOUSE
167 W 12th St   212 675-4984

The legendary James Beard had his roots in Oregon, so anything to do with his life is of special interest to this author. He was a familiar personality on the Oregon coast, where he delighted in serving the superb seafood that the region is famous for. When Beard died in 1985, his run-down Greenwich Village brownstone was put on the market, but it was not a very attractive buy. Now the home is run by the nonprofit James Beard Foundation as a food and wine archive, research facility, and gathering place; it is the nation's only culinary center. There are periodic dinners, which anyone can attend, where some of our country's best regional chefs come to show off their talents. For foodies, this is a great opportunity to have a one-on-one with some really interesting folks.

III. Where to Find It: Special Activities, Tours, and Other Experiences

Auctions

Whether you're in the market for rare antiques, a used car, or just a fun experience and don't want to pay set prices, an auction (or an auction preview) might be a good place to start. Look in the Weekend section of the Friday *New York Times* or the Arts and Leisure section of the Sunday *Times* for advertisements about auctions listed below and others. The classified section of the *New York Times* also has an auction section, and you can find all of Manhattan's auction houses listed under "Auctioneers" in the Manhattan Yellow Pages.

Before going you should know that no two auctions are alike. First, each has different rules about viewing merchandise. Most auctions produce catalogs, usually for a price, but the less fashionable ones may only include descriptions (like "Lot 75 – Books"). Second, every auction has different rules about payment. Some take credit cards and checks, others take cash only, and some require a deposit before they will allow you to bid. As with many other things, my advice is to call ahead and find out what you're getting into.

Finally, a word of warning: the people you will find at most auctions in New York are professionals. They know what they are looking for, they know what they want to pay, and sometimes they know each other. Auctions in New York are a one-of-a-kind experience and can be lots of fun. Just don't go expecting to beat the professionals.

Think of **high-class art and antique auctions** and you'll probably come up with two names: Christie's and Sotheby. I've added William Doyle Galleries to that list:

Christie's – Located at 502 Park Avenue (at East 59th Street), this British auction house specializes in antiques and art. For information about upcoming auctions and inspections, look for Christie's advertisements in the *New York Times,* call their 24-hour Auctionline at 212 371-5438, or talk to a representative at 212 546-1000 during business hours. For information about art courses and lectures, call 212 546-1092.

Christie's East – Located at 219 East 67th Street (between Second and Third avenues), this is the junior version of Christie's. It sells what the lady at the reception desk calls anything of value that "would not pass the clientele at the big Christie's." Christie's East also advertises its upcoming auctions and inspections in the *New York Times,* or you can call 212 606-0400 during business hours.

Sotheby Parke Bernet—Located at 1334 York Avenue (at East 72nd Street), Sotheby's is probably the most elite auction house in the world. Like Christie's, it is British and specializes in antiques and art. Sotheby's also has a junior version, Sotheby's Arcade, where the more affordable pieces are sold. For information about upcoming auctions, inspections, and exhibitions at both places, look for Sotheby's advertisements in the *New York Times.* For information about Sotheby's, call its 24-hour recording at 212 606-7245 or talk to a real person at 212 606-7000 during business hours. For information about Sotheby's Arcade, call 212 606-7409.

William Doyle Galleries—Located at 175 East 87th Street (between Lexington and Third avenues), this American-owned auction house tends to be American-oriented in its offerings. For information about upcoming auctions and inspections, look for advertisements in the *New York Times* or call 212 427-2730. Also take a look at the Tag Sale next door for estate pieces that are not sold at auction. The prices at this crowded place are terrific. The Tag Sale's phone number is 212 410-9285.

If you're looking for **collectibles** like old signs or carnival memorabilia, your best bet may be the auctions at **Guernsey's,** located at 108 East 73rd Street (between Park and Lexington avenues). Give them a call during the week at 212 794-2280 to find out when the next auction will be held.

Because New York is a major port, and because the number of people and warehouses is enormous, another kind of auction in and around the city involves **surplus and confiscated merchandise.**

New York City Department of General Services—If you want to be on the mailing list for the city's auctions of scrap metal, cartridge casings, and other industrial materials sold in bulk, call 212 669-8546. If you're interested in the city's commercial real-estate auctions, call the Division of Real Property at 212 566-7530 for information about schedules and procedures.

New York City Parking Violations Bureau—Auctions of impounded and abandoned cars are held at different locations throughout New York's five boroughs and at different times during the week. Look under "Auctions" in the classified section of the *New York Times* for specific information about where, when and what cars are being auctioned. (They include a list of makes, models, and even serial numbers.) In most cases, you can inspect the cars half an hour before the auction. You can also call 212 788-7800, but they'll probably direct you to their newspaper ads.

New York City Police Department—The Police Department also auctions off cars, trucks, and vans, as well as other impounded or abandoned goods. You must pay with cash or certified check. There are no guarantees, and all sales are final. Auctions are announced in the classified section of the Sunday *New York Times* and *New York Daily News* in advance. Inspections usually are held the day before auction at locations in other boroughs. (Catalogs are available at the inspection site.) The auctions take place in the auditorium of police headquarters, between Chambers and Centre streets, downtown. For more information, call the very informative recording at 212 406-1369.

Main Post Office — The post office auctions off a completely random assortment of stuff from time to time in its main buildings at 380 West 33rd Street (between Eighth and Ninth avenues). The typical schedule allows for viewing between 8 and 10:15 a.m., while bidding begins at 10:30. You must pay cash, and all sales are final. For information on upcoming auctions, call 212 330-2931 and ask to be connected to the auction hotline recording.

Customs Service and Internal Revenue Service — Edison, New Jersey, is just one of a number of sites around the country where the Customs Service and Internal Revenue Service hold auctions of **confiscated and abandoned merchandise**. Anything and everything is auctioned here: cars, houses, manhole covers, jukeboxes, and clothing that can only be sold for export. There's even a grab-bag section of abandoned personal property, like a suitcase that may contain the crown jewels or someone's dirty laundry. The hitch is that you won't know what's inside until you've bought it. For information about upcoming auctions, call 703 351-7887.

Films

Like any city, New York has lots of theaters for first-run movies. Unlike many other cities, however, New York also has theaters that show old movies, foreign films, and unusual documentaries. *The New Yorker, New York* magazine, and the *New York Times*' Friday "Weekend" are all good places to look for what is playing at any given time. If you are looking for something a little offbeat, you can also call and find out what is showing at:

Angelika Film Center 18 West Houston St, at Mercer St (212 995-2000)
Anthology Film Archives Second Ave and East 2nd St (212 505-5181)
Carnegie Hall Cinemas Seventh Ave bet West 56th and West 57th St (212 265-2520)
Cinema Village East 12th St and Third Ave (212 505-7320)
8th Street Playhouse 52 West 8th St (212 674-6515)
The Film Forum and **the Film Forum 2** 209 West Houston St (212 727-8110)
Florence Gould Hall at the French Institute 55 East 59th St (212 355-6160)
Japan Society 333 East 47th St (212 752-0824)

Lincoln Center Plaza Broadway bet West 62nd and 63rd St
 (212 757-2280)
Loews Festival 6 West 57th St (212 307-7856)
Loews Paris Fine Arts Cinema 4 West 58th St (212 980-5656)
Millennium Film Workshop 66 East 4th St (212 673-0090)
Museum of Modern Art 11 West 53rd St (212 708-9480)
Museum of Television and Radio 25th West 52nd St (212 621-6600)
NatureMax American Museum of Natural History (212 769-5650)
Public Theater 425 Lafayette St, just south of East 8th St (212 598-7171)
St. Mark's Place Theater 80 80 St. Mark's Place (212 254-7400)
"Sunday at the Met" Metropolitan Museum of Art (212 570-3756)
Walter Reade Theater at Lincoln Center 165 West 66th St
 (212 875-5600)
Whitney Museum of American Art 945 Madison Ave, at East 75th St
 (212 570-0537)

Most of the phone numbers connect you with a recording that will tell you what is playing, how much tickets cost, and how to get there. Like everything, the price of movie tickets in New York tends to be higher than anywhere else in the country. (Don't be surprised if your total for two adults eats up most of your $20 bill!) The second-run theaters, film societies, and museums usually charge a little less than the first-run theaters.

Flea Markets

Craft and street fairs pop up all over New York on the weekends in the spring, summer, and fall. If you hear about one or just stumble into it, by all means go. Real New Yorkers go to these, and you'll get a very different sense of the city and the people who live here at these fairs than you would walking around midtown on a weekday. You'll also find everything from woven baskets made by somebody's relatives in Nigeria to socks and underwear sold at steep discounts. You'll also find some great food. Watch your pockets, watches, and purses, however, as these fairs are often very crowded.

In addition to crafts and street fairs, New York also has several regularly scheduled **flea markets** as well as what are called **Greenmarkets.** Take cash, don't be embarrassed to haggle when it seems appropriate, and look around before you buy anything—sometimes you'll see the same thing at more than one place. Real bargain hunters go at the end of the day when the dealers may have lowered their prices.

Most flea markets either shrink or disappear entirely between the late fall and early spring. The following list includes both relatively well-established markets and some particularly good new ones, but these are all shoestring operations and may not be around next year or the year after that. You might want to look under "Flea Markets" in the special "Antiques" classified listing in the Friday *New York Times'* Weekend section before setting out.

Annex Antiques Fair and Flea Market — You'll find this popular, well-established market in parking lots on Sixth Avenue from West 24th to West 26th streets. It's open from 9 to 5 on both Saturdays and Sundays (although Sunday is the best day to go). Admission to half of it costs $1, while admission to the other half is free.

Bryant Park Crafts Show — Bryant Park is located behind New York Public Library on the south side of West 42nd Street, between Fifth and Sixth avenues. This craft show is held on Fridays from 11 to 6 in warmer months. Admission is free.

Canal West Flea Market — Cheap, cheaper, and cheapest describe this one. On Canal Street near West Broadway, it's open from 7 to 6 on Saturdays and Sundays. Look nearby for the Downtown Art and Antique Center (376 Canal Street) while you're in the neighborhood.

Greenwich Village Flea Market — Held in the schoolyard of Public School 41 on Greenwich Avenue (near Seventh Avenue and West 10th Street), this relatively small market is held on Saturdays from noon to 7 p.m.

Greenmarkets — Those city-sponsored farmers' markets offer all sorts of goodies: fresh vegetables and fruit, baked goods, jams and jellies, flowers, and whatever else happens to be in season. The locations of the ones open all year include Park Row in front of City Hall (Tuesday and Friday), Federal Plaza at Broadway and Fulton Street (Friday), and Sheffield Plaza at Ninth Avenue and West 57th Street (Saturday). Many others operate during the warmer months at locations throughout the city. Call 212 566-0990 for seasonal locations and more information.

Intermediate School 44 Flea Market — Held both inside and outside Public School 44 on Columbus Avenue between West 76th and 77th streets, this popular flea market is held on Sundays from 10 to 5:30. Look for one of the city's Greenmarkets here, too.

Public School 183 Flea Market — Open all year on Saturdays from 6 to 6, this decidedly upscale flea market is known for both antiques and produce. It's held at Public School 183, on East 66th Street between First and York avenues.

SoHo Antiques and Collectibles — Held at the intersection of Broadway and Grand Street, this market is open Saturdays and Sundays from 9 to 5.

Tower Market — Located at Broadway between West 4th and Great Jones streets, this market is held on Saturdays and Sundays from 10 to 7. The generally funky and crafty merchandise tends to be of higher quality than you'll find at a lot of other markets.

26th Street Indoor Antiques Fair — This newcomer to the market scene is held indoors on Saturdays and Sundays from 9 to 5 at 122 West 26th Street, between Lexington Avenue and Park Avenue South.

Union Square Farmers' Market—Held on Wednesday, Friday, and Saturday at the north end of Union Square (between Broadway and Park Avenue South, on East 17th Street), this popular market offers fresh produce, baked goods, jams, jellies, and seasonal flowers and greens.

West 53rd Street Market—For reasons I do not know, several artists and people selling wonderful African masks and jewelry are clustered along the sidewalk on the north side of West 53rd Street between Fifth and Sixth avenues during the day all week long. If you're interested in African masks, look for a man from Mali named Boubou—his collection is exceptional.

Yorkville Flea Market—Another decidedly upscale market, this one is located at 351 East 74th Street, between First and Second avenues. It's held on Saturdays from 9 to 4 (except in June, July, and August).

Galleries

When people think of art, they sometimes think only of museums. While the art museums in New York are exceptional, anybody interested in art ought to think about visiting some commercial galleries, too. Galleries are places where potential buyers and admirers alike can look at the work of what are usually contemporary and other 20th-century artists (a few galleries specialize in older work) at their own pace and without charge. Let me stress "admirers alike." A lot of people are afraid to go to galleries because they think they'll be expected to buy something or be treated poorly if they don't know everything there is to know about art. That just isn't true, and an afternoon of gallery hopping can be lots of fun.

If you want to go gallery hopping, you should first decide what kind of art you want to see. New York has long been considered the center of the contemporary art world, and it follows that the city is home to literally hundreds of galleries of all sizes and styles. In general, the more formal and conventional galleries are on and just off Madison Avenue on the Upper East Side, and on both East and West 57th streets. (You need to look up to find a lot of them, particularly on 57th Street.) The less formal, avant-garde galleries tend to be in SoHo: on West Broadway, between Broome and Houston streets; on Greene Street, between Prince and Houston streets; and on Prince Street, between Greene Street and West Broadway.

If you want to sample some of the best known and most prestigious galleries, try **ACA** (41 East 57th Street), **Andre Emmerich** (41 East 57th Street), **Hirscl & Adler** (21 East 70th Street), **Holly Solomon** (724 Fifth Avenue), and **Prakapas** (19 East 71st Street), all located in midtown or the Upper East Side. Down in SoHo, visit **Mary Boone** (417 West Broadway), **Leo Castelli** (420 West Broadway), and **Tony Shafrazi** (130 Prince Street). You might also drop by the **Stark Gallery** (594 Broadway, Suite 301) and other galleries in the same building. For a free directory of galleries that belong to the Art Dealers Association of

America (not all of the ones in New York do), write the association at 575 Madison Avenue, New York, NY 10022, or call 212 940-8590. You can also ask at any gallery for a free copy of the *Art Now Gallery Guide,* a monthly publication listing exhibits at several hundred galleries in Manhattan.

Galleries are typically known for the artists they showcase. If you are interested in the work of one particular artist, both the *New Yorker* and *New York* magazine contain listings of gallery shows by artists' names. (Be sure to look at the dates – shows sometimes change quickly.) *New York* magazine also lists galleries displaying the work of several artists, and the Sunday *New York Times'* Arts and Leisure section devotes several pages to advertisements from various galleries and reviews of new shows. The *Times'* Friday Weekend section also contains reviews. *Art in America* and *Arts* magazines also include reviews of new shows.

Most galleries are open Tuesday through Saturday from 10 or 11 in the morning to 5 to 6 in the evening. Some close for a couple weeks during the summer.

Museums

Even if you aren't a museum person, take a look through the following list. I can't imagine that you won't find at least one place that strikes a chord! For more information about museum and library gift shops, see the "Museum and Library Shops" section in Chapter 6. For a list of museums that are particularly good for children, see the "Manhattan for Children" section in Chapter 7. And for a complete list of museums that offer free admission and special free hours, see the "Manhattan for Free" section in Chapter 7. For museums that are off the beaten path, I've suggested how to get there.

ABIGAIL ADAMS SMITH MUSEUM
421 East 61st Street (bet First and York Ave)   212 838-6878

This little (and little-known) gem will transport you back to the days when midtown Manhattan was a country escape for New Yorkers living at the southern end of the island. Constructed in 1799 as a carriage house for a 22-acre estate and converted into the Mount Vernon Hotel in 1826, this stone building sits on land originally owned by Colonel William Smith and his wife, Abigail Adams Smith, daughter of President John Adams. The house is run by the Colonial Dames of America, the oldest women's genealogical society in the United States, and it is preserved in its hotel incarnation. It's staffed by professionals and volunteers who are as knowledgeable as they are enthusiastic. They will walk with you through the house and answer any questions about the hotel or the period. Anyone interested in social history or antiques ought to put this well-run and interesting museum at the top of their itinerary. **Hours:** Monday through Friday from noon to 4, Sunday from noon to 5. **Admission:** $3 for adults, $2 for senior citizens and children.

ALTERNATIVE MUSEUM
594 Broadway (bet Houston and Prince St)   212 966-4444

Located in Suite 402 of a building largely occupied by commercial galleries, this small, artist-run museum definitely merits a visit if you're spending time in SoHo and are interested in contemporary art. (Also check out the New Museum of Contemporary Art, across the street.) The Alternative Museum was founded in 1975 and is dedicated, to quote one of its brochures, to exhibiting "the work of emerging and mid-career artists who have been underrecognized or disenfranchised because of ideology, race, gender, or economic inequality." In addition to its changing exhibits, the museum sponsors a variety of concerts and other events. **Hours:** Tuesday through Saturday from 11 to 6. **Admission:** free (although contributions to this nonprofit museum are encouraged).

AMERICAN BIBLE SOCIETY
1865 Broadway (at West 61st St)   212 408-1200

The American Bible Society is an organization dedicated to making the Christian Bible readily available to people in this country and around the world. Since it was founded in 1816, ABS has distributed more than 5.8 billion Bibles and other portions of scripture in upward of 400 languages! If you're interested in religious history, the small gallery on the second floor of its headquarters is well worth the trip. In addition to Bibles and other materials printed in Amharic, Chiyo, Quichua, and other exotic languages, the gallery displays a portion of a Torah scroll that was found after the flooding of Kai Feng Fu in China in 1643. The second floor also houses a research library. **Hours:** weekdays from 9 to 5. **Admission:** free.

AMERICAN CRAFT MUSEUM
40 West 53rd St (bet Fifth and Sixth Ave)   212 956-3535

This is one of those museums you'll either love or wonder why you came. Its relatively new galleries are wide open and well lit, and the atmosphere is decidedly unhurried. Both its changing displays and permanent collection are dedicated to crafts of the 20th Century — quilts, baskets, pottery, and clay sculpture are just a few of the various media that fit under that umbrella. If your definition of art is limited to the great masters, stick to Museum Mile along Fifth Avenue or go out on a limb at the Museum of Modern Art across the street from here. But if your definition of art includes innovative crafts, or if you just want to expand your horizons, by all means make time for a visit here. Half-hour docent tours of the museum are offered Saturday at 11 and 11:30 and Tuesday at 6:30 and 7. Make sure to ask about the schedule of upcoming lectures, films, and family workshops. **Hours:** Tuesday from 10 to 8, Wednesday through Sunday, 10 to 5. **Admission:** $4.50 for adults, $2 for senior citizens and students with ID cards, free for children under 12.

AMERICAN MUSEUM OF NATURAL HISTORY
Central Park West (bet West 77th and 81st St)   222 769-5100

If ever there were a perfect answer for what to do with children on a rainy day, this sprawling collection of 30 million (yes, *million*!) artifacts and specimens is it. You could spend an entire day on any one of the museum's three floors. (The main entrance puts you on the second floor.) I suggest asking for a floor plan at the information desk and then planning what you want to see if time is limited. The exhibits include ocean life, complete with a whale suspended from the ceiling; African mammals, complete with elephants; gems and minerals; and fascinating displays about different cultures from all over the globe. An exhibit on human evolution is expected to open in mid-1993, and one on fossils is planned for 1994. A guided tour of the museum's highlights begins at quarter after the hour between 10 and 3 and lasts a little more than an hour. You'll find a cafeteria and a restaurant on the lower level. Request information about the Hayden Planetarium (212 769-5920) and the NatureMax Theater (212 769-5650) at the information desk. They cost extra, but the shows in both places are excellent. **Hours:** Sunday through Thursday from 10 to 5:45, Friday and Saturday from 10 to 8:45. **Admission:** $5 for adults and $2.50 for children between 2 and 12 is "suggested," although you can pay whatever you feel is appropriate.

ASIA SOCIETY GALLERY
725 Park Ave (bet East 70th and East 71st St)   212 288-6400

The Asia Society is a nonprofit organization founded in 1956 to foster mutual understanding between Asian nations and the United States. One of the ways it reaches out to the public is through changing art exhibitions. Its very classy gallery is located in the Asia Society's elegant, modern building. (Call ahead to make sure they aren't in the process of changing exhibitions.) Gallery talks are held Tuesday through Saturday at 12:30 and Sunday at 2:30. For information about concerts, lectures, and other special programs, drop by the information desk in the lobby or call the society's event line at 212 517-6397. The Asia Society also runs a shuttle service on Saturday to and from the impressive Isamu Noguchi Garden Museum in Long Island City (call that museum at 718 204-7088 for details). **Hours:** Tuesday, Wednesday, Thursday, and Saturday from 11 to 6; Friday from 11 to 8; Sunday from noon to 5. **Admission:** $2 for adults, $1 for students and senior citizens, free for children under 12 accompanied by an adult, and free for everybody from 6 to 8 on Friday evening.

BLACK FASHION MUSEUM
155 West 126th St (bet Adam Clayton Powell, Jr. and
Malcolm X Boulevards)   212 666-1320

Dedicated to recognizing and showcasing the contribution of African-Americans to American fashion, this museum and the Harlem Institute of Fashion are open by appointment. You'll see thousands of garments spanning almost 200 years, from a slave's dress and an exact replica of Mary Todd Lincoln's inaugural gown to costumes from *The Wiz.* The only frustration is that you usually need to call, leave a message, and wait for it to be returned before you can visit. Take the M101 bus up Third Avenue from midtown to West 125th Street and Malcolm X Boulevard, and walk the two blocks to the museum. (The same bus will take you back to midtown on Lexington Avenue.) **Hours:** by appointment only on weekdays between noon and 8. **Admission:** $1.50 for adults, $1 for students and senior citizens, 50 cents for children.

CHILDREN'S MUSEUM OF MANHATTAN
212 West 83rd St (bet Broadway and Amsterdam Ave)
212 721-1234

On paper, this place sounds wonderful, and children will definitely find some fun and interesting things to do on the several floors of this museum. Just don't go expecting too much. There are buttons to push, ladders to climb, all sorts of things to examine, a rain forest to walk through, and even a media center with audio-visual equipment and other communication technologies. You'll find an Early Childhood Center, where children under four can play with blocks, paint, and do other things on the second floor, with storytelling, workshops, and other events occurring throughout the day. But the museum's space is lousy, its layout can be confusing, and things seem to be breaking all the time. Also be forewarned that the museum gets very crowded and unpleasantly warm on weekends and rainy days. **Hours:** Monday, Wednesday, and Thursday from 1:30 to 5:30; Friday, Saturday and Sunday from 10 to 5. **Admission:** $5 for adults and children, $2.50 for senior citizens, free for children under two. (Many workshops and performances cost an additional dollar or two.)

CHINA HOUSE GALLERY
125 East 65th St (bet Lexington and Park Ave)
212 744-8181

This extremely small but interesting gallery is run by the nonpolitical China Institute in America and is housed on the first floor of the institute's lovely brownstone. In addition to changing exhibits of Chinese art and artifacts, the gallery has a tiny gift shop specializing in books about China and Chinese art. **Hours:** Monday through Saturday from 10 to 5. **Admission:** a "suggested contribution" of $3.

THE CLOISTERS
Fort Tryon Park (in upper Manhattan)   212 923-3700

Perhaps the finest medieval art museum in the world, the Cloisters is also one of the quietest and most beautiful places in all of Manhattan.

Built on land donated by John D. Rockefeller, Jr., in the late 1930s, the museum incorporates large sections of cloisters and other pieces of buildings brought to the United States from southern France by sculptor George Grey Barnard. Barnard's collection was purchased by the Metropolitan Museum of Art with money donated for that purpose by Rockefeller in 1925, and the Cloisters is still part of the Metropolitan. (This means you can pay admission to one and visit the other without charge on the same day.) The truly spectacular collection also includes carved wood and ivory, tapestries, and sculptures. The museum is rarely crowded, and its outdoor terrace offers a great view of the Hudson River. If you're wondering how to get there, the M4 bus takes you to the front entrance from Madison Avenue in midtown and back again via Fifth Avenue. **Hours:** Tuesday through Sunday from 9:30 to 5:15 (4:45 in the winter). **Admission:** $6 for adults, $3 for students and senior citizens, free for children under 12 when accompanied by an adult. Fee includes same day admission to the Metropolitan Museum of Art.

COOPER-HEWITT
2 East 91st St (bet Fifth and Madison Ave)   212 860-6898

Founded by three granddaughters of Peter Cooper (their last name was Hewitt) as the Cooper Union Museum for the Arts of Decoration just before the turn of the century, this exceptional museum became part of the Smithsonian Institution in 1967 and moved into Andrew Carnegie's mansion on Fifth Avenue in 1976. Drawing from a permanent collection of almost a quarter million pieces involving every imaginable aspect of design, the museum's exhibitions change frequently. A recent one on the making of maps illustrated the diversity of the collection as well as the talent of the curators for making the collection interesting and accessible to the general public. Lectures and special gallery talks are developed around the exhibitions. They often are free but usually require advance reservations. Part of the pleasure of a visit to the Cooper-Hewitt is seeing the Carnegie Mansion itself. (For 25 cents, you get a booklet detailing the history of the mansion, with pictures from when the Carnegies lived there.) **Hours:** Tuesday from 10 to 9; Wednesday through Saturday from 10 to 5; Sunday from noon to 5. **Admission:** $3 for adults, $1.50 for senior citizens and students over 12. Free for children under 12 accompanied by an adult, Smithsonian Associates, and everybody on Tuesday evening between 5 and 9.

DYCKMAN HOUSE
4881 Broadway (bet West 204th and West 205th St)
212 304-9422

This is the last surviving farmhouse in Manhattan and a real treat for anybody interested in the city's history or the Revolutionary War period. The Dyckman family emigrated to what were then the American colonies from the Netherlands in the 17th century and had a thriving farm in this area before the Revolutionary War. They were forced to flee during the war, however, and both their home and farm were occupied and ultimately destroyed by British troops. When they returned to the area in 1784, the Dyckmans built this home. The adjoining buildings housing slave quarters and an outdoor kitchen no longer exist, but the house itself has been preserved much as it was then. You'll find several rooms with period furniture (some of which actually belonged to the Dyckmans) on the first and second floors and a kitchen in the basement. Probably the most interesting thing in the house is the "relic room" display of Revolutionary War artifacts, including a general's uniform, a tattered American flag with 13 stars, cannon balls, and bayonets. All were excavated from around the house at the beginning of this century. The cherry tree and flowers on the lovely grounds surrounding the house come alive during the spring and early summer. You can get to the Dyckman House from midtown by taking the M1 bus up Madison Avenue to East 125th Street and transfering to the M100. The M100 will drop you off in front of Dyckman House and pick you up again on the corner of West 204th Street and Broadway. **Hours:** Thursday through Sunday from 11 to 4. **Admission:** free.

EL MUSEO DEL BARRIO
1230 Fifth Ave (nr East 105th St)   212 831-7272

El Museo del Barrio — Spanish for "the Museum of the Neighborhood" — is the only museum in the United States outside Puerto Rico devoted exclusively to the art and culture of Latin America. Located at the southern end of Spanish Harlem and the northern tip of museum mile, El Museo is housed in the northern part of an old and rather odd building that runs the length of the block between East 104th and 105th streets. The museum features both permanent and changing exhibitions of contemporary and traditional art. Perhaps the most valuable holdings in the museum's 10,000-piece collection — artifacts created by the Arawak Tainos, Indians who lived in the Caribbean basin when Columbus and other European explorers began arriving in the region — unfortunately are not on display. However, the curatorial staff is working on a possible exhibit. El Museo also sponsors film festivals, lectures, and educational programs for children. **Hours:** Wednesday through Sunday from 11 to 5. **Admission:** $2 for adults, $1 for students and senior citizens, and free for children under 12 accompanied by an adult.

ELLIS ISLAND MUSEUM OF AMERICAN IMMIGRATION
Ellis Island   212 363-7620

Think of immigration to the United States, and you'll probably think of Ellis Island. An estimated 40% of all Americans today have at least one relative among the 12 million people who came through the immigration-processing center on the island between 1892 and 1954.

Located in New York Harbor, in the shadow of the Statue of Liberty, Ellis Island was all but abandoned until it was restored and opened as a museum in 1990. While a few glitches—including decay in the "American Immigrant Wall of Honor" running along the periphery of the island—still are being worked out, this museum is as interesting as it is moving. Overhearing older people telling children or grandchildren about what they brought with them and why they came while walking through a display of photographs and artifacts brought by other immigrants is overwhelming! One display retraces the steps immigrants took once they arrived on the island, and another discusses immigration in the U.S. up through the present. An Academy Award-winning film by Charles Guggenheim, *Island of Hope, Island of Tears,* is shown frequently and is well worth watching. To get to Ellis Island, take a Circle Line ferry from Battery Park. (The ticket booth is in Castle Clinton.) The best time to go is on a weekday, as the lines get long on Saturday and Sunday. The least expensive and most efficient way to get to Battery Park is on the 1 or the 9 subway line. (Be sure to get in one of the front cars, as only a few doors open at the Battery Park stop.) For more information about the ferry, call 212 269-5755. **Hours:** 9:30 to 5 in the winter and 9:30 to 5:30 in the summer. The last ferry to both Ellis Island and the Statue of Liberty leaves at about 3. **Admission:** $6 for adults, $5 for senior citizens, $3 for children from 3 to 17, and free for children under 3 (includes both Ellis Island and the Statue of Liberty).

FORBES MAGAZINE GALLERIES
62 Fifth Ave (bet West 12th and 13th St)   212 206-5548

What do 10,000 toy soldiers, 12 Fabergé eggs, documents written by Abraham Lincoln and other American presidents, and an Imperial Russian diadem have in common? They're in the Forbes Magazine Galleries (on the first floor of the Forbes magazine building). Assuming you're among the 900 people allowed in on a first-come, first-served basis every day, you can view them for free. The small galleries can get a little cramped on Saturday, but the collections assembled over the years by the late Malcolm Forbes and his sons definitely have something for everyone. Children under 16 are not allowed in without an adult, and no more than four children can accompany one adult. **Hours:** Tuesday through Saturday from 10 to 4. Thursday is reserved for guided tours, call 212 206-5548 for reservations or more information. **Admission:** free.

FRAUNCES TAVERN MUSEUM
54 Pearl St (at Broad St)   212 425-1778

If you're interested in Colonial and early U.S. history and culture, you'll really enjoy this often overlooked museum. The site of General George Washington's farewell address to his officers in 1783 and an anti-British meeting place before and during the Revolutionary War, this tavern has seen many generations and a lot of history come and go through its doors.

You have not gone to the wrong place if you open the front door of the Fraunces Tavern to find yourself in a restaurant. The first floor of the building is home to one of Wall Street's more pleasant places to eat. Just proceed straight past the host and up the stairs. You'll find period rooms (including the one in which Washington gave his address) with marvelous antique furniture and excellent explanations; a fascinating collection of newspapers, glasses, a cider mill, and even a wine press from the late 18th and early 19th centuries; as well as changing exhibitions on the second and third floors. Make sure to ask about movies, special events, and walking tours. **Hours:** weekdays from 10 to 4:45, Saturday from noon to 4. **Admission:** $2.50 for adults, $1 for students, senior citizens, and children under 12.

THE FRICK COLLECTION
1 East 70th St (bet Fifth and Madison Ave)   212 288-0700

The home of the late Henry Clay Frick is an exceptionally elegant and peaceful mansion displaying Frick's collection of paintings, sculpture, rugs, furniture, porcelain, and other artwork. While wandering around, look at the mansion itself—the moldings, the floors, the ceilings, the light fixtures, and the stairs—as well as the art. It's hard to believe anybody actually lived like this! Unlike the guards at a lot of other museums, the sentinels here are very knowledgeable and obviously proud of the collection. If you ask, they'll even tell you about the giant heat lamps that are brought out every night for the plants and flowers in the inner garden! Because the museum's temperature is kept at a constant 70 degrees, you'll be glad they require you to check your coat (at no charge). A special exhibition is held downstairs two or three months each year, so be sure to ask about it. Although not a place to take small children, this exceptionally beautiful and uncrowded museum is a real treat for art buffs and oglers alike. **Hours:** Tuesday through Saturday from 10 to 6; Sunday from 1 to 6. **Admission:** $3, although I suggest spending an extra $1 for the printed guide to the collection, as very few pieces are marked.

THE GUGGENHEIM MUSEUMS
1071 Fifth Ave (bet East 88th and 89th St)
575 Broadway (at Prince St)   212 360-3500

Housed in an enormous white spiral designed by Frank Lloyd Wright, the original Guggenheim (formally known as the Solomon R. Guggenheim Museum) is as famous for its building as for its collection. That is saying a lot, given its collection of 20th-century art is arguably the best in the world. A second Guggenheim (formally known as the Guggenheim Museum SoHo) opened in 1992 to showcase parts of the museum's permanent collection, as well as special exhibitions designed to complement those at the Fifth Avenue location. A third Guggenheim museum, the Peggy Guggenheim Collection, is located in Venice—but that's another trip! The works displayed at these museums offer a who's who of 20th century art: Chagall, Miro, Calder, Kandinsky, Picasso, Gauguin, and Mondrian are just a few of the artists represented. Both museums offer gallery talks and other special events. (Call 212 423-3600 to ask about current and upcoming events.) The café, operated by Dean & DeLuca at the Fifth Avenue location, is well worth a visit. **Hours:** The Fifth Avenue location is open daily (except Tuesday) from 10 to 8, while the SoHo location is open Sunday, Monday, and Wednesday from 11 to 6 and Thursday, Friday, and Saturday from 11 to 10. **Admission:** $7 for adults, $4 for senior citizens over 65 and students with identification at the Fifth Avenue location, and $5 for adults, $3 for senior citizens over 65 and students with identification at the SoHo location. Children under 12 are admitted free at both places. For $10 ($6 for senior citizens and students), you can purchase a two-day pass to both museums.

HISPANIC SOCIETY OF AMERICA
Audubon Terrace (Broadway bet West 155th and West 156th St)
212 926-2234

Founded as a public museum and research library in 1904, this little-known place is home to one of the most diverse and impressive collections in the world of art and artifacts from the Iberian Peninsula (Spain and Portugal). The building itself, located directly across from the dramatic El Cid statue in the middle of Audubon Terrace, is beautiful, but the lighting is awful and most descriptions are less than complete. That said, however, the Hispanic Society is well worth a visit. You'll find seals from the Roman Empire, a 15th-century silver processional cross from Barcelona, and paintings by Goya, Valazquez, and El Greco. Make sure to look at the beautiful tiles and mosaics in the walls on your way up the stairs between floors. A small "sales desk" selling reproductions of the society's holdings in post-card and print form is located in the Sorolla Room (so named for Joaquin Sorolla y Bastida's dramatic murals on the walls) at the far right end of the first floor. You can take either the M4 bus up Madison Avenue or the M5 bus up Sixth Avenue from midtown to get to the museum, and then take either back. **Hours:** Tuesday through Saturday from 10 to 4:30; Sunday from 1 to 4. **Admission:** free.

INTERNATIONAL CENTER OF PHOTOGRAPHY
1130 Fifth Ave (at East 94th St)   212 860-1777
1133 Sixth Ave (at West 43rd St)   212 768-4682

Anyone interested in photography should put the International Center of Photography (ICP) galleries at the top of their list of places to visit. Devoted to displaying photography both as art and as records of history, these galleries have changing exhibits of photographers from all over the world, as well as changing exhibits drawn from the center's permanent collection. The main ICP gallery on Fifth Avenue is relatively small, but its unhurried, quiet atmosphere allows you to take in the exhibits at your own pace. The newer gallery in midtown is almost twice the size, but the atmosphere is every bit as pleasant. **Hours:** Tuesday from 11 to 8; Wednesday through Sunday from 11 to 6. **Admission:** $4 for adults, $2.50 for senior citizens and students, $1 for children under 12.

INTREPID SEA-AIR-SPACE MUSEUM
Pier 86 (West 46th St and the Hudson River)   212 245-0072

The water is not particularly inviting and you'll find few pedestrians in this area, but a trip down here can be lots of fun if you're interested in aircraft carriers, submarines, space exploration, and the like. The centerpiece of this museum is the giant *U.S.S. Intrepid,* an aircraft carrier that served in both World War II and the Vietnam War. The *U.S.S. Edison,* a destroyer, and the *U.S.S. Growler,* a guided-missile submarine, are also here. You must go on a guided tour to see the *Growler,* but you can choose between a tour or wandering around by yourself to see everything else. Galleries, display halls, and theaters are scattered throughout the complex. You won't have much trouble finding the museum, as the *Intrepid* dominates this part of the river. The ticket booth and gift store are right inside the main entrance, past the tanks. The best way to get to the museum from midtown is either by taxi or M42 bus (make sure it says "Piers" on the front) all the way to the end of West 42nd Street. **Hours:** every day between Memorial Day and Labor Day from 10 to 5; Wednesday through Sunday from 10 to 5 during the rest of the year. (The ticket booth closes at 4, and the last tours finish at 6.) **Admission:** $7 for adults, $6 for senior citizens, $4 for children under 12. Free for active-duty military personnel and children under six accompanied by an adult.

JAPAN SOCIETY GALLERY
333 East 47th St (bet First and Second Ave)   212 832-1155

Founded in 1907, the Japan Society is an American organization dedicated to fostering better understanding between Japan and the United States. Its building, designed by Japanese architect Junzo Yoshimura, is an interesting blend of traditional and modern Japanese architecture and is home to everything from film festivals to conferences and classes. Up the staircase, in the main lobby on the second floor, is a quiet and relatively small gallery that hosts changing exhibits from Japan and other parts of the Pacific Rim. For more information about events at the Japan Society, call 212 752-3015. **Hours:** Tuesday through Sunday from 11 to 5. **Admission:** free, but a $2.50 contribution is suggested.

THE JEWISH MUSEUM
1109 Fifth Ave (at East 92nd St)   212 423-3200

Operated by the Jewish Theological Seminary of America and housed in yet another elegant Fifth Avenue mansion, the Jewish Museum displays the largest collection of Jewish art and Judaica in the United States. Much of the museum's collection was rescued from European synagogues before World War II, and all of it is extremely well displayed. The museum moved to temporary quarters for two years so its building could be renovated and expanded. As this is being written, the museum is behind schedule in reopening but will no doubt have done so by the time you read this. **Hours and admission:** call ahead for information about hours, admission, and special programs.

LOWER EAST SIDE TENEMENT MUSEUM
97 Orchard St (bet Delancey and Broome St)   212 431-0233

This unique museum was founded in 1988, and it is still in the process of defining itself. But it's already made an enormous contribution to the preservation of American social history and the urban immigrant experience. Housed in a tenement building that was home to as many as 10,000 people from more than two dozen nations between 1863 and the 1935, the museum features both changing and permanent exhibits. Perhaps most fascinating is the preserved hallway, which gives a glimpse of what life in one of these incredibly crowded places must have been like. Exciting plans are now underway to restore the entire second floor to its original condition. Make a point to strike up a conversation with one of the docents. Most of them are older people who once lived in this area, and all have stories to tell. **Hours:** Tuesday through Friday from 11 to 4; Sunday from 10 to 5. **Admission:** free on weekdays (although contributions are encouraged and desperately needed), $3 for adults and $1 for children 17 and under on Sunday. Special programs, including exceptionally well-conceived tours and slide shows, are offered on Wednesday and Sunday for an extra charge.

METROPOLITAN MUSEUM OF ART
Fifth Ave (bet East 80th and 84th St)   212 535-5500

The Met, as it is known to New Yorkers (not to be confused with the Metropolitan Opera) is one of those places you can visit 100 times and never see the same thing twice. Whether you're interested in Egyptian tombs, Greek or Roman coins, paintings by the great Renaissance masters, African masks, Tiffany windows, or arms and armor from the Crusades, the Met has a lot you'll want to see. Start by getting a floor plan at one of the information desks in the main hall, and then map out your visit. Although the Met often has excellent but very crowded special exhibits, I sometimes head for places with fewer people and just wander and gaze at my own pace. The best time to go is on a weekday morning. The worst time to visit the museum and its gift shops is right before Christmas. Self-guided audio tours in English and several other languages are available at an extra charge. The Met also sponsors an incredible number of films, lectures, gallery talks, concerts and other special programs. Call the Public Programs department at 212 570-3756 for information on upcoming schedules, or pick up a seasonal program at one of the information desks. If you come to New York frequently and like to visit the Met and its gift shops, you ought to think about becoming a National Associate. For a $35 annual fee, people who live outside a 200-mile radius of New York City can get free admission to both the Met and the Cloisters and a 10% discount on anything they buy, as well as receiving calendars and the Met's magazine. **Hours:** Sunday, Tuesday, Wednesday, and Thursday from 9:30 to 5:15; Friday and Saturday from 9:30 to 8:45. **Admission:** $6 for adults, $3 for senior citizens and children. Fee includes same-day admission to the Cloisters.

MORRIS-JUMEL MANSION
160th St (bet Edgecombe Ave and Jumel Ter)   212 923-8008

Built in 1765 as a summer house for Col. Roger Morris and his wife, this graceful old mansion sits atop a hill overlooking the East River. It briefly served as General George Washington's headquarters in 1776 and later was home to Madame Eliza Jumel and her second husband, Aaron Burr. (They were married in the parlor to the left of the front door.) Throughout the house you'll find exceptional period furniture, including a 19th-century French mahogany *directoire* sleigh-bed said to have belonged to Napoleon Bonaparte when he was First Consul of France. A hand-woven American flag from 1790 hangs upstairs, just outside the room used as a study by Washington. The surrounding neighborhood is pretty dicey and the mansion itself is not in the best condition, despite ongoing renovations, but it's worth a trip up if you're interested in the period surrounding the American Revolution. The grounds are particularly pretty in the spring and early summer. You can take the M2 bus up Madison Avenue to the front of the mansion on Edgecombe Avenue, but getting back to midtown is a little more complicated. I recommend taking a taxi or going on a tour. (Look under Harlem Spirituals in the "Tours" section of this chapter.) **Hours:** Tuesday through Sunday from 10 to 4. **Admission:** $3 for adults, $2 for senior citizens over 65 and students with identification, free for children under 12.

MUNICIPAL ART SOCIETY
457 Madison Ave (bet East 50th and East 51st St)
212 935-3960

The Municipal Art Society is a nonprofit organization dedicated to urban planning and historic preservation. In addition to sponsoring marvelous walking tours, lectures, and other public programs, the Society maintains several small galleries on the first and second floors of its headquarters on the left side of the New York Palace. You can learn a great deal about the city from the changing displays relating to the city, its people, and its architecture. If you're interested in architecture and urban planning, make sure to stop by Urban Center Books adjacent to the galleries on the first floor. You can also pick up tour schedules and other information in the lobby. **Hours:** Monday through Thursday from 11 to 7; Friday and Saturday, 10 to 6. **Admission:** free.

MUSEUM FOR AFRICAN ART
593 Broadway (bet Houston and Prince St)   212 966-1313

Although both the Metropolitan Museum of Art and the American Museum of Natural History have African collections on display, this is the only museum in New York devoted exclusively to African art. In a renovated space designed by Vietnam War Memorial architect Maya Lin, the museum's two floors house changing exhibits from all over the continent. You walk in through part of the eclectic gift shop and bookstore. (Check out the magnificent coffee-table books and the children's books to the right of the reception desk.) The museum also sponsors gallery talks and other events. **Hours:** Wednesday, Thursday, and Sunday from 11 to 6; Friday and Saturday from 11 to 8. **Admission:** $3 for adults, $1.50 for children, senior citizens, and students.

MUSEUM OF AMERICAN FOLK ART
2 Lincoln Square (Columbus Ave bet West 65th and 66th St)
212 595-9533

You'll find a lot of Americana here: weathervanes, quilts, whirligigs, and even a wooden carousel horse, as well as some paintings. The gallery is quite small but has lots of benches and can be a very pleasant place to just sit and think. Best of all, it's free. The museum sponsors lots of educational programs and demonstrations. **Hours:** 9 to 9 every day. **Admission:** free.

MUSEUM OF AMERICAN ILLUSTRATION
128 East 63rd St (bet Park and Lexington Ave)
212 838-2560

Adjacent to the main offices of the American Society of Illustrators, this gallery houses changing exhibits of advertising, artistic, and other work by professional illustrators. Call ahead to make sure they aren't in the midst of changing exhibits. **Hours:** weekdays from 10 to 5. **Admission:** free.

MUSEUM OF THE AMERICAN INDIAN
Audubon Terrace (Broadway bet West 155th and West 156th St)
212 283-2420

This incredible museum is one of several hidden treasures located at Audubon Terrace, a beautiful marble complex built on the grounds of the summer home of John James Audubon (now in the midst of what is now one of Manhattan's less appealing neighborhoods). "American" means just that—North, Central, and South. The museum's vast collection of clothing, baskets, tools, and other artifacts spans the entire continent, from northern Canada and Alaska to Tierra del Fuego. It also spans more than 10,000 years. There is so much here that the displays on the museum's three floors sometimes seem a little overwhelming, and the descriptions are not always as informative as you wish they were, but people interested in native Americans or the history of this conti- nent definitely ought to stop at this museum. If you've always meant to visit but never quite got around to it, go soon. The museum is now run by the Smithsonian Institution and will move to a new building on the Mall in Washington, D.C., by the end of the decade. You'll find the museum to your left immediately inside the gates of Audubon Terrace. (The fascinating Hispanic Society of America is a little further inside the Terrace on the same side.) You can take the M4 bus up Madison Avenue or the M5 bus up Sixth Avenue from midtown to get to the museum, and then take either back. **Hours:** Tuesday through Saturday from 10 to 5; Sunday from 1 to 5. **Admission:** $3 for adults, $2 for students and senior citizens, free for children under seven and Smithso- nian Associates.

MUSEUM OF THE CITY OF NEW YORK
1220 Fifth Ave (bet East 103rd and 104th St)   212 534-1672

Often overlooked by tourists and New Yorkers alike because of its location at the far north end of Fifth Avenue's "museum mile," this museum is a real treasure. Like the Cooper-Hewitt and the Frick, the Museum of the City of New York is housed in an old mansion. Part of the pleasure of a visit is imagining what it would have been like to live there. The museum is dedicated to the history of the city from the earliest European settlement through the present. Permanent exhibits in- clude period rooms, an exquisite silver collection, toys and dollhouses, a firefighting gallery, and an enormous number of model ships. Chang- ing exhibits cover everything from the history of theater in New York to the city's different ethnic groups. A short film, *The Big Apple,* is shown frequently in the basement theater. The museum also offers an excep- tionally diverse array of walking tours, children's programs, lectures, classes, and other events. Call the Education Department (ext. 206) for more information, or pick up a seasonal schedule at the information desk. **Hours:** Wednesday through Saturday from 10 to 5; Sunday, 1 to 5. **Ad- mission:** free, but contributions of $5 for adults, $3 for senior citizens, students and children, and $8 for families are strongly encouraged.

MUSEUM OF MODERN ART
11 West 53rd St (bet Fifth and Sixth Ave)   212 708-9480

Affectionately known as "MOMA" to New Yorkers, the Museum of Modern Art is among the most important museums in the world devoted to modern art. If it's not at one of the Guggenheims, chances are it's at MOMA. This is a big museum, and wandering through its many galleries will take some time. They are divided by artist, period, place, and medium. Architecture and design are on the fourth floor, American art from 1955 to 1963 is on the third floor, and a cubism display is on the second floor. MOMA does host some traveling exhibits (the recent one on Matisse was a smash hit), but its permanent collection alone is as enormous as it is impressive. If you need to rest, spend some time out in the sculpture garden (behind the front entrance on the ground floor) or head for the pleasant and not terribly expensive Garden Café (at the far northeast corner of the ground floor). MOMA also offers lectures, workshops, and films, as well as gallery talks on weekdays at noon, 1 and 3, and on Thursday evenings at 5:30 and 7. Information about all that and more is available at the information desk in the main lobby. **Hours:** Thursday from 11 to 9; Friday through Tuesday from 11 to 6. **Admission:** $7.50 for adults, $4.50 for students and senior citizens. Free for children under 16 accompanied by an adult and everybody on Thursday evening from 5 to 9.

MUSEUM OF TELEVISION AND RADIO
25 West 52nd St (bet Fifth and Sixth Ave)   212 621-6600

This is one of the most popular museums in Manhattan with adults and children alike! Its extensive collection includes thousands of radio and television programs and commercials, many of which are periodically shown to the public and all of which are available for individual viewing in private rooms. Several galleries display changing exhibits on every imaginable aspect of television and radio, from a recent one on *Star Trek: the Next Generation* to more serious displays on the evolution of advertising and the people who work in the telecommunications industries. Everything changes constantly, so check the schedule in the lobby or give the museum a call to find out what is going on at any given time. It gets pretty crowded on weekends, so I suggest going on a weekday if you can. **Hours:** Tuesday through Sunday from noon to 6. The theater stays open until 8 on Thursday and until 9 on Friday. **Admission:** free, but a contribution of $5 for adults, $4 for students, and $3 for senior citizens and children under 13, is strongly suggested.

NATIONAL ACADEMY OF DESIGN
1083 Fifth Ave (bet East 89th and 90th St)   212 369-4880

Founded in 1825, this museum and school was modeled after the Royal Academy in London. In addition to workshops and classes for artists, the Academy features changing exhibits of American and European paintings and other art. The museum is in a lovely townhouse, and wandering through its intimate galleries is a real pleasure. Winslow Homer, Thomas Eakins, and John Singer Sargent are just a few of the artists who have been members of the Academy and whose work is part of its permanent collection. **Hours:** Wednesday, Thursday, Saturday, and Sunday from noon to 5; Friday from noon to 8. **Admission:** $3.50 for adults, $2 for students, and senior citizens, free to everyone on Friday from 5 to 8.

NEW MUSEUM OF CONTEMPORARY ART
583 Broadway (bet Houston and Prince St)   212 219-1222

This museum is a showcase for contemporary artists and is definitely worth a visit if you're spending time in SoHo. Its changing exhibits feature both individual artists and thematic collections, and they tend to be unusually well displayed and conceived. The museum is known for its multidisciplinary approach to art. People from such diverse fields as anthropology, political economy, and urban history are often involved in developing exhibits. The museum offers gallery talks and group tours tailored to the age and interest of the participants. Call 212 219-1355 for recorded program information. **Hours:** Wednesday, Thursday, Friday, and Sunday from noon to 6; Saturday from noon to 8. **Admission:** $3.50 for adults, $2.50 for artists, students and senior citizens. Free for children under 12 and for everybody from 6 to 8 on Saturday.

NEW YORK CITY FIRE MUSEUM
278 Spring St (bet Hudson and Varick St)   212 691-1303

This museum, set in a turn-of-the-century firehouse, is dedicated to the history of fire prevention. In addition to a relatively modern fire engine, a quite old ladder truck, a hand-pulled hand pump from 1820, and other fire apparatus, the museum displays pictures from fire stations all over New York, a collection of 19th-century leather fire buckets, and an assortment of badges. Kids will love looking at the equipment, and most things are well displayed, but I wish they had at least one engine children could climb around in. The museum is a bit out of the way, but the neighborhood (technically part of SoHo) is as safe as it is quiet. **Hours:** Tuesday through Saturday from 10 to 4. You might want to call ahead to make sure your visit doesn't coincide with that of a big school group. **Admission:** free, although donations of $3 for adults and 50 cents for children are encouraged.

NEW YORK PUBLIC LIBRARY FOR THE PERFORMING ARTS
Lincoln Center (bet the Metropolitan Opera House and the Vivian Beaumont Theater)   212 870-1630

If you are interested in the performing arts, put this amazing place at the top of your list. First, you'll always find something interesting in its four galleries. An exhibit of programs and materials from the New York Philharmonic may be in one gallery, while an exhibit on the history of ballet is in another. Second, this is not just a book library. Its collection includes tens of thousands of recordings, videos, and printed materials from dance, theater, classical music, and other media – and you can listen to or watch whatever you choose without leaving the library! Finally, the library's Bruno Walter Auditorium is constantly being used for concerts, dramatic readings, and other performances. Call 212 870-1721 for recorded information on upcoming schedules or drop by the information desk inside the main entrance. **Hours:** Monday and Thursday from noon to 8; Wednesday, Friday, and Saturday from noon to 6. **Admission:** free.

NEW YORK TRANSIT MUSEUM
Boerum Pl and Schermerhorn St, Brooklyn   718 330-3060

Although it's located in Brooklyn, I couldn't resist including what the *New York Times* calls "a spectacular celebration of urban infrastructure." If you're interested in the history of the subway system and the technology that keeps it running today, this small museum is a must. Located on the platforms and mezzanines of the now-defunct Court Street Station, the New York Transit Museum contains several old subway cars; an exhibit on the design of the first IRT (Interborough Rapid Transit) line, opened in 1904; and a large number of artifacts relating to the entire system. It only seems fitting that you take the subway to get here. Follow the signs after taking the A or F train to Jay Street or the 2, 3, 4, or 5 to Borough Hall. The museum also offers lectures, workshops, and tours of used and unused subway stations throughout the city. **Hours:** Tuesday through Friday from 10 to 4; Saturday and Sunday from 11 to 4. **Admission:** $3 for adults, $1.50 for senior citizens and children under 17.

NICHOLAS ROERICH MUSEUM
319 West 107th St (off Riverside Dr)   212 864-7752

Located in an aged but quite elegant townhouse on this unusually pleasant block between Riverside Drive and Broadway, this museum is dedicated to the life and work of Russian-born artist-philosopher-author-educator Nicholas Roerich. History buffs may remember him as the author of the Roerich Pact, an agreement signed by President Franklin Roosevelt and the leaders of some 20 Latin American countries in 1935. It stipulated that a banner be flown over museums, monuments, and other cultural institutions in times of both war and peace. You'll find a number of books written by and about Roerich in several languages, but the real reason to come to this museum is the large collection of unusual paintings of the Himalayas, various religious scenes, and other subjects by Roerich. Very little is labeled and the displays are quite informal, but it's definitely a pleasant place off the beaten track. Seasonal schedules of poetry readings, concerts, and other events are available in the front hall, as are post cards with reproductions of some of Roerich's paintings. **Hours:** Tuesday through Sunday from 2 to 5. **Admission:** free.

PIERPONT MORGAN LIBRARY
29 East 36th St (at Madison Ave)   212 685-0008

Have you ever wondered where copies of the Guttenberg Bible are kept? Wonder no more. That Bible (one of several copies in the world) and one of the most remarkable collections of medieval and Renaissance manuscripts, books, drawings, and art are in the Pierpont Morgan Library. Built at the turn of the century by financier J. Pierpont Morgan to house his personal collection (which was impressive to begin with but has since grown by leaps and bounds), the library was open to the public by his son in 1924. It's now both a scholarly research center and a museum with changing and permanent exhibitions. By far the most exciting thing here for even the casual art fan is "Mr. Morgan's Library": a study and private three-story library connected by a rotunda. Pick up the separate brochure for these rooms at the reception desk in the front hall so you can identify the unbelievable collection of mostly Italian Renaissance carvings, furniture, paintings, tapestries, mosaics, and more in these rooms. Call 212 685-0610 for recorded information about current exhibits and special events. **Hours:** Tuesday through Saturday from 10:30 to 5; Sunday from 1 to 5. **Admission:** $5 for adults, $3 for students and senior citizens.

POLICE ACADEMY MUSEUM
235 East 20th St (bet Second and Third Ave)   212 477-9753

This small museum is on the second floor of the New York City Police Academy. If you're interested in antique firearms or the history of the police in New York City, you'll really enjoy this place. Collections of badges, shields, nightsticks, handcuffs, and trophies are also on display, as are exhibits on fingerprinting, mug shots, drugs, and youth gangs. When you arrive at the academy, you must check in at the desk inside the entrance and present identification before heading up to the museum. **Hours:** weekdays from 9 to 5. Call ahead to make sure of the hours and to sign up for a tour. **Admission:** free.

SCHOMBURG CENTER FOR RESEARCH IN BLACK CULTURE
515 Malcolm X Boulevard at West 135th St   212 491-2200

This incredible place is both yet another branch of the New York Public Library and one of the nation's premier African-American research centers. It has an enormous collection of manuscripts, books, photographs, maps, and other materials on the experience of African-Americans. You will also find changing exhibits on African art and history, as well as lectures, films, and other events. Take the M102 bus up Third Avenue to the center from midtown and then back down Lexington Avenue. **Hours:** Monday, Tuesday, and Wednesday from noon to 8; Friday and Saturday from 10 to 6. The exhibition areas are also open Sunday from 1 to 5. **Admission:** free.

SOUTH STREET SEAPORT MUSEUM
Fulton St (east end)   212 669-9400

This is not a museum in the traditional sense of the word but rather a collection of exhibits and ships spread throughout the South Street

Seaport complex. You can walk around and look at everything without paying a dime. But the museum includes the four-masted *Peking,* a lightship called the *Ambrose,* a tall ship called the *Wavertree* (which is now being restored), a gallery with changing exhibitions, and a children's center with hands-on workshops and displays. Stop by the visitor center a block and a half down Fulton Street from the main entrance on your right or the ticket booth on Pier 16 to get a map and information. On any given day, particularly in the warmer months, you'll find all sorts of special tours and activities throughout this fascinating and wildly successful complex. Call 212 669-9424 for recorded information about current exhibits, special activities, and other events. **Hours:** every day from 10 to 5 in the winter and 10 to 6 in the summer. Restaurants and some stores stay open longer in the summer. **Admission:** $6 for adults, $5 for senior citizens over 65, $4 for students with identification, $3 for children under 12. You can combine admission to the South Street Seaport Museum with a ride around New York Harbor on a paddle-wheeler called the *Andrew Fletcher* for $14 for adults, $13 for senior citizens, $12 for students, and $7 for children.

STUDIO MUSEUM IN HARLEM
144 West 125th St (bet Malcolm X and Adam Clayton Powell, Jr. Blvd)   212 864-4500

In a relatively new space, the Studio Museum offers changing exhibits of work by African-American, African, and Caribbean artists. In addition to more traditional media like paint and sculpture, you'll find crafts and other works here. This world-class museum recently celebrated its 25th anniversary, and it is a real force in Harlem's art community. The Studio Museum also offers demonstrations, films, lectures, and other events. Take the M101 bus up Third Avenue from midtown to the museum and then back down Lexington Avenue. **Hours:** Wednesday through Friday from 10 to 5; Saturday and Sunday from 1 to 6. **Admission:** $5 for adults, $3 for senior citizens and students, $1 for children under 12.

THEODORE ROOSEVELT BIRTHPLACE
28 East 20th St (bet Broadway and Park Ave)   212 260-1616

Tucked on a side street in an often overlooked neighborhood (although it was once among the city's most elegant residential streets), this wonderful brownstone is a rebuilt version of Theodore Roosevelt's childhood home. The buildings at 28 and 26 East 20th Street were both torn down in 1916, but they were rebuilt by the president's sisters and wife using original blueprints and were furnished and decorated largely as they had been in Teddy's childhood. You enter through what was once the servants' entrance, browse through a collection of pictures, clothing, and other things that belonged to the Roosevelt family in a wonderful wood-paneled room, then are taken through the living quarters on the second and third floors by a National Park Service guide. (This is a national historic site.) If you're interested in presidential history, the late 19th and 20th centuries, or just want to see how the wealthy lived in the 1850s and 1860s, make sure to put this museum on your list. **Hours:** Wednesday through Sunday from 9 to 5. Tours are given every half hour or on demand. **Admission:** $2 for adults, free for seniors and children under 17.

TRINITY CHURCH MUSEUM
Broadway and Wall St   212 602-0872

This small museum is to the left of the pulpit in historic Trinity Church, located at the foot of Wall Street in the old part of the Financial District. The sanctuary itself is something to behold. You enter through a gorgeous carved foyer to find a magnificent set of stained-glass windows. Remember this is a place of worship that happens to be a historic site with a museum, rather than the other way around. The museum houses the parish's original charter (dating back to 1697) and other precious pieces of Trinity Church's history, as well as changing exhibits. Make sure to ask about the short video presentation. **Hours:** Monday through Friday from 9 to 11:45 and from 1 to 3:45; Saturday from 10 to 3:45; Sunday from 1 to 3:45. **Admission:** free.

UKRAINIAN MUSEUM
203 Second Ave (bet East 12th and East 13th St)
212 288-0110

Sponsored by the Ukrainian Congress of the U.S. and housed on the fourth and fifth floors of its townhouse on the northern edge of the East Village, this out-of-the-way place is a real find for anybody interested in the Ukraine and the heritage of its people. The best time to visit is the roughly two-month period around Easter, when the museum displays its extraordinary collection of *pysanky,* the elaborately decorated Ukrainian Easter eggs that were once used as talismans to ward off evil spirits. The museum also sponsors demonstrations and classes during this period and around Christmas. You'll find Ukrainian costumes and crafts on display all year round and a small gift shop on the fifth floor. Everything here is conducted in both English and Russian, and you get the feeling that the museum is very much a part of New York's Ukrainian immigrant community. **Hours:** Wednesday through Sunday from 1 to 5. **Admission:** $1 for adults, 50 cents for senior citizens and students, free for children under 12.

WHITNEY MUSEUM OF AMERICAN ART
945 Madison Ave (at East 75th St)   212 570-3600

This museum has a decidedly modern focus, although the Whitney's collection includes works by American artists from throughout this country's history. Several exhibits are shown at any given time, some focusing on one artist and others built around a theme. The Whitney's Biennial Exhibit, which opens in March of odd years and runs for several months, has become a revered tradition in the New York art world and is eagerly awaited by the museum's many fans. If you're interested in gallery talks, special events, or finding out what's on display at any given time, you can pick up a weekly schedule outside the museum's main entrance. Sarabeth's Kitchen, long a popular East Side restaurant, has opened a branch on the museum's lower level. (See the "Restaurants" section.) **Hours:** Wednesday, Friday, Saturday, and Sunday from 11 to 6; Thursday from 1 to 8. **Admission:** $6 for adults, $4 for senior citizens over 62 and students with identification. Free for children under 12 and everybody between 6 and 8 on Thursday evening.

The small **Whitney Gallery and Sculpture Court** at Philip Morris is located in the lobby of the Philip Morris Building (120 Park Avenue, at East 42nd Street). The gallery is open weekdays from 11 to 6 (until 7:30 on Thursday evening), and admission is free. The sculpture court, which doubles as a pleasant sitting area, is open Monday through Saturday from 7:30 in the morning until 9:30 in the evening, and Sunday from 11 to 7. Call 212 878-2550 for more information.

YESHIVA UNIVERSITY MUSEUM
2520 Amsterdam Ave (at West 185th St)   212 960-5390

On the main campus of Yeshiva University, this museum has an exceptional collection of paintings, books, religious artifacts, and other things related to Jewish life and culture. It mounts one major exhibit each year in addition to smaller changing exhibits throughout the year. Ask about special holiday events and workshops for adults and children. Before heading up there, you ought to know that the campus is quite safe but the surrounding neighborhood can get rough after dark. (It's also full of steep hills, in case you're thinking about walking around.) The M101 bus goes up to the museum via Third Avenue from midtown and then back down Lexington Avenue. **Hours:** Tuesday, Wednesday, and Thursday from 10:30 to 5; Sunday from noon to 6. The museum closes for Passover and other Jewish holidays. **Admission:** $3 for adults, $1.50 for senior citizens and children over four.

Parks

Believe it or not, Manhattan has almost 2,600 acres of parkland. That means 17 percent of the city is grass, rocks, playgrounds, and walking trails. Central Park, spanning roughly 750 acres from 59th and 110th streets, between Fifth Avenue and Central Park West, is the biggest and certainly the most famous. Smaller ones like Carl Schurz Park and Lighthouse Park on Roosevelt Island can sometimes be more peaceful, however, precisely because fewer people know about them. Inwood Hill Park and Fort Tryon Park on Manhattan's northern tip are so wooded and hilly you won't believe you're in New York.

Unless you are going to a scheduled event such as a play or concert, you probably don't want to walk around in any park at night. If you are by yourself, stay away from isolated areas and dense shrubs even during the day. That said, however, the parks are there for you to explore and enjoy—and they can offer a wonderful respite from the concrete and chaos that sometimes is New York.

Battery Park—Named for the gun battery built along its old shoreline during the War of 1812, this 23-acre park sits at the very southern tip of Manhattan, below State Street and Battery Place. Castle Clinton, a national monument and the place to buy tickets for trips to the Statue of Liberty and Ellis Island, is in Battery Park, as are the Staten Island Ferry terminal and one of the last remaining kiosks for the original subway system. The park has lots of benches and pathways, and offers an excellent view of New York Harbor.

Bryant Park—Located behind the New York Public Library (between West 40th and 42nd streets and Fifth and Sixth avenues), this park has undergone major renovations in recent years. In its northwest corner you'll find a half-price outlet for tickets to various dance performances and concerts. The benches are great resting spots, and you'll find lots of street vendors and a lovely garden in the spring and summer. Bryant Park even has public bathrooms, complete with attendants.

Carl Schurz Park—Running between East End Avenue and the East River from East 84th to 90th streets, this is probably the safest public park in the city. It's no coincidence that this park, named for a German immigrant turned U.S. senator and secretary of the interior, includes Gracie Mansion, the official residence of New York's mayor. In addition to the great view of barge traffic along the East River, the park offers plenty of benches and playgrounds.

Central Park—Designed in 1858 by Frederick Law Olmsted, the same landscape architect who designed the U.S. Capitol grounds in Washington, D.C., this is the ultimate urban park. It runs for two and a half miles between 59th and 110th streets, bounded by Fifth Avenue and Central Park West. The park has ice-skating rinks, boat ponds, a lake, a zoo, jogging tracks, a reservoir, baseball diamonds and other playing fields, playgrounds, tennis courts, and lots of open space. Unless you just want to wander, stop by the Visitors Information Center at the Dairy (212 794-6564), near what would be West 65th Street and Sixth Avenue if those roads went through the park. (If you ever get lost, it might help to know that the first digits of the number plates on the park lampposts correspond to the nearest cross street.) In summer, Central Park is home to Shakespeare in the Park, various concerts on the "SummerStage," and free concerts by the New York Philharmonic and the Metropolitan Opera.

Fort Tryon Park—This 66-acre gift from John D. Rockefeller, Jr., extends from Riverside Drive to Broadway and from West 192nd Street to Dyckman Street. Home to the Cloisters, this hilly and wooded park offers magnificent views of the Hudson River. Take a friend or two along if you're going to go walking here.

Greenacre Park — One of what are known as vest-pocket parks, this was a gift from the daughter of John D. Rockefeller, Jr. It's located on East 51st Street, between Second and Third avenues. On a nice day during the work week, simply follow the lunchtime crowds.

Inwood Hill Park — The second largest park in Manhattan, Inwood Hill Park is at the northwest tip of Manhattan. Bordered by the Harlem River on the north and the Hudson River on the west, this rugged park is home to caves once used by Algonquin Indians. Hiking and climbing enthusiasts will love this park's relatively unspoiled wilderness, but I suggest going in groups.

Lighthouse Park on Roosevelt Island — If you really want to get away but only have a little time, this is the place to go. Located on the northern tip of Roosevelt Island in the middle of the East River, this park has picnic facilities and clean open space, as well as the lighthouse for which it is named. The view of the Manhattan skyline from the west side of the park is among the best in the city, and it's free — except for the cost of getting there. The tram, which leaves frequently from its own station at Second Avenue, between East 59th and East 60th streets, costs $1.40 each way, and the bus that takes you from the tram station most of the way to the northern end of the island costs 10 cents.

Riverside Park — Running between Riverside Drive and the Hudson River from West 72nd Street to West 159th Street, this is another one of Frederick Law Olmsted's creations. In addition to playgrounds, great paths for walking, jogging, and bicycling, and a terrific view of the Hudson River, the park is home to the Soldiers' and Sailors' Monument (at West 89th Street) and Grant's Tomb (at West 122nd Street).

Stuyvesant Square Park — This park was given to the city by Peter Stuyvesant, the last Dutch governor of Nieuw Amsterdam in the mid-17th century. It was once among the most elegant places in the city, though it still has a little of its charm and lots of benches besides. You'll find it on both sides of Second Avenue at the southern end of the Gramercy Park neighborhood, between East 15th and East 17th streets.

Washington Square Park — Long considered the emotional if not geographic center of Greenwich Village, this park sits at the foot of Fifth Avenue and is best known for the Washington Memorial Arch. The park was constructed in 1827, while the marble arch was not dedicated until 1895. (It replaced a wooden one.) The park is near New York University, and its chess tables, playgrounds, and other features are much used by students and other area residents. It's surprisingly dirty, however, and you probably don't want to wander around at night.

For recorded information on what's happening on any given day in the parks of Manhattan and other boroughs, call 212 360-3456. For specific information about parks in Manhattan, call the Manhattan Parks and Recreation Department at 212 316-8111. Finally, for information about free walking tours and workshops sponsored by the Urban Park Rangers in Central Park, Inwood Park, and other places, call 212 427-4040.

You also can find a little peace and quiet even in midtown at one of the many elaborate **water fountains** built inside or outside major office buildings. Some of my favorites include:

Crystal Pavilion, East 50th St bet Second and Third Ave (indoors, but not always on)

Exxon Garden, 1251 Sixth Ave, bet West 49th and West 50th St (outdoors)

Grand Hyatt Hotel, East 42nd St, next to Grand Central Station (right inside the front door)

Lincoln Center Plaza, Columbus Ave bet West 62nd and West 65th St (outdoors)

Metropolitan Museum of Art, Fifth Ave bet East 80th and East 84th St (outdoors)

McGraw-Hill Plaza, 1221 Sixth Ave, bet West 48th and West 49th St (outdoors)

Olympic Tower, East 51st and 52nd St bet Fifth and Madison Ave (indoors)

Paley Park, East 53rd St bet Fifth and Madison Ave (outdoors)

Park Avenue Plaza, East 52nd and East 53rd St bet Madison and Park Ave (indoors)

Tishman Building, 666 Fifth Ave, nr East 52nd St (indoors)

Trump Tower, 725 Fifth Ave, bet East 56th and East 57th St (indoors)

Finally, you can rest your feet at one of the many formal and informal **public sitting areas** in midtown and other parts of the city. Here are a few suggestions:

Crystal Pavilion, East 50th St bet Second and Third Ave (indoors)

Ford Foundation Gardens, East 42nd and East 43rd St bet First and Second Ave (indoors)

Galleria, East 57th and East 58th St bet Park and Lexington Ave (indoors)

Grace Plaza, Sixth Ave and West 43rd St (outdoors)

IBM Plaza, 590 Madison Ave, at East 56th St (indoors)

Vivian Beaumont Theater Plaza, off West 65th St bet Broadway and Amsterdam Ave (outdoors)

Margaret Mead Green, Columbus Ave bet West 79th and West 81st St (outdoors)

Metropolitan Museum of Art steps, Fifth Ave bet East 80th and East 84th St (outdoors)

Museum of American Folk Art, Columbus Ave bet West 65th and West 66th St (indoors)

New York Public Library steps, Fifth Ave bet West 40th and West 42nd St (outdoors)

Paley Park, East 53rd St bet Fifth and Madison Ave (outdoors)

Park Avenue Plaza, East 52nd and East 53rd St bet Madison and Park Ave (indoors)

Philip Morris Building, Park Ave at East 42nd St (indoors)

Sutton Place Park, Sutton Pl at East 57th St (outdoors)

Trump Tower Gardens, Fifth Ave bet East 56th and East 57th St (outside, on levels 4 and 5)

UN Plaza, First Ave bet East 45th and East 46th St (outdoors)

Vietnam Veterans Memorial Plaza, off Water St just north of Broad St (outdoors)

Places of Worship

Manhattan is home to some of the oldest, largest, and most famous churches and synagogues in the United States. Many of them allow people to come in and look around, but always remember that you are in a place of worship rather than a museum or gallery. My favorites are:

Abyssinian Baptist Church — Located at 132 West 138th Street (between Frederick Douglass and Adam Clayton Powell, Jr. boulevards), this church is one of the oldest in Harlem and boasts one of the largest congregations in the city. Made famous by the late U.S. Congressman, the Reverend Adam Clayton Powell, Jr., the church contains a display of pictures of Powell and memorabilia from his career. Call 212 862-7474 for information about services.

Cathedral Church of St. John the Divine — Facing Amsterdam Avenue at 112th Street, this magnificent Episcopal cathedral has been under construction for more than a century and will probably be the largest Christian house of worship in the world when (and if) it is completed in the mid-21st century. The stonework, art, and stained glass are exceptional, as is the combination of Gothic, Romanesque, and Byzantine architectural styles. Even if you are not particularly interested in cathedrals, architecture, or religion, this is really a must-see. The Cathedral Shop, off the main sanctuary (see the "Museum and Library Shops" section in Chapter 6), has an eclectic assortment of books and gifts. Call 212 316-7400 for information about services. (See the "Tours" section later in this chapter, or call 212 932-7314 for information.)

Central Synagogue — On the southwest corner of Lexington Avenue and East 55th Street, this reform synagogue is the oldest continuously used synagogue in the city. Completed in 1872, it was designed by Henry Fernbach. The beautiful Moorish Revival exterior and carved wooden doors make it hard to miss, and the red, gold, and blue stenciling inside are breathtaking. Call 212 838-5122 for information about services.

Church of the Holy Trinity — Up near Gracie Mansion at 316 East 88th Street (between First and Second avenues), this Episcopal church is a French Gothic marvel that dates back a hundred years. It's a favorite of classical-music lovers because of its frequent winter concerts. Call 212 289-4100 for information about concerts and services.

Church of the Transfiguration — On the north side of East 29th Street, between Fifth and Madison avenues, this Episcopal church is probably better known as "the little church around the corner." You'll find a lovely garden in front of this low-lying brick church and beautiful stained-glass windows inside. The church is open to the public from 8 to 6 daily. Call 212 684-6770 for information about services.

Grace Church — Situated on Broadway, between East 10th and East 11th streets, this exquisite Episcopal church was built in 1846 and is one of several in New York designed by James Renwick, Jr. An elegant Gothic presence in the neighborhood and one of the most important examples of early Gothic Revival architecture in the country, the church is known for its daily prayer services, carved pulpit, and outstanding music. It is open to the public from 10 to 5:30 on weekdays and from noon to 4 on Saturdays. Call 212 254-2000 for information about services.

Holy Trinity Greek Orthodox Cathedral — Located on the north side of East 74th Street, between First and Second avenues, this magnificent brick cathedral actually doesn't look like much from the outside. Walk inside the great wood doors, however, and you'll think you're in ancient Greece. Call 212 288-3215 for information about services.

Marble Collegiate Church — At the northwest corner of Fifth Avenue and West 29th Street, this stately church was designed by Samuel Warner in 1854 and made famous by Dr. Norman Vincent Peale. It is an example of Early Romanesque Revival and draws its name from the Tuckahoe marble used in its construction. The public is welcome to visit between 10 and 4 on weekdays. The entrance is around the corner at 1 West 29th Street. Call 212 686-2770 for information about services.

Riverside Church — A gift of John D. Rockefeller, Jr., this interdenominational church was inspired by Chartres cathedral in France and can seat up to 2,500 people. Its 22-story bell tower dominates the northern end of Morningside Heights, and the 74-bell carillon can be heard throughout the area. Known for its beauty as well as its social activism, the church is located at 490 Riverside Drive (between West 120th and West 122nd streets). Call 212 222-5900 for information about services.

St. Bartholemew's Church — Complete with a mosaic dome and a carved, triple-arched portico designed by architect Sanford White, this brick and stone Episcopal church sits between East 51st and 50th streets on Park Avenue. In addition to religious services, the church runs a community club with a pool, squash courts, and other facilities as well as a thrift shop on Tuesday through Friday from 11:30 to 3:30. Call 212 751-1616 for information about services.

St. Mark's in the Bowery – Constructed on the site of Peter Stuyvesant's personal chapel in 1799, this understated but elegant Episcopal church has lovely yards on either side. (Usually, though, a pretty downtrodden collection of people mills around them.) It is located on the northwest corner of East 10th Street and Second Avenue in what is now the East Village but what was once Stuyvesant's farm. ("Bouwerie" is *farm* in Dutch.) Call 212 674-6377 for information about services.

St. Nicholas Russian Orthodox Cathedral – This amazing Russian Orthodox cathedral, complete with onion domes, is nestled between apartment buildings at 15 East 97th Street (between Fifth and Madison avenues). Built at the beginning of this century with money collected in Russia, it was patterned after Baroque churches in Moscow. The cathedral is the diocesan seat of the Russian Orthodox Church in North America. Call 212 534-1601 for information about services.

St. Patrick's Cathedral – Designed by James Renwick, Jr., more than a hundred years ago, this astonishing building is the largest Roman Catholic church in the United States and the seat of the archdiocese of New York. The enormous building takes up an entire city block between East 50th and 51st streets and Fifth and Madison avenues. The main organ alone has 9,000 pipes! Its steps along Fifth Avenue are a great place to rest your feet and watch the world go by. Call 212 753-2261 for information about services.

St. Paul's Chapel – On Broadway, between Fulton and Vesey streets, this Episcopal parish is housed in the oldest church building in the city. Construction began in 1764, when New York was New Amsterdam and America was a British colony, as the dates on the gravestones in the surrounding cemetery attest. The interior is surprisingly plain but exceptionally elegant and lit by Waterford crystal chandeliers. Look for George Washington's pew in the north aisle. The chapel is open to the public from 9 to 3 on weekdays and from 7 to 3 on Sunday. Call 212 602-0874 for information about services.

St. Peter's Lutheran Church – The only really modern church on this list, St. Peter's is nestled under the towering Citicorp Center at the southeast corner of East 54th Street and Lexington Avenue. The church has an extensive program of jazz, opera, and other music on Sunday and during the week. Look for the posted schedule outside the main entrance. Call 212 935-2200 for information about services.

St. Thomas Episcopal – On the northwest corner of Fifth Avenue and West 53rd Street, this beautiful church is best known for its magnificent music programs. The incredibly ornate stone carvings on the church's exterior, its attractive doors, and its stately bell tower combine to make it a real presence on Fifth Avenue. Call 212 757-7013 for information about services.

Spanish and Portuguese Synagogue – Home of the Congregation Shearith Israel, founded in 1654 by descendants of Jews who fled the

Spanish Inquisition, this synagogue was built in 1897 but contains remnants from its congregation's original synagogue, built on the Lower East Side in 1730. The Tiffany stained-glass windows are particularly impressive. The synagogue is located at 8 West 70th Street, between Central Park West and Columbus Avenue. Call 212 873-0300 for information about services.

Temple Emanu-El – Built in 1929 and capable of seating 2,500 people, this is the largest Reform synagogue in the world. It is located at 1 East 65th Street (at Fifth Avenue). Stained-glass windows and mosaics grace the interior, while the limestone facade is a beautifully carved combination of Eastern and Western architectural styles. Call 212 744-1400 for information about services.

Trinity Church – In the heart of the financial district, at the intersection of Broadway and Wall streets, this is the third building of an Episcopal church founded in 1698 on land donated by King William III of England. This building was completed in 1846, although the oldest headstones in its 2.5-acre graveyard date back to 1681. Alexander Hamilton is among those buried here. The church offers a small museum (for more information, see "Museums" in this chapter), guided tours (see "Tours" in this chapter), and concerts, in addition to its daily services. Call 212 602-0800 for information about services.

If you want to find out when services are held, the first section of the Saturday *New York Times* includes advertisements for Catholic, Protestant, Ethical Culture, Hindu, and a few Jewish services under the heading "Religious Services." The Manhattan Yellow Pages include extensive listings under the headings "Churches," "Synagogues," and "Religious Organizations."

Sights and Other Pleasant Places

Some of the places in New York that make this city unique don't fit neatly into "Museums," "Places of Worship," or any of the other categories included in this book. Many can be visited without a guide or a formal agenda – indeed, the pleasure of most of them is simply in walking around and gazing. A diverse lot, the following list includes some of the most famous, interesting, or unusual sights and other pleasant places in Manhattan. Unless otherwise noted, admission is free.

Alwyn Court Apartments – Of all the magnificent apartment buildings in New York, this is my favorite one to look at from outside. For the best view, cross the street. Built between 1907 and 1909, it sits on the corner of West 58th Street and Seventh Avenue. You could spend hours looking at the elaborate carved terra cotta exterior. Keep an eye out for the dinosaurs (or are they salamanders?) at about the fourth floor.

Brooklyn Bridge – Spanning the East River between Manhattan and Brooklyn, this was the world's longest suspension bridge when it was built, and it remains one of the most spectacular. The 5,989-foot bridge took 15 years (1868–1883) to build, and two generations of Roeblings are responsible for it. After John Roebling, the engineer who designed the bridge, died from injuries sustained in an accident, his son, Washington, and his wife, Emily, finished the project. You can get an incredible view of New York Harbor and the city's skyline by taking a stroll on the bridge's historic promenade. To reach it, go through the Municipal Building just off Park Row on the southeast side of City Hall and follow the signs in the subway tunnel. Better yet, ask one of the many policemen patrolling the area for directions.

Carnegie Hall – On the corner of Seventh Avenue and West 57th Street, this magnificent concert hall opened in 1891 with the American conducting debut of Peter Ilyich Tchaikovsky. Named for steel magnate Andrew Carnegie, it has been renovated to accommodate an audience of more than 2,800. For information about daytime tours, see the "Tours" section later in this chapter. For box-office information, call 212 247-7800 or just drop by the lobby. **Hours:** daily from 11 to 6; Sunday from noon to 6.

Castle Clinton National Monument – Probably the best known of the seven national parks in Manhattan – it's the gateway to two others and headquarters for them all – Castle Clinton is a red circular building in Battery Park, at the very southern tip of Manhattan. Built on what was then an island as part of a series of forts defending New York Harbor at the beginning of the 19th century, Castle Clinton has been different things through the years: an entertainment center, an immigrant receiving station (8 million immigrants came through here between 1855 and 1890), and the home of the New York Aquarium. Castle Clinton may be best known to tourists today as the place to buy tickets for the short boat rides to Ellis Island and the Statue of Liberty, but take a few minutes to visit the small museum detailing the site's history inside the door to your right as you pass through the gate. If you're looking for books about the area, prints, and post cards, try the small kiosk to the left of the ticket kiosk. Unfortunately, its staff is as disinterested as its selection is disappointing. **Hours:** daily from 9 to 5. The shop closes at 4:30.

Chrysler Building – One of New York's most recognized sights, this art deco building at 405 Lexington Avenue (between East 42nd and 43rd streets) was built as the home of the Chrysler Corporation between 1928 and 1930 at the dawn of the automobile age. Its stainless-steel spire is easy to spot, but take a closer look at the radiator-cap gargoyles, based on the 1929 Chrysler, and the racing cars built into the relief. The Chrysler Corporation no longer has offices there, and the interior isn't much to see, but the lobby is open to the public.

Citicorp Center – Among the newer additions to the New York skyline, this 59-story building on Lexington Avenue (between East 53rd and 54th streets) opened in 1977. Its slanted roof and modern design make the

Citicorp Building stand out among its more traditional neighbors, and its diverse shops, restaurants, and food court make it a favorite with the midtown lunch crowd. You'll find tables both inside and outside on the lower level along Lexington Avenue.

City Hall – Located between Broadway and Park Row on the northern edge of City Hall Park, City Hall was built in the early 19th century and has served as the offices of the mayor and other city officials ever since. The neighborhood surrounding it is as dirty as it is busy, but the building itself is quite grand and well worth the trip. The Declaration of Independence was read to General George Washington and his troops in the park outside, and Abraham Lincoln lay in state inside the rotunda here. The desk Washington used as president when New York was the nation's capital, some exceptional portraits of Washington and other figures from his time, and other fine antiques are up the marble staircase in the Governor's Room. Although security has been tight since the World Trade Center bombing, the building is open to the public. **Hours:** weekdays from 10 to 3:30, but call 212 566-8681 to be sure.

Cleopatra's Needle – This 3,000-year-old Egyptian obelisk is 77 feet tall and inscribed with hieroglyphics. A gift of Khedive Ishmael Pasha to the City of New York in 1880, it now stands behind the Metropolitan Museum of Art in Central Park.

Commodities Exchange – Located in 4 World Trade Center (the smaller building on the left as you enter the complex from Church Street), the Commodities Exchange is not as big or exciting as the New York Stock Exchange, but that means it's not usually very crowded either. **Hours:** The visitors gallery on the eighth floor is open weekdays from 9:30 to 3. Call 212 938-2025 before going, however, as the exchange often talks about moving to New Jersey.

Conservatory Garden – The only formal garden in Central Park, Conservatory Garden is also one of only several designated "quiet zones" in the city. Located in the park off Fifth Avenue at East 105th Street, the garden is not much to see in the winter, but it is spectacular in the spring, summer, and fall. **Hours:** every day from 8 a.m. until dusk.

Empire State Building – When people think of New York, this 102-story building is often the first image that comes to mind, and the views from the top live up to every expectation (assuming it's a relatively clear day or night). Conceived as a great office building but almost bankrupted

---

Even though it is not the tallest building in Manhattan, the Empire State Building attracts the largest crowds. Over 1.7 million visitors a year take the famous elevator ride to view the wonders of the city from the 86th floor.

when it opened in 1931 because of the Great Depression, the Empire State Building soars above its neighbors on Fifth Avenue, between West 33rd and West 34th streets. For those who like a real challenge, there are 1,860 steps between the first floor and the observation deck — and hundreds of brave souls actually go up most of them during February's Empire State Building Run-Up! Call 212 736-3100 for more information. **Hours:** every day from 9:30 to midnight. The last tickets are sold at 11:30. **Admission:** Tickets to the observation deck cost $3.50 for adults, $1.75 for children and senior citizens. The ticket office is through the lobby, to the left and down an escalator — just follow the signs and the inevitable crowd.

Federal Hall National Memorial — This fine example of Greek Revival architecture was built in 1842 as the U.S. Customs House, but the history of the site goes back much further than that. Indeed, this was the site of the first U.S. capital. That's right. New York City was the nation's first capital, and the building on this site housed the entire federal government for a year. General George Washington took the oath of office, becoming the first president of the United States, and Congress debated the Bill of Rights here. Before that, the building on this site was New York's first city hall (dating back to 1703). Federal Hall, at the corner of Wall and Nassau streets, is now a national monument run by the National Park Service and featuring exhibits on the site's history. **Hours:** weekdays between 9 and 5.

Flatiron Building — This 22-story architectural oddity was built at the intersection of Fifth Avenue and Broadway (at about 23rd Street) in the very beginning of this century. The prow of the building is said to be on the windiest street corner in all of Manhattan. Its triangular shape and terra cotta exterior have made it a familiar landmark in New York, and the neighborhood around it — the Flatiron district — carries its name.

Ford Foundation Gardens — The plant-filled atrium of the Ford Foundation's headquarters rises more than ten stories and is open to the public between 9 and 5 on weekdays. This warm, multilevel garden is a wonderful place to get away from it all, especially in winter. The plants are watered with rain and steam condensation gathered in a cistern, and any coins thrown into the little pool are donated to UNICEF. The building is at 320 East 43rd Street (between First and Second avenues), although you also can enter the atrium from East 42nd Street.

Grand Central Terminal — This grand but fading *beaux-arts* station was built at the turn of the century during the great age of railroads. It replaced a station built on the spot by Cornelius Vanderbilt after steam engines were banned south of 42nd Street in 1854. Scores of commuter trains to Westchester County and Connecticut arrive and depart here, but Amtrak has moved all its operations to Penn Station. There are lots of shops on the multilevel concourses, but the real pleasure of a visit to Grand Central is gazing out over the main lobby. (For information about a free tour, see the "Tours" section of this chapter.) You can enter through several doors on East 42nd Street, but by far the most dramatic entrance is through the driveway off Vanderbilt Avenue (a small street that runs parallel to and just east of Madison Avenue) at East 43rd Street. **Hours:** daily, except closed between 1:30 and 5:30 in the morning.

Grant's Tomb — Formally called the General Grant National Memorial, this is the not very subtle resting place of Civil War General and U.S. President Ulysses S. Grant and his wife. Built after Grant's death in the late 19th century, the interior was inspired by Napoleon's tomb in Paris. It's run by the National Park Service. You'll find it in Riverside Park, between Riverside Drive and the Hudson River. It's across the street from Riverside Church, near West 122nd Street. **Hours:** Wednesday through Sunday from 9 to 4:30.

IBM Garden Plaza — Although a number of office buildings in midtown have public sitting spaces on the first floor, this one is particularly pleasant and safe. An atrium full of flowers, trees, and bamboo is dotted with tables and chairs for conversation, a little quiet contemplation, or just a brief rest for the weary. The building has several entrances, but the main one is on Madison Avenue, at East 57th Street. **Hours:** daily from 8 a.m. until 10 p.m.

Jefferson Market Library — I've included this courthouse turned public library because it looks just like a castle in a fairy tale and people are always wondering what it is. Built in 1877, it's now one of the city's nicest libraries, and it has a wonderful community garden during warmer months. You'll find it at 425 Sixth Avenue (at West 10th Street) in Greenwich Village.

Lincoln Center — This amazing but sometimes overwhelming complex sits along Columbus Avenue between West 62nd and West 65th streets. (Don't be confused by Broadway, which intersects Columbus at about West 65th Street.) Constructed between 1959 and 1969, Lincoln Center includes Avery Fisher Hall, the New York State Theater, Alice Tully Hall, a wonderful public library and museum devoted to the performing arts, the Julliard School of Music, the Guggenheim Bandshell, the Vivian Beaumont Theater, and the Metropolitan Opera House. An open plaza, complete with a fountain, sits in the center of the complex, and small parks and open spaces flank the Opera House. You can wander around by yourself or take a tour. (See the "Tours" section of this chapter for more information.) Make sure to visit one of the two specialty stores inside the opera house or eat at one of the center's two restaurants. Call 212 875-5400 for the Lincoln Center information hotline.

Madison Square Garden — The only real sporting arena in Manhattan, Madison Square Garden plays host to everything from the International Cat Show to the circus to the New York Knickerbockers. This particular building opened in 1968. (There were three Madison Square Gardens before it, but none at this location.) It covers most of the blocks between Seventh and Eighth avenues from West 31st to West 33rd streets. Oddly enough, Penn Station—the terminal for Amtrak and New Jersey Transit, with 750 trains a day coming and going—sits directly underneath "the Garden." (Plans are afoot for a new Penn Station, across the street in the old Post Office building.) To find out what's going on at any given time, call the box office at 212 465-6741.

National Debt Clock—You'll find this unnerving clock by looking up on the west side of Sixth Avenue near West 43rd Street. It keeps a running tally of both the total national debt and the amount of that debt owed by a family of four.

New York Public Library—The main branch of the extraordinary New York public-library system is a treasure trove for researchers. This beautiful building sits on Fifth Avenue between West 40th and West 42nd streets, next to Bryant Park. The marble stairs and open areas outside—a favorite brown-bag lunch spot for people who work in the area—are dominated by two wonderful lion statues. You'll find a gallery with changing exhibits and a terrific gift shop on the first floor. A nonprofit group, Friends of the New York Public Library, offers tours of the exhibits and the library itself. For more information, stop by their desk in the lobby to the right of the front entrance or see the "Tours" section of this chapter. A new $100 million science, industry, and business library will open in the old B. Altman Building (E 34th St and Madison Ave) in 1995. Call 212 869-8089 for recorded information about the library, as well as current exhibits and special events. **Hours:** Tuesday and Wednesday from 11 to 7:30; Thursday, Friday, and Saturday from 10 to 6.

New York Stock Exchange—Although the elegant home of the New York Stock Exchange is on the corner of Broad and Wall streets, the visitors entrance is at 20 Broad Street, between Wall and Exchange streets. Tickets are handed out right outside or immediately inside the door for entrance to the two-tiered visitors gallery on the third floor, overlooking the trading floor. You will be turned away at the elevators if you do not have one. When the place gets crowded they stagger the tickets, and there may be a little bit of a wait before you can get in. Once inside, however, you can move around at your own pace. Call 212 656-5168 for more infomation. **Hours:** weekdays (except federal holidays) between 9:10 and 3:30.

Plaza Hotel—On the south side of Central Park South, just west of Fifth Avenue, this elegant old hotel is a sentimental and architectural favorite. A stroll through the lobby is a stroll through pure class. You might even catch a glimpse of Eloise (or at least her portrait)!

Radio City Music Hall—This 6,200-seat art deco wonder was the largest theater in the world when it was built in the early 1930s as part of the

Rockefeller Center complex. Its murals and art alone are well worth a visit, but Radio City is best known for its long-running Christmas and Easter shows, featuring the Rockettes. Call 212 247-4777 or drop by its lobby at the corner of Sixth Avenue and West 50th Street to find out what's scheduled. You can also tour Radio City. (See the "Tours" section of this chapter for more information.) **Hours:** daily from 10 to 8; Sunday from 11 to 8.

Rockefeller Center — The 19 buildings that make up Rockefeller Center stretch from West 47th to West 52nd streets, between Fifth and Seventh avenues, but the heart of it all lies between West 49th and West 50th streets, just off Fifth Avenue. Interesting stores, the famed statue of Prometheus, the ice-skating rink, and the beautiful Channel Gardens (planted in the spring, summer, and fall) are all here, in the shadow of 30 Rockefeller Plaza. Long known as the RCA Building but now owned by General Electric, "30 Rock" is the home of NBC's network studios. (See information about the NBC Studio Tour in the "Tours" section of this chapter.) Call 212 632-3975 for more information.

Roosevelt Island — If you want an experience that even most New Yorkers haven't had, along with some of the best views of the city's skyline, take the tram to Roosevelt Island in the middle of the East River. It leaves regularly from its station on Second Avenue, between East 59th and East 60th streets, and costs $1.40 per person each way. Although they are only minutes away from midtown Manhattan, the 7,500 people who live over here might as well be on another planet. Their island, which was known for its debtors' prison at one time and its insane asylum at another, is quiet, unhurried, and almost crime-free. For 10 cents you can take one of the rather elderly red buses that traverse the island from the tram station through the small shopping area to just south of Lighthouse Park on the island's northern end. Buy a map (they cost a quarter) at the tram station, and see the sights or just wander around. Whatever else you do, however, make sure to walk along the sidewalk on the island's west side to get a view of the skyline that is not to be believed.

South Street Seaport — This is the only place I've included in both the "Museum" section and this "Sights" section, because it's a little of both. The main entrance to this popular area is on Water Street at Fulton Street. (Anybody who tells you, by the way, that the walk on Fulton Street from the financial district to the seaport is "charming" hasn't done it for awhile.) The area stretches for several blocks between Water Street and the East River. If you've ever been to Quincy Market in Boston, you'll recognize the concept immediately: upscale shops, food courts, restaurants, and history all wrapped into one. South Street was one of the city's most important ports for many years, and this district was created more than two decades ago to preserve that history. You can stroll through the cobblestone streets, look at the early 19th-century buildings along Schermerhorn Row, and gaze at the tall ships, or you can buy a ticket that entitles you to tours of the ships and entrance to the seaport galleries and children's center. (For a few extra dollars, you can also take a cruise of New York Harbor.) Start your trek at the visitors center a block and a half inside the main entrance on Fulton Street. Call 212 669-9424 for recorded information or 212 669-9400 to talk to a real person. **Hours:** The South Street Seaport Museum is open every day from 10 to 5 during the winter and from 10 to 6 in warmer months, although many shops and restaurants in the area stay open much later.

Statue of Liberty — This 151-foot gift from France was built on Liberty Island in New York Harbor in 1886, and it has been among New York's most recognized sights ever since. Generations of immigrants remember seeing Lady Liberty and her raised torch when they arrived at nearby Ellis Island, and the Emma Lazarus poem ("Give me your tired . . .") still expresses the most noble instincts of our country. It's more than a little touristy these days, but a climb or elevator ride up to her crown or a stroll around the grounds can be fun for children and adults alike. A small exhibit tells you about the statue's construction. To reach the Statue of Liberty, you must take a ferry from Castle Clinton in Battery Park. (Your ticket also admits you to Ellis Island.) For more information about the ferry, call 212 269-5755. For more information about the Statue of Liberty, call 212 363-3260. **Hours:** 9:30 to 5 in the winter, 9:30 to 5:30 in the summer (although the last boat out to the Statute of Liberty leaves at about 3:30). **Admission:** $6 for adults, $5 for senior citizens, $3 for children between 3 and 17. This includes admission to both the Statue of Liberty and Ellis Island.

Steinway Hall — I listed this as a museum in the last edition of the book, but it really isn't a museum in the strictest sense. It is first and foremost the main showroom and sales gallery for Steinway & Sons pianos. But it's also an exceptionally elegant building with the finest collection of Steinway pianos and related memorabilia in the world. (Look for the grand with morning glories done in inlay.) If you are in the market for a piano or are just a real music buff, definitely stop by. But think of it as the extremely upscale gallery it is, and don't bring the kids. It's located at 109 West 57th Street (between Sixth and Seventh avenues). Call 212 246-1100 for more information.

Times Square — One of New York's best-known areas, it's unfortunately also one of the city's raunchiest and not really a place to go wandering. Located around the intersection of Seventh Avenue and Broadway at West 43rd Street, this is the southern end of the theater district and the location of the main TKTS booth. (See the "Tickets" section in this chapter for more information.) The square was named for the *New York Times,* which is located just west of the square on West 43rd Street. Heaven knows how much electricity is used for the lights around here, but everything from the XXX-rated movie houses to the news ticker competes for your attention with enormous, bright signs. The billboards here are some of the biggest in the world and are often rather risque. The area west of Times Square (along 42nd Street and Eighth Avenue around the Port Authority Bus Terminal) just goes from bad to worse. Watch your wallet around here.

Trump Tower – This 66-floor building, named for Donald Trump, is one of the newest additions to Fifth Avenue in midtown. You'll find it on Fifth Avenue, between East 56th and East 57th streets. The six-story pink marble atrium – complete with galleries, shops, restaurants, outdoor gardens (on the fourth and fifth levels), and a dramatic waterfall – is open to the public and is almost always crowded. Apartments begin on the 30th floor, although tenants come through a separate entrance to avoid the perpetual crowds. **Hours:** daily from 8 a.m. to 10 p.m.

United Nations – The United Nations runs along First Avenue (called United Nations Plaza) between East 42nd and East 47th streets. The flags of all member nations fly along the entire length of the complex, and you'll hear all sorts of languages being spoken inside the UN and on surrounding streets. The main visitors entrance, between East 45th and East 46th streets, is well marked and manned by UN guards. The park and plaza inside the gate offer wonderful views of the East River and comfortable benches. You will go through a security checkpoint inside the main building. From here you can wander through the enormous lobby, eat in the Delegates' Dining Room, or go on a tour. (See information in the "Tours" section, later in this chapter.) Downstairs is the wonderful UN post office and a great assortment of shops. An information desk is located in the middle of the main lobby, providing daily schedules of meetings and other events. Remember that the people who work here are involved in some pretty important projects. Look around and ask questions, but be quiet and respectful. **Hours:** weekdays from 9 to 5; Saturday, Sunday, and holidays from 9:15 to 5.

U.S. Customs House – This grand old *beaux-arts* building is located right outside Battery Park, directly across from Castle Clinton National Monument on Bowling Green, between State and Whitehall streets. The park in front of the building, the first "ornamental green" in the city, was established in 1733 and was the site of the 1765 Stamp Act riots. The building now houses Federal Bankruptcy Court for the Southern District of New York. (The customs operations are now in the World Trade Center.) There isn't much for visitors to see, but a small museum is scheduled to open in the rotunda in the summer of 1994.

Vietnam Veterans Memorial – If you've been to the unforgettable Vietnam Veterans Memorial in Washington, D.C., this smaller one is somewhat of a disappointment. It's made of green glass etched with excerpts from speeches given during the war and letters written by soldiers during their tours. The plaza surrounding it is full of places to sit and offers terrific views of downtown Brooklyn and New York Harbor. You'll find the memorial and the plaza between two enormous office buildings on Water Street, just up from Broad Street. (The actual cross street is named Coenties Slip, but I defy you to find that on any map!)

Washington Arch — Thanks to scenes in movies like *When Harry Met Sally,* you probably already have a pretty good idea of what this triumphal arch looks like. Erected at the end of the 19th century at the foot of Fifth Avenue, just south of 8th Street in Washington Square Park, the marble arch replaced a wooden structure commemorating the inauguration of George Washington (who was sworn in as president in New York). The arch could use a bath, but it's really quite beautiful.

Woolworth Building — This national landmark is among the city's most impressive office buildings. The lobby is a definite "don't miss" if you're in the area. Dime-store king F. W. Woolworth paid $13 million in cash to have his namesake building erected in 1913, and it remained the world's tallest building for more than a decade. You'll find it near City Hall on Broadway, between Barclay Street and Park Place.

World Trade Center — Unfortunately now best known because of the horrible bombing that took place here early in 1993, the center is a complex of office buildings dominated by the twin stories of 1 and 2 World Trade Center. (They are the second tallest buildings in the world after the Sears Tower in Chicago.) You'll find eight acres of stores and restaurants on the lower levels, all sorts of outdoor markets and events around the complex during the spring and summer, and a stunning observation deck on the 107th floor of 2 World Trade Center. The complex sits between West, Vesey, Liberty, and Church streets. Look for a TKTS outlet on the mezzanine floor of 2 World Trade Center. (For more information, see the "Tickets" section of this chapter.) For more information about the observation deck, call 212 435-7377. For information about the World Trade Center itself, call 212 435-4170. **Hours:** daily from 9:30 to 9:30 (until 11:30 in the summer). **Admission:** Tickets to the observation deck cost $3.50 for adults, $1.75 for senior citizens and children between 6 and 12.

World Financial Center — In the heart of Battery Park City, between Vesey and Albany streets at the Hudson River, the World Financial Center is in the newer part of an area known as the financial district and is home to many of the nation's leading brokerage and financial firms. Often confused with its bigger neighbor, the World Trade Center, this complex of four buildings surrounding the exquisite and always lively Winter Garden does indeed have a life and character of its own.

Sports and Recreation

Some people associate New York with fine food and expensive stores, while others link the city with the New York Yankees, the New York Knicks, or one of the city's other professional sports teams. In fact, the New York area is home to a number of professional sports teams —

although only two, basketball's Knicks and hockey's Rangers, actually play in Manhattan. Home field for the city's two football teams is across the river in New Jersey. Diagrams of all the various stadiums appear near the front of the Manhattan Yellow Pages.

Tickets for most regular-season baseball games usually can be purchased as late as game day, while tickets for football's Giants and Jets are almost impossible to find unless you have a generous friend who happens to be a season-ticket holder. If you're planning a trip to New York during any season, however, it's worth finding out which team is in town and who they're playing.

A word of warning: New York sports fans are like no others. They are loud, rude, and typically very knowledgeable about their teams and the sport they're watching. I'm not sure which would be worse: being a referee or a fan of the opposing team at a New York sporting event. A friend from Oregon who went to see the Knicks play the Portland Trail Blazers at Madison Square Garden recently would argue the latter!

New York Giants—The 1991 Super Bowl champions, the Giants play in the National Football Conference of the National Football League. To give you some idea of how likely it is that you will get tickets for a Giants game: if you put your name on the waiting list for season tickets today, you would have a wait of roughly three decades! Individual tickets are sold at least a season in advance. If you're really planning ahead, write the Giants at the Meadowlands, East Rutherford, NJ 07073, or call the box office at 201 935-3900. If you happen to get tickets (and have no alternative), you can take a bus between the Port Authority Bus Terminal and the Meadowlands.

New York Jets—The team made famous by Joe Namath, the Jets play in the American Football Conference of the National Football League. Tickets for Jets games are easier to score than those for Giants games, but you still ought to plan well in advance. They also play at the Meadowlands, but you should write the Jets at 1000 Fulton Avenue, Hempstead, Long Island, NY. You can also call the Meadowlands box office at 201 935-3900. You can take a bus between Port Authority Bus Terminal and the Meadowlands.

New York Knickerbockers—The Knicks, who dominated the National Basketball Association in the 1970s with such famous players as Bill Bradley and Willis Reed, play at Madison Square Garden. The better the Knicks are doing, the harder it is to get tickets. Try calling Ticketmaster at 212 307-7171, the Knicks' hot line at 212 465-5867, or Madison Square Garden's box office at 212 465-6741. Unlike the Meadowlands, Madison Square Garden is easily accessible by public transportation—it sits right on top of Penn Station!

New York Mets—The Mets play in major league baseball's National League. Their home is Shea Stadium in Queens, an easy subway ride away from Manhattan. (Take the 7 line from 42nd Street to the Willets Point/Shea Stadium stop.) Tickets for games are usually easy to get and, relative to their football and basketball counterparts, not very expensive. Call Ticketmaster at 212 307-7171 for tickets. You can also write the Mets at Shea Stadium, 126th Street and Roosevelt Avenue, Flushing, NY 11368, or call 718 507-8499 for more information.

New York Rangers – Like the Knicks, the National Hockey League's Rangers play at Madison Square Garden. You can call Ticketmaster at 212 307-7171, the Rangers' hotline at 212 308-6977, or the Garden's box office at 212 465-6741 to find out about tickets.

New York Yankees – The Yankees, the team America loves to hate, play in major league baseball's American League. Except for games against such historic rivals as the Boston Red Sox, tickets for Yankees games are relatively easy to get. They play at Yankee Stadium in the Bronx, known to many as the House that Ruth Built, because Babe Ruth played there in the early part of this century. It's an easy subway ride from Manhattan. (Take the 4 line from the East Side or the C or D line from the West Side to the 161st Street/Yankee Stadium stop.) Call Ticketmaster for information about tickets at 212 307-7171. You can also write the Yankees at Yankee Stadium, 161st Street and River Avenue, The Bronx, NY 10451, or call 718 293-6000 for more information.

U.S. Open – The U.S. Open, one of professional tennis' four grand-slam tournaments, is held in late August and early September at the United States Tennis Center in Queens. The finals are held over Labor Day weekend. Tickets to the semifinals and finals sell out immediately, but tickets for earlier rounds can usually be purchased in the weeks leading up to the tournament. Call Ticketmaster at 212 307-7171, or write the U.S. Tennis Center, Flushing Park, Queens, NY 11365. You can also call 718 271-5100 for more information.

If you can't get tickets for a game or would rather play yourself anyway, New York offers plenty of opportunities for recreation. Many people think of New York as nothing more than concrete and can't imagine what New Yorkers do for exercise other than walking. Those who live here, however, know that you can do just about everything in New York that people do anywhere else – and then some! Whether its miniature golf, riding horses, or scuba diving, chances are that New York has got it, if you just know where to look. Unless otherwise noted, call the Manhattan Department of Parks and Recreation at 212 360-8111 for general information or 212 360-8133 for permits.

Badminton – For information about tournaments and clubs in Manhattan and elsewhere, call the U.S. Badminton Association (914 923-3300).

Baseball – There are seven baseball diamonds in Central Park and at least a dozen more elsewhere in Manhattan.

Basketball — Between schoolyards and city parks, you'll find more than 1,000 basketball courts in Manhattan.

Bicycling — You can go bike riding in Central Park, Riverside Park, and even on the city's streets if you have the nerve. You can rent bicycles at the Loeb Boathouse (212 517-2233) in Central Park for $6 an hour. Most bicycle shops in the city also rent bicycles, although they will probably require a sizable deposit. If you're looking for company, call the New York Cycle Club (212 242-3900).

Billiards — Julian Billiard Academy (212 475-9338) at 138 East 14th Street (between Third and Fourth avenues) comes as close as any of the several dozen billiards clubs in Manhattan to the kind of pool hall you've seen in the movies. If you're looking for something a little more upscale, try Jack's Billiards (212 315-5225) at 614 Ninth Avenue, between West 43rd and 44th streets, or the Amsterdam Billiard Club (212 496-8180) at 344 Amsterdam Avenue, between West 76th and West 77th streets. If they aren't open 24 hours, they certainly come close.

Birdwatching — Call the New York Audubon Society (212 691-7483) for information about upcoming outings.

Boating — You can rent rowboats at the Loeb Boathouse (212 517-2233) in Central Park, near Fifth Avenue at about 74th Street, between May and early October. Believe it or not, you can also find a Venetian gondola, complete with gondolier, here on summer evenings. (For information about bigger boats, see the "Manhattan on the Water" section of Chapter 7.)

Bowling — Try Bowlmor Lanes at 110 University Place, between 12th and 13th streets (212 255-8188) or Leisure Time Bowling, on the second floor of the Port Authority Bus Terminal (212 268-6909).

Bridge — Try the Beverly Bridge Club (212 486-9477) at 130 East 57th Street or the Gotham Bridge Club (212 874-2180) at 27 West 72nd Street.

Carriage Rentals — Horse-drawn carriages are lined up across the street from the Plaza Hotel at the southeast corner of Central Park, on Central Park South. A ride costs $34 for 30 minutes. Other prices are printed on the outside of the carriages.

Chess, Checkers, and Backgammon — For $2 an hour, you can play to your heart's content at the Backgammon Chess Club (212 787-4629) at 212 West 72nd Street. You can also find a game of chess at the Chess Shop (212 475-9580) at 230 Thompson Street. In warm weather, you can usually find a game of checkers going at Washington Square Park or in the Chess and Checkers House in Central Park.

Croquet — Call the New York Croquet Club (212 860-5347) for suggestions.

Fencing – Try Blade Fencing (212 620-0114) at 212 West 15th Street or the New York Fencers Club (212 874-9800) at 154 West 71st Street, after 5 p.m.

Fishing – To fish on the Hudson, Harlem, or East rivers, or anywhere else with fresh water, you'll need a permit from the New York State Department of Environmental Conservation (718 482-4999). If you want to do some saltwater fishing and are willing to spend a couple hundred dollars, call New York Harbor Sportfishing (201 941-1988). The company is in New Jersey but will pick you up for a day of fishing in the shadow of the Statue of Liberty at South Street Seaport or on the pier at East 23rd Street.

Golf – Manhattan does not have either a 9- or an 18-hole golf course, but you can play golf at some of the nation's great courses with video technology at the Midtown Golf Club (212 869-3636), at 7 West 45th Street. You also can try your hand at miniature golf at Hackers, Hitters & Hoops (212 929-7482), at 123 West 18th Street. And if you have your heart set on a real golf course, call 718 255-4653 for information on public golf courses in New York's other four boroughs.

Handball – Try Club La Raquette (212 245-1144) in the Meridian Hotel, at 119 West 56th Street, between Sixth and Seventh avenues.

Horseback Riding – If you know how to ride, you can rent a horse at the Claremont Riding Academy (212 724-5101) for $30 an hour. It's located at 175 West 89th Street, just off Amsterdam Avenue, and you can ride either in Central Park or the Academy's ring.

Ice Hockey – On weekend mornings in season, you can join the Sky Rink Adult Hockey League (212 695-6555) on the 16th floor of 450 West 33rd Street or the free-for-all game at the Lasker Rink (212 996-1184) in Central Park, near West 106th Street and Lenox Avenue.

Ice-Skating – The most famous rink in New York and probably the world is the one in front of Rockefeller Plaza (212 757-5730), off Fifth Avenue between West 49th and 50th streets. Central Park has two rinks: Lasker Rink (212 996-1184), near 106th and Lenox Avenue, and Wollman Rink (212 517-4800), near East 68th Street. For a small, uncrowded rink, try Rivergate Rink (212 689-0035), at 401 East 34th Street. The appropriately named Sky Rink (212 695-6555) is on the 16th floor of 450 West 33rd Street. All of the rinks rent skates, but only the Sky Rink is open all year as an ice-skating rink.

Kite-Flying – Try Sheep Meadow in Central Park, near West 67th Street.

Lawn Bowling – Call the New York Lawn Bowling Club (212 997-5754).

Marinas – Some of the biggest marinas in Manhattan include the 79th Street Boat Basin, off Riverside Park in the Hudson River

(212 362-0909); Dyckman Marina, at Dyckman Street and the Hudson River (212 567-5120); and New York Skyports, at East 23rd Street and the East River (212 686-4546).

Miniature Car Racing — Try Manhattan Raceway (212 673-4100), at 893 Broadway, between East 19th and 20th streets.

Model Boats — Model boats may be sailed in the Conservatory Water in Central Park, near Fifth Avenue and East 74th Street. Regattas are held on Saturdays during the summer.

Racquetball — Try the Manhattan Plaza Racquet Club (212 594-0554), at 450 West 43rd Street, or Club La Racquette (212 245-1144), in the Meridian Hotel at 119 West 56th Street.

Rollerblading — You can rent rollerblades by the hour or the day from a number of places, including Blades West (212 787-3911) at 105 West 72nd Street, between Amsterdam and Columbus avenues, and Blades East (212 996-1644) at 160 East 86th Street, between Lexington and Third avenues. Look in the Manhattan Yellow Pages under "Skating Equipment and Supplies" for more options.

Roller Skating — Try the Lezly Skate School (212 777-3232) at 622 Broadway.

Running — Some of Manhattan's most popular places to run are Riverside Park and the 1.58-mile trail around the reservoir in Central Park. If you want other ideas or some company (the latter is always a good idea), call the New York Road Runners Club (212 860-4455).

Sailing — The Manhattan Yacht Club (212 619-3656), the only public sailing club in Manhattan, is located at the southern end of South Street Seaport.

Scuba Diving — PanAqua Diving (212 496-2267), at 166 West 75th Street, runs certification courses at various sites throughout the city.

Shooting — Try the Downtown Rifle and Pistol Club (212 233-5420) at 24 Murray Street or the Seventh Regiment Rifle Club (212 772-7219) at 643 Park Avenue.

Soccer — Central Park contains four soccer fields, including one on the Great Lawn behind the Metropolitan Museum of Art and three in the North Meadow at the top of the park.

Squash — Try the Park Avenue Athletic Complex (212 686-1085), at 3 Park Avenue; Park Place Squash Club (212 964-2677), at 25 Park Place; or Club La Racquette (212 245-1144) in the Meridian Hotel at 119 West 56th Street, between Sixth and Seventh avenues.

Swimming — You can find lots of public beaches in the other boroughs and on Long Island, but swimming in Manhattan is limited to pools. Call the Manhattan Department of Parks and Recreation for information about locations, hours, and fees at the various pools throughout the city.

Tennis – Manhattan has more than 100 public tennis courts.

Volleyball – Call the New York Urban Professional League (212 877-3614) for times and locations of their games.

If you're planning ahead or are going to be here for more than a week or two, call the New York City Parks and Recreation Department's press office (212 360-8141) and ask for their 60-page "Green Pages" listing of addresses, phone numbers, and descriptions of the literally hundreds of programs and facilities they offer.

Finally, you can find a little bit of just about everything at the various Y's in Manhattan. They include the 92nd Street YMHA (212 427-6000) at 1395 Lexington Avenue, the West Side YMCA (212 787-4400) at 5 West 63rd Street, the YWCA (212 735-9755) at 610 Lexington Avenue, the Vanderbilt YMCA (212 755-2410) at 224 East 47th Street, and the McBurney YMCA (212 741-9216) at 215 West 23rd Street.

Tickets

No trip to New York would be complete without going to see at least one play, musical, ballet, concert, or opera. The trick, of course, is getting tickets. People have written entire books about how and where to get tickets, and others have made pretty good careers out of procuring them for out-of-towners. What I've tried to do here is give you a variety of approaches to getting theater tickets and some directions to help you find out about other performances (if you want tickets to sporting events, see the first part of the "Sports and Recreation" section in this chapter). Keep your eye out for student and other discounts, but be forewarned that good deals for the best shows and performances in town are few and far between.

Broadway

Different people have very different things in mind when they say they want to see a Broadway show. Some have their hearts set on great seats at a Saturday night performance of the hottest show in town, while others are willing to sit anywhere to see anything. A lot of people fall somewhere between those two extremes. In addition, some people are willing to pay whatever it takes to see the show they want, while others just won't go if they can't get a great discount. Depending on your approach, here are some potential strategies:

The Hottest Shows in Town – Look in the Sunday Arts and Leisure section or the Friday Weekend section of the *New York Times,* the front of a current *New Yorker,* or the back of a current *New York* magazine to find the name, address, and phone number of the theater where the play or musical you want to see is being performed. You can find a list of Broadway or off-Broadway theaters and a map of the theater district in the front section of the Manhattan Yellow Pages. If you want to save a little money and pick your seat, go directly to the theater's box office right when it opens with cash or a major credit card. Ask to see the diagram of the theater if it isn't posted, although most theaters are small enough that everybody has a pretty good view. The best time to try is the middle of the week. If you're willing to spend a little extra and let random chance (in theory, it's "best available") pick your seat, call the phone number listed and give them your credit card number. Most phone numbers listed will be for Telecharge (212 239-6200) or Ticketmaster (212 307-4100). Both services charge a handling fee in addition to the ticket price. You can also try calling the Broadway Line at 212 563-2929 if you have a touch-tone phone. People with American Express Gold Cards ought to call 800 448-8457 to find out about special reserved seating at certain hot shows on certain nights.

Be forewarned: if it's really hot, the play or musical you want to see may be sold out the entire time you're in New York. If it is but you still have your heart set on seeing it, ask the hotel concierge for help, or look under "Ticket Sales – Entertainment & Sports" in the Manhattan Yellow Pages for the name and phone number of a ticket broker. Either way, this approach is going to cost extra – and above and beyond the full price of a Broadway ticket is pretty pricey indeed.

If You're Flexible – If you want to see a Broadway (or off-Broadway) show but are willing to be a little flexible and have some time, go to one of the TKTS outlets in Manhattan. Run by the Theater Development Fund, these outlets sell whatever tickets happen to be left for various shows on the day of performance for half price. (Call 212 768-1818 for locations and other information.) The most popular TKTS outlet is in Times Square at West 47th Street and Broadway. It's open from 3 to 8 daily (matinee tickets are sold from 10 to 2 on Wednesday, Saturday, and Sunday), and you can't miss the line. A less crowded TKTS outlet with better hours is on the mezzanine level of 2 World Trade Center. It's open from 11 to 5:30 on weekdays and from 11 to 3:30 on Saturday. (Matinee tickets go on sale here on the day *before* performance.) You must pay with cash.

The Theater Development Fund also offers extremely good deals on tickets to theater and other performances to its members. If you're a student, member of the clergy, on active duty in the armed forces, a teacher, union member, retired or performing artist and are planning well in advance, send a stamped, self-addressed envelope to the fund for an application. The address is Theater Development Fund, 1501 Broadway, New York, NY 10036. (Write "Attention: Application" on the envelope.) You can also call the fund at 212 221-0013.

Twofers – If you just want to see something on Broadway and save some money too, keep your eye open for twofers. These are one of the ways theaters sell tickets to less-than-hot shows. By exchanging them at a given theater's box office, you can get two tickets for (almost) the price of one. Twofers look like actual tickets and can be found in hotel lobbies, restaurants, and at the New York Convention and Visitors' Bureau (2 Columbus Circle, across from the southwest corner of Central Park).

Opera and Classical Music

I think it's safe to say that no other city in the world has as much music from which to choose as New York. Look in the "Annual Events" section of Chapter 7 for information about some of the free concerts offered here or in the "Dancing and Other Clubs" section of Chapter 7 for information about rock, big band, and jazz clubs. The front section of the Manhattan Yellow Pages contains diagrams of the major music halls. If you're willing to pay for the service, ask the hotel concierge for help if you have a particular opera or concert in mind and tickets are sold out. Also try getting half-price tickets at the Music and Dance Booth (212 382-2323) on the corner of Sixth Avenue and West 42nd Street, in Bryant Park. If you call in advance, they'll tell you their hours and what tickets are available. Otherwise, here's how to find schedule and ticket information:

Carnegie Hall – You'll find individual musicians, out-of-town orchestras and chamber music ensembles performing in Carnegie Hall all year. If you're planning well in advance, write Carnegie Hall, 57th Street and Seventh Avenue, New York, NY 10019 for a schedule and ticket information, or just drop by the lobby for a current schedule. You can also call the box office (212 247-7800) for current information.

Lincoln Center Chamber Music Society – To get schedule and ticket information about the Lincoln Center Chamber Music Society and other performances, write Alice Tully Hall, Lincoln Center, New York, NY 10023. You can also call CenterCharge (212 721-6500) or the box office (212 875-5030) for current information.

Metropolitan Opera – The opera season runs from fall through spring, but ticket sales are broken into three different periods. If you're planning well in advance, write the Metropolitan Opera House, Lincoln Center, New York, NY 10023 for a schedule and ticket information. You can also call the box office (212 362-6000) or drop by the box office inside the Opera House between 10 and 8 (noon to 6 on Sunday) for a current schedule and ticket information.

New York City Opera – The opera season runs through summer and early fall. If you're planning well in advance, write the New York City Opera, New York State Theater, Lincoln Center, New York, NY 10023 for a schedule and ticket information. You can also call the box office (212 870-5570) for current information.

New York Philharmonic – The Philharmonic's season runs from September through June. If you're planning well in advance, write the

New York Philharmonic, Avery Fisher Hall, Lincoln Center, New York, NY 10023 for a schedule and ticket information. You can also call Center-Charge (212 721-6500) or the box office (212 875-5030) for current information.

Dance and Ballet

New York is home to several world-class dance and ballet companies. Many of them (the American Ballet Theater and the New York City Ballet are exceptions) spend at least part of their season performing at the City Center Theater, at 131 West 55th Street (212 581-1212), and each has a slightly different season. Look for a diagram of the City Center Theater in the front section of the Manhattan Yellow Pages. Try getting half-price tickets for different performances at the Music and Dance Booth (212 382-2323) on the corner of Sixth Avenue and West 42nd Street, in Bryant Park. If you call in advance, they'll tell you their hours and what tickets are available. Otherwise, I suggest you write or call the specific company to get schedule and ticket information:

Alvin Ailey 211 West 61st Street, New York, NY 10023 (212 767-0590)
American Ballet Theater: The Metropolitan Opera House, Lincoln Center, New York, NY 10023 (212 362-6000)
Dance Theater of Harlem: 247 West 30th Street, New York, NY 10001 (212 967-3470)
New York City Ballet: The New York State Theater, Lincoln Center, New York, NY 10023 (212 870-5580)
Paul Taylor Dance Company: 522 Broadway, New York, NY 10012 (212 431-5562)

Tours

No matter what your interest, price range, or schedule, chances are that New York has a tour for you. I've divided the tours into four categories: tour organizers (largely for groups and corporate clients), tours of New York, tours of specific places, and walking tours. Some simply require you to show up and pay a couple of dollars, while others require reservations in advance and can be pretty costly. Some are well established and reliable, while others are either new or eccentric and may not be around by the time you read this. As with just about everything else, my advice is to write for a brochure or at least call ahead.

Tour Organizers

Art Horizons International — If your group is serious about art and you would like to meet some gallery owners or museum curators, give Art Horizons International a call and they'll help you arrange it. Their guides are extremely well qualified, and individuals can sometimes hook up with previously scheduled group tours. Call 212 888-2299 for more information or a brochure.

Brooks Country Cycling and Hiking Tours – If you like to ride a bike and want to explore what lies beyond the city for a weekend or during the week, give these folks a call and find out what they have scheduled. Brooks Country organizes tours of varying lengths, prices and levels of difficulty to Long Island, the Catskills, the Berkshires, and other nearby areas. (They also take trips to Europe and more distant parts of the U.S.) Accommodations and meals are included in the price. Call 212 874-5151 for more information or a brochure.

Dailey-Thorp Cultural Tours – In addition to organizing tours for opera and music lovers around the world, Dailey-Thorp teams up with the Metropolitan Opera Guild in New York to put together spectacular "deluxe" and "Opera Express" tours to New York involving the Metropolitan Opera, the New York Philharmonic, and the New York City Opera, as well as Broadway shows. People on the deluxe tours usually stay at the Peninsula or the Plaza hotels and have just about every need and want taken care of by a staff of real professionals. The "Opera Express" tours are a bit more down-scale (and cheaper) but run just as well. Call 212 307-1555 for more information or a brochure.

Doorway to Design – If you're organizing a trip to New York for people interested in high fashion, art, or interior design, Sheila Sperber and her staff can take you behind the scenes into private homes, gardens, galleries, and studios. Whether you want to spend a couple of hours or a couple of days, Doorway to Design can customize tours that are just right for your group of ten or more. Call 212 221-1111 for more information or a brochure.

Inside New York – Groups interested in gaining entree to wholesale lofts and other fashion showrooms regularly closed to the public ought to call these folks. Inside New York is staffed by fashion professionals, and their behind-the-scenes tours and special events are carefully designed for groups of 20 or more. Call 212 861-0709 for more information or a brochure.

Manhattan Passport – Run by Ina Lee Selden, this terrific company organizes customized trips and tours to New York and other places in the region for corporate clients and special-interest groups from the U.S. and other countries. Whether you're thinking ultimately elegant or a little offbeat, chances are Ina and her staff can make it happen. Call 212 832-9010 for more information or a brochure.

Viewpoint International – Whether you're organizing a gala event for thousands or just want a first-class customized tour put together for a couple of people, these very competent folks can help. Their extraordinary client list speaks volumes about the professional, reliable, and creative service you'll get here. While they're best known for corporate event work, Viewpoint International offers lots of interesting tours, too. Call 212 355-1055 for more information or a brochure.

Tours of New York

Circle Line – Particularly on warm days, the three-hour boat trip around the entire island of Manhattan on one of Circle Line's boats is a real treat. In addition to nice breezes, you'll get a good sense of how Manhattan is laid out and what neighborhoods are where. A guide offers commentary as you make your way down the Hudson River, into New York Harbor, up the East River, across the top of the island in the Harlem River and back down the Hudson. The boats leave from Pier 83 (at West 43rd Street and the Hudson River) and make at least several trips a day (almost a dozen at the height of the season) between mid-March and December. Tickets cost $18 for adults and $9 for children under 12. Call 212 563-3200 for more information or a brochure.

Gray Line – If you're feeling overwhelmed by New York and want to be completely anonymous as someone shows you the highlights, this may be your answer. Gray Line offers partial-day and full-day bus tours to a variety of areas: Lower Manhattan, Upper Manhattan, and just about everywhere in between. Most of the tours operate at least once a day, and some are offered in French, German, Italian, and Spanish, as well as English. Gray Line also offers package tours to places like West Point, factory outlets in Connecticut, Niagara Falls, and even Washington, D.C. The prices vary for different tours and for adults and children. Call 212 397-2600 for more information or a brochure.

Island Helicopter – One of several helicopter tours in Manhattan, this one takes off from the heliport at the eastern end of East 34th Street. Prices range from $55 to $119, depending on the flight pattern you choose. (For inexplicable reasons, you can save $5 per ticket if you purchase them from the hotel concierge rather than at the heliport.) They operate daily but require at least two passengers per flight. Call 212 683-4575 for more information or a brochure.

Liberty Helicopter Tours – This helicopter tour takes off from the heliport at the western end of West 30th Street. If you don't mind heights and are willing to pay the steep price (from $55 to $99, depending on the flight pattern you choose), this is a great way to see the city. They operate daily but require at least three passengers per flight. Call 212 629-5370 for more information or a brochure.

New York Double Decker Tours – This newcomer on the scene offers a combination of 12 optional stops (at places like the South Street Seaport, the United Nations, and Rockefeller Center) and a narrated tour of the city while you're on board. The buses, just like the double-decker ones in London (and just like the ones that used to run up and down Fifth Avenue in years past), operate every day between 10 and 5, making six stops at each sight. For $15 per adult ($10 for children and senior citizens), you can get on and off as many times as you want for two full days. Tickets can be purchased on the bus or at the company's offices in Suite 825 of the Empire State Building. Call 212 967-6008 for more information or a brochure.

Short Line Tours — These tours are big and institutional but with a twist — they use buses, boats, and helicopters. You can see a little or a lot, depending on the pre-established itinerary you choose. All tours leave from the Short Line headquarters in Times Square, and the cost depends on both the mode of transportation and the length of your tour. Call 212 354-5122 for more information or a brochure.

Tours of Specific Places and Areas

Backstage on Broadway — If you're interested in how a play or musical is put together or want to see what goes on behind the scenes (literally and figuratively), you won't want to miss this tour. The tour guides are actors, directors, and other theater professionals. Unfortunately, it's only offered for groups of 25 or more, but you ought to call and see if you can hook up with another group. Call well in advance, as reservations are required. The tour costs $8 for adults and $7 for senior citizens and students. Call 212 575-8065 for more information or a brochure.

Carnegie Hall — Lincoln Center may have the Metropolitan Opera and the New York Philharmonic, but Carnegie Hall is still synonymous with classical music. If you want to take a look around during the day, hour-long tours are offered on Monday, Tuesday, and Thursday at 11:30, 2, and 3. The tour costs $6 for adults, $5 for students and senior citizens, and $3 for children under 12. There's also a package that combines the tour with afternoon tea at the nearby Russian Tea Room. Call 212 903-9790 for more information or drop by the "House Manager" window inside Carnegie Hall's lobby at 153 West 57th Street, just off Seventh Avenue. The tours meet inside the lobby.

Cathedral Church of St. John the Divine — If you're even remotely interested in Gothic architecture or just want to see one of the most amazing and beautiful places in all of New York, I strongly encourage you to take a tour of this cathedral-in-progress. Located on Amsterdam Avenue at West 112th Street, this is technically an Episcopal church, but it makes a real effort to welcome people of all faiths. Regular tours cost $2 per person and meet at a table in the back of the narthex, inside the main doors at 11 on Tuesday through Saturday and after morning services at 1 on Sunday. The new "vertical tour" is definitely not something for small children or people who are afraid of heights. (You must sign a waiver at the outset.) It costs a little more but is as interesting as it is popular. Schedules vary and reservations are required. If you can get ten people together, the folks here will organize a tour tailored to your particular interests. Call 212 932-7314 for more information.

Central Park — This incredible park is so big that you may want to get the lay of the land by taking a 90-minute guided trolley tour run by the

Central Park Conservancy. It leaves at 10:30, 1, and 3 from the information booth at East 61st Street and Fifth Avenue on weekdays. The price is $14 for adults, $12 for senior citizens and students, and $7 for children under 11. Call 212 360-2727 for recorded information. You might also check with the city's Urban Park Rangers (212 427-4040) to see if they have any free walking tours scheduled.

Eldridge Street Synagogue — This beautiful synagogue was built by Eastern European immigrants between Canal and Division streets on the Lower East Side in 1887. Tours are offered every Sunday on the hour between noon and 4 (and by appointment on other days). Admission is $5 for adults, $4 for senior citizens, and $2.50 for students and children. Tours of the whole area and one involving Ellis Island are also offered. Call 212 219-0880 for more information or a brochure.

Federal Reserve Bank — Free tours of the gold vaults (which contain almost 11,000 tons of monetary gold) and other parts of this incredible place are given twice in the morning and twice in the afternoon on weekdays (except major holidays). You must make reservations at least one week in advance and have tickets mailed to you. Write to the Public Information Department at 33 Liberty Street, New York, NY 10045 or call 212 720-6130 to find out whether they have space on a day that works for you. You'll find the Federal Reserve Bank on Liberty Street between Nassau and Williams streets. No free samples!

Gracie Mansion — This historic mansion is located in Carl Schurz Park, overlooking the East River (at about East 88th Street and East End Avenue). It is the official residence of the city's mayor. Two morning and two afternoon tours are offered on Wednesday. (Special tours for large groups are available on other days.) The mansion only recently was opened to the public, and these tours are very popular. To make advance reservations, call 212 570-4751. A contribution of $3 for adults and $2 for senior citizens is suggested.

Grand Central Station — In addition to all sorts of walking tours, the Municipal Art Society conducts a free tour of Grand Central Station on Wednesday at 12:30. This schedule is always subject to change, and I encourage you to call before heading down there (212 935-3960). The tour meets at the Chemical Bank Commuter Express on the main concourse.

Harlem Renaissance Tours — If you want to go to the Harlem Jazz Festival, the Black Theater Festival, or other events in Harlem but would like some company and a well-informed guide, give Harlem Renaissance Tours a call. They can develop specialized tours of cultural events and just about anything else you want to see in Harlem. Prices vary. Call 212 722-9534 for more information or a brochure.

Harlem Spirituals — This extremely friendly company runs a variety of tours in and around Harlem. Whether you want to visit a jazz club, stop by historic buildings like the Morris-Jumel Mansion and the Apollo Theater, or go to church on Sunday morning to hear a gospel choir, Harlem Spirituals has a tour that's right for you. They also offer tours in Italian, German, Spanish, and French. All tours are by bus and begin at their offices in midtown. Prices vary depending on your itinerary. Call 212 757-0425 for more information or a brochure.

Lincoln Center — If the incredible Lincoln Center complex seems a little overwhelming but you are interested in seeing its magnificent auditoriums and concert halls, one-hour tours are given every day between 10 and 5. The tour costs $7.75 for adults, $6.75 for students and senior citizens, and $4.50 for children. (If that seems steep to you, check out the prices of opera and philharmonic tickets!) Lincoln Center stretches between West 62nd and West 65th streets along Columbus Avenue, and the tour office is on the lower level of the Metropolitan Opera House, directly in back of the main square. Call 212 875-5350 for more information or a brochure.

Lou Singer's Noshing Tour — This is the treat to end all treats. For $25 (plus food), you get a real taste of New York's Lower East Side and other areas, as well as the wonderful company of Brooklynite Lou Singer. I hesitated to include Lou's tour for years, because he's based in Brooklyn. (He offers some wonderful tours of that borough, if you want to venture out a bit.) But this tour is too good to leave out. Call 718 875-9084 in the evening for more information or a brochure.

Lower East Side Tenement Museum — In addition to visiting the museum itself, you can take fascinating guided walking tours of the Lower East Side, sponsored by the museum on Sunday afternoon. The tours cost about $12 per person and are worth every cent. Call 212 431-0233 for information about upcoming tours.

Metropolitan Opera — The Metropolitan Opera Guild offers 90-minute tours of this extraordinary place between the end of September and June on weekday afternoons and Saturday mornings. You should make reservations well in advance, but you can always call at the last minute to see if space is available. Tickets cost $7 for adults and $4 for full-time students. Call 212 769-7020 for more information or a brochure.

NBC Studios — Children under six are not admitted, but anybody else can take an hour-long tour of NBC's television studios for $8 per person. The quality of the tour varies dramatically depending on both chance (what famous person happens to be getting off the elevator when you're getting on) and whether some big news event is breaking. The tour leaves every 15 minutes between 9:30 and 4:30 daily from NBC's lobby on West 50th Street, between Fifth and Sixth avenues. Call 212 664-4000 for more information.

New York Public Library — An informative tour of the grand New York Public Library is offered free of charge Tuesday through Saturday at

11 and 2. It leaves from the Friends of the Library desk, to the right of the main entrance on Fifth Avenue, directly across from East 41st Street. Tours of the changing exhibits in the library's Gottesman Hall are also offered free of charge on Tuesday through Saturday at 12:30 and 2:30. Call the library's volunteer office at 212 930-0501 for more information.

Old Merchant's House — This Greek Revival row house was built in 1823 and now serves as a time capsule of 19th-century New York. The furniture and decorations are a real treat for anyone interested in antiques. Tours of the house, located at 29 East 4th Street in Greenwich Village, are offered between 1 and 4 on Sunday. (Large groups can arrange for tours at other times and days.) Call 212 777-1089 for more information.

Police Academy — You can take a free tour of the New York City Police Academy on weekdays, but you must schedule it in advance and arrive with identification. The Police Academy is located at 235 East 20th Street, between Second and Third avenues. Call 212 477-9753 for more information.

Post Office — Free tours of the main branch of the New York City Post Office can be arranged by calling 212 330-3605 or by writing the Manager of Communications, New York Post Office, Room 3023, New York, NY 10199. Children under 5 are not allowed on the tour, and children between 5 and 12 are not allowed in areas with mechanized equipment.

Radio City Music Hall — If you want to see inside this art deco treasure but don't want to attend a concert or other event, try one of the daily tours. Schedules vary depending on activities going on here, but the tour runs about an hour and costs $8 for adults and $4 for children under 6. Call 212 632-4041 for more information. Radio City Music Hall is located on the corner of Sixth Avenue and West 50th Street, and tours meet inside the main lobby.

Schapiro's House of Kosher Wines — It's not exactly the Napa Valley, but Schapiro's Winery on the Lower East Side offers one of the most interesting and certainly one of the most unusual tours in all of Manhattan. The tour is offered every hour on Sunday afternoon and costs $1 (samples included). This kosher winery is located at 126 Rivington Street, at Essex Street. Call 212 674-4404 for more information.

Trinity Church — A guided tour of this historic church at the intersection of Broadway and Wall streets leaves from the pulpit inside the sanctuary at 2 every afternoon. It's free, although donations are accepted. Call 212 602-0800 for more information.

United Nations — If you want to peek inside the chambers of the United Nations General Assembly and learn a little about this incredible organization, tours begin every 20 minutes between 9:15 and 4:45 every day of the week. Don't bring small children—if they are under 5, they will be turned away. The tours costs $6.50 for adults and $4.50 for senior citizens and students from high school age on up, and $3.50 for children between 5 and 14. The tours last between 45 minutes and an hour and are offered in languages other than English if visitors request it. The visitors entrance to the UN is on First Avenue, between East 45th and East 46th streets, and the tour desk is directly across from the entrance, past the main lobby and down the hall. Call 212 963-7713 for more information (or 212 963-7539 for information about tours in languages other than English).

Yankee Stadium—Groups of 12 or more can tour the dugout, press box, and other parts of "the House that Ruth Built" on weekdays, but advance reservations are required and tours are not given on game days during baseball season. Special rates are available for senior citizens and student groups, but the regular cost is $6 per adult and $3 per child. Call 718 293-6013 for more information or a brochure.

Most museums offer tours of specific galleries or their entire collection. Look under specific entries in the section on "Museums" in this chapter, or call particular museums of interest for more information.

Walking Tours

Adventures on a Shoestring—The name pretty much sums up this organization. For a $40 membership fee, you can go on any and all of the offbeat tours of the city and surrounding areas they put together for free. If you're just visiting, you can go along on most of their scheduled wanderings for $5. Call 212 265-2663 for more information or to get on their mailing list.

Big Onion Walking Tours—Seth Kamil and Ed O'Donnell are two enterprising and engaging doctoral candidates at Columbia University who share their vast knowledge of New York through a wide array of walking tours in different parts of the city. George Washington's New York, Historic Catholic New York, and the Civil War and Draft Riots are just a few of their many topics. These are the only people I know who offer a tour of Governor's Island! Prices vary, but none of the tours is very expensive. Call 212 439-1090 for more information or to get on their mailing list.

Citywalks—For $12 a person, you can take one of John Wilson's guided walking tours of the Lower East Side, Greenwich Village, or one of lower Manhattan's other neighborhoods. Most of his tours are on the weekend and last for two hours. Call 989-2456 for more information or to get on his mailing list.

Municipal Art Society—This terrific advocacy group offers a wide array of thematic and area-specific walking tours for people interested in the city's architecture and history. Most of the tours are led by historians. Topics include Midtown Lobbies, Immigrant New York, and Downtown Public Art. Tours are offered on different days and meet at different places, but all of them last about 90 minutes and cost $10 for adults and $8 for students and senior citizens. Call 212 935-9360 for more information or to get on their mailing list.

Museum of the City of New York — This museum makes a real effort to be part of the city rather than an aloof observer, and its walking tours are very much in keeping with that spirit. Typically held every other Sunday from April to October, the tours are led by experts and cost $15. Registration is required. Call the museum's education department at 212 534-1672, ext. 206, for information or to get on their mailing list.

New York City Cultural Walking Tours — Is there a neighborhood in New York that you've always wondered about and wanted to explore with a guide who can answer your questions? Call Alfred Pommer. For $25 an hour for four or more ($15 an hour for three or less), he'll meet you anywhere in the city and show you the sights. He also offers more than a dozen walking tours of different areas on Sunday afternoon all year long for $10 per person. Call 212 979-2388 for more information or to get on his mailing list.

92nd Street YMHA — This amazing institution often offers walking tours to complement its frequent lectures and other programs, as well as open houses in historic areas. Prices vary, but the guides are always very knowledgeable and the tours well run. They fill up quickly, and reservations are required. Call 212 415-5599 for more information or to get on their mailing list.

River-to-River Downtown Walking Tours — Ruth Alscher-Green, a retired high-school teacher and lifelong New Yorker, doesn't come cheap. (A two-hour tour costs $35 for one person and $50 for two, although she does offer special rates for groups and senior citizens.) I don't know of a better guide for a "river to river" walk in lower Manhattan. Call 212 321-2823 for more information or to get on Ruth's mailing list.

Sidewalks of New York — Even when these tours cover the conventional areas, they are anything but conventional. Ye Olde Tavern Tour, for example, takes you to historic bars and taverns in Greenwich Village, while another takes you to the homes of famous writers in the areas and sights mentioned in their works. The most unconventional of these tours is not a walking tour at all but rather a visit to some of the city's most famous murder sites in the "Murdermobile." (Call 212 388-2286 for information about that tour.) The walking tours cost $10 per person. Call 212 517-0201 for more information or to get on their mailing list.

Urban Explorations — Landscape architect Patricia Olmstead offers walking tours of Battery Park City, SoHo, Chinatown, the flower district, and just about any other neighborhood or district you want to see. She is the only person I know who offers a tour of Islamic Architecture and the dramatic 96th Street Mosque. She will happily design an itinerary if nothing in her current repertoire of well over a dozen different tours suits you. Most tours are held on weekends and cost $12 for adults and $10 for children. Call 718 721-5254 for more information or to get on her mailing list.

Urban Park Rangers — No, you didn't misread that. The City's Department of Parks and Recreation employs urban park rangers, and they give wonderful weekend walking tours and talks in Central Park and other parks throughout Manhattan and the city's other four boroughs. These tours are free, and many are geared to children. All of them are both fun and educational! Call 212 427-4040 for more information or to get on their mailing list.

A Week in New York

You could spend your entire life in New York and still never have time to see and do (and eat) everything this fabulous city has to offer. If you're here for a week or two, you obviously have a lot of choices to make.

The first thing you need to know when planning an itinerary is that some areas are best on certain days (SoHo on Saturday and the Lower East Side on Sunday, for example), while others shut down on the weekend (the financial district), Saturday (the Lower East Side), Sunday (SoHo and most of midtown), or Monday (many major museums). If your time is limited, I suggest you pick a couple of things you really want to do or places you really want to see and build your days around them. Check the hours of the places you're planning to visit, and plan your days accordingly, so you can make the most of your time here.

If you're at a loss — you want to see everything but don't know where to start — I've sketched an outline of the possible itineraries for seven days in New York that might at least give you some ideas or a place to start. In so doing, however, I do not mean to imply that the places I've included are necessarily better than others. Moreover, I do not recommend trying to do everything on every day, lest you drop dead of exhaustion!

Monday — Upper West Side
- Cathedral Church of St. John the Divine (Amsterdam Ave at West 112th St)
- Columbia University main campus (entrance off W 116th St, at Broadway and Amsterdam Ave)
- American Museum of Natural History (Central Park W, bet W 77th and W 81st St)
- Zabar's (2245 Broadway, at W 80th St)
- late lunch at Tavern on the Green (just off Central Park W, inside the park at W 67th St)

- Lincoln Center (Columbus Ave, bet W 62nd and W 65th St)
- Museum of American Folk Art (Columbus Ave, bet W 65th and W 66th St)
- dinner at Andiamo (in back of Café Bel Canto, 1991 Broadway at W 67th St)

Tuesday — Midtown

- Macy's (151 W 34th St, bet Broadway and Seventh Ave)
- Pierpont Morgan Library (29 E 36th St, at Madison Ave)
- New York Public Library (Fifth Ave, bet W 40th and W 42nd St)
- Saks Fifth Avenue (611 Fifth Ave, bet E 49th and E 50th St)
- lunch at the American Festival Café (in front of 30 Rockefeller Plaza, nr Fifth Ave and W 50th St)
- Rockefeller Center (bet Fifth and Sixth Ave and W 49th and W 51st St)
- Museum of Television and Radio (25 W 52nd St, bet Fifth and Sixth Ave)
- Museum of Modern Art (11 W 53rd St, bet Fifth and Sixth Ave)
- Trump Tower (Fifth Ave, bet E 56th and E 57th St)
- Bergdorf Goodman (Fifth Ave and 58th St)
- dinner at Docks (633 Third Ave, at E 40th St)
- Empire State Building observation deck (Fifth Ave bet W 33rd and W 34th St)

Wednesday — Museum Mile

- Conservatory Garden in Central Park (Fifth Ave at E 105th St)
- Museum of the City of New York (1220 Fifth Ave, bet E 103rd and E 104th St)
- Jewish Museum (1109 Fifth Ave, at East 92nd St)
- Solomon R. Guggenheim Museum (1071 Fifth Ave, bet E 88th and E 89th St)
- lunch at the Dean & DeLuca Cafe, in the Guggenheim
- Metropolitan Museum of Art (Fifth Ave, bet E 80th and E 84th St)
- Frick Collection (1 E 70th St, bet Fifth and Madison Ave)
- Bloomingdale's (1000 Third Ave, bet E 59th and E 60th St)
- dinner at Sette Mezzo (969 Lexington Ave, at E 70th St)

Thursday

- United Nations (First Ave, bet E 45th and E 46th St)
- Ford Foundation Gardens (320 E 43rd St, bet First and Second Ave)
- early lunch at Tropica (Met Life Building, 200 Park Ave)
- The Cloisters (Fort Tryon Park)
- Dyckman House (4881 Broadway, bet W 204th and W 205th St)
- Museum of the American Indian (Audubon Terrace, off Broadway, bet W 155th and W 156th St)
- Hispanic Society of America (Audubon Terrace, off Broadway bet W 155th and W 156th St)
- dinner in Harlem at Sylvia's (328 Malcolm X Blvd, bet W 126th and W 127th St)

Friday — Financial District
- Battery Park to Statue of Liberty and Ellis Island
- World Trade Center observation deck (2 World Trade Center)
- pick up half-price tickets for the theater (TKTS booth on the mezzanine of 2 World Trade Center)
- lunch at Delmonico's (56 Beaver St)
- New York Stock Exchange (20 Broad St, bet Wall and Exchange St)
- Trinity Church (Broadway at Wall St)
- Fraunces Tavern Museum (54 Pearl St, at Broad St)
- pre-theater dinner at La Resérve (4 W 49th St, bet Fifth and Sixth Ave)
- theater

Saturday — SoHo
- early lunch at Café (210 Spring St, at Sixth Ave)
- "gallery hopping" on and around W Broadway
- Alternative Museum (594 Broadway, bet Houston and Prince St)
- Museum for African Art (593 Broadway, bet Houston and Prince St)
- Contemporary Museum (583 Broadway, bet Houston and Prince St)
- Guggenheim Museum SoHo (575 Broadway, at Prince St)
- dinner at Provence (38 MacDougal St, bet Houston and Prince St)

Sunday — Lower East Side
- brunch at Katz's Delicatessen (205 E Houston, at Ludlow St)
- Lower East side shopping
- Lower East Side Tenement Museum (97 Orchard St, bet Delancey and Broome St)
- dinner in Chinatown at the Golden Unicorn (18 E Broadway at Catherine St)

IV. Where to Eat It: New York's Best Food Shops

Bakery Goods

A. ORWASHER BAKERY
308 E 78th St (nr Second Ave)   212 288-6569
Mon-Sat: 7-7

This family business has been in existence for over 75 years, and many of their breads are from recipes handed down from father to son. You'll find Old World breads that used to exist in the local immigrant bakeries and have become extremely rare. Over 30 varieties are always available. Hearth-baked in brick ovens and made with natural ingredients, the breads come in a marvelous array of shapes and sizes — triple twists, cornucopias, and hearts, just to name a few. Be sure to sample the onion boards, cinnamon-raisin bread, and challah, available on Fridays. It's almost as good as the home-baked variety. Best of all is their raisin pumpernickel, which comes in small rolls or loaves. When warm, it's moist, delicious, and sensational.

A. ZITO AND SON'S BAKERY
259 Bleecker St (bet Sixth and Seventh Ave)
212 929-6139
Mon-Sat: 6 a.m.–6:30 p.m.; Sun: 6–2

Those in the know, know Zito's. They flock here at sunrise to buy bread straight from the oven. Among Zito's fans are Frank Sinatra and numerous Village residents. They love Zito's because the bread crust is crunchy perfection, a sharp contrast to the soft, delicate inside. Two of the best sellers are the whole-wheat loaf and the Sicilian loaf. Anthony John Zito is proudest of the house specialties: Italian, whole-wheat, and white breads. The latter two come in sizes of 4, 7, and 13 ounces.

BONTE PATISSERIE
1316 Third Ave (bet 75th and 76th St)   212 535-2360
Mon-Sat: 9–6:30; closed Aug

Mrs. Bonte serves a delicious line of pastries and cakes. The style is decidedly French, but the taste has earned universal appreciation. The pastry is flaky smooth, the chocolates creamy satin, and the croissants and eclairs – well, they're perfection. Mrs. Bonte personally supervises the operation, and everything sold here bears the hallmark of a tremendously accomplished pastry chef. Her husband is just as talented.

BREAD SHOP
3139 Broadway (at La Salle St)   212 666-4343
Daily: 8 a.m.–9 p.m.

This tiny, out-of-the-way bakery, under the tracks at 123rd Street, supplies some of the best handmade, untainted-by-preservatives bread in the city. Their customers are mostly local stores and New York's better food shops, but if you arrive between 10 a.m. and 3 p.m., one of the house specialties will be available fresh from the oven. (A gastronomic treat unique to New York is walking into the neighborhood bagel shop and sampling "whatever's hot.") Jenny Buchanan and Jim Fitzer, who run the shop, are big on healthy, natural ingredients, so the bread is not only delicious but good for you.

BUDAPEST PASTRY
207 E 84th St (bet Second and Third Ave)
212 628-0721
Mon.-Sat: 7:30-7:30; Sun: 9:30-5:30

In 1985, Al Maghrebi, a Syrian baker, bought Budapest Pastry from its Hungarian owners. The resulting mixture of baking styles was a success. Of course, they had a few things in common. The Hungarians stuff the thin, flaky babka, strudel, and baklava dough with cabbage or apples, while Middle Easterners stuff the same kinds of dough with spinach or eggplant. They also make cakes for birthdays and other personalized cakes. Nowadays the bakery resounds with a mix of Syrian bakers, Hungarian pastry lovers, and all kinds of falafel fans who come together to form a model of foreign relations the UN would envy.

CAFÉ LALO
201 W 83rd St (at Amsterdam Ave)   212 496-6031
Mon-Thurs: noon–2 a.m.; Sat: 11 a.m.–4 a.m.;
Sun: 11 a.m–2 a.m.

This is the best dessert shop in town, in my opinion. You will think you are in a fine European pastry shop as you enjoy fine cappuccino, espresso, cordials, and a large selection of delicious desserts. I know good cakes and pastries, as I judge them at the state fair every year. At Café Lalo there are 38 kinds of cake, 12 flavors of cheesecakes, and 18 different pies! Yogurt and ice cream are also available, and soothing music makes every calorie go down sweetly.

CHELSEA BAKING COMPANY
259 W 19th St (bet Seventh and Eighth Ave)
212 242-7692
Daily: 7-7

The Chelsea Baking Company is a wholesale source for restaurants, caterers, and gourmet stores, but it's also open to retail customers who call in advance. I rate David Talbot's deep-dish apple pie the very best in New York. The food is divided into three lists to accommodate wholesale customers. The top is the Signature line, which, Talbot says, offers the finest ingredients, style, and presentation available. The layer-cake line features a renowned cheesecake, a Mandarin cream cake, and a real Key lime pie, while the breakfast line includes all-butter Danishes and croissants. Chelsea Baking also specializes in custom orders; you can get superb wedding cakes, birthday cakes, or other special-occasion cakes—all made to order.

COLETTE'S FRENCH PASTRIES
1136 Third Ave (bet 66th and 67th St)   212 988-2605
Mon-Fri: 7:30–7; Sat: 7:30–6

Some of the best restaurants in the city buy cakes from Colette's, knowing that the French pastry made and sold here is unexcelled. A mail-order following developed from former New Yorkers and tourists. (They ship anywhere within the United States.) The star is the Trianon (a dark, heavy chocolate), but the croissants, brioche, mousse cakes, fruit and chocolate charlottes, specialized cakes, petit fours, tarts, and cheesecakes are just as good. Colette's is not the place to start a diet, but it's the place for a restaurant-quality dessert. Takeout foods are available.

CREATIVE CAKES
400 E 74th St (at First Ave)   212 794-9811
Tues-Fri: 8–4:30; Sat: 9–11

Being in the "creative cake" business myself, I know about the fun involved in making all kinds of unusual concoctions. Creative Cakes knows how to have fun, using fine ingredients and ingenious patterns. Cake lovers are fans of the fudgy chocolate with frosted buttercream icing and the sensational designs. Bill Schutz, the boss, has designed Bella Abzug's hat on a platter and even made a copy of the U.S. Customs House for a Fourth of July celebration. Prices are reasonable, and the results are sure to be a conversation piece at any party.

DUFOUR PASTRY KITCHENS
808 Washington St   212 929-2800
Mon-Fri: 7–5; call for Sat hours

The location is not the handiest. The air is full of pastry dough, so you shouldn't wear your best black outfit. And all items are frozen, so you'll have to bake them yourself (instructions included). But these are the only drawbacks! You'll find delicious and creative pastry items of high quality at sensible prices at Dufour, which counts many fancy up-town restaurants among its regular customers. Chocolate and regular puff-pastry dough is available in sheets and in bulk. Wonderful hors d'oeuvres can be ordered in quantity: bite-size, hand-filled "party lites" in flavors like fresh-mushroom pâté, Swiss and spinach, Southwestern black bean, smoked salmon, Caribbean pâté, Indian curry, and ratatouille. Enchilada corn cups are a delicious melt of green chilies, tomatoes, and cheeses in a tasty corn shell. Try the apple and spice turnovers for desserts. Great lunch puffs—chili with fresh vegetables, tuna melt, smoked salmon, broccoli-spinach gratin, and more—provide a satisfy-ing and light meal. Holiday strudels are also available. And all ingre-dients are natural.

ECCE PANIS
1120 Third Ave (bet 65th and 66th St)   212 535-2099
Mon-Fri: 9–8; Sat, Sun: 9–6

1260 Madison Ave (off 90th St)   212 348-0040
Mon-Fri: 9–7; Sat, Sun: 9–6

Evelina, the boss, says that bread is their passion, and it shows. The varieties are creative, to say the least. Come take a look, then take home a loaf of chocolate bread! Breads include dark and light sourdough, neo-Tuscan, whole-wheat currant, double walnut, Sunday raisin, and more. The chocolate *biscotti* is superb! Unusual gift baskets are a specialty.

EROTIC BAKER
582 Amsterdam Ave (bet 88th and 89th St)
212 362-7557
Mon-Sat: 11–7

In keeping with the spirit of the times, this shop is not as erotic as it used to be. Yes, they still make and stock X-rated cookies, cakes, and chocolates, but now they also make cakes for advertisers. Well, as long as they don't mix up the deliveries, everything should be okay. I'd hate to think what would happen if they sent out the wrong kind of cake!

FERRARA PASTRIES
195 Grand St (bet Mulberry and Mott St)   212 226-6150
Daily: 8 a.m.–midnight

This store in Little Italy is probably one of the largest "little grocery stores" in the world. The business deals in wholesale imports and several other ventures, but it is easy to believe that the sheer perfection of their confections and groceries could support the whole business. Certainly, the atmosphere would never suggest that this is anything but a very effi-ciently run Italian grocery store. Their Old World Caffe is famous for its numerous varieties of pastry, gelati, and coffee.

GERTELS
53 Hester St   212 982-3250
Sun-Thurs: 7–5:30; Fri: 7–2

The customers who come here are almost evenly divided between those who call this place Ger*tells* (accent on the last syllable) and those who call it *Girt*ils (as in girdles), but all agree that the cakes and breads here are among the best in New York. Locals prefer the traditional babkas, strudels, and kuchens, but I find the chocolate rolls and chiffon blackout cake to be outstanding. For those who want to sample the wares, there are tables where customers can enjoy baked goods, coffee, or a light lunch. From the regulars at these tables, one can glean the choicest shopping tidbits on the Lower East Side. A final tip: every Thursday and Friday, Gertels makes a potato kugel that is unexcelled. People have come all the way from California for a Thursday kugel! During a slow week, you can occasionally find one left over on a Sunday. It's good then, too. (Note: They will ship anywhere in the United States.)

GLASER'S BAKE SHOP
1670 First Ave (bet 87th and 88th St)   212 289-2562
Tues-Sat: 7–7; Sun: 7–4
Closed July and half of Aug

If it's Sunday, it won't be hard to find Glaser's. The line frequently spills outside as people queue up to buy the Glaser family's fresh cakes and baked goods. And *one* isn't enough of anything here. Customers always walk out with arms bulging. The Glasers run their shop as a family business and pride themselves on their breads, cakes, cookies, and wedding cakes. Try their chocolate-chip cookie!

GROSSINGER'S UPTOWN
570 Columbus Ave (at 88th St)   212 874-6996, 800 479-6996
Mon-Fri: 8–6; Sun: 9–5

Grossinger's was once known as Grossinger's on Columbus Avenue, when that street was plain and drab, a far cry from today's trendy boulevard. Since 1935 Grossinger's has also been known for top-quality cheesecakes and ice-cream cakes—and a great homey aroma. The uptown operation is the only on-premises kosher bake shop on Columbus Avenue.

H&H BAGEL
2239 Broadway (at 80th St)   212 595-8000
Daily: 24 hours

H&H starts baking fresh bagels at 2 a.m., an hour at which you can get a piping hot bagel without having to wait on H&H's long daytime line. But the biggest plus is that you can satisfy your bagel craving at *any* hour of the day or night at H&H. Another only-in-New-York special, they are the best in Manhattan.

KOSSAR'S BIALYSTOKER KUCHEN BAKERY
367 Grand St   212 473-4810, 212 674-9747
Daily: 24 hours

Tradition has it that the bialy derives its name from Bialystoker, where they were first made. Kossar's brought the recipe over from Europe almost a century ago, but the bialys, bagels, horns, and onion boards are as fresh as the latest batch from the oven. The taste is Old World, and those who have never had one should try these authentic versions.

LET THEM EAT CAKE
287 Hudson St (at Spring St)   212 989-4970
Mon-Fri: 7:30–5

Just talking to Gloria Tarigo, who runs Let Them Eat Cake, makes one hungry. She will describe to you the great desserts of the house: carrot cake, chocolate velvet cake, bourbon pecan pie, triple chocolate layer cake, raspberry nut torte, and many more. All are made on the premises and are of top quality. The retail shop is open to the public, and it serves sandwiches, soups, a few hot dishes, and the house specialty desserts, which can be eaten here or taken out. Catering for corporate events or parties is available.

LITTLE PIE COMPANY
424 W 43rd St (at Ninth Ave)   212 736-4780
Mon-Fri: 8–8; Sat: 10–6; Sun: noon–5

Former actor Arnold Wilkerson started baking apple pastries for restaurants and food stores when he was working in his own kitchen. Now he and Michael Deraney operate a unique attraction—a shop that makes handmade pies and cakes using fresh seasonal fruits. Although they specialize in apple pie (available every season), they also make fresh peach, cherry, blueberry, and other all-American fruit pie favorites. Stop by for a hot slice of pie à la mode, along with a cup of cider. There also are delicious brownies, bars, and muffins. Yankee Doodle never had it so good!

MOISHE'S HOME MADE KOSHER BAKERY
181 E Houston St (bet Orchard and Allen St)   212 475-9624
Sun-Thurs: 7 a.m.–6:00 p.m.; Fri: 7–4

115 Second Ave   212 505-8555
Sun-Thurs: 7 a.m.–8:45 p.m.; Fri: 7–5

Jewish bakery specialties are legendary, and they are done to perfection at Moishe's. The corn bread is prepared exactly as it was in the old country (and as it should be now). The pumpernickel is dark and moist, and the ryes are, well, simply scrumptious. The house specialty is the black Russian pumpernickel, which probably cannot be bested in an old-fashioned bakery in Russia. But by no means should you ignore the cakes and pies. Owners Mordechai and Hymie are charming and eager to please, and they run one of the best bakeries in the city. There is the usual complement of bagels, bialys, cakes, and pastries. Most of all, try the challah on Thursday and Friday; Moishe produces the best. The chocolate layer cakes are also superb.

NEW FIRST AVENUE BAKERY
121 First Ave (at 7th St)   212 674-5699
Mon-Sat: 6 a.m.–7 p.m.

This is an old-fashioned bakery with one of the best reputations in town. The diverse ethnic makeup of the neighborhood is reflected in the variety of breads made here. The quality is endorsed by the local natives from Italy, Poland, the Ukraine, and Russia, who claim the bread tastes as good as grandma's, if not great-grandma's! There is so much to recommend: The pumpernickel is dark and moist, and it tastes nothing like the commercial variety. The babka smells irresistible, and it is. And the Italian breads are so authentic they include a pizza dough. The Jewish contingent is represented by bagels and bialys. Each group thinks New First Avenue is *their* bakery. Could there be a higher compliment?

PALERMO BAKERY
213 First Ave (bet 12th and 13th St)   212 254-4139
Mon-Sat: 7–7, Sun: 7–3

A made-in-the-back specialty is featured here each day. The best is the pork bread—huge slices of pork inside a delicate dough, topped with a crackling crust. Palermo Bakery routinely produces bread in the most unusual and contorted shapes you can imagine, and they taste wonderful. Some of the exotic baked goods include the prosciutto bread, which contains bits of Italian salami, ham, and Lucatelli cheese. Then there's the French-style butter cookies, breadsticks, challah, and babka. Don't miss this very inexpensive gourmet tour of the Old World.

PARISI BAKERY
198 Mott St (bet Broome and Kenmare St)   212 226-6378
Mon-Sat: 7:30–6

If you want to taste Italian bread that has been made the same way for untold generations, then hurry to Parisi. Joe Parisi dispenses whole-wheat bread, peasant bread, meat bread, *focaccia,* rolls, homemade salads, sandwiches, knishes, and more. Prices are really in the bargain range, and the same quality standards have been passed on to customers since 1928!

PATISSERIE LANCIANI
271 W 4th St (bet Perry and W 11th St)   212 929-0739
Tues-Thurs: 8 a.m.–11 p.m.; Fri, Sat: 8 a.m.–midnight;
Sun, Mon: 8 a.m.–10 p.m.

For those who haven't yet observed the delicacies at Patisserie Lanciani, a quick review of Joseph Lanciani's extensive credentials is in order. For starters, you have certainly seen Joseph's work. While chief pastry chef at the Plaza (enough of a recommendation in itself), he was the creator of Julie Nixon's wedding cake. He is also a certified expert in spun-sugar creations, and is one of the best pastry chefs in the city. Results of this experience can now be sampled firsthand in Lanciani's own shop. The cakes, pastries, tortes, mousses, and breads defy description, and for those too impatient to wait, there are tables.

PATISSERIE LES FRIANDISES
972 Lexington Ave (bet 70th and 71st St)   212 988-1616
Mon-Fri: 8–7; Sat: 8–5:30

665 Amsterdam Ave (bet 92nd and 93rd St)   212 316-1515
Tues-Sat: 8–6; Sun: 8:30–3

Owner Jean Kahn has refined her pastry talents on both sides of the Atlantic. Now she offers New Yorkers wonderful breakfast specialties (like really sticky sticky buns), super tarts (try the apple almond), and pies (like the mile-high Granny Smith apple pie). There is also a selection of other delectables, like double chocolate truffles and chocolate-chip walnut brownies. The east side location has a place for specialty teas and coffees, and Jean offers outstanding desserts for tasty occasions.

POSEIDON GREEK BAKERY
629 Ninth Ave (bet 44th and 45th St)   212 757-6173
Tues-Sat: 9–7; Sun: 10–4

Poseidon is a family-run bakery that endlessly and effortlessly produces Greek specialties. Tremendous pride is evident here. When a customer peers over the counter and asks, "What is that?" the response is usually a long description and sometimes an invitation to taste. There is homemade baklava, strudel, *kataif, trigona, tiropita* (cheese pie), *spanakopita* (spinach pie), *saragli,* and phyllo. Poseidon was founded in 1922 by Greek baker Demetrios Anagnostou. Today it is run by grandsons John and Anthony Fable to the same exacting standards. Poseidon's specialty is handmade phyllo pastry, which is world-renowned. Any and all Greek specialties using phyllo are turned out here.

RIGO HUNGARIAN VIENNESE PASTRY
318 E 78th St (bet First and Second Ave)   212 988-0052
Tues-Sat: 8–6; Sun: 9–4; closed Aug

Many European-type pastry shops have products that look great, but when you taste them, it's a different story. Not this one. Delicious homemade strudels, sacher torte, petit fours, linzer tortes, coffee cakes, and cookies of all kinds are first-rate. No preservatives are used. Wedding and birthday cakes are a specialty.

ST. FAMOUS BREAD
796 Ninth Ave (at 53rd St)   212 245-6695
Daily: 7 a.m.–8 p.m.

You can tell from the minute you walk in this shop that everything is baked fresh; their kitchen is busy all night. You get to choose from a real international selection: sourdough breads, homemade muffins, corn bread, *focaccia,* orange poppyseed, banana-walnut bread, Irish soda bread, all kinds of croissants, and many daily specials. The folks here seem to be genuinely happy to see you, and I guarantee you will not leave empty-handed!

STREIT MATZOTH COMPANY
150 Rivington St   212 475-7000
Sun-Thurs: 9–5

Matzoth, for the uninitiated, is a thin, waferlike square cracker, which, according to tradition, came out of Egypt with Moses and the children of Israel when they had to flee so swiftly there was no time to let the bread rise. Through the years, matzoth was restricted to the time around Passover, and even when matzoth production became automated, business shut down for a good deal of the year. But not today and not in New York. In a small building with a Puerto Rican mural stretching the length of one side, Streit's matzoth factory pours forth matzoth throughout the year, pausing only on Saturday, Jewish holidays, and to clean the machines. Streit's factory not only allows a peek at the actual production—which is fascinating, because it is both mechanized and extremely primitive at the same time—but it also sells matzoth to the general public. It is baked in enormous thin sheets that are later broken up. The matzoth is so fresh that if you ask for a batch that happens to be baking, they will often break it off the production line for you.

SYLVIA WEINSTOCK CAKES
273 Church St (bet Franklin and White St)   212 925-6698
Mon-Fri: 9–6

Sylvia Weinstock has been in the cake business for over a decade, so she knows how to satisfy customers who want the very best. Her trademark is floral decorations: they are almost lifelike! Although weddings are a specialty, she will produce a masterpiece for any occasion. The next time you are interviewed by Barbara Walters, ask her about Sylvia. She made Walters' wedding cake!

VESUVIO BAKERY
160 Prince St (bet W Broadway and Thompson St)
212 925-8248
Mon-Sat: 7–7

Tony Dapolito was born and bred (no pun intended), in his family's store in SoHo. Since that time, the family's expertise in baking has grown along with the bakery's claim to fame as SoHo's common green. When he's not manning the ovens, Tony serves stints on the community planning board and disperses SoHo lore to customers. Visitors unaware of Dapolito's status (it doesn't remain a secret long) come for the bread, biscuits, and rolls. They all have a reputation that reaches far beyond SoHo. After all, it isn't every commercial bakery that eschews sugar, shortening, and preservatives and still manages to produce the tastiest Italian bread around. Try the *biscotti,* the pepper biscuits, or the wholewheat brick oven-baked bread. And if you have any questions about the bread or SoHo, Tony will supply you with a slice of SoHo life.

WHOLE EARTH BAKERY & KITCHEN
70 Spring St (bet Broadway and Lafayette St)   212 226-8280
Mon-Sat: 8 a.m.–9 p.m.; Sun: 9–6

This is the only bakery in Manhattan that makes baked goods using exclusively organic flours. No animal products, no honey, no egg whites are used here, and all of their products are sugar free. For the health conscious, this is a good bet.

YONAH SCHIMMEL
137 E Houston St   212 477-2858
Daily: 8–6

Yonah Schimmel has been selling perfect knishes for so long that his name is legendary, and national magazines have written articles about him. Schimmel started out dispensing knishes among the pushcarts of the Lower East Side, and a Yonah Schimmel knish is still a unique experience. It doesn't, incidentally, look or taste anything like the massproduced things sold in supermarkets, at lunch stands, or at New York ballgames. A Yonah Schimmel knish has a very thin, flaky crust—almost like strudel dough—surrounding hot, moist filling. The best-selling filling is potato, but there is also kasha (buckwheat), spinach, and a halfdozen others. No two knishes come out exactly alike, since each is handmade, but if a particular batch is not up to par, the man behind the counter won't sell it.

Beverages

B&E QUALITY
511 W 23rd Ave   212 243-6559
Mon-Sat: 9-7

If you are planning a party and want to make a quantity purchase of beer and soda, this is a good place to go. They are a wholesale distributor but will also pass along savings to retail customers.

RIVERSIDE BEER AND SODA DISTRIBUTORS
2331 Twelfth Ave   212 234-3884
Mon-Sat: 9-6

Run by Hector Borrero, this place mainly supplies wholesalers and large retail orders, but he's not averse to serving retail customers. The only reason most orders aren't small is because once you've shlepped up there, you might as well take advantage of the good discount. He guarantees that his prices are at least as low as any supermarket's.

British

MYERS OF KESWICK
634 Hudson St (bet Horatio and Jane St)   212 691-4194
Mon-Fri: 10-7; Sat: 10-6; Sun: noon-5

In case you haven't noticed, the British are coming—again! According to the British Information Services, the number of expatriate Brits in the city has topped 100,000. Two of them, Peter and Irene Myers, are now doing with English food what Burberry, Church, and Laura Ashley have done with English clothing. They've made it possible for you to visit "the village grocer" for imported staples and fresh, home-baked items you'd swear came from a kitchen in SoHo—the London neighborhood, that is. Among the tins, a shopper can find Heinz treacle sponge pudding, trifle mix, ribena, mushy peas, Smarties, Quality Street toffee, lemon barley water, chutneys, jams and preserves, and all the major English teas. The fresh goods include sausage rolls, kidney pie, Scotch eggs, Aberdeen kippers, and sides of salmon. There are also cheeses (the double Gloucester is outstanding) and chocolates. For Anglophiles and expatriates alike, Myers of Keswick is a *luverly* treat.

Candy

CHOCOLATE PHOTOS/
CHOCOLATE CROSSWORDS
637 W 27th St (9th Floor)   212 714-1880
Mon-Fri: 9-6

Chocolate Photos was founded on the premise that nearly anything can be created in chocolate . . . and taste good, too. Unique items are ideal for gifts of all kinds, company logos, and you-name-it novelties. They are all custom-molded chocolate, with a minimum of 100 units packaged per order. The newest item is "Chocolate Crosswords": chocolate letters and numbers arrayed on a board to spell out any message.

ECONOMY CANDY
108 Rivington St 212 254-1531, 800 352-4544 (outside NY)
Sun-Fri: 8–6; Sat: 10–5

The same family of owners has been selling everything from penny candies to beautiful gourmet gift baskets since 1937. What a selection of dried fruits, nuts, candies, coffees, teas, jams, spices, cookies, crackers, and chocolates! The best part is the price. You can get gourmet items like caviars and pâtés without exceeding your party budget. Mail orders are filled efficiently and promptly.

ELK CANDY
240 E 86th St   212 650-1177
Mon-Sat: 9–6:45; Sun: 10–5:45

Elk Candy Company is a glorious kingdom of chocolate. Every conceivable kind of chocolate can be bought in at least two different forms. It's the one sure place to find old-fashioned European chocolate specialties. Elk Candy is known locally as a haven for the marzipan lover. If you don't favor marzipan, then sink into the florentines— thin chocolate layered over cream, fruit, nuts, honey, butter, and more. If that's not a hit, the little "cats' tongues" chocolate bars are bound to be. It's hard to select a favorite, but the most commonly overheard comment is, "Gee, I haven't had that in years."

LEONIDAS
485 Madison Ave (bet 51st and 52nd St)   212 980-2608
Mon-Fri: 9–7; Sat: 10–7; Sun: 12–6 (closed Sun in summer)

I guarantee you that Leonidas' pralines are sumptuous. This is the only U.S. franchise of the famous Belgian confectionary company, and it is a haven for those who appreciate good things. Over 60 varieties of confections—milk, white, and bittersweet pieces, chocolate orange peels, solid chocolate medallions, fabulous fresh cream fillings, truffle fillings, marzipan—are flown in fresh every week. Jacques Bergier, the genial owner, makes one hungry just describing his treasure trove. You'll be happy to know that the prices are in the affordable range!

LI-LAC CANDY SHOP
120 Christopher St (at Bleecker St)   212 242-7374
Tues-Sun: 12–8 (summer hours vary)

Since 1923, Li-Lac has been *the* source for fine chocolate in the Village. The most delicious creation is Li-Lac's own chocolate fudge, which is made fresh every day. If you tire of the chocolate, there is maple walnut fudge, which is every bit as good. And there are pralines, mousses, French rolls, nuts, dried fruits, hand-dipped chocolates, and more.

MONDEL CHOCOLATES
2913 Broadway (at W 114th St)   212 864-2111
Mon-Sat: 11–7; Sun: 12–5

This is one of the very best! Mondel has been a tasty word in the neighborhood for about a half century. It was founded by the father of its present owner, Florence Mondel. The aroma here is fantastic! The wonderful chocolate-covered ginger, orange peel, nut barks, and turtles are special winners. They also offer a dietetic chocolate line.

NEUCHATEL CHOCOLATES
Plaza Hotel   212 751-7742   60 Wall St   212 480-3766
Daily: 9–9   Mon-Fri: 9–6

Neuchatel Chocolates is a class act—and you pay for it. Neuchatel offers a discount for orders of over $1,000, and it's easy to earn that discount! To create the finest Swiss chocolate from family recipes, the chocolates are prepared by hand with natural ingredients. The taste has been likened to velvety silk. There are 70 varieties of chocolate, with the house specialty being handmade truffles. But that shouldn't keep anyone from trying the marzipan or pralines with fruit or nuts. Neuchatel's origins are Swiss, but perhaps its greatest virtue is that the chocolates are not flown-in daily but created fresh in New York.

NEUHAUS CHOCOLATES
Saks Fifth Avenue
611 Fifth Ave (at 50th St)   212 753-4000
Mon-Wed, Fri, Sat: 10–6; Thurs: 10–8

In 1857, the same year that my great-grandfather started his one-man store on the riverfront in Portland, Jean Neuhaus settled in Belgium and established a pharmacy and confectionery shop. Succeeding generations have produced some of the finest handcrafted, enrobed, and molded-design bittersweet and milk chocolates in the world. They are still imported from Belgium. The showpiece is the Astrid Praline, named after the beloved late Queen of Belgium; it is a sugar-glazed butter delight! Candy is sold in bulk, bars, pre-packs, and also by private label.

ROCKY MOUNTAIN CHOCOLATE FACTORY
11 Fulton St (South Street Seaport, Fulton Market)
212 393-1270
Daily: 10–9; Summer: 10–10

What is a store with "Rocky Mountain" in its name doing in a place like the South Street Seaport? The answer is simple. The first Rocky

Mountain Chocolate Factory was started high in the Rocky Mountains in a town called Durango. Each batch of chocolate was handmade and hand-dipped according to generations-old recipes. Word soon spread, and within a very short time, the concept was franchised across the country. But the popularity hasn't affected the quality of the chocolate. Forty percent is made on the premises, and it still meets the standards established in Durango. What to try? The chocolates should be your top choices, especially the fudge and truffles. But in season don't miss the dipped fresh fruit, the glazed fruit, the blueberry and raspberry clusters, and the candy or caramel apples. The fudge is available in a slew of exotic flavors, from Irish Cream to coffee crunch. Your teeth will squeak just thinking about it!

TEUSCHER CHOCOLATES OF SWITZERLAND
25 E 61st St (at Madison Ave)   212 751-8482
Mon-Sat: 10–6

620 Fifth Ave (Rockefeller Center)   212 246-4416
Mon-Sat: 10–6; Thurs: 10–7:30

If there were an award for the most elegant chocolate shop, it would have to go to Teuscher. Theirs are not just chocolates; they're imported works of art. Bernard Bloom, who owns these Teuscher stores, imports chocolates once a week from Switzerland. The chocolates are packed into handmade boxes so stunning that they add to the décor of many a customer's home. The truffles are almost obscenely good. The superb champagne truffle has a tiny dot of champagne cream in the center. The cocoa, nougat, butter-crunch, muscat, orange, and almond truffles each have their own little surprise. Truffles are the stars here, but Teuscher's marzipan, praline chocolates, and mints (shaped like sea creatures) are of similar high quality.

Cheese

ALLEVA DAIRY
188 Grand St (at Mulberry St)   212 226-7990
Mon-Sat: 8:30–6; Sun: 8:30–3

Alleva, founded in 1892, is the oldest Italian cheese store in America. The Alleva family has operated the business since the start, always maintaining meticulous high standards. Robert Alleva is the current boss, overseeing the production of over 4,000 pounds of fresh cheese a week: *parmigiano, fraschi, manteche, scamoize,* and *provole affumicale.* The ricotta is superb, and the mozzarella tastes like it was just made on some little side street in Florence.

BEN'S CHEESE SHOP
181 E Houston St (bet Allen and Orchard St)   212 254-8290
Sun-Thurs: 8:15–5:30; Fri: 8:15–3:30

About half the varieties of cheese sold here are made in the back of the shop. The locals swear by the farmer's cheese in any of its forms. Favorites include homemade farmer's cheese embedded with such tasty ingredients as strawberries, scallions, raisins, pineapple, and – my personal favorites – almonds and pistachios. Don't miss the baked farmer's cheese. There is homemade cream cheese, also!

EAST VILLAGE CHEESE
34 Third Ave (bet 9th and 10th St)   212 477-2601
Mon-Fri: 9–6:30; Sat, Sun: 9–5:30

Value is the name of the game here. For years this store has prided itself on selling cheese at just about the lowest prices in town. Now in larger quarters, they claim the same for bean coffee, fresh pasta, extra virgin olive oil, quiche, pâté, and a wide selection of fresh bread. An added reason to shop here: this is not a self-service operation!

IDEAL CHEESE SHOP
1205 Second Ave (at 63rd St)   212 688-7579
Mon-Fri: 9–6:30; Sat: 9–6

This is the cheese connoisseur's cheese shop. Ideal has hundreds of varieties of cheese, both imported and domestic, and a staff that will educate you on the fine points of their delicious offerings. Since 1954 these folks have scoured the markets of Denmark, Canada, England, France, Germany, Holland, Italy, Norway, Switzerland, Belgium, Bulgaria, and Ireland for the very best. You name it, they have it. There are also pâtés, mousses, smoked salmon, specialty meats, smoked turkey breasts, smoked ham, jambon, olives, pickles, cheese sticks, and all the other yummy things that go with the wordly flavor of cheese. Some incidental information: a one-ounce serving of delicious Jarlsberg cheese from Norway has only 80 calories. So there!

Chinese

CHINESE AMERICAN TRADING COMPANY
91 Mulberry St (at Canal St)   212 267-5224
Daily: 9–8

If an authentic Chinese dinner is on your itinerary, there may be no better source than this store in Chinatown. Chinese American Trading boasts that 95% of its business is conducted with the Chinese community. In any case, they have an open and friendly attitude here, and great care is taken to introduce you to the wide variety of imported Oriental foodstuffs.

FUNG WONG BAKERY
30 Mott St   212 267-4037
Daily: 7 a.m.–9:30 p.m.

Fung Wong is the real thing, and everyone from the local Chinatown residents to the city's gourmands extol its virtues. The pastries and baked goods are traditional, authentic, and downright delicious; flavor is not compromised to appeal to Western taste. The bakery features a tremendous variety (enough so that Fung Wong sells wholesale all over town), and it has the distinction of being the oldest and largest "real" Chinese bakery. In surveys, Fung Wong is rated number one, and a visit is the surest way to see why.

KAM MAN FOOD PRODUCTS
200 Canal St (bet Mott and Mulberry St)   212 571-0330
Daily: 9–9

A trip to Kam Man is cheaper than one to China, and there's very little available overseas that Kam Man doesn't have here. It's the largest Oriental grocery store on the East Coast. They also carry Japanese, Vietnamese, Philippine, Thai, and Singapore products. Even native Chinese will feel at home in this shop, where you can find every possible ingredient for a Chinese meal. Speaking Chinese is not a requirement for shopping at Kam Man—some of the best English in Chinatown is spoken by the people who work here, and the amenities are totally familiar to those who patronize the city's other gourmet delis and supermarkets. The difference is that at Kam Man the shopping carts wheel past produce displays of water chestnuts, bok choy, winter melon, and tofu; 50 types of Oriental delicacies (like shark's fin); and butcher and fish counters offering duck, sausages, pork dumplings, and shrimp. Desserts and tea round out the selection, and the prices—even for American tangerines and oranges— are the least expensive anywhere.

LUNG FONG CHINESE BAKERY
41 Mott St   212 233-7447
Daily: 7:30 a.m.–9 p.m.

English is definitely a foreign language here, but you can place your order simply by pointing to the authentic Chinese cookies and pastries of your choice. Molded cookies are in abundance, as are rice cakes and pastries covered with sesame or lotus seeds—or perhaps it's something else. The truth is, these are not your everyday fortune cookies; they almost defy description. Nevertheless, it's all authentic, and none of it is ordinary. Don't bother asking how anything tastes, because Lung Fong's explanation is liable to be, "Is good. Is good." And it is.

QUON JAN MEAT PRODUCTS
79 Chrystie St (bet Hester and Grand St)   212 925-5175
Daily: 10–7

William Chan, one of Quon Jan's owners, studied Chinese cooking in Hong Kong, and he devoted two years solely to seasoning and cooking barbecued meats. He is just as meticulous with his staff, making sure that his store is the best Chinese barbecue place in the city. And it is. (The *New York Daily News* concurs.) It is just outside of Chinatown, even by the standards of the ever-expanding borders. Oriental is definitely the theme; most of the business is conducted either in Chinese or sign language. But sign away. Prices are reasonable, and the taste is authentic and delicious. The best seller is the Mandarin duck, but don't overlook the pork, sausages, and roast chicken. They are excellent and exotic.

Coffee, Tea

BELL-BATES HEALTH FOOD CENTER
107 W Broadway (at Reade St)   212 267-4300
Mon-Wed: 9:30–6; Thurs, Fri: 9:30–6:30; Sat: 11–5

Bell-Bates is a hot-beverage emporium, specializing in all manner of tea and coffee for the retail customer. Their selection is extensive and prices are competitive. Bell-Bates considers itself a complete food center, stocking health food, vitamins, nuts, dried fruit, spices, herbs, and gourmet food, along with freshly ground coffees and teas. Ask for Mrs. Sayage; she's marvelous.

THE COFFEE GRINDER
348 E 66th St (bet First and Second Ave)   212 737-3490
Mon, Fri: 9:30–7; Sat, Sun: 9:30–6

If it has anything to do with coffee or tea, you can find it here. The selection of custom-blended coffees and teas (and coffee makers) is excellent. They will also arrange gourmet gift baskets for the coffee lover.

EMPIRE COFFEE AND TEA COMPANY
592 Ninth Ave   212 586-1717
Mon-Fri: 8:30–7; Sat: 9–6:30

Midtown java lovers have all wandered in here at one time or another. There is an enormous selection of coffee (75 different types of beans), decaffeinated coffee, tea, and herbs. Because of the aroma and array of the bins, making choices is almost impossible. Empire's personnel are very helpful, but perhaps most helpful of all is a perusal of their free mail-order catalog *before* entering the shop. Dave Mottel pointed out that fresh coffee beans and tea leaves are available in bulk, along with fresh peanut butter and spices. Everything is sold loose and can be ground. Empire also carries a small selection of appliances.

McNULTY'S TEA AND COFFEE COMPANY
109 Christopher St (bet Bleecker and Hudson St)
212 242-5351
Mon-Sat: 10–9; Sun: 1–7

McNulty's has been supplying choosy New Yorkers with coffee and tea since 1895. Over the years, they have developed a complete line that includes spice and herb teas and coffee blends ground to order. They have a reputation for personalized, gourmet coffee blends, and they work hard to maintain it. That reputation will take its toll on the pocketbook, but their blends are unique and their personal service is highly valued. McNulty's maintains an extensive file on customers' special blends.

M. ROHRS
1692 Second Ave (bet 87th and 88th St)　　　212 427-8319
Mon-Sat: 9–7

Dennis Smith owned a candy store in Manhattan before he bought M. Rohrs, which was established in 1896. The tradeoff of candy for coffee beans was primarily for better working hours, but Smith is always on the premises long before the store opens and stays long after it closes. If he uses his coffee to stay awake, he's not telling. But he is willing to expound on the various types of beans and teas that the store stocks. His guidance is needed, because there are hundreds of varieties of tea, coffee, coffee beans, and honey in the store, as well as accessories. While not a coffee shop, it is possible to get a cup of coffee and sample the wares. Incidentally, Smith is one of the most relaxed proprietors in the city. So either he doesn't drink coffee or he's right when he says that all the studies on caffeine don't amount to a hill of beans.

PORTO RICO IMPORTING COMPANY
201 Bleecker St　　212 477-5421
40½ St. Marks Pl　　212 533-1982
107 Thompson St　　212 966-5758
Mon-Sat: 9:30–9

In 1907, Peter Longo's family started a small coffee business in the Village. Primarily importers and wholesalers, they were soon being pressured to serve the local community around them, so they opened a small storefront as well. That storefront gained a reputation for having the best and freshest coffee available and developed a loyal corps of customers. Since much of the surrounding neighborhood consisted of Italians, the Longo family reciprocated the neighborhood loyalty by specializing in Italian espressos and cappuccinos, as well as "health" and medicinal teas. Dispensed along with such teas are folk remedies and advice to mend whatever ails you. Today, the store remains true to its tradition. Peter has added a coffee bar, so now it is possible to sit and sip 60 various coffees and 120 loose teas while listening to the folklore or trying to select the best from the bins. (Hint: The inexpensive house blends are every bit as good as some of the more expensive coffees.)

SCHAPIRA COFFEE COMPANY
117 W 10th St   212 675-3733
Mon-Fri: 9–6:30; Sat: 9–5

Schapira, also known as the Flavor Cup Shop, has been run by the same family since 1903. Joel and Karl Schapira and Ron Bowen offer

---

Good Coffee Drinks:

Caffè Reggio (119 MacDougal St)
Caffè Roma (385 Broome St)
Cooper's Coffee & Espresso Bar (2151 Broadway, at 75th St)
Daily Caffè (1221 Sixth Ave, at 49th St and Rockefeller Plaza)
Daily Grind (605 Third Ave, nr 39th St)
Pasqua Coffee Bar (165 Broadway and 250 Vesey St)

ESPRESSO: A coffee beverage produced by using pressure to infuse the ground coffee beans with boiling water very rapidly. Here are some variations:

Americano: A two-ounce shot of espresso with hot water. This drink substitutes for drip coffee.

Caffè Latte: A popular version of espresso combining a two-ounce shot of espresso with steamed milk and a spoonful of milk froth on top.

Caffè Mocha: A latte with an ounce of chocolate flavoring (either powder or syrup).

Cappuccino: A two-ounce shot of espresso with equal parts steamed milk and milk froth.

Flavored Caffè: A latte with an ounce of Italian syrup. Almond, hazelnut, and vanilla are a few of the more common flavors. Some like their espresso flavored with liqueurs.

Granita: Made with a granita machine, or *granitore*, these Italian frozen drinks can be made with espresso and milk, or with fresh fruits and juices.

Note: A **tall** is any 12-ounce espresso drink, while a **grande** is any 16-ounce espresso drink. A **double** is any espresso drink with a second shot added. Finally, a **skinny** is any drink that uses non-fat milk.

advice on tea or coffee selections to any customer who asks. Many coffee shops disdain tea, but Schapira is fair to connoisseurs of both and is equally well-versed in either field. They will happily send you a mail-order price list and tuck in answers to any question you might have as well. (Hint: Try Flavor Cup's own brand of tea or coffee.) Coffee is roasted every morning on the premises and is available in bulk, bean form, or ground to personal specifications. Tea is sold in bulk or bags. There are also coffee and tea brewing accessories.

TIMOTHY'S COFFEES OF THE WORLD
1285 Sixth Ave (near 51st St)   212 956-0690
Mon-Fri: 7–6

Timothy's purchases its own coffee crops to insure that their customers get the very best-tasting bean. All of their coffees are fresh-roasted and shipped directly to the store. No product is over two weeks old. Coffees and teas are all self-service; however, a full service cappuccino and espresso bar is available. They carry a good selection of accessory items like mugs, pitchers, teapots, and coffee makers, all reasonably priced.

Dairy Products

HARRY WILS & CO
182 Duane St   212 431-9731
Mon-Fri: 6–3

For nearly three-quarters of a century and through three generations, this venerable outfit has been supplying the food needs of New York's better restaurants. Butter, cheese, and eggs are the mainstays of the business, and they are sold in quantity to commercial buyers. But here is an inside hint: The individual customer will probably not be turned away for orders of a reasonable amount of cheese or butter. For eggs, you would have to purchase at least 15 dozen. But the quality and the prices can't be beat!

Delis, Catering, Food to Go

AGATA & VALENTINA
1505 First Ave (at 79th St)   212 452-0690
Mon-Sat: 7 a.m–8:30 p.m.; Sun: 7 a.m.–8 p.m.

This is a very classy new gourmet shop with an ambience that will make you think you're in Sicily. There are all kinds of good things to eat, with one counter more tempting than the next. A great selection of gourmet dishes, bakery items, magnificent fresh vegetables, meats, candies, gelati, and everything in between. One specialty of the house is extra-virgin olive oil (a secret family recipe). Don't expect bargain prices; everything about the place is first-class. Come instead for quality!

BALDUCCI'S
424 Sixth Ave (at 9th St)   212 673-2600
Daily: 7 a.m.–8:30 p.m.

No visit to the Village is complete without a stop at Balducci's, one of the premier food emporiums in the city. When Balducci's opened in Greenwich Village as a greengrocer in 1947, Mom and Pop tended a single cast-iron register, answered questions, serviced customers, and kept pencil accounts for their neighbors. To this day you will see members of the family in the store helping customers. Under one roof they sell nearly everything: coffee, pastries, fine cheese, smoked salmon, fresh pasta, aged beef, hearth-baked breads, prepared entrees, and the largest selection of quality produce in the city. They produce many traditional specialties like *focaccia,* fresh-cut pasta and ravioli, sauces, *taralli,* country breads, and fresh-fruit tarts. Special services include personal shopping, catering, gift baskets, and seasonal catalogs from which you can mail-order many Italian home-cooked specials. Free delivery is available between Houston, 15th Street, and Broadway to West Street. Half the fun of shopping here is the crowded aisles and family atmosphere. Village residents and city-wide fans jostle for space in this yummy emporium.

BARNEY GREENGRASS
541 Amsterdam Ave (bet 86th and 87th St)   212 724-4707
Tues-Sat: 8:30–5:45; Sun: 8:30–5
Closed Passover and first three weeks in Aug

Dick Scharp says: "Without my order from Barney Greengrass, I'd never survive Sundays!" Barney Greengrass is synonymous with sturgeon to New Yorkers. This family business has been located at the same place since 1929. Barney has been succeeded by his son, Moe, and Moe's son, Gary, but the same quality gourmet smoked fish is still sold over the counters, just as it was in Barney's day. The Greengrasses lay claim to the title of "sturgeon king," and there are few who would dispute it. While sturgeon *is* king here, Barney Greengrass also has schools of other smoked-fish delicacies. (And he could start a school on preparing and selling them.) There is Nova Scotia salmon, belly lox, white fish, caviar, and pickled herring in the fish lines. The dairy-deli line — including vegetable cream cheese, homemade salads and borscht, and a smashing Nova Scotia salmon with scrambled eggs and onions — is world-renowned. In fact, because so many customers couldn't wait to get home to unwrap their packages, Greengrass started a restaurant next door. Devotees claim that the Greengrass brunch is the example par excellence of what brunch should be. How could it be otherwise when the kitchen, which is just a step away, has been producing the ideal brunch menu for more than 60 years? Their smoked-fish delicacies can be shipped anywhere in the U.S. overnight. Great for a party!

BENNIE'S
321½ Amsterdam Ave (at 75th St)   212 874-3032
Daily: 8 a.m.–10 p.m.

Bennie's was founded by Dr. Bennie, a Lebanese plastic surgeon, with his partner and compatriot, a pediatrician. And while a takeout food business usually wouldn't hold a candle to a medical career, here it's a tossup. And that's a pun. Bennie's, you see, specializes in salads, and they're among the best anywhere. Homage is paid to Bennie's Lebanese roots with the best tabbouleh in the city (it may also be the cheapest) and a plate that speaks with a definite Middle Eastern and European accent. The health aspect is not ignored, either. Besides three sensational chicken salads, Bennie's boasts the biggest selection of vegetarian foods in the neighborhood. A prime example is the *muda-data* (a salad of rice, onions, and lentils). It, too, is reasonably priced and excellent. If you see Dr. Bennie, he may tell you business is healthy. Don't be surprised if he doesn't say anything, though. English is not spoken fluently here, but with all these goodies, who cares?

BROADWAY FARM
2339 Broadway (at 85th St)   212 787-8585
Daily: 7 a.m.–midnight

Upper West Side shoppers will enjoy this quality food outlet, which features a full deli, excellent coffee and cheese selection, smoked fish, specialty beers, and unusual imported items. There is free delivery from Central Park West to Riverside Drive, and from 70th to 93rd streets.

CANARD AND COMPANY
1292 Madison Ave (at 92nd St)   212 722-1046
Daily: 7 a.m–9 p.m.

It seems as though you are in a rural country store when you step inside Canard and Company. The atmosphere is homey, and the personnel are eager to show you the fabulous selection of prepared gourmet foods, specialty jams and jellies, rich desserts, custom gift baskets, fine candies, and some of the best sandwiches to be found in Manhattan. Also available are the finest beluga and ossetra caviars and smoked salmon. Catering is a specialty here. No big-time hustle-and-bustle, but a truly enjoyable shopping experience.

CAVIARTERIA
29 E 60th St   212 759-7410, 800 4-CAVIAR
Mon-Sat: 9–6

Caviarteria, the largest distributor of caviar in the U.S., operates out of a small store. That is sufficient, since most of the business is done by phone or by mail. Because of the wholesale business, prices are as reasonable as they can be for caviar, and the quality is top-notch. The

staff is friendly and helpful, and they assure safe delivery by shipping
on ice. Caviarteria also stocks pâté de foie gras, Scotch and Swedish
smoked salmon, homemade *biscotti,* and New Zealand smoked eels.

CHARLOTTE'S
146 Chambers St (bet Greenwich St and W Broadway)
212 732-7939
Mon.-Fri: 10–6

Just thinking about Charlotte's makes me hungry! They have developed
an outstanding reputation for catering, with no detail too small for their
careful attention. Their client list reads like a who's who, including Sony
USA, Miramax Films, and Lehman Bros. Charlotte's is a full-service
catering establishment, from menus and music to flowers and waiter's
outfits. This is the place to come when you want real experts to do the
work for wedding receptions, dinner dances, teas, luncheons, business
meetings or dinners, and so forth.

CHELSEA FOODS
198 Eighth Ave (at 20th St)   212 691-3948
Mon-Fri: 9–9; Sat, Sun: 9–8

The Upper West Side has Zabar's. The Village has Balducci's. The
Upper East Side has Grace's Marketplace. SoHo has Dean & Deluca.
And Chelsea has its own gourmet emporium—Chelsea Foods. The owner
is a neighborhood resident who combines a love of the area with the
experience and skill necessary to run a really first-rate establishment.
Catering is also available.

COUCH CUISINE
1593 Second Ave (bet 82nd and 83rd St)
212 439-0750, 212 439-0699
Mon-Fri: 12–10:30; Sat, Sun: 10 a.m.–10:30 p.m.

This is one of the most complete catering, delivery, and take-home
establishments in the city. If you can't find what you want here, you
must be a very picky eater! There are soups, salads, a dozen different
appetizers, five kinds of potatoes, entree dishes (fish, chicken, meat),
brunch selection, desserts, and beverages. Free delivery is offered from
East 72nd to East 92nd streets. Prices are reasonable, with a three-course
prix fixe special available. Strangely, their burgers are the only overpriced item on the menu!

CROSSING DELANCEY
1367 Third Ave (at 78th St)   212 734-1420
Daily: 10–9

If you don't want to go all the way down to the Lower East Side to
get your specialty food items, try this uptown version! Here you will

find many tastes of Old New York, like fresh bagels, smoked fish, Hester Street sandwiches (sturgeon with cream cheese, chopped herring, and the like), deli items, appetizers, Delancey Street sandwiches (hot pastrami, hot corned beef, turkey breast), Hebrew National franks, knishes, hot strudel, soups from Ratner's, homemade cream cheese, Essex Street pickles, and made-to-order egg creams!

DANIEL'S MARKET
179 Prince St   212 674-0708
Daily: 9–8

What a selection! Under one roof there is a vast assortment of prime meats (beef, fresh American lamb, veal, and pork), poultry (turkey, Bell & Evans chicken, duck, quail, rabbit, squab, pheasant, and goose), bakery items, cheeses, condiments, drinks, and special *plats du jour.* Specialties include beef fillet with sun-dried tomatoes, veal shoulder stuffed with spinach, roast pork with prunes, stuffed lamb Florentine, duck confit, homemade pâtés and charcuteries, and homemade sausages. A catering service is available.

DEAN & DELUCA
560 Broadway (at Prince St)   212 431-1691
Mon-Sat: 8–8; Sun: 9–7

This is one of the great gourmet stores in the country. Long a tradition for smart food buyers, Dean & Deluca is now housed in a store that is four times as large as their original location. The temptations here are extraordinary: wonderfully fresh produce; a huge selection of cheeses; fresh bakery items; takeout dishes; every kind of meat, poultry, or fish product you could want; coffees; magnificent pastries and desserts; housewares; books; and much more. A very popular espresso and cappuccino bar greets the customer at the door. Now this part of the operation has been expanded into small and convenient locations on Wall Street, University Place, the Paramount Hotel in midtown, the Guggenheim Museum, 121 Prince Street (the store's old location), and Rockefeller Center. Professional kitchen equipment is available to both wholesale and retail customers, and a special catering kitchen is located on-premises.

DELMONICO GOURMET FOOD MARKET
55 E 59th St (bet Park and Madison Ave)   212 751-5559
Daily: 24 hours

This is a very handy store in an area that does not have a wide choice of gourmet food operations. In one stop, you can find deli items, gourmet breads and coffees, candies, cheeses, and a hot and cold salad bar. A breakfast menu is featured; at noontime a great selection of sandwiches is available, and an authentic French charcuterie is first-class. They do special catering, charge accounts are welcome, and free delivery (with a minimum order) is offered in a ten-block radius. There is also an indoor seating area.

FAIRWAY
2127 Broadway (at 74th St)   212 595-1888
Daily: 7 a.m.–midnight

When you take care of over 50,000 customers a week, you must be doing something right. Fairway is a west side institution originally known for its fresh fruit and vegetables. But now it has so much more: pasta, cheese, bread, and all kinds of deli items. They offer 30 varieties of olive oil, for example. Fairway has carved out its own niche in the food business, leaving the household items to their busy and aggressive neighbor, Zabar's. Fairway operates its own farm on Long Island, and they have developed relationships with the best produce dealers throughout the state, which has enabled them to capitalize on the trend for healthier items on the dinner table. There is no place like Zabar's for prepared food, but if you want to prepare it yourself, start with the ingredients at Fairway. Prices are right at both places.

FINE & SCHAPIRO
138 W 72nd St   212 877-2874, 212 877-2721
Daily: 9 a.m.–10 p.m.

Ostensibly a kosher delicatessen and restaurant, Fine & Schapiro offers some of the best dinners for at-home consumption in the city. Perhaps because of their uptown location, but more likely as homage to the quality of their foods, they term themselves "the Rolls-Royce of delicatessens." That description is cited here only because it is very apt. Fine & Schapiro dispenses a complete line of cold cuts, hot and cold hors d'oeuvres, Chinese delicacies, catering platters, and magnificent sandwiches. Everything that issues from Fine & Schapiro is perfectly cooked and artistically arranged. The sandwiches are masterpieces; it seems a shame to eat them, but the aroma and taste are irresistible. Chicken in the pot and stuffed cabbage are two of their best items.

FISHER & LEVY
875 Third Ave (at 53rd St; concourse level)   212 832-3880
Mon-Fri: 7–6 (call before 3 p.m. for dinner orders)

Chip Fisher has put together what may well be the best office-catering operation in the city. This is a quality operation, taking care of big parties and providing pizza for solitary diners alike. Fisher & Levy begin the day with delicious breakfast items. How does a fresh doughnut sound? Your choices include plain topped with cinnamon, white glaze, coconut almond crunch, chocolate, and many other sinful flavors. Delivery hours throughout midtown and Wall Street are 7 a.m. to 6 p.m., Monday through Friday. In addition to delicious pizzas, menu selections include a wide assortment of sandwiches and salads, great desserts, and appetizer platters for every occasion. Special low-cholesterol entrees from the Canyon Ranch Spa in Tucson, Arizona, are available.

FRASER MORRIS FINE FOODS
1264 Third Ave (at 73rd St)   212 288-7716
Mon-Fri: 9–6; Sat: 9–5

Fraser Morris was a gourmet-to-go source eons before the neighborhood knew there was such a thing, and certainly long before the Upper East Side became the center of all such operations. The result was a carriage-trade store offering gourmet delicacies at not-inconsiderable prices. With a virtual monopoly on the whole idea, Fraser Morris was the definitive such stop and set the standard for the breed. These days the gourmet shop still stocks the finest fruit, cheese (500 different kinds), candy, caviar, chocolate, delicatessen items (imported sliced ham and pâté de foie gras), quiche, canned gourmet items, ice cream, cheesecake, caviar, and coffee beans. A catering department offers such delicacies as salmon and crown roast of lamb. A bakery department features fruit tarts, Hungarian pastry, scones, and an international variety of goodies. Food baskets are a specialty. Finally, for the true gourmet-to-go, there's a sandwich department. This is an old spot that has gracefully and successfully entered the modern age.

GOURMET GARAGE
47 Wooster St   212 941-5850
Daily: 12–6

This is a strictly no-frills operation, from which many catering outfits and restaurants buy their foodstuffs at wholesale prices. The same savings are available to you. There are LaBelle Rouge free-range chickens, fruits, vegetables, bakery items, seafood, flowers, and much more. Quality is high, prices are low, and variety is somewhere in-between!

GRACE'S MARKETPLACE
1237 Third Ave (at 71st St)   212 737-0600
Mon-Sat: 7 a.m.–8:30 p.m.; Sun: 8–7

At last the Upper East Side has a first-class food store. You won't find a better assortment of fine fruits and vegetables, as well as cheese, pastry, bread, candy, coffee, and preserves. In addition, they also have one of the best selections of smoked meat, smoked fish, caviar, foie gras, and pâtés. The gourmet takeout dishes, catering department, gift-basket selections, and everyday items are of first-rate quality, and the selection is almost overpowering. Displays seduce you into that "I want one of each" frame of mind. Grace and her family have deep roots in the food business, and their experience shows in every phase of this outstanding operation.

GREAT PERFORMANCES CATERERS
125 Crosby St   212 219-2800 (catering),
212 925-9090 (personnel)
Daily: 9–5 (phone orders only)

Liz Neumark, the owner of Great Performances, should know the business from the bottom up. She is a former photographer who supported herself by working as a waitress in a help-for-hire agency. She soon realized that there were quite a number of moonlighting artists in the city, so she decided to organize her own agency, which supplies New Yorkers with party help from the city's artistic community. Her company is a full-service caterer, handling all kinds of affairs, from small dinner parties to gala dinners for thousands. The permanent staff includes party planners, an executive chef, and a professional kitchen crew. The party planners will arrange all the details of your event and provide the necessary personnel. (Corporate clients include top names like AT&T, Coca-Cola, and American Express.) Each of their personnel carries a survival kit, which includes such tools of the trade as aspirin, Band-Aids, a corkscrew, and even a coffee measure. The folks at Great Performances are the kind you want to have around. Good show!

HALE & HEARTY
849 Lexington Ave (bet 64th and 65th St)   212 517-7600
Mon-Thurs: 8–8; Fri: 8–7; Sat: 10–5:30

For those who look closely at the scale and the mirror each morning, here is the answer to your needs. Hale & Hearty offers soups, salads, sandwiches, pastas, entrees, side dishes, and desserts low in cholesterol, fat, and sodium. Their desserts taste great, even though they are made without butter, egg yolks, and cream! Local delivery service is available.

H&H BAGELS EAST
1551 Second Ave (bet 80th and 81st St)   212 734-7441
Daily: 24 hours

The initials H&H have long been synonymous with the best bagels on New York's Upper West Side. Now east-siders can feast upon this fresh, delicious New York specialty, along with a choice of homemade croissants, pastries, super sandwiches, tasty salads, salmon, lox, and sturgeon. Pickled herring is another specialty. Although this is mainly

---

Advance Notice!

Be on the lookout for a retail outlet to be opened soon by David Bouley (of Bouley Restaurant fame). You can expect exceptional (and unusual) good things to eat.

a takeout operation, there are a few tables for those who just can't wait to start noshing.

INDIANA MARKET & CATERING
80 Second Ave (at 5th St)
212 505-7290 (store); 212 228-1196 (catering)
Mon-Sat: 8 a.m.–9:30 p.m; Sun: 11–8:30
(closed Sun in July and Aug)

Indiana Market offers a takeout service, as well as a full-service catering operation. They will take care of staffing, rentals, insurance, unique party sites, music, photography, flowers, and all the incidentals necessary for a successful event. Their FAX menu is sent out on a daily basis to clients who want to know the specials of the day. Menu items include a wide choice of soups, salads, entrees (poultry, meat, seafood, and vegetarian), side dishes (like corn casserole and wild-rice pancakes), and great desserts. Call and ask to be put on their newsletter.

INTERNATIONAL GROCERIES AND MEAT MARKET
529 Ninth Ave (bet 39th and 40th St)   212 279-5514
Mon-Sat: 8–6

Ninth Avenue is one great wholesale market of international cookery, resplendent with exotic spices. So what would an international market on Ninth Avenue be if not a retailer of exotic spices at wholesale prices? The International Groceries and Meat Market is that, but it is also an excellent source for rudiments on which to sprinkle the spices. Food is displayed in huge, open burlap bags, and while this may be disconcerting to some, you will sacrifice the frills for some of the best prices in town and the assurance that the turnover is rapid enough to insure freshness. The meat market is a gourmet market for aficionados of baby lamb and kid. It comes seasoned, prepared, and sliced. If you're unsure about what to do with it, ask!

MAISON GLASS DELICACIES
111 E 58th St (bet Lexington and Park Ave)   212 755-3316
Mon-Sat: 9–6; closed Sat in July, Aug

This is *the* source of gourmet supplies for New Yorkers in the know, and it has been since it was founded by Ernest Glass in 1902. Nowadays, the store is run by Marvin Goldsmith, who has only enhanced the mystique. The house specialties are caviar, foie gras, truffles, Virginia ham, smoked salmon, freshly roasted nuts and coffees, fine chocolates and candies, teas, herbs, spices, vinegars, and jams. Goldsmith says that they stock the largest selection of imported and domestic delicacies in the country, and possibly the world. In addition to catering, services include gift baskets, package deliveries, and a catalog for gourmet subscribers.

MANGIA
54 W 56th St (bet Fifth and Sixth Ave)   212 582-3061
Mon-Thurs: 7:30–6:30; Fri: 7:30–6; Sat: 9–5
(closed Sat in summer)
16 E 48th St   212 754-7600
Mon-Fri: 7:30–6

At Mangia the old European reverence for ripe tomatoes and brick-oven bread endures. This outfit offers three distinct services: corporate catering, with anything you need for an office breakfast or luncheon; a carry-out shop, with an antipasto bar, sandwiches, entrees, and cappuccino; and a restaurant, with pastas made to order. Prices are competitive, and delivery service is offered.

MISS GRIMBLE
909 E 135th St   212 665-2253
Mon-Fri: 7–2

Old-time New Yorkers drool when they hear the name "Miss Grimble." Long famous for the goodies at her café, she now operates uptown with the same delectables, priced a bit above wholesale. There are great cheesecakes made without preservatives or fillers (classic vanilla, chocolate chip, marble, raspberry marble, chocolate, strawberry, and orange), wonderful pies (chocolate pecan, apple, apple crumb, Key lime. French open apple), and more. Don't leave without sampling the double chocolate fudge cake. It's worth the trip!

M. SCHACHT OF SECOND AVENUE GOURMET DELI
99 Second Ave (at Sixth St)   212 420-8219
Daily: 7 a.m.–12 a.m.

This is a self-professed "old-time Lower East Side appetizing store," which is almost totally unknown outside the neighborhood or among non-caterers. Without a doubt, some of the best smoked fish anywhere is served here, New York-style. The emphasis is on salmon, salads, gourmet deli, and any elegant fish. Schacht's slices it, platters it, smokes it, caters it, and even ships it worldwide. A really unique item is a Scotch salmon, presented on a board with a knife and instructions for slicing. It makes an impressive gift and a mouth-watering centerpiece. Those lucky enough to drop in at Schacht's can sample all kinds of fish, cheese, caviar, and gourmet delicatessen meats.

NEUMAN & BOGDONOFF
1385 Third Ave (bet 78th and 79th St)   212 861-0303
Mon-Fri: 7 a.m.–8:30 p.m.; Sat: 7 a.m.–7:30 p.m.; Sun: 8–6:30

There is a whole new look at this popular, appetizing gourmet shop. The place has been expanded, with a bigger selection of all manner of good things to eat. If there is one area where owners Stacy and Paul shine, it is the specialty-catering dishes. It is no wonder the store does a big business for luncheons, dinners, office parties, and every other kind of occasion. Paul has a family history in the fish business, with the Rosedale Fish and Oyster Market, so of course you can find excellent seafood here also. Muffins, scones, and other bakery items are baked right on premises. Free delivery is offered on the Upper East Side; there is a slight charge to other areas of the city. Don't come here if you are hungry, because you might buy out the place!

PETAK'S
1244 Madison Ave (bet 89th and 90th St)   212 722-7711
Daily: 7:30 a.m.–8 p.m.; Sun: 9–8

158 Pearl St (corner of Wall St)   212 558-6000
Mon-Fri: 7:30–5

Richard Petak, third-generation member of a family that has owned appetizing businesses in the South Bronx and New Jersey, has made the leap to New York, offering the first "appy shop" the Carnegie Hill neighborhood has seen in a long time. (As housing has gotten scarcer, Carnegie Hill has emerged as a prime neighborhood. Ten years ago, it was on the outskirts of Spanish Harlem.) In any event, no neighborhood could be assessed as truly having arrived without a gourmet takeout shop, and now Petak's fills that need. So there are all the "appy" standbys, such as salads (60 of them!), corned beef, pastrami, smoked fish, and all sorts of takeout foods. The stores offer full corporate catering, gift baskets, picnic hampers, and box lunches. And don't forget the sesame snow peas, baked salmon salad, cheeses, vinegars, oils, preserves, breads, and other staples of gourmet food emporiums.

PIATTI PRONTI
34 W 56th St (bet Fifth and Sixth Ave)   212 315-4800
Mon-Fri: 8–5; Sat: 11–4

If you are staying at a hotel in midtown or live nearby, note this phone number. This is the greatest alternative to room service in the city, and it's cheaper, to boot! At Piatti Pronti, you'll find an outstanding fresh salad bar, gourmet pizzas, dozens of pasta dishes, and a daily breakfast special. I recommend any of them for a quick, wholesome meal at a small price. Since they do corporate catering *(on one hour's notice!)* and delivery, they should be first and foremost considered an alternative to cooking at home. They are faster, better, and cheaper—even counting the tip! Incidentally, David Snedden, one of the owners of Piatti Pronti, is also a co-owner of Fairway Fruits and Vegetables, one of the city's best markets. Fairway supplies the ingredients for the shop, as well as for restaurants around town owned by the other partners.

PRANZO
1500 Second Ave (at 78th St)   212 439-7777
Mon-Sat: 7:30 a.m–10 p.m.; Sun: 8 a.m.–9 p.m.

In addition to delicious food, there are two special reasons to shop at Pranzo: the extended hours and the free delivery service (from East 57th to East 96th Streets, and from the East River to Fifth Avenue). Prices are not inexpensive, but the quality is apparent in the wide selection of appetizers and entrees. Their custom-made sandwiches, served on a variety of specialty breads, are excellent. Table service in the retail store and catering are available.

RUSS & DAUGHTERS
179 E Houston St   212 475-4880
Daily: 9–7

A family business in its third generation, Russ & Daughters has been a renowned New York shop since it first opened its doors. There are nuts, dried fruits, pâté de foie gras, lake sturgeon, pickled herring, Gaspé salmon sliced and replaced on the skin, and a number of fancy fish dishes, including caviar, smoked fish, sable, and herring. Russ & Daughters has a reputation for serving only the very best. Caviar comes in five different varieties, all sold at low prices. They sell both wholesale and over the counter, and many a Lower East Side shopping trip ends with a stop at Russ & Daughters. Their chocolates are premium quality. They also ship anywhere. If I were to give a five-star rating, this shop would qualify. It is clean, first-rate, friendly—what more could you ask?

SABLE'S SMOKED FISH
1489 Second Ave (bet 77th and 78th St)   212 249-6177
Mon-Sat: 8–8; Sun: 9–5

Kenny Sze was the appetizers manager at Zabar's for 11 years, and he learned the trade well at that famous gourmet store. Now on his own, he has brought his knowledge to the Upper East Side, where he offers wonderful smoked fish, caviar, cold cuts, cheeses, salads, fresh breads, and prepared foods. A catering service is available (smoked fish platters, cold-cut platters, cheese platters, jumbo sandwiches, whole hams, cured meat, and more), and free delivery service is offered in the immediate area. Cold cuts and various chicken dishes are specialties.

SALUMERIA BIELLESE
376–378 Eighth Ave (at 29th St)   212 736-7376
Mon-Sat: 7–6

This Italian-owned grocery store is the best (and the only) French charcuterie in the city. If that isn't contradiction enough, get this: The loyal lunchtime crowd thinks it's dining at a hero shop when it's really enjoying the fruits of a kitchen that serves many good restaurants in the city.

To understand how all this came about, a lesson in New York City geography is necessary. In 1945 when Ugo Buzzio and Joseph Nello came to this country from the Piedmontese city of Biella, they opened a shop a block away from the current one in the immigrant neighborhood called Hell's Kitchen. (Today, it's gentrified and known as Clinton.) The two partners almost immediately began producing French charcuterie. Word spread rapidly among the chefs of the city's restaurants that Salumeria Biellese was producing a quality product that could not be duplicated anywhere. (Buzzio's son Marc is one of four partners who run the business today.) Friendly service is not a trademark, however.

SARGE'S
548 Third Ave (bet 36th and 37th St)   212 679-0442
Daily: 24 hours

It ain't fancy, but Sarge's could feed an army, and there's much to be said for the taste, quality, and price. Sarge's will cater everything from hot dogs to a hot or cold buffet for almost any size crowd. Prices are gauged by the number of people and type of food, but there are several package deals, and all are remarkably reasonable. Even one of the more expensive buffets—the deluxe smoked fish version—runs about $15 per person, and that includes cream cheese and bagels, as well as sturgeon, sable, and stuffed smoked whitefish. Sarge's also caters deli items and has an excellent selection of cold hors d'oeuvres platters, which offer everything from canapes of caviar, sturgeon, and Nova Scotia salmon to shrimp cocktail. To make the party complete, Sarge's can supply serving pieces, condiments, and staff. My favorite is the guy who slices hot pastrami in front of the guests. The carver, cutting board, knife, pastrami, warming oven, and table can all be obtained from Sarge's.

THE SILVER PALATE
274 Columbus Ave (nr 73rd St)   212 799-6340
Mon-Fri: 7 a.m.–9:30 p.m.; Sat-Sun: 7:30 a.m.–9 p.m.

There are picnic baskets, and then there are *picnic baskets*. The Silver Palate gourmet gift baskets are of a caliber that has prompted stores like Bloomingdale's and Macy's to feature them in their gourmet sections. You can go directly to the source and have the Silver Palate prepare anything from a light picnic lunch to a full-course meal with a decadent dessert. The baskets can be filled with such gourmet specialties as mousses, pâtés, imported cheeses, and fresh homemade desserts. A professionally made basket from the Silver Palate is perfect for any occasion. The owner prides himself on the reputation of the gourmet shop, a reputation built on unique takeout food and gift baskets, as well as their own bottled mustards, chutneys, salad splashes, toppings, and so on. Moreover, the Silver Palate offers fine foodstuffs at good prices. Their catering department will handle anything from a basket for two to a splendid sit-down dinner for 2000.

TAYLOR'S PREPARED FOODS AND BAKE SHOP
523 Hudson St (bet W 10th and Charles St)   212 645-8200
Mon-Thurs: 6 a.m.–9 p.m.; Fri: 6 a.m.–10 p.m.;
Sat, Sun: 8 a.m.–9 p.m.

This is a cheery country store in the West Village. It is like visiting your neighbor's home and finding warm hospitality. They sell delicious pies and cakes: specialty baked items, like scones, muffins, and bagels; assorted salads; and hot takeout entrees. Breakfasts are a specialty. A catering service for both informal and elegant affairs is available, and production companies may pick up their items as early as needed.

TODARO BROTHERS
555 Second Ave (bet 30th and 31st St)   212 532-0633
Mon-Sat: 7:30 a.m.–9 p.m.; Sun: 8–8

This is food heaven! Great lunch sandwiches, fresh homemade mozzarella, and authentic *panettone* are offered daily. Todaro carries the very best in imported and domestic gourmet food. Just about everything here is irresistible and will wreak havoc on pocketbook and diet alike. There is imported stuffed pasta, fresh fish (over 40 selections), pâté, jams, coffees, cheeses, homemade sausages, and a half-dozen gourmet items, all top quality. Todaro even stocks fresh truffles, a delicacy seldom seen this side of a haughty restaurant. Then, to top it off, Lucien Todaro imports the very best chocolates from Europe.

WORD OF MOUTH
1012 Lexington Ave (bet 72nd and 73rd St)
212 734-9483 (store); 212 249-5351 (café)
Mon-Fri: 10–7; Sat: 10–6; Sun: 11:30–5:30
Closed Sun in Aug

The history of Word of Mouth is actually the gastronomic history of Manhattan—or at least the Upper East Side. When Christi Finch (an Oregonian—they pop up everywhere!) opened her tiny shop in 1976, she was one of the first establishments to offer home-style prepared foods for at-home or picnic use. Success was almost instantaneous, and by 1979 the shop had moved around the corner and became incorporated. Today, she enjoys a reputation as one of the finest sources for pasta, soups, vegetable and chicken salads, quiches, baked goods, and specialty meat dishes. The aim is still the same, however. Nothing is catered per se (although Word of Mouth does work with professional and amateur caterers), and everything is geared for at-home consumption. There is no ethnic orientation, though there are worldwide influences, and the philosophy is still home-style cooking that makes use of the very finest ingredients. There is now a café on the second floor, open daily for breakfast, lunch, and afternoon tea. A wonderful brunch menu is offered on Saturday and Sunday.

ZABAR'S
2245 Broadway (at 80th St)   212 787-2000
Mon-Fri: 8–7:30; Sat: 8 a.m.–midnight; Sun: 9–6
Mezzanine: 9–6 daily

This is America's most unique gourmet, appetizer, and housewares shop. Zabar's is not just another food emporium; it is a New York institution. Don't expect neat aisles and fancy fixtures. That is not the way the store is merchandised by one of the last of the real hands-on operators, Murray Klein. The genius of the place is that it is like a permanent carnival. However, this carnival features top-quality food items in every category, with broad selections and enormous quantities, at what are arguably the best prices in the city. You can find a huge selection of bakery goods, candy bargains you won't believe (they buy in large lots), every kind of cheese you could ask for, an appetizer section that has to be the busiest in the city, and a coffee department that sells more than any other store in the country. In between, there are all the staple grocery items, pots and pans hanging from the ceiling, and aisles stacked high with daily specials and demonstrations. Upstairs you will find the city's best bargains on housewares—everything from toasters to ice cream machines and carving knives. Next door is an informal café, where weary shoppers can be refreshed with orange juice, coffee, yogurt, and baked delicacies. For native New Yorkers, a visit to Zabar's is a normal routine; for visitors, don't leave the Big Apple without a look!

Fruits, Vegetables

GREENMARKET
130 E 16th St (office)   212 477-3220

These unique, open-air markets in various city neighborhoods are sponsored and overseen by a nonprofit organization. Because there is no overhead, prices are more reasonable than at a supermarket. Another great advantage is that all produce (over 600 varieties) is very fresh, as it is brought directly to the location by farmers. When the supply is gone, the stand closes for the day. Lesson: come early. I'd suggest calling the above number to find out the address nearest you, and the day and time when that particular market will be open. (Most are seasonal, operating from 8 a.m. to 6 p.m.).

LA MARQUETA
Park Ave (under the tracks from 110th to 116th St)
212 534-4900

Tucked under the train tracks in Harlem, this is one of the most fabulous shopping places in the city. La Marqueta is famous, and the early-morning babble of voices here is proof that its customers are not only the local residents of Spanish Harlem. Although the accent is definitely Latin

American, there is nothing that isn't sold here. Each building contains several individual businesses that hawk whatever is fresh and reasonable that day. It's a friendly, informal place to get bargains.

Gift Baskets

MANHATTAN FRUITIER
210 E 6th St (at Third Ave)   212 260-2280
Mon-Fri: 9-5:30

Most fruit baskets are pretty bad, but this outfit makes some great-looking (and great-tasting) masterpieces using fresh seasonal and exotic fruits exclusively. And you can add comestibles such as hand-rolled cheddar-cheese sticks, *biscotti,* and individually wrapped chocolates. Locally handmade truffles and flowers are also available for inclusion. Delivery charges in Manhattan are very reasonable.

SANDLER'S
212 279-9779, 800 75-FRUIT
Daily: 9-6

Sandler's is a key source for scrumptious candies, delicacies, and some of the best chocolate-chip cookies in New York. But Sandler's is best known for its gift baskets (filled with fancy fresh fruit, natural cheeses, and gourmet delicacies), which are perfect for any number of occasions. No one does it better!

Greek

LIKITSAKOS
1174 Lexington Ave (bet 80th and 81st St)
212 535-4300, 212 535-4313, 212 535-0474
Mon-Fri: 8 a.m.-9 p.m.; Sat, Sun: 8-8

Likitsakos is one of the better places in New York to find all kinds of Greek specialties, including salads, grains, dips, and appetizers.

Health Foods

COMMODITIES
117 Hudson St (at N Moore St)   212 334-8330
Daily: 10-8

Commodities is the largest natural-food store within a 100-mile radius, according to the store's staff. In addition, they are considered the best by virtually everyone in the health-food market. Their produce is of excellent quality, and the prices are comparable to those of local super-markets. They've earned that "largest" reputation with a very well-rounded stock of canned and processed health foods, including vegetable and meat substitutes and a full line of health-food products. They are able to serve everyone from macrobiotics to those who are only marginally interested in chemical-free food. The staff is helpful without being fanatical, and the store is so large that you might assume it is just another grocery. It isn't. Commodities is the very best!

DOWN TO EARTH
33 Seventh Ave (bet 12th and 13th St)   212 924-2711
Mon-Fri: 9 a.m.–9:30 p.m.; Sat: 10–8:30; Sun: 11–8:30

This is probably the Village's most complete, best run, and most ap-pealing health-food store. Look over the vitamins, packaged health foods, vegetables, frozen meats, cheeses, and sprouts. All are top quality. The takeout sandwiches are filling and wholesome. And they have made their price structure competitive.

GOOD EARTH FOODS
1334 First Ave (bet 71st and 72nd St)   212 472-9055
Mon, Wed, Thurs: 10–7; Tues, Fri: 10–8; Sat: 10–6

167 Amsterdam Ave (at 68th St)   212 496-1616
Mon-Fri: 9:30–7:30; Sat: 9:30–6:30; Sun: 12–6

The Good Earth has the reputation of being the finest and best-stocked health-food store in New York—and one of the most expensive. The helpful and knowledgeable sales personnel will vehemently deny they are overpriced, but a quick comparison of prices shows they are. Just as surely, a quick visit will confirm their reputation for having one of the largest and freshest stocks. In addition to their enormous selection, the Good Earth offers delivery anywhere within the city.

INTEGRAL YOGA NATURAL FOODS
229 W 13th St (bet Seventh and Eighth Ave)
212 243-2642
Mon-Fri: 10–9:30; Sat: 10–8:30; Sun: 12–6:30

Selection, quality, and health are the order of the day in this clean, attractive shop, which features a complete assortment of natural foods. Vegetarian items, packaged groceries, organic produce, bulk foods, juice bar, salad bar, deli, and baked items are all available at reasonable prices for the health-conscious shopper. They are located in the same building as a yoga center that offers classes in yoga, meditation, and philosophy. A vitamin and health food store is located across the street.

Hungarian

PAPRIKAS WEISS, IMPORTER
1572 Second Ave (bet 81st and 82nd St)
212 288-6117, 212 288-6903
Mon-Fri: 9–7; Sat: 9–6

Paprikas Weiss is more than a century old, and it is still a family owned and operated business. Paprika, spices, and Hungarian staples built their business, but this fine store now offers a complete line of coffee and tea, pâtés, foie gras, pastries, imported candies, and pastas. Many professional cooks use this store as a source, as they carry imported items from France, Italy, Spain, China, India, and South America, as well as the Hungarian basics. If you are in the market for old-fashioned meat grinders, nut grinders, and poppyseed mills (or ground poppyseed itself), this is a good place to look. Hard-to-find items are a specialty. A free mail-order catalog is available.

Ice Cream

CHELSEA ICE
259 W 19th St (bet Seventh and Eighth Ave)   212 242-7692
Daily: 7–7

For a time, you had to go to an expensive restaurant or eat in an executive dining room to enjoy top-quality sorbet, gelati, ice cream, and frozen desserts from this outfit. Now you can go to West 19th Street for such special flavors as espresso, white chocolate, cassis, passion fruit, and champagne. It is a good idea to call ahead, as they mainly deal with the trade.

MINTER'S ICE CREAM KITCHEN
Pier 17, South Street Seaport   212 608-2037
4 World Financial Center   212 945-4455
Daily: during regular Seaport and World Financial Center hours

Minter's became famous dispensing ice-cream mixes—combinations of 16 homemade ice cream flavors sprinkled with a choice of over 20 assorted candy, cookie, fresh fruit, and nut toppings. They are kneaded on a marble slab and dispensed as ice cream scoops, sundaes, milkshakes, malts, and sodas. At the World Financial Center wonderful yogurt shakes, smoothies, and Belgian-waffle sundaes complement a lunch menu of salads, stuffed potatoes, soups, quiches, and stuffed entree croissants.

PRAVINIE GOURMET ICE CREAM
193 Bleecker St (bet MacDougal St and Sixth Ave)
212 475-1968
Mon-Fri: noon–midnight; Sat, Sun: noon–1 a.m.

Pravinie offers gourmet ice cream and much, much more, none of which will reduce the waistline. But the calories are well worth it. Ice cream comes in over 30 exotic flavors, both American and Oriental. Pravinie, dedicated to sweet indulgence, also offers tofutti (in unusual-for-tofutti flavors, of course), cookies, Fruitage, Skimpy treats, and non-fat frozen yogurt. The locals claim that Pravinie offers the best milkshake in town. Needless to say, their help looks as if they never eat the goodies, or maybe this stuff isn't as fattening as it looks!

Indian

K. KALUSTYAN
123 Lexington Ave (bet 28th and 29th St)   212 685-3451
Daily: 10–8

In 1944, Kalustyan opened as an Indian spice store at its present location. After all this time, Kalustyan is still a great spot. Everything is sold in bins or bales rather than pre-packaged containers, and everything is available in bulk or wholesale sizes for retail customers. The difference in cost, flavor, and freshness compared to that of regular grocery stores is extraordinary. The best indication of the latter two points is a simple whiff of the store's aroma! Kalustyan is not strictly an Indian store, but rather an Orient export trading corporation with a specialty in Middle Eastern and Indian items.

Italian

ITALIAN FOOD CENTER
186 Grand St (at Mulberry St)   212 925-2954
Daily: 8–7

Joseph De Mattia, the proprietor, serves a tantalizing array of Italian food that's a credit to his prime location in the heart of Little Italy. The Italian Food Center is truly that: It stocks fresh and cured Italian meats and cheeses, delicious fresh-baked breads, roasted coffee beans, barbecued chicken, Italian-American cold cuts, Italian salads, delicacies, groceries, and dry goods. If it's Italian, it's here.

MELAMPO
105 Sullivan St (bet Spring and Prince St)   212 334-9530
Mon-Sat: 11–8

In a tiny store not much larger than an oversized closet, Melampo manages to display a sizable variety of the best in Italian food items. The specialty, however, is the sandwich. This is the place to go for super special combinations like Battigota (salami, provolone), Ruben (prosciutto, provolone), Cristina (mozzarella, artichoke), and Alessandro (tuna, peppers, bel paese). All sandwiches are served on individual-sized white or whole-wheat loaves of bread. A treat you'll never forget: the Bombolo Tricolore, made of fresh mozzarella, Jersey tomato, basil, special dressing, and served on *focaccia* bread. Yum, yum!

Japanese

KATAGIRI AND COMPANY
224 E 59th St (bet Second and Third Ave)   212 755-3566
Mon-Sat: 10–7; Sun: 11–6

Planning a Japanese dinner? Do you have some important clients from across the Pacific that you would like to impress with a sushi party? Katagiri features all kinds of Japanese food, sushi ingredients, and utensils. They also provide wholesale items for major hotels and restaurants. You can get some great party ideas from the helpful personnel here, and the prices are more reasonable than in Tokyo.

Kosher

LEIBEL'S KOSHER SPECIALTIES
39 Essex St   212 254-0335
Sun-Thurs: 9:30–6:30; Fri: 9:30–1

Here's a handy place to buy all of your kosher food items, including cheese, fish, jams, and frozen goods. Almost every kosher specialty is available at this personable, family-operated store on the Lower East Side. Prices reflect the neighborhood; translated, that means there are bargains by the dozen.

SIEGEL'S KOSHER DELI AND RESTAURANTS
1435 Second Ave (bet 74th and 75th St)   212 288-2094
1646 Second Ave (bet 85th and 86th St)   212 288-3632
Mon-Thurs: 11–10; Fri-Sun: 10–10

If you are looking for a top kosher deli and gourmet appetizer store on the Upper East Side, you can't do better than Siegel's. Not only do they keep long hours (Sundays, too), but they also deliver from 10 a.m. to 9 p.m. Featured are fresh, decorated turkey dishes; overstuffed sandwich platters; barbecue, roasted, and fried chicken platters, hors d'oeuvre selections; smoked fish platters; fresh baked breads and salad trays; and a large selection of cakes, cookies, and fresh fruit platters. The number of selections is awesome, with nearly two dozen sandwiches on the menu, ten different soups, dozens of salads, and side dishes ranging from potato and meat knishes to kugel and kishka.

Liquor, Wine

CROSSROADS WINES AND LIQUORS
55 W 14th St (at Sixth Ave)   212 924-3060
Mon-Sat: 9–9

This store may have the best selection of wine (over 3,000 different kinds) in the city, featuring a complete selection from all the great wine-producing countries. There are rare, unique, and exotic liquors as well.

"Insider special" mailings every month or two are available. Crossroads will special-order items, deliver, and help with party and menu planning. Finally, they are not in a snobby neighborhood, and their prices are as low as their attitude is low-key.

FAIRFAX LIQUOR
211 E 66th St   212 734-6871
Mon-Sat: 10-8

Since you can't pick a liquor supplier by price (although Fairfax promises their markup is a mere 12%, the absolute minimum allowed by law), you might as well pick one by the company it keeps and the service it offers. You'd be hard-pressed to beat this store on either count. The selection is vast; there's hardly a vintage that's not represented. And the price is guaranteed lowest in town. Fairfax claims to supply David Rockefeller, Richard Nixon, and Ronald Reagan, among others. This is the place to go if you want to be able to place a bottle on the table and say, "Oh, the Rockefellers recommended this label."

GARNET LIQUORS
929 Lexington Ave (bet 68th and 69th St)
212 772-3211, 800 USA-VINO (out of state)
Mon-Sat: 9-9

Don't you love that "800" number? You'll love Garnet's prices even more. This may be the most inexpensive place in the city for specialty wines. If you're in the market for champagne, bordeaux, burgundy, or other imported wine, check out the prices here first. They're equally good on other wines and liquors, too. This is a first choice for choice spirits.

K&D FINE WINES AND SPIRITS
1366 Madison Ave (bet 95th and 96th St)   212 289-1818
Mon-Sat: 9 a.m.-10 p.m.

On the Upper East Side, K&D is an excellent wine and spirits market. There are hundreds of top brands and top wines, with prices that are more than competitive. Major ads in local newspapers occasionally highlight K&D's special bargains, but even on a regular basis the values here are outstanding.

MORRELL AND COMPANY
535 Madison Ave (bet 54th and 55th St)   212 688-9370
Mon-Fri: 9-6:45; Sat: 9:30-6:30

Charming and well-informed, Peter Morrell is the wine adviser at this small, jam-packed store, which carries every possible type of wine and liquor. The stock is really overwhelming; since there isn't room for displaying everything, a good portion is kept in the wine cellar. All of it is easily accessible, however, and the Morrell staff is knowledgeable and amenable to helping you find the right thing. The stock consists of spirits, including brandy liqueurs, and many vintages of wine, from rare and old to young and inexpensive.

QUALITY HOUSE
2 Park Ave (bet 32nd and 33rd St)
212 532-2944, 212 532-2945
Mon-Fri: 9–6:30; Sat: 9–5; closed Sat in July, Aug

Quality House boasts one of the most extensive assortments of French wine in the city, an equally fine offering of domestic and Italian wines, and selections from Germany, Spain, and Portugal. Oenologist Willie Gluckstern claims that Bernie Fradin (Quality House's owner) and his son Gary have the best wine palates in the city. This is a quality house, not a bargain house. Delivery service is available and almost always free.

SOHO WINES AND SPIRITS
461 W Broadway (bet Prince and Houston St)   212 777-4332
Mon-Thurs: 10–8; Fri, Sat: 10–9

Stephen Masullo's father ran a neighborhood liquor store on Spring Street for over 25 years. When his local neighborhood evolved into the SoHo of today, his sons expanded the business and opened a stylish SoHo establishment for wine. The shop is lofty. In fact, it looks more like an art gallery than a wine shop. The various bottles are tastefully displayed, with classical music playing in the background. Every advantage is made of the enormous floor space, and Stephen boasts that SoHo Wines also has one of the largest selections of single malt Scotch whiskeys in New York. Again, in keeping with the neighborhood, SoHo Wines and Spirits offers several unique services. Among them are party planning, wine-cellar advice, and specialty items of interest to the neighborhood. Note that this is *not* a liquor store (as Mr. Masullo Sr.'s was), but a wine and spirits shop.

WILLIAM SOKOLIN
178 Madison Ave (bet 33rd and 34th St)   212 684-3827
Mon-Fri: 9:30–6:30; Sat: 10–5:30

This is a unique wine store, featuring a huge inventory of fine wines at attractive prices. They also have a special program for storing wine in climate-controlled conditions in Bordeaux; they offer this service free for four years. (You can also opt to have your wines shipped to the United States or Moscow!) Many of these wines are tradable, and they offer that service, too. They have been in the wine business since 1934, claim to have a $20 million cellar, and are constantly making new discoveries. They will show you the best domestic and imported brands (especially whites), evaluate your wine cellar, and arrange for you to attend a tasting.

YORKVILLE WINE AND LIQUOR
1393 Third Ave (at 79th St)   212 288-6671
Mon-Sat: 9:30 a.m.–10 p.m.

This fair-sized store has carved out a niche for itself as the best source
for kosher wines and liquors. The selection is incredible; they are frequently the first to introduce a new label or variety of wine. They are
a good source (with very good prices) for non-kosher wines as well.
Hungarian wines and spirits are a specialty, as well as California boutique wines.

Meat, Poultry

CITY WHOLESALE MEATS
305 E 85th St (bet First and Second Ave)   212 879-4241
Mon-Fri: 6–3

The name and the hours are indicative of the wholesale aspects of this
business. The many services offered belie the fact that this is a briskly
professional place, but the result is that the individual retail customer
at City Wholesale Meats receives the same quality and price that is
available to hotels and restaurants. Personalized services include delivery,
freezer-wrapping, and cutting to order.

FAICCO'S PORK STORE
260 Bleecker St (at Sixth Ave)   212 243-1974
Tues-Sat: 8–6; Fri: 8–7; Sun: 9–2

An Italian institution, Faicco's has delectable dried pepperoni, cuts of
pork, and sweet and hot sausage. They also sell an equally good cut for
barbecue and an oven-ready rolled leg of stuffed pork. The latter, a house
specialty, is locally famous. Note Faicco's full name: the shop really
specializes in sausage and cold cuts rather than meats. There is no veal
or lamb — and no steaks. But if you're into Italian-style deli, try Faicco's
first. And if you're a lazy cook, take home some ready-to-heat chicken
rollettes: breast of chicken rolled around cheese and then dipped in a
crunchy coating. It's the perfect introduction to Faicco's specialties.
Already prepared hot foods to take home, like eggplant parmesan and
veal marsala, are also available.

H. OPPENHEIMER
2606 Broadway (bet 98th and 99th St)
212 662-0246, 212 662-0690
Mon-Sat: 8–6:55

Oppenheimer is one of the first names mentioned for prime meats in
New York. Harry Oppenheimer has run the same meticulous shop for
over 40 years. It's an old-fashioned butcher shop with the kind of ser-

vice that used to be expected (and that supermarkets have never had). The supermarkets never had this quality, either. There's milk-fed veal, fresh poultry, and game, sold at competitive prices. Oppenheimer is so reliable and trustworthy that over half his customers never even bother to visit the shop in person; they leave the choices and cuts for their dinners in his capable hands.

JEFFERSON MARKET
455 Sixth Ave (at 10th St)   212 675-2277
Mon-Sat: 8 a.m–9 p.m.; Sun: 9–8

Quality is the byword here. Originally a prime-meat and poultry market, Jefferson has expanded into an outstanding full-line store. Second-generation family management insures hands-on attention to service. Prime meats, fresh seafood, select produce, fancy groceries, Bell and Evans chicken, and fresh salads are all tempting. There are expanded deli and smoked-fish sections, and delivery service is available. If you don't feel like cooking dinner, come by Jefferson, and let Louis Montuori send you home with some delicious hot or cold prepared foods.

KUROWYCKY MEAT PRODUCTS
124 First Ave (bet 7th and 8th St)   212 477-0344
Mon-Sat: 8–6; closed Mon in July, Aug

Erast Kurowycky came to New York from the Ukraine in 1954. He opened this tiny shop the same year, and almost immediately it became a mecca and bargain spot for the city's Poles, Germans, Hungarians, Russians, Lithuanians, and Ukrainians. Many of these nationalities still harbor centuries-old grudges, but they all come to Kurowycky's, where they agree on at least two things – the meats are the finest, and the prices are the best available. Erast's son, Jaroslaw ("Jerry"), now runs the shop he grew up in, and he maintains the same traditions and recipes his father handed down. Come taste the thick black bread, sausages, and ham (ask Jerry for a sample). Hams, sausages, meat loaves, and breads are sold ready to eat, as well as in various stages of preparation. There are also condiments, including a homemade Polish mustard, honey (imported directly from Poland), sauerkraut, and a half-dozen other Ukrainian specialties imported or reproduced from the area. On any given day, Kurowycky plays host to native sons, second generations being introduced to the old-country flavor, and foreigners seeking the real thing. Jerry treats them courteously and efficiently, and all come back for more.

M. LOBEL AND SONS
1096 Madison Ave (bet 82nd and 83rd St)   212 737-1373
Mon-Sat: 9–6: closed Sat in summer

Lobel's has periodic sales on some of the best cuts of meat in town (poultry and veal, too). Because of Lobel's excellent service and reasonable prices, there are few human carnivores in Manhattan who haven't heard of the shop. The staff has published four meat cookbooks, and they are always willing to explain the best use for each cut. It's hard to go wrong here, since the store carries nothing but the best.

OTTOMANELLI'S MEAT MARKET
285 Bleecker St (bet Seventh Ave and Jones St)
212 675-4217
Mon-Fri: 8–6:30; Sat: 7–6

With renewed attention to federally inspected meats, Ottomanelli's now has an on-site inspector. The stock in trade here is rare gourmet fare. Among the regular weekly offerings are such meats as boar's head, whole baby lambs, game rabbits, and pheasant. This is *not* a place to act naive. Quality is good, but being served by the right person can make the difference between a good cut and an excellent cut. Other family members run similar operations in other sections of town, but this is the original store, and it's noteworthy. They gained their reputation by offering full butcher services and a top-notch selection of prime meats, game, prime aged steaks, and milk-fed veal. The latter is available as prepared Italian roast, chops, and steaks, and its preparation by the Ottomanellis is unique. Best of all, they will sell it by the piece for a quick meal at home.

PREMIER VEAL
555 West St (off West Side Hwy, two blocks south of 14th St)
212 243-3170
Mon-Fri: 5 a.m.–1 p.m.

Mark Hirschorn worked in various business jobs from Albany to Aspen before deciding to join the family wholesale veal distribution center. As a result, he is better attuned to the needs of both wholesale and retail customers than most distributors. Or, as he says, he's been on both sides of the counter. This translates as a wholesaler who has a good eye for what sells in restaurants and institutions and who has a business that is friendlier than most to small, individual customers. Premier Veal offers veal and lamb stew, Italian cutlets, shoulder or leg roasts, and veal pockets for stuffing, all at wholesale prices with no minimum order. Of course, if you're trekking to West Street, it might be economical to make the order as large as possible. Hirschorn suggests that three or four customers get together to order a few loins. Less than that leaves too much waste and is not profitable for him or the customer. A loin weighing 26 pounds breaks down to 16 or 24 steaks and chops, and the price is a fraction of that at a butcher shop.

SCHALLER & WEBER
1654 Second Ave (bet 85th and 86th St)   212 879-3047
Mon-Fri: 9–6; Sat: 8:30–6

Once you've been in this store, the image will stay with you for a long time because of the sheer magnitude of cold cuts on display. The store is simply incredible. It is a *Babes in Toyland* for delicatessen lovers, and there is not a wall or a nook that is not covered with deli meats. Besides a complete line of delicatessen items, Schaller & Weber also occasionally stocks game and poultry, and they claim to be a butcher shop as well. Try the sausage and pork. They will bake, prepare, smoke, or roll it for you, and that's just the beginning.

YORKVILLE PACKING HOUSE
1560 Second Ave (at 81st St)   212 628-5147
Mon-Sat: 7–6; Sun: 11–5

Yorkville used to be a bastion of Eastern European ethnicity and culture before it became the Upper East Side's swinging singles playground. Here and there, remnants of Old World society remain, and within a four-block stretch on Second Avenue, there are three Hungarian butchers, each of whom offers the best in Hungarian provisions. Yorkville Packing House is patronized by Hungarian-speaking little old ladies in black, as well as some of the city's greatest gourmands. And the reason is simple: except for its neighbors, these prepared meats are available nowhere else in the city and possibly nowhere else on the continent. The shop offers almost 40 different kinds of salami—and that's just for starters. Goose is a mainstay of Hungarian cuisine, so there is goose liverwurst, smoked goose, and goose liver. Fried bacon bits and bacon fried with paprika (another Hungarian staple) are other offerings. Ready for on-the-spot consumption is a selection of preserves, jams, jellies, prepared delicacies, and breads, as well as takeout meals. All of it is authentic.

Middle Eastern

TASHJIAN'S
123 Lexington Ave (bet 28th and 29th St)   212 683-3451
Mon-Sat: 10–8; Sun: 11–7

One of the oldest food stores in the city (founded over a century ago), Tashjian is Armenian in origin, but it's been in the melting pot long enough to encompass all of the Middle East. Indian, Pakistani, and Bangladesh items are available. The shelves are jammed with groceries and foodstuffs, and the counters display appetizers. There's even a catering service. Tashjian claims to be an import business as well. It would have to be in order to get some of the items it stocks!

Nuts

KADOURI IMPORT
51 Hester St (at Essex St)   212 677-5441
Sun-Fri: 9–5

Kadouri is a wholesale-retail store, operating out of burlap bags. Everything here is natural and healthful. The main staples are nuts and dried fruits. The almonds and their derivatives are especially good. Kadouri carries spices as well, but only the more popular varieties. Still, they are extremely fresh, and prices are wholesale, no matter how small the purchase. A number of specialty items from Israel—like pickles, jams, and soups—are available.

YES INTERNATIONAL FOOD COMPANY
165 Church St (at Reade St)   212 227-4695
Daily 9–7

Yes is a Middle Eastern food shop, but it's the nuts that attract their clientele. The nuts are freshly roasted and simply sensational. As a staff member said, "We're nuts about nuts." Also check out the dried fruits and confections—though nothing compares with those nuts!

Pasta

RAFFETTO'S CORPORATION
144 W Houston S (bet Sullivan and MacDougal St)
212 777-1261
Tues-Sat: 8–6

You could go to a gourmet place for pasta, or you could go straight to the source. Raffetto's is the source and has been since 1906. Since that time, they have made all kinds of pasta and stuffing. Though most of the business is wholesale, Raffetto's will sell anyone fresh noodles in 12 different flavors, fresh ravioli, tortellini, manicotti, gnocchi, and fettuccine with no minimum order. Variations on the theme include Genoa-style ravioli with meat and spinach, Naples-style with cheese, and a non-geographic cheese-and-spinach ravioli. Seven kinds of sauces, daily fresh bread, dry pasta, and bargain-priced olive oils and vinegars are featured. Prices generally reflect the fact that this is indeed *the* source.

Pickles

GUSS PICKLES
35 Essex St (bet Grand and Hester St)   212 254-4477
Sun-Thurs: 10–6; Fri: 10–3

Two legendary rival businesses started decades ago, with Guss and Hollander each dispensing pickles, tomatoes, sauerkraut, pickled peppers, and watermelon rinds from barrels on the sidewalk. They have since merged into one business that operates at Hollander's store. Pickles still come sour or half sour, with a half-dozen gradations in between, and the business is still conducted out on the street, with the stock taking up the interior of the store. Customers can actually glimpse a semblance of order and even a refrigerator inside. That refrigerator is stocked with such items as watermelon rind (in season), hot peppers, fresh-ground horseradish, sauerkraut, and whole pickled melons. But what's really important to remember is that this enterprise is still the best place in the world for fresh-from-the-barrel pickles. Pickled celery and carrots are a new and welcome addition.

Seafood

CATALANO'S FRESH FISH
1652 Second Ave (at 86th St)   212 628-9608
Mon-Fri: 9–7; Sat: 9–6

Add youth, consumer interest, and healthy eating to the ancient craft of the fishmonger, and you have Catalano's Fresh Fish market. Owner Joe Catalano is a rare blend of concern, knowledge, and youth. His customers—including many local restaurants—rely on him, as often as not, to select the best items for the dinner menu. And this he does with a careful eye toward health, price, and cookery. He feels strongly that a fish store should not be intimidating and that the only way to attract new customers is to educate them. Catalano's also has a good selection of poached fish and fish cakes. On cold, wintry days, don't miss the Manhattan clam chowder. Joe Catalano is too young to have concocted the recipe, but he deserves credit for the abundance of clams, ham chunks, and vegetables that go into it.

CITARELLA
2135 Broadway (at 75th St)   212 874-0383
Mon-Sat: 8:30–7; Sun: 10–6

Long a fixture on the Upper West Side, Citarella isn't as great as it used to be, but they still offer a wide selection of fillets and whole fish from well-known species to exotics like pompano and sea urchin. Clams and oysters are now available for takeout only; the shellfish bar is history.

CENTRAL FISH COMPANY
527 Ninth Ave (bet 39th and 40th St)   212 279-2317
Mon-Sat: 7:30–6:30

Central doesn't look like much from the outside, but the stock is so vast that it's easier to list what is *not* available than what is. They have 35 species in stock at any given time, including fresh imported sardines from Portugal and live carp. Conducting customers through this whale of a selection are some of the friendliest and most knowledgeable salespeople I've encountered anywhere. Louis and Anthony Riccoborno and Calogero Olivri are skillful guides; they clean and fillet fish. They stock fresh and frozen fish and seafood products. There are fish that even the most devoted seafood lover would have trouble identifying, and the prices are among the most reasonable in town.

LEONARD'S FISH MARKET
1241 Third Ave (bet 71st and 72nd St)   212 744-2600
Mon-Fri: 8–7; Sat: 8–6; Sun: 12–6

Leonard's, a family-owned business since 1905, is operated by three family members who display the same exacting standards the store has maintained throughout the years. It's a neighborhood store that gears its selection to the locals' menus. Thus, the better, smaller-portioned seafoods are always in stock. There are oysters, crabs, haddock, scampi, striped bass, halibut, salmon, live lobster, and squid. The latter is usually purchased by people who know what they are doing, but if they don't, the Leonards are happy to assist. They also run specials on whatever happens to have been a good buy that day at the Fulton Fish Market. This is not to say that Leonard's is a bargain establishment. Leonard's is class all the way. Their takeout seafood department includes codfish cakes, deviled crabs and lobsters, and a super Manhattan clam chowder. Leonard's also carries a full range of imported appetizers. Yes, there is caviar, and you can also find filet mignon, smoked meats and fish, and canned delicacies. Barbecued poultry, cooked and prepared foods, and prime meats round out Leonard's selection.

MURRAY'S STURGEON SHOP
2429 Broadway (bet 89th and 90th St)   212 724-2650
Sun-Fri; 8–7; Sat: 8–8

The reason Ira Goller is the owner of a place called Murray's Sturgeon Shop is that he bought Murray's several years ago. That is of interest to every appetizer lover in New York, because Murray's is the definitive place to buy fancy and smoked fish, dispensing the finest in appetizing products. There is sturgeon, Eastern and Norwegian salmon, whitefish, kippered salmon, sable butterfish, pickled herring, schmaltz herring, and caviar. Quality is magnificent and prices are fair.

ROSEDALE FISH AND OYSTER MARKET
1129 Lexington Ave (at 79th St)   212 861-4323
212 288-5013, 212 734-3767
Mon-Sat: 8–6

Rosedale has quality seafood in good supply at all times, plus a selection of takeout fish dishes and salads that are tasty, unusual, and noteworthy. All are individually prepared. They are not inexpensive; their high quality is accompanied by equally high prices. But according to many of the city's restaurants and caterers, they are the best fish source in New York. Free delivery is offered.

Spices

ANGELICA'S TRADITIONAL HERBS & FOODS
147 First Ave (at E 9th St)   212 677-1549
Mon-Sat: 10–7:45; Sun: 11–6:45

The scent of Anglica's is heavily organic and home-remedy medicinal. This East Village shop caters to folks who want fresh, high-grade spices, teas, and coffees, but the bulk of the business is in medicinal herbs, organic produce and fruit, and related books. They claim to be the largest and best-stocked herb retailer in the country.

APHRODISIA
264 Bleecker St (bet Sixth and Seventh Ave)   212 989-6440
Mon-Sat: 11–7; Sun: 12–5; closed Sun in July and Aug

Aphrodisia is stocked from floor to ceiling with nearly every herb and spice that exists. Seven hundred of them are neatly displayed in glass jars. Some of the teas, potpourri, dried flowers, and oils are really not what one might expect. The general accent is on folk remedies, but most every ingredient for ethnic cooking can be found here. Prices depend upon scarcity. Aphrodisia also conducts a mail-order business.

MEADOWSWEET HERBAL APOTHECARY
77 E 4th St (bet Second and Third Ave)   212 254-2870
Fri, Sat: 12–7; closed Aug

Arcus and Dorothy Flynn believe in the power of herbs and herbal medicine. They offer a complete assortment of their own mixtures, oils, ointments, medicines, and formulas to aid a variety of ailments from alcoholism to tranquilizer addiction. In addition to herbal remedies, they have expanded their gift department to include potpourri, unusual incense, incense burners, candles, dream pillows, smudge sticks, stained-glass hanging pieces, musical tapes, massage oils, crystals, and crystal jewelry. The folks here like to share their own experiences, which helps to make your visit particularly interesting.

> The first part of the great street called Fifth Avenue opened above what was to be Washington Square in 1824. By 1825, Chickering Hall was well established at the corner of Fifth Avenue and 18th Street as the focal point of the city's musical world.

V. Where to Find It:
New York's Best Services

Animal Services

ANIMAL MEDICAL CENTER
510 E 62nd St (bet FDR Dr and York Ave)   212 838-8100
Daily: 24 hours

If your pet should become ill in New York, try the Animal Medical Center first. This nonprofit organization handles all kinds of veterinary work reasonably and competently with board-certified specialists. The care here is far better than it is anywhere else in the city. They suggest you call for an appointment. Emergency care costs more.

CAROLE WILBOURN
299 W 12th St   212 741-0397
Mon-Sat: 9–6

Want to talk to the author of *Cats on the Couch?* Carole Wilbourn is an internationally known cat therapist who has the answer to most of your cat problems. She writes a monthly column for *Cat Fancy* magazine and seems to have a special way with her furry patients. Carole makes house calls from coast to coast and can take care of many cat problems with just one session and a follow-up phone call. She also does consultations by phone and letter.

CAT GROOMING IN YOUR HOME
BY HOWARD
240 E 35th St, #5A   212 889-1729
Daily: 8 a.m. – whenever!

Grooming can be a traumatic experience for your cat, so why not do it where your cat is the happiest . . . in his or her own home. If your cat wants queenly treatment, give professional groomer Howard Bedor a call. No tranquilizers are used, just tender loving care.

EAST VILLAGE VETERINARIAN
241 Eldridge St (just off Houston St)   212 674-8640
Mon, Tues, Thurs, Fri: 9–7; Wed, Sat: 9–3

This is the only practicing homeopathic veterinary hospital in New York City. Doctors and a licensed animal health technician reside on the premises to insure monitoring of hospitalized cases. They feature one of the most complete homeopathic dispensaries in New York, with over 1,000 remedies in stock. Boarding, grooming, and nutritional advice for birds and reptiles are provided in a friendly atmosphere.

FIELDSTON PETS   212 796-4541
Mon-Sat: 9–7

Bash Dibra, a friendly, zeppelin-shaped man who was born in Albania, is an "animal behaviorist." Have you ever met one of those before? Or has your dog? Well, if your pet has bad manners, Bash is the person to teach both you and your dog how to behave. People and pets are trained together. This gentleman identifies himself as "dog trainer to the stars." Would you believe he got his start in a Yugoslavian camp, where he and his family were interned after fleeing their native country? There, five-year-old Bash befriended the attack dogs! Dog and cat grooming is also available.

LE CHIEN DOG SALON
1461-A First Ave (at 76th St)   212 861-8100
Mon-Fri: 8:30–7; Sat: 9–7

Le Chien is known for their tiny A.K.C. puppies, all bearing very distinguished credentials! All dogs and cats at this establishment drink and are bathed in chlorine- and bacteria-free water. How many of us can make that same claim? Dresses. Coats. Sweaters. Fourteen-karat gold identification tags. Cultured pearls. Mink coats. Special brand-name perfumes. Lisa Gilford runs this classy establishment as an elegant spa for small and large breeds – sort of a finishing school for the canine set! A separate business grooms and trains cats and dogs, and boarding is provided for some breeds.

MANHATTAN PET HOTEL
312 E 95th St (bet First and Second Ave)   212 831-2900
Mon-Fri: 7–6:30; Sat: 8–4:30

This place sounds so good you may want to check in yourself! It's the only venture in Manhattan that boards pets as a primary business. They use the best commercial foods available, have separate exercise areas for cats to sun and play (and scratch), and have luxury suites for those cats and dogs that are used to living in Trump Tower. Dog and cat grooming is part of their service.

PET CARE NETWORK
251 E 32nd St (at Second Ave)   212 889-0756
Daily: 9–6 and by appointment

Evelyn McCabe and her crew of pet sitters and trainers will take care of your companions while you are away, and you can be sure they are in expert hands. They have 30 locations around the city, and they will also come to your residence for service. All personnel are bonded. No cages, please, and one pet or set of pets at a time per location. These folks will walk, groom, feed, pick up, clothe, and deliver your pet. Transportation and vet care are available, and service is around the clock. What more could Fido ask for?

Antique Repair

MICHAEL J. DOTZEL AND SON
402 E 63rd St (at York Ave)   212 838-2890
Mon-Fri: 8–4:30

Do you want a chandelier wired or assembled? Dotzel specializes in the repair and maintenance of antiques and precious heirlooms. Dotzel won't touch modern pieces or inferior antiques, but if your antique is made out of metal and needs repair, he's the man for the job. He pays close attention to detail, and he will hand-forge or personally hammer metal work, including brass. If an item has lost a part or if you want a duplication of an antique, he can re-create it. Although Dotzel also does stripping and replating, he feels it isn't always good for an antique, and he'll probably try to talk you out of it.

SANO STUDIO
767 Lexington Ave, Room 403 (at 60th St)   212 759-6131
Mon-Fri: 10–5; closed Aug

Mrs. J. Baran presides over this fourth-floor antique repair shop, and she has an eye for excellence. That eye is focused on the quality of the workmanship and the quality of the goods brought here to be repaired. Both must be the best. Sano is a specialist who limits herself to repairing porcelain, pottery, ivory, and tortoise-shell works and antiques, and she has many loyal adherents.

Art Services

A. I. FRIEDMAN
25 W 45th St   212 243-9000
Mon-Fri: 9–5:30

Those who want to frame it themselves can take advantage of one of the largest stocks of ready-made frames in the city at A.I. Friedman. Nearly all are sold at discount. In addition to fully assembled frames, there are ones that can be put together and come equipped with glass and/or mats.

ELI WILNER & COMPANY
1525 York Ave (bet 80th and 81st St)   212 744-6521
Mon-Fri: 9:30–5:30; Sat: by appointment

Eli Wilner runs two separate businesses. One offers the unique service of positioning, grouping, and hanging artwork—a real art in itself. But his main business is period (or antique) framing, mirror framing, and framing restoration. He keeps 2,000 19th- and early 20th-century American and European frames in stock. He can locate any given size or style with advance notice and is a handy guy to call. His frame exhibitions at the Metropolitan Museum of Art and the Parrish Museum have met with great success.

GUTTMANN PICTURE FRAME ASSOCIATES
180 E 73rd St (bet Lexington and Third Ave)   212 744-8600
Mon-Thurs: 9–5, Fri: 9–12

Though the Guttmanns have worked on frames for some of the nation's finest museums, including the Metropolitan, they stand apart from other first-class artisans in that they are not snobby or picky about what work they will take. They will restore, regild, or replace any type of picture frame. While they are masters at working with masterpieces, they are equally at home restoring or framing a Polaroid snapshot. Even better, they are among the few experts who don't price themselves out of the market. Bring a worn-out frame to them, and they will graciously tell you exactly what it will cost to fix it.

JINPRA NEW YORK PICTURE FRAMING
1208 Lexington Ave (at 82nd St)   212 988-3903
Tues-Thurs: 11–7; Fri, Sat: 11–7

The proprietor of Jinpra New York Picture Framing has the intriguing name of Wellington Chiang, and his service is as unique as his name. Jinpra handles art services (cleaning, restoration, and gilding) in general, and picture framing in particular. Chiang makes the high-quality frames himself, and they often outshine the pictures they frame. Chiang's artistry is evident in every piece he creates. His frames are the perfect complement to great artwork. They will frame lesser works as well, but because of the price and fine workmanship, it would be a waste.

JULIUS LOWY FRAME AND RESTORING CO.
28 West End Ave   212 586-2050
Mon-Fri: 9–5

223 E 80th St (bet Second and Third Ave)   212 861-8585
Mon-Fri: 9–5; Sat: noon–5 p.m. (Sept-May)

There are many firms in the city that specialize in art restoration and framing, but this is the definitive place for both services. Julius Lowy's seems to have no space that isn't heaped with frames. Many look as though they've been there since opening over 80 years ago. It's obvious any kind of frame could be unearthed somewhere on their two floors. There is, then, no framing job they cannot do. Clients include the Metropolitan Museum of Art and the White House. As a byproduct of having done some really odd jobs, a sideline was developed in art restoration, antique-frame reproduction, and frame rearrangement. (*Rearrangement* means enlarging or reducing existing frames to match new artwork.) All work is done impeccably. Prices are not as high as might be expected, and brand-new, custom-made frames are available.

Babysitters

BABYSITTERS GUILD
60 E 42nd St, Suite 912   212 682-0227
Daily: 9–9

Established in 1940, the Babysitters Guild charges high rates, but their professional reputation commends them. All of their sitters have passed rigorous scrutiny, and only the most capable are sent out on jobs. There is a four-hour minimum here, but as members of the New York Convention and Visitors Bureau, they will sometimes relax the rule for tourists. Among their sitters, 16 languages are spoken.

BARNARD COLLEGE BABYSITTING SERVICE
3009 Broadway (Milbank Hall), Room 12   212 854-2035
Mon, Wed, Thurs, Fri: 10–5; Tues: 12–5

Barnard College, the undergraduate women's college of Columbia University, has an unusually large number of kids following their grad-student and instructor moms around campus. To keep watch on them, the Barnard Babysitting Service was started by the Office of Career Services. The service is a nonprofit organization, wholly run by students who become mother's helpers (usually in exchange for room and board) and full-time or part-time babysitters. Most of the young women prefer one-time or occasional babysitting arrangements, though.

C.A.S.H./STUDENT EMPLOYMENT OFFICE
New York University
21 Washington Pl, 3rd floor (at Greene St)   212 998-4433
Mon-Fri: 9–5

Perhaps because of its location in the Village, New York University has always been known for its free and easy attitude. Its babysitting service is no different, and it's certainly refreshing after the lists of restrictions imposed elsewhere. At NYU, rates are reasonable and there are no minimum fees. Rates are negotiated between parents and students. With such a large student body, there is usually someone willing to sit, even on short notice. No further commitment is necessary. C.A.S.H.

(Collective Agency for Student Health) combines all the student employment offices, so this is also the place to hire student bartenders, tutors, housesitters, and odd-jobbers.

Beauty Care and Consultation

BORJA AND PAUL
805 Madison Ave (at 67th St)   212 734-0477
Mon: 9–5; Tues, Wed, Fri, Sat: 9–5:30; Thurs: 9–7

Pierre Henri, formerly of Saks, is in residence here on Tuesday, Wednesday, and Thursday, from 9 to 3:30. Though the other operators are good, Pierre is exceptional. He has a long list of clients who follow him wherever he moves. Indeed, this shop relies on steady clients. The service is courteous and old-fashioned, but the cuts are stylish and up-to-date—that is, up to a point. "Our makeup girl does elegant, chic makeup to complement our hair coloring," said one operator. "We're not into the punk-rock look." The salon also does manicures, haircuts, setting, and pedicures—everything you'd expect from a traditional salon.

CATHERINE ATZEN DAY SPA
856 Lexington Ave (bet 64th and 65th St)   212 517-2400
Mon-Sat: 9–8

If you are in need of a real pick-me-up, a visit to this spa can be just the ticket. A lymphobiology facial can do big things for you. Perhaps one could even make you look a bit younger, to which no one would object! Catherine herself is available for consultation. You can choose from a wide variety of services: a full day of beauty, a shape-up day for men and women, hair services, makeup lessons, manicuring, or pedicuring.

CORNELIA'S NAIL DESIGN
151 E 71st St (corner Lexington Ave)   212 535-5333
Mon-Sat: 9:30–8

Take your malnourished nails to Cornelia's Nail Design for a healthy transformation. Cornelia Margaret Evans will create beautiful plastic or paper nail wrapping, all the while making sure you end up with healthy nails of your own in the long run. Tender loving care is regularly administered to help a client maintain healthy nails. While you're there, you may want to try body-waxing, eyelash-tinting services, or paraffin treatments for hands and legs.

JOSEPH MARTIN
717 Madison Ave (bet 63rd and 64th St)   212 838-3150
Mon, Tues, Fri, Sat: 9–5; Wed, Thurs: 9–7

Often there is need for beauty care in a home, apartment, or hotel. Joseph Martin will perform services on an out-call basis. Hair coloring, nail care, cutting, and makeup are available, but you will, of course, pay extra away from the premises.

KENNETH
Waldorf-Astoria Hotel
301 Park Ave, lobby floor   212 752-1800
Mon-Sat: 9–7 (Wed until 9)

You may remember Kenneth as *the* White House hairdresser during the Kennedy years. He is still considered one of the best, and now anyone can make an appointment with Kenneth himself by booking three to four weeks in advance. It's also possible to get an appointment with one of his associates the same day that you call. Some staff members will make appointments as early as 8 a.m. They do everything from leg-waxing to hair-dying. Men may take advantage of all the services of the salon in their own area, and a Kenneth for Kids is available.

LINDA TAM BEAUTY SALON
680 Fifth Ave, 2nd floor   212 757-2555
Mon-Wed, Fri, Sat: 8–7; Thurs: 8–8

The specialty here is hair-coloring. Linda Tam, a native of China, has been working in this field for over a quarter of a century, and she has assembled a staff of experts who give full service to men and women. Private rooms and the latest hair-treatment machines are available.

MAKE-UP CENTER
150 W 55th St (bet Sixth and Seventh Ave)   212 977-9494
Mon-Wed, Fri: 10–6; Thurs: 10–8; Sat: 10–5

The Make-Up Center counts everyone from teenage girls to the rock group Kiss among its clientele. What makes that range interesting is the Center's credo that makeup should be natural and easy to apply and not wash away at night. The Center is set up to serve stage stars, formal events (such as weddings), and everyday folks alike. All of their makeup is individually geared to customers' lifestyles and packaged with instructions on how to achieve the look at home. Private one-hour sessions that feature the latest makeup techniques are tailored to the customer and cost around $25. It may well be the best bargain in town, for in addition to the personalized expertise, the lesson is given with the expectation that the client won't be back for quite a while. There's only minimal pressure for you to buy Make-Up cosmetics, and lessons can even be videotaped and purchased.

MAKEUP SHOP
131 W 21st St (bet Sixth and Seventh Ave)   212 807-0447
Tues-Sat: 10–6

Now you can get the same kind of professional service that stage, screen, and political celebrities enjoy. Tobi Britton and her crew provide makeup lessons and application, aroma-therapy facials and body wraps, hair-coloring and -styling, nail work, and body massages. Work is done on location or at the shop. It's a great place to get made up for some special party or masquerade!

NARDI SALON
143 E 57th St (bet Lexington and Third Ave)   212 421-4810
Mon-Fri: 9:30–5:30; Sat: 9:30–4:30

Vincent and Fred Nardi wrote a book called *How to Do Your Hair Like a Pro,* and their two salons (one of which is in Manhattan) live up to that title. These are full-service salons, handling the clients from head (hairstyling, cutting, perming, coloring, etc.) to toe (pedicures). Makeup classes and demonstrations, as well as application, waxing, and accessory products, are also available. The aim is a total look, but it is a look less known for its professional gloss than its ability to be *almost* re-created by a client at home. Nardi services both men and children, as well. It is all well worth paying for, but those who wish to avoid 57th Street prices can do so by attending classes at 6 p.m. on Tuesday and Wednesday evenings. At that time, free haircuts by students are offered.

Here is a quick listing of other reliable outfits offering particular beauty services:

Hair care:
Frederic Fekkal Beauty Center, at Bergdorf Goodman, 1 W 57th St (212 753-9500) – Elegant
John Frieda, 30 E 76th St, 2nd floor (212 879-1000) – Very much "in"
John Sahag, 18 E 53rd St (212 371-4777) – Trendy
La Beaute, 142 E 49th St (212 754-0048) – Reasonably priced
Private World of Leslie Blanchard, 19 E 62nd St (212 421-4564) – Excellent value
Roger Thompson, of Barney's New York, Seventh Ave and 17th St (212 924-8500) – Ultra-low maintenance specialists
Rose Reti, 673 Madison Ave, nr 61st St (212 355-3152) – Hair-coloring experts
Vidal Sassoon, 767 Fifth Ave, at 59th St (212 535-9200) and 90 Fifth Ave, nr 15th St (212 229-2200) – You know him! Very popular for both men and women.

Hair removal:
Alise Spiwak, 20 E 68th St (212 535-6878)
Allana of New York, 160 E 56th St (212 980-0216)

Skin care:
Anushka, 241 E 60th St (212 355-6404)

Georgette Klinger, 501 Madison Ave, at 51st St (212 838-3200)
and 978 Madison Ave, at 76th St (212 744-6900)
Lia Schorr, 686 Lexington Ave, at 57th St (212 486-9670)

Also check the Chanel and Estee Lauder counters at **Bloomingdale's,** 1000 Third Ave, at 60th St.

Bookbinding

TALAS
213 W 35th St   212 736-7744
Mon-Fri: 9–11:30, 1–5

Here you'll find tools, supplies, and equipment, as well as books for artists, restorers, collectors, bookbinders, museums, archives, libraries, calligraphers, and retail customers. Elaine Haas presides over a wealth of services for bibliophiles. Should a book be in need of repair and you want to attempt it yourself, there is no better place to come. After all, if Haas can service professional book repairers, she can certainly help amateurs. The attitude here is briskly professional.

WEITZ, WEITZ & COLEMAN
1377 Lexington Ave (bet 90th and 91st St)   212 831-2213
Mon-Thurs: 10–7; Fri: 9–5; Sat: 12–5

Weitz is a highly respected name in the rare-book field. Leo Weitz began a rare-book business in New York in 1908, becoming so well known that he did work for the Rockefellers, DuPonts, Firestones, and other famous families. Today, Herbert Weitz (his son) and partner Elspeth Coleman continue the tradition of fine bookbinding. Weitz and Coleman restore and rebind books and family heirlooms. They also design and create albums, guest books, archival boxes, presentation folders, and special gift books. Coleman's specialty is custom-designing to clients' specifications. Weitz and Coleman also buy and sell rare books.

Calligraphy

CALLIGRAPHY STUDIOS
106 Franklin St (bet Church St and W Broadway)
212 226-4056
By appointment

Nothing sets off a card or a letter like calligraphy. Many claim to be experts, but if you really want first-class work, let Linda Stein and her crew customize your order. She is able to do work in any language you desire. This studio is considered *the* expert in protocol.

Camping Equipment

DOWN EAST
73 Spring St   212 925-2632
Mon-Fri: 11–6

Owner Leon Greenman provides a phenomenal range of services to outdoors people. He started Down East as a service center for hiking, camping, and outdoor equipment. He has excellent credentials, having owned another camping equipment store and been a veteran hiker, camper, and trailblazer. During those years, he came to recognize the lack of service centers for camping equipment, and when he was ready to run a store again, Down East was the result. This store is a godsend for campers. It offers guidebooks, hiking maps, and USGS topographic maps. Outdoor gear can be modified, repaired, and customized.

Carpentry

WOODSMITH'S STUDIO
220 E 67th St   212 879-4300
Mon-Fri: 9:30–4:30

Jerry Gerber ran a carpentry business-cum-woodworking school until he was forced to move when his old location was demolished. Instead of merely relocating, Gerber reappraised the entire operation. When he went back into business, he stressed aspects of the craft that most appealed to him. Nowadays Gerber spends his time on custom cabinetry, particularly bookcases, wall units, tables, turnings, and carvings.

Carriages

CHATEAU STABLES/CHATEAU THEATRICAL ANIMALS
608 W 48th St   212 246-0520
Daily: 9–5

How would you like to arrive at your next dinner party in a horse-drawn carriage? Well, Chateau is the place to call. They have the largest working collection of horse-drawn vehicles in the United States. Although they would like advance notice, they can take care of requests at any time for weddings, group rides and tours, theater connections, movies, and overseas visitors. There is nothing quite as romantic as a ride in an authentic hansom cab.

Cars for Hire

CAREY LIMOUSINE NY
212 599-1122 (reservations)
718 898-1000 (office)
24 hours

Carey is considered by many to be the grandfather of car-for-hire services. They provide chauffeur-driven limousines and sedans at any time, and they will take clients anywhere in almost any kind of weather. They will accept last-minute reservations on an as-available basis.

COMPANY II LIMOUSINE SERVICE
718 430-6482
24 hours

Steve Betancourt provides a responsible, efficient, and confidential service at reasonable prices. His reputation for reliability is well earned.

Chair Caning

CHAIRS CANED
371 Amsterdam Ave, 2nd floor (bet 77th and 78th St)
212 724-4408
Wed-Sat: 11–7; Sun: 1–5

Jeffrey Weiss is an unusual, and an unusually good, craftsman. He does hand- and machine-caning, rush- and splint-seating, and wicker repair. A new addition to his business is re-gluing and repairing furniture.

VETERAN'S CANING SHOP
550 W 35th St   212 868-3244
Mon-Fri: 8–4:30; Sat: 9–12
(closed Sat in summer)

Veteran's owner, John Bausert, has written a book about chair-caning, and he claims his shop is one of the oldest in the world. Certainly, his prices and craftsmanship are among the best in town, and Bausert believes in passing along his knowledge. Customers are encouraged to repair their own chairs. The procedure is outlined in his book, and the necessary materials are sold in the shop. If you don't want to try or have had disastrous results on your own, the shop will repair the chair. For a slight charge, they'll even pick it up from your home. Since chair-caning is such a specialized and limited industry, a company often has a monopoly in its neighborhood. It's remarkable, then, that Bausert offers his services at such good prices. Equally remarkable are the stacks of cane! In addition to caning, Veteran's also stocks materials for chair and furniture repair. He will encourage you to tackle these jobs, too.

China and Glassware Repair

CENTER ART STUDIO
250 W 54th St, Room 901   212 247-3550
Mon-Fri: by appointment

"Fine art restoration and display since 1919" is the motto here. The word *fine* should be emphasized, for owners of really good crystal, porcelain, china, or bronze art should make Center Art Studio *the* place to go for repairs. The house specialty is the restoration of antiques. They will restore or repair porcelain, terra cotta, shells, and precious stones. They will also restore antique furniture and decorative objects, using original materials whenever possible. They'll even design and install display bases and cases. Finally, they will pack and crate articles for shipment. Probably the oldest and most diverse art-restoration studio in the city, Center Art offers a multitude of special services, like designs and sketches by FAX, and multilingual personnel for overseas shoppers. The owner, Lansing Moore, has a superbly talented staff.

EARTHWORKS POTTERY/M. SIMONDS STUDIO
1705 First Ave (bet 88th and 89th St)   212 534-9711
Tues-Thurs: 12–8; Fri-Sun: 12–5:30 (Earthworks)
Tues, Thurs, Sat: 12–5:30 (M. Simonds)

Margaret Simonds ran the M. Simonds Studio for more than 15 years. It was the best place in New York for the restoration of fine-art objects. In 1979, she bought Earthworks—then located around the corner—and the merger created a comprehensive shop that caters to stoneware, pottery, and porcelain pieces from the kiln to "beyond hope" stages. The Earthworks section of the business is both a retail shop and a pottery school. The front of the shop has a fine selection of one-of-a-kind porcelain and stoneware pieces made by potters from all over the U.S. (They're great for gifts!) The shop also conducts classes in pottery making, taking advantage of the on-site studio equipment. During the later part of the week (note the hours), Ms. Simonds is in residence. Her specialty is the restoration of pottery, porcelain, cloisonné, clay, and fine-art objects.

GEM MONOGRAM
628 Broadway (bet Hudson and Bleecker St)   212 674-8960
Mon-Fri: 9–5

Junior was playing with the prized Steuben crystal apple, thinking it was a baseball? Then it's time to call Martin Noren at Gem, who can repair chipped or damaged Steuben and Baccarat pieces. They must see the piece before they will undertake the job. Remember they only work with fine crystal objects, like chandeliers!

HESS RESTORATIONS
200 Park Ave S (at 17th St)   212 260-2255, 212 979-1143
Mon-Fri: 10:30–4; by appointment for later times

Hess has been in business since 1945, providing a restoration service so professional that previous damage is unnoticeable. Their emphasis is on restoration of fine European porcelains, ivory, tortoise shell, sculptures, and objets d'art. They are recommended by the leading museums, auction houses, and galleries in Manhattan. The replacement of blue glass liners for antique silver salt dishes is unique. Hess accepts parcel post-insured shipments of items to be repaired, and they will send an estimate for restoration work.

Clock and Watch Repair

FANELLI ANTIQUE TIME
1131 Madison Ave (bet 84th and 85th St)   212 517-2300
Mon-Fri: 10–6; Sat: 11–5

In a beautiful new clock gallery, Cindy and Joseph Fanelli specialize in the care of high-quality "investment-type" timepieces, especially carriage clocks. They have one of the nation's largest collections of rare and unusual early-American grandfather clocks and vintage wristwatches. They do both sales and restorations, will make house calls, give free estimates, rent out timepieces for special assignments, and purchase single pieces or entire collections. Granddad would be happy to see his prize in the hands of these exceptionally able folks.

FOSSNER TIMEPIECES CLOCK SHOP
1057 Second Ave (at 56th St)   212 980-1099
Sun-Fri: 10–6; Sat: 11–5

In Europe, fine-watch repairing is a family tradition, but this craft is being slowly forgotten in our country. Fortunately, in Manhattan there is a four-generation family, the Fossners, who have passed along this talent from father to son. You can have complete confidence in their work on any kind of watch. They will guarantee their work for six months, and in most cases, they will get a job done within a week. Besides, it's a treat to meet this outstanding Czechoslovakian family.

SUTTON CLOCK SHOP
139 E 61st St (at Lexington Ave)   212 758-2260
Mon-Fri: 11–5

While Sutton's forte is selling and acquiring unusual timepieces, there is an equal interest in the maintenance and repair of antique clocks. Some of the timepieces—even the contemporary ones—are truly outstanding, and there's a long list of satisfied customers endorsing their repair work. They sell and repair barometers as well.

TIME PIECES
115 Greenwich Ave (at W 13th St)   212 929-8011
Mon-Fri: 11–7; Sat: 11–4:30; closed Mon in summer

Grace Szuwala services, restores, repairs, and sells antique timepieces. Her European training makes her particularly expert on antique watches and clocks, with a strong sensitivity for pieces that have more sentimental than real value. This amazing Grace can really do wonders with keepsakes from another time.

Clothing Repair
MAGIC MENDERS
118 E 59th St, 2nd floor (bet Park and Lexington Ave)
212 759-6453
Mon-Thurs: 9–3:30; Fri: 9–1:30

If you have a clothing emergency while in the vicinity of 59th Street, head over to Magic Menders. They will repair almost any type of wearing apparel, from monogrammed A's to zippers, on the spot. Of course, they prefer to be given time to work, but their reputation rests on emergency repairs. Their vast repertoire includes glove- and umbrella-mending, and handbag and zipper repairs. If you would like to keep a relative's linens, although the monogram is all wrong, Magic Menders can fix that, too. Their mending really is invisible. They will mail your item anywhere in the country.

Craft Instruction
CRAFT STUDENTS LEAGUE
YWCA of the City of New York
610 Lexington Ave   212 735-9731

The Craft Students League offers programs in crafts and fine arts. The curriculum is wide ranging and includes bookbinding, jewelry, pottery, woodworking, drawing and painting, and a great one for do-it-yourself types on decorative finishes. For anyone yearning for a creative outlet, this school's convenient midtown location and excellent professional teaching staff is a winner.

Currency Conversion

FREEPORT CURRENCIES
132 W 45th St   212 730-8339
49 W 57th St   212 223-1200
708 Seventh Ave   212 840-2266
Daily: 9–7

If you want to make sure you have enough French francs for a weekend in Paris, this is the place to go. Usually their rates are better than most banks or hotels, and they will exchange currency for any country. Freeport will also buy and sell traveler's checks and make cash advances.

Delivery, Courier, Messenger Services

AIRLINE DELIVERY SERVICES
60 E 42nd St (bet Park and Madison Ave)   212 687-5145
24-hour service, 7 days a week

Before the big guys got in the business, this outfit was doing round-the-clock local and long-distance deliveries. If you have some time-sensitive material, give them a call. Not only will they promptly pick up your item (whether it is in the middle of the night or the middle of a snowstorm), they will also try to beat an amazing 97% on-time delivery rate for the more than 60 years they have been operating.

JIMINY SPLIT DELIVERY SERVICES
147 W 46th St   212 354-7373
Daily: 7–7

Jiminy Split can hand-deliver a package from New York to Washington, D.C., in less than five hours. That's remarkably fast; Federal Express can't match that, and the U.S. mail is not even in the running. (It once took three weeks for a package of mine to go from New York to Washington, D.C.—it went by way of Washington, North Carolina!) If you want a fast, reliable, and personal service, Jiminy Split can deliver anywhere within the continental U.S. as fast as a plane or train can deliver the messenger. (Rates include travel fare, plus delivery expense.) Within the city, rates depend upon distance traveled (the city is divided into zones) and how long delivery takes. There are several Jiminy Split branches around the city.

KANGAROO COURIER
120 E 32nd St   212 684-2233
Mon-Fri: 8–6 (scheduled services all the time)

Messenger services range from bicycle couriers to international shipping firms. Some of them are fly-by-night operations (and I am not referring to the hours that they travel). We have personally run the gamut from rushing galleys between editors to having literally tons of books shipped cross-country. I wish I could tell you that our experience has been wonderful. Suffice it to say that no previous edition ever recommended an all-around company until we met Michael Cohen of Kangaroo Courier. Part of the problem is that no company really does it all. If you are used to sending envelopes crosstown, then you are at sea on warehouse distribution cross-country. And so are the companies you usually deal with. Kangaroo's idea is that *all* shipping is in-house, and the same company oversees the entire job. Thus, Cohen boasts that he can do everything from a rush letter (delivery completed within an hour) to a 10,000-pound shipment, while tracking the entire job.

NOW VOYAGER
74 Varick St, Suite 307   212 431-1616
Mon-Fri: 12–5

Voyager runs an international courier service, and you can be a part of it. The firm has a schedule of flights to various areas, mostly Europe, South America, and the Far East, and you can go at a fraction of the regular fare if you have only carry-on luggage. Usually the flights are booked some weeks ahead, and it is a good idea to call or write as early as possible to see what might be available. Who knows, you might be able to take an exciting trip and save enough money to buy this book for all your relatives at Christmas!

Doll Repair

NEW YORK DOLL HOSPITAL
787 Lexington Ave, 2nd floor (bet 61st and 62nd St)
212 838-7527
Mon-Sat: 10–6

New York Doll Hospital has been fixing, mending, and restoring dolls to health since 1900. Owner Irving Chais has been operating in this cramped, two-room "hospital" since 1947. That was the year he took over from his grandfather, who had begun fixing the dolls of his clients' children in his hair salon. Originally, the children wanted the dolls' hair done along with theirs. When the senior Chais obliged by keeping a supply of doll wigs, he discovered that he had a better business with the dolls than with the women. So he abandoned the hair salon and created the doll hospital. Irving Chais came into the business one Christmas season when his father was ailing and needed help. Several flipped wigs later, Chais was the latest family member in the business. He has replaced antique fingers, reconstructed China heads and German rag dolls, and authentically restored antique dolls. Additional services include appraisals, made-to-order dolls, and buying and selling antique dolls. He will also work on teddy bears and talking dolls with computer chips.

Dry Cleaners, Laundries

CLEANTEX
2335 Twelfth Ave (at 133rd St)   212 283-1200
Mon-Fri; 8–4

Cleantex specializes in cleaning draperies, furniture, balloon and Roman shades, vertical blinds, and Oriental and area rugs. They provide a free pickup and delivery service. Top museums, churches, and rug dealers use their facilities, underscoring the fact that they offer top-grade work.

HALLAK CLEANERS
1232 Second Ave (at 65th St)   212 879-4694
Mon-Fri: 7–6:30; Sat: 8–3; closed Sat in July, Aug

Hallak is a family business run for four decades by Joe Hallak and his sons, John-Claude and Joseph, Jr., which probably accounts for the exceptional pride they take in personal service. Much of their work comes from referrals by designers of delicate fabrics and patterns (like Giorgio Armani, Valentino, and Gucci). In addition, they now have a shirt laundry and fine linen service. Their specialty is working with wedding gowns. For those (like your author) who have trouble with salad dressing landing in the middle of a beautiful necktie, Hallak is the place to go for help. Their skilled work takes time, but they will give 48-hour emergency service.

LEATHERCRAFT PROCESS OF AMERICA
212 W 35th St   212 564-8980, 800 845-6155
Mon-Fri: 7:30–6:30

Leathercraft is all things to all suedes, sheepskins, and leathers. They will clean, re-dye, re-line, repair, and lengthen or shorten any suede or leather garment brought in. That includes boots, gloves, clothing, and handbags, as well as odd leather items. Because leather is extremely difficult to clean, the process can be painfully expensive. However, Leathercraft has a reputation dating back to 1938, and their prices have remained competitive. It now shares space with Marvel Cleaners.

MIDNIGHT EXPRESS CLEANERS
212 921-0111
Mon-Sat: 9 a.m–midnight

Put this number in a prominent spot near your phone. What a handy place to know about! It is 11 p.m. and you want some dry cleaning picked up? No problem. Midnight does dry cleaning, shirt laundry, luggage repair, leather and suede cleaning and repair, shoe and boot repair, and bulk laundry. Best of all, they will pick up and deliver, day or night, with a small minimum. Prompt return is assured. They specialize in dry cleaning restoration for smoke, fire, and water-damaged goods.

MME. PAULETTE DRY CLEANERS
1255 Second Ave (bet 65th and 66th St)   212 838-6827
Mon-Fri: 7:30–6:30; Sat: 7:30–3 (closed Sat in summer)

Where do folks from Henri Bendel take their cleaning? Here, at Mmme. Paulette. This full-service establishment has been in business for over 35 years. They do dry cleaning (including knits, suedes, and leathers), tailoring (including reweaving and alterations), laundry, household and rug cleaning, and they provide fur and box storage. In addition, they will correct water- and fire-damaged garments, bleach-stained materials, do wet cleaning, and clean upholstery and tapestry by hand. Mme Paulette offers free pickup and delivery service throughout the city, has charge accounts, and will provide one-day service upon request. If only they offered service on Sundays, they would do it all!

NEW YORK'S FINEST FRENCH CLEANERS
16 Hudson St (bet Duane and Reade St)   212 791-3859
Mon-Thurs: 7:30–6:30; Fri: 7:30–7:30; Sat: 8:30–6

Three generations of the same family have operated this quality business, featuring pickup and delivery and one-day service. Tailoring and storage, as well as care for fine silks and leathers, is available.

TIECRAFTERS
252 W 29th St   212 629-5800
Mon-Fri: 9–5

Old ties never die or even fade away here; instead, they're dyed, widened, straightened, and cleaned. Tiecrafters is dedicated to the philosophy that a tie can live forever, and they provide services to make that possible. In addition to converting tie widths, they will restore soiled or spotted ties and clean and repair all kinds of neckwear. Perhaps most impressive is Andy Tarshis' willingness to discuss tie maintenance so that frequent visits to the shop won't be necessary. Tiecrafters offers several pamphlets on the subject, including one that tells how to take out spots at home. Tiecrafters accepts business via any carrier, and their charge for cleaning a tie is reasonable. They also make custom neckwear. (Hint: If you roll your tie at night, wrinkles will be gone by morning.)

Electricians

MICHAEL ALTMAN
212 681-2900
Daily: 24 hours

Usually, electrical emergencies happen at the most inconvenient times, as we all know. Fortunately, Michael Altman's licensed crew will respond immediately with emergency service. They are available around the clock, every day of the year. This outfit will take care of everything from small problems to big wiring jobs. They give free estimates and are very reliable, having been in business for over half a century.

Exterminators

ACME EXTERMINATING
460 Ninth Ave (bet 35th and 36th St) 212 594-9230
Mon-Fri: 7–5

Are you bugged? I'm referring to the type that crawls around and causes screams when you open the kitchen closet. Well, Acme is expert at debugging private homes, offices, stores, museums, and hospitals. Acme is state of the art in pest control, employing integrated pest management.

Eyeglass Repair

DELL AND DELL
19 W 44th St (at Fifth Ave) 212 575-1686
Mon-Fri: 9–6; Sat: 9–1
July, Aug: Mon-Fri: 9–5:30; closed Sat

If you desperately need Dell and Dell, you probably can't read this. No need to worry. They do on-the-spot emergency repair on glasses, even if they were purchased in Peoria. This is *the* place to go for eyeglass emergencies in the city. They also repair binoculars. Of course, Dell and Dell won't mind if you stop by for regular optical needs.

Fashion Schools

FASHION INSTITUTE OF TECHNOLOGY
Seventh Ave at 27th St
212 760-7675 (admission), 212 760-7654 (placement)

The Fashion Institute of Technology (FIT) has assumed the position as the world's premier institute serving the fashion industry. The school was founded more than 40 years ago, and it includes a graduate roster that reads like "who's who" in the fashion world. (Jhane Barnes, Calvin Klein, and Norma Kamali are just a few.) The school offers a multitude of majors like accessories, advertising, display and exhibit, toy, jewelry, interior, textile and fashion design, illustration, photography, fine arts, fashion buying and merchandising, apparel production management, patternmaking, and marketing. FIT maintains a student placement service. All students are of top caliber. The Edward C. Blum Design Laboratory is the world's largest repository of the history of fashion, with over one million articles of clothing. It is open to the public, as are the galleries at FIT. Call 212 760-7848 for information about exhibits and shows.

WOOD TOBE-COBURN SCHOOL FOR
BUSINESS & FASHION CAREERS
8 E 40th St   212 460-9600
Mon-Fri: 8:30–5:30; Sat: 10–3

When these people talk fashion, they mean business! Tobe Coller Davis and Julia Coburn were two of the top names in the fashion industry when they jointly founded the Tobe-Coburn school in 1937 as a training ground for careers in fashion marketing and management. Tobe was a personal friend of mine, and I had the privilege of attending many of her spectacular fashion clinics when I was in the retail business. She was an incredible person! Today, Patricia Niemi and her crew are keeping up the outstanding professional reputation of the great lady. Wood Tobe-Coburn students receive an intensive two-year course in all aspects of the garment industry. Even the liberal-arts courses are oriented to industry application. Universal business-skills courses stress advertising and public-relations writing, and history courses deal with retailing and merchandising history, as well as fashion trends. Over the years, the school has established a better than 95% placement record and a reputation as one of the best schools for training in the merchandising, marketing, and management aspects of fashion. The school has co-op programs and internships with the top names in the business, and when students graduate, they know the city as well as they know the inside of Seventh Avenue. Secretarial and accounting courses are now available.

Formal Wear Rental and Sales

A. T. HARRIS
11 E 44th St, 2nd floor (bet Madison and Fifth Ave)
212 682-6325
Mon, Tues, Wed, Fri: 8:30–6; Thurs: 8:30–7
Sat: 10–4 by appointment

A.T. Harris has been in the business of outfitting gentlemen correctly since 1892. They have serviced ten U.S. presidents! This store sells and rents only current formal wear "of the better kind." You will find proper cutaways, tails, and tuxedos rather than iridescent disco wedding outfits. Shoes and accessories run in the same categories. The cut is decidedly English. In addition to imported shirts, Chesterfield topcoats, stud and cuff-link sets, and kid and suede gloves, Harris completes the outfit by renting their own Rolls-Royce Silver Spur. They not only dress you in style, they make sure you get there in style. A class act!

BALDWIN FORMALS
52 W 56th St (bet Fifth and Sixth Ave)
212 245-8190, 212 246-1782
Mon, Thurs: 8:30–7; Tues, Wed, Fri: 8:30–6; Sat: 10–4

If you are suddenly called to a state dinner at the White House, Baldwin will take care of all the dressing details. These folks rent and sell all types of formal attire, suits, overcoats, top hats, shoes, and everything in between. There is free pickup and delivery to many midtown addresses, and a slight charge for other addresses. Same-day service is guaranteed for orders received by early afternoon. Rapid alteration service is available.

Fur Rental

ABET RENT-A-FUR
231 W 29th St, Suite 304 (bet Seventh and Eighth Ave)
212 268-6225
Mon-Fri: 9:30–5:30

Abet is one of the few places in the country that operates a fur-rental business on a full-time basis. Beautiful fur coats, capes, jackets, and stoles are all available for your grand entrance at that special occasion. Many furs you see on television commercials have come from this shop, which numbers its satisfied customers in legions.

Furniture Rental

AFR (The Furniture Rental People)
711 Third Ave (bet 44th and 45th St)   212 867-2800
Mon-Sat: 9–6

AFR is a major relocation service, providing furnishings for a single room, entire apartment, or a business office. They show accessories as well, and all furnishings (including electronics) are available brand-new for rent, purchase, or renting with an option to purchase. An apartment locator service is offered, free professional decorating is available, and an international staff speaking multiple languages is at your service. A specialty part of their business is working with Japanese clients. The stock is large, delivery and setup can often be done within 48 hours, and all styles of furniture and accessories are shown.

CHURCHILL-WINCHESTER FURNITURE RENTALS
6 E 32nd St (bet Fifth and Madison Ave)   212 686-0444
Mon-Thurs: 9–7; Fri: 9–6; Sun: 11–5

Say Churchill, and you think of staid old England, right? Well, *this* Churchill is starkly contemporary, as well as traditional. They can fill any size order for business or residence, and they offer free interior-decorating advice and a lease-purchase plan. A customer simply selects whatever is needed from stock or borrows from the loaner program until special orders are processed. Churchill also offers a comprehensive package, including housewares and appliances, if needed, and they specialize in executive locations, both corporate and personal. They will rent out anything from a single chair to entire homes. They have done so for sports-team managers, executives on temporary assignment, and actors on short-term contracts.

INTERNATIONAL FURNITURE RENTALS
345 Park Ave (at 51st St)   212 421-0340
Mon-Fri: 9–5:30; Sat: 10–2

International claims to be the largest firm renting home and office furniture in the metropolitan area. They offer a free decorating and design service, which includes on-site evaluation and layout by a design specialist. The firm carries accessories to coordinate with the furnishings, and the quality of all items is very good. Quick delivery from their own warehouse is a real plus.

Furniture Repair and Restoration

ANTIQUE FURNITURE WORKROOM
225 E 24th St (at Third Ave)   212 683-0551
Mon-Fri: 8–4

For years Antique Furniture Workroom was the traditional place of choice for French polishing, chair repair, and woodwork restoration. William Olsen added antique furniture restoration (especially American, English, Oriental, and continental originals), gold-leafing, building of furniture, and caning. Now Max Schneider and Son Antiques has become part of the family, so even more expertise and experience has been added. If a piece of furniture in your apartment or home needs special attention, this is a very reliable place to go. Estimates are given in the home.

SACK CONSERVATION COMPANY
730 Fifth Ave   212 933-6562
Mon-Fri: 9:30–5; Sat: 10–3;
closed Sat in July, Aug (call for appointment)

This is a class act. If your favorite sofa is valuable enough for the exclusive attention given pieces from the White House and countless museums, this is the place. The firm deals only in 17th- and 18th-century American Colonial furniture. The work is first-rate, and not inexpensive.

General Services

TOP SERVICE
845 Seventh Ave (bet 54th and 55th St)   212 765-3190
Mon-Fri: 8–6; Sat: 9–1

Shoe repair is the big business here, but there is much more. Their specialty is working on dance shoes, and they are used by many Broadway theater groups. In addition, Top Service will make rubber stamps, cut keys, engrave anything, do luggage and handbag repair, and dye and clean shoes. They are great people to know in case of last-minute emergencies.

VIDEO TOWN LAUNDRETTE
217 W 80th St (bet Broadway and Amsterdam Ave)
212 721-1706
Daily: 7 a.m.–12 midnight

Talk about one-stop convenience; just about the only thing missing here is someone to balance your checkbook! Under one roof you have wash, dry, and fold facilities; a video rental library of 5,000 titles; tanning facilities; FAX service; mailbox rentals; full-service copier; and lottery tickets. If you get worn out from all this activity, there is even a place to sit and relax.

Gift and Regular Wrapping Services

Single gift packages: **Party Bazaar,** 390 Fifth Ave (at 36th St), 212 695-6820 or 800 286-6869; Mon-Wed: 8–6:30; Thurs: 8–8; Fri: 8–7; Sat: 9:30–6.

Multiple gift packages: **Enfra Trading,** 381 Park Ave S (at 27th St), 212 684-3072; by appointment.

UNITED SHIPPING & PACKAGING
147 Second Ave (bet 9th and 10th St)   212 475-2214
Mon-Fri: 9–8; Sat: 10–5

United Shipping will ship anything anywhere in the world. They also sell all kinds of paper wrapping supplies and boxes. Additional services include FAX capability, mailboxes, office supplies, messenger services, and moves of relatively short distances (like to Boston or Washington).

Haircuts

Children

MICHAELS' CHILDREN'S HAIRCUTTING SALON
1263 Madison Ave (at 90th St)   212 289-9612
Mon-Sat: 9–5; closed Sat in July, Aug

Since 1910, Michael's drawing card has always been rapport with children and consistency of personnel and style. Nick Di Sisto, the salon's owner, is living proof of this. He worked for Michael for years, and when Michael retired, he bought him out. Many of the hairstylists have worked under both owners. Appointments are unheard of, and lollipops, seats shaped like toy cars, and comic books are *de rigueur.* This place is totally dedicated to children, but a sprinkling of mothers get their hair cut at children's prices.

Family

ASTOR PLACE HAIR STYLISTS
2 Astor Pl (at Broadway)   212 475-9854
Mon-Sat: 8–8; Sun: 9–6

Does your hairstylist shop have a DJ on staff? They do here! Astor Place doesn't need its address listed here. Just follow the mob to the spot in Manhattan where getting a haircut is an event not unlike being admitted to the hallowed halls of the latest "in" nightspot. The personnel inside what was once a modest neighborhood barbershop give the trendiest, wildest, and most unusual haircuts on the scene. How did this all get started? Well, it seems that the Vezza brothers inherited a barbershop from their father in the East Village at a time "when not even cops were getting haircuts." Enrico took note of the newly gentrified neighborhood's young trendies and their sleek haircuts and changed the name of the shop to "Hair Stylists." Now, the shop is staffed with a resident manager, a doorman (how many barbershops need one of those?), a loft, and an ever-increasing number of barbers. A haircut at this unique barbershop is among the city's cheapest, most fun-filled souvenirs.

ATLAS BARBER SCHOOL
32 Third Ave   212 475-1360
Mon-Fri: 9–9; Sat: 9–6

Atlas is the only barber school in the city. Haircuts here are as cheap as they come, and students, under close supervision, work on customers. Custom grooming it's not, but for the price, it's excellent.

PAUL MOLE FAMILY BARBERSHOP
144 E 74th St (at Lexington Ave)   212 535-8461
Mon-Fri: 7:30–6:30; Sat; 7:30–5:30

Paul Mole is a find. This barbershop does a super job on kids' hair without a super price tag. During holidays, Saturdays, and after school, the place is jammed, so appointments are suggested.

Men

Before getting into haircuts, first a note about shaves. Yes, gentlemen, it is still possible to get shaved at a barber shop, even if the price has gone up a bit. Most hotel barbers will perform this luxury. You can also try **Astor Place Hair Stylists** (2 Astor Place, 212 475-9854), **Broadway Barber Shop** (2713 Broadway, 212 666-3042), **Paul Mole Barbershop** (144 E 74th St, 212 535-8461), or **Feature Trim** (1108 Lexington Ave, 212 650-9746).

FEATURE TRIM
1108 Lexington Ave (bet 77th and 78th St)   212 650-9746
Tues-Fri: 11-7; Sat: 10-6

This neighborhood establishment recently underwent a major facelift but maintains its standard of basic hair care for men, women, and children. Low maintenance is the key to Feature Trim's haircuts. Easy care, reasonable prices, friendly faces, and over 50 years combined experience keep the impressive clientele asking for proprietors Victor and Joe. Appointments are encouraged, but walk-ins are also welcome. Feature Trim is a rare gem of a shop on Manhattan's Upper East Side — a barber shop for the 90's.

PEPPE AND BILL
Plaza Hotel, mezzanine (Fifth Ave and Central Park S)
212 751-8380
Mon-Sat: 9-6

When you pay the kind of prices charged here, you expect the best. And that is exactly what you get with highly professional hairstyling by Jacques and equally first-rate manicure work by his wife, Marie. You can be confident using the services of the other personnel here, also.

Hardware Installation

SABER'S HARDWARE ARNESTO
15 Avenue A (bet 1st and 2nd St)   212 473-6050, 212 473-6977
Mon-Fri: 9-6; Sat: 9-5

This store is a general housewares emporium with an emphasis on kitchen and bathroom fixtures. Ceramic tile, medicine cabinets, shower doors, kitchen cabinets, and hardware are house specialties, and they can install all of these items. They also have a good display of gates and locks. But where Saber's really shines is service; as their motto says, "We hang the impossible." Mirrors and shower doors are a matter of course. Locksmith emergencies are answered routinely. They even stock and hang drapery hardware. Regular customers can get Saber's to do almost any kind of handiwork. At this time, in this city, that's rare indeed. Think of Saber's, despite its location, as the city's general store and all-around handyman.

Health Clubs and Fitness Training

With all the interest in keeping fit, health clubs have sprung up all over Manhattan. Some do not last long, and it is wise to be careful about long-term financial arrangements with any but the largest and most secure operations. Prices and facilities vary. For those who live in the city, watch newspaper and television ads for special introductory offers. For visitors, many clubs will honor reciprocal memberships or allow one- or two-day guest memberships. A number of newer hotels have excellent facilities, including the Peninsula, Holiday Inn Crowne Plaza, Four Seasons, the Intercontinental, Vista International, Parker Meridien, United Nations Plaza, and Rihga Royal. The New York Health and Racquet Club, the Vertical Club, and the New York Sports Club are the most highly recommended. Following are the better clubs, by districts.

Downtown
Executive Fitness Center, Vista International Hotel, 22nd floor (212 466-9266)
New York Health and Racquet Club (39 Whitehall St, 212 269-9800; 24 E 13th St, 212 924-4600)

Midtown
Atrium Club (115 E 57th St, 212 826-9640)
Club La Raquette, Parker Meridien Hotel (119 W 56th St, 212 245-1144)
Manhattan Plaza Health Club (482 W 43rd St, 212 563-7001)
New York Health and Racquet Club (132 E 45th St, 212 986-3100; 20 E 50th St, 212 593-1500; 110 W 56th St, 212 541-7200)
New York Sports Club (614 Second Ave, 212 213-5999; 541 Lexington Ave, 212 838-2102; 404 Fifth Ave, 212 594-3120)
Sports Training Institute (239 E 49th St, 212 752-7111)
Vertical Club (335 Madison Ave, 212 983-5320; 139 W 32nd St, 212 465-1750; 350 W 50th St, 212 265-9400)
YWCA (610 Lexington Ave, 212 735-9755) and **YMCA** (215 W 23rd St, 212 741-9210)

Upper East Side
New York Health and Racquet Club (1433 York Ave, 212 737-6666)
New York Sports Club (151 E 86th St, 212 860-8630)
92nd Street Y Health and Fitness Center (1395 Lexington Ave, 212 415-5700)
Vertical Club (330 E 61st St, 212 355-5100)

Upper West Side
New York Sports Club (61 W 62nd St, 212 265-0995)
Paris Health Club (752 West End Ave, 212 749-3500)
West Side YMCA (5 W 63rd St, 212 787-4400)
World Gym (1926 Broadway, 212 874-0942)

EXUDE
1173-A Second Ave   212 753-0656
By appointment

There are more fitness experts — both male and female — in New York than you can shake a barbell at! One has to be careful in choosing who to work with, as many are not qualified or have severe attitude problems. It is reassuring to know there is an outfit that really takes you, your mind, and your lifestyle seriously. The founder and head motivator is Edward Jackowski, a gentleman completely absorbed by his calling. He will do a fitness assessment, provide an individualized program, give nutritional advice, and then turn you over to one of his expert assistants. Prices are very reasonable. Exude works with both men and women, and their client list reads like a "who's who"! There's no fooling around here; if you really want to get and stay in shape, give Edward a call!

Recommended personal trainers:

Ron Filippi (212 753-9700)
Bruce Mark (212 860-8635)
Jonathan Urla (212 472-6976)

Help for Hire

A.E. JOHNSON EMPLOYMENT AGENCY
681 Lexington Ave (bet 56th and 57th St)   212 644-0990
Mon-Thurs: 8:30–4:30; Fri: 9–4

Dating from 1890, Johnson is the oldest employment agency in the world dealing exclusively with household help. They specialize in providing affluent clients with highly qualified butlers, cooks, housekeepers, chauffeurs, valets, maids, and couples. Both temporary and permanent workers are available, many on a moment's notice.

COLUMBIA BARTENDING AGENCY
212 854-4537
Mon-Fri: 9–5

The Columbia Bartending Agency uses students so apt at bartending that one wonders what profession they could possibly do as well after college. The service has been around a long time, and there is none better. Columbia also supplies waiters, waitresses, and hat checkers.

DIRTBUSTERS
20 W 64th St, #39N   212 721-4357
Mon-Sun: anytime

Boy, are these handy folks! They will clean apartments, residences, and small offices for flat rates. Their staff, hours, and rates are flexible, and they are bonded. Dirtbusters can arrange upholstery and window cleaning, walk your dog, wax your floors, serve as party waiters, paint your rooms, and perform a homemaker's service for new mothers and invalids. They will also videotape the contents of your home for insurance purposes. A Dirtbusters certificate makes a great gift.

LYNN AGENCY

250 W 57th St   212 582-3030
Mon-Fri: 9–5

The Lynn Agency is keeping up with current needs. They have developed a child-care system division, which offers on-site customized child-care programs for conventions, corporate facilities, meetings, and hotels. They are a full-service agency that can supply baby nurses, bartenders, butlers, geriatric care, chauffeurs, cooks, companions, couples, governesses, maids, nursing aides, and housekeepers. There is also a party-planning service. The agency can supply help for any kind of function, from a small dinner party to a formal corporate affair. The owners claim that Lynn's biggest virtue is the ability to mold its services to a clients' needs. Rates are reasonable, personnel are reliable, and they will serve outside Manhattan.

Hotels

New York Hotel Taxes

Most New York City hotel guests pay a staggering 21.25% in taxes each night. Sales tax is 8.25% (state, 4%; city, 4%; MTA, 0.25%). City Hotel Occupancy Tax is 6%, plus $2 per night. State Hotel Occupancy Tax is 5%, and is levied on rooms over $100/night. Whew!

Ripoffs (a few favorites)

- Carefully check your in-room refrigerator.
- Check the rate posted in your room against the quoted price.
- Keep your hotel key with you at all times.
- Put your luggage tag (with name and address) on inside of bag.
- Watch personnel put stamps on your letters and post cards.
- Don't change foreign currency at hotels; exchange rates are poor.
- Ask taxi drivers the approximate fare; watch the amount of bridge and tunnel and extra-baggage charges.
- Cash traveler's checks at banks, where there is no service charge.
- Leave your real jewelry at home; if you must bring along the family jewels, keep them in the room safe or a hotel safe.
- Don't give out your room number to anyone you don't know.

Telephone charges

Carefully examine the telephone charges at your hotel. Many outfits find this a handy way to pad the bill. A few hints:

- Don't bill calls to your room.
- Ask for your own long-distance carrier.
- Beware of the phrase "standard AT&T operator-assisted rates."
- Check your bill.
- Have friends and associates call you whenever possible.
- Don't hang up after completing a call; tap the receiver button for next call.

Getting the best hotel rate

- Call the hotel directly, not a 800 number.
- Ask for a special rate: weekend, corporate, senior, or whatever.
- Don't book hotels through travel agents.
- Never pay "rack" or published room rates.
- Weekend rates are often offered Thursday through Sunday nights.
- Negotiate hotel contract rates only with the general manager.
- Don't pay for an extra night until you know the hotel won't offer you a late checkout.

These outfits can help get good hotel rates:

Central Reservation Service (800 950-0232) – Best with two-star hotels.

Express Hotel Reservations (800 950-6835) – The emphasis is on luxury hotels, but good deals are available on rooms under $100.

Hotel Reservations Network (800 964-6835) – They reserve big blocks of rooms and can usually offer substantial savings.

Quickbook (800 221-3551) – As part of the largest convention housing travel company in the nation, they can usually offer an individual traveler up to 40% off the rack rate, with no fee or service charge.

Reasonably Priced Digs

In the write-ups that follow are a number of places that give excellent value for money. In addition, there are several hotels that are not fancy but do provide clean and comfortable rooms at a good rate.

Excelsior (45 W 82nd St, 212 362-9200) – Quiet and roomy, overlooks American Museum of Natural History

Gramercy Park Hotel (2 Lexington Ave, at 21st St, 212 475-4320) – Renovated, right on Gramercy Park, kitchenettes

Hotel Olcott (27 W 72nd St, 212 877-4200) – Strictly utilitarian, safe, spacious

Roger Williams Hotel (28 E 31st St, 212 684-7500) – In Murray Hill area, kitchenettes

Washington Square Hotel (103 Waverly Pl, 212 777-9515) – Get a front room in this Greenwich Village residence.

Concierge

A concierge is the handiest person in the hotel if you want special services: restaurant reservations, massage, car and driver, theater tickets, shopping hints. There is no charge for services, and any fees will be added to your hotel bill. Tipping is expected: $10 is about right for the average service, more if a request takes an unusual amount of time. For requests above and beyond the call of duty, 15% of the value of a service is a good guideline. If you are a regular guest, it's valuable to keep on the good side of these very helpful folks.

Hotels Near Airports

JFK: Hilton JFK (718 322-8700); Holiday Inn JFK Airport (718 659-0200); JFK Plaza Hotel (718 659-6000); Kennedy Inn at JFK (718 276-6666); Travelodge International JFK (718 995-9000)
La Guardia: Days Inn La Guardia (718 898-1225); King's Inn at La Guardia (718 672-7900); La Guardia Marriott (718 565-8900); Ramada Inn at La Guardia (718 446-4800)

All are conveniently located, provide transporation service to the airports, have restaurants, and are reasonably priced (ask for corporate rates), and some have recreation facilities such as fitness gyms and pools.

Hotel Specialties

Dancing, nightclubs: Carlyle, Kimberly, New York Hilton, Marriott Marquis, Paramount
Offbeat: Morgans, Paramount, Royalton
Pets allowed: Dorset, Essex House, Gramercy Park, Holiday Inn Crowne Plaza, Plaza Athenee, Intercontinental, Lowell, Mayflower, New York Hilton, Marriott Marquis, Vista, Pierre, Plaza, Rihga Royal, Royalton, Sheraton Park Avenue, Westbury

ALGONQUIN
59 W 44th St (bet Fifth and Sixth Ave)   212 840-6800
Moderate

The Algonquin is truly legendary; it has been designated by the city of New York as a Historic Landmark. The elegance of years past is reflected in the property, as the result of a $20 million restoration. This home of the famous Round Table, where Dorothy Parker, Harold Ross, Robert Benchley, and other literary wits sparred and dined regularly, now reflects the same charm and character as it did in the Roaring Twenties! There are only 165 rooms, so the atmosphere is intimate and friendly. The lobby is the best place in the city for people watching, and the Oak Room still features renowned cabaret artists.

CHELSEA INN
46 W 17th St (bet Fifth and Sixth Ave)   212 645-8989
Moderate

In the true sense of the word *inn,* the Chelsea is a small, informal, European-style operation. Most rooms have kitchenettes. The two attached, refurbished townhouses offer studio rooms, guest rooms (with shared bath at a very modest price), and one and two-bedroom suites. For those with business in the Flatiron district, this is a handy destination. Check it out with Mindy Goodfriend Chernoff. (Now isn't that a great name for an innkeeper?)

DORAL TUSCANY
120 E 39th St   212 686-1600
Moderate

The Tuscany has a fine reputation for service, with the personal attention only a small hotel can offer. Large rooms, personal exercycles, and free overnight shoeshine service add to the attractiveness of this well-located midtown hotel. The in-house restaurant, Time and Again, provides excellent meals. Kids under 12 stay free in their parents' room. Guests here can enjoy newly renovated rooms at a sensible price in comfortable and safe surroundings.

ESPLANADE
305 West End Ave   212 874-5000
Moderate

For those wishing to stay on the Upper West Side near Lincoln Center, this completely renovated hotel is ideal. Room rates for single or double occupancy are reasonable, with a small charge for extra persons. The hotel is clean, the kitchens include all necessary equipment (but no cooking utensils), all rooms have color cable TV and air conditioning, and on-premises dining and room service are available. Suites are also available at prices you'd pay for just one room in many other hotels.

ESSEX HOUSE
160 Central Park S   212 247-0300
Moderate to expensive

With a great new look in a great old location, the new Essex House is open after a two-year renovation program. The lobby and public areas have been restored to their original art deco grandeur. The restaurants offer outstanding dining. The number of rooms has been cut down to make the newly decorated units more spacious. The rooms feature classic French and English Chippendale themes; all offer marble bathrooms, two-line telephones, remote-control television, and individual climate control. A new fitness center offers a full array of services, including exercise equipment, massage, herbal wraps, and personal training.

FOUR SEASONS HOTEL
57 E 57th St (bet Madison and Park Ave)   212 758-5700
Expensive

In the hotel world, no name elicits higher praise or wins more awards than Four Seasons. All over the world, they are considered the best in the business. Now visitors to the Big Apple have an elegant 52-story limestone building to call their home away from home. The Four Seasons (designed by I.M. Pei and Frank Williams) provides 367 rooms and suites, several fine eating places (including a lobby lounge for light snacks and tea); a fully equipped business center, complete with freestanding computer terminals and modem hookups; a 5,000 square-foot fitness center (with all the latest equipment); and numerous meeting rooms. The main attraction, however, is the larger-than-usual guest rooms. They average 600 square feet, offer spectacular views of the city, and feature huge, luxurious marble bathrooms with separate dressing areas. A classy staff is determined to make this rising star another award-winning property for the world's largest operator of luxury hotels and resorts.

GRAND HYATT
E 42nd St (Park Ave at Grand Central Terminal)
212 883-1234, 800 233-1234
Moderate to moderately expensive

This centrally located hotel provides safety, comfort, and large rooms for good value. The lobby, complete with a waterfall, is a popular meeting place. Several good restaurants provide informal and formal dining. The hotel's Regency Club rooms are top of the line, featuring a host of amenities like complimentary continental breakfast, cocktails and appetizers in the evening, terrycloth robes, and wall-mounted hair dryers. Special rooms are provided for handicapped guests.

HERALD SQUARE HOTEL
19 W 31st St (at Fifth Ave and Broadway)   212 279-4017
Inexpensive

Located right in the heart of Manhattan, next door to Macy's and the Empire State Building, this 100-year-old hotel has been given a facelift but still excludes the charm of the past. Rooms have been remodeled, color televisions installed, and air conditioning made available in the summer. Best of all, the price is just right for the budget-minded. In the lobby and in some rooms the works of some of our country's most noted illustrators are displayed.

LOWELL
28 E 63rd St   212 838-1400
Moderate to expensive

This small, classy, well-located hotel features 48 suites and 13 deluxe rooms. There is a 24-hour multilingual concierge service, at least two phones per room, VCRs and outlets for personal computers and FAX machines, marble bathrooms, complimentary shoeshine service, and all the rest that goes with a top operation. Thirty-three suites have wood-burning fireplaces, ten have private terraces, and one has a separate gym room with treadmill, stationary bicycle, weights, a Nautilus system, and a compact-disc stereo with built-in speakers. (Oh, yes, the latter also has *seven* telephones!)

MANHATTAN EAST SUITES HOTELS

Beekman Tower Hotel
3 Mitchell Pl (at 49th
and First Ave)
212 355-7300

Dumont Plaza
150 E 34th St
212 481-7600

Eastgate Tower
222 E 39th St
212 687-8000

Lyden Gardens
215 E 64th St
212 355-1230

Lyden House
320 E 53rd St
212 888-6070

Moderate

Plaza Fifty
155 E 50th St
212 751-5710

Shelburne Murray Hill
303 Lexington Ave
(at 37th and 38th St)
212 689-5200

Southgate Tower
371 Seventh Ave (at 31st St)
212 563-1800

Surrey Hotel
20 E 76th St
212 288-3700

These all-suite hotels are among the nicest, most reasonably priced, and conveniently located in New York. Each features 24-hour attendants, and there are modern kitchens in every apartment. Nearly 2,000 suites in all — studio suites, junior suites, and one- or two-bedroom suites — are available at very attractive daily, weekly, or monthly rates. These are particularly convenient accommodations for long-term corporate visitors and traveling families. Families can economize by putting the kids on the pull-out couches and by using the fully equipped kitchens. Additional attractions: fitness centers at Eastgate Tower and Plaza Fifty, renovated rooms at Dumont Plaza and Plaza Fifty. Women especially like these accommodations when they must travel and dine alone. A great buy!

THE MARK

Madison Ave (at E 77th St)   212 744-4300
Moderately expensive

Here's a winner! An older residency building (the Hyde Park, built in 1926) has been converted into one of the most charming hotels in New York. There are 125 guest rooms, 26 junior suites, and 34 one- and two-bedroom suites, all decorated in exquisite taste. Every room has cable TV, FAX capability, and two-line phones, and most have pantries. The suites (which I strongly recommend) have separate vanities and marble baths. Some even have libraries, wet bars, and terraces with views of Central Park. The location is terrific, the personnel are extremely nice, and an excellent restaurant just off the lobby serves all meals, plus tea and brunch. If you really want to be pampered, ask for a suite with heating lamps and heated towel racks. Everyone gets Frette linens, down pillows, umbrellas, and Molton Brown of London soaps!

MARRIOTT MARQUIS
1535 Broadway   212 398-1900
Moderate to moderately expensive

The opening of this 50-story showplace in the center of Times Square in the summer of 1985 represented a major step in the rejuvenation of the area. Along with over 1,800 rooms, huge meeting and convention facilities, and the largest hotel atrium in the world, guests can enjoy a 700-seat, three-story revolving restaurant and lounge at the top of the hotel; a revolving lounge overlooking Broadway on the eighth floor; a legitimate Broadway theater on the premises; a fully equipped health club; suites with walk-in wet bars and refrigerators; oversized rooms; and a sky lounge. There are nine restaurants and lounges in all. A concierge level offers special amenities, including 24-hour room service. All rooms overlook Manhattan on the exterior and open directly to the atrium on the interior.

MAYFLOWER
15 Central Park W (at 61st St)   212 265-0060, 800 223-4164
Moderate

If you are coming to New York for cultural events at Lincoln Center or Carnegie Hall, this is an ideal place to stay. Overlooking Central Park, with most accommodations recently redecorated, this is a safe, comfortable hotel with spacious rooms. There are a number of two- and three-bedroom suites and several terraced penthouses, all with refrigerators and video message features. A health club is on the property. Room service is available from 7 a.m. until midnight.

MERCER
99 Prince St   212 478-7878
Moderate to moderately expensive

The Mercer is SoHo's first hotel; it is a small, rather chic hotel that caters to the international set. The guest rooms (numbering only 78) are decorated in the 1940s *art moderne* style. The bathrooms are large, and there is a state-of-the-art sound system throughout. The building is a renovation of a Romanesque Revival structure, with all of the interior redone. There is a restaurant on premises.

MILFORD PLAZA
270 W 45th St (bet Seventh and Eighth Ave)
212 869-3600, 800 221-2690
Inexpensive to moderate

Value is the key word here. The Milford Plaza, a Best Western operation located at the edge of the theater district in midtown Manhattan, offers extraordinarily reasonable rates that are partially offset by its location. But the hotel has extremely tight security, which lessens the need to be concerned. Rooms are small yet clean, and late-night dining is available. Very attractive rates are available on weekends and for groups. The Milford was recently refurbished, with all new bathrooms and attractive wall coverings in guest rooms.

MILLENIUM
55 Church St (bet Fulton and Dey St)   212 693-2001
Moderate to moderately expensive

For the traveler who has business appointments in the financial area, the new 58-story Millenium is a good bet. Most rooms are king-size, nonsmoking accommodations are available, each room has two telephone lines, and every modern amenity (robes, umbrellas, etc.) is standard. The Taliesin restaurant features American cuisine in an elegant atmosphere. Weekend packages, with reasonable parking fees, are featured. Additional attractions include an up-to-date fitness center with swimming pool, and complimentary limo service to midtown.

MORGAN'S
237 Madison Ave (at 37th St)   212 686-0300, 800 334-3408
Moderate

If a downtown location and a boutique atmosphere are what you're looking for, this is it. Formerly the Executive Hotel, Morgan's was completely redone by a French designer, and the result is calm, comfort, and convenience. 24-hour room service is available, and room rates include continental breakfast. There is a stereo system in each room.

NEW YORK PALACE
455 Madison Ave (at 51st St)   212 888-7000
Moderately expensive to expensive

This used to be the Helmsley Palace, but then you know the story of the Helmsleys. It is now the New York Palace. Located close to Saks Fifth Avenue, one block off of Fifth Avenue, it's enchanting in the evening! The public rooms are exceptionally attractive, encompassing the 100-year-old Villard Mansion, one of New York's legendary landmarks. (The Villard House used to be the chancery office of the archdiocese of New York.) There are no convention facilities here, although meeting rooms are available. The New York Palace has several hundred apartments and suites, and even some triplex apartments.

THE PENINSULA HOTEL
700 Fifth Ave (at 55th St)   212 247-2200
Expensive

Quality is the word here. The Peninsula Hotel has a lot going for it. A prime location in the heart of the city's best shopping, right off Fifth Avenue. A completely remodeled building, with rooms done in *art nouveau* style and featuring king-sized marble bathrooms. A superior staff, who make every effort to please guests. A superb restaurant, Adrienne, that pampers diners and their taste buds. A lounge that serves afternoon tea and goodies. And best of all, a trilevel, glass-enclosed fitness center that offers a superb view and even a swimming pool. It is one of the finest facilities in the city. Peninsula Hotels are known worldwide as superior properties, and New York is no exception.

PIERRE HOTEL
2 E 61st St (at Fifth Ave)   212 838-8000
Expensive

At a Four Seasons operation, you expect top quality, and that is exactly what you get. The Pierre is quiet, modest, luxurious, and expensive. There are beautiful suites, excellent meeting and banquet facilities, and a three-to-one ratio of guests to staff. Some of the rooms and suites are part of a residential co-op. Even if you don't stay here, a meal in the elegant Café Pierre or tea in the Rotunda is a special experience.

PLAZA HOTEL
Fifth Ave and Central Park   212 759-3000
Expensive

In every city there is a perfect location; in New York it is the corner of Central Park and Fifth Avenue, home of the Plaza Hotel. Besides the prime setting, this grande dame of Manhattan exudes the physical charm and grace that has made it the center of activity in the city for decades. It is now a historic landmark, polished and shined by Donald Trump to the tune of over $100 million. The guest rooms and suites (many with fireplaces), the public spaces, the restaurants, and the shops all have a new look of comfort and convenience, along with a slight tinge of nostalgia for how it used to be. The result is a gorgeous matron with a world-class facelift. Magnificent floral arrangements adorn the lobby, newly gilded ceilings shine in lobbies and rooms, and fabulous chandeliers glitter in the famous Palm Court. Polite bellmen, some of whom have been there for a quarter of a century, guide you to your comfortable digs, where king-sized towels await in marble bathrooms. Special linens with the Plaza crest enhance the beds. If you really feel like celebrating, ask for an English suite. There are horse-drawn carriages at the front door, and Eloise, the Plaza's most famous inhabitant, still stares down from her lobby painting. In case you do not want to jog in nearby Central Park, you can work out in the new fitness center.

PLAZA ATHENÉE
37 E 64th St (bet Park and Madison Ave)   212 734-9100
Expensive

A recent survey rated this hotel at the top of the heap in New York
in several categories, including service. Most of the rooms are furnished
with a pantry, and all have marble bathrooms. Some of the suites on
the higher floors feature solariums and roof terraces. Additional amenities
include a workout facility, 24-hour room service, and an outstanding
restaurant, Lé Regencé.

RADISSON EMPIRE
44 W 63rd St (bet Broadway and Columbus Ave)
212 265-7400
Moderate

A $30 million renovation has injected new life into this 1923 building,
located directly across from Lincoln Center. Special features include CD
players, color television, two-line phones, and a voice-mail messaging
service. There is a four-story health club, a complimentary continental
breakfast (in the Empire Club), and 24-hour room service for guests.

RIHGA ROYAL HOTEL
151 W 54th St (bet Sixth and Seventh Ave)   212 307-5000
Moderately expensive

The Rihga Royal is the newest and tallest all-suite hotel — and one of
the best deals in New York! It features over 500 suites, 24-hour suite
dining, late supper, full business center, meeting and banquet rooms,
fitness facility with sauna, and valet services, as well as six "royal" suites
that are truly special (and expensive). The concierge is one of New York's
most pleasant and talented. Halcyon, the hotel dining room, is a superb
place for a classy meal. Foreign travelers will appreciate the fact that
the staff speaks over 25 languages.

ROYALTON
44 W 44th St   212 869-4400
Moderate to moderately expensive

Run by the same people as Morgan's, the Royalton is a historic hotel
that's been reborn into a high-tech facility. It's sure to appeal to some
modern travelers. A French designer has created stark rooms, furnished
with low beds, VCRs, and finished with mahogany accents. Many of
the rooms have working fireplaces, and the bathrooms are king-sized
and very attractive. There is a lobby restaurant and an attractive small
bar near the hotel entrance. The helpful staff offers 24-hour room service and will gladly change pieces of art in the bedrooms.

ST. REGIS
Fifth Ave at 55th St   212 753-4500
Expensive

After a three-year, $100 million restoration, this historic hotel reopened as the crown jewel of the ITT Sheraton operation. With 236 oversized rooms and 86 suites, the hotel provides luxury accommodations with beautiful appointments. Each room has a refrigerator, classy bathroom, and all the fine extras you expect. A private butler is assigned to each floor. Gourmet French dining is available at Lespinasse, the showpiece restaurant. Old-timers will be pleased to learn that the St. Regis Roof, the only hotel-roof ballroom in the city, is still in full swing. With a superb location and a grand history, the St. Regis exudes class.

SALISBURY
123 W 57th St   212 246-1300
Moderate

The Salisbury is clean and intimate, with just over 300 rooms. Most have been redecorated, and many are outfitted with butler's pantries and refrigerators. Suites are large, comfortable, and reasonably priced. This is a favorite of lady travelers. If you want to be in the vicinity of Carnegie Hall and other midtown attractions, this hotel is for you. If you've waited until the last minute for reservations, the Salisbury is a good place to call, as it is not very well-known among out-of-towners and rooms are usually available. Rooms are also available for meetings and banquets.

SHERATON MANHATTAN
790 Seventh Ave (at 51st St)   212 581-3300, 800 325-3535
Moderate

The Sheraton folks have pumped nearly $50 million into redoing the former Sheraton City Squire, and it shows. The lobby, rooms, and eating facilities all have a bright, friendly, attractive look. An indoor swimming pool (a rarity in Manhattan) is a special attraction; so are the rates. Bistro 790 is a convenient place to dine when exploring midtown.

SHERATON NEW YORK
811 Seventh Ave (at 52nd St)   212 581-1000
Moderate to moderately expensive

You won't know this hotel, which has a classy new look! A stylish renovation of all rooms and public facilities has taken place. A great location, a nationwide referral service, and a wide selection of restaurants and lounges add up to a convenient and pleasant place to stay. The Sheraton Towers—the more expensive top floors—offer exclusive digs for the business or pleasure traveler. Amenities include terrycloth robes and butler service. The Sheraton New York also has a wide selection of package deals, and the price is right.

STANHOPE
995 Fifth Ave (at 81st St)   212 288-5800
Moderate to moderately expensive

The Stanhope is a quiet and refined hotel just right for those who are touring museums or who like to be away from the throngs. The hotel has about 150 rooms (79 of which are very spacious and attractive suites), a new health club and business center, and a wonderful park view from many rooms. Eating here is exceptionally agreeable, with three excellent restaurants and an outside garden for tea and snacks in nice weather. Managing Director Neil Trubowitch is a helpful and congenial gentleman; he directs a competent and helpful staff. VCRs and FAX machines are available upon request.

UNITED NATIONS PLAZA
1 United Nations Plaza (bet First and Second Ave, at 44th St)
212 355-3400
Moderate to expensive

This is a fashionable facility in the United Nations area, and therefore a prime gathering spot for the international set. The hotel is modern but executed in good taste. United Nations Plaza has a health club and restaurant, and it features nicely appointed rooms and international-style service. The suites are particularly attractive. The 288 rooms and suites offer spectacular views, since they begin on the 28th floor.

WALDORF-ASTORIA
301 Park Ave (at 50th St)   212 355-3000
Moderately expensive

For many years the Waldorf stood as *the* symbol of class in Manhattan. Sadly, over a period of years the place rested on its laurels. Now Hilton has invested more than $180 million to restore their flagship— and the work shows! The lobby, bedecked with magnificent mahogany wall panels and hand-woven carpets, is rich and impressive. In response to complaints about the size of some guest rooms, renovations created larger spaces by reducing the number of rooms. All-marble bathrooms and butler pantries were installed in some suites. An event at the Waldorf is sure to be something special.

WALDORF TOWERS
100 E 50th St   212 355-3100
Expensive

Peter Wirth presides over the Waldorf Towers, a palace in the middle of Manhattan. Guests of the Towers have their own entrance elevators, concierge, and all the other services you would expect from a first-rate operation. All rooms and suites, ranging from very comfortable to deluxe, are above the 28th floor, offering commanding views. I can remember visiting former President Herbert Hoover in his suite here; this hotel within a hotel provides the privacy and quiet many public figures desire. All the amenities of the Waldorf-Astoria are just an elevator ride away.

WALES
1295 Madison Ave (bet 92nd and 93rd St)   212 876-6000
Moderate

The Wales is a small, European boutique hotel that has recently been restored to its original condition. It was built in 1901 as the Chastaigneray, and it is now family-owned and operated — unusual in this day of major chains. There is a free continental breakfast, the uptown Madison Avenue address is good (and safe) for shoppers, and the Roof Garden overlooking the Central Park reservoir is attractive. Busby's (a bistro) and Sarabeth's Kitchen (an excellent restaurant) are on the ground floor.

WESTBURY
Madison Ave at 69th St   212 535-2000
Moderate to expensive

The Westbury is ideal for the solo traveler. The rooms are comfortable, modern, and offer every convenience, including closet safes and refurbished bathrooms. There is 24-hour room service; a new health club with saunas and steam rooms, plus state-of-the-art exercise equipment; and an excellent restaurant, the Polo, on the premises. The top-of-the-line suites are superbly tasteful and not a bit ostentatious. If you like refined living, check out this one.

WYNDHAM
42 W 58th St (at Fifth Ave)   212 753-3500
Moderate

This charming hotel is more like a large home where the owners rent out rooms. Many guests are folks who regularly make the Wyndham their Manhattan headquarters. The advantages are numerous: great location, uniquely decorated rooms and suites, complete privacy, individual attention, and no business conventions. On the other hand, the hotel is always busy, and reservations for the newcomer may be difficult. No room service is available; however, there is a small restaurant, and the suites have refrigerators. John Mados has created a winner!

Alternative Housing

. . . AAAH! BED & BREAKFAST #1
212 246-4000

The principal market this outfit serves is the small business person who is more interested in the comforts of home than a fancy address.

They also have a following among tourists who like to have a host clue them in about what to do and what not to do in the big city. William Salisbury, the manager, was a butler for many years, and he knows the hospitality business. Hosted or unhosted apartments are available. It is desirable to contact the firm two to four weeks in advance of your stay.

ABODE BED & BREAKFAST
P.O. Box 20022, New York, NY 10028   212 472-2000
Mon-Fri: 9–5; Sat: 11–2

Do you have your heart set on staying in a delightful old brownstone apartment? How about a contemporary luxury apartment in the heart of Manhattan? Abode selects their hosts with great care, and all homes are personally inspected to insure the highest standards of cleanliness, attractiveness, and hospitality. Shelli Leifer, the director, can provide clients with a maid, conference or meeting space, and whatever else is necessary for a perfect stay. Hosted accommodations with complimentary breakfast begin at $65 for singles, $80 for doubles; unhosted accommodations (minimum stay of two nights) are as low as $90 per night.

BED AND BREAKFAST NETWORK OF N.Y.
134 W 32nd St (bet Sixth and Seventh Ave)   212 645-8134
Mon-Fri: 8–6

Would you like to stay in a million-dollar high-rise condo? Or are you more comfortable in an artist's loft? This outfit can fix you up with either, for one night or several months. They offer over 300 accommodations, mostly in Manhattan, and guests can choose to stay with a host or have their own furnished apartment. Leslie Goldberg has been in the business since 1986 and is sensitive to the needs and desires of her guests.

CITY LIGHTS BED & BREAKFAST
P.O. Box 20355, Cherokee Station, New York, NY 10028
212 737-7049
Mon-Fri: 9–5; Sat: 9–12

Over 400 apartments and bed-and-breakfast accommodations all over Manhattan are available through these folks. Prices depend on length of stay and size, ambience, and location of the accommodation chosen. The approximate price range is $40–$70 per night for one person and $60–$95 for two people per night. Complimentary continental breakfast is included with all hosted apartments; hosts are carefully screened and their homes are inspected regularly. Be sure to specify the area of the city you are interested in, and chances are you will be able to save about 50% over commercial hotel rates. (Special business rates are available.) Ask for Yedida Nielsen when you call.

INTERNATIONAL HOUSE
500 Riverside Dr   212 316-8434
Moderate

This is a residence for 700 graduate students, interns, and other travelers from over 80 countries who are spending a day or several years in New York. It is located on the Upper West Side, near Columbia University and Manhattan School of Music. There are all sorts of special features: low-budget cafeteria, pub with dancing, gymnasium, computer room, and self-service laundry. Free programs include ballroom dancing, lectures, films, recitals, and organized sports. Single-room occupancy, with a shared bath on the floor, or suites with a kitchen run $25 per night but drop to $18 per night for stays of two to four weeks. Rates are less still by the semester.

LEO HOUSE
332 W 23rd St   212 929-1010, 800 732-2438
Inexpensive

This is the answer to one of the major questions people ask about New York: Where can a visitor find an inexpensive, safe, and clean place to stay in the city? You should have no qualms about the Leo House, a Catholic hospice. A secure, refined, and quiet place, it is still run by the Sisters of St. Agnes. Reservations are required and may be made as much as a year in advance. All guests are expected to follow very reasonable house rules. A small deposit is required. (It is refundable if cancellation is made 24 hours prior to scheduled arrival.) The maximum length of stay is two weeks. No smoking is allowed in guest and meeting rooms, and although the outside doors are locked at midnight, registered guests may still get in after that hour. Breakfast, featuring homemade bread, is available at a moderate price. It is a great place for the single student!

NEW WORLD BED AND BREAKFAST
150 Fifth Ave (Suite 711)   212 675-5600, 800 443-3800

New World offers accommodations in over 150 personally inspected locations in Manhattan. Prices start at $50 for single and $65 for double hosted apartments, $100 for unhosted studio rooms, and $120 for unhosted one-bedroom units.

NEW YORK INTERNATIONAL AMERICAN YOUTH HOSTEL
891 Amsterdam Ave (at W 103rd St)   212 932-2300
Inexpensive

Don't let the name mislead you; this facility is available to visitors of all ages. The hostel provides over 480 beds in a newly renovated, century-old landmark. They offer meeting spaces, catering, tours, self-service kitchens, and laundry facilities to individuals as well as large groups. Best of all, the price is right!

92ND ST Y (DE HIRSCH RESIDENCE)
1395 Lexington Ave   212 415-5650
Mon-Thurs: 9–6; Fri: 9–5; Sun: 10–5
Inexpensive

This facility offers convenient, inexpensive, and secure housing for men and women between the ages of 18 and 26. There are special discounts for Y health-club memberships, and both single and double rooms are available. Lengths of stay range from several days to several months. Admission is by application, and it is nontransient.

SHORT TERM HOUSING
862 Lexington Ave (at E 64th St)   212 570-2288
Mon-Fri: 10–6; Sun: 1–5
Summer: Mon-Fri: 10–8; Sat, Sun: noon–5

Short-term housing is the solution to all sorts of problems, such as marital separation, roommate problems, and extended visits from relatives or business executives. This agency serves as the go-between for those looking for an apartment and those who will not be using one for an extended length of time. Most of the clients are from North America, Europe, or the Orient, and all are individually matched to their needs. Terms are usually between one month and one year, and almost always involve sublets. One interesting wrinkle is that the fee is paid by the tenant taking occupancy, which means that Short Term works for the renter, not the owner, as most agents do.

URBAN VENTURES
P.O. Box 426, New York, NY 10024   212 594-5650
Mon-Fri: 9–5

Mary McAulay founded this service in 1979, modeling it after Britain's famous bed-and-breakfast rooms, because she felt something needed to be done about Manhattan's lack of reasonably priced lodging. After being carefully screened, 650 hosts, who live either in apartments, townhouses, brownstones, or lofts, signed up with Urban Ventures. Hosts range from older people living in big apartments to young artists. Both groups need a little help with the rent, and they are friendly and interested in their guests. The spare bedrooms are found on the Upper West Side, in the Village, in midtown, on the east side, in SoHo and TriBeCa, and even in Brooklyn. Security is good — after all, this is someone's home — and the B&B's, as they are known, are concentrated in areas heavily populated by sons and daughters trying their wings in Manhattan. Hence, these rooms are convenient for visiting parents, since their child's apartment is rarely large enough to accommodate a visitor. Accommodations ranging from studios to three-bedroom and three-bath apartments are available from two nights to two months or more without hosts. The price is right, and this is a first-rate chance to get a sense of what it's really like to live in Manhattan.

WEBSTER APARTMENTS
419 W 34th St (at Ninth Ave)   212 967-9000
Inexpensive

This place has to be one of the best buys in the city for working women with moderate incomes. It is *not* a transient hotel but operates on a policy developed by Charles B. Webster, a first cousin of Rowland Macy (of the department-store family). Webster left the bulk of his estate to found these apartments, which opened in 1923. Residents include college students, designers, actresses, secretaries, and other business and professional women. Facilities include dining rooms, recreation areas, a library, and lounges. The Webster also has private gardens for its guests, and meals can be taken outdoors in nice weather. Rates at press time were $120-$165 per week, which includes two meals a day plus maid service. Visitors must be sponsored by a current guest. The Webster is a secret find, known mainly to residents and readers of this book.

Interior Decorators

DAVID WAYNE INTERIORS
324 E 93rd St, #2W (bet First and Second Ave)   212 996-2134
Mon-Fri: 8–6 (summer, Mon-Thurs: 10–6)
After hours, weekends upon arrangement

Have you seen something in a decorative accessory that caught your eye? Many times it is difficult to get a large firm interested in small projects. No worry. Call David Wayne and he will put your idea into reality or copy something you like. Maybe it is custom-making a special picture frame in fabric or perhaps putting together a set of table linen to go with your china. He will do slipcovers, headboards, valances, shower curtains, pillows, decorative tiebacks, and small accessory items, but he does not undertake large upholstery pieces like sofas and club chairs.

DESIGNER PREVIEWS
212 777-2966

Having problems finding the right decorator? Designer Previews has information on over 100 of Manhattan's most trustworthy and talented designers, architects, and landscaping experts, and they will present it to you by way of slides and photographs. They will also discuss the designers' fees. Karen Fisher, the genius behind this handy service, was the decorating editor at *Cosmopolitan* and the style editor at *Esquire*. She charges $100 for her services.

MARTIN ALBERT INTERIORS
288 Grand St (corner Eldridge St)   212 226-4047
Sun-Fri: 9:30–5

Martin Albert specializes in window treatments, and they really know their business. They measure and install their products at prices that are considerably lower than most decorators. With over 30 home furnishings shops in their immediate vicinity, any store has to be good to survive in this highly competitive field. Martin Albert offers thousands of fabric samples ranging from $3 to $900 a yard. Services include upholstery and slipcovers; a large selection of drapery hardware is also available.

NEW YORK METROPOLITAN CHAPTER OF THE AMERICAN SOCIETY OF INTERIOR DESIGNERS
212 685-3480
Mon-Fri: 9–3

This is not a decorating service; it's a self-monitoring professional association to which most ethical and qualified interior designers belong. After an interview—during which you must specify your needs, taste, and budget—ASID will recommend up to three members who would be suitable and available for the job. They are not snobbish, and they treat a small job just as seriously as a large one. Even if you don't go this route, be sure the interior designer you *do* choose is ASID-affiliated.

PARSONS SCHOOL OF DESIGN
66 Fifth Ave (at 13th St)   212 229-8950
Mon-Fri: 9–5

Parsons, a division of the New School for Social Research, is one of the two top schools in the city for interior design. Those who call will get their request posted on the school's board, and every effort is made to match clients with prospective decorators. Individual negotiations determine the price and length of job, but it will be considerably less than what a not-so-recent student charges. The disadvantage is that most of these students don't have a decorator card. (One can always be borrowed.) This is a good place to contact if you just want a consultation.

RICHARD'S INTERIOR DESIGN
1325 Madison Ave (at 93rd St)   212 831-9000
234 E 75th St (bet Second and Third Ave)   212 734-4488
Mon-Wed, Fri, Sat: 10–6; Thurs: 10–7; Sun: 11–5

Here you will find over 10,000 decorator fabrics, including tapestries, damasks, stripes, plaids, silks, velvets, and floral chintzes. These are all first-quality, with competitive prices to boot. They will do upholstered furniture, reupholstery, slipcovers, draperies, top treatments, shades, bedroom ensembles, and wall coverings. Design services, in-home consultation, and installation are all available.

Jewelry Services

GEM APPRAISERS LABORATORY
608 Fifth Ave   212 333-3122
Mon-Fri: 9–5; closed first two weeks of July

Leopold Woolf, who owns Gem Appraisers Laboratory, is a graduate gemologist. He is also an officer and director of the Appraisers Association of America. As such, he is entrusted with the appraisals for major insurance companies, auction houses, banks, and the New York City Department of Consumer Affairs. In an area where it can't hurt to be too careful, this is a very safe bet. In addition to doing appraisals and consultations for estate, bank, insurance, and tax purposes, Woolf also runs Gem Appraisers Laboratory Designs, which manufactures and designs jewelry. A better appraiser would be hard to find.

RISSIN'S JEWELRY CLINIC
4 W 47th St (at Fifth Ave)   212 575-1098
Mon, Tues, Thurs: 9:30–5 (closed first two weeks of July)

This is indeed a clinic! The assortment of services is staggering: jewelry repair and design, antique repair, museum restorations, eyeglass repairs, pearl stringing, redoing of old necklaces, stone identification, and appraisals. Joe Rissin and his wife, Toby, now run the place. Joe's father was a master engraver, so the family tradition has been passed along for decades. *Honesty* is the byword here, and customers can rest assured merchandise will be returned in excellent condition. Estimates are gladly given, and all work is guaranteed.

ZDK COMPANY
48 W 48th St, Room 1409   212 575-1262
By appointment only

Most of his work has been the creation of rare and original pieces for neighbors in the diamond district, but in his free time Zohrab David Krikorian will do the work he does professionally for you, too. In addition to making jewelry, ZDK will mend and fix broken jewelry as only a professional craftsman and artist can. He makes complicated repairs look easy and has yet to encounter a job he can't handle. If he can't exactly match the stones in an antique earring, he'll redo the whole piece so it looks even better than before. He loves creating the latest designs from traditional materials, and his prices are quite reasonable.

Leather Repair

ARTBAG CREATIONS
735 Madison Ave (at 64th St)   212 744-2720
Mon-Fri: 9–5:45; Sat: 9–4; closed Sat in summer

Artbag will make, sell, or repair any type of handbag, and they do it well. The range goes from mounting needlepoint bags to relining heirloom bridal bags, as well as making leather, reptile, and beaded evening bags. Messrs. Moore and Price are European craftsmen who modestly advertise themselves as "understanding, genteel, and good listeners. They know their business." Any one of their customers could have said the same thing. Artbag is also known for its sense of style. They carry the latest and best designs, and they frequently refashion old handbags into chic trendsetters. It isn't every day you come across men who know more about handbags than women, but these gentlemen certainly know and keep up with the latest styles.

CARNEGIE LUGGAGE
1392 Sixth Ave (bet 56th and 57th St)   212 586-8210
Mon-Fri: 8:30–5:45; Sat: 9–5

Carnegie is handy to most major midtown and Central Park hotels. Service can be fast, if you let them know you're in a hurry. They are responsible in their dealings and offer reliable work at competitive prices.

JOHN R. GERARDO
30 W 31st St (bet Broadway and Fifth Ave)   212 695-6955
Mon-Fri: 9–5; Sat: 10–2; closed Sat in July, Aug

Dan Gerardo manages to dispense luggage and luggage repairs at John R. Gerardo that rival Crouch and Fitzgerald's (minus the glamour). Gerardo carries the standard brands in almost all kinds. There are sample cases, overnighters, two-suiters, and drawers with seemingly endless spare parts. There are zippers, handles, locks, and patches of fiber and material for emergency patching. Gerardo does quick, professional repairs. They also have a pickup and delivery service for a nominal fee.

SUPERIOR REPAIR CENTER
133 Lexington Ave   212 889-7211
Mon-Wed: 10–7; Thurs: 10–8; Fri: 10–6; Sat: 10–3;
Closed Sat in summer

Leather repair is the highlight of the service at Superior. Many major stores in the city use them for luggage and handbag work. They are experts in the repair or replacement of zippers on leather items. They will work on sporting equipment and fix tents and backpacks. If there is a leather problem, Superior has the answer.

Locksmiths

AAA LOCKSMITHS
44 W 46th St (at Sixth Ave)   212 840-3939
Mon-Thurs: 8–5:30; Fri: 8–5

You can learn a lot from trying to find a locksmith in New York. For one thing, as a profession it probably has the most full-page ads in the Manhattan Yellow Pages. For another, this particular "AAA" is *not* the place to call about a dead battery. However, in an industry that has little company loyalty or recommendations, AAA Locksmiths has been in the business for over a half-century, and that says a lot right there.

NIGHT AND DAY LOCKSMITH
1335 Lexington Ave (at 89th St)   212 722-1017
Mon-Sat: 9–6:30 (24 hours for emergencies)

Just in case you're ever locked out, Night and Day is a number you should be carrying close to your heart. New Yorkers, even those who are in residence for a short time, become experts on locks and cylinders. Cocktail-party conversation is frequently peppered with references to dead bolts, Medeco, and Segal. If you haven't the vaguest idea what all the talk is about, you obviously don't live in the city, where a locksmith is as revered a professional as there can be. He's got to stay ahead of the cocktail-circuit fads, as well as the local burglar's latest expertise, and be able to offer fast, on-the-spot service for a variety of devices designed to keep people out. (After all, no apartment has just *one* lock.) Mena Sofer, Night and Day's owner, fulfills these rigid requirements. The company answers its phone 24 hours a day; posted hours are for the sale of locks, window gates, intercoms, car alarms, safes, and keys. Inside and outside welding is a specialty. If you buy a lock here, you can be sure they'll be willing to help you out (or *in,* as the case may be) when the time comes.

Marble Works

NEW YORK MARBLE WORKS
1399 Park Ave (at 104th St)   212 534-2242
Mon-Fri: 8–4:30; closed July 1–10

Three generations of Louis Gleicher's family have run this business at the same location since 1900, and they know the marble business cold (sorry for the pun!). Gleicher will create and custom-design marble pieces and furniture for bathrooms, fireplaces, tables, and mantels. They also repair broken marble, do repolishing, and craft consoles, pedestals, and tabletops. They have the largest selection of floor and wall marble, granite, onyx, and slate tiles in the country. A full line of marble-care supplies is available. They will ship anywhere in the world.

PUCCIO MARBLE AND ONYX
232 E 59th St (gallery and showroom)   212 688-1351
661 Driggs Ave, Brooklyn (factory warehouse showroom)
718 387-9778

Puccio's factory and warehouse are in Brooklyn, but they qualify for
a listing since they have a showroom in Manhattan, which is open only
by appointment. Paul Puccio runs both as a showcase for his sculpture
and furniture designs, which range from traditional to sleekly modern.
It is almost incongruous to see an angular, free-flowing sculpture made
of formal marble, when Roman busts on pedestals are what comes to
mind. But John Puccio boasts that his tables are found in décors that
are strictly modern and very chic. "We strive for plain but luxurious,"
he says. He succeeds, and the results are startling as well as elegant.
Interior furnishings include dining and cocktail tables, chairs, chests of
drawers, buffets, desks, consoles, and pedestals. Custom-designed installations include foyer floors, complete bathrooms, kitchens, bars, staircases, fountains, and fireplaces. A project takes from 6 to 16 weeks for
delivery, since it is custom-manufactured, but a commission is not even
accepted (even though there is a ready-made line) if it is not received
through a decorator or designer. Puccio is just not equipped to deal with
retail orders, but a visit to the factory will enable you to see the line
for yourself.

Massage

JUDY MARKOVA
212 737-0247

The top concierges in town call Judy Markova for professional, reliable
massage service. She has been a licensed massage therapist for over 15
years, specializing in Swedish massage.

LEWIS HARRISON
40 W 72nd St   212 724-8782

Lewis Harrison has been an instructor at the respected Swedish
Massage Institute in New York, and he is recognized as an expert in
the field. He has written several books on massage and is absolutely
reliable. He works on both men and women, does shiatsu, Swedish, and
sports massage, and will take appointments at his place of business, plus
home and hotel calls.

Matchmaking

FIELD'S EXCLUSIVE SERVICE
41 E 42nd St   212 391-2233

The motto "New York lives by this book!" is a big challenge, but I
can't let anyone down, so this edition even includes a hint on matchmak-

ing. Dan Field's company has been playing Cupid for three quarters of a century. If Dan is successful for you, how about a testimonial for *Where to Find It, Buy It, Eat It in New York* – the Romance Edition, of course!

Medical Services (See also Manhattan at Night, Emergency Rooms, Chapter VII)

DOCTORS ON CALL
718 238-2100

This service answers a real need in the city. In the past, hotels always had staff doctors on call. Medical and dental associations would arrange for doctors to cover the city during off hours, and, of course, hospital emergency rooms are open 24 hours a day. But private doctors have stopped making house calls, even to regular patients. Doctors on Call was created to take care of that problem. Though most calls are to people who don't have regular city doctors (usually visitors), many calls are made on residents. The fee in Manhattan is $60–125, which covers the cost of transportation and parking, and most calls are completed within two hours of your phone call. All members of Doctors on Call are licensed, and further tests or treatments can be arranged, if necessary.

OLSTEN HEALTH CARE
30 Rockefeller Plaza, Room 25   212 586-1790
24 hours

Olsten is a nationwide service that provides fully screened, bonded, supervised, and trained home health aides. The type of person sent and the subsequent bill depend upon the level of care needed, but they are capable of supplying registered nurses, licensed practical nurses, home health aides, and companions. In-home IV therapy is offered. They will supply complete home-nursing service, as well as hospital support.

QUALITY CARE
350 W 34th St   212 563-2100
Mon-Fri: 8:30–5, on-call 24 hours a day

Quality Care is a nationwide organization dedicated to providing temporary health-care personnel on all levels. It was created to meet the changing needs of medical care. Formerly, the sick were treated at home, but today they are sent to institutions. That isn't always what patients want, so there is a need for professionals who will work at a patient's home. Quality Care supplies registered and licensed practical nurses, home health aides, homemakers, companions, physical-occupation and speech therapists, and just about every other kind of home-care specialist imaginable. These professionals will adapt their program to special needs, such as kosher cooking and small rooming accommodations, as well as providing health screening tests and guidance to clients. They also do IV therapy. Here's hoping you won't need them, but it's nice to know that Quality Care is there and that a national organization stands behind it.

UNION SQUARE DRUGS
859 Broadway (bet 17th and 18th St)   212 242-2725
Mon-Fri: 7:30–6; Sat: 9–3

This store consistently offers the best prices on prescription drugs, industrial first-aid supplies, and vitamins, and is equally well-known for its reliability. The service is so conscientious that the pharmacist will call — long-distance if necessary — to verify prescriptions. (And you know how most salespeople react to the very *thought* of making a long-distance call.) Union Square will fill union prescriptions.

Metal Work

AMEROM
212 675-4828
Mon-Fri: 7:30–5; Sat by appointment

Florin Carmocanu is a Romanian artisan whose metal workshop originally focused on welding and cutting metal to size. Not terribly exciting or demanding of Carmocanu's considerable talent. But then word of his handiwork got out to loft dwellers, co-op remodelers, and interior decorators, and suddenly Amerom is one of the hottest places in town. And no wonder. Carmocanu is a genius with decorative metal, structural steel, and wrought-iron furniture and gates. His spiral staircases are awesome. Amerom can even replace original artwork and wrought-iron designs of old brownstones. As for the name, which doesn't exactly come tripping off the tongue, could it be a combination of the words *Ame*rican and *Rom*anian?

RETINNING AND COPPER REPAIR
525 W 26th St (at Tenth Ave)   212 244-4896
Mon-Fri: 9–6

Jamie Gibbons has taken over a long established Manhattan business whose specialty is retinning (which is basically copper repair). Gibbons, who has over 10 years experience in the field, restores brass and copper antiques; designs and creates new copperware (almost all copper pots in use today are heirlooms); restores lamps, chandeliers, and brass beds; and sells restored copper pieces.

Movers

IKE BANKS
718 527-7505

Ike Banks probably breaks every rule for inclusion in this book. He's not bonded or licensed, nor is he a resident of Manhattan (he lives in Queens), but he never breaks anything, and I trust him more than anyone else listed here. He was first recommended to me by an appliance store, when a delicate and temperamental washing machine needed to be delivered. Since then, he has moved pianos, households, and dining rooms for friends. Several years ago, estimates for moving a nine-piece dining room ran from $100 to $300. Banks did it perfectly for $25. He will travel anywhere in the city, sometimes further, and will work odd hours (unless he's taking his nephew to a ballgame). He's a super guy. The only complaint I have is that he's so careful that he can be very slow. (It's a good thing he doesn't charge by the hour!) Ike also has a used wood-furniture store.

MOISHE'S MOVING SYSTEMS
212 439-9191

Moishe learned the business from the bottom up, packing boxes and handling them personally to make sure the customers were satisfied. He learned well and quickly, and soon parlayed his experience into organizing one of the largest and most successful moving and storage companies in the area. He now has dozens of bright red trucks, and several hundred bright, red-clad employees. Moishe Mana, a Tel Aviv University Law School dropout, claims he did it the hard way—from nothing to a business that now grosses millions. Document storage in modern facilities is just one feature of the storage side of his operation. Boxes and packing materials in all sizes are available for purchase.

MOVING STORE
644 Amsterdam Ave (bet 91st and 92nd St)   212 874-3800
Mon-Fri: 8–6; Sat: 9–3

Steve Fiore started West Side Movers in the kitchen of his studio apartment more than 20 years ago. Business was so good that he soon moved into a storefront. He was happy there until he realized the magnitude of requests he was getting from people who wanted to rent and buy dollies and boxes of all sizes. A man who knows a good business opportunity when he sees one, Fiore moved into a brownstone storefront on Amsterdam Avenue in order to sell nothing but moving aids and paraphernalia. The main stock-in-trade is still boxes. They come in more sizes than seem possible, including three different sizes just for mirrors. He now rents and sells dollies, in addition to moving pads. Since all items are built to the specifications of professional movers, they are durable.

WEST SIDE MOVERS
644 Amsterdam Ave (bet 91st and 92nd St)   212 874-3800
Mon-Fri: 8–6; Sat: 9–4; Sun: 9–3

We came to West Side Movers via their Moving Store. But such ecumenical and diverse groups as the Union Theological Seminary and Tiffany & Company came to West Side Movers by recommendation and have added their accolades to the file. A company with a subdivision that specializes in helping people move themselves (by selling boxes and moving supplies) has to be top-notch. West Side Movers pays particular attention to efficiency, promptness, care, and courtesy. Customer after customer has called their staff the most courteous they've dealt with — and they don't dent the furniture, either!

Newspaper Delivery

LENOX HILL NEWSPAPER DELIVERY
502 E 74th St   212 879-1822

Lenox Hill Newspaper Delivery is an excellent door-to-door service. For a slight charge, they will deliver the New York papers, the *Christian Science Monitor,* the *Washington Post, Women's Wear Daily,* the *Sunday Observer,* or whatever else the customer wants. All of these, Lenox Hill claims, can be delivered "earlier than subscriptions reach your mailbox." For many people, that makes it worth the service charge.

Office Services

AMAL PRINTING AND PUBLISHING
630 Fifth Ave, concourse level (at 51st St)   212 247-3270
Mon-Fri: 9–5:30 (evenings and weekends by appointment)

Run out of business cards on the day you have an appointment for a big deal? Well, don't worry, you can get them done in a day (for a bit extra) at Amal, located on the concourse level of the International Building. They do all kinds of printing, from flyers to business forms to invitations, and if the order is large enough, they'll work on weekends. Overnight and while-you-wait service is available, as well as pickup and delivery. This is a good spot to remember for just about any kind of printing need.

SEEFORD ORGANIZATION
75 Varick St (bet Canal and Watts St)   212 431-4000
Mon-Fri: 8:30–5

Not too many outfits can say they have dealt with one special customer since the day they opened . . . over 43 years ago! Seeford does quality general commercial printing and advertising specialties of all kinds. They can handle printing jobs from concept and design right through printing, binding, and delivery. The boss, Sam Goldstein, is on the job himself, and the quality of the work and service shows that personal concern. Besides, he is one of the nicest individuals in New York.

WORLD-WIDE BUSINESS CENTRES
575 Madison Ave (bet 56th and 57th St)
212 605-0200, 800 296-9922
Mon-Fri: 9–5:30; Sat, Sun: by request

Alan Bain, a transplanted English lawyer, has created a highly profitable business that caters to executives who need more than a hotel room when in New York on business. The operation grew out of Bain's own frustrations in trying to put together a makeshift office, write and get out reports, answer telephones, and still attend to matters that brought him to the city in the first place. Services by on-premises word processors and typists are available. Desk space, private offices, and conference rooms may be rented on a daily, weekly, monthly, or quarterly basis. The daily rate includes telephone answering, receptionists, and a private office. The company also operates a full-service travel agency that specializes in corporate travel and travel-management service to small and medium-sized companies, as well as corporate meeting planning.

Party Services (See also Party Places, Chapter VII)

BALOOMS
147 Sullivan St   212 673-4007
Mon-Fri: 10–6; Sat: 12–6; Sun: available for parties

Balooms differs from most balloon services in that customers are not only invited but requested to visit the office. That is because Balooms is a legitimate, albeit small, store that encourages browsing and spur-of-the-moment sales. While there are still skeptics who feel *no one* impulsively buys a balloon, Balooms' sales prove otherwise. In addition to the standard balloon bouquet, they offer party decorating and custom-designed bouquets with names, logos, and even portraits on each balloon. Balooms will deliver in Manhattan and the boroughs, and they will ship anywhere. The store also has helium rental. As befits this lighthearted business, owners Marlyne Berger and Raymond Baglietto are delightful.

LINDA KAYE'S BIRTHDAYBAKERS, PARTYMAKERS
195 E 76th St (bet Lexington and Third Ave)
212 288-7112
Parties seven days a week

Linda Kaye likes to say that she arranges fun times for those aged one right up to one hundred plus. It all started in 1976, when she needed some entertainment for her daughter's sixth birthday party and came up with the idea of kids baking and decorating a birthday cake. Now her operation has expanded into one of the most unique party services in Manhattan, with headquarters in a townhouse where there is a party room for children's events. There are dinosaur parties, magic-tea parties, square-dancing parties, ice-skating parties . . . and for the oldsters there are belly dancers, hayrides, stilt walkers and much more. Linda offers themed paper party items by mail, rents kiddie tables and chairs, and offers a wide variety of custom-styled cakes for any occasion. You decide who you want to honor, and Linda and her crew will do the rest with style and imagination.

NEW YORK PARTIES
22 E 13th St   212 777-3565
Daily: 10–6

When you are thinking big, Jean-Michel Savoca's New York Parties is a great name to remember. These folks take charge of everything including food, liquor, equipment rentals, tents, flowers, lighting, music, and trained personnel. When people like Frank Sinatra, Paine Webber, and Chase Manhattan use a service, you know it has to be first-rate. They can offer prime locations, such as grand ballrooms or spacious yachts, if that is what you have in mind.

PARTY POOPERS
104 Reade St (bet W Broadway and Church St)
212 587-9030
Mon–Fri: 10–6 (hours may vary depending on party schedule)

Party Poopers are really entertainers who make sure they never do the same party twice. They have excellent facilities and even include a "spoofhouse" in their attractions. They can arrange a carnival, a fairy tale experience, a disco, or a spookhouse/monster bash. They will come to your place, if you want, and will bring costumes, puppets, wigs, and everything else to make the occasion an unforgettable one for your child.

PROPS FOR TODAY
121 W 19th St (bet Sixth and Seventh Ave)   212 206-0330
Mon–Fri: 9–5

This is the handiest place in town when you are preparing for a party. Props for Today has the largest rental inventory of home decorations in New York. Whether you want everyday china and silver or unique antiques going back as far as a hundred years, they have the goods in stock. There are platters, vases, tablecloths, and everything in between. There is a Christmas section, children's items, books, fireplace equipment, artwork, garden furniture, foreign items, and ordinary kitchenware. Over a million items are available, to give you an idea of the selection! Phone orders are taken, but it is a good idea to call for an appointment and see for yourself. Ask for Dyann Klein, the proprietor.

Pen and Lighter Repair

AUTHORIZED REPAIR SERVICE
30 W 57th St   212 586-0947
Mon, Tues, Thurs, Fri: 9–5; Wed: 9–6

When a business' specialty is the repair of fountain pens and cigarette lighters in this day of disposable ball points and no-smoking campaigns, you might not think it would be a viable concern. But you would be wrong. Morton Winston first started the business over two decades ago, and it is still incredibly busy — perhaps because it is almost without competition. Those who use fountain pens are devoted customers. Authorized Repair sells and services nearly every brand, and the shop can refill lighters, as well as all kinds of ball point, cartridge, and fountain pens. Authorized also sells, repairs, and services electric shavers. Tourists can even pick up 220-volt appliances or adapter plugs, and the extremely polite and helpful staff is well versed in the fine points of each brand.

FOUNTAIN PEN HOSPITAL
10 Warren St (across from City Hall)   212 964-0580
Mon-Fri: 8–6

This establishment is one of the few in town that repairs fountain pens. The Fountain Pen Hospital sells and repairs pens of all types, and other writing implements as well. They are probably the most experienced shop around at what they do.

Personal Services

BIG APPLE GREETER
1 Centre St (at Chambers St)   212 669-2896
Office: Mon-Fri: 9:30–5:30;
Greeter appointments, daily, daytime

More than 400 volunteers from all five boroughs will meet individuals and small groups and show them familiar neighborhoods. Notice is requested for those who need special language greeters. Greeters will come to a visitor's hotel and arrange a special itinerary for things that will be of interest. This is a wonderful way to get an inside view of a city that can be very intimidating. Tipping, home visits, and use of private transportation are considered inappropriate. Visitors are provided with transportation maps, site and attraction information, calendars of events, and arts and entertainment data. It is sort of like a new friend showing you the wonders of their city!

CATHERINE VAN ORMER
238 Madison Ave   212 532-4446

Image-wardrobe-fashion consultant Catherine Van Ormer not only associates with diplomats, socialites, executives, and show-business personalities, but she dresses them. As more people began demanding her fashion-shopping expertise, she closed her boutique and went into personal shopping full-time. She is quite simply the best in the business. Most of her clients have neither the time nor talent to put together a top-notch wardrobe, and they benefit from her close association with the city's top clothing designers. She scouts lines and then shows the best to her clients. Clothes can be purchased at Catherine's wholesale cost, which is roughly 50% less than retail, and the fashions reflect her eye for couture lines and natural fibers. Her fee is a mere pittance for those who simply must have this service. (There are those who simply can't keep all those cocktail parties straight.) Van Ormer offers a similar service for custom-made bridal gowns and accessories. The gowns are magnificent, and the prices do not reflect the superb quality of the work. Her one-hour consultation fee is included in the price of a wedding gown. A full range of bridal planning is also available.

Doula Agencies

Doula comes from a Greek word meaning "mothering the mother." These ladies, usually mothers themselves, are trained to provide all kinds of help for new mothers, including cooking, shopping, feeding, and emotional support. A few of the best:

In a Family Way (212 877-8112)
Motherlove (201 358-2703)
Mother Nurture (718 631-BABY)
N.Y. Nurse (212 989-3036)

EMILY CHO
212 289-7807, 201 784-3325
By appointment

Emily Cho is a lady whose job it is to make her clients "look and feel terrific!" She is a clothing psychologist and has been doing this kind of work for a quarter of a century. The process begins with an in-depth interview at your home or hotel, where your wardrobe is reviewed. She will then organize and update your clothes, and escort you on a personal shopping tour. Emily finds new resources every year, and she promises to stay on her client's budget plans. Corporate services and an intensive two-day course in personal image consulting are also available. This talented professional has had prior experience at Bloomingdale's, the Ford Model Agency, and *Seventeen* magazine.

FASHION UPDATE
718 377-8873
Daily: 9–5

Sara Gardner is a mother of three who naturally wants to make sure she gets the best value out of every clothing dollar spent. She found she could get apparel for her family at wholesale prices from some manufacturers, so she decided to share her discovery with others. Thus she started *Fashion Update,* a quarterly publication that uncovers bargains in women's, men's, and children's designer clothing and accessories available in the garment district. She even conducts special shopping expeditions to designer showrooms.

GLENN BRISTOW
218 W 10th St (at Bleecker St)   212 243-0571
Hours: by appointment

Financial consultant Glenn Bristow claims she can demystify the process of managing money and paperwork. Her clients include homemakers, dentists, designers, restaurant operators, and horticulturists. She has had over 20 years of experience in business administration, is computer literate, and comes highly recommended for bookkeeping and budgeting advice.

THE INTREPID NEW YORKER
1230 Park Ave (bet 95th and 96th St)   212 534-5071
Daily: 24 hours

Kathy Braddock, founder and owner of this service, is indeed "the Intrepid New Yorker." She was born, bred, and educated in the Big Apple. Like your author, she delights in trying to help folks unravel the hassles and confusion of this great city. She provides one of the most complete personal-service businesses in the area and is available at any time. Kathy can take you on private guided tours, shopping expeditions, help you find a place to live, and take care of your decorating or refurbishing needs. She also offers a membership that will give clients referrals and 10% off her regular hourly rates. This is handy for those who need quick and complete information. Of course, you could first look in this book, but calling Kathy is the next best alternative.

IT'S EASY
10 Rockefeller Center   212 586-8880
Mon-Fri: 9–6

Some time ago, David Alwadish found himself trying to remain cool amid an angry crowd of people at the passport office in Rockefeller Center. When someone in line told him that they would pay anything to get off that line, Alwadish took him literally, and a new business was born. Over the next decade, Alwadish did so well as a stand-in and gofer that he went national and branched out into doing research for attorneys and businesses, auto leasing, and even motor-vehicle inspection. His com-

---

After John D. Rockefeller, Jr., graduated from college, he was immediately put on his father's payroll. He was made a board member of 17 different corporations, including U.S. Steel, and received a yearly salary of $10,000. When the market crashed in 1929, Rockefeller lost a fortune but saved a 24-year lease (at $3.3 million a year) for the site of the future Rockefeller Center.

pany will help with passports, visas, and "bureaucratic transactions." Indeed, if there is any occupation or line or work where someone else can wait in line for a client, then It's Easy will do it. Incidentally, they haven't lost the personal touch, even though the company is now owned by Alwadish's sister, Leslie Shapiro. She guarantees that no one will wait on line for reservations at It's Easy!

LET MILLIE DO IT!
212 532-8775
Daily: 10 a.m. to whenever

Millie Emory has been in business for over 15 years as a professional organizer, saving people time, money, and stress. She especially likes working for theatrical folks but will help anyone with a broad variety of tasks. She will organize and unclutter apartments, desks, files, closets, libraries, attics, basements, garages, and storage rooms; pay bills; reconcile checkbooks; and get your papers in order for a tax accountant or IRS audit. She can help with paper flow, time management, and space problems. Millie is also good at finding things: antiques, out-of-print books and records, and so on. She assists seniors in dismantling their homes before entering nursing facilities. When loss of a loved one strikes, she will handle estate liquidations, selling, donating, and leaving the space "broom clean." She is a real problem solver! Millie charges by the hour.

SAVED BY THE BELL CORP
11 Riverside Dr   212 874-5457
Mon-Fri: 9–7 (or by appointment)

Susan Bell (get it?) is the genius behind this organization. Her goal is to take the worry out of planning virtually any type of job for people who are too busy or disorganized to do it themselves. Bell says "doing the impossible is our specialty," and you can believe her. Specialties include weddings, fundraising and charity benefits, party planning, tag sales, corporate relocations, shopping, delivery arrangements, and service referrals.

SMARTSTART
334 W 86th St   212 580-4924

There is always someone alert enough to fill a special niche or need. Such a person is Susan Weinberg. By her own experience, she learned that many expectant mothers and fathers were too busy to plan for the arrival of the bundle from heaven. So she started Smartstart, a consulting service to aid folks in pulling everything together. Her service provides the basics of what the new arrival will need, as well as room design, gifts, and personal shopping. In addition, Susan sells hand-painted children's furniture, from table and chair sets to coat hooks and toy chests. She is truly the stork's number one assistant.

Photographic Services

A.A. IDENTIFICATION SERVICE

698 Third Ave (bet 43rd and 44th St)   212 682-5045
Mon-Fri: 8–6

A.A.'s main virtue is their ability to do passport and identification photos competently and quickly. This is no small matter, as some photo shops near passport offices can be very unreliable. A.A. has a good reputation for laminating, doing one-day business portraits, and providing one-hour photo-lab services.

DAN DEMETRIAD

119 W 57th St, 2nd floor   212 245-1720
Mon-Fri: 9–6:30; Sat: 11–3

These folks were trained as commercial photographers, and now they have parlayed their experience into photo restoration. They are pros at making a copy negative when the original is missing, retouching, and doing quantity work at special prices. Everything is hand-done, and you can be assured of top quality.

FRED MARCUS PHOTOGRAPHY

245 W 72nd St (bet Broadway and West End Ave)
212 873-5588
Mon, Fri: 9–5; Tues-Thurs: 9–7 (by appointment)

Half a century in the photography business has made this firm a favorite for weddings, parties, or any kind of business event. Children's portraits are a specialty, and Marcus offers videotaping services in a most professional manner.

GALOWITZ PHOTOGRAPHICS

50 E 13th St   212 505-7190
Mon-Fri: 8:15–5:30; Sat: 10–4

In a city that has two button shops, two seashell shops, and a dozen pet groomers, you would think there would be a number of photographic restoration establishments. No, sir. This very exacting art is a rare bird, and I am happy to recommend Galowitz as a fine practitioner whose specialty is making old photos look presentable and worth more than sentimental value. One of their specialties is large blowups that can be used for parties or business events. Galowitz is a quality, full-service photo lab.

NEW YORK FILM WORKS
928 Broadway (at 21st St)   212 475-5700
Mon-Fri: 8–8; Sat: 10–4

Need a copy of a slide or print? These folks can produce a color photograph in one hour, with prices that are extremely competitive.

PHOTOGRAPHICS UNLIMITED/
DIAL-A-DARKROOM
17 W 17th St, 4th floor (bet Fifth and Sixth Ave)
212 255-9678
Mon-Fri: 9 a.m.–11 p.m.; Sat: 10–7; Sun: noon–7

Here's another only-in-New York idea. Photographics Unlimited offers photographers of limited physical means a full range of photographic darkroom equipment and a place to work on a rental basis. The shop has everything from the simplest equipment to an 8x10 Saltzman enlarger, including all manner of printing paper and film supplies, as well as a lab for on-the-spot developing of black-and-white and color. They also do custom processing and printing. Ed Lee claims his center is a complete one for amateurs and advanced professional photographers alike, and he aims to prove it. Darkrooms can be rented, and they come with advice and suggestions from the owner. Whatever could be desired in a personal darkroom can be rented. A technical hotline is available to answer questions.

PROFESSIONAL CAMERA REPAIR SERVICE
37 W 47th St (bet Fifth and Sixth Ave)   212 382-0511
Mon-Fri: 8:30–5

Rush jobs are the specialty here, so there's no need to spoil your vacation because your camera is on the blink. Professionals will work on still cameras from 35mm up. They will also do modifications and adaptations for special camera equipment.

STAT STORE DIGITAL EXCHANGE
1 W 20th St   212 929-0566
Mon-Fri: 9–6:30; Sat: 10–4

In medical parlance, *stat* means "fast." In photo jargon, *stat* is short for photostat, and it has come to mean virtually any kind of copy. The Stat Store specializes in both meanings of the word: rapid copying and photo duplication, and it offers Xerox copying, Kodaliths, color stats, cibaprints, custom transfers, photo posters, and photo murals, as well as photostats. A new electronic publishing division offers high-resolution computer output and design services. They also assist clients in design, illustration, technical support, and production management of projects.

Plant Consultation

COUNCIL ON THE ENVIRONMENT OF NEW YORK CITY
51 Chambers St, Room 228   212 788-7900
Mon-Fri: 9–5

It's a little-known fact that the city will loan tools to groups involved in community sponsored open-space greening projects. Loans are limited to one week, but the waiting period is not long, and for the price (nothing!) the wait is worth it. You can borrow the same tools several times a season, as long as there is no one ahead of you on the list. A group can be as few as four people. The council will also design office waste prevention and recycling service programs for commercial businesses. They will do tree labeling for a fee, and they have a number of interesting free publications.

Plumbers

KAPNAG HEATING AND PLUMBING
212 289-8847

As an out-of-towner, I'm not often in need of a local plumber, so there's a story behind how I learned that Kapnag is a really first-rate operation. A while ago, I was visiting a friend who was having a plumbing problem. She called Kapnag but got no response. When she called a second time, Kapnag apologized profusely and came out immediately to fix it. There was even a follow-up call to make sure the problem had been completely corrected. Ask any New Yorker, and you'll learn what a rare virtue this story illustrates. Brett Neuhauser, Kapnag's president, is the impetus behind all this kindness and competence. When we first published this story, Neuhauser wrote to tell us that the sudden surge in sales was due to his mother "supplying the Northeast region with our books." May they both continue to thrive!

Postal Services

MAIL BOXES ETC. USA
212 629-6200 (information on nearest facility)

Mail Boxes Etc. has over 24 locations in New York, and they can provide convenient FAX and telex service in all time zones. They also represent all major carriers and will do professional packaging and shipping. Handy services (not all of them available at every location) include stamps and envelopes, mail forwarding, packing supplies, business cards, office stationery, notary and secretarial services, passport photos, laminating, key duplication, and computer letters. Who needs a secretary?

Reweaving

FRENCH-AMERICAN REWEAVING COMPANY
119 W 57th St   212 765-4670
Mon-Fri: 10–6; Sat: 11–2

For more than 60 years, this company has been repairing and mending knit, lace, linen, silk, and wool fabrics with an almost invisible mending process that makes the new threads indiscernible from the originals. Even when an item is badly – and seemingly irreparably – damaged, the people at French-American claim that if they can't completely mend the wound, they can at least repair it so that their work is the next best thing to invisible. Needless to say, one doesn't submit a $3 tie to these costly procedures. But if an item is worth saving, it's almost a sure bet that these people can pull it off. They repair suede and leather, also.

Rug Cleaning

A. BESHAR AND COMPANY
611 Broadway (Cable Building)   212 529-7300 (gallery),
212 292-3301 (rug cleaning)
Mon-Fri: 9–5

Lee Howard Beshar's family has run this carpet and Oriental rug business for three generations. Consequently, there is little he doesn't know or hasn't seen in the carpet business. He can handle any kind of request competently. His expertise and experience are the basis of the Besharizing Cleaning Process, which is received by all floor coverings submitted for correction. Naturally, if a rug needs only cleaning, you're ahead of the game. Beshar does pickup and delivery, and all carpets are cleaned at the company's warehouse. This can be expensive, so if your carpet isn't very valuable, you might be better off buying a new one. Here, too, Beshar can come to the rescue with a large range of Oriental and antique rugs. All are of good quality and value, and Beshar stands behind – and sometimes on – them all!

Scissors and Knife Sharpening

HENRY WESTPFAL AND COMPANY
105 W 30th St   212 563-5990
Mon-Fri: 9–6

A Japanese gentleman once brought in his prized Samurai sword for repair at Henry Westpfal's, so you know this place has to be expert at what it does. They've been in business since 1874, and the same family has been in charge all that time. They do all kinds of sharpening and repair, from barber scissors and pruning shears to cuticle scissors, plus all kinds of work on light tools. Tools for leather workers, cutlery, shears, and scissors are all for sale. And for you southpaws, they also sell those hard-to-find left-handed scissors.

Shoe Repair

B. NELSON SHOE CORPORATION
1221 Sixth Ave (C-2 level, McGraw-Hill Bldg)   212 869-3552
Mon-Fri: 7:30–5:15

When several luggage dealers recommend the same shoe-repair out-fit, you know that it must be pretty good. This is exactly how I heard about B. Nelson. When I finally found the establishment, imagine how red-faced I was when I saw a previous write-up from my own book on their wall! The explanation is that B. Nelson branch outlets go under the name General Shoe Repair. They are very good at repair of dress, leisure, or athletic shoes. Other outlets (look for General Shoe Repair) are on the plaza concourse level at 30 Rockefeller Plaza (the General Electric Building), 1285 Sixth Ave (the Paine Webber Building), and 630 Fifth Ave (the International Building).

JIM'S SHOE REPAIR
50 E 59th St (bet Madison and Park Ave)   212 355-8259
Mon-Fri: 8–5:45; Sat: 9–3:45; closed Sat in summer

This operation offers first-rate shoe repair, shoeshine, and shoe sup-plies. Shoe repair is a field that is rapidly losing its craftsmen, and Jim is one of the few who upholds the tradition. Jim's owner is Joseph A. Rocco, who specializes in orthopedic work and boot alteration.

MANHATTAN SHOE REPAIR
6 E 39th St   42 E 41st St   212 683-4210
Mon-Fri: 7:30–5:45

Manhattan Shoe Repair offers a large range of fashion repairs. In ad-dition to resoling and heel repairs, Manhattan does rebinding, re-dyeing, and bag repair. Their motto is "Work that lasts," and 45 years in the business bears that out.

Silver Repair

BRANDT & OPIS
46 W 46th St, 5th floor   212 302-0294
Mon-Thurs: 8–5; Fri: 8–2

If it has anything to do with silver, Roland Markowitz can fix it. This includes silver repair, silver polishing, buying and selling estate silver, repair of silver-plated items, and fixing silver tea and coffee services. Gold-plating, lamp restoration, and plating of antique bath and door hard-ware are other specialties. Brandt & Opis are, in short, specialists in metal restoration.

THOME SILVERSMITHS
49 W 37th St, Room 605 (bet Fifth and Sixth Ave)
212 764-5426
Mon-Fri: 8:30–5:30

Thome cleans, repairs, and replates silver, in addition to buying and selling some magnificent pieces. They have a real appreciation for the material, and it shows in everything they do. They will repair and polish brass and copper, and they also perform restorations of antique silver and *objets d'art,* silver and gold plating, pewter repair and cleaning, restoring the velvet backs of picture frames and velvet box linings, lacquering, and refining. (Incidentally, *don't* attempt pewter repair yourself; pewter is an alloy and must be handled delicately.) Thome also specializes in brass and is one of the very few still engaged in that business.

Stained-Glass Restoration

VIC ROTHMAN FOR STAINED GLASS
212 255-2551, 914 965-1196

Victor Rothman has over 20 years experience in stained-glass restoration and new fabrication. He worked on St. Paul's Chapel at Columbia University, and he helped restore the magnificent Lalique glass windows at Henri Bendel. He also does work in private residences.

Tailors

CLAUDIA BRUCE
140 E 28th St (bet Lexington and Third Ave)   212 685-2810
By appointment

You just can't part with that beautiful but outdated dress you got ten years ago on your honeymoon in Paris? Or perhaps you don't want to send that special gown you wore to your daughter's wedding to the dry cleaner to get a new look? Don't worry. Just call Claudia Bruce, a talented lady who has been taking care of such problems with finesse for over a decade. Not only will Claudia repair and rejuvenate garments, she also will tailor made-to-order clothing. Home-fitting appointments and wardrobe consultations are also available.

MARSAN TAILORS
897 Broadway, 2nd floor (at 20th St)   212 475-2727
Mon, Tues, Wed, Fri: 10–6:30; Thurs: 10–8; Sat: 10–6;
Sun: 12–4

Before Saint Laurie—one of the biggest emporiums of men's clothing in Manhattan—established its own tailor shop, all of its alterations were done by Marsan. Any tailor who survives in the middle of the men's wholesale garment area must be good, and Marsan is among the best. All work is done by hand.

SEBASTIAN TAILORS
767 Lexington Ave, Room 404 (at 60th St)   212 688-1244
Mon-Fri: 8:30–5:30; Sat 9–4:30

Tailors are a peculiar breed in New York. In a city that is the home of the garment industry, most professionals who repair garments build their trade as "custom alteration and design specialists," or else they're dry-cleaners who incidentally mend whatever bedraggled outfit has been brought in for cleaning. Sebastian Tailors is one of the few shops in the city that is exactly what it says it is: a tailor shop. The custom alterations for men and women are quick, neat, and (wonder of wonders) reasonable. Sebastian also does reweaving. Best of all, everything is accomplished without the usual ballyhoo most such New York establishments seem to regard as their due.

Television Rental

TELEVISION RENTAL COMPANY
13 E 31st St, 2nd floor   212 683-2850
Mon-Fri: 9–5

Ted Pappas runs a rental service that is fast, good, and efficient. He will rent televisions for long or short-term periods, and will happily deliver and pick up the sets. He also rents big-screen TVs, VCRs, camcorders, and other audio-visual aids. The prices are among the best in the city, and in a business like this, his solid reputation is a formidable recommendation in itself.

Translations

BERLITZ
257 Park Ave S   212 777-7878
Call for hours

If you do business or travel overseas, this is a handy address to know. Berlitz provides translations of technical, advertising, legal, and commercial documents for (and on) software and audio-visual materials such as film, video, and slides. In addition, they operate 324 language centers in 32 countries, where they teach people to speak new languages via live instruction. There are 12 such centers in Manhattan, and information about them can be obtained from this address.

Travel Services

MOMENT'S NOTICE
425 Madison Ave (at 49th St)   212 486-0500
Daily: 9–5:30

Moment's Notice is the place to call for last-minute travel arrangements. They are a clearinghouse for a number of leading tour operators, airlines, and cruise lines that are often faced with undersold or canceled bookings. This outfit provides sizable discounts on all types of vacation destinations, including European air tickets, Caribbean packages, and international cruises. Discounts are offered for travel within 30 days prior to departure. Membership is required. Moment's Notice is not some new fly-by-night outfit but has been in the travel business for over 30 years.

PASSPORT PLUS
677 Fifth Ave, 5th floor   212 759-5540, 800 367-1818
Daily: 9:30–5:30

Larry Marsiello was another person struck by inspiration while waiting in that infamous line at the passport office at Rockefeller Center. His passport-fetching was one of the first such services, and though he has expanded nationwide, he has remained a purist, concentrating on the procurement of travel documents. With the expansion, Passport Plus now offers a very personalized and complete document service. They will take care of visas; birth, death, and marriage certificates; international licenses; passport photos (while you wait); and airline ticket pickups. If you've ever waited months for an errant passport or crucial certificate, you'll understand how valuable Passport Plus is. Imagine not ever having to deal with a passport office again!

Travel Bargains
Here are some of the best places to call for discount fares:
Access Travel (212 465-0707)
Travel Bargains (800 872-8385)
800 FLY-CHEAP (no name) – Yes, I know, one too many numbers!
Unitravel (800 325-2222)

TRAVEL COMPANION EXCHANGE
516 454-0880
Mon-Fri: 8:30–4:30

Tired of traveling alone? These folks can help. Now you can find a compatible travel companion or partner. They are a nationwide service, have been in business over a dozen years, and serve individuals from 20 to 80 years of age. (It's never too late!) A newsletter gives tips for solos, so you can make contacts with others in the same position in other cities. One of the nicest services is the opportunity to have company for a meal in New York; although there are a number of good "single" places listed in the "Manhattan à la Carte" section at the front of the book, having someone to share the dining experience is a lot more fun.

Uniform and Costume Rental

ALLAN UNIFORM RENTAL SERVICE
152 E 23rd St, 5th floor (bet Lexington and Third Ave)
212 529-4655
Mon-Fri: 9–5

Because you will probably use a costume only once, it is far less expensive to rent than buy. At this establishment you can rent contemporary, period, animal, Santa, or any number of other costumes. They also provide a uniform rental service.

Upholstering

RAY MURRAY INCORPORATED
121 E 24th St, 2nd floor (bet Park and Lexington Ave)
212 838-3752
Daily: 8:30–5

Here's the good news: Ray Murray is a reliable, capable, talented reupholstering company. Now the bad news: it costs just as much to reupholster your furniture as it does to replace it. Murray's specialty is creating custom-made furniture. Cheap it isn't, but the quality is superb. They can copy any design you want (including heirloom pieces or furniture from museum exhibits), but they specialize in classic and contemporary furniture. Big, overstuffed sofas are their forte. If you're redecorating and your furniture is generally in good condition, Murray can coordinate all the work, fabric, and patterns. They can make drapery and accessory pieces to match the re-covered furniture, and the total cost will be substantially less than it would be to throw everything out and start from scratch. Joe Sinis, a very talented craftsman, has taken over the Ray Murray business, carrying on the tradition of excellence.

Even at age 73 the legendary Cornelius Vanderbilt was an energetic fellow. He had complete control of all rail traffic between New York and the Great Lakes. He enjoyed fat black cigars, loved racing his horses, and thrived on the company of beautiful women. Even before his wife died, housemaids at the Vanderbilt mansion on Washington Place spent as much time dodging the Commodore's advances as picking up after him!

VI. Where to Buy It: New York's Best Stores

Shopping Hints

1. Watch for periodic sales at major stores.
2. Try to catch Nordstrom's start-of-season sale.
3. Comparison-shop—If labels don't mean much to you, you can usually save a bundle.
4. Try on clothing items before leaving the store.
5. Always save receipts for returns or to check bills.
6. Stay away from street vendors, particularly those peddling watches and jewelry.
7. Stay away from midtown electronics stores; prices are inflated, and merchandise can be outdated.
8. Special sales in the garment district *can* be great; check ads, "elevator starters" in garment area buildings, flyers, or call your favorite designer.
9. Cash prices are usually better on the lower East Side, so don't be afraid to do a bit of haggling here.
10. Check this book carefully; there is a bargain listing for practically every item of merchandise!

How to Shop and Save Month After Month

Here are the best times to find bargains.

January: Men's shirts, linens, white sales, appliances, furniture
February: China, glass, silver, mattresses, bedding
March: Spring clothing, ski equipment
April: After-Easter clothing sales
May: Carpets, rugs, household cleaning supplies
June: Furniture
July: Inventory clearances, sportswear, sporting goods, garden supplies
August: Patio furniture, lawn mowers, barbecues, camping items
September: School clothes (end of month)
October: Fall sales (do your holiday shopping)
November: Wool clothing for men and women
December: Christmas merchandise (after Dec. 25th)

Pricing

Retail: This is the price the consumer usually pays. The markup (from 100% and up) is adjusted according to what the market will bear.

Wholesale: This figure is about double what it costs to produce the item but about half of what the retail customer usually pays.

Cost: The actual cost to the manufacturer of an item.

Bargains

Every month there are special bargain sales, closeouts, factory specials, and what have you. It is handy to have reference guides that tell you of these events, as many are announced just days ahead of time. Two good sources are *New York Magazine* and the *S&B Report,* published monthly by Elyse Lazar, 112 E 36th St (4th floor), New York, NY 10016, 212 679-5400. A sales and bargain hotline for S&B is 900 820-SALE.

Special note: If you want big-time shopping help, you might call Marjorie Stokes (212 753-0033). She is known as *the* person to get special prices on elite designer merchandise for elite shoppers (read: those with deep pockets). Be sure to ask about her commission, but be discreet about it!

The Best (and Some Not So Good) Places to Find Specific Items in New York: An Exclusive List

Please note: space limitations preclude detailed listings of some of these stores.

Things for the Person (Men, Women, Children)

Accessories, discount: Bernard Krieger & Son (316 Grand St)
Albert Nippon apparel, discounted: Lea's (119 Orchard St)
Aprons: Apron and Bag Supply Company (47 Second Ave)
Attitude-adjustment needed: Polo-Ralph Lauren (867 Madison Ave)
Attitude, insulting: Gucci (683 Fifth Ave)
Baby gift ensembles: Ovations (World Financial Center)
Baby gift service, mail-order: Life's Little Treasures (516 937-0511)
Bags, antique: Sylvia Pines Uniquities (1102-B Lexington Ave)
Boots, Western: Lord John Bootery (428 Third Ave)

Boots and shoes, men's, handmade: E. Vogel Boots and Shoes (19 Howard St)

Bridal gowns and accessories, expensive: Vera Wang Bridal House (991 Madison Ave)

Briefcases: Jobson's (666 Lexington Ave)

Brushes: Smalley & William (806 Lexington Ave)

Buttons: Tender Buttons (143 E 62nd St)

Cancer, breast, survivor needs: Underneath It All (444 E 75th St)

Caps: Detente (60 Wooster St)

Carriages, baby: Albee's (715 Amsterdam Ave)

Cartoon, clothing, jewelry, and accessories: Mouse 'n' Around (A&S Plaza, Sixth Ave and 33rd St)

Clothing, African design: Kasondoro (411 E 9th St)

Clothing, antique: Antique Boutique (712–714 Broadway) and Alice Underground (380 Columbus Ave)

Clothing, children's: Wicker Garden's Children (1318 Madison Ave) and Glad Rags (1007 Madison Ave)

Clothing, children's discounted: Jack's Bargain Store (2 W 14th St)

Clothing, children's French: Jacadi (1281 Madison Ave)

Clothing, classic men's and women's: Peter Elliot (1383 Third Ave)

Clothing, custom-made men's clothing, shirts, and ties: Ascot Chang (7 W 57th St)

Clothing, designer, men's & women's: Fowad (2254 Broadway)

Clothing, dressy, teens: Farnaz (1193 Lexington Ave)

Clothing, embroidered cartoon characters: Too Cute (113 Prince St)

Clothing, evening: Lucille Chayt (214 W 39th St)

Clothing, imported designer: India Cottage Emporium (1150 Broadway)

Clothing, infant, elegant: La Layette Et. Plus (170 E 61st St)

Clothing, Italian, men's: Manitalia (24 W 55th St)

Clothing, men's custom-made: Alan Flusser (16 E 52nd St)

Clothing, men's discounted brand-name: L.S. Men's Clothing (19 W 44th St)

Clothing, men's good value: Saint Laurie (897 Broadway), Gorsart (9 Murray St and 10 E 44th St), and Oliver Grant (222 Columbus Ave)

Clothing, men's resale: Exchange Unlimited (563 Second Ave)

Clothing, men's, ridiculous prices: Bijan (699 Fifth Ave)

Clothing, school: Off Campus (1137 Madison Ave)

Clothing, small-sized women's: Piaffe (212 869-3320)

Clothing, unusual: The Gallery of Wearable Art (43 E 63rd St)

Clothing, vintage: Gene London (897 Broadway)

Clothing, women's (be careful of pricing): S&W (165 W 26th St)

Clothing, women's designer sportswear, discounted: PRG (307 Seventh Ave)

Clothing, women's discounted: Simply Samples (150 W 36th St, 3rd floor)

Clothing, women's, good prices: Miriam Rigler (14 W 55th St)

Clothing, women's trendy: Betsey Johnson (248 Columbus Ave and 251 E 60th St)

Clothing, women's ultrasuede, discounted: Irving Katz (209 W 38th St)

Coats, lambskin: Spanish Shearling Center (345 Seventh Ave)

Coats, suits, and jackets, petite, junior, and half-sizes: Rain Barrel Coat Factory (101 Orchard St)

Condoms: Condomania (351 Bleecker St)

Cosmetics, discounted: Apple Cosmetics (135 Canal St), Kris Cosmetics (1170 Broadway)

Cosmetics, discounted designer: Almaya Cosmetics (1214-B Broadway)

Diamonds: Rennie Ellen (15 W 47th St)

Dresses, evening and wedding, made-to-order: Jane Wilson-Marquis (124 Thompson St)

Dresses, silk/party: Sam's Knitwear (93 Orchard St)

Dresses, special occasion, for teens: Sweeteen (675 Madison Ave, 2nd floor)

Earrings, custom-designed: Sheri Miller (578 Fifth Ave)

Eyewear, discounted: Superior Optical (1133 Broadway, Suite 223)

Eyewear, elegant: Morgenthal-Frederics Opticians (685 Madison Ave)

Fabrics, decorator, discounted: Harry Zarin (72 Allen St)

Fabrics, discounted: A&N Fabrics (268 W 39th St)

Fabrics, imported: Far Eastern Fabrics (171 Madison Ave)

Fabrics, Oriental: Oriental Dress Company (38 Mott St)

Fans, antique hand: Lune (Place des Antiquaires, 125 E 57th St)

Footwear, women's small sizes: Giordano's (1150 Second Ave)

Fragrances: Scentsitivity (8701–8702 Lexington Ave)

Fragrances, discounted brand-name: Kris Cosmetics (1170 Broadway)

Fur scarves and hats: Aaron Weining (348 Seventh Ave)

Furs: G. Michael Hennessy (333 Seventh Ave)

Gifts, spiritual: The Hero's Journey (489 Columbus Ave)

Gloves, discounted leather: Bernard Krieger (316 Grand St)

Gowns, couture, secondhand: Irvington Institute Thrift Shop (1534 Second Ave)

Hair accessories: Head Master (37 W 39th St)

Handbags: Fine and Klein (119 Orchard St)

Handbags, discounted eelskin: New Star Handbags (1010 Sixth Ave)

Hats, custom fur: Lenore Marshall (235 W 29th St)

Hats, custom-made: Victoria DiNardo (68 Thompson St)

Hats, men's: Young's Hat Store (139 Nassau St)

Herbs: Meadowsweet Herbal Apothecary (77 E 4th St)

Hosiery, discounted brand-name: D&A Merchandise Co (22 Orchard St)

Jeans, antique 501: The Antique Boutique (712–714 Broadway)

Jeans, discounted: Classics (15 Third Ave)

Jeans, good prices: Alaska Fashions (41 Orchard St)

Jewelry: Fortunoff (681 Fifth Ave) and Hidden Treasures (Grace Garfinkel, 450 E 63rd St)

Jewelry, custom-made: Eurocraft Custom Jewelry (42 W 48th St)

Jewelry, fine: Stuart Moore (128 Prince St)

Jewelry, gold and silver: Gold and Silver Man (2142 Broadway)

Jewelry, handmade, discounted: Bonnie and Toni (81 Orchard St)

Jewelry, Indian: David Saity (48 E 57th St)

Jewelry, special designs: Eurocraft Custom Jewelry (42 W 48th St)

Jewelry, 24-carat gold: Fu Zhou Jewelry (170–172 Canal St, Booth 15)

Jewelry, vintage costume: Norman Crider Antiques (Trump Tower, 725 Fifth Ave, Level D-5)

Kimonos: Kimono House (120 Thompson St) and East East (230 E 80th St)

Knit suits, sportswear: Sam's Knitwear (93 Orchard St)

Knitwear: Knit Couture (800-B Madison Ave)

Leather goods and accessories: Daniel Mode (184 W 4th St) and FOMO (317 Grand St)

Lingerie, best values: Goldman and Cohen (55 Orchard St)

Lingerie, fine: Village Bra Smyth (179 W 4th St)

Lingerie, sexy: Samantha Jones (1074 Third Ave) and Victoria's Secret (34 E 57th St)

Loungewear: Enelra Uptown (309 E 9th St) and Enelra Downtown (481–482 E 7th St)

Massage oils: The Fragrance Shoppe (21 E 7th St)

Millinery: Victoria DiNardo (68 Thompson St)

Millinery, custom-made: Don Marshall (212 758-1686) and Lola (2 E 17th St)

Outdoor wear: Eastern Mountain Sports (20 W 61st St)

Outerwear: Down Generation (725 Columbus Ave)

Pearls: Sanko Cultured Pearls (45 W 47th St)

Perfume: Parisian (123 Fifth Ave) and Warwick Chemists (1348 Sixth Ave)

Perfume copies: Essential Products Company (90 Water St)

Perfumes, discounted: Round House Fashions (256 W 36th St), La Femme (110 W 40th St), and Hema Cosmetics (313 Church St) Perfumania (1 Times Sq)

Piece goods, men's: Beckenstein (121 Orchard St)

Prescriptions: J. Leon Lascoff & Sons (1209 Lexington Ave)

Scarves: Wraps (Pier 17, South Street Seaport)

Shirts, custom-made: Seewaldt and Bauman (17 E 45th St)

Shirts, men's, great prices: Acorn Shirts (11 E 47th St)

Shirts, sport: Sosinsky's (143 Orchard St)

Shoes, athletic: The City Athlete (132 Orchard St)

Shoes, big and wide: Tall Size Shoes (3 W 35th St)

Shoes, bridal: Peter Fox (105 Thompson St)

Shoes, discounted: Aly's Hut (85 Hester St) and Stapleton Shoe
  Company (68 Trinity Pl)

Shoes, discounted children's party: Trevi Shoes (141 Orchard St)

Shoes, discounted designer: Designer Eye Shoes (93 Nassau St)

Shoes for millionaires: Susan Bennis/Warren Edwards (22 W 57th
  St)

Shoes, kids' upscale: Shoofly (465 Amsterdam Ave)

Shoes, men's discounted: J. Sherman (121 Division St) and
  Statesman Shoes (6 E 46th St)

Shoes, women's custom-made: Mathia (20 E 69th St)

Shoes, women's, petite: In Step (1230 Second Ave)

Silk blouses and dresses, wholesale prices: Omanti Designs (530
  Seventh Ave, 9th floor)

Sneakers, men's and women's discounted: Shoe City (133 Nassau
  St)

Sportswear: C.P. Company (175 Fifth Ave)

Sportswear, discounted brand-name: Athlete's Choice (1 Times
  Sq)

Sportswear, discounted (sizes 2–12): Joseph Vincent (575 Seventh
  Ave)

Sportswear, men's and women's mod: Poco Loco (106 Wooster
  St)

Sportswear, Swedish-designed: Marc O'Polo (44 W 69th St)

Sportswear, women's, good prices: M. Friedlich (196 Orchard St)
  and Giselle (143 Orchard St)

Sunglasses: Shades of the Village (167 Seventh Ave S)

Sweaters, Austrian: Geiger of Austria (505 Park Ave)

Sweaters, cashmere, men's and women's: David Berk (781
  Madison Ave)

Sweaters, college: Off Campus (2151 Broadway)

Swimsuits: New York Body Shop (49 W 57th St and 1195 Third
  Ave)

Tailoring, custom: Mr. Ned (22 W 19th St)

Ties, made-to-order: De Casi (37 W 57th St)

Ties, Nicole Miller copies: Tie Moda (143½ Orchard St)

Tuxedo shirts and accessories, discounted: Ted's (83 Orchard St)
  and Allen Tie & Shirt Center (146 Allen St)

Umbrellas: Uncle Sam (161 W 57th St)

Umbrellas, discount: Unitec Umbrella Co (250 Fifth Ave)

Underwear, pantyhose and socks, discounted: Universal Hosiery Corp (100 Orchard St) and D & A Merchandise (22 Orchard St)

Uniforms: Dornan (653 Eleventh Ave) and Ja-Mil (92 Orchard St)

Vests, kimonos: Nicolina (247 W 46th St)

Vitamins, natural: New York Apothecary (469 Sixth Ave)

Watchbands: George Paul Jewelers (51 E 58th St)

Watches: Mostly Watches (200 W 57th St) and M.A.G. Time (60 W 22nd St)

Watches, discounted (Seiko, Casio): Foto Electric Supply Co (31 Essex St)

Watches, vintage: Aaron Faber (666 Fifth Ave), Time Will Tell (962 Madison Ave), and Fanelli Antique Timepieces (1131 Madison Ave)

Wigs: Theresa's Wigs (217 E 60th St) and Jacques Darcel International (50 W 57th St)

Zippers: A. Feibusch (30 Allen St)

Things for the Home

Air conditioners: Elgot Sales (937 Lexington Ave)

Antiques, Chinese: Jackson Chu Arts & Products (825 Broadway)

Antiques, decorative: Karen Warshaw (167 E 74th St)

Antiques, French: French Country Store (35 E 10th St)

Antiques, turn-of-the-century English: J. Zacker (97 Spring St)

Antiques, Victorian: Somethin' Else Antiques & Needle Arts (182 Ninth Ave)

Appliances, discount: LVT Price Quote Hotline (800 582-8884), Dembitzer Bros. (5 Essex St), Kaufman Electrical Appliances (365 Grand St), Sam Diamond (94 Fulton St), Price Watchers (718 470-1620 or 516 222-9100), and Bloom and Krup (206 First Ave)

Appliances, kitchen: Zabar's (2245 Broadway)

Appliances, overseas: Appliances Overseas (276 Fifth Ave, Suite 407)

Art, ancient, European, Oriental, and pre-Columbian: Athena Galleries (153 E 57th St)

Art, antique Oriental: Imperial Fine Oriental Art (760 Madison Ave)

Art deco, French: Maison Gerard (36 E 10th St)

Art, decorative: Susan Meisel Decorative Arts (133 Prince St)

Art, Mexican (Bustamonte): Pavo Real Gallery (Pier 17, South Street Seaport)

Art, primitive: The Lands Beyond (1218 Lexington Ave) and Eastern Arts (365 Bleecker St)

Art, Western, 19th-century: J.N. Bartfield Galleries (30 W 57th St)

Artifacts: Jacques Carcanagues Gallery (106 Spring St)

Artist and drafting materials: The Amber Palette (444 Madison Ave)

Bakeware, discounted: Broadway Panhandler (520 Broadway)

Baskets, dried-flower: Galerie Felix (968 Lexington Ave)

Baskets, fruit: Macres (173 W 57th St)

Bathroom accessories: Elegant John (812 Lexington Ave)

Batteries: Global Imports (160 Fifth Ave)

Bedding, Korean embroidered: Seoul Handicraft (284 Fifth Ave)

Beds, antique: Alice's Antiques (505 Columbus Ave)

Beds, Murphy: Murphy Bed Center (110 W 17th St, 2nd floor)

Bird cages: Lexington Gardens (1008 Lexington Ave)

Boxes, wooden: An American Craftsman Galleries (317 and 321 Bleecker St)

Butcher-block counters, tables, and chairs: Alexander Butcher Blocks & Supply (176 Bowery)

Candles: The Candle Shop (118 Christopher St)

Candles, illuminating: Imprescia (1407 Broadway)

Ceramics: Contemporary Porcelain (105 Sullivan St)

Chests, Oriental: Min Yea (79 Madison Ave)

China, Amari: Bardith (901 Madison Ave)

China and glass, discounted: Lanac Sales (73 Canal St)

China, French hand-painted: Solanee (138 E 74th St)

China, odds-and-ends, bargains: Fishs Eddy (551 Hudson St)

Christmas decorations, discounted (mid-November through Christmas): Kurt Adler's Santa's World (1107 Broadway)

Clocks, cuckoo: Alfry Co (48 W 46th St, 5th floor) and Time Pieces (115 Greenwich Ave)

Clocks, English antique: Hymore Hodson Antiques (903 Madison Ave)

Closet fixtures: Hold Everything (1311 Second Ave)

Coca-Cola merchandise: Coca-Cola (711 Fifth Ave)

Collectibles: Gargoyles Ltd., of Philadelphia (138 W 25th St)

Comic books: Village Comics (163 Bleecker St, 2nd floor)

Cookware, French: Lamalle (36 W 25th St)

Crystal: Crystal Shop (551–552 Greene St)

Dinnerware, Chinese: Wing On Wo & Co. (26 Mott St)

Dinnerware, Fiesta: Mood Indigo (181 Prince St)

Dinnerware, porcelain: Bernardaud (777 Madison Ave)

Displays, jewelry: Premier (33 W 46th St)

Ecological products: Terra Verde Trading Co. (72 Spring St)

Electronics, good values: The Wiz (12 W 45th St and other locations) and Vicmarr (88 Delancey St)

Engravings, Irish: Irish Books and Graphics (580 Broadway)

Environmental goods: Greenlife (400 W Broadway)

Fans, ceiling: Modern Supply (19 Murray St)

FAX machines: Fairfax (145 W 45th St)

Figurines, discounted: East Side Gifts and Dinnerware (351 Grand St)

Floor coverings: ABC Carpets (888 Broadway)

Floral designs, Ikebana: Frank Luisi (42 E 49th St)

Flowers, silk: United States Flower Co. (131 W 28th St)

Folk art: Country on Columbus (281-A Columbus Ave) and Folk Art Gallery (1187 Lexington Ave)

Frames, picture: SR Glass (1196 Lexington Ave), Ready Frames (14 W 45th St), and Framed on Madison (740 Madison Ave)

Frames, hand-carved picture: D. Matt (223 E 80th St)

Furnishings, traditional hand-carved: Devon Shops (111 E 27th St)

Furniture, antique pine: Wendover's (6 W 20th St)

Furniture, butcher-block: J&D Brauner (316 E 59th St, 302 Bowery, 1522 Second Ave, and 181 Amsterdam Ave)

Furniture, custom-made: Navedo Woodcraft (179 E 119th St)

Furniture, department store: Bloomingdale's (Third Ave at 59th St)

Furniture, fine mica: Room Plus (1555 Third Ave)

Furniture, French country: Pierre Deux Antiques (870 Madison Ave)

Furniture, leather: Leather Center (44 E 32nd St)

Furniture, modular: Room Plus Furniture (1555 Third Ave)

Furniture, pine: Better Times Antiques (500 Amsterdam Ave) and Evergreen Antiques (120 Spring St)

Furniture reproductions: G. Carderelli (205 W Houston St) and Foremost (8 W 30th St)

Furniture, Swedish antique: Eileen Lane (150 Thompson St)

Gadgets: Brookstone (18 Fulton St)

Glass: Simon Pearce (385 Bleecker St and 500 Park Ave)

Glass and tableware: Avventura (463 Amsterdam Ave)

Glassware, Steuben, used: Lillian Nassau (220 E 57th St)

Globes and maps: E. Forbes Smiley (16 E 79th St)

Hardware: Barson Hardware (35 W 44th St)

Home accessories: Carole Stupell (29 E 22nd St)

Housewares, unusual: D.F. Sanders and Co. (952 Madison Ave)

Judaica: Hecker Corporation (164 E 68th St)

Kilims (Oriental rugs): Le Monde Des Kilims (407-A Broome St)

Kitchen and bath fixtures: Windsor World (240 E 59th St)

Kitchens, custom: Regba Diran New York (1100 Second Ave)

Lamp finials: Grand Brass (221 Grand St)

Lampshades: Just Shades (21 Spring St)

Lightbulbs: Just Bulbs (938 Broadway)

Lightbulbs, discounted: Wiedenbach-Brown (435 Hudson St)

Lighting fixtures: New York Gas Lighting Company (145 Bowery)

Linens, antique: Jean Hoffman-Jana Starr (236 E 80th St)

Locks: Lacka Lock (253 W 46th St)

Lucite: Acrylium International (955 Third Ave)

Marble, Greek: SG Marble (900 First Ave)

Marble and stone: Petrafina (964 Third Ave)

Mattresses, good values: Town Bedding & Upholstery (205 Eighth Ave)

Movie-star photos: Movie Star News (134 W 18th St)

Movie and TV pictures and posters, good prices: Movie Material (242 W 14th St)

Perfume bottles, vintage: Gallery #47 (1050 Second Ave)

Pictures, animation: New York Animation Gallery (324 Columbus Ave)

Plants: Farm and Garden Nursery (2 Sixth Ave)

Plants, cactus: Grass Roots Garden (131 Spring St)

Plants, orchids: Robert Lester (280 W 4th St)

Plumbing parts: George Taylor Specialties (100 Hudson St)

Poster originals, 1880-1940: Philip Williams (60 Grand St)

Posters, best selection: Poster America (138 W 18th St)

Posters, international theater: Triton Gallery (323 W 45th St) and Jerry Ohlinger (242 W 14th St)

Posters, vintage: La Belle Epoque (282 Columbus Ave)

Potpourri: Victor Decorators (260 Madison Ave)

Prints, botanical: W. Graham Arader (29 E 72nd St)

Prints, contemporary wildlife and sporting: Sportsman's Edge (136 E 74th St)

Quilts: Hands All Around (986 Lexington Ave) and Down Quilt Shop (1225 Madison Ave)

Quilts, antique: Kelter/Malce (361 Bleecker St), Quilts of America (431 E 73rd St), and Susan Parrish (390 Bleecker St)

Rugs, old: Doris Leslie Blau (15 E 57th St)

Rugs, Oriental: Momeni International (36 E 31st St)

Safety merchandise: Safety Store (Columbus Ave at 83rd St)

Screens, shoji: Miya Shoji (109 W 17th St) and Katsura Studio (389 Broome St)

Security devices: REM Security (11 E 20th St)

Shells: The Shell Center (South Street Seaport, Pier 17, East River)

Shelves: Shelf Shop II (1295 First Ave)

Silver and wedding gifts: Rogers and Rosenthal (22 W 48th St)

Silver, unusual: Jean's Silversmiths (16 W 45th St)

Silverware and holloware, good values: Eastern Silver (54 Canal St)

Software: Electronics Boutique (A&S Plaza, Third Ave and 71st St)

Stationery, discounted home and office: Tunnel Stationery (301 Canal St)

Stationery, personalized: Jamie Ostrow (876 Madison Ave)

Stone pieces: Modern Stone Age (111 Greene St)

Tableware: Fishs Eddy (889 Broadway)

Tapestries: Lovelia Enterprises (356 E 41st St) and Saint-Remy (818 Lexington Ave)

Textiles, antique: Cora Ginsburg (19 E 74th St)
Tiles: Tiles (42 W 15th St)
Tiles, ceramic, and marble and wall coverings: Quarry Tile, Marble & Granite (192 Lexington Ave)
Tools, garden: Zona (97 Greene St)
Vacuum cleaners: Desco (1236 Lexington Ave)
Wallpaper, discounted: Pintchik (278 Third Ave)

Things for Leisure Time

Albums, out-of-print: Golden Disc (239 Bleecker St)
Art supplies: Pearl Paint Company (308 Canal St)
Athletic gear: Modell's (109 E 42nd St)
Athletic gear, team: Yankee Clubhouse (110 E 59th St)
Baseball cards, best selection: Card Collectors (105 W 77th St)
Bibles (in every language): International Bible Society (172 Lexington Ave)
Bicycles: Gene's Bike Shop (242 E 79th St)
Binoculars: Clairmont-Nichols (1016 First Ave)
Books, art: Jaap Rietman (134 Spring St) and Hacker Art Books (45 W 57th St)
Books, astrology and artificial intelligence: New York Astrology Center (545 Eighth Ave)
Books, children and parents: Bank Street (2875 Broadway)
Books, children's: Barnes & Noble Jr (128 Fifth Ave and 120 E 86th St)
Books, decorative arts: Archivia (944 Madison Ave)
Books, exam-study and science-fiction: Civil Service Book Shop (89 Worth St)
Books, gay and lesbian: A Different Light (548 Hudson St)
Books, military: Soldier Shop (1222 Madison Ave)
Books, mystery: Foul Play Books of Mystery & Suspense (13 Eighth Ave)
Books, mystical and religious: Quest Bookshop (240 E 53rd St)
Books, old and rare: Imperial Fine Books (790 Madison Ave, 2nd floor)
Books, rail and motor: Albion Scott (48 E 50th St)
Books, rare: Martayan Lan (48 E 57th St)
Books, religious: Paraclete Book Center (146 E 74th St)
Books, sports: James Cummings (859 Lexington Ave)
Books, theater: Theatre Arts Bookshop (405 W 42nd St)
Books, tribal art: Oan-Oceanie-Afrique Noire (9 E 38th St, 4th floor)
Books, used and review copies: Strand Book Store (828 Broadway)
Books and magazines on aviation and military subjects: Sky Book International (48 E 50th St)
Cameras: Grand Central Camera (420 Lexington Ave)

Cameras, professional movie: Cine 60 (630 Ninth Ave)

Cigarettes, luxury: Nat Sherman (500 Fifth Ave)

Comic books: Village Comics (163 Bleecker St, 2nd floor)

Compact discs, rock and roll: Smash Compact Discs (33 St. Marks Pl)

Computer printers, discounted: Tri State Computer (160 Broadway)

Computers: Village Computer (7 Great Jones St)

Crafts, contemporary: Civilisation (78 Second Ave)

Decoys: Grove Decoys (36 W 44th St)

Diving equipment: Pan Aqua Diving (166 W 75th St)

Dollhouses: Tiny Doll House (1146 Lexington Ave)

Drums: Drummer's World (147 W 46th St)

Educational Gifts: Tenzing & Pema (956 Madison Ave)

Films, music: Coconuts (Grand Central Terminal and elsewhere)

Films, videotape (classics): Evergreen Video (228 W Houston St)

Fishing tackle: Orvis (355 Madison Ave)

Fly-fishing equipment: Hunting World (16 E 53rd St)

Games, war: Compleat Strategist (11 E 33rd St, 630 Fifth Ave, and 320 W 57th St)

Golf equipment, reasonably priced: New York Golf Center (29 W 36th St)

Guitars: The Guitar Salon (45 Grove St, 212 675-3236; by appointment only)

Holographs: Holographic Studio (240 E 26th St)

Home Entertainment: J&R (23 Park Row)

Horseback-riding equipment: Miller's Saddlery (117 E 24th St) and H. Kauffman and Sons Saddlery (419 Park Ave)

Jukeboxes: Back Pages Antiques (125 Greene St)

Kaleidoscopes: After the Rain (149 Mercer St)

Kites: Big City Kite Company (1201 Lexington Ave)

Luggage: Roebling Leather Goods (207 E 43rd St)

Luggage, antique: Gargoyles (138 W 25th St)

Luggage, soft: The Bag House (58 E 8th St)

Magazines: Eastern Newsstand (Met Life Bldg, 42nd St and Park Ave) and Magazine Store (30 Lincoln Pl)

Magazines, back issues: A&S Book Company (304 W 40th St)

Maps: Richard B. Arkway (538 Madison Ave) and Hammond Map Store (57 W 43rd St)

Marine supplies: Goldberg's Marine (12 W 37th St)

Movie-star photos: Movie Star News (134 W 18th St)

Music (all publishers): Music Store at Carl Fischer (62 Cooper Sq)

Musical instruments: Music Inn (169 W 4th St) and Sam Ash Music Store (160 W 48th St)

Musical items: Yamaha (142 W 57th St)

Needlecraft: The Yarn Co (2274 Broadway)

Needlepoint: 2 Needles (1266 Madison Ave)
Newspapers, out-of-town: Hotalings News Agency
(142 W 42nd St)
Papers, elegant: Il Papiro (1021 Lexington Ave and
World Financial Center)
Paper, sheet: Kate's Paperie (561 Broadway)
Pens, antique: Arthur Brown & Brother (2 W 46th St)
Pens, discounted: Altman Luggage (135 Orchard St)
Pens, Mont Blanc, discounted: The Write Stuff (1089 Third Ave)
Photographic equipment, discounted: Tri State Photo (60 Broad-
way and 2 Cortlandt St)
Photo supplies: Ben Ness Camera & Studio (114 University Pl)
Pipes: Connoisseur Pipe Shop (Paine Webber Bldg, 1285 Sixth
Ave)
Records: Tower Records (692 Broadway and 1961 Broadway)
Records, Broadway show: Footlight Records (113 E 12th St)
Records, old rock and roll: Strider Records (22 Jones St)
Records, opera: Music Masters (25 W 43rd St)
Records, out-of-print: Dayton's (799 Broadway)
Records, used: St. Marks Sounds (20 St. Marks Pl)
Science fiction: Forbidden Planet (821 Broadway)
Sci-fi gifts: Star Magic (745 Broadway)
Skating equipment: SoHo Skateboards (19 E 7th St) and Blades
(105 W 72nd St)
Snorkeling equipment: Scuba Network (116 E 57th St)
Soccer supplies: Soccer Sport Supply (1745 First Ave)
Soldiers, lead: Second Childhood (283 Bleecker St)
Soldiers, toy, rare: Classic Toys (69 Thompson St)
Stamps: Subway Stamp Shop (111 Nassau St)
Stereo equipment, discounted: 6th Ave Electronics City (1024 and
1030 Sixth Ave)
Tennis equipment: Jay Schweid's Grandstand (588 Columbus Ave)
Theater items: One Shubert Alley (346 W 44th St)
Tobacco: J.R. Tobacco (11 E 45th St)
Toys, discounted: Park Row Novelty (248 Grand Ave)
Toys, handmade: Dinosaur Hill (302 E 9th St)
Toys, museum quality (1900–1940): Bizarre Bazaar Antiques
(Place des Antiquaries, 125 E 57th St)
VCRs, discounted: Sound City (58 W 45th St)
Videotapes: RKO Video (1608 Broadway, 168 W 96th St, 1309
Lexington Ave, 507 Third Ave, and 93 Greenwich Ave) and
New Video (941 First Ave and 90 University Pl)
Videotapes, Betamax: Beta Only Store (202 W 49th St)
Videotapes, hard-to-find (for sale or rent): Evergreen Video (213
W 35th St, 2nd floor)
Winemaking supplies: Milan Home Wine and Beers (57 Spring St)

Things from Far Away

Afghan imports: Nusraty Afghan Imports (215 W 10th St)
African handicrafts: Craft Caravan (63 Greene St)
Brazilian products: Coisa Nossa (46 W 46th St, 2nd floor)
British imports: 99X (84 E 10th St)
Buddhas: Leekan Designs (93 Mercer St)
Caribbean clothing: Island Trading Co (15 E 4th St)
Chinese antiques: Jackson Chu Arts & Products (825 Broadway)
Chinese goods: Chinese American Trading Company (91 Mulberry St)
Crafts, imported: Il Mercato (341 E 9th St)
English antiques, turn-of-the-century: J. Zacker (97 Spring St)
European pottery: La Terrine (1024 Lexington Ave)
Guatemalan gift items: Artesania (274 Columbus Ave)
Hawaiian crafts: Radio Hula (169 Mercer St)
Himalayan craft items: Himalayan Crafts and Tours
  (1228 Lexington Ave)
Indian imports: Katinka (303 E 9th St)
Indonesian art: Eastern Arts (107 Spring St)
Irish gifts: Grafton Shoppe (22 E 54th St)
Irish imports: Shamrock Imports (A&S Plaza, Sixth Ave and 33rd St,
  6th level)
Japanese books, records, and art: New York Kinokuniya Bookstore
  (10 W 49th St)
Japanese gift items: Five Eggs (436 W Broadway) and Katagiri
  (224 E 59th St)
Lambskin coats: Spanish Shearling Center (345 Seventh Ave)
Leather items, imported: Il Bisonte (72 Thompson St)
Mexican furnishings and crafts: Amigo Country (19 Greenwich Ave)
Scottish kilts and tartans: Scottish Products (133 E 55th St)
Tibetan treasures: Do Kham (51 Prince St), Tibetan Handicrafts
  (144 Sullivan St), and Vision of Tibet (167 Thompson St)

Other Things

Astrology items: New York Astrology Center (545 Eighth Ave)
Bargains (all kinds): Unredeemed Pledge Sales (64 Third Ave)
Bird and kennel merchandise: Belmont (30 Rockefeller Plaza)
Birds: Bird Jungle (401 Bleecker St)
Bottles, perfume: Gallery #47 (1050 Second Ave)

Now here's a first: a do-it-yourself ceramic housewares company. At Pull Cart (31 W 21st St, 7th floor, 212 727-7098), anyone can select shapes of unglazed ceramicware and transform them into bright and colorful housewares of their own design! There is an hourly rate, plus the cost of the ware.

Butterflies: Mariposa, the Butterfly Gallery (128 Thompson St and Pier 17, South Street Seaport)
Canvas goods: Matera Canvas Products (5 Lispenard St)
Covert surveillance equipment: Counter Spy Shop (630 Third Ave, 5th floor)
Fire memorabilia: New York Firefighter's Friend (263 Lafayette St)
Fish, tropical: American Aquarium (810 Lexington Ave)
Flags, banners: Art Flag Co. (8 Jay St)
Flowers, silk, discounted: Holland Flowers (800 Sixth Ave)
Fun shopping: Orchard Street on Sundays
Gifts, good prices: Jompole (330 Seventh Ave) \
Hologram watches, pendants, and pyramids: Baggy Pants Express (345 Sixth Ave)
Holographs: Holographic Studio (240 E 26th St)
"Ladies of the evening": Sixth Ave at 58th St (Be careful!)
Office furniture, discounted: Frank Eastern Company (599 Broadway, 6th floor)
Office supplies: Menash (2305 Broadway)
Parrots: Urban Bird (177 W Broadway)
Pet supplies, discounted: Petland (132 Nassau St)
Pharmacy, complete: Windsor Pharmacy (1419 Sixth Ave)
Postcards: French Kisses (144 Bleecker St)
Quartz, minerals: Crystal Gardens (21 Greenwich St)
Stone items: Modern Stone Age (111 Greene St)
Thrift store: Everybody's Thrift Shop (261 Park Ave S)
Travel items: The Civilized Traveller (1072 Third Ave, 2003 Broadway, and World Financial Center)
Typewriter ribbons: Abalon Office Equipment (227 Park Ave)

Special Places to Shop (with Exciting Values) Outside of Manhattan: An Exclusive Listing!

Adirondack Store: Traditional wooden lawn chairs, hickory furniture, rustic knickknacks (109 Saranac Ave, Lake Place, NY; 518 523-2646)
AMS Shoe: Generic-looking shoe outlet offers up to 25% off retail on big footwear names. (Industrial Park at 20 Aquarian Dr, Secaucus, NY; 201 866-4835)
Antique Hardware Store: Vintage and reproductive plumbing fixtures (9730 Eastern Road, Route 611, Kintnerville, PA; 715 847-2447)
Antiques at Dales: Antique furniture for much less than most places in Manhattan (683 Coney Island Ave, Kensington, Brooklyn, NY; 718 941-7059)
Antiques at Traders Cove: They rent luxurious dresses and newer knockoffs at reasonable rates. (230 Traders Cove, Port Jefferson, Long Island, NY; 516 331-2261)

Ardsley Musical Instrument Service: Affordable drums, violins, and clarinets, new and secondhand (212 Sprain Rd, Scarsdale, NY; 914 693-6639)

Argold International: Fireplace equipment manufacturer's warehouse features tool sets and baskets at a discount. (110 BiCounty Blvd, Suite 122, Farmingdale, NY; 516 293-5779)

Argyles Custom Clothier: Argyle's tailors will visit your home or office and create impeccable custom suits, shirts, ties, underwear, and shoes. (P.O. Box 352, Brielle, NJ; 800 727-9665)

Arne Smith: Smith custom-designs the rustic twig furniture sold at most upstate country stores. (7599 Saulsbury Rd, Tully, NY; 315 696-5776)

Artemide Inc. Outlet: They sell overstocks and discontinued models of bargain lamps that look expensive (including Tizio) for up to 75% off retail. (1980 New Highway, Farmingdale, Long Island, NY; 516 694-9292)

Asiatic Hosiery Company: Men's and boys' socks (195 Paterson Ave, P.O. Box 31, Little Falls, NJ; 201 256-7701)

Bally Outlet Store: Bally goods discounted up to 60% off retail (20 Enterprise Ave, Secaucus, NJ 07094; 201 864-3444)

Bare Necessities: Just about every brand of bra sold under one roof (American Way Mall, Fairfield, NJ; 201 227-8871)

Barry's Formalwear: At least 30% to 60% off retail on tuxedos by Perry Ellis, Ralph Lauren, Christian Dior, and Pierre Cardin (315 Monroe St, Passaic, NJ; 800 648-0116)

Blair: Everything big men need for their wardrobes (Route 662, Warren, PA; 800 458-6057)

Brimfield Outdoor Antique Shows: It's worth a car, bus, or train ride. (Route 20, Brimfield, MA; 413 283-6149)

Calico Corners: Enormous selection of first- and second-quality fabrics and window treatments (323 Route 10, East Hanover, NJ; 201 887-3905)

Casella Brothers: Specialize in office furniture from Tiffany (198 Market St, Elmwood Park, NJ; 201 791-0757)

Chatham Jewelers: Beautiful custom pieces (94 Main St, Chatham, NJ; 201 635-9100)

Christoffer's: Spectacular flower baskets and dried arrangements (860 Mountain Ave, Mountainside, NJ; 908 233-0500)

Coach Bag Outlet: Irregular and discontinued Coach items at 30% to 50% off retail (Main St, Amagansett, NY; 516 267-3340)

Crib Outlet: Bassett, Simmons, Childcraft, Perego, and Aprica cribs discounted 15–30% (163-A Route 22W, Union, NJ; 908 686-6733)

Crown Discount Office Products: Reliable source for office furniture, computer peripherals, copy machines, and supplies (4773 Sunrise Highway, Bohemia, NY; 800 222-PENS)

Crowning Glory Headpieces: For bridal headpieces, this is one of the area's best sources. (21-A Ridgeway Ave, White Plains, NY; 914 686-9072)

Dan Howard's Maternity Factory: Inexpensive nursing aids, lingerie, and maternity wear (5077 Merrick Rd, Massapequa, NY; 516 799-1242)

Dan River Outlet: Secret source for Dan River and Yves St. Laurent bedding supplies (1001 W Main St, Danville, VA; 804 799-7256)

Deckers: Country's largest selection of men's and women's cashmere sweaters (666 West Ave, So. Norwalk, CT; 203 866-5593)

Decorators Walk Outlet: Barely touched floor samples from decorator's showrooms (141 S Service Rd, Plainview, NY; 516 249-0003)

Deer Chase Antiques: These people can copy any piece of antique furniture. (P.O. Box 194, Morris Plains, NJ; 201 538-6186)

Designer's Room: Clones of designer wedding gowns (5 Sunrise Plaza, Valley Stream, NY; 516 561-5761)

Designs by Maurice Jewelry Outlet: All that glitters in this factory outlet costs much less than retail. (31–00 47th Ave, Long Island City, NY; 800 225-2580)

Dial-a-Mattress: The same day you phone in your mattress order, they'll deliver and assemble it. (31–10 48th Ave, Long Island City, NY; 718 473-1200)

Dollhouse Factory: Dollhouses, furniture, and accessories (157 Main St, Lebanon, NJ; 908 236-6404)

Dunham: Solid, handsome boots, boat shoes, and walking shoes for less than retail (P.O. Box 813, Brattleboro, VT; 800 544-4202)

Elegant Brass Beds: You can actually watch them make your bed. (1460 65th St, Brooklyn, NY; 718 256-8988)

Enchanting Alternatives: Well-priced rentals of bridal gowns, mother-of-the-bride dresses, cocktail dresses, and prom gowns (1860 Wantaugh Ave, Wantaugh Village, Long Island, NY; 516 785-1430)

Etienne Aigner: Classy shoes, handbags, blouses, and leather coats (47 Brunswick Ave, Edison, NJ; 908 248-1945)

Fabric Alternative: Invaluable source for decorating or refurbishing (78 Seventh Ave, Park Slope, Brooklyn, NY; 718 857-5482)

Factory Outlets at Norwalk: Mall's 26 stores include Bed Bath & Beyond, Company Store, and Old Mill; men's, women's, and kidswear outlets, too. (East Ave, Norwalk, CT; 203 838-1349)

Fancy Footwork: Bridal party shoes and custom evening shoes (Cobble Hill, Brooklyn, NY; 718 855-4592)

Fieldcrest Store: Fieldcrest and Cannon towels, comforters, and bedding at deep discounts (Highway 14, Eden, NC; 800 841-3336)

Flemington Fur Company: The fur-lover's mecca (8 Spring St, Flemington, NJ; 908 782-2212)

Frankel's Boots: Justin and Dan Post cowboy boots, Timberland and Doc Martens shoes, Ray-Ban and Vuarnet sunglasses (3924 Third Ave, Brooklyn, NY; 718 788-9402 and 718 768-9788)

French Creek Sheep & Wool Company: Solid shearlings and wool sweaters (Elverson, PA; 215 286-5700)

Furniture Connection: High-end, traditional furniture discounted up to 50% (Holmdel, NJ; 908 946-2378)

Furniture Expo Inc: Find the name and model number of the furniture or bedding you want; they'll get it, discounted 30–50%. (1 Bruce Ave, Stratford, CT; 203 575-6686, 800 969-EXPO)

G&J Van Dam Inc: Basic kitchen table set (3414 Church Ave, Brooklyn, NY; 718 469-7216, 718 327-4907, and 718 327-4993)

Gordon's Warehouse Outlet: Discounted air conditioners, TVs, stereo equipment, jewelry, watches, and scratched or dented appliances (10 Prospect St, Madison, NJ; 201 377-5000)

Harmon Cove Outlet Center: Fifty high-end stores, from American Tourister luggage to Bally shoes (20 Enterprise Ave, Secaucus, NJ; 201 348-4780)

Harvé Benard: Sharp suits, sport coats, and casual wear (225 Meadowland Pkwy, Secaucus, NJ; 201 319-9780)

Hickory and Tweed: Ski-and-sports shop bargains (410 Main St, Armonk, NY; 914 273-3397)

Hobensack and Keller: Museums shop here for antique garden appointments. (P.O. Box 96, Bridge St, New Hope, PA; 215 862-2406)

Hong Kong Custom Tailors: These people will come to your home or office for fittings. (72 Narrows Rd S, Staten Island, NY; 718 447-7653; appointment only)

Ideal Department Store: Boy and Girl Scout supplies and school uniforms (1814–16 Flatbush Ave, Brooklyn, NY; 718 252-5090)

Island Bridal Gown Rental: They rent gowns and headpieces. (148 Broadway, Route 107, Hicksville, Long Island, NY; 516 681-5816)

Jamar: Secret source for famous-name silver, china, crystal, stainless, flatware, and ceramics (1714 Sheepshead Bay Rd, Brooklyn, NY; 718 615-2222)

Kerekes Bakery and Restaurant Equipment: Higher-end professional equipment (7107 Thirteenth Ave, Brooklyn, NY; 718 232-7044)

Kids At Large: Cool clothes for hard-to-fit children, ages 4–14 (Endicott St, Bldg 32, Norwood, MA; 617 769-8575)

Kids Plus: Tremendous discounts on names like Osh Kosh, Bugle Boy, Levi's, and Tickle Me (70 Highway 10, Whippany, NJ; 201 386-1005)

King's Chandelier Co: Manufacturer's prices on exquisite lighting fixtures (P.O. Box 667, Eden, NC; 919 623-6188)

Knickerbocker Shop: Big men and husky boys should check here for dressy and casual clothes. (370 Knickerbocker Ave, Brooklyn, NY; 718 452-8000)

Kolson: Classy bathroom accessories and fixtures (653 Middle Neck Rd, Great Neck, NY; 516 487-1224)

Krug's Big & Tall: Names like Adolfo, Nino Cerutti, Bill Blass, and Palm Beach (16 N Washington Ave, Bergenfield, NJ; 201 387-0100)

Lamps and Shades Unlimited: Favorite designer's source for hand-sewn and custom lampshades (44 Elm St, New Canaan, CT; 203 966-1314)

Large and Lovely: Larger-size women who have had trouble finding stylish bridalwear should drop by this place. (381 Sunrise Highway, Lynbrook, Long Island, NY)

L'eggs Brand: Discounts from brands you'll recognize (P.O. Box 748, Rural Hall, NC; 919 744-1790)

Leonie Power: Christening and prom dresses in classic styles from $200 (1735 Madison Pl, Brooklyn, NY; 718 339-3540)

Lewis of London: Whimsical furniture and accessories (175 Route 4 W, Paramus, NJ; 201 843-8224)

Liberty Village: Anne Klein, Joan and David, Calvin Klein, Corning/Revere, Villeroy & Boch, Jones New York, and Bass (1 Church St, Flemington, NJ; 908 782-8550)

Liz Claiborne: Marked-down versions of her women's wear (2 Emerson Ln, Secaucus, NJ; 201 319-8411)

Marcia Kahan: Invitations at great prices (46 Rose Ln, East Rockaway, NY; 516 374-1167)

Markell Jewelers: Special-occasion jewelry (100 Woodbridge Mall, Woodbridge, NJ; 908 855-1600)

Mikasa Outlet: The same tableware you've eyed in department stores at prices you won't believe (25 Enterprise Ave, Secaucus, NJ; 201 867-6805)

Miss Vicki's Millinery and Gift Shop: Antique furniture, frames, vintage jewelry, and dazzling custom-made hats (430 Anderson Ave, Cliffside Park, NJ; 201 945-1023)

Modern Hatters: Stetson, Borsalino, Adolfo, Mr. John, and Sylvia hats up to 50% off retail (313 Third St, Jersey City, NJ; 201 659-1113)

More Furniture: Big-name household furniture from Stanley and Broyhill (309 Route 32, Central Valley, NY; 914 923-7799)

Murray's: This place carries clothes and shoes for large-size men, women, and kids from designers like Pierre Cardin and Sergio Tacchini. (160–13 Northern Blvd, Flushing, NY; 718 463-6644)

National Wholesale Company: Terrific bargains on pantyhose and undergarments (400 National Blvd, Lexington, NC; 704 246-5904)

Norman Hilton: Handmade suits for men and clothes for women (35 E Elizabeth Ave, Linden, NJ; 908 486-2610)

Norman's: Gigantic selection of kids' furniture, tot to teenage (1714 S Second St, Philadelphia, PA; 215 334-0632)

Nostalgia Oak Warehouse: Lots of solid oak bedroom, dining-room, and kitchen sets, plus curios, rockers, and hutches (2075 Jericho Turnpike, New Hyde Park, NY, 516 328-1711; 353-B Englishtown Rd, Jamestown, NJ, 908 446-4333; 1 Jake Brown Rd, Old Bridge, NJ, 908 679-1700; 1057 Route 46 East, Clifton, NJ, 201 777-9112)

Outlet for Leather: Terrific prices on contemporary leather pieces from around the world (4014 Promenade Shops at Main St, Voorhees, NJ; 609 751-9111)

Outlet of the Bridal Center: One-of-a-kind designer bridal samples for $200 and under (381 Sunrise Highway, Lynbrook, NY; 516 599-8556)

Outlet Store: Mostly American labels at this menswear discounter (77 Metro Way, Secaucus, NJ; 201 601-8700)

Outlets at the Cove: Fenn Wright & Manson, Harvé Benard II, Jones New York, Van Heusen (45 Meadowlands Pkwy, Secaucus, NJ; 201 866-3516)

Patchogue Floral's Fantasy Land: One of the East Coast's largest silk flower outlets (10 Robinson Ave, East Patchogue, NY; 516 475-2059)

Patricia, Inc.: Custom gowns from around $200; sample gowns for as low as $50 (534 West Side Ave, Jersey City, NJ; 201 433-1884)

Pattern Finders: If they don't stock the elusive piece of silver you want, they'll trace it for a fee. (P.O. Box 206, Port Jefferson Station, Long Island, NY; 516 928-5158)

Pero Originals: Hand-painted shoes and custom-dyed women's footwear (9747 Shore Rd, Brooklyn, NY)

Price Watchers: Discounts on TVs, video equipment, and large appliances (718 470-1620, 516 222-9100)

RDM (Rina Di Montella) Factory Outlet: Fabulous selection of evening dresses in silks, laces, sequins, and beads (2nd and Fayette St, Conshohocken, PA; 215 834-0367)

Reading Outlet Center: In all, 75 stores—from Bass Shoes and Dooney & Burke handbags to Kitchen Collection (801 North 9th St, Reading, PA; 215 373-5495)

Red Balloon: Kids' furniture and clothing on consignment (409 Main St, Ridgefield, CT; 203 438-8606)

Renovator's Supply: They can track down any type of plumbing or lighting fixture (Cinema Plaza, Flemington, NJ; 908 788-5340)

Rock-Bye-Baby: Kiddie department store with strollers, high chairs, car seats, and bedding (4150 Merrick Rd, Massapequa, Long Island, NY; 516 799-2229)

Rose Marie Reid Outlet: Bill Blass, Rose Marie Reid, and Esther Williams swimsuits and sportswear at $20 or less (3350 Liberty Ave, North Bergen, NJ; 201 867-2020)

Roy Electric: Fabulous designer source for bathroom lighting fixtures (1054 Coney Island Ave, Brooklyn, NY; 718 434-7002)

Rubie's Costume Company: America's largest costume manufacturer (One Rubie Plaza, Richmond Hill, NY; 718 846-1008)

Seaport Fabrics: More than 200,000 yards of home-decorating fabrics (203 536-8668)

Second Chance: Antique linens, jewelry, china, and glassware (40 W Main St, Southhampton, NY; 516 283-2988, 516 283-0495)

Sepco Industries: Bathroom fixtures and best prices for bathroom and kitchen accessories (491 Wortman Ave, Brooklyn, NY; 800 227-1598, 718 257-2800)

Sig Greenbaum: Chunky industrial kitchen equipment (38 Davey St, Bloomfield, NJ)

Smart Shades Co: One of the last Tiffany stained-glass manufacturers (127–03 20th Ave, College Point, NY; 718 358-8454)

Status: These people can copy any bridal gown for a fraction of retail. (747 Fulton St, Brooklyn, NY; 718 596-6333)

Stonehenge Mill Store: Designer upholstery and window fabrics (30 Canfield Rd, Cedar Grove, NJ; 201 239-9710)

Swan Creek Architectural Center: Worth the drive for architectural antiques and rustic-looking, handcrafted outdoor furniture (333 N Main St, Lambertville, NJ; 609 397-4884, 800 927-3004)

Swim and Cruisewear Outlet: First-quality women's cruisewear, sportswear, and swimwear (590 Smith St, Farmingdale, NY; 516 420-1400)

UFO Used Furniture Outlet: Refurbished, good-as-new office furniture, deeply discounted (259 North Henry St, Brooklyn, NY; 718 389-1144)

Underworld Plaza: Terrific source for lingerie, discounted up to 75% (1421 62nd St, Brooklyn, NY; 718 232-6804)

United Status Apparel: Real name-brand women's wear here from Evan-Picone, J.H. Collectibles, and Jones New York at deep discounts (25 Enterprise Ave, Secaucus, NJ; 201 867-4455)

U.S. Box Corporation: Every kind of packaging (126 Lombardy St, Brooklyn, NY; 718 387-1510)

Valley Furniture: Solid copies of Williamsburg, Newport, Sturbridge, and Mission-style pieces (20 Stirling Rd, Watchung, NJ; 908 756-7623)

Value Hosiery: Stock up on socks at this underwear emporium. (272 Fifth Ave, Park Slope, Brooklyn, NY; 718 499-6721)

Vesture: High-design hats and hatboxes for much less than what you'd pay in Manhattan. (141 Atlantic Ave, Brooklyn, NY; 718 237-4126)

Wallach's Outlet: Deals on high-end name-brand menswear (3100 47th Ave, Long Island City, NY; 718 482-8442)

Wearables International Apparel: High-quality hosiery for men, women, and kids at cheaper-than-cheap prices (P.O. Box 8521, Saddle Brook, NJ)

Woodbury Common Factory Outlets: A total of 95 outlets, including Adidas, Carlos Falchi, and Tahari Carole Little (Route 23, Tower Bldg, Central Valley, NY; 914 928-7467)

Young Elegance: Over 100 manufacturer's made-to-measure and ready-to-wear prom, homecoming, bar mitzvah, junior bridesmaid, and flower-girl dresses (433 Chestnut Ridge Rd, Woodcliff, NJ; 201 930-0949)

Yours Alone Swimwear: Custom bathing suits that flatter where they should (14 Roosevelt Ave, Chatham, NJ; 201 701-1777)

Anatomical Supplies

MAXILLA & MANDIBLE LTD.
451–5 Columbus Ave (bet 81st and 82nd St)   212 724-6173
Mon-Sat: 11–7; Sun: 1–5

Henry Galiano grew up in Spanish Harlem, and on the days his parents weren't running their beauty parlor, the family often went to the American Museum of Natural History. His interest in things skeletal increased when Galiano got a job at the museum as a curator's assistant. He soon started his own collection of skeletons and bones. That, in turn, led to his opening Maxilla & Mandible (the scientific names for the upper and lower jaw, respectively), the first and only such store in the world. That's understandable. How many people need complete skeletons – or even a single maxilla? Apparently more than you would think. The shop started by supplying museum-quality preparations of skulls, skeletons, bones, teeth, horns, skins, butterflies, beetles, seashells, fossils, taxidermy mounts, and anatomical charts and models to artists, sculptors, painters, interior decorators, jewelry manufacturers, prop masters, medical personnel, scientists, and educators. The real business is in the basement storerooms and laboratory. They also carry natural-history books, African art, Papua New Guinea art, bronze skeletal models, and scientific equipment. It seems only natural that an anatomical supply company and bone shop should have catacombs beneath Columbus Ave.

Animals, Fish, and Accessories

BIDE-A-WEE HOME ASSOCIATION
410 E 38th St   212 532-4455 (adoption shelter),
212 532-5884 (clinic)
Mon-Sat: 10–7; Sun: 10–6 (adoption)
Mon-Fri: 8:30–4:30; Sat: 9–2 (clinic)

Bide-a-Wee is the only shelter I know of in Manhattan that does not kill animals it can't place for adoption. For this alone, it deserves special mention. Dogs, cats, puppies, and kittens are available for adoption at nominal fees. Bide-a-Wee also has a veterinary clinic open to the public, and it provides a pet bereavement program.

DEDE'S DOG-O-RAMA
161 Seventh Ave S (bet Perry and Waverly St)   212 627-3647
Daily: 8:30–6

Dede Goldsmith wants everyone to understand that this is a pet *boutique*. That means your favorite companion can find the right turtleneck sweater, designer fabric bed, or fanciful toy to make his or her life more pleasant. They also offer more mundane things like dog grooming, leashes, collars, bowls, parkas, and (naturally) deli platters, with bagels and pizza. After all, doggies are into "junk food," too!

PACIFIC AQUARIUM & PET
46 Delancey St (bet Forsyth and Eldridge St)   212 995-5895
Daily: 10–8:30

Goldfish are the specialty of the house, but there is much more. Pacific Aquarium & Pet carries all types of freshwater and saltwater fish, parakeets and other exotic birds, and every kind of aquarium and supply you could imagine. With adequate notice they will even come to your home and take care of aquarium maintenance.

PET DEPARTMENT STORE
233 W 54th St (bet Broadway and Eighth Ave)
212 489-9195
Mon-Sat: 10–7; Sun; 1–5

A pet department store? Having grown up in the department-store business, I thought I had heard of everything . . . guess not! Leigh Westbrook and Roger Appleby claim this is really one-of-a-kind, and they must be right. They started out as designers and manufacturers of pet fashions, and have gone in all directions since then. For pets there are fashions and food; for people, one can find everything related to dogs, cats, fish, and birds. Dog birthday parties. "Pup" corn. Coffee and tea for weary pet owners. Pet books. A photo studio so you and Fido can pose together. You get the picture. . . .

PETLAND DISCOUNTS

132 Nassau St	212 964-1821
7 E 14th St	212 675-4102
2675 Broadway	212 222-8851
304 E 86th St	212 472-1655
404 Third Ave	212 447-0739
976 Second Ave	212 755-7228

Mon-Fri: 9–7; Sat: 10–6; Sun: 11–5

The folks at the New York Aquarium recommend this chain of stores for fish and accessories. Petland also carries birds and discount food and accessories for all pets, including dogs and cats.

Antiques

Some of New York's more interesting antique stores are described below. However, if you are an antique buff, you might want to tour various areas in Manhattan where other antique stores are located. Here is a list of stores, by neighborhood.

Second Avenue Area
Manhattan Art & Antiques Center (1050 Second Ave): General

57th Street and Fifth Avenue Area
Place Des Antiquaires (125 E 57th St): General
James Robinson (15 E 57th St): Silver Flatware
Doris Leslie Blau (15 E 57th St): Rugs
Israel Sack (15 E 57th St): Colonial furniture
Dalva Brothers (44 E 57th St): French furniture
Ralph M. Chait Galleries (12 E 56th St): Chinese art
À La Vieille Russle (781 Fifth Ave): Russian art

Madison Avenue Area
Art of the Past (1242 Madison Ave): East Asian
Marco Polo (1135 Madison Ave): Silver
Bernard & S. Dean Levy (24 E 84th St): Colonial Americana
Fanelli Antique Timepieces (1131 Madison Ave): Watches
Barry Friedman (1117 Madison Ave): Art deco
Eagles Antiques (1097 Madison Ave): English country
Guild Antiques II (1095 Madison Ave): English country
Linda Horn (1015 Madison Ave): Diverse
Navin Kumar Gallery (1001 Madison Ave): Asian art
Ursus Books and Prints (981 Madison Ave): Books
Florian Papp (962 Madison Ave): Furniture
Time Will Tell (962 Madison Ave): Watches
DeLorenzo (958 Madison Ave): Art deco
Julian Graham-White (956 Madison Ave): Diverse
Stair & Company (942 Madison Ave): Furniture
Cora Ginsburg (19 E 74th St): Fabrics

Leigh Keno (19 E 74th St): American furniture
20th Century Antiques (878 Madison Ave): Art nouveau
Macklowe Gallery & Modernism (667 Madison Ave): Tiffany
Gorevic & Gorevic (635 Madison Ave): Jewelry
J.J. Lally (41 E 57th St): Chinese Art

Lexington Avenue Area

Japan Gallery (1210 Lexington Ave): Japanese art
Stubbs Books & Prints (153 E 70th St): Books
Sylvia Pines Uniquities (1102 Lexington Ave): Diverse
L'Art de Viere (978 Lexington Ave): Early 20th century
Evergreen Antiques (1249 Third Ave): Furniture
S. Wyler (941 Lexington Ave): Silver, china
Philippe Farley (157 E 64th St): Furniture
Victor's Antiques (223 E 60th St): Furniture
Newel Art Galleries (425 E 53rd St): Furniture

SoHo

Alan Moss (88 Wooster St): Furniture
Michael Carey (77 Mercer St): Arts and crafts
Lost City Arts (275 Lafayette St): Architectural items
Cynthia Beneduce (281 Lafayette St): Eclectic
Eileen Lane Antiques (150 Thompson St): Refurbished art deco

University Place

Philip Colleck (830 Broadway): Diverse
Howard Kaplan Antiques (827 Broadway): *Belle époque*
Hyde Park Antiques (836 Broadway): English antique furniture
Kentshire Galleries (37 E 12th St): English antiques
Florence Sack (813 Broadway): Furniture
Kensington Place Antiques (80 E 11th St): Furniture
Little Antique Shop (44 E 11th St): Formal antiques
Fifty/Fifty (793 Broadway): Furniture
Karl Kemp & Associates (29 E 10th St): Furniture
L'Epoque (30 E 10th St): Armoires
Maison Gerard (36 E 10th St): French art deco

Bleecker Street Area

Susan Parrish (390 Bleecker St): Quilts
Pierre Deux Antiques (367 Bleecker St): French country

James Fenimore Cooper on New York (1930): "New York belongs already more to the country than she does to the State, and every day has a tendency to increase this catholic disposition among the votaries of commerce."

ANTIQUARIUM, FINE ANCIENT ARTS GALLERY
948 Madison Ave (at 75th St)   212 734-9776
Tues-Fri: 10–6; Sat: 10–5; closed Sat in summer

Antiquarium is a magnificent gallery for those who appreciate museum-quality antiquities and can afford to own them. This gallery specializes in classical and ancient Near Eastern items, with a particular emphasis on ancient glass and jewelry, marble, stone statuary and reliefs, bronzes, pottery, and coins. This is definitely not the place to take your three-year-old or the Merrill Lynch bull. On the other hand, you may need Merrill Lynch's help in order to send a piece home!

BACK PAGES ANTIQUES
125 Greene St   212 460-5998
Mon-Sat: 11–6; Sun: 12–6

You provide the guests, and proprietor Alan Luchnick will see to it that everyone is royally entertained. He has a fine stock of classic Wurlitzer jukeboxes, pool tables, old Coca-Cola vending machines, Edison and Victor phonographs (remember the dog?), and Regina music boxes. If nothing else, a visit here will spark a lot of pleasant memories.

CHARLOTTE MOSS
1027 Lexington Ave   212 772-3320
Mon-Thurs: 10–5:30; Fri: 10–5; Sat: 11–5, closed Sat in summer

Charlotte Moss left a successful Wall Street career to open a shop that offers products and interior-design services under one roof, like it is done in London. Her place is filled with attractive decorative accessories and antiques, including two furniture lines and a home fragrance line ("Virginia") developed by Moss herself.

COBWEB
116 W Houston St (bet Thompson and Sullivan St)
212 505-1558
Mon-Fri: 12–7; Sat: 12–5 (closed bet Christmas and New Year's Day and Sat during July and Aug)

Isn't that a great name for an antique shop? The stunning collection of country furniture and formal antiques from Europe includes armoires, brass beds, tables, chairs, benches, trunks, chests, wooden bowls, earthen olive-oil urns, and even water jugs. The merchandise is distinctive, original, and authentic. Cobweb offers customized refinishing of its own furniture.

DARROW'S FUN ANTIQUES
309 E 61st St (bet First and Second Ave) 212 838-0730
Mon-Fri: 12–7; Sat: 11:30–4:30; Sun: by appointment

Darrow's specializes in whimsical antiques for all ages. So expect to
find toys (the valuable and collectible, as well as the merely nostalgic),
slot machines, original animation art, jukeboxes, old pay phones, Mickey
Mouse watches, cast-iron banks (remember them?), and toy soldiers.
Gary Darrow, the proprietor, says that at any given time there are more
than 5,000 items in stock. He has customers all over the world who swear
he's the best. The store was founded by Gary's father in 1964, and they've
since earned a reputation as the prime source for buying and renting props
and "fun" antiques. Gary has now been joined by sister Virginia and
brother George so it is a *real* family fun business! Darrow's also sells
carefully labeled reproductions that would fool most people.

HOME TOWN
131 Wooster St (bet Houston and Prince St) 212 674-5770
Tues-Sun: 11–7

Here you'll find an outstanding collection of genuine American
antiques, both furniture and accessories. There are cupboards, kitchen
tables, chairs, quilts, game boards, vintage toys, benches, stools, andirons, lamps, and much more. Most items date from 1890 to 1940 and
are in reasonably good shape. The place is fun to visit even if you aren't
in a collectible mood!

HYDE PARK ANTIQUES
836 Broadway (bet 12th and 13th St) 212 477-0033
Mon-Fri: 9–5; Sat: 10–2:30; closed Sat in summer

This gallery has the largest inventory of genuine 18th- and 19th-century
English furniture in the world. William and Mary, Regency, and other
old English periods are represented. To accompany the furniture, there
are accents, mirrors, paintings, and porcelains. If that isn't enough, Hyde
Park maintains a fine workroom for restoring their own furniture.

JAMES ROBINSON
15 E 57th St 212 752-6166
Mon-Sat: 10–5; closed Sat in summer

Collectors and specialists in antiques (particularly silver from the 17th
and 18th centuries) are familiar with James Robinson, and many have
dealt with the store, if only by mail. James Robinson is the best at what
they do, but be warned that what they do *not* do is run an establishment
where tourists can pick up knickknacks. Even the Victorian period, which
is best known for its knickknack style of decorating, is represented with
only the finest, most silvery, and expensive pieces. James Robinson

specializes in antique silver and antique jewelry, porcelains, and glass. If something exists but is not available in the store, they will comb the world for it. What is no longer in existence will be perfectly reproduced in handmade silver. Other antique specialties include 17th- through 19th-century English bone china and porcelain (many in complete services), jewelry, and glass. None of it is inexpensive.

KURLAND-ZABAR
19 E 71st St (at Madison Ave)   212 517-8576
Tues-Fri: 11–6; Sat: 11–5

Worth browsing, if nothing else, this is the only gallery specializing in British arts and crafts in this country. And what a show it is! There are outstanding pieces of British and American furniture, silver and decorative art pieces spanning 1840 to 1940, including Gothic revival, the aesthetic movement, Renaissance revival, the arts and crafts movement, and modernist styles. Special services include locating particular pieces, bidding at auction in New York or London for a customer (for a fee, of course), and helping develop a collection. Pricey!

LITTLE ANTIQUE SHOP
44 E 11th St (at Broadway)   212 673-5173
Mon-Fri: 10–5

In a neighborhood that is borderline Village and is often referred to as "Strand territory," the Little Antique Shop stands out as a gem. This small store specializes in Oriental and European antiques, large and small. These are fine, delicate antiques, priced accordingly. There are small accent pieces, as well as large screens. All of them are quality pieces, and you'll never believe you found them on East 11th Street.

MANHATTAN ART & ANTIQUES CENTER
1050 Second Ave (bet 55th and 56th St)   212 355-4400
Mon-Sat: 10:30–6; Sun: 12–6

This is the oldest (1976) and largest (104 dealers) antique center in the country. Offered in this bazaar of small boutiques are 18th- and 19th-century English, French, Oriental, and continental furniture, silver, porcelain, decorations, bronzes, clocks, and tapestries. The careful browser can also find some fine pieces of Tiffany glass, Japanese ivory, American quilts and folk art, and colorful lacquerware. Special services include repair of clocks, watches, silver, lacquer, and ivories; jewelry design; expert appraisals; rentals to commercial photographers; interior-design consultations; rug and tapestry restorations; and packing, crating and shipping.

PLACE DES ANTIQUAIRES
125 E 57th St (bet Park and Lexington Ave)
212 755-5377
Mon-Sat: 11–6

Although a far cry from the extensive showing offered here when the facility opened, there are still several dozen galleries that display different antique specialties, with an emphasis on furniture and accessories, some serving as showrooms for larger collections housed elsewhere. As this is in the high-rent district, you are not going to find many bargains. There is a café on the concourse level for weary shoppers.

URBAN ARCHAEOLOGY
285 Lafayette St (bet Houston and Prince St)   212 431-6969
Mon-Fri: 8–6; Sat: 10–4, closed Sat July, Aug

Nowadays people are collecting almost anything and calling it antique. Urban Archaeology offers the best trims and pieces of New York architecture from the 1880s to the 1920s. While the business specializes in house artifacts, bathroom items, lighting fixtures, and display cases, owners Leonard Schechter, Gil Shapiro, and Allen Reiver display entire mood settings as well. You might find furnishings from barbershops, ice-cream parlors, saloons, and who knows what else!

Art Supplies

CHARRETTE
215 Lexington Ave   212 683-8822
Mon-Fri: 8:30–7; Sat: 10–5; Sun: 12–5; closed Sun in summer

This branch of a Massachusetts company is for serious architects, engineers, draftsmen, graphic designers, and artists. The stock includes more than 36,000 items, which means that a practitioner in any of these fields would be hard-put *not* to find what he or she needs. Charrette offers quality supplies and good advice. Professionals will be pleased to find anything they need; amateurs might want to study the catalog first.

LEE'S ART SHOP
220 W 57th St (nr Broadway)   212 247-0110
Mon-Fri: 9–7; Sat: 9:30–6:30; Sun: 12–5:30

No shortage of stock here! Ricky, the boss lady, offers her customers expanded stock of all manner of materials for both the amateur and professional artist; a section for architectural and drafting supplies; lamps, silk screens, and art brushes; a large selection of paper goods, stationery, pens, cards, and gifts; plus much more. Same-day on-premises framing is available, along with catalog ordering and free delivery. Designer lighting equipment and good-looking furniture is available at Lee's other stores (1755 Broadway and Third Ave at 63rd St).

NEW YORK CENTRAL
62 Third Ave (at 11th St)   212 473-7705
Mon-Sat: 8:30–6:15

For many years artists have looked to this firm for fine-art materials, especially unique and custom-made items. There are two floors of fine-art papers: one-of-a-kind decorative papers in various designs and colors, and over a hundred special Oriental papers from Bhutan, China, India, Japan, Thailand, Taiwan, and Nepal. Amateur and skilled artisans can find a full range of decorative paints and painting materials.

PEARL PAINT CO.
308 Canal St (bet Broadway and Church St)
212 431-7932, 800 221-6845
Mon-Wed, Fri, Sat: 9–5:30; Thurs: 9–7; Sun: 10–5:30

If you can't find it here, it probably does not exist! Ten retail selling floors contain a vast selection of art, graphic, and craft merchandise; fabric paint; silk-screening and gold-leaf items; drafting and architectural goods; as well as a fine-writing department. They specialize in providing every facet of fine-art supplies at some of the best prices in town.

SAM FLAX
425 Park Ave (at 55th St)   212 620-3060
12 W 20th St   212 620-3038
Mon-Fri: 9–6; Sat: 10–5

Sam Flax is one of the biggest and best in the art-supply business. The stock here is enormous, the service special, and the prices competitive. They carry a full range of art and drafting supplies, gifts, pens, drawing-studio furniture, and photographic products. Framing services are offered at both stores, and even one-day framing is available. The store at 12 W 20th Street is primarily devoted to furniture.

UTRECHT ART AND DRAFTING SUPPLIES
111 Fourth Ave (at 11th St)   212 777-5353
Mon-Sat: 9–6

We once mused about the name of this art-supply outlet, and we received a letter from a reader who pointed out that Utrecht is a large city in Holland with a long tradition of arts and crafts. Fair enough, but we initially raised the question because this shop used to be called Utrecht *Linens*. In any case, Utrecht is a major manufacturer of paint, art, and drafting supplies, with a large factory in Brooklyn. At this retail store, factory-fresh supplies are sold at factory discounts, and the Utrecht name stands behind every purchase. Quality is superb, as are discounts. Utrecht also carries other manufacturers' lines at impressive discounts.

Autographs

ANNA SOSENKO
25 Central Park W (bet 62nd and 63rd St) 212 247-4816
Mon-Sat: by appointment

This lady is in love with the showbiz, music, and literary worlds, and it shows. She has assembled a fine collection of letters, photos, and autographs of leading figures in these fields, offering them for sale from her home. There are plenty of stories to go with the collections.

JAMES LOWE AUTOGRAPHS
30 E 60th St (bet Madison and Park Ave, Suite 907)
212 759-0775
Mon-Fri: 9–5

James Lowe is one of the most established autograph houses in the country. Catalogs, published several times a year, make a visit to the gallery unnecessary, but in-person inspections are fascinating and invariably whet the appetite of autograph collectors. There is no one specialty; the gallery seems to show whatever superior items are in stock, though there is a particular interest in historic, literary, and musical autographs, manuscripts, documents, and 19th-century photographs. The offerings range from autographed pictures of Buffalo Bill to three bars of an operatic score of Puccini's. It all depends on what a buyer finds intriguing. Perhaps that explains why James Lowe prefers that you drop by.

KENNETH W. RENDELL
989 Madison Ave (at 77th St)   212 717-1776
Mon-Sat: 11–6 or by appointment

Kenneth Rendell has been in the business for over 30 years, and he offers a fine collection of pieces from famous personages in literature, arts, politics, and the sciences. Rendell shows autographed letters, manuscripts, documents, and signed books and photographs. All are authenticated, attractively presented, and priced according to rarity. Rendell evaluates collections for tax purposes and arranges the purchase or sale of items on a consulting basis.

TOLLETT AND HARMAN
175 W 76th St   212 877-1566
By appointment only

Autographs used to be a big business in New York, perhaps because of the number of celebrities in the city. Lately, however, there are less than a handful of reliable dealers. Tollett and Harman is one of the best. They carry or will obtain original autographs, manuscripts, signed books, maps, and vintage photographs. Collectors of specific items can leave requests with them. (I collect presidents of the U.S. and of the Continental Congresses.) When they come across an item, they will notify you. Each item is carefully authenticated. Ask for a catalog!

Baskets

BASKETFULL
1133 Broadway (at 25th St)   212 255-6800, 800 645-GIFT
Mon-Fri: 9–5:30

When you want a basket crafted with unique and innovative ideas, this is the place to call. These folks custom-design their gift items year-round for parties, anniversaries, and special occasions. For example, you could send a sinful collection of indulgences that includes chocolate-covered potato chips and orange croissants, David Glass chocolate-mousse balls and chocolate-mousse cake, chocolate truffles and cookies, and even some fabulous Manon chocolate candies from Belgium! There are breakfast baskets, Southwest baskets, fitness baskets, and even a spa basket, complete with a book on massage! How about a basket full of theater-sized boxes of good things to nibble on? Same-day hand-delivery is available in Manhattan, and arrangements can be made for shipment anywhere in the world.

Bathroom Accessories

A. F. SUPPLY CORPORATION
22 W 21st St (bet Fifth and Sixth Ave)   212 243-5400
Mon-Fri: 8–5 and by appointment

Some might argue that the bathroom is the most important room in the house, and the folks at A. F. Supply would definitely agree. They offer a great selection of luxury bath fixtures, whirlpools, faucets, bath accessories, door and cabinet hardware, saunas, steam showers, shower doors, medicine cabinets, and spas from top suppliers.

ELEGANT JOHN
812 Lexington Ave (bet 62nd and 63rd St)   212 935-5800
Mon-Wed, Fri, Sat: 10–6; Thurs: 10–7

After getting over the initial awkwardness of entering a store that displays prominently labeled "john seats" on its walls, you'll be amazed at the array of shower curtains, dressing tables, coordinated accessories, soap dishes, and (of course) seats, all sold with the aim of creating a bathroom that is every bit as comfortable and striking as the rest of the house. Wicker furniture for the bathroom and bedroom are a recent addition to their stock.

SHERLE WAGNER INTERNATIONAL
60 E 57th St (at Park Ave)   212 758-3300
Mon-Fri: 9:30–5

Sherle Wagner takes a topic that even the Elegant John skirted and places it in the most elegant location in the city, where it rubs elbows with silversmiths, art galleries, and exclusive antique shops. However, the luxurious bathroom fixtures are almost works of art and are deserving of their 57th Street location. Fixtures come in every possible material, and some are so striking that they make a glass display case seem like a natural setting. Prices are high, as might be expected. One warning! The displays are in the basement, and what seems like the world's slowest elevator will give you a good case of claustrophobia.

Beads

THE BEAD STORE
1065 Lexington Ave (at 75th St)   212 628-4383
Mon-Wed, Fri: 10–7; Thurs: 10–8; Sat, Sun: 10–6

Can you imagine over 1,500 varieties of beads on display in one store? You'll find that many here, with types ranging from imported beauties and hand-painted beads to colored-glass beads from Japan to cloisonné pieces. There is a complete selection of jewelry findings, leather and silk cording, workshops and classes, and a nice selection of semiprecious stones. Prices are reasonable, and the place is so neat and attractive you will want to spend an afternoon here stringing that special necklace!

Books

American Indian

BOB FEIN BOOKS
150 Fifth Ave (at 20th St, Room 841)   212 807-0489
Mon-Fri: 12–6

Bob Fein claims that his is the only shop devoted to the literature of American Indians. Within this boundary, he also includes pre-Columbian art and Eskimos as subjects, and he has on hand more than 4,000 books and journals on those topics. Many of his items are out-of-print or one-of-a-kind, and Fein is considered the primary source for such material. There is also a good percentage of what Fein terms "scholarly material," along with Smithsonian publications and reports. Most of the stock is unique and rare, and if any new literature is published about Fein's specialties, chances are he'll have it first.

Architecture

URBAN CENTER BOOKS
457 Madison Ave (at 51st St)   212 935-3595
Mon-Thurs: 11–7; Fri, Sat 10–6

Urban Center Books, the retail arm of the Municipal Art Society, practices what it preaches. The society was founded in 1892 to preserve the best of New York's historical architectural facades. That the society should be located in the north wing of the Villard Houses—historic homes that make up the base of the New York Palace Hotel—is only fitting. Since most of the rooms in those buildings have been refurbished to resemble drawing rooms and libraries, it is equally appropriate that the society decided to sell publications on its interests in a suite that is a real library. If nothing else, a visit to Urban Center Books offers a chance to further explore the public rooms of the houses. Although only the physical amenities are left (wide doorways, parquet floors, painted ceilings), it is still a stunning look back into times gone by. The store specializes in architecture, history, and the city's physical plan. Publications on the topics of urban planning, design, and historic preservation are available.

Art

HACKER ART BOOKS
45 W 57th St   212 688-7600
Mon-Sat: 9:30–6

There can only be one "largest" in any field, and Hacker is it in art books. You'll find books on fine arts, decorative arts, architecture, and much more. They have been in business for nearly half a century; if Hacker doesn't have it, it probably doesn't exist!

JAAP RIETMAN
134 Spring St (bet Greene and Wooster St)   212 966-7044
Mon-Fri: 9:30–6; Sat: 10:30–6

If paintings, sculpture, photography, or any of the fine arts are in your field of interest, you will find this a wonderful shop for browsing. This is a complete fine-arts book store with top-quality merchandise and very accommodating personnel.

PRINTED MATTER
77 Wooster St   212 925-0325
Tues-Sat: 10–6

The name Printed Matter is almost a misnomer, since the store is the only one in the world devoted exclusively to artists' books—a trade term for a portfolio of artwork in book form. They stock 5,000 titles by over 2,500 artists. The result is inexpensive, accessible art that can span an entire artist's career or a particular period or theme. The idea is carried further by Printed Matter's selection of periodicals and audio work in a similar vein. Nearly all featured artists are contemporary, so just browsing through the store would bring you up-to-date on what is going on right now in the art world. They sell both wholesale and retail.

Biography

BIOGRAPHY BOOKSHOP
400 Bleecker St (at 11th St)   212 807-8655
Mon-Fri: 12–8; Sat: 12–10; Sun: 12–6

Here's a New York specialty shop that deals only with books of a biographical nature. If one is researching a particular person, or if you have an interest in someone's life story, this is the place to find it. There are biographies, books of letters, autobiographies, diaries, journals, biographies for children, and even fiction.

Children's

BOOKS OF WONDER
132 Seventh Ave (at 18th St)   212 989-3270
Mon-Sat: 11–7; Sun: 12–6

464 Hudson St (at Barrow St)   212 645-8006
Mon-Sat: 11–7; Sun: 12–6

Books of Wonder established its reputation as a prime source for rare, collectible, and out-of-print children's books at its store on Hudson Street. Owners Peter Glassman and James Carey stocked the store with their own favorites and established the largest selection of Oz books for sale in the world. Books of Wonder opened a second and much larger store across the street from the clothing store Barney's. Together they have the largest number of children's book titles in the city.

STORYLAND
1369 Third Ave (at 78th St)   212 517-6951
Mon-Sat; 10–6; Sun: 11–6

Storyland is the ultimate bookstore for children. Genial owner Jeff Bergman has created an atmosphere that children will love and parents will enjoy while shopping for children's books, videos, and cassette tapes. Every Wednesday and Sunday (except during summer) a writer or illustrator is on hand for story hour. (The hours are 12:10 p.m. on Wednesday, and 1:30 p.m. on Sunday.) A carnival atmosphere reigns at this first-class bookstore.

Comic

ACTION COMICS
1724 Second Ave (bet 89th and 90th St)   212 249-7344
Mon-Sat: 11–8; Sun: 12–6

Here you will find just about the best selection of comic books and more in the city. There are new comics from all publishers, collector's comics from the 1930s to the present, new and collector's baseball cards, posters, T-shirts, original comic art, and collecting supplies.

ST. MARK'S COMICS
11 St. Mark's Pl (bet Second and Third Ave)   212 598-9439
Mon, Tues, Wed: 10–11; Thurs, Fri, Sat: 10–1; Sun: 11–11

This unique store carries small-press and underground comics that are not easy to find elsewhere. They have a large selection of back issues available and claim that "if it's published, we carry it." Ask for Mitch Cutler; he is very service-oriented and will hold selections for you. The neighborhood will provide you with some comic relief, too!

SUPERSNIPE COMIC BOOK EUPHORIUM
P.O. Box 1102, Gracie Station, New York, NY 10028
212 580-8843
By appointment and mail order
Call Fri, Sat: 10–4:30

The ultimate comic-book emporium. Supersnipe now deals only by phone and mail order. It is well worth your time, however, because their stock is unequaled.

VILLAGE COMICS
163 Bleecker St, 2nd floor (bet Sullivan and Thompson St)
212 777-2770
Mon-Wed: 10–8:30; Thurs-Sat: 10–9:30; Sun: 11:30–7:30
940 Third Ave, 2nd floor   212 759-6255
Mon-Sat: 10:30–7:30

Village Comics brags that they carry *everything* in the comic-book field, with merchandise for every taste and age. They have collector's items, old and new books, limited editions, new sports cards, and an outstanding selection of science-fiction and horror books. Regular customers may even get into a rebate program. If you hear about something special soon to be published, they will take advance orders.

Food

KITCHEN ARTS & LETTERS
1435 Lexington Ave (at 94th St)   212 876-5550
Mon: 1–6; Tues-Fri: 10–6:30; Sat: 11–6;
closed Aug and Sat in July

Cookbooks traditionally are best sellers in bookstores, and with the renewed interest in health, fitness, and natural foods, that rule of thumb is more operative than ever. So it should come as no surprise that Nachum Waxman's Kitchen Arts & Letters should be an immediate success as a store specializing in books, literature, photography, and original art about food and its preparation. Imported books are a specialty. Waxman claims that his store is the only one like it in the city and one of less than ten in the entire country. Waxman is a former editor at Harper & Row and Crown publishing companies, where he supervised several cookbook projects. Bitten with the urge to start a specialty bookshop, he discovered almost immediately that there was a huge demand for out-of-print and original cookbooks. So while the tiny shop stocks more than 7,000 titles, as well as a gallery of photography and original art, much of the business is in finding out-of-print and want-listed books.

Foreign

BOOK-FRIENDS CAFE
16 W 18th St   212 255-7407
Mon-Fri: 10–9; Sat, Sun: 12–7

Should this entry appear in the "Stores" or "Restaurants" section of this book? Both, really, but I decided to list it here because of the unusual combination of activities available. You can feast upon delicious chili or beef stew, pâté, salads, cheeses, scones, and wonderful desserts. You can have afternoon tea. You can meet and chat with interesting authors. You can choose from a large selection of attractive teapots. Best of all, you can browse a fine collection of books centered around Europe in general and Paris in particular from the 1890s through the 1940s.

LIBRAIRIE DE FRANCE
LIBRERIA HISPANICA
610 Fifth Ave (bet 49th and 50th St)   212 581-8810
Mon-Sat: 10–6:15

115 Fifth Ave (at 19th St)   212 673-7400
Mon-Sat: 10–6

A short stroll through the Rockefeller Center promenade takes you by the Librairie de France and Libreria Hispanica, where they have been located since 1934. Inside, you will find an interesting collection of French and Spanish newspapers, magazines, tourist guides, and light reading. There are more than a million French and Spanish books and records in stock, and *all* of them are neatly cataloged and easily found. At least several books in French or Spanish are available on seemingly every topic, including a collection of books in Spanish about French literature and vice versa! A partial list of the available categories includes textbooks, dictionaries and encyclopedias, children's books and records, bilingual and bicultural educational records and tapes, games, greeting cards, posters, audiovisual aids, newspapers, magazines, French popular music (on CDs and LPs), French and Spanish films on video (with English subtitles), and Haitian and African literature. A special division stocks dictionaries and cassettes in over a hundred languages.

NEW YORK KINOKUNIYA BOOKSTORE
10 W 49th St (at Fifth Ave)   212 765-1461
Daily: 10–7:30

Kinokuniya is Japan's largest and most esteemed bookstore chain. An American branch, located in Rockefeller Plaza, has two floors of books about Japan. The atmosphere is the closest thing in New York to Tokyo. On the first floor there are 20,000 English-language books, which leave no part of Japanese culture neglected. Art, cooking, travel, language, literature, history, business, economics, management techniques, martial arts—they're all here. The rest of the floor is rounded out with books on the same subjects in Japanese, and there are paperbacks on the second floor. Kinokuniya has the largest collection of Japanese books in the city—and possibly outside of Japan.

UNIVERSITY PLACE BOOK SHOP
821 Broadway, 9th floor   212 254-5998
Mon-Fri: 10–5

In this out-of-the-way, dust-covered loft may be the largest collection of books on Africa and the West Indies in the world. After climbing up to its ninth-floor location, it's disconcerting to find piles of books that seem to be arranged by chance. But there are some great finds here, and the salespeople are friendly and knowledgeable. The selection includes literature in more than 35 African dialects. Compensating for the fact that many African dialects have never been written down, University stocks 200 to 300 books about them; almost every subject or group is covered. University also carries many old, rare, and out-of-print books on Africa and the West Indies. The newer books are involved with current black America. William French, the owner and manager, seems to know every book in the store—an amazing feat. The books he personally values most are the early printed books from the 15th to the 17th centuries, and the rare and out-of-print books on Africa, the West Indies, and Afro-Americans.

General

BARNES AND NOBLE
Branches throughout the city   212 807-0099
Hours vary by store

These are the big guys in the book business! Barnes and Noble and their affiliated stores offer unexcelled opportunities for book buyers and browsers, no matter what area of the city one lives in. Generations of New York students have bought their texts at the main store (105 Fifth Avenue, at 18th Street). Now Barnes and Noble has opened a number of magnificent superstores, with enormous stocks of staples and bargains, comfortable shopping conveniences (even a café), a large selection of discounted magazines, and best of all, their traditional discounts on best sellers and other popular books. New Barnes and Noble Jr. stores appeal to youngsters, with stocks that are as exciting and complete. For value and selection, you can't beat these folks!

B. DALTON BOOKSELLER
212 247-1740 (main store)
Branches throughout city
Hours vary by store

The B. Dalton shop on Fifth Avenue, among the largest bookstores in the city, is the flagship for one of the largest and best bookselling operations in the nation. Dalton has access to huge lots of remainders and reprints, due to its nationwide buying power. There are sections for children, technical subjects, special interests, and the arts. Dalton doesn't excel in any one particular area, but it deserves an "A" for presentation. Their window displays are always must-sees for the latest in the publishing world.

BURLINGTON BOOK SHOP
1082 Madison Ave (bet 81st and 82nd St)   212 288-7420
Mon-Fri: 9:30–6; Sat: 10–6; Sun: 12–5

Burlington functions as a small-town bookstore in the big city. Their business card still lists their phone number as "Butterfield 8"! (John O'Hara would love it.) The store specializes in art books and literature, and they offer friendly, neighborly service. Two specialties of this unique operation: downstairs is a fabulous collection of Burlington Antique Toys, and on the mezzanine, a shop called "Compulsive Collector" features an out-of-print book department.

DOUBLEDAY BOOK SHOPS
724 Fifth Ave (bet 56th and 57th St)   212 397-0550
Mon-Sat: 9–10; Sun: 12–6

Citicorp Center (Lexington Ave at 53rd St)   212 223-3301
Mon-Fri: 8–7; Sat: 11–6

Doubleday, the granddaddy of the Fifth Avenue bookstores, has it all. There probably isn't a topic or title they don't stock or can't get; they are particularly proud of their back list. The Fifth Avenue store is the prototype of what a bookstore should be—particularly a bookstore in the city. The first floor of the 57th Street store is known for its selection of current and best-selling books and for a great travel department. If a title is newly released, Doubleday's main section often has it before publication date. Other floors in the 57th Street store concentrate on art books, cookbooks, political issues, and backlisted publications—and that is only a partial list. But the quintessential bookstore relies heavily on its personnel, and it is in this area that Doubleday really excels. They still give service with a capital S. The store crew are real professionals.

The Citicorp branch blends perfectly with its locale. Philosophical works are basically nonexistent, but gift books, coffee-table books, and light fiction are runaway favorites. Doubleday stores have a large selection of light reading: fiction, mysteries, self-improvement books, and cookbooks. They have the largest selection of books on tape in Manhattan. My good friend, the talented Don Rieck, is the manager of the flagship store. He knows everything there is to know about books!

GOTHAM BOOK MART
41 W 47th St   212 719-4448
Mon-Fri: 9:30–6:30; Sat: 9:30–6

The Gotham is a New York institution founded by the late Frances Steloff, a legend herself. Steloff founded the store nearly 73 years ago as a small, personal, theatrically inclined bookstore. In the early days, as is true today, there was a heavy emphasis on poetry and the arts, because those were Steloff's passions. Steloff, who could never understand how a book could be banned, once smuggled 25 first editions of Henry Miller's *Tropic of Cancer* into the country from Paris via Mexico. She developed a deep personal interest in authors and clients alike, and even as she grew older she would always make one daily visit downstairs to the shop around 2 p.m. Steloff lived to reach the century mark; her influence on this charming store will probably live on for another century. An exceptional search service is a special attraction.

McGRAW-HILL BOOKSTORE
1221 Sixth Ave (bet 48th and 49th St)   212 512-4100
Mon-Sat: 10–5:45

This huge shop, located downstairs in the McGraw-Hill Building (at Rockefeller Center), is limited in fiction and general titles, but for anything published by McGraw-Hill or written with a business, technical, or scientific bent, it is excellent. They're all sold at list price, and the wide selection of books would make any engineer happy. One-third of their books is about computers. A fine, well-run, and professional store.

RIZZOLI
31 W 57th St (bet Fifth and Sixth Ave)   212 759-2424
Mon-Sat: 9–8; Sun: 10:30–7:30
Branches at the World Financial Center, in SoHo
(on West Broadway), and at Bloomingdale's

When you talk class in the book business, Rizzoli is right on top of the list. They have managed to maintain the elegant atmosphere that makes a patron feel he or she is browsing a European library rather than a midtown Manhattan bookstore. The emphasis here is on art, literature, photography, music, dance (particularly ballet), and foreign languages. There is also a good selection of paperbooks. Upstairs you will find Italian books, a music department, and children's books. Art objects are shown throughout the store. The SoHo store has been greatly expanded, and the Bloomingdale's department is a great place to shop for gift books. Besides that, they always feature New York's best guidebook! (I wonder what that could be?)

SPRING STREET BOOKS
169 Spring St   212 219-3033
Mon-Thurs: 10–11; Fri: 10–12; Sat: 10–1; Sun: 11–10

In addition to the fun of browsing through an interesting bookstore, one of the joys of shopping here is observing the cast of characters who are your fellow customers! Stocks are complete, they ship anywhere, do special ordering, and feature free gift-wrapping.

STRAND BOOK STORE
828 Broadway (at 12th St)   212 473-1452
Mon-Sat: 9:30–9:30; Sun: 11–9:30;

Strand at South Street Seaport
159 John St   212 809-0875
Daily: 10–10

For book lovers, no trip to New York is complete without a visit to this fabulous bookstore, one of the largest in the world. For New Yorkers, this is surely the place to start looking for that volume you must have. There are carts full of real bargains outside and eight miles of books inside, tagged at up to 85% off list price. These crowded quarters house secondhand, rare, and out-of-print books at reduced prices, as well as thousands of new books at 50% off the publisher's list price. Upstairs in the rare-book room, where a signed first edition of James Joyce's *Ulysses* sold for $30,000, you can find books in the four- to five-figure range, including an early, signed, hand-colored Andy Warhol book, *Wild Raspberries,* for $7,000. There is also a fine selection of more moderately priced books, including 20th-century first editions, limited signed editions, fine bindings, and art books. The store also imports English remainders, sells to libraries, and does a booming mail-order business. Be sure to meet owner Fred Bass, one of the nicest and most knowledgeable individuals in the book business. This is definitely a must-visit!

TOWER BOOKS
383 Lafayette St (at 4th St)   212 228-5100
Daily: 11–11

The highly successful Tower chain has now gotten into the book business in a big way. Their first bookstore on the East Coast houses over 100,000 titles (including a large selection of children's books), 1,200 magazine titles, and national and international magazines. All paperbacks are discounted 10%; best sellers are 30% off.

WALDENBOOKS
57 Broadway (at Exchange Pl)   212 269-1139
Mon-Fri: 8–6

While the other major bookstores have their flagship outlets on Fifth Avenue, Walden chose the Wall Street area for its major operation. And what an operation it is! The store literally overflows with titles in almost every category. Befitting its location, Walden offers one of the largest selections of business and investment books in the country. They also publish the *Walden Street Journal,* a free monthly newsletter, featuring new and noteworthy business and investment titles. But no matter what you are looking for, Waldenbooks can satisfy your need. The selection in this store is so vast (around 50,000 titles) that fiction browsers in one area may not realize that nearby is housed a comprehensive selection of computer and reference books, as well as travel guides and maps. In keeping with their reputation as a full-service bookstore, Walden will special-order and gift-wrap free of charge, send merchandise anywhere, and provide expert answers to a multitude of readers' questions. They also specialize in corporate purchasing, with bulk discounts.

Irish
IRISH BOOKS
580 Broadway, 11th floor (bet Prince and Houston St)
212 274-1923
Mon-Fri: 11–5; Sat: 1–4

Angela Carter has changed the name of her shop from Keschcarrigan (that was a mouthful) to Irish Books, but she has not changed the great selection of new and used Irish books, posters, old maps, and engravings. Books are offered in both Irish Gaelic and in English.

Military
MILITARY BOOKMAN
29 E 93rd St   212 348-1280
Tues-Sat: 10:30–5:30

The inventory here is limited to books of a military nature. The specialty is out-of-print and rare books on military, naval, and aviation history. At any given time, there are 10,000 such titles in stock. Topics run the gamut from Attila the Hun to atomic warfare. The Military Bookman also has a large mail-order business and maintains a subscription mail-order catalog. The proprietors are Harris and Margaretta Colt.

SOLDIER SHOP
1222 Madison Ave (bet 88th and 89th St)   212 535-6788
Mon-Fri: 10–6; Sat: 10–5; Sat: 10–3 in July, Aug

The military is a deadly serious business here. Many of the books are extremely rare and valuable. The general specialty, however, is the military in all of its ramifications, and as a result, the Soldier Shop stocks current as well as rare military books concerning history, battles, theory, and biography. Their catalog lists 166 pages of military history books, antique soldiers, arms, and armor.

Mystery

FOUL PLAY BOOKS OF MYSTERY & SUSPENSE
13 Eighth Ave (at W 12th St)   212 675-5115
Mon-Sat: 11–9:45; Sun: 11–7

1465-B Second Ave (at 76th St)   212 517-3222
Mon-Fri: 12–10; Sat: 11–11; Sun: 11:30–6:30

In addition to mystery, suspense fiction, and out-of-print paperbacks, Foul Play stock large sections on true crime. Both stores are open late. ("Where To" mystery hint: Ask to see the secret door!)

MURDER INK®
2486 Broadway (bet 92nd and 93rd St)   212 362-8905
Mon-Wed, Fri, Sat: 10–7:30; Thurs: 11–9; Sun: 11–7

Murder Ink® was the first mystery bookstore in the city. When Dilys Winn founded Murder Ink,® she started not so much a bookstore as a way of life. Today, Jay Pearsall runs the store, which still claims to stock every murder or mystery book in print and several thousand selections no longer in print. You'll find rare books and other artifacts, but the emphasis is on good, entertaining mysteries.

MYSTERIOUS BOOK SHOP
129 W 56th St   212 765-0900
Mon-Sat: 11–7

Otto Penzler is a Baker Street Irregular, a Sherlock Holmes fan extraordinaire (an elementary deduction!), and the Mysterious Book Shop's owner. As a result, the shop is run as a friendly business, and spontaneous conversations among customers are the norm. On the ground floor (actually, a few steps below street level), Mysterious stocks new hardcover and paperback books that deal with any genre of mystery. ("But *not* science fiction," says the store manager. "Science fiction is not mystery.") Upstairs, via a winding circular staircase, the store branches out to the width of two buildings and is stocked floor-to-ceiling with out-of-print, used, and rare books. Amazingly, they seem to know exactly what is in stock, and if it is not on the shelves, they will order it. There is as much talk as business conducted here, and you can continue the conversation at the store's next autograph party.

New York

CITYBOOKS
61 Chambers St (bet Broadway and Centre St)   212 669-8245
Mon-Fri: 9–5

This city-government bookstore has access to more than 120 different official publications, all of which are dedicated to helping New Yorkers cope with their complex lives. *The Green Book* is the official directory of the City of New York, listing phone numbers and addresses of more than 900 government agencies and 6,000 officials. It includes state, federal, and international listings; the courts; and a section on licenses. There is also a unique collection of New York memorabilia: city-seal ties, pins, and rare New York photographs reproduced in calendars, posters, and much more.

NEW YORK BOUND BOOKSHOP
50 Rockefeller Plaza (lobby)   212 245-8503
Mon-Fri: 10–6; Sat: 12–4

Barbara Cohen and Judith Stonehill have assembled a printed ode to New York. The older and more esoteric a view of New York a publication has, the more these ladies covet it for their shop. The specialty is old, rare, out-of-print, and unusual ephemera (their word) relating to New York. History buffs will have a field day with the eyewitness accounts of early life in the Big Apple. Check out the photographs or browse through the current catalog, but definitely visit. Old New York is alive and well at New York Bound. Of course, there are *new* books on the Big Apple, too.

Occult

SAMUEL WEISER
132 E 24th St (nr Lexington Ave)   212 777-6363
Mon-Wed, Fri: 9–6; Thurs: 10–7; Sat: 9:30–5:30; Sun: 10:30–5

For stocking all kinds of publications on metaphysics, religion, and the occult, Samuel Weiser has a worldwide reputation that is well deserved. The shop is clean and modern, and its selection includes the eeriest titles found anywhere. The specialties cover almost any topic that is otherworldly: witchcraft, astrology, alchemy, magic, mysticisim, ESP, flying saucers, Zen, and herb medicine. These are explored in books, magazines, periodicals, and foreign publications. Some of the best in the field seem to be printed in foreign languages; many are translated and sold here in both versions. Finally, Samuel Weiser is one of the most obliging shops in town. They maintain a waiting list for out-of-print titles, and when the title arrives (by whatever mystical means), they will ship it anywhere in the world. The shop also sells topical videos, incense, and music tapes.

Out-of-Print

ACADEMY BOOK STORE
10 W 18th St (nr Fifth Ave)   212 242-4848
Mon-Sat: 9:30–9; Sun: 11–7

Academy has one of New York's largest selections of used, rare, and out-of-print books, records, and CDs. The emphasis here is on literature, the arts, photography, architecture, philosophy, psychology, history, music, cinema, dance, and drama. In the music area, you will find a good choice of jazz recordings and a concentration on opera, contemporary classical, and early music.

CHARLOTTE F. SAFIR
1349 Lexington Ave, Apt 9B, New York, NY 10128
212 534-7933
Phone any time

If you want to add to a book collection or find out more about that special author you enjoy so much, here is a lady who can save you a lot of time and effort. Charlotte Safir provides a search service for out-of-print books by mail or phone only. She has a fantastic network of contacts and can locate any kind of book, although she specializes in out-of-print cookbooks and children's books. Charlotte is efficient, persistent, and a pleasure to deal with.

Paperback

CLASSIC BOOK SHOP
World Trade Center, concourse level   212 466-0668
Mon-Fri: 7:30–7; Sat: 10–5; Sun: 12–6

Classic Book Shop pursues unusual, rare, and esoteric paperbacks, and its selection is among the best. Although *paperback* at one time meant "inexpensive," this is no longer always true. The 25-cent "pocketbook" is a thing of the past. Classic's forte is paperback backlist titles, and it claims to have the best collection in the area. Classic also carries hardcover books and has a good selection of children's titles.

Photography

A PHOTOGRAPHERS PLACE
133 Mercer St (at Prince St)   212 431-9358
Mon-Sat: 11–6; Sun: 12–5
Mail-order address: P.O. Box 274, Prince Street Station, New York, NY 10012

There is no doubt that photography is an art form to Harvey Zucker and the people who run A Photographer's Place. The shop is a temple to photographers, past and present. It is *not* a supply shop. Rather, it pays homage to great pictures of various eras and the people who took them. The owners claim to be "the only all-photographic book shop in the city and perhaps the country." They're interested in being the best they can be; it's a credo they feel is shared by every photographer. The shop excels at offering inspiration, history, advice, and the latest in technological advances. A super catalog is free for the asking.

Rare

BAUMAN RARE BOOKS
Waldorf-Astoria Hotel Lobby, 301 Park Ave (at 50th St)
212 759-8300
Mon-Sat: 10–7

Bauman offers a fine collection of books and autographs dating from the 15th through the 20th centuries. Included are works in literature, history, economics, law, science, medicine, nature, travel, and exploration. They also provide full services, from designing and furnishing libraries to locating books for customers.

IMPERIAL FINE BOOKS
790 Madison Ave, 2nd floor (nr 66th St)   212 861-6620
Mon-Fri: 10–5:30; Sat: 10–5 (closed Sat in summer)

If you are in the market for books that *look* as great as they read, Imperial is the place to visit. Here you will find fine leather bindings, illustrated books, vintage children's books, unique first editions, and some magnificent sets of prized volumes. Their inventory includes literary giants like Twain, Dickens, Bronte, Churchill, and Shakespeare. Services include complete restoration and binding of damaged or aged books. A search office will locate specific titles and make appraisals.

J.N. BARTFIELD GALLERIES AND FINE BOOKS
30 W 57th St, 3rd floor   212 245-8890
Mon-Fri: 10–5; Sat: 10–3 (summer hours vary)

This shop is a spectacular hunting ground for lovers of fine paintings and rare books. Since 1937 they have specialized in the masters of the American West, and 19th- and 20th-century American paintings and sculptures. I have purchased outstanding collections of leatherbound books from them and can vouch for their expertise. First editions, sporting books, and high-quality antiquarian books are featured. Who wouldn't be excited to browse through elegantly bound volumes by famous authors that once graced the shelves of old family libraries?

PAGEANT PRINT AND BOOK SHOP
109 E 9th St (bet Third and Fourth Ave)   212 674-5296
Mon-Thurs: 10–7; Fri: 10–8; Sat: 11–7:30

This shop might be as old and rare as the stock it carries. A holdover from the days when this area was the rare- and old-book capital of the world, it displays and sometimes sells antiquarian books, maps, prints, and first editions from the 15th to the 20th centuries. I doubt that anyone inside could readily tell me what year it is today (let alone the date), but then again the shop is as timeless as its attitude. Pageant carries virtually every kind of printed matter. There are etchings and early printed items; it would require several days just to admire the prints. But remember this is a print and book shop, and the emphasis is on the latter. In the old days, this would have been one of a dozen shops. Today, it may be one of the very few places left where you can have an authentic rare book-buying experience.

XIMENES RARE BOOKS
19 E 69th St   212 744-0226
Mon-Fri: 9–5 (appointment advisable)

In a profession whose proprietorship immediately calls to mind a stooped Dickensian character peering through a pince-nez in a paneled library, Stephen Weissman of Ximenes stands alone. He has an understanding and knowledge of rare books that would seemingly come only after years of burial under dusty volumes. Furthermore, Ximenes' collection is among the more affordable (prices start at about $100), and Weissman will happily discourse on his trade, if asked. His specialties include English-language first editions printed between 1500 and 1890. In that field, he is a primary source.

Religious

CHRISTIAN PUBLICATIONS BOOK STORE
315 W 43rd St (bet Eighth and Ninth Ave)   212 582-4311
Mon-Fri: 9:30–5:45; Thurs: 9:30–6:45; Sat: 9:30–4:45

This is the largest Christian bookstore in the metropolitan area. It has over 20,000 titles in stock, along with religious CDs, tapes, videos, and church and school supplies. A large number of these items are also available in Spanish, as befits the Latin neighborhood.

J. LEVINE BOOKS & JUDAICA
5 W 30th St   212 695-6888
Mon-Wed: 9–6; Thurs: 9–7; Fri: 9–2; Sun: 10–5

The history of the Lower East Side is reflected in this store. Started back in 1902 on Eldridge Street, it was a fixture in the area for many years. Now things have changed, and J. Levine has moved uptown into expanded quarters, just off Fifth Avenue. Being one of the oldest Jewish bookstores in the city, they are a leader in the Jewish-book marketplace. They have added a second floor with many gift items, tapes, coffee-table books, and thousands of items of Judaica, though the emphasis is still on the written word.

NEW YORK BIBLE SOCIETY
172 Lexington Ave (bet 30th and 31st St)   212 213-5454
Mon-Fri: 10–6

The New York Bible Society sells the world's most popular book in over 30 languages and in all kinds of editions. They can fill large church orders or special gifts. They have the greatest variety of low-cost New International Version scriptures in the city. There are all kinds of Bibles here, from pocket-sized to giant print. It's on audio and videotapes, and there's even a children's Bible storybook.

STAVSKY HEBREW BOOKSTORE
147 Essex St   212 674-1289
Sun-Thurs: 9–5; closed Sun in summer

This store supplies synagogues and schools with religious books and objects. While they will fill an order for ten coloring books, they are more accustomed to outfitting entire congregations, and they do it well. Their prices are fair, and service is excellent. Stavsky has the best collection of Jewish books, cassettes, CDs, Jewish videos, and everyday religious objects in the city.

Science Fiction

FORBIDDEN PLANET
821 Broadway (at 12th St)   212 473-1576
Mon-Wed: 10–7; Thurs, Fri: 10–7:30; Sat: 10–7; Sun: 12–7

When Mike Luckman started a science-fiction book-cum-toy shop in his native London, he quickly discovered that a good percentage of his customers were Americans clamoring for a similar shop at home. So Luckman obliged and opened a satellite store at 12th Street and Broadway, directly across from the Strand. Many pilgrimages have been made to this shrine of science-fiction literature and artifacts. While most of the stock is devoted to sci-fi comic books and publications, Luckman discovered in London that devotees are not catholic in taste. First-edition collectors love Chewbacca face masks and bookends, and Darth Vadar fans browse the vintage comic books and fantasy art. In between, there are enough toys and games to entertain the crew of *Star Trek's Spaceship Enterprise* during a trip to Saturn. There is seemingly at least one copy of every science-fiction title ever written.

SCIENCE FICTION SHOP
163 Bleecker St   212 473-3010
Mon-Fri: 11:30–6:45; Sat: 11–6: Sun: 12–6

While there are other sci-fi stores, this is the only one devoted totally to science-fiction literature. Their stock of books and magazines in the field includes rare and want-listed literature. This is a special place for people interested in a special subject.

Theater

ACTOR'S HERITAGE
262 W 44th St (bet Eighth Ave and Broadway)
212 944-7490, 800 446-6905
Mon-Sat: 9:30 a.m.–11:30 p.m.; Sun: 11–7

Actor's Heritage has an enormous stock of books, T-shirts, cards, recordings, scripts, and vocal selections relating to the theater at prices less than the theaters themselves charge. They claim to surpass every other store in the city in those areas. It certainly is worth browsing. Actor's Heritage also deserves a nod for being part of the effort to spruce up the Times Square area with interesting, legitimate businesses.

APPLAUSE THEATER & CINEMA BOOKS
212 W 71st St (at Broadway)   212 496-7511
Mon-Sat: 10–8; Sun: 12–6

Quite simply, this store offers the best selection of theater and cinema books in the world. There is great interest these days in theater literature, and these folks are on the cutting edge. They specialize in British plays and claim to have the scripts for all British productions.

Special Hint:

Be sure to pick up a copy of *Applause: New York's Guide to the Performing Arts*. It tells you all you need to know about the theater, dance, music, opera, performance-art festivals, jazz, cabaret, and children's activities. It provides ticket and discount information, seating plans, and bus and subway directions. Invaluable!

DRAMA BOOK SHOP
723 Seventh Ave, 2nd floor (bet 48th and 49th St)
212 944-0595
Mon, Tues, Thurs, Fri: 9:30–7; Wed: 9:30–8; Sat: 10:30–5:30; Sun: 12–5

This shop probably has the largest selection of drama books assembled outside of the Library of Performing Arts in Lincoln Center. Nearly everything in the shop relates to the written word. There are works on theater (both American and foreign), performers, scenery, props, makeup, lighting, staging, puppetry, magic, and all aspects of music and dance. A scholarly shop, they provide a catalog for each area of entertainment. The Drama Shop is best known for having the most complete selection of scores, accent tapes, film and published screenplays, librettos, arrangements, scripts, and plays in the world. While it is not always the least expensive, it is the largest and one of the oldest (established in 1923) theater-oriented bookstores in the country.

RICHARD STODDARD-PERFORIMING ARTS BOOKS

18 E 16th St, Room 305 (bet Fifth Ave and Union Sq)
212 645-9576
Mon, Tues, Thurs-Sat: 11–6

Richard Stoddard runs a one-man operation dedicated to rare, out-of-print, and used books, and to memorabilia relating to the performing arts. Equipped with a Ph.D. from Yale in theater history and more than 15 years of experience as a dealer and appraiser of performing arts materials, Stoddard is determined to offer a broad range of items. So while there is an extensive collection of rare books, playbills, souvenir programs, original scenic and costume designs, and back issues of performing-arts magazines, Stoddard also stocks a case of paperback plays that are within the financial reach of the most impoverished actor. There is a similar table of bargain books. Stoddard's pride is his collection of scenic and costume designs. The sole agent for the estate of the late Jo Mielziner, the Broadway designer, Stoddard is also in possession of the drawings of a half-dozen other set designers. In fact, this is the only shop in the country that regularly sells such designs.

THEATREBOOKS

1600 Broadway, Room 1009 (bet 48th and 49th St)
212 757-2834
Mon-Thurs: 10:30–5; Fri: 10:30–1:30

Theatrebooks is just another example of the growing demand for theater literature. One of the only stores in the city with a selection of out-of-print and used books on the performing arts, it is also the only store with a search service for books not in stock. But the staff is proudest of being, in their own words, "the most trivia-laden staff of any theater bookstore in town." They really love the theater here! Two-fer theater tickets are available at the counter, and the staff couldn't be more helpful in discussing the current status of the Broadway theater. With their location and stock, the folks at Theatrebooks have a keen eye on it all.

Travel

COMPLETE TRAVELLER BOOKSTORE

199 Madison Ave (at 35th St)   212 685-9007
Mon-Fri: 9–7; Sat: 10–6; Sun: 12–5

Do you want to read all about an African safari? How about the Seychelles? How does one get around in China? Now in expanded quarters, the Complete Traveller specializes in travel guides and literature, tapes, language materials, books, maps, and other travel-related accessories. They also have a fine collection of rare travel books. The store is intimate, and they encourage browsing. You can obtain their excellent catalog—which lists many travel series, travel books, maps, and accessories—in the store or by mail for only two dollars.

TRAVELER'S BOOKSTORE
22 W 52nd St (75 Rockefeller Plaza, bet Fifth and Sixth Ave, lobby of Time-Warner Bldg)   212 664-0995, 800 755-8728
Mon-Fri: 9–6; Sat: 11–5

This is the store for travelers who read, and readers who travel. Diana Wells has collected an outstanding assortment of travel guides, maps, accessories, and international fiction and nonfiction books. They publish catalogs in the spring and fall.

Butterflies

MARIPOSA
South Street Seaport, Pier 17   212 233-3221
Daily: 10–9

At Mariposa, the Butterfly Gallery, butterflies are regarded as art. Designer Marshall Hill is probably the most famous in the world at this medium. Butterflies are unique, and Mariposa (the Spanish word for butterfly) displays them separately, in panels, and as parts of groups. There are even butterfly farms, which breed and raise butterflies. They live their full one-month life span under ideal conditions for creating this art. I admit that sounds a little coldhearted, but it would be impossible to appreciate so many beautiful specimens during their extremely fleeting lifetimes. A free catalog is available upon request.

Buttons

GORDON BUTTON COMPANY
222 W 38th St (near Seventh Ave)   212 921-1684
Mon-Fri: 9–5

Peter Gordon's extensive collection of old, unusual, and antique buttons is fascinating, but I would mainly come to Gordon for its new buttons. The enormous stock is used by all of the neighboring garment manufacturers. Gordon's quality, selection, and variety are that good! Belt buckles, components, chains, and brass rings are also sold here at excellent discounts. *Courtesy* is the byword here. Most garment-center manufacturers cannot be bothered with small retail customers, and their attention varies in direct proportion to the size of your order. But at Gordon, which also accepts mail orders, the size of the order is irrelevant.

TENDER BUTTONS
143 E 62nd St   212 758-7004
Mon-Fri: 11–6; Sat: 11–5:30; closed Sat in July, Aug

Owners Diana Epstein and Millicent Safro have assembled a retail button store that is complete in variety as well as size. One antique wooden display cabinet shows off Tender Buttons' selection of natural, original buttons, many imported or made exclusively for them. Here are buttons of pearl, wood, horn, Navajo silver, leather, ceramics, bone, ivory, pewter, and precious stones—many of them antique. Today buttons are as valuable as artwork; a French enamel button can cost almost as much as a painting! Many unique pieces can be made by Tender Buttons into special cuff links—real conversation pieces for the lucky owner. They also have a fine collection of antique and period cuff links and men's stud sets. As a cuff-link buff, I have purchased some of my best pieces from this shop.

Candles

CANDLE SHOP
118 Christopher St (bet Bleecker and Hudson St)
212 989-0148
Mon-Thurs: 12–8; Fri, Sat: 12–9; Sun: 1–7

Thomas Alva Edison's inventions haven't made a flicker of an imprint on the folks at the Candle Shop. Ivan Smith has assembled a collection of beeswax, paraffin, and stearin candles in an assortment of sizes and colors for every need. It's positively illuminating to learn that candles are available in so many configurations! The shop also carries candle holders and incense.

Canvas

MATERA CANVAS PRODUCTS
5 Lispenard St (one block south of Canal St off W Broadway)
212 966-9783
Mon-Fri: 10:30–5:30; closed Christmas week

John Matera is an expert with canvas. His store covers the canvas scene, from the raw product to elaborate finished items. Since he manufactures as well as sells, he has a firm hand on the quality of everything the shop handles. There are custom-made boat covers, navy tops, automobile covers, artists' canvases, tarpaulins, and pool covers. Matera also turns out custom-made products for items that require canvas and nylon materials. If you need canvas, particularly large pieces, make Matera your first choice.

China, Glassware

Madison Avenue has become a showplace for the very best, not only in clothing but also in fine china and glassware. The following stores are almost like museums, but goods are for sale—for those with very deep pockets, that is.

Daum (694 Madison Ave, at 62nd St)
Lalique (680 Madison Ave, at 61st St)
Puiforcat (811 Madison Ave, at 68th St)
Villeroy & Boch (972 Madison Ave, at 76th St)

EASTSIDE GIFTS & DINNERWARE
351 Grand St (bet Essex and Ludlow St)   212 982-7200
Sun-Thurs: 10–6; Fri: 10–2

If you have been drooling over beautiful china in the department stores but hesitated because of price, head down to the Lower East Side to Eastside Gifts. Here you will find Mikasa, Fitz and Floyd, Royal Doulton, Wedgwood, Haviland, Hutchenreuther, Lalique, and many others at great savings. In addition to dinnerware and crystal, they also carry a wide selection of stemware and flatware. Come here to replace those broken pieces of your best set!

FISHS EDDY
889 Broadway (at 19th St)   212 420-9020
Mon-Sat: 10–8; Sun: 11–7

551 Hudson St   212 627-3956
Mon-Sat: 11–8; Sun: Noon–7

Besides being a treasure trove for bargain hunters, Fishs Eddy is a fun place to browse for some of the most unusual china and glassware items available anywhere. Everything here is made in America, and the stock changes on a regular basis. For young people setting up a new residence, or for a business looking for unique pieces, try here first.

GREATER NEW YORK TRADING
81 Canal St (bet Eldridge and Allen St)
212 226-2808, 212 226-2809, 212 226-8850, 800 336-4012
Mon-Thurs: 10–6; Fri: 10–3; Sun: 9:30–6

The big attraction here is a good selection of brand-name china, silver, crystal, and stainless that is rarely discounted at other stores. This business has been in the same family for nearly 70 years, and sometimes the place looks like it hasn't been cleaned up since opening day! If Royal Doulton, Lenox, Minton, Baccarat, Waterford, Lalique, or Noritake is on your shopping list, head down this way. Personnel are unusually friendly for this part of town. Prices are quoted over the phone or by mail.

LANAC SALES
73 Canal St (at Allen St)   212 925-6422
Mon-Thurs: 9–6; Fri: 9–2; Sun: 10–5

Lanac is a great source for chinaware, cut glass, silverware, and gifts at discount prices. They have a reputation for excellent discounts on everything in stock, and that stock includes some of the finest domestic and imported tableware and crystal in the city. *Lanac,* incidentally, is *Canal* spelled backward!

ROBIN IMPORTERS
510 Madison Ave (bet 52nd and 53rd St)   212 752-5605
Mon-Fri: 9:30–5:30; Sat: 10–5; closed Sat in July, Aug

If you don't want to travel way downtown to take advantage of discount bargains in silverware, crystal, china, cutlery, dinner cloths, and giftware, this is a good place to shop. Prices are not as low as the Lower East Side stores, but the selection and quality are very adequate. They will guarantee their lowest prices for 30 days after purchase or refund the difference. Be sure to ask how long it will take for delivery of your purchase, as some suppliers are notorious for lengthy waiting periods.

Clothing and Accessories

Antique

ANTIQUE BOUTIQUE
712–714 Broadway (at Washington Pl)
227 E 59th St (bet Second and Third Ave)
212 460-8830
Mon-Thurs: 11–10; Fri, Sat: 11–12 midnight; Sun: 12–8

Despite the name, clothing at Antique Boutique is more vintage than antique. Translated, this is the place to find recently recycled clothing, as opposed to a Victorian wedding gown. Prices reflect the fact that these clothes are not one-of-a-kind antiques. The selection is excellent; they carry everything from argyle socks to suede jackets and incredible sweaters in alpaca, mohair, and moth-free wools. Rack after rack of clothing is designed to make their customers legends in any time.

HARRIET LOVE
126 Prince St   212 966-2280
Mon-Sat: 12–7; Sun: 12–6; closed Mon in Jan, Feb

Harriet Love is right on the front line in the field of vintage apparel and accessories. Her shop overflows with beautiful alligator purses, jackets, and jewelry from Victorian days to the 1950s. Harriet also buys from vendors who interpret vintage pieces to create new treasures that have an old feeling. Harriet takes especially good care of gentlemen who want to purchase vintage jewelry for the ladies in their lives.

JEAN HOFFMAN
236 E 80th St (at Jana Starr Antiques)   212 535-6930
Mon-Sat: 12–6 or by appointment

In a tiny space, Jean Hoffman offers one of the best selections of quality vintage items in the city. She has laces and trims, linens, jewelry, and all kinds of old clothing. For the bride-to-be who wants something special, the stock of vintage wedding gowns is without equal in the country.

REMINISCENCE
74 Fifth Ave (nr 13th St)   212 243-2292
Mon-Sat: 11–8; Sun: 12–7

It's fun to go back to the 1950s and 1960s at this "cool" emporium, which Stewart Richer created on lower Fifth Avenue. Although he is

SIZE COMPARISON CHART FOR CLOTHES

Children's clothing

						3	4	5	6	6x
American						3	4	5	6	6x
Continental						98	104	110	116	122
British						18	20	22	24	26

Children's shoes

American		8	9	10	11	12	13	1	2	3
Continental		24	25	27	28	29	30	32	33	34
British		7	8	9	10	11	12	13	1	2

Ladies' dresses, coats and skirts

American	3	5	7	9	11	12	13	14	15	16	18
Continental	36	38	38	40	40	42	42	44	44	46	48
British	8	10	11	12	13	14	15	16	17	18	20

Ladies' blouses and sweaters

American				10	12	14	16	18	20
Continental				38	40	42	44	46	48
British				32	34	36	38	40	42

Ladies' stockings

American			8	8½	9	9½	10	10½
Continental			1	2	3	4	5	6
British			8	8½	9	9½	10	10½

Ladies' shoes

American			5	6	7	8	9	10
Continental			36	37	38	39	40	41
British			3½	4½	5½	6½	7½	8½

Men's suits

American		34	36	38	40	42	44	46	48
Continental		44	46	48	50	52	54	56	58
British		34	36	38	40	42	44	46	48

Men's shirts

American		14	15	15½	16	16½	17	17½	18
Continental		37	38	39	41	42	43	44	45
British		14	15	15½	16	16½	17	17½	18

Men's shoes

American		7	8	9	10	11	12	13
Continental		39½	41	42	43	44½	46	47
British		6	7	8	9	10	11	12

a child of this era, most of Richer's customers are between the ages of 13 and 30. The finds here are unusual and wearable, with large selections of colorful vintage clothing and attractive displays of jewelry, hats, shoes, and all kinds of accessories. Richer's goods, although vintage in style, are mostly new, and he has become a manufacturer who sells to outlets all over the world. Because of his large distribution, Richer is able to produce huge quantities and sell at low prices.

SCREAMING MIMI'S
22 E 4th St (bet Lafayette St and Bowery)   212 677-6464
Mon-Fri: 11–8; Sat: 12–8; Sun: 1–7

Owners Biff Chandler and Laura Wills, two fashion stylists, have located their landmark-upper West Side shop in NoHo (that is, north of Houston!). Their selections feature styles from the 1950s, 1960s, and 1970s, as well as current trends. A vintage housewares department, a shoe department, Katy K Western Boutique, and the store's own line of sportswear round out a fun and exciting place to shop. Recently added is a children's department, featuring selections from innovative downtown designers. Choices range from party dresses to see-through vinyl motorcycle jackets.

TRASH AND VAUDEVILLE
4 St. Mark's Pl (bet Second and Third Ave)   212 982-3590
Mon-Thurs: 12–8; Fri: 11:30–8; Sat: 11:30–9; Sun: 1–7:30

This place is hard to describe, since the stock changes constantly and seems to have no boundaries. The store describes its stock as new and antique clothing, accessories, and original designs. "Antique clothing" here seems to mean rock and roll styles from the 1950s to the 1980s, including some outrageous footwear, although there are some older items. There are some real finds here, but perhaps because this is a wholesale as well as retail business, you get the feeling that someone else has already escaped with the best values. They also carry new clothing from Europe.

Bridal

I. KLEINFELD AND SON
8202 Fifth Ave	8209 Third Ave
Brooklyn, NY	Brooklyn, NY
718 833-1100	718 238-1500

Tues, Thurs: 11–9; Wed, Fri: 11–6; Sat: 10–6
(and by appointment)

The bridal business has changed a great deal. Today there are very limited collections at some specialty stores (like Bergdorf and Saks), but there is only one true bridal complex. I use the word *complex* because two separate buildings are involved. The half-century-old operation is called I. Kleinfeld and Son. The bridal gown collection (800 to 1,000 models in stock at all times) is located at 8202 Fifth Avenue in Brooklyn. Yes, I know, this is a book about Manhattan, but there is no store anywhere that can match Kleinfeld. The mother of the bride can find a special section called Kleinfeld's P.M., which specializes in evening wear. (Wedding guests will find this selection helpful, also.) Kleinfeld carries every major name in bridal wear, including Priscilla of Boston, Caroline Herrera , and Scassi. One-fifth of the collection is of international origin. A separate store for bridesmaids' gowns is located several blocks away at 8209 Third Avenue. The store prefers to operate by appointment; they can handle over a hundred a day with their specialized personnel. This is *the* place to come when wedding bells will soon be ringing.

Children's — General

BEN'S FOR KIDS
1380 Third Ave (bet 78th and 79th St)   212 794-2330
Mon-Wed, Fri: 10–5; Thurs: 10–8; Sat: 11–5

Ben's is really a kids' department store! For youngsters up to age three you can find cribs, strollers, car seats, and playpens, as well as layettes, clothing, toys, nursing accessories, and more. This is one of New York's best juvenile outlets.

M. KREINEN SALES
301 Grand St (at Allen St)   212 925-0239
Sun-Thurs: 9–5; Fri: 9–4

No sense in spending extra dollars to keep your kids in the most fashionable clothes. This Lower East Side establishment carries only brand-name goods, girls' sizes from infant to 14, and boys' sizes from infant to 20. Discounts average about 25%, and the quality as good as those at higher-priced specialty and department stores.

PETIT BATEAU
930 Madison Ave (at 74th St)   212 288-1444
Mon-Sat: 10–6

From France comes some of the most charming outfits for kids. Petit Bateau specializes in French-designed clothing for infants, children, and teens. Most of the designs are exclusive, and the quality is absolutely top-notch.

PUSHBOTTOM FOR KIDS
252 E 62nd St (bet Second and Third Ave)   212 888-3336
46 E 59th St   212 759-6200
Mon-Sat: 11–7

With a name and reputation like Pushbottom's, the goods have to be special. And indeed they are. If your kid is something special (and whose isn't?), get the young ones outfitted here. Pushbottom specializes in sportswear, and they can outfit your child from newborn to size 7. All designs are originals.

RICE AND BRESKIN
323 Grand St (at Orchard St)   212 925-5515
Sun-Fri: 9–5

Rice and Breskin is probably the Lower East Side's top-quality shop for children's clothing. Wrapped in plastic, the merchandise includes good brand names at a 20% discount or more. They specialize in infant clothing and baby gifts. Despite its Lower East Side location, the sales help is charming, even motherly.

WICKER GARDEN
1318 Madison Ave (at 93rd St)   212 410-7000
Mon-Sat: 10–5:30; closed Sat in July and first two weeks of Aug

Want to meet an archetypal New Yorker? Pamela Scurry of Wicker Garden fits that category. Besides having two children and a husband who is CEO of a real-estate company, she operates a successful business. The Wicker Garden was established as a prime source for wicker furniture and antique hand-painted adult furniture, plus accessories displayed in a Victorian garden setting. When Pam needed furniture for her children, she created the Wicker Garden's Baby (1327 Madison Ave). When her children needed clothing to match their antique bedroom suites, she set up the Wicker Garden's Children (1327 Madison Ave) to outfit them and other lucky kids. The infant's furnishings department has museum-quality wicker furniture and accessories, including antique quilts, linens, and lace infant furnishings, along with a line of hand-painted furniture.

Children's — Used

ONCE UPON A TIME
171 E 92nd St (bet Lexington and Third Ave)
212 831-7619
Mon-Sat: 10–6

This children's resale shop on the Upper East Side has clothing from infants to sizes 10–14 for boys and girls. Some of the items have never been worn, and all are in almost-new condition and attractively priced. At the end of each season, the previous season's clothing goes for a fraction of what it would sell for in department stores. In addition, the seasons are realistically timed, meaning you can buy a bathing suit in July.

SECOND ACT CHILDREN'S WEAR
1046 Madison Ave (bet 79th and 80th St)   212 988-2440
Tues-Sat: 9–5

The best buys here are the clothes that were bought and used for only one or two occasions, such as communion dresses, Easter outfits, and flower-girl gowns. Some of the other items don't seem worth the price tag, even at one-third of the original cost, but everything is kept in A-1 condition. All clothing is washed and ironed or cleaned before it is put up for sale, and it is indeed in "like new" condition. Clothing is consigned to separate rooms according to sex, and within these rooms everything is sized in order. Sizes run from girls' infant to 14 and boys' infant to 20. In addition to clothing, there are ice skates, riding apparel, ski boots, books, and toys.

Costumes

ABRACADABRA
10 Christopher St   212 627-5745
Mon-Sat: 11–7

Abracadabra! There is nothing but fun here. You can transform yourself into almost anything at this unique emporium. They rent and sell costumes, have every kind of costume accessory, provide theatrical makeup, and even have all the props for magic tricks. Oh yes, if you are a gagster, the place is a blast!

Dance Wear

CAPEZIO'S
locations all over Manhattan

The various Capezio stores are the definitive outlets for dance parapher-nalia, including athletic wear and fashion shoes. The shop at 1650 Broad-way (at 51st St; 212 245-2130) is the largest dance-theater retail store in the world, with a special section for men in addition to departments for ballet companies and theatrical shoes. Capezio East (136 E 61st St, at Lexington Ave; 212 758-8833) reflects the east side neighborhood and includes a well-stocked children's area. The most interesting shop is the one in the Village (17 MacDougal St; 212 477-5634), which also has a men's department. There is also a Capezio's at Steps (2121 Broad-way, at 74th St; 212 799-7774) and a store called Capezio at Alvin Ailey (211 W 61st St, 3rd floor; 212 767-0940). Hours vary, but all stores are open on Saturday. Capezio East and Capezio at Steps are both open on Sunday afternoons.

FREED OF LONDON
922 Seventh Ave (at 58th St)   212 489-1055, 800 835-1701
Mon-Sat: 10–6:45 (phone orders: 10–4)

The venerable English establishment Freed of London has landed in New York, bringing with it a tradition of supplying the best and finest in dance supplies. There is virtually no piece of dance gear that Freed does not carry or cannot order. The store keeps leg warmers, leotards, ballet shoes, skirts, and tutus in stock. A list of the shop's clientele reads like a who's who of stars that have danced in London. The store carries, as a matter of course, the complete line of regulation wear for the Royal Academy of Dancing. For those who can't stop in, a measuring chart and mail-order catalog are available. For dancers, this store is a must.

Furs

FURS BY DIMITRIOS
130 W 30th St (bet Sixth and Seventh Ave)   212 695-8469
Mon-Fri: 9–6; Sat: 10–4; Sun: 10–4

This store is the best source for men's fur coats at wholesale prices. The racks are shaggy with furs of all descriptions and sizes for both genders. Prices are wholesale but go up slightly if the garment has to be specially ordered. This shouldn't be necessary, though, since the off-the-rack selection is the most extensive and of the best quality in the city.

G. MICHAEL HENNESSY FURS
333 Seventh Ave, 5th floor (bet 28th and 29th St)
212 695-7991
Mon-Fri: 9:30–5; Sat: by appointment

Furs are one item you want to be very sure of when you buy. By this, I mean you want to be sure of the people you are buying from. They must also be knowledgeable and have the proper stock, and they must be reliable and honest. This firm strongly fits the mold. Michael Hennessy started as an international fur trader, ran a salon in Beverly Hills, and later became fur director of Bonwit Teller and president of Maximilian Furs. His talented and charming wife Rubye is a former editor of *Seventeen* magazine and the *Philadelphia Inquirer.* These folks manufacture high-quality designer furs for women that are sold to stores around the world; these same items are also available direct to the public at great values. Best prices are for in-stock furs, particularly mink, the house specialty. Wonderful buys are available for ladies who want a mink coat made to order. There are two new specialties: large-size furs and cashmere-with-fur coats, excellent for use from fall through spring. Hundreds of my readers have been well-taken care of by Rubye and Michael, and every one has been a satisfied customer.

GUS GOODMAN
333 Seventh Ave, 10th floor (bet 28th and 29th St)
212 244-7422
Mon-Fri: 10–6; Sat: 10–2 (Sat by appt in summer)

Since 1918 the Goodmans have been creating fine fur styles. Now father (Gus) and two sons (David and Mark) are carrying on in the family tradition, offering a quality collection of fur-lined and reversible fur coats and jackets for both men and women. An unusually complete selection of outerwear fabrics is available: silk, poplin, microfiber, ultrasuede, leather, and cashmere. If you have a musty old fur coat in the closet that you never wear any more, these folks will bring it back to life with a trendy design. Goodman has a full-time designer on staff and specializes in custom designs.

HARRY KIRSHNER AND SON
307 Seventh Ave (bet 27th and 28th St)   212 243-4847
Mon-Fri: 9–6; Sat: 10–5

Kirshner should be one of your first stops for any kind of fur product, from throw pillows to full-length mink coats. They re-line, clean, alter, and store any fur at rock-bottom prices. They are neither pushy nor snobbish. Harry Kirshner offers tours of the factory, and if nothing available appeals to the customer, a staff member will try to draw a coat to specifications. Often, however, the factory offers a collection of second-hand furs that have been restored to perfect and fashionable condition. Many customers come in for a new fur and walk out with a slightly worn one for a fraction of what they were prepared to spend.

H.B.A. FUR
150 W 30th St, 3rd floor   212 564-1080
Mon-Fri: 8:30–5; Sat (Oct-Jan): 9–1

H.B.A. was one of the first fur-industry garment lofts to open to the public. As a result, they are more experienced and better attuned to customer requests than some of their neighbors. The stock includes all kinds of furs but tends to avoid trends and stick to more classic styles. As a result, this year's fads, while available, are not singled out as the *only* thing to wear. There's a good selection of timeless furs, which can be taken off the racks or made to order at wholesale prices.

RITZ THRIFT SHOP
107 W 57th St   212 265-4559
Mon-Sat: 9–6

Down the block and across the street from Carnegie Hall, the Ritz Thrift Shop is as much a New York institution as its neighbor, and its clientele is just as loyal. The Ritz Thrift Shop seems to have been in business forever, buying and selling used furs to smart shoppers. All those years of experience have made the management as knowledgeable and fashion-conscious as the finest retail operations. The Ritz buys used furs outright. Half of the stock is purchased from individual customers, and the rest comes from furriers who took them as trade-ins. Because they are not usually a consignment operation, and perhaps because they offer free repairs and storage for as long as a client owns a coat, they are very picky about what they will buy. So if your coat is passe, damaged, or not very good to begin with, the Ritz won't be interested—unless your coat is so outdated it's "in." (Jackets from the 1940s and longhaired and silver-fox furs fall in this category; the Ritz can't get enough of them!)

Customers are offered an incredible array of modern, stylish furs at prices roughly one-third of the original cost. A good portion of their business is with people who trade in their furs every two years or so. The Ritz also sells 1980s men's furs.

Hosiery

FOGAL
680 Madison Ave (bet 61st and 62nd St)   212 759-9782

510 Madison Ave (at 53rd St)   212 355-3254
Mon-Sat: 10–6

Before Fogal came to New York from Switzerland, the thought of a Madison Avenue boutique devoted to hosiery was, well, foreign. But since opening in 1982, it's hard to imagine Manhattan without it. If it's new, fashionable, and different leg wear you're after, Fogal has it. Plain hosiery comes in over a hundred hues, at last count; the designs and patterns make the number of choices almost incalculable. You might say that Fogal's has a leg up on the competition, but there have never even been any serious contenders.

LOUIS CHOCK
74 Orchard St   212 473-1929
Sun-Thurs: 9–5; Fri: 9–1

It's hard to find a classification for this store. It seems to stock a little of everything, but perhaps the old-fashioned term "dry goods" sums up the stock sold here. Louis Chock sells dry goods for the home, school, and the entire family from some of the nation's best: Berkshire, Burlington, Carter, Calvin Klein, Hanes, Duofold, and Munsingwear. They appear to specialize in hosiery and underwear. Children's nightwear is available in a large choice of colors and sizes, and there is something in the hosiery section for every member of the family. Furthermore, everything in the store is sold at a discount that begins at 25%. There is an even larger discount on items bought in quantity. Louis Chock also has a mail-order department, offering a 25% to 30% discount on everything in stock. A catalog can be obtained for $1.

M. STEUER HOSIERY COMPANY
31 W 32nd St (nr Fifth Ave)   212 563-0052
Mon-Fri: 7:45–5:20

By walking one block from Herald Square, hosiery buyers can save a bundle. M. Steuer is a wholesale operation that treats each retail customer as a wholesaler, no matter how small the order. They even speak a half-dozen languages—the better to welcome visitors to New York. They stock a huge inventory of name-brand hosiery, socks, pantyhose, and dance wear, and they will fill unusual requests with aplomb.

Jeans

CANAL JEANS

504 Broadway (off Spring St)   212 226-3663, 212 226-1130
Sun-Thurs: 11–7; Fri, Sat: 10–8

From the moment you walk past the bins full of sweaters, you know Canal Jeans is not an ordinary store. Canal Jeans buys, sells, and wholesales the latest SoHo look and has made itself a popular place. The look is certainly casual. Even their best new clothing stretches the meaning of sportswear, but if it's motorcycle jackets, brightly colored pants, tops, and outfits you want, this is the place to shop. A large percentage of customers are Europeans and Japanese who stock up on as many pairs of jeans as they can hoard in their suitcases and backpacks. They can sell them back home and make enough profit to pay for their trip. Other clothing items include grunge outfits, bins of junk clothes (don't bother—they're just that), and close-outs.

Leather

BARBARA SHAUM

63 E 4th St   212 254-4250
Wed-Fri: 1–8; Sat: 1–6

Barbara Shaum does magical things with leather. She's a wonder with sandals, bags, sterling-silver buckles, belts (with handmade brass, nickel-silver, inlaid wood, and copper buckles), jewelry, attaché cases, and briefcases. Everything is designed in the shop, and Barbara Shaum meticulously crafts each item using only the finest materials.

NORTH BEACH LEATHER

772 Madison Ave (at 66th St)   212 772-0707
Mon-Fri: 10–6; Sat: 10–6; Sun: 12–5

If leather wear connotes "home on the range" or some biker bar on the Village waterfront, then you are obviously unaware that leather is the flip side of fur and can be just as elegant. With stores in Houston, Los Angeles, and San Francisco, North Beach Leather's locations are proof of that, and the fashions are further evidence. If you need a leather ensemble for an outing in the Mercedes, then North Beach is the place to look. The emphasis is on jackets, coats, and outerwear, but there are also suits and even skirts and dresses for women. Their leather jackets for men are just the thing to round out an outfit. But they aren't cheap.

Men's and Women's — General

A/X ARMANI EXCHANGE

568 Broadway (at Prince St)   212 431-6000
Mon-Fri: 11–7; Sat, Sun: 11–6

When does a brand name become overexposed? Does seeing a certain designer's merchandise everyplace you turn make the items a bit less attractive? Armani is everywhere; new boutiques have opened up at Bloomingdale's and Saks, and now there is a junior version just across the street from Dean and Deluca. At A/X you will find lower-priced, casual Armani items like jeans and sport shirts at reasonable prices in an easy-to-shop atmosphere. The place really looks like a military PX, but Uncle Sam's items just don't have the same class as Giorgio's!

BARNEY'S

106 Seventh Ave (at 17th St)   212 929-9000
Mon-Thurs: 10–9; Fri: 10–8; Sat: 10–7; Sun: 12–6

660 Madison Ave (bet 60th and 61st St)   212 826-8900

World Financial Center (225 Liberty St)   212 945-1600
Mon, Tues, Wed, Fri: 10–7; Thurs: 10–9; Sat: 10–6; Sun: 12–6

At one time Barney's was *the* place for clothing and accessories for boys and men. Barney Pressman was a great merchant, offering a huge selection of quality goods at his emporium; the third generation is doing the same, and more! But now there's a big difference: they have opened a women's section, and it has become an important part of their operation, especially in sportswear. Men will find huge selections of the best brands in both domestic and imported clothing. But be forewarned: this is a difficult store to shop in. Merchandise is arranged for the store's convenience, not the customer's. The main store at 17th Street has just about anything you want; the new store on Madison Avenue does not stock all the fancy labels, due to conflicts with nearby outlets. The World Financial Center outlet is really a poor country cousin when it comes to assortments. Salespeople are pushy or disinterested, prices (except for sales) are in the high range, paperwork is prehistoric, but tailoring is excellent, and you know you are getting the best goods available.

CASHMERE-CASHMERE

840 Madison Ave (bet 69th and 70th St)   212 988-5252

595 Madison Ave   212 935-2522
Mon-Fri: 10–6; Sat: 12–6

Thanks in part to the growth of Silk Surplus, silk is no longer a luxury fabric in this city. Not so cashmere! At this shop, every possible type of clothing from all over the world is available. The weights vary, so that it is possible to wear cashmere year round. The styles vary as well, reflecting different lifestyles. There's clothing for men and women, as well as cashmere accessories for the home. A visit here will make cashmere a necessity in one's life!

CHARIVARI

Locations and phones noted within review
All stores open daily, late Thurs nights, and Sun until 6

The Upper West Side was a fashion desert until Selma Weiser arrived on the scene with her first Charivari. With a smart merchant's sense of location and fashion, Selma and her family have guided the growth of this organization into a six-store chain. Mother Selma still has a major hand in most of the operation, while daughter Barbara and son Jon do most of the buying. Charivari for women (2315 Broadway, bet 83rd and 84th St; 212 873-1424) carries women's clothes. The sports store (201 W 79th St, at Amsterdam Ave; 212 799-8650) is brimming with fun play clothes at reasonable prices. The Workshop (441 Columbus Ave, at 81st St; 212 496-8700) features avant-garde Japanese-designed merchandise for both men and women. Charivari 72 (257 Columbus Ave, at 72nd St; 212 787-7272). Charivari 57 (18 W 57th St; 212 333-4040) and Charivari Madison (1001 Madison Ave; 212 650-0078), feature high-fashion designer clothing for both men and women. The 72nd Street store is more intimate; the 57th Street store is cold and uninviting. Running an operation as spread out as this one is difficult at best. The Weisers, who possess a unique flair for the dramatic in merchandise presentation, might well concentrate on passing on that same expertise to their salespeople, some of whom have a severe attitude problem.

COCKPIT
595 Broadway (bet Houston and Prince St)   212 925-5455
Mon-Sat: 11–7; Sun: 12:30–6

This is a fascinating store for anyone interested in flying. A fabulous collection of flight jackets, Flying Tiger shirts, China-Burma baggies, athletic jerseys, T-shirts, coveralls, trench coats, European jeans, flight boots, sweaters, insignias, books, watches, bags, flight suits, and dozens of gift items are displayed to create an attractive, aviational atmosphere. There is also a good selection of Western wear.

DAFFY'S
111 Fifth Ave (at 18th St)   212 529-4477
Mon-Sat: 10–9; Sun: 11–6

335 Madison Ave (at 44th St)   212 557-4422
Mon-Fri: 10–9; Sat: 10–6; Sun: 11–5

Daffy's describes itself as a bargain clothing outlet for millionaires. Since a lot of folks got to be millionaires by saving money, perhaps they have something going for them. But millionaire or not, you can find great bargains here in better clothing for men, women, and children. Fine leather items are a specialty. This is not your usual "off-price" store; they have done things with a bit of flair.

EMPORIO ARMANI
110 Fifth Ave (at 16th St)   212 727-3240
Mon-Wed, Fri, Sat: 11–7; Thurs: 11–7:30; Sun: 1–6

In the lower canyons of Fifth Avenue, where lofts feature off-priced men's clothing, you can now walk into one of the classiest designer showrooms in the city. Emporio Armani clothes for both men and women are shown with style and taste, befitting the hefty price tags. The sportswear, dress-up wear, accessories, and jeans all bear the distinct Armani look. It well could be this boutique is the forerunner of a move from pricey Madison Avenue for some of the better-known names in the ready-to-wear business. Don't miss this one, especially if you're "just looking!"

MATSUDA
461 Park Ave (at 57th St)   212 935-6969
Mon-Fri: 11–7; Sat: 11–6
156 Fifth Ave   212 645-5151
Mon-Fri: 11–7; Sat: 11–6; Sun: 12–5

Mitsuhiro Matsuda is one of Japan's most successful fashion designers. He designs lines of business, casual, and active sportswear for men and women. There is also a line of apparel and accessory basics, including bath items, nightwear, hats, glasses, jewelry, ties, gloves, belts, socks, and shoes. Madonna and Cher are customers, so you know the place is at the forefront of fashion.

NICOLE MILLER
780 Madison Ave (at E 67th St)   212 288-9779
Mon-Fri: 11–7; Sat: 10–6

Nicole Miller was just another fashion designer until she hit upon theme ties, which have made her a household word for both men's and women's fashions. For ladies she shows classic sports and evening wear and accessories, mainly in unique prints. For men there are the famous ties, socks, plus shirts and jackets—all very distinctive. Prices are very distinctive (read: expensive), too. Knockoffs are everywhere.

OTTO PERL
HOUSE OF MAURIZIO
18 E 53rd St, 5th floor   212 759-3230
By appointment only

Otto and Susanne Perl cater to women who like the functional and fashionable tailored look of suits. Although they can copy almost any kind of garment, the Perls are known for their coats, two- to four-piece suits, and mix-and-match combinations. Unusually, this look is favored by busy executives, artists, or journalists who have to look well-dressed but don't have hours to spend dressing. Perl creates blazers (or suits) in a range of 2,000 fabrics, and those in silk, linen, cotton, and solid virgin wool are sensational. In addition to women's garments, the Perls can design and create coats and suits for men in the same broad range of fabrics. They promise fast service, expert tailoring, and moderate prices on everything they do, but no alterations. Custom shirts and ties are a recent addition.

POLO-RALPH LAUREN

867 Madison Ave (at 72nd St)   212 606-2100
Mon-Sat: 10–6; Thurs: 10–8

Ralph Lauren has captured the mood of the times, and I admit to being a Ralph Lauren fan. He has probably done as much as anyone in this period to bring a classic look to American fashion and furnishings. His showpiece store in Manhattan, housed in the magnificent remodeled Rhinelander mansion, is fabulous. There are four floors of merchandise for men, women, and the home, beautifully displayed and expertly accessorized. You will see a much larger selection here than in any of the specialty Polo boutiques in the stores. There are several things to be aware of, however. One is an attitude problem of the help. I'm sure that Ralph himself would not put up with the above-it-all way some of his people greet customers who don't look like they have big bucks to spend. Then again, although the clothes and furnishings are stylish and classy, one can find items of equal or better quality elsewhere at considerably lower price tags. But then, shopping elsewhere is not nearly as stylish as carrying your item out in one of those popular green bags. And that little monogrammed horse says something about your taste and lifestyle. A new sportswear store is located across the street.

Men's Formal Wear

JACK AND COMPANY FORMAL WEAR

128 E 86th St   212 722-4609, 212 722-4455
Mon-Fri: 10–7; Sat: 10–4

Jack and Company rent and sell men's ready-to-wear formal wear. They carry an excellent selection of sizes and names (After Six, Lord West), and they have a good reputation for service since 1925. In sales

---

How to tie a bow tie:

1. Start with end in left hand, extending 1½" below that in right hand.

2. Cross longer end over shorter and pass up through loop.

3. Form front loop of bow by doubling up shorter end (hanging) and placing across collar points.

4. Hold this front loop with thumb and forefinger of left hand. Drop long end down over front.

5. Place right forefinger, pointing up, on bottom half of hanging part. Pass up behind front loop.

6. Poke resulting loop through knot behind front loop. Even ends and tighten.

or rentals, Jack's can supply head-to-toe formal wear. The people here are excellent at matching outfits to customers, as well as knowing exactly what is socially required for any occasion. Same-day service is available, and the full rental price will be applied toward purchase!

ZELLER TUXEDOS
201 E 56th St (at Third Ave)   212 355-0707
Mon-Fri: 9–7:45; Sat: 10–4:45

1010 Third Ave (at 60th St)   212 688-0100
Mon-Fri: 9–7:45; Sat: 10–4:45; Sun: noon–4:45

Zeller Tuxedos is tops in sales and rentals of tuxedos, formal shirts, capes, overcoats with fur collars, and all the accessories necessary for a big night on the town. Merchandise from Canali, Belvest, Bill Kaiserman, Bally, Valentino, and Burberry is featured. Zeller even provides made-to-order service for those who require special attention.

Men's — General

CAMOUFLAGE
141 Eighth Ave (at 17th St)   212 741-9118
Mon-Fri: 12–7; Sat: 11–6; Sun: 1–5
(Sun hours in April, May, Nov, Dec only)

If you've got patriotic tastes, this may be the store for you. It is one of the few shops that eschews foreign designers, selling only American clothing. New resources are Jeffrey Banks, Pendleton, Ruff Hewn, New Republic, and Heartland, plus private-label trousers, shirts, ties, and accessories. Prices range from reasonable (their chinos may be one of the best buys in the city) to good, considering those pricey designer names. But one of Camouflage's best virtues is the ability to dress its customers with a dignified but special appearance. There's nothing at Camouflage that will blend into the wallpaper!

EISENBERG AND EISENBERG
85 Fifth Ave, 6th floor   212 627-1290
Mon-Wed, Fri: 9–6; Thurs: 9–7; Sat: 9–5:30; Sun: 10–4

The Eisenberg and Eisenberg style is a classic one that dates from 1898, the year they opened. E&E consistently offers top quality and good prices on suits, tuxedos, coats, and sportswear. They also stock outerwear, slacks, name-brand raincoats, cashmere sport jackets, and 100% silk jackets. All are sold at considerable discounts, and alterations are available. London Fog coats are featured; no label is better known for wet-weather needs.

GILCREST CLOTHES COMPANY
900 Broadway (at 20th St)   212 254-8933
Mon-Fri: 8–5; Sat: 8:30–5; Sun: 9:30–4

These days buying a suit means laying out a lot of dough, so it is a good idea to shop around. Gilcrest provides savings on quality brands like Ralph Lauren, Perry Ellis, Ungaro, Andrew Fezza, Louis Feraud, and Profilo. Their own line of clothing is available at sensible prices. The sport coat stock is worthy of inspection, and if you are in the market for a tux, the selection is enormous. There is no charge for alterations.

GORSART
9 Murray St   212 962-0024
10 E 44th St   212 557-0200
Mon-Wed, Fri: 9–6; Thurs: 9–7; Sat: 9–5:30

Gentlemen! If you are the natural-shoulder type, read on. And if you find the style and quality of Brooks Brothers or Paul Staurt appealing but the prices appalling, head to this little-known jewel. In 1921, two brothers started catering to the financial community with what was then a new twist: quality merchandise at a discount. Moe Davidson and Neil Roberts purchased the store from its founders in 1975, and they carry on the same tradition. They offer classy suits made at prices that will make you smile. These are not seconds or markdowns. In addition to suits, there is a nice selection of sportswear and furnishings, all discounted. The reason for the great prices? Simple: low overhead. You can pick up a tux for about half the department store price, and you don't pay for tailoring unless it's a complete restructuring. They have 35 in-house tailors on the job all the time. These are special stores, fellows, and you will enjoy shopping here. No high-pressure selling, no gimmicks, just value and service.

IRVING BARON CLOTHES
343 Grand St (at Orchard St)   212 475-1718
Mon-Thurs: 9:30–6; Wed: 9:30–7:30; Sat, Sun: 9–5:30;
summer: Sun-Fri: 9:30–6

Once inside, a customer at Irving Baron might think he's in a posh Fifth Avenue store. Such brand names as Groshire, Marzotto, Corneliani, Yves St. Laurent, Halston, Le Baron, Louis Roth, London Fog, Mondo, Torras, Countess Mara, Damon, and Calvin Klein are part of the stock. The staff say they can dress a man from top to bottom. (Shoes are an exception.) It is only when the bill is presented that the customer realizes that this is indeed a Lower East Side store, for the discount starts at 25%. Suits, sport jackets, pants, overcoats, raincoats, outerwear, shirts, sweaters, and ties are carried to attire men sized from 36 short to 50 long. The salespeople are excellent.

J. PRESS
7 E 44th St (bet Fifth and Madison Ave)   212 687-7642
Mon-Sat: 9–6

As one of New York's classic conservative men's stores, J. Press prides itself on its sense of timelessness. Its salespeople, customers, and attitude have changed little from the time of J. Press to that of Richard Press today. Styles are impeccable and distinguished. Blazers are blue, and shirts are button-down and straight. Even in the days when button-down collars were out, Press was such a bastion of support that it went so far as to make them available in colors other than blue.

LESH CLOTHING
115 Fifth Ave (at 19 St), 6th floor   212 255-6893
Mon-Fri: 9–6; Sat: 9–4; Sun: 10–3

Irving Lesh claims that his family business was one of the first (if not *the* first) wholesale men's clothing lofts. He takes a certain pride in the bare-piped surroundings, and the quality of the suits, sport jackets, slacks, and outerwear seems designed to prove that here the dollar goes for the merchandise rather than the décor. Lesh manufactures its own suits. The selection and quality of suits, tuxedos, and sport coats is great. Lesh has been manufacturing them since 1935, and they adhere to the fine nuances of tailoring.

LOUIS BARALL AND SON
58 Lispenard St (bet Canal St and Broadway)   212 226-6195
Mon-Fri: 9:30–6; Sat: 9:30–5; closed Sat in July, Aug

Although it has been in existence for 75 years, this store is one of the best-kept secrets in town. The only possible reason is that the savvy Wall Street types who shop here have no desire to share the market with anyone else. Styles are conservative and traditional at best. But that doesn't mean old-fashioned or even out of season; it simply bypasses the ultratrendy. If your style runs to the tried and true, try Barall. Prices *begin* at one-third off list price and go down from there. Name-brand garments come in first-quality or clearly marked irregulars, with the latter going for about 50% off list price and more.

L.S. MEN'S CLOTHING
19 W 44th St, Room 403   212 575-0933
Mon-Thurs: 9–7; Fri: 9–4 (Sun: 10–4 at 19 W 44th St)

L.S. Men's Clothing bills itself as "the Executive Discount Shop," but I would go further and call them a must for fashion-minded businessmen. For one thing, their midtown location precludes a trip downtown to Fifth Avenue in the teens which is the usual area for finding men's discount clothing. Better still, as owner Israel Zuber puts it, "There are many stores selling $200 suits at discount, but we are one of the few that discount the $475 to $975 suits *and* are located in mid-Manhattan." The main attraction, though, is the tremendous selection of executive-class styles. Within that category a man could almost outfit himself entirely at L.S. The natural and soft-shoulder designer suits are available in all sizes. A custom-order department is now available. This is one of the top spots for top names. I would make it number one on the midtown shopping itinerary.

MANO A MANO
580 Broadway (bet Houston and Prince St)   212 219-9602
Mon-Thurs: 11–7:45; Fri: 11–8:45; Sat: 11–7:45;
Sun: 11:30–6:45

There are monkeys in cages, hip salespeople, and a carnival atmosphere here, but don't let that keep you from investigating the huge selection of stylish sportswear, leather items, suits, and accessories for men. If you have seen it in one of the men's fashion magazines, you no doubt will find it here at less than uptown prices.

NAPOLEON
Trump Tower (Fifth Ave at 57th St)   212 759-1110
Mon-Sat: 10–6

Trump Plaza
1048 Third Ave (at 62nd St)   212 308-3000
Mon-Fri: 10–7; Sat: 10–6:30

Plaza Hotel Lobby
768 Fifth Ave   212 759-8000
Mon-Sat: 10–6:30

This is one of the top men's boutiques in the city—or anywhere, for that matter. The customer is emperor here, and what an empire he has! Napoleon stocks only the finest in haberdashery. The style is set by modern Italian designers. There are extensive lines by Brioni, Mila Schon, Stefano Ricci, and Ermenegildo Zegna. Its superb quality and style are matched only by an incredibly personalized service that makes each person who enters feel that he or she is someone special. Prices are in the if-you-have-to-ask-you-can't-afford-it class, but the merchandise and ambience make it all worthwhile. Napoleon really does carry clothes fit for a king and his consort.

PAN AM SPORTSWEAR AND MENSWEAR
50 Orchard St (bet Grand and Hester St)   212 925-7032
Sun-Wed: 9–6; Thurs: 9–8; Fri: 9:30–3 (winter); 9–5 (summer)

With more stores like this, the Lower East Side could become synonymous with class as well as bargains. From the shiny glass windows (as opposed to the clutter of hangers that usually denotes an entrance) to the extremely fine stock, Pan Am is distinctive enough to be on Madison Avenue, except for its prices. They are nothing short of super! Perry Ellis, Mani by Giorgio Armani, Polo by Ralph Lauren, and Andrew Fezza are but a few of the names that adorn the racks in all their glory *sans* the excessive price tag. (Prices are at least a third off that of the uptown shops.) What's more, styles are *au courant;* they often preview here first, and they're in classic good taste. Finally, the sales help is a major exception to the Lower East Side norm. They are prompt and courteous, although they may be a little too quick to pounce on any customer who walks through the door. But at these prices, that's a minor annoyance.

PARKWAY
30 Vesey St   212 962-7500
Mon-Fri: 8:30–7; Sat: 10–5

Parkway carries most major brands for men, including Pierre Cardin, Oleg Cassini, Alexander Julian, Manhattan, Botany, Chaps, Perry Ellis, Bill Blass, and Halston. Prices are excellent, reflecting an average discount of 40%. The stores are noted for their selection of outerwear, sportswear, dress shirts, and ties as well.

PAUL SMITH
108 Fifth Ave (at 16th St)   212 627-9770
Mon-Wed, Fri, Sat: 11–7; Thurs: 11–8; Sun: 12–6

Paul Smith is an English menswear designer, and his shop would be right at home on Bond Street in London. The suits, coats, slacks, and sportswear bespeak quality and exude a classic look. If the sales personnel were half as classy, this would be a top place to shop.

PAUL STUART
Madison Ave (at 45th St)   212 682-0320
Mon, Thurs: 8–7; Tues, Wed, Fri: 8–6; Sat: 9–6

This is the store for you if you are the kind of shopper who doesn't really know what you want, has trouble putting things together to make a "look," or who worries about quality. You would be hard pressed to find a better selection of fine men's and women's apparel and accessories. But there is little excitement here, either in the presentation or merchandise. The men's suits and sports jackets are first-class, as is the collection of handmade English shoes.

ROTHMAN'S
200 Park Ave S (at Union Sq)   212 777-7400
Mon-Wed, Fri: 10–7; Thurs: 10–8; Sat: 9–6; Sun: 12–5;
closed Sun in summer

Forget your mental picture of the old Harry Rothman store. Harry's grandson, Ken Gidden, runs this classy new men's store, which offers a huge selection of quality clothes at discount prices of up to 40% in a contemporary and comfortable atmosphere. He carries top names like Gieves and Hawkes, Hugo Boss, Burberry, Hickey-Freeman, Norman Hilton, Perry Ellis, Polo by Ralph Lauren, and Alexander Julian, all at off-prices. Gentlemen, be sure to check out the Alexander Julian clothes in particular; no designer has more interesting fabric and color combinations. They have also added Italian clothing like Canali and Lubiam. Sizes at Rothman range from 36 to 50 in regular, short, long, and extra long. Raincoats, slacks, sport jackets, and accessories are stocked in-depth at the same attractive prices. It's great to see the third generation just as eager and as capable as Grandpa himself!

SAINT LAURIE
897 Broadway (at 20th St)   212 473-0100
Mon-Wed, Fri, Sat: 10–6:30; Thurs: 10–8; Sun: 12–5

If you want selection, quality, and value, this is the place to go first. Saint Laurie is a manufacturer that distributes entirely outside Manhattan and does not sell its retail line anywhere else in the city. Consequently, the customer can take advantage of the missing middle man and choose from thousands of garments in sizes 35 to 48, regular, short, long, and extra long. Custom-made clothing at truly reasonable prices is offered, all arranged for easy looking and selection. The professional salespeople are informed but not pushy. Saint Laurie also manufactures women's classic business suits made of 100% worsted wool. They are outstanding. Custom shirts made in-house are first-class. The relatively new building has a "living museum," demonstrating Saint Laurie's production of its clothing as well as a tour of the workrooms and an exhibit showing various suit styles over the years.

SOSINSKY'S
143 Orchard St (bet Delancey and Rivington St)   212 254-2307
Mon-Thurs: 10–5; Fri: 10–3; Sun: 9–5;
closed Friday July and Aug

Three generations of the Sosinsky family have been in business at this same location for over 75 years. This says something for the bargains offered here on men's dress and sport shirts, sweaters, and robes by such famous names as Arrow and Alexander Julian. Unlike many of their neighbors, these folks are polite and helpful and will provide first-quality or irregular (always marked) merchandise at one-quarter to one-half or more off uptown prices. The Julian sport shirt selection is especially impressive, both in variety and value.

Men's Hats

J.J. HAT CENTER
310 Fifth Ave (at 32nd St) 212 239-4368, 800 622-1911
Mon-Sat: 8:45–5:45

If you can't find the piece of headgear you want here, it probably does not exist. This outfit stocks over 15,000 pieces of major-brand merchandise from all over the world. Founded in 1911, it is New York's oldest hat shop. Special services include free brush-up, free hat-stretching or -tightening, and custom orders. For those with really swollen heads, hats and caps up to size 8 are available.

VAN DYCK HATTERS
94 Greenwich Ave 212 929-5696
Mon-Fri: 7:30–6; Sat: 9–4

The quintessential hatter, Van Dyck is the first choice for anything that has to do with men's hats in New York. Since 1940, Van Dyck has been known for the quality of its own brand, which it manufactures and sells. Prices and quality can't be beat, but should you not trust its brand (New Yorkers do), Van Dyck also discounts Stetson hats at a minimum of 25%. No matter what the brand, Van Dyck can also clean, block, restyle, reband, or renovate any hat brought in.

Men's Large Sizes

IMPERIAL WEAR
48 W 48th St 212 719-2590
Mon-Wed, Fri, Sat: 9–6; Thurs: 9–8

Among New York's specialty shops, several are devoted exclusively to clothing in extra-large and extra-tall sizes. The salespeople at this one are well trained in the problems that large men usually encounter, and quality is not sacrificed in garments that require more material. It is this, perhaps, that has won Imperial its clientele. Many stores cater to big men, but having a captive audience causes some stores to relax their standards. The many regular customers who return to Imperial prove this is not the case here. The new line of designer fashions for big men is a major attraction, as is the shoe stock (sizes 12–16).

Men's Shirts

PENN GARDEN GRAND SHIRT CORPORATION
63 Orchard St (at Grand St) 212 431-8464
Sun-Wed, Fri: 9–6; Thurs: 9–8

G&G INTERNATIONAL
62 Orchard St (bet Grand and Hester St) 212 431-4530
Sun-Wed: 9–6; Thurs: 9–8; Fri: 9–6 (summer), 9–4 (winter)

If you thought the Lower East Side pickle business was inbred, it's got nothing on the local men's haberdashery dynasties. These stores are probably the most typical of the breed. Each considers itself a distinct entity, to the point that the people at Penn Garden will not tell you to go next door to G&G if you can't find what you want at their store. (Tell you? Ha! They won't even give out the other's phone numbers!) Taken separately, however, each store is a gem, and the sales help can sometimes be charming.

SHIRT STORE
51 E 44th St (bet Vanderbilt and Madison Ave)   212 557-8040
Mon-Fri: 8–6:30; Sat: 10–5

The attraction here is that you buy directly from the manufacturer, with no middle man to increase the price. The Shirt Store offers 100% cotton shirts for men, from the smallest (14x32) to the largest (18½x37). Although the ready-made stock is great, they will also do custom work and even come to your office with swatches. Imagine excusing yourself from the rest of the office crew to have your shirt-maker take some measurements! How's that for status? Additional services include home-order visits, alterations, and monogramming.

VICTORY SHIRT COMPANY
96 Orchard St (bet Delancey and Broome St)
212 677-2020, 800 841-3424
Sun-Thurs: 9:30–5:30; Fri: 9:30–4

Victory manufactures and retails their own 100% cotton ready-to-wear and made-to-measure shirts. They have the facilities to taper, shorten, alter, or monogram any shirt to individual specifications. Sizes run from 14x32 to 18½x36. There is also a good assortment of ties, cuff links, and belts. Periodic sales make their already reasonable prices even more attractive.

Men's Underwear

UNDER WARES
1098 Third Ave (bet 64th and 65th St)
212 535-6006, 800 237-8641
Mon-Fri: 10–7; Sat: 10–6; Sun: 12–5

It used to be that the average fellow couldn't tell you what kind of underwear he wore and probably didn't even buy it himself. All that changed with the ads featuring Jim Palmer and other celebrity jocks. These days a man's underwear makes a fashion statement. Ron Lee was on top of the trend and opened a fashionable shop that sells over a hundred styles of briefs and boxer shorts—the largest selection of men's undergarments in the whole world, many with top labels. There are also T-shirts, hosiery, robes, pajamas, workout wear, swimwear, and gift items. If you are shy about browsing all the sexy styles, call for one of their free catalogs.

Men's Western Wear

BILLY MARTIN'S
812 Madison Ave (at 68th St)   212 861-3100
Mon-Fri: 10–7; Sat: 10:30–6; Sun: 12–5

If Western wear is on your shopping list, head right to Billy Martin's, where you will find a great showing of deerskin jackets, shirts, riding pants, skirts, Western hats, and parkas. They also have one of the best collections of boots in the city for both men and women. Great accessory items like bandannas, jewelry, buckles, and belt straps complete the outfit. The items are well-tooled and -designed, and priced accordingly.

Outerwear

C.P. COMPANY
175 Fifth Ave (bet 22nd and 23rd St)   212 260-1990
Mon-Sat: 10–7 (Thurs: 10–8); Sun: 12–5

In a spectacular location in the historic Flatiron Building, noted Italian designer Massimo Osti has put together one of the classiest collections of unisex sportswear in the city. The space presently occupied by his C.P. Company was originally a cigar store. The whole area is making a comeback, and this store is sure to add to the interest. There are shirts and jackets that spell style and comfort, but with true lasting appeal. You can find jackets with built-in goggles in the hood and special built-in watch windows on the sleeve. An "ice jacket" that changes colors when exposed to the cold is both unusual and extremely stylish. This is one store that shouldn't be missed by anyone interested in the fashion picture. It is just another indication that Italians are Number One when it comes to design. Besides the quality of the merchandise (price tags are hefty), the ambience is first-class and the personnel exceptionally friendly and helpful.

Shoes – Children's

LITTLE ERIC SHOES
590 Columbus Ave (bet 88th and 89th St)   212 769-1610
Mon-Sat: 10–6; Sun: 1–6

Little people want shoes just like those worn by big people and this is the place to find them. They are comfy, with many lined in soft leather. You'll note that most of the "in" styles are made in Italy. The staff here are just as colorful as the shoes they sell!

RICHIE'S DISCOUNT CHILDREN'S SHOES
183 Avenue B (bet 11th and 12th St)   212 228-5442
Mon, Tues, Thurs-Sat: 10–5; Sun: 10–4

Richie's offers your children's feet a one-of-a-kind experience. Inside the décor is old, but the stock includes the very latest shoes at a fraction of the prices found anywhere else. Brands include Stride Rite, Jonathan Bennett, Babybotte, Blue Star, Jumping Jacks, and Keds sneakers, and the clincher is that the fit will be extraordinary. Considerable time is spent with each customer, and for each pair of shoes sold here, another pair has also not been sold. Reasons for the latter include the customer's being told that the child's old ones are still good. (Has that ever happened elsewhere?) Salesmen have even admitted that the quality desired just wasn't in stock or that Richie's would not sell lesser quality to a customer. The one drawback is the neighborhood. Gentrification hasn't quite reached this block of the East Village.

SHOOFLY
465 Amsterdam Ave (bet 82nd and 83rd St)   212 580-4390
Mon-Sat: 11–7; Sun: 12–6

This store is included for two special groups! Shoofly carries attractive and reasonably priced shoes for the younger set, infants to 14-year-olds. But there are lots of women with tiny feet who have a difficult time finding an adequate selection of footwear. As a matter of fact, this is one of the most common questions I am asked on call-in radio talk shows. Look no further, my petite friends. Shoofly will take care of your needs with delightful styles and sizes.

Shoes—Family

BUFFALO CHIPS BOOTERY SOHO
116-A Greene St (bet Spring and Prince St)   212 274-0651
Mon-Sat: 11–7; Sun: 12–6

The best of the West comes East! You'll be all set for a dude-ranch visit or plain old Western comfort and ambience with the wall art, Indian and contemporary Western jewelry, leather items, artifacts, pottery, rugs, and blankets from this attractive outlet. Best of all are the unique Western boots, all designed by the store's own personnel. If you have ever fantasized about having a pair made especially for you, they can produce custom-made boots in about 12 weeks.

THE CITY ATHLETE
131, 132-A, 132-B Orchard St (three stores)   212 475-4875
Daily: 9–6

What used to be separate stores have now been combined into three outlets with the same name, offering good prices on brand-name sneakers, casual and rugged footwear, and children's shoes. Featured brands include Bally, Zodiac, Timberland, Adidas, Nike, Puma, Reebok, and New Balance, among many others. These stores are usually so crowded that you'll need a new pair of shoes after all the bargain-hunting customers step on your toes. Family management insures a hands-on operation.

KENNETH COLE
353 Columbus Ave (bet 76th and 77th St)   212 873-2061
Mon-Sat: 11–8; Sun: 12–7

This is not a run-of-the-mill shoe store. For one thing, the walls are adorned with clever, irreverant posters poking fun at well-known personalities. But the real treats are the fashionable and trendy shoes for men and women at sensible prices. Cole is a master of public relations, and he has developed a deserved reputation for a quality product. I suggest you browse the high-style shops like Susan Bennis-Warren Edwards, where prices are absurd, and then come here to buy.

LEACH-KALE
1261 Broadway, Suite 815–816 (at 31st St)   212 683-0571
Mon-Fri: 9–5

While some custom-shoe craftsmen are determined to prove that their product can and should be owned by every man, Andre S. Feuerman of the Leach-Kale Company is not among them. Perhaps he has been burned by too many bargain hunters who thought the gap between a high-class shoe salon and Leach-Kale couldn't be as great as it is, or by customers who think that at Leach-Kale's price the shoes should cure all their orthopedic problems for life. Feuerman is careful to point out this is not the case. The business has customers who have been loyal patrons for 25 to 30 years, and these are the people Feuerman would rather court. They have neither unrealistic expectations nor impossible dreams but appreciate the quality items that Leach-Kale produces. Leach-Kale specializes in orthopedic work, which is probably why many customers pay the price without batting an eye. They have no choice. Shoes start at about $700 for the first pair, but some first orders and all subsequent orders can be substantially less.

LESLIE'S BOOTERY
319 Grand St (bet Orchard and Allen St)   212 431-9196
Sun-Wed, Fri: 9:30–6; Thurs: 9:30–7

For over 20 years this business has been selling top-name ladies' and men's shoes at discount prices. Normal prices reflect a 20% discount. At sales times in January and July, prices are even better on Bally, 9 West, Enzo, Liz Claiborne, Cole-Haan, Timberland, Reebok, Bass, Rockport, Bostonian, Clark's of England, and other name brands.

LORD JOHN BOOTERY
428 Third Ave (bet 29th and 30th St)   212 532-2579
Mon-Fri: 10–7; Sat: 10–6; closed Sat in July, Aug

Now here's a real "shoe dog" store. John Kyriannis and two generations of his family have been happily working together for four decades, and this happiness spills over to their customers. They carry Dan Post and Justin Western boots in all kinds of leathers for men and women, discounted by 20% to 30%. They also carry discounted Timberland and Dexter boots and shoes, as well as imported brands like Evan Picone, Nickels, Joan and David, and many more. They even sell clogs! It's refreshing to be helped by people who really know the business.

MANUFACTURERS SHOE OUTLET
537 Broadway (bet Spring and Prince St)   212 966-4070
Mon-Fri: 8–6; Sat: 9–5; Sun: 10–6

The hours and phone number are nebulous, and the attitude is "go help yourself, don't bother me." But if a lack of amenities doesn't bother you, then run to this dirty store in SoHo. It carries a wide variety of shoes, slippers, and hosiery, and the sizes range from infants' to large men's. If that isn't inducement enough, there are top brand names at a discount. Finally, note the hours. If your son breaks a buckle at 9 a.m. or the heel falls off a shoe an hour before a business meeting, this is the place to go for a quick replacement at discount prices. They claim to keep these hours because "everyone else here does." Now you know another difference between SoHo and the Village!

T.O. DEY
9 E 38th St   212 683-6300
Mon-Fri: 9–5; Sat: 9–1

For years I have included T.O. Dey, because they are a good, fancy, jack-of-all-trades operation. Though their specialty is custom-made shoes, they will also undertake any kind of repair on any kind of shoe. They will create both men's and women's shoes, based on a plaster mold taken of a customer's feet; their styles are limited only by the customer's imagination. They also make arch supports and will cover shoes to match your garment.They sell sports shoes for football, basketball, cross-country, hockey, boxing, and running, as well as downhill ski boots.

VOGEL BOOTS AND SHOES
19 Howard St (one block north of Canal St, bet Broadway and Lafayette St)   212 925-2460
Mon-Fri: 8–4:30; Sat: 8–2
Closed Sat in summer and first two weeks of July

The Vogels—Hank, Dean, and Jack Lynch—are the third and fourth generations to join this 110-year-old family business. They will happily fit and supply made-to-measure boots and shoes for any adult who can find the store. Howard is one of those streets that even native New Yorkers don't know exists. The many who have found Vogel beat a path to the door for top-quality shoes and boots, personal advice, excellent fittings, and prices that, while not inexpensive, are reasonable for the service involved. The fit is not to be taken lightly, for made-to-measure shoes do not always fit properly. At Vogel, they do. Once you have a shoe pattern on record at Vogel, they can make new shoes without a personal visit and will ship anywhere. For top craftsmanship, this spot is top-drawer. There are more than 600 Vogel dealers throughout the world, but this is the grandfather store, and the people here are super.

Shoes — Men's

ADLER SHOE SHOPS
141 W 42nd St (bet Sixth Ave and Broadway)   212 382-0844
Mon-Sat: 10–7

Adler's is a chain of men's shoe stores in New York, featuring Weyenberg, Hush Puppies, Timberland, Rockport, Elevator, Stacy Adams, and Nunn-Bush brands. At this store, all of the rejects, overruns, and odd lots are sold at big reductions.

CHURCH ENGLISH SHOES
428 Madison Ave (at 49th St)   212 755-4313
Mon-Fri: 9–6; Sat: 9–5:30

Anglophiles have a ball here, not only because of the *veddy* English atmosphere, but for the pure artistry and "Englishness" of the shoes. Church has been selling English shoes for men since 1873 and is known for classic styles, superior workmanship, and fine leathers. The styles basically remain unchanged year after year, although one or two new designs are occasionally added as a concession to fashion. All are custom-fitted by shoe salesmen. If a style or size does not feel right, Church's will craft a customized special order for approximately $150 more than the regular price. The salesmen are very professional. For foot problems, this is the place to come for competent advice.

J. SHERMAN SHOES
121 Division St (bet Orchard and Ludlow St)   212 233-7898
Mon-Thurs: 9:30–5:30; Fri: 9:30–3:30; Sun: 9–5:30

Upholding the Lower East Side tradition, J. Sherman has excellent prices on merchandise. But its shoes are not less than top-of-the-line quality, so here's the place to pick up Bally, Bruno Magli, Polo, Rockport, Clarks, Zodiac, Timberland, Frye, New Balance, and other brand-name shoes for 20% to 60% off list price. J. Sherman boasts that they have the best buys on brand-name shoes in the city. They may be right.

McCREEDY AND SCHREIBER
213 E 59th St (bet Second and Third Ave)   212 759-9241
Mon, Thurs: 9–9; Tues, Wed, Fri, Sat: 9–7; Sun: 12–6

37 W 46th St (bet Fifth and Sixth Ave)   212 719-1552
Daily: 9–7

How about a department store for shoes and boots? Here is one that features Lucchese, Tony Lama, Frye, Justin, and Timberland boots, as well as Bass and Allen-Edmonds shoes. There are boots in large sizes (like 14 and 15), prices are competitive, and made-to-order footwear is available.

STAPLETON SHOE COMPANY
68 Trinity Pl (at Rector St)   212 964-6329
Mon-Thurs: 8–6; Fri: 8–5

Their motto is "better shoes for less," but that doesn't begin to cover the superlatives that Stapleton deserves. Gentlemen, here is the place to get Bally, Alden, Allen-Edmonds, Cole-Hahn, Timberland, Rockport, Johnston Murphy, and a slew of other top shoe names at a discount. Stapleton is located on the same block as the American Stock Exchange. With the money saved here, there should be enough left over to take a flyer in the stock market. There probably isn't a better source for quality shoes anywhere.

TO BOOT
256 Columbus Ave (at 72nd St)   212 724-8249
Mon-Fri: 12–8; Sat: 12–8; Sun: 1–6

Bergdorf-Goodman Men
Fifth Ave (at 57th St), 3rd floor   212 339-3335
Mon-Wed, Fri, Sat: 10–6; Thurs: 10–8

To Boot presents high-quality men's footwear for the sophisticated urban man. They carry casual, dressy, and business shoes in fine leathers, suedes, and exotics, with designer collections by Armani, Ralph Lauren, and Cesare Paciotti. Western boots are also featured. Higher-priced shoes (including Ferragamo) are available at Bergdorfs.

Shoes — Women's

ANBAR SHOES
60 Reade St (bet Church St and Broadway)   212 227-0253
Mon-Sat: 8:30–6

Shoe bargain hunters rejoice! After years of searching through the dusty décor at their former store, Anbar customers can find the same great bargains on brand-name styles at discounts as high as 50%, but now in a clean setting! A good place to save money.

GIORDANO'S SHOES
1150 Second Ave (at 60th St)   212 688-7195
Mon-Fri: 11–7; Sat: 11–6

Susan Giordano has a very special clientele. Giordano stocks a fine selection in a range of tiny sizes of women's shoes (a range that is nonexistent in regular shoe stores). If you're a woman with a shoe size in the 3½ to 6 medium or 5½ to 6½ AA range, learning about Giordano's will make the purchase of this book more than worthwhile. Most women in this category shop in children's shoe departments or have shoes custom-made, either of which can cramp your style. For these women, Giordano's is a godsend. A selection of small-size clothing and accessories is also available.

IN STEP
1230 Second Ave (bet 64th and 65th St)   212 734-7484
Mon: 11–5:30; Tues-Fri: 11–7; Sat: 11–6

Petite ladies take note! "In Step" carries fashion footwear catering to sizes 3½ to 6½ medium and 5½ to 6½ narrow. Dale Feinblatt, the owner, comes from a family with small feet, so she knows well the frustrations of trying to find fashionable footwear in small sizes. Her store not only carries stylish name brands (like Stuart Weitzman, Bally, and Amalfi, among others), but also has work shoes, evening shoes, and boots, plus coordinated handbags and gloves. Pumps may be special-ordered in a variety of colors, and mail orders are encouraged. Their mail-order catalog is available twice yearly.

LACE UP SHOE SHOP
110 Orchard St (at Delancey St)   212 475-8040, 800 488-LACE
Sun-Fri: 9–5:30

The unusual thing about Lace Up is that it's a full-service shoe store in an area where such a thing isn't supposed to exist! The folks at Lace Up actually help customers put on their shoes. They will special-order a particular style, if available, and will discount your purchase. They carry a large selection of top-name, current-season merchandise for both men and women. You will find Mephisto, Arche, Cori, Karl Langfeld, Bruno Magli, Evan Picone, and many other designer names. If your young ones gets bored while you are trying on some super styles, "Shoo-Guy"—their mascot, a yellow nape parrot—will entertain them.

PETER FOX SHOES
105 Thompson St (bet Prince and Spring St)   212 431-6359
378 Amsterdam Ave (at 78th St)   212 874-6399
Mon-Sat: 11–7; Sun: 12–6

Peter Fox was the downtown trailblazer for women's shoes. Everything sold in the shop is exclusive, limited-edition designer footwear. Perhaps because of the store's original location, Fox's designs seem more adventurous than those of its uptown competitors; the look seems younger and more casual than it does with other designers. For those looking for shoes to be seen in, Cedric (uptown) and Jacques (downtown) are the people to see. Bridal and special-occasion shoes are available next door (from Linda) to the Thompson Street store.

TALL SIZE SHOES
3 W 35th St (at Fifth Ave)   212 736-2060
Mon-Wed, Fri, Sat: 9:30–6; Thurs: 9:30–7

Finding comfortable shoes if you are "tall size" is not easy. This store can solve the problem, as they carry a broad selection of wide and extra-wide styles in sizes 5 to 14. There are narrow to extra-wide-width shoes from Bandolino, Nickels, Via Spiga, Liz Claiborne, Amalfi, Evan Picone, and Zodiac. They will take phone orders and ship anywhere.

Sportswear

GERRY COSBY AND COMPANY
Madison Square Garden
3 Pennsylvania Plaza (at 32nd St and Seventh Ave)
212 563-6464
Mon-Fri: 9:30–6:30; Sat: 9:30–6; Sun: 12–5

There's a lot to like about this company. Although it will be difficult for an out-of-towner to find them, they are a briskly professional business that is located at the most appropriate spot for its wares. And those wares are team sportswear—as in what people active in sports *wear*. In particular, Gerry Cosby designs and markets protective equipment and covers for both bodies and sports gear. The protective equipment and bags are designed exclusively for professional use but are available to the general public as well. Gerry Cosby's designs are coveted and frequently copied, but why not get an original? They accept mail and phone orders for all equipment, including personalized jerseys and jackets.

HOWRON SPORTSWEAR
295 Grand St (bet Eldridge and Allen St)   212 226-4307
Sun-Fri: 9–5

Howron was transformed from a typical Lower East Side shop into a fashionable boutique without sacrificing Lower East Side prices. They carry an excellent selection of men's sportswear and women's wear, including top names like Damon, Countess Mara, Members Only, and Pierre Cardin. For women, choose from Hanes, Bali, Warners, Maidenform, and Jockey.

WOMEN'S WORKOUT GEAR
121 Seventh Ave (at 17th St)   212 627-1117
Mon-Fri: 11–7; Sat: 11–6; Sun: 1:30–5:30

Here is a store that specializes in clothes for today's health-conscious woman. Paula Shirk, an avid runner herself, has put together a great collection of women's aerobic and running wear; walking, running, and aerobic shoes; bathing suits and goggles; sports bras; and weights and exercise mats. Paula and her crew give professional advice to their customers, along with brand-name merchandise from Baryshnikov, S.E. City Lights, Gilda Marx, Reebok, Saucony, Speedo, and Triangle. Almost everything is specially designed for women, and careful shoppers can find outstanding bargains in off-season merchandise.

Surplus

59th STREET ARMY AND NAVY
221 E 59th St (bet Second and Third Ave)　　212 755-1855
Mon, Thurs: 10–7:45; Tues, Wed, Fri: 10–6:45; Sat: 10–6; Sun: 1–5:45

328 Bleecker St (at Christopher St)　　212 242-6665
Mon-Thurs: 10–7:45; Fri, Sat: 10–8:45; Sun: 1–6:45

110 Eighth Ave (bet 15th and 16th St)　　212 645-7420
Mon-Fri: 9–6:45; Sat: 10–6:45; Sun: 1–5:45

SECOND AVENUE ARMY NAVY
1598 Second Ave (at E 83rd St)　　212 737-4661
Mon-Sat: 10–7:45; Sun: 12–6

I have long sung the praises of so-called army-navy stores, although the genuine outlets for surplus military supplies have been gone for years. These shops are the best source for camping supplies, as well as durable and practical clothes and equipment. Instead of navy dress pants and sailor uniforms, this chain specializes in rugged outdoor wear, including the largest inventory of 501 Levi's on the East Coast. There are sweat outfits; top-brand sneakers at excellent prices; Timberland, Nike, and Rockport shoes; Schott leather jackets; and Champion and Russell Athletic sportswear.

KAUFMAN SURPLUS
319 W 42nd St (bet Eighth and Ninth Ave)　　212 757-5670
Mon-Wed, Fri, Sat: 10–6; Thurs: 10–7

Kaufman's has long been a favorite among New Yorkers and visitors alike for its extensive selection of genuine military surplus from around the world. Over the last half-century, Kaufman's has outfitted dozens of Broadway and TV shows and supplied a number of major motion pictures with military garb. The store is a treasure trove of military collectibles, hats, helmets, dummy grenades, uniforms, and insignias. Over a thousand military pins, patches, and medals from armies the world over are on display.

Sweaters

BEST OF SCOTLAND
581 Fifth Ave (bet 47th and 48th St), penthouse　　212 644-0403
Mon-Sat: 10–6

Who doesn't like the luxury of cashmere? Best of Scotland offers beautiful sweaters at sensible prices. In the spring they carry a good assortment of made-in-Scotland silk/merino wool sweaters for ladies. There is also a vast showing of Scottish cashmere capes and stoles, available in over 100 colors!

GRANNY-MADE
381 Amsterdam Ave (bet 78th and 79th St)   212 496-1222
Mon-Fri: 11–7:30; Sat: 10–6; Sun: 12–5

Grannie Bert Levy has passed on to her reward, but she must be looking down with pleasure on the very appealing selection of handiwork that grandson Michael Rosenberg has assembled. He carries an extensive collection of sweaters for young people, from infants to size 14. Handmade cable-knit sweaters from Uruguay sit beside ones that are hand-loomed right here at home. The selection of women's sweaters, knitwear, suits, dresses, skirts, slacks, and accessories is unique, as are the men's sweaters and novelty T-shirts.

Thrift Shops

ARTHRITIS FOUNDATION THRIFT SHOP
121 E 77th St (bet Lexington and Park Ave)   212 772-8816
Mon-Sat: 10:30–4:45

This very friendly store carries donated clothing, furniture, bric-a-brac, and oddities that will appeal to bargain hunters. Their donors include people whose family members have suffered from arthritis.

ENCORE
1132 Madison Ave (bet 84th and 85th St), upstairs
212 879-2850
Mon-Wed, Fri, Sat: 10:30–6; Thurs: 10:30–7:30; Sun: 12:30–6;
closed Sun from July to mid-Aug

Encore is a very professional thrift shop. It is so chic and select that it prefers to be billed as a "resale shop of gently worn clothing." When one sees the merchandise and the caliber of the clientele at this three-decades-old shop, Encore can be forgiven its conceit. For one thing, it is a consignment boutique, not a charity thrift shop. Its donors receive a portion of the sales price, and according to owner Carole Selig, many of the donors are socialites and other luminaries who can't afford to be seen in the same outfit twice. Selig can afford to be picky, and so can you. The fashions are up-to-date, and if Jackie O doesn't mind dropping off her better items here, why should a customer mind grabbing these top fashions at 50% to 70% off original retail prices? At any time, there are over 6,000 items in stock. Prices range from reasonable to astronomical, but just think how much more they sold for originally!

EVERYBODY'S THRIFT SHOP
261 Park Ave S   212 355-9263
Mon-Fri: 10–5; Sat: 10–4; closed Sat in July and Aug

This shop was founded in 1921 to support the "Bundles for Britain" program, one of the recovery efforts after World War I. Today it serves as the umbrella organization for six charities and has an impressive list of supporters. Knowing who they are and when they donate is the reason a queue forms outside the store on some mornings. (The list of donors includes many manufacturers and retail stores.) Everybody's Thrift Shop features designer clothing, bric-a-brac, jewelry, furniture, and donations from large corporations.

MEMORIAL SLOAN-KETTERING CANCER CENTER THRIFT SHOP
1440 Third Ave (at 82nd St)   212 535-1250
Mon-Sat: 10–4:30

Because of its location on the affluent Upper East Side, this thrift shop benefits from big-name donors. Try it for accessories, and don't miss its designer room, which is better stocked than some retail stores.

MICHAEL'S
1041 Madison Ave (bet 79th and 80th St)   212 737-7273
Mon-Sat: 9:30–6; Thurs: 9:30–8; summer: Mon-Fri: 9:30–6

It's not common to find bargain prices on designer clothes along trendy, expensive Madison Avenue. Michael's is an exception. You can find an excellent selection of quality merchandise in sizes 4–12 at very substantial discounts in this consignment shop.

REPEAT PERFORMANCE
220 E 23rd St (bet Second and Third Ave)   212 684-5344
Mon-Fri: 10–5:45; Thurs: 10–6:30; Sat: 10–5

Repeat Performance is run for the benefit of the New York City Opera, a cause near and dear to the hearts of wealthy donors and major department and specialty stores. So while there are the usual thrift-shop furniture, jewelry, and bric-a-brac, plus occasional paintings, the strong suit here is brand-new, designer-name, often store-labeled clothing at ridiculously inexpensive prices.

There is more at the new **Barney's** (Madison Avenue at 61st St) than just things to please the body's exterior. A variety of food offerings – several café's, two restaurants, a wine bar, a catering service, and a food complex with an espresso bar – will satisfy any appetite.

T-Shirts

EISNER BROS.
75 Essex St (bet Grand and Delancey St)
212 475-6868, 800 426-7700
Mon-Thurs: 9–6:30; Fri: 9–3; Sun: 9–5

In expanded showroom facilities, you will find all sports-licensed team merchandise, from the NBA and NHL to collegiate teams. There are caps, sweatshirts, jackets, bandannas, and the largest selection of T-shirts around. You'll also find police, fire, emergency and sanitation-department logos, as well as those of Disney and Harley-Davidson. Personalizing is available on all items. Sizes include infants through adult 5XL, and prices are very competitive.

Umbrellas

UNCLE SAM
161 W 57th St (bet Sixth and Seventh Ave)
212 247-7163, 212 582-1976
Mon-Fri: 9:30–6; Sat: 10–5

This is a New York specialty store at its very best. Uncle Sam sells canes and services, re-covers, and customizes umbrellas. There are umbrellas for children, golfers, fashion models, travelers, chauffeurs, doormen, and beach goers. All are carved, sewn, and assembled by hand. Uncle Sam also sells umbrella accessories and remakes old umbrellas and canes.

Uniforms

DORNAN
653 Eleventh Ave (bet 47th and 48th St)
212 247-0937, 800 223-0363 (outside New York State)
Mon-Wed, Fri: 8:30–4; Thurs: 8:30–6

Dornan is the largest supplier of chauffeur uniforms in the country, and they carry many other lines of work uniforms as well. This includes outfits for butlers, maids, beauticians, hospital workers, doormen, bellboys, bartenders, chefs, stewards and stewardesses, pilots, firemen, police, doctors, nurses, and . . . you get the picture. They have been in the business for nearly 70 years, so they know what they are doing. They are capable of setting up a uniform program, screen-printing, customizing, and distributing the outfits anywhere.

JA-MIL UNIFORMS
92 Orchard St (at Delancey St)   212 677-8190
Mon-Fri, Sun: 10–5

This is *the* bargain spot for those who wear uniforms and do not want to spend a fortune on work clothes. There are outfits for doctors, nurses, and technicians, as well as good values on white nursing-duty shoes.

Women's Accessories

BERNARD KRIEGER & SON
316 Grand St   212 226-1929
Mon-Thurs, Sun: 8–4:30; Fri: 8–3;
Sun hours may vary in summer

The assortment of items here is limited, but they do have one of the best selections anywhere of millinery, handkerchiefs, scarfs, accessories, and gloves. It also looks as though they have more berets than any store in Paris. The price tags are certainly a lot more reasonable, because everything is discounted.

FINE AND KLEIN
119 Orchard St (at Delancey St)   212 674-6720
Sun-Fri: 9–5

The finest handbag store for value and selection is not located in Rome, Paris or London. It is not even located on Fifth Avenue in New York. It is on the Lower East Side, and the name is Fine and Klein. What a selection! There is a bag for every purpose, for any time of day, and in any fabric. Top labels are sold for a fraction of what you would pay uptown. Besides, shopping at Fine and Klein is fun. The crowds, especially on Sundays and holidays, are so great that the number of persons allowed to enter is controlled! One Saudi princess bought $9,600 worth of bags here. My good friends Julius Fine and Murray Klein are the epitome of old-time merchants. Tell them I sent you, and you will be delighted with the service.

HYUK BAGS
39 W 29th St   212 685-5226, 212 685-5399
Mon-Thurs: 7:30–6; Fri: 7:30–5; Sat: 7:30–1

Hyuk K. Kim runs an importing company exclusively dedicated to handbags. Importing and wholesaling companies are common in this area. What is uncommon is the courtesy and selection Kim gives individual retail customers. She has a knack for making everyone feel like a valued customer and does not take offense when a finicky lady picks through the entire stock in search of the right handbag. Besides, it shouldn't be too hard to find, within certain guidelines. *Imported* here usually refers to origins from points west rather than east. Hyuk seems to import every type of handbag—leather, vinyl, canvas, and nylon. Most of this is average, serviceable stuff. But there are a few stars in the line, and prices border on magnificent. Spoken English is at a premium here.

J.S. SUAREZ
26 W 54th St (bet Fifth and Sixth Ave)   212 315-5614
Mon-Fri: 9:30–6; Sat: 10–5:30

J.S. Suarez has been in business for over 42 years. In that time, he has made his reputation by selling name-brand bags at a 30% to 50%

discount, and copies of name-brand bags at even better prices. For years, Suarez was the source for unlabeled Gucci bags that sold for less than half the price and were identical to the real thing (naturally, since they came from the same factory). And, unlike Gucci, Suarez doesn't have some of the most obnoxious clerks this side of Italy. In fact, Suarez and his people are downright pleasant. He discounts name brands as well as "fake" (read "unlabeled") Bottega Veneta, Celine of Paris, Chanel, Fendi, and Hermes items. There is also a great selection of exotic skins. Suarez takes it as a matter of course that you are *supposed* to deliver top quality, great service, good selection, and excellent prices to all customers. Gucci could learn a few things from J.S. Suarez!

MICHAEL KLEIN'S FOMO
317 Grand St   212 925-6363
Mon-Fri, Sun: 9:15–5:30

The name Klein is world-famous because of Fine and Klein. A second-generation Klein wanted to continue the family tradition of being in the handbag business, but he wanted to flap his own wings. Thus Michael Klein's FOMO. And what does FOMO stand for? *Finally On My Own!* Michael offers an outstanding collection of briefcases and bags, including such top names as Givenchy of Paris, Carlos Falchi, and Cosci of Italy. Prices reflect a 25% to 50% discount, and the imported merchandise includes belts and wallets, as well as handbags.

ST. REGIS DESIGNS
58 E 7th St (bet First and Second Ave)   212 533-7313
Mon-Sat: 10–7:30; Sun: 12–6:30

From this unlikely spot in the East Village, Andrew Pelensky — who used to work for a top handbag designer — turns out handmade, original custom-designed handbags and belts from the finest leathers, including snake and alligator skins. The workmanship is both unique and magnificent, and items can be custom-ordered. For the quality, prices are outright cheap. George Pelensky is listed as being in charge of "sales." I hope this doesn't mean they are going into mass production. Right now, it's the personal touch, like a final fitting before a belt leaves the premises, that makes St. Regis so special.

Women's Evening Wear

ONE NIGHT STAND
905 Madison Ave (bet 72nd and 73rd St)   212 772-7720
Mon-Fri: 10–6:30 by appointment; Sat: 11–5 by appointment; closed Sat in July, Aug

Now here's a great idea. You are invited to a gala, but you "don't have a thing to wear." Don't buy, rent. One Night Stand has over 700 pieces of ladies' evening wear for rent from sizes 2 to 16. Jewelry, evening bags, and cloaks are also available for hire. You can even select your outfit and pick it up the same day. Sure beats shelling out big bucks for a dress you may not need for another two years, if ever.

TAMARA BOUTIQUE
134 E 70th St (bet Park and Lexington Ave)   212 628-0902
Mon-Sat: 9:30–5:30 (closed Sat in July and Aug)

If you are looking for a place to find dinner, cocktail, evening, or other special-occasion apparel that you will not see in every other store in town, then Tamara is worth a try. Individual attention in the choice of garments and alterations is a tradition here. Naturally, you pay for the personal interest and the exclusive designs, but if it is a once-in-a-lifetime event, why not go for the best?

Women's — General

ATELIER/45
347 Madison Ave   212 687-6877
Mon-Fri: 10–7:30; Sat: 11–6

ATELIER/55
101 W 55th St (at Sixth Ave)   212 245-3650
Mon-Wed, Fri: 10–7; Sat: 11–6; Thurs: 10–7:30

ATELIER/86
144 E 86th St   212 427-2211
Mon-Fri: 10:30–8; Sat: 10:30–7; Sun: 12–6:30

When a store down the street from ABC and Burlington calls itself a "small family kind of place," it may be a little hard to believe. But Atelier, a chain with great fashions from American designers, is just that. Atelier claims that the 86th Street store attracts browsers and a tourist clientele, while the 55th Street shop has loyal and devoted customers who, with all of the midtown Manhattan stores to choose from, pick their wardrobes from Atelier season after season. The reason is simple: Atelier's prices on brand-name garments are excellent.

BEN FARBER
212 W 35th St, 15th floor   212 736-0557, 800 223-6101
Mon-Fri: 9–5:30; Sat: 9–4

The recession took its toll on this operation, but they survived! What was at one time one of the largest and very best women's fashion discount houses in the city has now been downsized into a much different operation that specializes in after-five dresses. However, there are also some good suit and coat buys available. The quality is superior, the merchandise mainly fresh and seasonal, and you have Don Farber and sidekick Joe Halperin around to provide personal service. It's sad to see a great operation lose a bit of luster, but this is still a good place to shop.

BETSEY JOHNSON

248 Columbus Ave (bet 71st and 72nd St)   212 362-3364
130 Thompson St (bet Prince and Houston St)   212 420-0169
251 E 60th St (at Second Ave)   212 319-7699
1060 Madison Ave (at 80th St)   212 734-1257
Mon-Sat: 12–7; Thurs: 12–8; Sun: 12–7

In the 1960s and 1970s, Betsey Johnson was *the* fashion designer. Her designs appeared everywhere, as did Betsey and her personal life. As an outlet for those designs not sold to exclusive boutiques, Betsey co-founded Betsey Bunky Nini, but her own pursuits led to more designing and ultimately her own store in SoHo. The SoHo store proved so successful that Betsey moved first to larger quarters and then up and across town, as well as into department stores such as Bloomingdale's. While her style has always managed to be avant-garde, it has never been way-out. Johnson believes in making her own statement, and each store seems unique, despite the fact that over 500 outlets carry her line. Prices, particularly at the SoHo store (which started as an outlet), are bearable and wearable. Incidentally, it's hard to overlook the shop—it's pink, with pink neon accents and what she simply refers to as "great windows."

BEVERLY M.

30 E 67th St (at Madison Ave)   212 744-3726
Mon-Fri: 11–5

Beverly Madden has been in the clothing business for a quarter of a century. The special edge here is that she will make and design clothing just for you, from skirts and blouses to jackets and evening pants. Delivery usually takes from ten days to two weeks (depending on fabric availability), but the waiting time can be shortened if you are a Manhattan visitor. Personal interest and patience are the rules of the house.

CHELSEA DESIGNERS

128 W 23rd St (bet Sixth and Seventh Ave)   212 255-8803
Mon-Sat: 10–7; Sun: 12–6

Chalk one up for comfort! This unusual store sells comfort in a big way. They design, make, and sell one-size-fits-all clothing for women. Best of all, their items have no buttons, zippers, or any other kind of closures. Great items in sizes 6–20 for maternity and post-maternity moms, and for those who just like to be able to expand a bit after a big dinner or a chocolate binge. Everything is made in natural fabrics, like crepe de Chine silk, raw silk, cotton, rayon, and wool. You really have to put on their clothes to grasp the appeal, because on hangers they don't look like much!

EILEEN FISHER
314 E 9th St   212 529-5715
521 Madison Ave (bet 53rd and 54th St)   212 759-9888
341 Columbus Ave (bet 76th and 77th St)   212 362-3000
103 Fifth Ave (at 18th St)   212 924-4777
1039 Madison Ave (at 79th St)   212 879-7799
Open every day, hours vary by store

For the lady who likes her clothes cool, loose, and casual, look no further than Eileen Fisher. This talented designer has put together a collection of easy-care, natural-fiber outfits that will travel well and be admired for their simple and attractive lines. The colors are very earthy. From a small start in the East Village to five units all over Manhattan and space in some of the area's best stores, Eileen has produced a winner.

FORMAN'S
82 Orchard St (bet Grand and Broome St)
FORMAN'S PETITE
94 Orchard St
FORMAN'S PLUS SIZES
78 Orchard St   212 228-2500
Sun-Wed: 9–6; Thurs: 9–8; Fri: 9–3
FORMAN'S
59 John St   212 791-4100
Mon-Wed: 7:30–6:30; Thurs: 7:30 a.m.–8 p.m.; Sun: 12–5

Forman's bills itself as "the fashion oasis of the Lower East Side." While you can determine for yourself if that overstates the case a bit, it is true they have enjoyed a good reputation for years and years. By Lower East Side standards, the store is enormous. It is laid out in such a way that a teenage daughter, mother, and grandmother can all head for sections designed for their needs and not meet for hours. Even then, it might be at one of the dozen dressing rooms or the cash register. Denim reigns here, but so does casual sportswear, separates, and trendy outerwear. The main floor dazzles the customer with designer sportswear (Calvin Klein must have a direct line here) and such better-made separates as Jones of New York and Adrienne Vittadini. The lower level is dedicated to young, suburban-type separates and sportswear. Forman's made its reputation outfitting these images. Prices reflect the obligatory Lower East Side discount. Read that to mean very good.

GALERIES LAFAYETTE
Trump Tower (E 57th St bet Fifth and Madison Ave)
212 355-0022
Mon-Sat: 10–6:30; Sun: 12–6

This first American branch of the famous French store carries only women's clothing and accessories, placed in a number of boutiques in a space that once housed Bonwit Teller. There are no *haute couture* clothes; the store carries "better," "bridge," and "designer" fashions. "Bridge" means clothes priced in between "better" and "designer." Only French designers are featured. It is *not* an exciting store.

GALLERY OF WEARABLE ART
43 E 63rd St   212 425-5379
Tues-Sat: 10–6

The best phrase to describe this innovative business is "anti-trendy." The Gallery of Wearable Art carries what is probably the largest collection of unusual clothing, jewelry, and accessories from all over the world that one can find in New York. It is primarily a cottage industry, with a specialty in creating and designing special-occasion and bridal wear, plus all the accessories that go with the main item. If you are looking for unusual evening gowns, cocktail suits, bridal alternatives for non-classic weddings, attractive jewelry, one-of-a-kind art jackets in antique textiles, lace collage ensembles, and antique collaged suede suits, make this your destination. One thing is for sure: you won't see similar apparel on a friend or relative!

LAURA ASHLEY
21 E 57th St (bet Fifth and Madison Ave)   212 752-7300
Mon-Fri: 10–7; Sat: 10–6; Sun: 12–5

398 Columbus Ave (at 79th St)   212 496-5110
Mon-Wed, Fri, Sat: 11–7; Thurs: 11–8; Sun: 12–6

4 Fulton St (at South Street Seaport)   212 809-3555
Mon-Sat: 10–8:45; Sun: 11–7

714 Madison Ave (bet 63rd and 64th St)   212 735-5000
Mon-Wed, Fri, Sat: 10–6; Thurs: 10–7; Sun: 12–6

The Laura Ashley look is now available in nearly 200 exclusive shops around the country—a far cry from when Laura and husband Bernard turned out their first dress on the kitchen table several decades ago. Most of the dresses are in a small print fabric that seems to come from the mills looking well-worn. The theme is distinctive, sort of a romantic Victorian-Edwardian look. In spring, you can find silks and rayons; in summer, the fabrics are 100% cotton; in winter, a light woolen tweed. Dresses for infants and children are a sure grandma pleaser. An annual bridal collection has become very popular. There are also home furnishings, fabrics for wallpapers and curtains, and loose fabric at the Madison Avenue store.

LEA'S DESIGNER FASHION
119 Orchard St   212 677-2043
Sun-Thurs: 10–5:30; Fri: 10–3

You don't have to pay full price for your Louis Feraud, Albert Nipon, or other famous designer dresses and suits if you head to this popular Lower East Side outlet. Lea discounts her merchandise up to 30% and sells the previous season's styles for as little as $50. Don't expect much in the way of amenities, but you'll save enough here to afford a special dinner to show off your new outfit!

LUCILLE'S
33 W 55th St (Hotel Shoreham, Suite 2B)   212 245-7066
Mon-Sat: 11–5:30; closed July 1–Aug 15

Women who wear sizes 6–20 can save substantial sums on designer fashions at Lucille's, a shop that specializes in classic designer clothing at good discount prices. The best part of all is Lucille, who presides over her beautifully organized emporium with taste and style. Exactly where Lucille gets her merchandise is uncertain, but somehow she obtains fantastic designer clothing in striking colors, patterns, and ensembles. And the labels are intact, unlike nearly every other designer outlet I can think of. Lucille also has an instinct for the needs of her customers. Most are middle-aged, very well-dressed, and classically fashionable rather than fad-conscious. So Lucille's styles show a prejudice for the larger sizes. They start at 6, and the higher you go (including a very unusual designer 20), the more varied the selection is. Lucille's concern is shown in her selection of summer outfits with coordinating sweaters (to wear when there's air conditioning), jerseys that pack easily, and three-piece ensembles in striking patterns that can be interchanged for various occasions. Finally, don't miss Lucille's formal wear; her dressy outfits are really special. And did I mention that all of these fashions are sold at a 20% to 40% discount?

M. FRIEDLICH
196 Orchard St (bet Stanton and Houston St)   212 254-8899
Daily: 9:30–5:30

Another typical Lower East Side boutique, Friedlich has the usual fabulous finds in both quality and price, as well as the usual abrasive service people. Starting with the good points, Friedlich stocks women's fine imported sportswear in sizes 3–14, a range that includes misses and juniors sizes and is somewhat limited on the larger sizes. M. Friedlich seems to favor imports from France and Italy—perhaps because they are the best—but there is a healthy assortment of better-quality American sportswear as well. Another plus is Friedlich's selection of coats and outerwear, which consists of great designer coats and better-brand offerings from both Europe and America. The only problem with a visit here is what one would facetiously call ambience. Perhaps the sales help are always too swamped with customers, or maybe handling all those good-looking fashions while wearing a smock gets to them. In any event, *surly* is a polite way to describe their behavior.

MIRIAM RIGLER
14 W 55th St   212 581-5519
Mon-Sat: 10–6 (Thurs: 10–7)

Miriam Rigler is the quintessential ladies' dress shop. They seem to have it all—personal attention, expert alterations, wardrobe coordination, custom designing, and a large selection in everything from sportswear to knits to evening gowns, in sizes from 4 to 20. Despite the location, all items are discounted, including specially ordered outfits that are not in stock. This store meets all of my criteria for one of the very best. Don't miss the costume jewelry!

NICOLINA OF NEW YORK
247 W 46th St   212 302-NICO
Mon-Sat: 10–8; Sun: 12–6

Theater people love it! This unique store, located in the midst of the theater district, features modern copies of old pieces made with charm and imagination. Vests made of old kimonos are a special feature of a stock that includes all manner of accessories and novelty ready-to-wear. An added incentive is the staff, who are as much fun and as consumer-friendly as the clothes.

S&W
Coats:
287 Seventh Ave (at 26th St)

Bags, Shoes, Accessories:
283 Seventh Ave (at 26th St)

Dresses, Sportswear:
165 W 26th St (at Seventh Ave)

212 924-6656
Mon-Wed: 10–6:30; Thurs: 10–8; Fri: 10–4; Sun: 10–6

Each location of S&W features a specialty, as indicated above. While the source of supply isn't entirely clear, S&W is one of the best places in the city for ladies' designer clothing. Clothing orders include elegant—the suedes and leathers in the coats and suits are magnificent—and top-of-the-line garments only. Unlike so many other discount boutiques, S&W maintains a consistent level of quality. It is *not* the place to uncover the buy of the year; the discount is a minimum of 40%, but 40% off a $300 suede suit still takes a bite out of a working girl's budget. Two serious drawbacks: prices are not marked for the customer to read, and rudeness seems to be a way of life.

SHULIE'S
175 Orchard St (bet Stanton and Houston St)   212 473-2480
Sun-Fri: 9:30–5:30

You probably don't think of Orchard Street as the place to come for designer clothes or shoes, but think again. Look uptown in some of the fancier shops for top-label clothing and accessories, then phone or come down to Shulie's. The merchandise will be the same, but the shopping bag, the ambience, and (most important) the price will be very different. A full line of Tahari designer clothing is available at comfortable prices. Special orders are taken, and service is above the norm for this area.

SPITZER'S CORNER STORE
101 Rivington St   212 477-4088
156 Orchard St   212 473-1515
Sun-Thurs: 9–5:30; Fri: 9–2:30

Spitzer on Rivington is a Lower East Side landmark. There are two good reasons for shopping at these stores: excellent selection and the best prices. On the down side, you have to put up with less than helpful salespeople, unmarked merchandise, and, at the Rivington store, three rooms jammed with goods. Be especially careful in any store that does not mark its merchandise; make sure you're getting the best price possible. A bit of "bargaining" may be necessary. Now that you know both sides of shopping here, you'll be able to get some great bargains and have a memorable shopping experience. Good luck.

THREE WISHES
355 W Broadway   212 226-7570
Sun-Fri: 12–7; Sat: 11–7

Not too many stores in SoHo are true discount operations all year round, but Three Wishes is just that. They feature knit suits, dresses, sweaters, separates, silk dresses, blouses, and evening wear at sizable savings. This is not a sample or overstock store; their merchandise is first-quality and fashion-current.

Women's Knitwear

SCALERA KNITS
796 Madison Ave (at 67th St)   212 988-3344
Mon-Fri: 10–6; Sat: 10:30–5:30

In this store devoted entirely to knitwear, women can pick up outfits in silk, wool, cashmere, cotton, or blends of those materials in sizes from 6 to 20. If that isn't impressive enough, Scalera is the only direct importer of Italian silk knits in the city.

Women's Large Sizes

ASHANTI
872 Lexington Ave (bet 65th and 66th St)   212 535-0740
Mon-Wed, Fri, Sat: 10–6; Thurs: 10–8

Its name is a throwback to the days when ethnic boutiques were popular in Manhattan, but Ashanti's current image couldn't be more in vogue. Today, Ashanti carries better dresses, clothing, and accessories solely for the "larger woman." What they can't buy, they will have made to order. In fact, says Bill Michael, 75% of his merchandise is of Ashanti's own design and manufacturing. The craftsmen who work exclusively for Ashanti, adds Sandra Michael, are often supplied with patterns as well as designs, since the field is so new. There is more to large sizes than letting out seams or sewing up caftans in polka-dot polyester. For the first time boutiques are operating on the belief that big ladies deserve a positive, stylish fashion image. Ashanti will do alterations and ship anywhere. It may be the only place that carries classic, quality clothing to size 28. There is even a bargain basement.

FORGOTTEN WOMAN
888 Lexington Ave (at 66th St)   212 535-8848
60 W 49th St   212 247 8888
Mon-Wed, Fri, Sat: 10–6; Thurs: 10–7:30

Nancye Radmin, a former partner in the Farmer's Daughter Boutique, was so appalled by the dearth of size 20 clothes that she opened her own boutique. The Forgotten Woman thus became the first store in New York devoted exclusively to the larger-size woman and, in the process, became a trailblazer for Seventh Avenue manufacturers as well. The selection was so small in the beginning that Nancye designed much of her own merchandise. (She still creates about 25% of what is sold.) Eventually, manufacturers followed her lead, and the Forgotten Woman now stocks most everything. As a "forgotten woman" herself, Nancye knows what looks good and what styles have become almost a uniform for large women. Nicest of all, sizes range from 14–24. The Forgotten Woman is one place where the well-endowed woman will truly feel wanted.

Women's — Maternity

THE EXECUTIVE MOTHER
60 E 56th St (bet Park and Madison Ave)
212 753-4993
Open seven days a week

The busy business woman who is going to have a new addition at home will find this store a real help. Business suits, conservative dresses, sportswear, lingerie, nightwear, infant apparel, and toys are all available in one convenient location. This is definitely an upscale operation. They will assemble clothing for you, deliver it anywhere in the country, provide alteration services, and make and deliver baby baskets. Christine LaBastille, herself a successful investment analyst, knows what the busy mother-to-be needs, and she has put together a first-class operation.

FORMAL EXPECTATIONS
142 Washington Ave, Pleasantville, NY 10570   212 675-4859
By appointment only

Located 34 miles north of New York City in Westchester County, this is the only formal maternity-wear rental company servicing the tri-state area. They offer top-of-the-line formal wear at a fraction of the retail price, with individualized attention. They will even send out-of-town customers a videotape to give them an idea of what is available.

LADY MADONNA
793 Madison Ave (at 67th St)   212 988-7173
Mon-Wed, Fri, Sat: 10–6; Thurs:10–7; Sun: 12–5

I'd like to reaffirm that I have personally visited nearly every one of the stores listed in this book—even the maternity shops. I wasn't exactly a regular customer, but my visits were pleasant and informative. Lady Madonna started with the premise that most pregnant women are adults who would like to dress as adults rather than as Raggedy Ann or Pollyanna. The idea took off beyond anyone's imagination. It was helped along by the rising number of women who combine careers with families and therefore need good clothing that is stylish even in the advanced stages of pregnancy. Old-fashioned ideas fell by the wayside. One such idea was that a pregnant woman should be hidden, either by staying home or by being swathed in voluminous clothing. Another was that maternity clothes should be inexpensive, since no one wants to pay a lot of money for an outfit worn a maximum of five months. Lady Madonna helped banish these concepts once and for all with fashionable, functional maternity clothing.

MANOLA MATERNITY
1040 Lexington Ave (bet 74th and 75th St)   212 861-1227
Mon-Sat: 11–7

Manola doesn't just design clothes, she cuts them to the required maternity measurements. This is why celebrity clients like Caroline Kennedy and Kathie Lee Gifford make this store their maternity headquarters. There really is a Manola; she is Manola Dominguez, a native of Spain, who has become the doyenne of maternity chic in Manhattan. She shows a fine collection of silk, wool, and cotton garments, specializing in custom-made dresses for special occasions and business wear.

Women's Millinery

DON MARSHALL
120 E 56th St, Suite 640   212 758-1686
Mon-Sat: 10:30–5; closed Sat from April to Sept

Personal milliners are a rare breed, even in fashion-conscious New York. In fact, Don Marshall, who's been in business over 40 years, says his is a dying art, and he can see the writing on the wall. "It's too bad," he says. "This is a beautiful profession. Years from now, people will look at these hats and be amazed at the care that was taken to make each piece." He's right, although it shouldn't take years for Marshall's work to be appreciated. All of Marshall's hats and clothing (often in matching ensembles) are custom-made. Your purchase could well be an instant heirloom, while its quality and style will always keep it fashionable. Marshall, who could be a crabby old craftsman or even a fashion snob, is actually one of the friendliest guys you'll ever meet.

HATS IN THE BELFRY
Pier 17 Pavilion, South Street Seaport   212 406-2574
Mon-Thurs: 10–9; Fri, Sat: 10–10; Sun: 11–8

The Pier 17 Pavilion, an addition to the South Street Seaport, is a popular gathering place for the young financial district crowd, as well as tourists. Many of the shops have sister stores in Rousse-inspired redevelopment projects in other cities, and Hats in the Belfry is among them. So if you're from Washington, Baltimore, Philadelphia, Annapolis, St. Louis, or New Orleans, you may already be familiar with the shop, which has a stock as cute as its name and a reputation that's unusual for such a location. Novelty hats for children and adults (the Statue of Liberty, animals) and theatrical-style hats are lined up alongside ladies' designer hats and some of the sharpest men's hats found anywhere. They're also one of the few places that will still steam, brush, and stretch hats. First-rate service and selection, all at the charming seaport.

MANNY'S MILLINERY SUPPLY COMPANY
26 W 38th St   212 840-2235
Mon-Fri: 9–5:30; Sat: 9–3:30

Manny's is another New York institution. They carry millinery supplies, and that's an understatement. There are row after row of drawers, built against the walls, and each is dedicated to a particular aspect of head adornment. The section for ladies' hatbands alone takes up almost 100 boxes and runs the gamut from thin pearl lines to wide leather Western-style belts. They have rhinestone banding and an enormous selection of artificial flowers and feathers. The center of the store is lined with tables that display accumulated odds and ends, as well as several bins of larger items that don't fit in the wall drawers. At the front, hat forms can be found on hat-tree stands. The front, incidentally, displays sample hats in no particular order. Manny's will help fix up any hat and play with interchangeable decorations for it. Manny's also sells completed hats, close-outs, and samples, and they will even re-create an old hat.

PAUL'S VEIL AND NET
66 W 38th St (bet Fifth and Sixth Ave)   212 391-3822
Mon-Fri: 8:30–4; Sat: 8:30–2

It is inconceivable that the mob scene here is repeated up and down the block, and that even *that* is a mere fraction of the bridal business nationwide. Despite the competition from its neighbors (or perhaps because of it), Paul's would be a first-choice recommendation for any bride-to-be who wants to put together her own bridal headpiece. Although they deal in illusion (lace, that is), they are one of the few stores on the block that does not maintain the illusion that they are a wholesale-only outfit, doing the lowly retail customer a big favor by unbarring the doors. The staff at Paul's seems genuinely glad to see you—glad to share your joy and help you create a truly unique bridal veil or crown. The store stocks all the equipment needed for the rest of the bridal party, as well as unusual accessories, bridal supplies, and a great collection of imported headpieces created from flowers. The lucky bride will find both the outfit and the savings extraordinary.

Women's Small Sizes

PIAFFE PROFESSIONAL
512 Seventh Avenue, 39th floor   212 869-3320
Mon-Fri: 9–5, by appointment

This is a personalized shopping service for the petite woman who is five feet four inches and under, size 2–12. They will search out fashionable and unique merchandise for the "little lady."

Women's Undergarments

A. W. KAUFMAN
73 Orchard St (bet Broome and Grand St)
212 226-1629, 212 226-1788
Sun-Thurs: 10:30–5; Fri: 10–2

With three generations in the business, Kaufman handles only the finest in ladies' lingerie and lounge wear at prices that are substantially less than what uptown stores charge. Kaufman's discounts are so good that top-quality merchandise here is competitively priced with lesser quality available elsewhere. Kaufman's line includes practical wear, such as lounge wear, hostess gowns, pajamas, slips, bikini briefs, terry robes, bridal sets, quilted velour robes, and flannel gowns, plus items such as pure silk underwear and hand-embroidered accessories that are both luxurious and downright frivolous. Underwear, gowns, and robes from France, Switzerland, and Belgium are also available at sensible prices.

BRIEF ESSENTIALS
1407 Broadway (bet 38th and 39th St)   212 921-8344
Mon-Fri: 8:30–5:30

Don't expect pleasant service at this one! Shop here for no other reason than to brag that you got your sensational lingerie and exercise wear at 1407 Broadway—that veritable bastion of inaccessibility in the wholesale garment center. No matter that Brief Essentials is off the lobby and is a legitimate store; if you can buy anything in this building, you've arrived! Not incidentally, the selection is great, if only slightly risqué. "Sensuous lingerie for the sensual woman" is their boast, and you'd better believe that a women's lingerie store doing business in a building full of men who wholesale women's fashions has got to offer the best in terms of quality, fashion, and price.

GOLDMAN AND COHEN
55 Orchard St   212 966-0737
Sun-Fri: 9–5

Goldman and Cohen specializes in name-brand underwear and lingerie for women at a great discount. The lines include almost anything that falls within those two categories. This is one of the best!

IMKAR COMPANY
(M. KARFIOL AND SON)
294 Grand St (bet Allen and Eldridge St)   212 925-2459
Sun-Thurs: 10–5; Fri: 9:30–2; Sun (summer): 10–3

Imkar carries pajamas, underwear, and shifts for both men and women at about one-third off retail prices. A full line of Carter's infants' and children's wear is also available at good prices. The store has a fine line of women's lingerie, including dusters, gowns, and layettes. Featured names include Model's Coat, Vanity Fair, Arrow, Jockey, Hanes, Lollipop, and Munsingwear.

MENDEL WEISS
91 Orchard St (at Broome St)   212 925-6815
Sun-Thurs: 9:30–5:30; Fri: 9:30–4

Mendel Weiss is one of the stalwarts in the Lower East Side tradition of selling ladies' undergarments and lounge wear at sizable discounts. Depending on the dates of the merchandise, prices can range from wholesale (10% above cost) to markdowns of as much as 75%. Weiss includes T-shirts and bathing suits in his collection. Trained specialists are available to aid mastectomy fittings. This is not a glamorous shopping environment, but lingerie styles don't change much from season to season, and you can save money here.

SAMANTHA JONES
1074 Third Ave (bet 63rd and 64th St) 212 308-6680
Mon-Sat: 11–7; Sun: 1–5

Samantha Jones, the owner and operator of her own namesake boutique, specializes in contemporary and glamorous lingerie. Her collection consists of art-deco styling in robes, gowns, teddies, and camisoles, and an interesting collection of undergarments, silk scarfs and wraps, and Samantha Jones fragrances. When you're in trouble at home, fellas, this is the place to come for something special for a special lady.

SCHACHNER FASHIONS
95 Delancey St (bet Orchard and Ludlow St) 212 677-0700
Sun-Fri: 9–5:30

For over 35 years Schachner has been a Lower East Side institution, selling brand-name robes, sleepwear, underwear, and lounge wear at discount prices. They are still doing what they do best!

VICTORIA'S SECRET
34 E 57th St (bet Park and Madison Ave)
212 758-5592, 800 888-8200
Mon-Wed, Fri: 10–7; Thurs: 10–8; Sat: 10–6; Sun: 12–5

This has to be one of the sexiest stores in the world, in terms of ambience. The beautiful lingerie and bedroom garb, bridal peignoirs, exclusive silks, and accessories are displayed against the most alluring backdrops. Combine all of this with absolutely charming personnel and, gentlemen, this is *the* place to buy the most personal gifts for your lady.

Coins, Stamps

HARMER ROOKE NUMISMATISTS
3 E 57th St, 6th floor 212 751-1900
Mon-Fri: 9:30–5; Sat: 10–2:30

Harmer Rooke is a virtual cornucopia of coins, antique items, and fine collectibles, all stocked in abundance and available in hundreds of different styles and price ranges. Howard Rose, one of the managers, says: "In antiquities alone, we have thousands of items on display, priced from a few dollars to $10,000." They feature Greek, Roman, Judaic, pre-Columbian, Egyptian, and Middle Eastern coins, jewelry, and artifacts. There are also collections of American antiques, paper money, and tribal arts, among others. Each collection can stand among its peers throughout the country. Taken together, under one roof, it's positively staggering. The personnel behind the counters are knowledgeable and helpful, even if you don't make a purchase.

STACKS RARE COINS
123 W 57th St (nr Sixth Ave)   212 582-2580
Mon-Fri: 10–5

Stacks, established in 1858, is the country's oldest and largest rare-coin dealer. With a specialty in rare coins, medals, and paper money of interest to collectors, Stacks has a solid reputation for individual service, integrity, and knowledge of the field. In addition to walk-in business, Stacks runs ten public auctions a year. Both neophyte and experienced numismatists will do well at Stacks.

SUBWAY STAMP SHOP
111 Nassau St (bet Ann and Beekman St)
212 227-8637, 800 221-9960
Mon-Fri: 9:30–5:30

Subway has operated a subterranean stamp shop for over half a century, offering discounts to collectors and becoming the largest mail-order stamp and coin-supply company in the world. A look at their 50-page catalog (obtainable for $1 postage) will explain why they are so successful. The prices are right for all their merchandise, including reference books, stamps, and stamp products; there is even a new-issue service.

Computers
(See also Electronics section)

COMPUTERS
7 Great Jones St (bet Broadway and Lafayette St)
212 254-9000
Mon-Fri: 10–6:30 (Thurs till 7); Sat: 11–6

This outfit has been in business since 1978, before computers had become a way of life. They are particularly expert in movie-industry software and CAD systems, as well as entry-level systems for beginners. They offer expert training and a good selection of point-of-sale systems and software, as well as desktop publishing systems and software. The folks here are patient and easy on beginners and those who are still afraid of these machines. Prices are very competitive.

Where did the name "Brooklyn Dodgers" come from? *"Dodgers"* was an abbreviation for trolley dodgers. The name became common during the early part of the 20th century, when trolley cars were familiar sights in Brooklyn. It was said that you were a trolley dodger if you were able to weave your way through traffic; it was only natural to relate that to the agility needed on the playing field!

SOFTWARE, ETC.

101 Fifth Ave (bet 17th and 18th St)   212 727-3280
Mon-Fri: 9:30–8; Sat: 9:30–6:30; Sun: 11–6

1120 Ave of the Americas (at 44th St)   212 921-7855
Mon-Fri: 9:30–7; Sat: 10–6; Sun: 11–5

162 E 53rd St   212 753-7780
Mon-Fri: 9–6:30; Sat: 12–5

666 Fifth Ave (at 52nd St)   212 315-4744
Mon-Fri: 8:30–7; Sat: 9:30–6:30; Sun: 11:30–5

2300 Broadway (bet 83rd and 84th St)   212 362-3460
Mon-Thurs: 10–8; Fri, Sat; 10–10; Sun; 12–8

Software, Etc. is the largest resource for computer accessories, books, and software in the area, with highly competitive prices. Their staff are very knowledgeable, and their return policy is generous. Customers may make use of computer demonstration equipment, and they will special-order any book or piece of software.

Cosmetics, Drugs

BOYD'S OF MADISON AVENUE

655 Madison Ave (at 60th St)   212 838-6558, 212 838-5524
Mon-Fri: 8:30–7; Sat: 9:30–6; closed Sat in July, Aug

Boyd is a drugstore in a city full of drugstores, so it has to have something special to be worthy of mention. Naturally, it does. In addition to a drug and prescription service, Boyd carries a complete line of cosmetics, soaps, jewelry, and brushes. The latter range from the common to the esoteric: i.e., nail brushes and mustache combs in a variety of sizes and shapes. I started my retailing career in the drug department of the family store and can vouch that Boyd has one of the most complete selections of drugs, cosmetics, and sundries. But shopping in this store is not always pleasant, because of an attitude problem. A new boutique department carries handbags, gloves, jackets, and hair accessories.

COSMETIC WORLD AND GIFT CENTER

393 Fifth Ave, 2nd floor (bet 36th and 37th St)   212 213-4047
Mon-Fri: 10–6 (Sat only during Christmas holidays)

Right in the heart of the city you can find cosmetics, crystal pieces, figures, handbags, jewelry, ties, and men's and women's fragrances at discounts that range from 15% to 50%. You will not find every major brand in stock at all times, but there are excellent buys on such well-known names as Chanel, Opium, Estee Lauder, Calvin Klein, Krizia, and Albert Nipon. Cosmetic World has a multilingual staff, a corporate gift program, and telephone and mail-order facilities.

ESSENTIAL PRODUCTS
90 Water St (bet Wall St and Hanover Sq)   212 344-4288
Mon-Fri: 9–6

Essential Products has been manufacturing flavors and fragrances for nearly a hundred years. They know that an enormous percentage of the price of colognes and perfumes pays for advertising and packaging, so they set out to see how closely they could duplicate expensive scents at cheap prices. They describe their fragrances as "elegant interpretations" of designer names sold at a small fraction of the original's price. Essential features 49 sensual perfumes and 20 men's colognes, and they offer a money-back guarantee. If you send a self-addressed stamped envelope, they will send you scented cards and ordering information.

KAUFMAN PHARMACY
557 Lexington Ave (at 50th St)   212 755-2266
Daily: 24 hours

I hope Kaufman's is one phone number in New York you will never need, but it's wonderful to know it's there. In addition to the usual drugstore operation—soda fountain, sundries, cigarettes, electrical goods, and traveling needs—Kaufman's has a prescription department that's always open. Should the nightmare of being ill in a New York City hotel room actually happen to you, it's nice to know a pharmacy is open and ready to deliver your prescription by cab. Bless them! (Incidentally, should you need a doctor to write that prescription, check this book's special telephone numbers.)

KIEHL'S
109 Third Ave (bet 13th and 14th St)   212 677-3171
Mon-Fri: 10–6:30; Sat: 10–6

Kiehl's has been a New York institution since 1851. It is a fourth-generation, family-owned company unlike any you have ever visited. Their special treatments and preparations are made by hand and distributed internationally. Natural ingredients are used in the full lines of cleansers, scrubs, toners, moisturizers, eye-area preparations, men's creams, masks, body moisturizers, bath and shower products, sports items, ladies' leg-grooming formulations, shampoos, conditioners, and treatments. Customers can also enjoy an unusual collection of memorabilia related to aviation and motorcycles—interests of the Aaron Morse family, which runs this famous shop.

PARISIAN PERFUMES & COSMETICS
123 Fifth Ave (bet 19th and 20th St)   212 254-5300
Mon-Fri: 9–5; Sat: 9–4

Are your tired of paying big prices for your favorite perfumes and colognes? Looking for some really nice gifts? Parisian stocks a large selection of top domestic and European brands, at discount.

Crafts

ALLCRAFT TOOL AND SUPPLY COMPANY
45 W 46th St, 3rd floor   212 840-1860
Mon-Thurs: 9–4:45; Fri: 9–4

If there is a definitive jewelry-making supply store, Allcraft is it. Allcraft's catalog is so all-inclusive that it's impossible to describe. There is a complete line of tools and supplies for jewelry making, silversmithing, metal smithing, lost-wax casting, and much more. Out-of-towners usually deal with the mail-order catalog, but New Yorkers don't miss an opportunity to visit this gleaming cornucopia. (For a catalog, write them at 666 Pacific Street, Brooklyn, NY 11217.)

CERAMIC SUPPLY OF N.Y. & N.J.
534 La Guardia Pl (bet Bleecker and 3rd St)   212 475-7236
Mon-Fri: 9–6; Sat: 10–5

Ceramic Supply runs the whole wheel of pottery. They have a school, sell supplies and equipment, and hand-make pottery, all from the same location. These people eat and breathe pottery, and their enthusaism shows in all of their projects. If classes aren't convenient, Ceramic Supply carries books and materials for self-starters. One can do everything from buying an ashtray to casting a mold at this location.

CLAYWORKS
332 E 9th St (bet First and Second Ave)   212 677-8311
Mon-Thurs: 3–7; Fri: 3–8

Clayworks is a place where true handmade American crafts and crafts-people are appreciated. All of Clayworks' pottery is lead-free and dishwasher- and microwave-safe. You can watch a talented artist, Helaine Sorgen, at work and ask questions about what is going on. Small classes in wheel throwing are given for adults. Everything here is individually produced, from teapots to casseroles, mugs, and saké sets. Decorative pieces include vases, platters, and bowls. You won't see them duplicated anywhere else!

COMMON GROUND
19 Greenwich Ave   212 989-4178
Mon, Tues, Thurs, Fri: 11:30–7:30; Wed: 11–7; Sat: 11–7;
Sun: 12–6

Coming from Oregon, where a multitude of artifacts and crafts are made and sold by native Indians, I am familiar enough with this kind of merchandise to know that Common Ground has an excellent selection of American Indian jewelry, furniture, rugs, baskets, and the like. The folks in the shop are proud of their stock and will take time to explain the origin of each item. Please note, however, that the address is

Greenwich *Avenue,* not Greenwich *Street.* Greenwich Avenue is a crosstown street in the Village, while Greenwich Street runs north-south from the Village down into TriBeCa.

ELDER CRAFTSMAN
846 Lexington Ave (bet 64th and 65th St)   212 535-8030
Mon: 11–5:30; Tues-Fri: 10–5:30; Sat: 11–5:30
Closed Sat in July, Aug

The Elder Craftsmen epitomizes all that is great about New York. It is strictly a nonprofit organization at which everything sold is certifiably handmade by a senior citizen at least 55 years old. Often in desperate need of both money and something to do, these talented people are able to satisfy both needs, keeping half of the purchase price for everything they make. (The remaining money goes to operating expenses for the shop.) Most work is of a higher quality than that of machine-made items.

ERICA WILSON
717 Madison Ave (at 63rd st), 2nd floor   212 832-7290
Mon-Wed, Fri, Sat: 10–6; Thurs: 10–7

Erica Wilson is a lady of many talents. This British émigré not only writes books and newspaper columns about needlework, but also finds time to run a store that supplies almost anything a needlework enthusiast might require. There is a huge stock of knitting yarns, ranging from alpaca to cashmere, and you'll find the city's finest selection of hand-painted needlepoint patterns from London and elsewhere. You can select hand-knitted sweaters or beautiful accessories from Erica's stock. Her chintz bags are very special. Blocking, padding, mounting, finishing — and classes in these skills — are available but not inexpensive.

IL MERCATO
341 E 9th St (bet First and Second Ave)   212 260-6329
Mon-Fri: 12:30–8:30; Sat: 12:30–9; Sun: 1–7:30

"Il Mercato" means "the Market," and that is exactly what you will find here. The prices are right at this international crafts bazaar, where you will find beautiful jewelry, antique furniture, and home furnishings, as well as unusual gift items from all over the world. This house will also rent items you might want to use for a party, television show, or other special event.

LOVELIA ENTERPRISES
356 E 41st St (in Tudor City)   212 490-0930
Mon-Fri: 9:30–5 (by appointment only)

Lovelia F. Albright's establishment is one of New York's great finds. From a shop in Tudor City, overlooking the United Nations, she dispenses the finest European Gobelin and Aubusson machine-woven tapestries at prices that are often one-third that of any other place. The tapestries are exquisite. Some of the designs depict the ubiquitous unicorns cavorting in a medieval scene; others are more modern. They come in all sizes. The latest additions include tapestries for upholstery, wool-pile miniature rugs for use as mats under *objets d'art,* and an extensive line of tapestry-woven borders. They're designed by Albright and made exclusively for her in Austria. Write for a very impressive mail-order catalog.

PERFORMERS OUTLET
222 E 85th St   212 249-8435
Tues-Thurs: 12–7; Fri: 3–7:30; Sat: 11–5:30

Performers Outlet was started as a cooperative venture to market the non-show business talents of show-business people who have lots of time and little money on their hands. The concept worked so well that several would-be performers gave up the lively arts to develop full-time crafts careers. Today, very few of the crafts are of amateur quality, and standards are so high that performers are barely even represented. Most items are made by professional craftsmen from this country and France, and the evolution has been such that the gallery now goes by the name of Francophilia Americana Gallery, as well as Performers Outlet. Craftsmen can be commissioned for specific projects, and a search service is offered. There is also color-coordinating of glass, pottery, rag rugs, picture frames, candles, flowers, and other decorating accessories. The atmosphere is still homey.

RADIO HULA
169 Mercer St (bet Houston and Prince St)   212 226-4467
Tues-Sat: 12–7

This is the only retail gallery on the East Coast dedicated to the native culture of Hawaii and the South Pacific. They carry traditional and contemporary Hawaiian arts and crafts, including woodcarving, weaving, clothing, gourmet foods, jewelry, books, and other unusual items.

SCULPTURE HOUSE
30 E 30th St (nr Madison Ave)   212 679-7474
Mon-Fri: 10–4

In 1918 Bruner F. Barrie's family established a small sculpture and pottery workshop in Manhattan. The business grew and grew, and today, after a move further downtown, it offers everything necessary for the serious sculptor. Note the word *serious,* because Sculpture House, while pleasant and informative, hasn't the time or space to initiate neophytes. It's assumed that customers know exactly what they want. Sculpture House offers 16 different types of clay bodies, tools for ceramics and pottery, and more than a thousand woodcarving tools that the Barrie business manufactures itself. While sculpture normally implies ceramics and clay, Claire Brush says that 40% of the business is related to woodcarving. Sculpture House also offers a wide variety of services, and while there are no formal classes, every conceivable related book can be found here.

SUNRAY YARN
349 Grand St (bet Essex and Ludlow St)   212 475-0062
Sun-Fri: 9:30–5; closed one week in July and Dec

Sunray is another of the Lower East Side needlework shops, featuring the wide selection and hefty discounts characteristic of the area. In addition to the best prices on DMC and precut rug yarns, Sunray also has yarns for knitting (hand and machine), needlepoint kits and components, stitchery, latch-hook and punch rugs, and crocheting. They also do a brisk business in custom pillow design and needlework framing. Instructors write out knitting- and crocheting-pattern instructions for customers and help with any difficulties.

WOMEN'S EXCHANGE
1095 Third Ave (at 64th St)   212 753-2330
Mon-Sat: 10–6

The Women's Exchange was started over a hundred years ago to provide a marketplace for the crafts of women widowed by the Civil War. Over the years it evolved into a source of income for retired governesses, housekeepers, and down-at-the-heels gentlewomen. In recent years it has regrouped and moved, but the tradition as a showcase for women's crafts continues. They are particularly known for their hand-smocking on children's clothing. Every item is one-of-a-kind. There are dolls, shawls, mittens, fabrics, pillows, handbags, accessories, and model furniture for sale. While prices are not cheap, they are certainly competitive. The women receive 75% of the sale, so you are helping to support them while dressing your children.

YARN CENTER
1011 Sixth Ave   212 719-5648
Mon-Fri: 10–6

The New York Yarn Center has become a discount establishment that concentrates on needlecraft items and accessories. They have one of the largest selections of DMC yarns in the area—over 3,000 colors and textures in all. You'll find Persian and tapestry yarns; cross-stitch books; kits for cross-stitch, embroidery, and crewel; and a tremendous assortment of wools for knitting and crocheting.

Dance Items

BALLET SHOP
1887 Broadway (bet 62nd and 63rd St)   212 581-7990
Mon-Sat: 11–7:30

This shop is a mecca for ballet fans. While the name presupposes an inundation of tutus and leotards, the store has only a few decorating the walls. The entire display area of the store is devoted to books, records, and other memorabilia. Available are gift and novelty items, rare and out-of-print books, limited editions, new books, albums, programs, posters, art, collector's items, ballet and opera videotapes, and autographs of stars. There are no ballet supplies, but now you know where to get T-shirts featuring stars of the dance in several poses.

Department Stores and Malls

At the start of this section you will find a listing of special factory-outlet type shopping in the greater New York and surrounding area. If you have time, some absolutely great bargains can be grabbed from this unique compilation of the very best in discount shopping.

After several tumultuous years, the department-store scene in Manhattan has settled down. We have lost some great old names like Alexander's, Bonwit Teller, and B. Altman, while witnessing major changes in many of the remaining stalwarts.

Bloomingdale's and **Macy's** are still the largest and most complete department stores. Both have had their fiscal problems, but now they are back on sound footing. Bloomie's primarily features merchandise found only in their store, while Macy's appeals to a more price-conscious buyer. You will find nearly every famous name in both of these establishments; watch for periodic sales events, and you will do well at the cash register. Service can be frustrating, as much part-time help is used, due to extended hours.

For tops in fashion, the two great stores are **Saks Fifth Avenue** and **Bergdorf Goodman.** Saks has undergone an almost complete facelift, with sparkling new sections on every floor. Deep stocks of fine merchandise for both men and women can be found here. Bergdorf Goodman remains an oasis of class in a sea of upheaval. Top names and service are the bywords. Well-dressed women will find the world's smartest clothes, while men now have their own equally impressive digs across the street. The home-accessories sections at Bergdorf are especially appealing.

Henri Bendel has a magnificent new store on Fifth Avenue, just around the corner from their previous home. It is a very attractive emporium where shoppers are enticed by unique displays and diverted into special corners. **Lord & Taylor** has long been a favorite for fashion-conscious shoppers, and it still is. American designers are featured.

Although it's not really a department store, **Barney's** offers a vast array of clothing and accessories for men, women, and boys in their three stores. The legendary main store downtown is difficult to shop in but offers huge selections. The newest one uptown brings increased retail competition to the Upper East Side.

There are four major malls in Manhattan, although they differ from the typical suburban mall because of space limitations.

Trump Tower (Fifth Avenue near 56th Street) is a vertical mall filled with upscale stores. Many of them serve as showrooms for leading overseas manufacturers and retailers. There are eating facilities, lots of marble, and even a waterfall! It is definitely a tourist stop.

A&S, a busy and well-managed store that appeals to middle America, is the main tenant at **A&S Plaza** (Sixth Avenue and 33rd Street). Floor after floor of specialty shops and a bustling food fair have brought new life to the Herald Square area.

Next door is the remnant of **Herald Center**, a much less successful mall that never really got off the ground (although it is a pretty big place). **Toys 'R' Us** and **Kids 'R' Us** are the main attractions in the building at the present time.

Further downtown you can relax, eat, and shop at the mall in the **World Financial Center** (Battery Park City). The centerpiece here is the magnificent Winter Garden. What a place for a party! The waterfront setting is special for looking, resting, or whatever. A number of classy stores make up the complex.

The **South Street Seaport,** a picturesque and historic area, attracts more tourists than residents. Pier 17 has some interesting shops, but the eating establishments in the area leave a lot to be desired. In nice weather there is outdoor entertainment, and the various harbor activities are popular.

Department Store Clearance Centers

Abraham & Strauss: 155 Glencove Road, Carleplace, Long Island, NY (516 742-8500): Home furnishings

Bloomingdale's: 155 Glencove Ave, Carleplace, Long Island, NY (516 248-1400): Home furnishings

Lord & Taylor: 3601 Hempstead Ave, Levittown, Long Island, NY (516 731-5031) and 839–60 New York Ave, Huntington, Long Island, NY (516 673-0009): Clothing

Macy's: 174 Glencove Road, Glencove, Long Island, NY (516 746-1490): Home furnishings

Most of these centers are open every day, but it is best to call for hours and specific merchandise.

Department Stores

BERGDORF GOODMAN
754 Fifth Ave (at 58th St)   212 753-7300
BERGDORF GOODMAN MEN
745 Fifth Ave (at 58th St)   212 753-7300
Mon-Wed, Fri, Sat: 10–6; Thurs 10–8

Sitting in a prime location on Fifth Avenue, just off a corner of Central Park, Bergdorf is the epitome of class. The operation has broadened its appeal in recent years, reaching out to young and affluent customers scared away by the cold atmosphere of previous years. Many sections of the store have been redone into smaller boutiques. Lines have been expanded, and an efficient transportation system has been completed. Dollar sales per square foot are among the highest in the nation. Bergdorf emphasizes top fashion names in all departments; many of the styles shown are found exclusively in this store. Their windows usually display a fine selection of this apparel. The top floor presents an exciting array of home-accessory merchandise, carefully selected and beautifully displayed. Several trendy eating places allow shoppers to spend more time in the store. Personnel here are great if they know you; if not, don't appear in your grubbies. A separate men's store is located across the street. There you'll find top names for men, along with prices to match. If you're looking for a special men's gift, or if you are a gentleman intent on appearing in the best-of-the-best, Bergdorf Goodman Men is the place to go.

BLOOMINGDALE'S
1000 Third Ave   212 355-5900
Mon, Thurs: 10–9; Tues, Wed, Fri, Sat: 10–6; Sun: 12–6

For visitors to the Big Apple, a trip is not complete without a day at Bloomie's. For residents, it is an institution. Folks either love the store or won't set a foot inside. Since 1879, Bloomingdale's has been a major force on the national retailing scene. There is no other store quite like it. If you are looking for something new, chances are it will be here first. Major designers choose Bloomie's to present their latest styles. Cosmetics outfits will launch new products in the store's huge, busy street-floor beauty bars. The fashion floors are filled with top labels from all over the world. The children's floors (8 and 9) have a great new look, and the selection of moderate and career apparel on 2 is outstanding. The men's furnishings areas are a treasure trove for gentlemen who want to see what is currently in style, but the men's clothing area is just so-so. The furniture department and home-accessories areas are New York's best. No visit to the store is complete without a stroll down the "Main Course" on the 6th floor. If you are hungry, Le Train Bleu (classy dining in a simulated railroad diner) or Forty Carrots (counter-style, excellent salads, sandwiches, and yogurt) are first-class. On the down side, crowds can be overwhelming, prices are not in the bargain category (except for some excellent sales events from time to time), and service leaves a bit to be desired. There are a number of services available, however, including personal shoppers and decorators. A visit here is more than a shopping trip; it is an experience. (P.S. Don't miss the great Martine's daily handmade chocolates on 6!)

CENTURY 21 DEPARTMENT STORES
22 Cortlandt St (at Broadway and Church St)　　212 227-9092
Mon-Fri: 7:45–7; Sat: 10–6:30

　Ask anyone who works in the Wall Street area where they like to shop best, and the answer you will get most often is Century 21. Why? Because its 16 departments carry an amazing selection of quality merchandise for men, women, children, and the home at discounts that run from 25% to 75% off normal retail prices. Outstanding areas include the housewares, women's shoes, and children's departments, where the brand names are tops and the prices comfortable. Don't expect fancy fitting rooms and the special amenities that cost uptown stores more money. But service is informed and courteous, and you won't be disappointed.

HENRI BENDEL
712 Fifth Ave (bet 55th and 56th St)　　212 247-1100
Mon-Sat: 10–6:30 (Thurs: 10–8); Sun: 12–6

　Having spent a major portion of my adult life in the retail business, I know stores pretty well. There are not many fine stores in this country or abroad that I have not visited. I can say, without equivocation, that the Henri Bendel store on Fifth Avenue is one of the classiest around. Founded in 1896 as a millinery store, Bendel's was a fixture on West 57th Street for years. In a boutique setting, the store catered to high-fashion women's apparel for the upwardly mobile New Yorker. The new store, in the former Coty Building, keeps the same boutique atmosphere but expands it into a series of shops that exude fashion, quality, and excitement. You will want to buy something in every section you visit; it is that colorful and attractive! Wood is used prominently throughout, and the magnificent original windows by Rene Lalique have been incorporated into the store design in a most appealing manner. The store recreates the ambience of Paris in the 1920s. Don't miss the Parfumerie, the "Kidz" section, the Salon de Thé (sandwiches, salads, pastries, and more by Les Delices Guy Pascal), and the Tabletoppings by McIntosh. A concierge service is provided, and the store includes the only American branch of the Institut Jeanne Gatineau, a French spa. Bendel's "stylists" can take you from boutique to boutique by oval staircases. (There are, happily, no escalators in the building!) Top billing is given to young, up-and-coming designers, and today's shopper will find a spectacular setting for her wardrobe selections.

LORD & TAYLOR
424 Fifth Ave (at 39th St)   212 391-3344
Mon, Tues, Fri, Sat: 10–7; Wed, Thurs: 10–8:30; Sun: 12–6

"Red, white, and blue" might be an appropriate way to describe this long-time player on the New York merchandising scene. For many years, this was *the* store for the working girl, an image that the legendary Dorothy Shaver cultivated when she headed Lord & Taylor. Today the store is owned by the May Company, successful merchants who have carved out a middle territory – price and fashion-wise – for their stores. So far, the strategy has been to strive for high volume with popularly priced goods that are actively promoted. If there is an underlying image, it is an emphasis on American designers. The store showcases good lines from local sources both in their ads and window displays. No longer is there a significant home-furnishings showing, and the men's areas have never been strong. But for the average woman who is looking for good value on clothing (and who does not want to put up with discount-store shopping), Lord & Taylor is an ideal alternative. What the store lacks in physical attractiveness (the first floor is one of the city's dullest), it makes up for in aggressive merchandising.

MACY'S
151 W 34th St (at Herald Square)   212 695-4400
Mon, Thurs, Fri: 10–8:30; Tues, Wed, Sat: 10–7; Sun: 11–6

The heart of New York might just be the giant Macy's store at Herald Square, "the world's largest department store." At one time this was certainly the heart of the retail world, as Macy's and Gimbel's fought it out across the street, with Saks 34th Street in between. In the battle, Macy's emphasized quantity rather than quality, and the store began to slip. Enter Ed Finkelstein, who brought his successful Macy's California formula to Manhattan, spruced up the store (beautiful new main floor, redone departments throughout), brought back top names and top-quality goods, and set out to reclaim the Macy's heritage. Now the retail battle pits Macy's and Bloomie's. A new element has been added, however, with the nearby arrival of A&S, which has brought back traffic to the area. Macy's excels in home furnishings and offers good values on children's merchandise, a great "Cellar" for fine foodstuffs and accessory items, and a dazzling main-floor cosmetics section. Numerous eating nooks are available, as is most every customer service known in the industry. At Easter time, the store is a magnificent garden scene, with live plants, flowers, and fountains. Macy's sale events offer special values and large selections. Shopping here is an experience; if you are addicted to the pastime, you'll love this place.

SAKS FIFTH AVENUE
611 Fifth Ave (at 50th St)   212 753-4000
Mon-Wed, Fri, Sat: 10–6:30; Thurs: 10–8; Sun: 12–6

Now there is even more of Saks to drool over! A 36-floor office and retail tower adjoins the original store, and 15,000 square feet of merchandising space has been added behind the escalators on each of the store's nine floors. The main floor has been completely and attractively redone. A new designer's shop for women has opened on level 3, and an expanded section for men's European clothing has been added on level 6. Cafe S.F.A., on the 8th floor, provides a rest stop for your feet and pocketbook. With a Bahrain-based holding company as a parent, financing here is not a problem. The store remains a quality institution of the highest order, where men and women and kids can be outfitted with the top names in the business. The career woman, the well-heeled young matron, and the society dowager will all find a huge selection of sportswear, dresses, formals, coats, suits, furs, and accessories with moderate to very expensive tabs. The men's clothing section is one of the best in the city. Ask for Dennis Weiner in this department; he is one of the last of the breed of truly concerned salesmen! (Hint: Smart shoppers save their dollars until Saks has a sale.)

TAKASHIMAYA
693 Fifth Ave (bet 54th and 55th St)   212 350-0100
Mon-Sat: 10–6 (Thurs till 8)

There is one thing you can say for sure about this new Manhattan store: it is different. Whether or not it will survive in Manhattan's hell-bent-for-shopping atmosphere is another question. Located on prestigious Fifth Avenue, right in the middle of the Tiffanys and Guccis, this store is as much a museum and gallery as it is a retail establishment. Old-line merchants will cringe to see the empty and underutilized spaces on the lower floors (galleries, garden items), but upstairs there are beautiful Japanese-made clothing and accessory items, home furnishings, and gifts. Downstairs is a Japanese café for rest and meditation.

Display Accessories

NIEDERMAIER DISPLAY DIVISION
138 W 25th St   212 645-0171
By appointment

Niedermaier designs and creates all kinds of displays, and they are considered the best. Although most of the business is conducted at trade shows, if you talk nicely (and mention this book) they will probably take care of an individual customer.

Domestics

AD HOC SOFTWARES
410 W Broadway (at Spring St)   212 925-2652
Mon-Sat: 11–7; Sun: 11:30–6

The name of this store means just what it says: soft textures for modern living. There is furniture, luggage, table-top items (china, glassware), robes, dressing gowns, pajamas, sheets and towels, blankets, and table linens. You will also find shower curtains, bathroom hardware, and steel occasional tables. You'll have a soft spot in your heart after you visit this unusual establishment!

D. PORTHAULT
18 E 69th St   212 688-1660
Mon-Fri: 10–5:30; Sat: 10–5

Porthault, the French queen of linens, needs no introduction. Custom-made linens are available in a range of 600 designs (more, if you count custom designs), scores of colors, and weaves of super luxurious density. Wherever the name Porthault appears—e.g., some fancy hotels—you know you're at a top-notch operation. The folks here are definitely top-notch. Their printed sheets seem to last forever; they're passed along from one generation to another. Porthault can handle custom work of an intricate nature for odd-sized beds, baths, and showers. Specialties include signature prints; printed terry towels; decorative accessories like trays, wastebaskets, tissue-box covers, drawer liners, and room sprays; and a large selection of other unusual gift items.

J. SCHACHTER'S
5 Cook St, Brooklyn
212 533-1150, 800 INTOBED
Mon-Thurs: 9–5; Fri: 9–2; Sun: 9–4

J. Schachter's is the foremost purveyor of quilts in the New York area and perhaps the entire continent. At some point, almost all quilts but those found in museums have been to Schachter's. Maybe it was purchased, restuffed, mended, or sewn anew there. Schachter's is the oldest quilting firm in New York, and they know everything there is to know about quilts and their making. They also do work in polyester, lamb's wool, and cotton. The talented staff can make a quilt in any size and in 20 different quilting patterns from any fabric given to them. Schachter's has a complete line of linens as well. Some of their bed linens come from Europe, and are offered at discount prices. Custom pillows can be made while you wait. When both lines are combined, entire bedrooms or bathrooms, from rugs to ceiling and wall coverings, can be coordinated.

PONDICHERRI
454 Columbus Ave (at W 82nd St)   212 875-1609
Mon-Sat: 11–7; Sun: 12–6

This is one of those stores that some people pass right by because the beautiful window displays make you think you'll never be able to afford anything inside. If you like exotic cotton prints and are looking for pillows, pillowcases, sheets, tablecloths, quilts, and the like, however, by all means do go in—both the selection and the prices are excellent. Keep an eye out for unusual small area rugs and interesting knickknacks, too. Because the selection is large and most things are folded on shelves, you might want to ask for help if you're looking for something specific.

PRATESI LINENS
829 Madison Ave (at 69th St)   212 288-2315
Mon-Sat: 10–6

Pratesi says it carries the best linens the world has to offer, and they're probably right. Families hand them down for generations, because they don't wear out. Customers who don't have affluent ancestors will wish to avail themselves of the two new collections that come out in the spring and fall. The Pratesi staff is unexcelled in coordinating linens to décor or creating a custom look. Nearly all of the linens are of natural fiber cloth (the upstairs maid can always do the ironing!), although there are some easy-care versions of late. The three-story store boasts a garden, which sets the mood for the luxurious linens. Towels are made in Italy exclusively for Pratesi and are of a quality and thickness that has to be felt to be believed. Bathrobes are magnificent—in natural fibers, plush, and quietly understated. (So are the price tags.) The baby boutique has been expanded.

Electronics, Appliances, FAX Machines

Don't say I didn't warn you! When visiting the numerous electronics, camera, and stationery-supply stores along Fifth Avenue and in the 50s along Sixth Avenue, don't be misled by the discounts quoted off the marked retail figure. In many cases, those prices are grossly inflated. It is a wise idea to shop around at reputable stores before deciding on your purchase.

BERNIE'S DISCOUNT CENTER
821 Sixth Ave (bet 28th and 29th St)   212 564-9431
Mon-Fri: 9–5:30; Sat: 11–3:30; closed in July, Aug

Bernie is nowhere to be seen, but the *discount* in the store's name is certainly apt. If you want to get first-class treatment, ask for George Vargas. Bernie's was the first appliance dealer in the country to discount the RCA Selectavision video recorder *before* the machine officially came out and at a time when it was the most popular item in town. Bernie's stocks electrical appliances, TVs, videogames, phone machines, refrigerators, washers, dryers, radios, tape recorders, and air conditioners from the finest names in the business (e.g., Mitsubishi, Sony, Panasonic, and Norelco). The discount may be better at some of the other stores mentioned in this section, but Bernie's is more conveniently located. Besides, Bernie's also services what it sells.

DEMBITZER BROS.
5 Essex St (at Canal St)   212 254-1310
Mon-Thurs: 10–5; Fri: 10–2; Sun: 10–5

Dembitzer was one of the first discount appliance stores on the Lower East Side, and it was so successful that it spawned many imitators. This is good for the consumer. With a host of competitors nearby, Dembitzer is constantly alert to keep the business it has garnered so far. They specialize in appliances that work in 220-volt, 50-cycle applications for overseas use. However, they also have appliances for domestic use. Dembitzer's motto is, "If it plugs in, we have it," but even that doesn't do justice to the stock. Left out of that description are pens, luggage, soda makers, cameras, film, *ad infinitum.* Dembitzer also breaks the Lower East Side rudeness code. Between them, the brothers speak 8 or 11 languages (depending on whom you ask). While they clearly don't have time to traffic with people who are "just looking" or comparing prices, they can be charming to real customers in any of those languages.

HARVEY ELECTRONICS
2 W 45th St (nr Fifth Ave)   212 575-5000
Mon-Fri: 9:30–6; Sat: 10–6

Not everyone understands all the fine points of the new technology flooding the markets these days. For those who need advice and individual attention, Harvey's is the place to shop for state-of-the-art consumer electronics. Home theater is their specialty. They offer top-of-the-line audio and video components and fully integrated audio and video systems. Harvey has developed an in-home design and installation division for both new and existing residences.

J&R MUSIC WORLD
15, 23, 27 Park Row (one block south of City Hall)
212 732-8600
Mon-Sat: 9–6:30; Sun: 11–6

These folks bill themselves as New York's most complete electronics and home-entertainment department store, and I believe them. You can find cameras, radios, televisions, speaker systems, VCRs, cassette and CD players, personal electronics, records, tapes, compact discs, computer systems, telephone answering machines, telephones, typewriters, microwave ovens, and even bread makers. The place is well organized but gets rather hectic at times. The prices are very competitive, and all merchandise is guaranteed.

PHONE BOUTIQUE
828 Lexington Ave (at 63rd St)   212 319-9650
Mon-Sat: 10–6:30

In my opinion, the breakup of Ma Bell was one of the saddest episodes in American corporate history. The confusion with the phone system since then has overwhelmed nearly everyone. Fortunately, there is a place in Manhattan where, under one roof, you can buy or rent new and antique-style phones, have them repaired, browse all kinds of answering machines, FAX machines, and telephone-related accessories, and even have your phone painted. They now also rent cellular phones and beepers to visitors.

SHARPER IMAGE
4 W 57th St (at Fifth Ave)   212 265-2550
900 Madison Ave   212 794-4974
Mon-Wed, Fri: 10–7; Thurs: 10–8; Sat: 10–6; Sun: 12–5

If you are a gadget freak (like me), you'll go wild at the Sharper Image. This is truly a grown-up's toy store! The very latest in electronic gadgets, household helpers, sports items, games, novelties, and clothing makes browsing this fascinating emporium a unique experience. There's also a branch on Pier 17 at the South Street Seaport.

SPECTRA RESEARCH GROUP
762 Madison Ave (bet 65th and 66th St)
212 744-2255, 800 342-0456
Mon-Sat: 9–6

Spectra offers consumers electronic solutions to contemporary problems. If that problem includes being overheard on the telephone, not being able to find or work a pocket-sized computer, or having difficulty spelling *deceive* (is it *ei* or *ie*?), then Spectra can be of great help. While the unreliable Fifth Avenue electronics stores major in customer deception and price ripoffs, these people have a one-price policy and offer only state-of-the-art items. Specialties include surveillance items and night-vision devices.

VICMARR STEREO AND TV
88 Delancey St   212 505-0380
Sun-Fri: 9–6

In the middle of famed Delancey Street on the Lower East Side, Mal Cohen presides over a treasure house of electronics, including microwave ovens, stereo and hi-fi equipment, multi-voltage items, telephones, answering machines, and camcorders, as well as such other items as organs, sunglasses, and fans. Unlike many electronics outfits, this place has everything on display, well organized and marked, with none of the high-pressure selling you often encounter. Best of all, the prices are right, and you can be assured of not getting secondhand merchandise. Vicmarr is one of the largest JVC outlets in the area. You can save yourself some time by calling for prices.

WAVES
32 E 13th St (bet University Pl and Fifth Ave)   212 989-9284
Tues-Fri: 12–6; Sat: 12–5

The past lives on at Waves, and Bruce and Charlotte Mager are trying to make it last forever with their collection of vintage record players, radios, receivers, and televisions. They have scorned the electronics age in favor of the age of radio. Their shop is a virtual shrine to the 1930s and before. Here you'll find the earliest radios (still operative) and their artifacts. There are even radio promotion pieces, such as a radio-shaped cigarette lighter and recording discs for crank-handled phonographs. Gramophones and anything dealing with the radio age are available, and Waves is capable of repairing privately owned instruments. Waves also rents phonographs, telephones, neon clocks, and "photographica" [*sic*] for media shoots. They also make appraisals and will answer any questions on repair, sales, or rental.

Environmental Interest

FELISSIMO
10 W 56th St   212 247-5656
Mon-Wed, Fri-Sat: 10–6; Thurs: 10–8; Sun: 12–5

This place is a must-see, even if you don't buy a thing. The theme of this magnificent four-story building, which was formerly a private residence, is the delicate balance between man and nature. All merchandise has been chosen to delight one's senses, and this it does in spades! Each of the eight rooms in this turn-of-the-century townhouse displays beautiful items like jewelry, scarfs, cashmeres, outdoor-living items, plants and flowers, gardening tools, and all sorts of antique accessories. There are sections for bed and bath products, clothing for men and women, toiletries, and unusual furniture. On the top floor you can relax and enjoy a tearoom dedicated to serving fine full-leaf teas like cinnamon plum, vanilla almond, mango Ceylon, Earl Grey, or ginger peach. Take your pick of black teas, green teas, and herbal teas. A visit here is an experience, believe me!

Fabrics, Trimmings

A.A. FEATHER COMPANY
(GETTINGER FEATHER CORPORATION)
16 W 36th St, 8th floor (bet Fifth and Sixth Ave)   212 695-9470
Mon-Thurs: 9–5; Fri: 9–3

Suppose you've made a quilt and want to stuff it with feathers? What if your latest outfit simply has to have an ostrich plume, feather fan, or feather boa? Well, you're in luck with A.A. Feather (a.k.a. Gettinger Feather Corporation). The Gettingers have been in the business since 1915 and have passed the trade down from grandfather to father to Dan Gettinger, who is the first Gettinger grandson. There aren't many such family businesses around now, and there are even fewer sources for really fine-quality feathers. This is a find!

A. FEIBUSCH—ZIPPERS & THREADS
30 Allen St   212 226-3964
Mon-Fri: 9–5; Sun: 9–4; closed Sun in summer

Would you believe a large store dedicated entirely to zippers? Well, in New York, nothing is impossible. One of the many amusing aspects of my visit here was hearing the boast, "We have one of the biggest selections of zippers in the USA." It's as if they really think there are zipper stores throughout the country! Feibusch does have zippers in every size, style, and color (hundreds of them), and if it's not in stock, they will make it to order. I saw one woman purchase tiny zippers for doll clothes! Should you need matching thread to sew in a zipper, Feibusch carries that as well. A selection of threads rivaling the number of zippers is available in all varieties. Eddie Feibusch assured me that no purchase is too small or too large, and he gives each customer prompt, personal service.

ART MAX FABRICS
250 W 40th St   212 398-0755, 398-0754, 398-0756
Mon-Fri: 8:30–6; Sat: 9–5

The fabric wholesale district is conveniently adjacent to the garment district, and the usual retail-shopper traditions of that area apply here. Some stores welcome retail customers, some don't, and some fluctuate with the market. Art Max is dedicated to the retail customer. Most languages are expertly spoken. The three floors are filled to overflowing with outstanding fabrics for clothing. They now carry full lines of fabric for everyday wear: linens, wools, cotton prints, solids, and silks. The really striking brocades, metallics, and laces require an experienced touch; it would be a shame for a novice to ruin such beautiful fabrics. The real specialty here, however, is bridal fabrics. When the fabrics mentioned above are made into gowns, the wedding party could rival a *Vogue* layout. There are a dozen different types of nets for bridal veils and infinite combinations of heavier materials. Try to get a peek at the basement, which looks like the catacombs!

B&J FABRICS
263 W 40th St (bet Seventh and Eighth Ave)   212 354-8150
Mon-Fri: 8–5:45; Sat: 9–4:45

B&J started in the fabric business in 1940 and is now run by the second and third generations of the Cohen family. There are three complete floors of fashion fabrics, many imported directly from Europe. Specialties of the house: natural fibers, designer fabrics, bridal fabrics, and silk prints. (There are over a thousand of the latter in stock.) Swatches are sent free of charge, upon request.

BECKENSTEIN MEN'S FABRICS
121 Orchard St   212 475-6666, 800 221-2727
Sun-Fri: 9–6

Simply put, this is the finest men's fabric store in the nation. These folks sell to about 90% of all custom tailors in the country, and also to many of the very finest manufacturers of men's clothing, so you know the goods are top quality. Their customer list reads like a who's who: Warren Beatty, Al Pacino, all three *Godfather* movies, Robert DeNiro, numerous diplomats and politicians, Magic Johnson, Wayne Gretsky, and on and on. You will find every kind of fabric, from goods selling for $10 a yard to fabulous pieces at $1000 a yard. There are pure cashmere, fine English suitings (super 120s and 150s), pure silks, camel hair, and much more. This is a professional operation that is not typical of most Lower East Side stores.

CINDERELLA FLOWER AND FEATHER COMPANY
60 W 38th St   212 840-0644
Mon-Fri: 9–5:15; Sat: 9–4:15

A few years back, in the midst of a particularly cold and dreary winter, Seventh Avenue fashions began to blossom with artificial flowers as the "in" look for spring. The department stores quickly got the message, and in just a few weeks, people were removing their fur-lined gloves to hand $10 over the counter for a single flower for their lapel. Many of these transactions were made along 34th Street or Fifth Avenue, and only a few wise New Yorkers walked an extra two blocks to the "trimmings district," where they could buy an identical flower for 35 cents. There were even buyers of the $10 variety who *knew* of the district and assumed that they couldn't get in! Cinderella Flower and Feather Company is for them. Jonathan Wolff, Cinderella's president, brags that they have the country's largest selection of feather trimmings, decorations, craft supplies, and conversation pieces, as well as silk and other artificial flowers. "Since we're the importer" he adds, "our prices are unbeatable."

FAR EASTERN FABRICS
171 Madison Ave (at 33rd St)   212 683-2623
Mon-Fri: 9–5

Far Eastern Fabrics is a small company that imports some lush fabrics from some of the world's most exotic places. From India, there are cotton prints, madras cottons, brocades, silks, and even silk saris and stoles. From China, there are more brocades and silks, plus damasks and woven and Jacquard tussah silk. Indonesia is represented by batiks, weavings, and cotton sarongs. Japanese pongee is among the least expensive silks Far Eastern offers, while Thailand is represented with a selection of cotton prints, silk scarfs, and stoles. There are even striking wax and java-print cottons from the Netherlands. Prices for these often unique fabrics are excellent. Far Eastern is really global in its intent to pick the finest.

GAMPEL SUPPLY
39 W 37th St (bet Fifth and Sixth Ave)   212 398-9222
Mon-Fri: 8:30–4

This is the kind of esoteric business New York does best. The sole stock in trade here is beads, and they know more about them than you will ever need to know. Just make a request, and you'll find that they have it—at a cheap price, too. While single beads go for a dollar each at a department store one block away, Gampel sells them in bulk for a fraction of that price. Though they prefer to deal in bulk and at wholesale, individual customers are treated as courteously as institutions, and the wholesale prices remain the same for all. As for the stock, well, a visit to Gampel is an education. Pearlized beads alone come in over 20 different guises, and they are used for everything from bathroom curtains to earrings and flowers. Since many of its customers are craftspeople, Gampel diverges slightly from its specialty to sell a few supplies for bead-related crafts. They stock needles, cartwheels, cord (in enough colors to match each bead), threads, poly bags, glues, jewelry tools, jewelry findings, and costume-jewelry parts and pieces.

HANDLOOM BATIK
214 Mulberry St (at Spring St)   212 925-9542
Wed-Sat: 12–7; Sun: 1–6; Mon, Tues by appointment

At Handloom you'll find one of the largest collections of batik outside a crafts museum. Carol Berlin runs Handloom Batik with near reverence for her merchandise. All of the fabrics are handmade, and she is quick to show how each can be set off to best advantage. Imported hand-woven and hand-batiked fabrics (primarily from India and Indonesia) are sold by the yard as fabric or are made up as clothing, napkins, tablecloths, and handiwork. Handloom Batik will also use its own fabrics for custom-made shirts and other garments. In addition, a gift selection features handicrafts of wood, stone, brass, and paper from the aforementioned countries. Pillows, bed covers, curtains, and napkins can be custom-made from the store's cotton *ikat* and batik.

HARRY ZARIN CO.
72 Allen St (at Grand St)   212 925-6112
Daily: 9–5:30

Imagine a city block full of upholstery- and drapery-fabric bargains! Harry Zarin has been in business for over a half century and shows one of the largest selections in the area at this outlet on the Lower East Side. Many of Manhattan's top decorators use this source.

HYMAN HENDLER AND SONS
67 W 38th St (bet Fifth and Sixth Ave)   212 840-8393
Mon-Fri: 9–5:30

Although Hyman Hendler has passed away, the store that proudly bears his name is in the capable hands of his sons and niece. In the middle of what may be the trimmings center of the world, Hyman Hendler is one of the oldest businesses (established in 1900) and probably the crown head of the ribbon field. This organization manufactures, wholesales, imports, and acts as a jobber for every kind of ribbon imaginable. It's hard to believe as many variations exist as are jammed into this store.

INTERCOASTAL TEXTILE CORPORATION
480 Broadway (at Broome St)   212 925-9235
Mon-Thurs: 9–6; Fri: 9–5; closed first two weeks in July;
Sun: 10–4 (Oct to Dec)

Intercoastal is an eight-story shop that carries decorator fabrics at wholesale prices. You must buy ample amounts of a particular item and know what you want when you come. The employees are accustomed to dealing with large department stores and decorators. Bloomcraft, Scalamandre, and Schumacher are some of the name brands that can be found here.

ISLAND FABRIC WAREHOUSE
406 Broadway (bet Canal and Walker St)   212 431-9510
Mon-Wed, Fri: 9–6; Thurs: 9–7:30; Sat, Sun: 10–5

Island Fabric Warehouse has three *very* full floors of every imaginable kind of fabric and trimming. Since all of it is sold at discount prices, it's one of the best places to buy fabrics. Some of the attractions include an extensive wool collection and such dressy fabrics as chiffon, crepe, silk, and satin. Most amazing are the bargain spots, where remnant and odd pieces go for so little it's laughable. Since Island Fabric Warehouse isn't exactly in the heart of the city, they sell an excellent selection of patterns, notions, and trimmings at the same low prices, so that customers don't have to make several stops.

LEATHER FACTS
262 W 38th St (bet Seventh and Eighth Ave)   212 382-2788
Mon-Fri: 9:30–6; Sat by appointment

François George dispenses all manner of leather, suede, and exotic skins. He concentrates upon custom-made actual skin clothing.

PARON FABRICS
60 W 57th St (bet Fifth and Sixth Ave)   212 247-6541
PARON II
56 W 57th St, 2nd floor
PARON WEST
239 W 39th St
SEW . . . NEW YORK
56 W 57th St, 3rd floor
Mon-Sat: 9–6; Sun: 11–3 (closed Sun in Dec-Feb, July, Aug)

Amazingly, you can find an excellent selection of designer fabrics uptown at discount prices! Paron carries the very latest, and many of the goods are available only in their stores. At their outlets (Paron II and Paron West) you can find a large selection of quality goods priced at 50% off. Their new sewing center, Sew . . . New York, offers classes, seminars, sewing-machine sales and service, and hard-to-find patterns. This is a family operation, so personal attention is assured.

PIERRE DEUX–FRENCH COUNTRY
870 Madison Ave (at 71st St)   212 570-9343
Mon-Sat: 10–6

Pierre Deux, the French Country home-furnishings company, specializes in authentic, handcrafted products from the provinces of France. Everything from 18th-century antique and reproduction furniture to fabrics, brightly colored pillows, faience, table linens, glassware, and bed linens can be found here. A personalized bridal registry and custom orders are also available.

SHERU ENTERPRISES
49 W 38th St (nr Fifth Ave)   212 730-0766
Mon-Fri: 9–6; Sat: 9:30–5

Sheru is almost impossible to describe. If you're into hobbies, crafts, or do-it-yourself decorating, Sheru has what you need. If you are an incurable bargain hunter, Sheru will satisfy your wildest dreams. And if you are none of these things, Sheru will guide, teach, and instruct you. Sheru is a wholesaler and retailer of beads and trimmings. Its stockpile includes bases for clips, shoe clips, ear posts, trimmings, artificial flowers, cords, ribbons, notions, buttons, and stringing supplies. You will need help from the friendly personnel, because these treasures are thrown about. Without a guide, many may well be overlooked. Antiquated and unwanted things are stored haphazardly in the basement.

SILK SURPLUS/TOWNHOUSE
235 E 58th St (bet Second and Third Ave)   212 759-1294
THE ANNEX
223 E 58th St   212 759-1294
Mon-Sat: 10–5:30

Silk Surplus is the exclusive outlet for Scalamandre close-outs of fine fabrics, trimmings, and wallpaper, as well as its own line of imported and domestic informal fabrics and trimmings. Scalamandre is sold for half of retail price, and there is a choice selection of other equally luxurious fabrics at similar savings. There are periodic sales, even on fabrics already discounted, at this elegantly run fabrics store.

TINSEL TRADING
47 W 38th St   212 730-1030
Mon-Fri: 10–5; Sat: call for hours

The personnel at Tinsel Trading claim it is the only firm in the United States specializing in antique gold and silver metallics, and they have everything from gold thread to lamé fabric. Tinsel Trading offers an amazing array of tinsel threads, braids, fringes, cords, tassels, gimps, medallions, edging, banding, gauze lamés, bullions, tinsel, fabrics, ribbons, soutache, trims, and galloons. All are genuine antiques, but many customers buy them for the accents they lend to modern clothing. The collection of military gold braids, sword knots, and epaulets is unexcelled anywhere in the city.

Fans

MODERN SUPPLY COMPANY
19 Murray St (bet Broadway and Church St), 2nd floor
212 267-0100
Mon-Fri: 10–5; Sat: 12–5

Modern Supply conducted business for 42 years at a site now usurped by the World Trade Center. Today, however, it's hard to reconcile *modern* with a store that sells fans and only fans. But Leo Herschman is not about to change his habits of over 50 years, so he still maintains the business name and a firm conviction that fans are the best way to keep cool and comfortable. From un-air-conditioned offices on the second floor, Herschman dispenses all kinds of fans. The floors are overcrowded with them, and they hang from the ceiling in abundant formations.

Fireplace Accessories

DANNY ALESSANDRO
307 E 60th St (Alessandro Building)   212 759-8210
Mon-Fri: 10–1, 2–5

New Yorkers have a thing for fireplaces, and Danny Alessandro caters to that infatuation. Just as New York fireplaces run the gamut from antique brownstone to ultramodern blackstone, Danny Alessandro's fireplaces and accessories range from antique pieces to a shiny new set of tools that look like plexiglass and silver. (They're really chrome. Do you know what would happen to silver in front of a fireplace?) The expanded two-store shop also stocks salvaged marble and sandstone mantelpieces, antique andirons, and an incredible display of screens and tool kits. In the Victorian era, paper fans and screens were popular for blocking fireplaces when not in use. Alessandro's collection of surviving pieces is great for modern decorating. Danny Alessandro will also custom-order mantels, mantelpieces, and accessories. This is primarily a fireplace *accessory* source, however; neither advice nor information is given on how to put a fireplace in working order. Danny Alessandro has been in business for over a hundred years, and he assumes every New Yorker who has a fireplace knows how to use it.

WILLIAM H. JACKSON
210 E 58th St   212 753-9400
Mon-Fri: 9–4:30

"WBFP" in the real-estate ads stands for "wood-burning fireplace," and they are the rage in New York. William H. Jackson is reaping the harvest of this resurgence in fireplace usage. In business since 1827, the company is familiar with the various types of fireplaces in the city. In fact, many of the fireplaces were originally installed by the company. William H. Jackson has hundreds of mantels on display in its showroom. The variety ranges from antique and antique reproductions (in wood or marble combinations) to stark modern. There are also andirons, fire sets, screens, and excellent advice on enjoying your own fireplace. Jackson does some repair work (removing and installing mantels is a specialty) but is better known for fireplace paraphernalia. A handy item: a reversible hanging sign that reads "Damper is open"/"Damper is closed."

Flags

ACE BANNER AND FLAG COMPANY
107 W 27th St   212 620-9111
Mon-Fri: 7:30–4

Rally round the flag, boys, and if you need a flag, Ace is the place to go. Established in 1916, Ace prides itself on having the flag of every country in the world readily available; other flags can be ordered. They range in size from lapel pins to bridge-spanning banners. (For those who don't know, the largest flag flown in the world is the Stars and Stripes that hangs from the New Jersey side of the George Washington Bridge every holiday.) For those who are not flag-waving types, Ace also sells custom banners, buttons, pins, patches, and pennants. If you're running for any kind of office, campaign paraphernalia can be ordered with a promise of quick delivery. Carl Calo, Ace's owner, does not subsist on flags and campaigns alone, however. A large part of his business consists of outfitting grand openings and personalizing equipment with such items as boat flags. If your boat already has a flag and you're not planning to run for office, you can always try the T-shirts. There's a full line, and all are custom-printed.

Floor Coverings

COUNTRY FLOORS
15 E 16th St   212 627-8300
Mon-Wed, Fri: 9–6; Thurs: 9–8; Sat: 9–5; closed Sat in summer

Country Floors is one of New York's biggest success stories, probably because they offer a magnificent product. Begun in 1964 in the tiny, cramped basement under the owner's photography studio, Country Floors has grown to include huge stores in New York, Philadelphia, Miami, and Los Angeles; Sydney and Melbourne, Australia; and 35 affiliated stores nationwide. Customers from across the country have learned that Country Floors carries the finest in floor and wall tiles. Their sources include a wide variety of styles and artisans from all over the world. All are unique, and a visit—or at least a look at their catalog—is really necessary to appreciate the fineness and intricacy of each design. Some of the more complex patterns are hard to imagine as a whole when one concentrates on individual tiles. The common denominator is that even the simplest solid-color tiles are beautiful.

DESIGNED WOOD FLOORING CENTER
281 Lafayette St (bet Prince and Houston St)   212 925-6633
Mon-Fri: 9–5; Sat by appointment

A couple of decades ago, the epitome of good decorating was wall-to-wall carpeting. Even 10 years ago, industrial carpeting covered floors, walls, and even seating in the most modern homes. But nowadays bare floors are in, and people who can provide and care for these floors are as successful as can be. It's no wonder that Designed Wood Flooring Center is in demand. Conventional homes are installing, finishing, or refinishing wood floors, while DWF's neighbors in former lofts have to deal with industrial flooring totally unacceptable for residential use. With the latter customer, the store can lay subfloor preparations as well as some magnificent wooden floors. These people are experts, and the floors come in almost as many varieties and patterns as that old-time wall-to-wall carpeting. And don't worry about their expertise. Despite the fact that they will accept the smallest private job, they are the choice of several major museums and department stores, as well as major show-rooms and building lobbies. From now on, I won't walk over a wood floor without noticing it.

ELIZABETH EAKINS
21 E 65th St   212 628-1950
Mon-Fri: 10–5:30

Collectors choose Elizabeth Eakins' shop as a first-class source for hand-woven rugs. Here they custom-design and make their hand-woven rugs in standard and hand-dyed colors. To complete the look, they offer coordinated upholstery fabrics, throws, and pillows. Custom-designed, hand-hooked wool rugs are also available.

KAMDIN DESIGNS
1020 Lexington Ave (bet 72nd and 73rd St)   212 772-2140
Mon-Fri: 10–6; Sat: 12–5

Have you always had a mental picture of what kind of rug you want, but you can't find it anywhere? Look no further. With hundreds of design plates, Kamdin specializes in custom-designing rugs with individualized colors, patterns, and sizes. Dhurries, needlepoints, chain stitches, kilims, and ambussons manufactured in Portugal, Madeira, and India are all available here. High-quality antique rugs are a feature of the store.

LE MONDE DES KILIMS
470-A Broome St (entrance on Greene St)   212 431-9064
Tues-Sun: 11–7

Kilims are flat-woven Oriental rugs that come mainly from Turkey, Caucasus, Russia, Iran, and Afghanistan. Le Monde, the only store in New York dealing in kilims, is part of a Belgian company that has its own studio and workshops in Brussels and Istanbul. Because they im-port directly, they have beautiful merchandise available at reasonable prices. The selection is fantastic, with over 600 antique and decorative kilims on display in their gallery. Victor Antiques (223 E 60th St) also features products from Le Monde.

MOMENI INTERNATIONAL
36 E 31st St, 2nd floor   212 532-9577
Mon-Fri: 9–5

The people here will tell you they are wholesale only, but don't let the stated policy scare you. Those who do visit will be rewarded by what may be the single best source for Oriental rugs in the city, because Momeni is a direct importer. Since they don't officially suffer individual retail customers, their prices reflect wholesale rather than retail business.

That doesn't make them cheap (good Oriental rugs never are), but it does assure the very best quality at the best price. Besides, they're really pussycats—but don't tell them I said so!

PASARGAD CARPETS
105 Madison Ave (at 30th St)   212 684-4477
Mon-Sat: 9–6; Sun: 11–5

Pasargad is a fifth-generation family business, established in 1904. They know what they are talking about when it comes to antique, semi-antique, and new Persian and Oriental rugs. They have one of the largest collections in the country, and they provide decorating advice, repair and cleaning, and a pickup and delivery service. Pasargad will also buy or trade quality antique rugs.

PILLOWRY
132 E 69th St   212 308-1630
Mon-Fri: 11:30–5:30; Sat: by chance or appointment; closed Aug

Marjorie Lawrence specializes in Oriental rugs and kilims. She has been doing so since 1971, and she is the best in the business. The name of the shop comes from the pillows made of tapestries, old rugs, and old textiles on the premises. Customers can select fabric from the kilims, knotted rugs, and Oriental carpets lying around the shop, or they can have them made to order. Her fabrics are old, authentic, and come from all parts of the world. The Pillowry does expert rug restoration, as well as pillow creations from old textiles, needlepoints, and rugs. You might say Lawrence has the subject covered!

RUG WAREHOUSE
220 W 80th St (nr Broadway)   212 787-6665
Mon-Sat: 10–6; Thurs: 10–8; Sun: 11–5

One of the largest collections of antique and semi-antique Oriental rugs in the city is available at the Rug Warehouse. The current owners come from a family tradition of five decades in the rug business. A huge inventory of over 5,000 antique and contemporary rugs includes creations from 13 countries. A recent modernization has provided an attractive setting for the rugs that are offered (often at good discount prices). The word *warehouse* is, in fact, hardly applicable to the tony new digs!

SAFAVIEH CARPETS
153 Madison Ave (at 32nd St)   212 683-8399
Mon-Fri: 9–6; Sat: 10–6; Sun: 12–6

There was a time when it was possible to visit the teeming markets of Tehran and find some real bargains in rugs. No more. But one is still able to see a vast selection of these beautiful works of art, even if the setting is a little less glamorous. Safavieh has one of the finest collections of Iranian, Indian, Pakistani, and Chinese rugs in this country. They're displayed in a showroom spacious enough for you to visualize how the prized pieces would look in your own home or place of business. These rugs are truly heirlooms, and you will want to spend time with the folks here while they tell you of their exotic products. Prices, although certainly not inexpensive, are competitive for the superior quality represented, and it doesn't hurt to do a little haggling.

Flowers, Plants, Gardening

CLAYCRAFT
101 W 28th St   212 242-2903
Mon-Fri: 7–4:30; Sat: 10–5
Hours vary by season; call ahead.

Claycraft claims to have the largest selection of planters, fiberglass display pieces, garden ornaments, and pottery for plants in the city. With a location in the wholesale flower market, they operate on a wholesale-retail basis as well. (This is supposed to mean wholesale prices for retail customers.) Owner Robert Lapidus claims that his years in the business have made him an expert at supplying the best planter and vase for any plant. With such a selection and location, he really does have an excellent vantage point. If Claycraft does not have the piece you're looking for, Lapidus will search for and usually locate any type of planter. Any plant that needs a new home can find one here!

FARM AND GARDEN NURSERY
2 Sixth Ave (bet White and Walker St)   212 431-3577
Daily: 9–6; Jan, Feb: Tues-Sat: 10–5

This is one of New York's most unusual enterprises. First, a little background. The towering buildings in this neighborhood are the two spires of the World Trade Center. However, the surrounding area used to be made up of 50-year-old buildings housing government offices, while the site of the future trade center was occupied by tiny and dirty electronics, job-lot, and gardening shops. When construction began on the World Trade Center, the small businesses were dislocated. Some retired. Many vanished. Those that relocated have done remarkably well. Of the garden centers, Farm and Garden Nursery was the only one to remain in the area. It operates like a suburban nursery, dispensing grass seed, fruit trees, vegetables, and sprays, and yet its nursery is, in its own terms, an "outdoor lot," while its customers' lawns are usually six-foot terraces. Oblivious of this fact, the nursery blissfully sells all manner of garden plants, indoor tropical plants, and trees under the assumption that they will grow anywhere. Usually, they do. One holdover from the old days is the prices, which are cheaper than uptown.

GRASS ROOTS GARDEN
131 Spring St (bet Wooster and Greene St)   212 226-2662
Tues-Sat: 9–6; Sun: 12–6

Larry Nathanson's grass-roots movement began 21 years ago when
he turned his hobby into a full-time vocation. The possessor of a genuine green thumb, Nathanson couldn't understand why city pavement had
to be an inhibiting factor for would-be urban farmers. So he blithely
set up his Grass Roots Garden, paying no mind to the boutique atmosphere or cutesy merchandising that marked the shops of his peers. Every
square inch in Nathanson's shop is crammed with a sprouting green plant.
The business is evenly divided between indoor and outdoor plants, and
no one here blinks an eye at the sale of a six-foot orange tree or a quarter-
inch-tall cactus. Somewhere in this city, it will make someone happy.
And if having to prune and water plants infringes on your happiness,
Grass Roots can handle that, too. In addition to soil, plants, lighting units,
insecticides, fertilizers, gardening tools and equipment, garden furniture,
and a consulting business, Grass Roots makes house calls "all over town"
and runs a plant-maintenance service. They also show one of the largest
stocks of pottery in Manhattan.

NEW YORK BOTANICAL GARDEN'S SHOP IN THE GARDEN
590 Madison Ave (bet 56th and 57th St)   212 980-8544
Mon-Sat: 10–6

Right in the center of the city, in the plaza of the grandiose IBM castle,
you can find one of the most colorful and interesting garden shops around.
This small shop is overflowing with plants and flowers, seeds, garden
books, tools, and all the other things that green thumbers (and the rest
of us) need in dealing with nature! The Botanical Garden also operates
a plant-information service, where folks can get telephone or walk-in
advice five days a week for gardening, plant, and other horticultural questions (718 817-8681). Incidentally, if you have time, a visit to the Botanical Garden itself is well worth the trip. If you are driving from Manhattan, take the Triboro Bridge and Bruckner Expressway east to Bronx
River Parkway north; then take the exit marked "Botanical Garden" to
Southern (Kazimiroff) Blvd. You can also go by train, via Conrail's
Harlem line, from Grand Central to the Botanical Garden station.

PUBLIC FLOWER MARKET
152 Fulton St   212 684-2850
Daily: 9–6

The Public Flower Market is not *the* flower market, but it is open to
the public. It specializes in supplying flowers to retail florists, as well
as creating lavish floral decorations for its own retail sale. Most of the
latter are destined for weddings or funerals—which, while occupying

opposite ends of the emotional spectrum, are pretty much the same thing to florists. Ordering in advance assures top quality, and Public Flower guarantees wholesale prices to retail customers.

RENNY
159 E 64th St   212 288-7000
Mon-Sat: 9–6

Renny's headquarters is a brownstone with an enclosed courtyard, complete with an antique fountain filled with a spectacular array of orchids and other exotic plants. Although primarily a florist, Renny Reynolds really specializes in party pieces. Renny also runs a plant-maintenance and landscaping service, and he carries materials for centerpieces, bouquets, sprigs, and plain flower decorations.

RIALTO FLORISTS
707 Lexington Ave (bet 57th and 58th St)   212 688-3234
Daily: 8 a.m.–midnight

Rialto is one of the few florists in New York that will make deliveries until midnight. Great for patching up late-night quarrels!

SIMPSON & COMPANY
852 Tenth Ave (at 56th St)   212 772-6670
Daily: 8–8

In new quarters, Simpson offers unusual flowers, plants, and beautiful freeze-dried arrangements of flowers, fruits, and vegetables. These are very lifelike; you can only tell the difference from fresh flowers by touching them. The fourth floor houses an orchid greenhouse, the only one of its kind in the city. These folks can handle gatherings of all sizes, and their prices are very competitive.

SURA KAYLA
55 Vandam St   212 941-8757
By appointment

This talented lady does wonders with dried, fresh, and silk flowers. Custom arrangements for parties and weddings are a specialty.

TREILLAGE
418 E 75th St (nr York Ave)   212 535-2288
Mon-Sat: 10–6

Many people forget that New Yorkers have gardens, too, although they are small. Many times they are just patios, but still they add a special dimension of charm to city living. Along comes Treillage to help make an ordinary plot of outside living into something special. There are all sorts of garden items, including furniture and accessories, with a great selection of unusual pieces that will set your place apart from your neighbors. The prices are not exactly inexpensive, but why not splurge and enjoy the blue sky when you do get a chance? Ask for some expert help from Carolyn Gregg.

Furniture, Mattresses

AMERICANA WEST
386 W Broadway   212 966-WEST
Daily: 12-6

Paralleling the current interest in foods from the Southwest, Americana West shows New York's best selection of furniture and accessories from that part of the country. Color and style are the name of the game; the merchandise will light up any dreary corner. Nearly everything is made in Santa Fe, New Mexico. There are tables, chairs, beds, cabinets—just about everything a cowboy (or girl) needs when away from the saddle!

ARISE FUTON MATTRESS COMPANY
Numerous locations throughout city
Mon-Sat: 11-7; Sun: 1-5

Futons are thick sleeping mats popular in Japan. They look like upholstered cushions with cotton batting and unbleached muslin casings. Arise claims to have introduced them in 1970, and their success has been substantial. There are four different styles currently available, ranging from the standard futon to the "Living Health Imperial" models. So while the classic futon has all-cotton batting, Arise's other models incorporate cores of various fibers for greater resiliency. In addition, the adaptation to New York has been made with the introduction of folding futon beds and even convertible sofas. These don't pull out; they simply drape the furniture. Frames are also available. All products are American-made.

AU CHAT BOTTE
903 Madison Ave (bet 72nd and 73rd St)   212 772-7402
Mon-Sat: 10-6

Here you will find some of the finest imported sleeping comforts and clothing for babies and children in town. But there is more: bassinets and linings, towels, linens, and quilts. Very special little ones can be outfitted in a very special way in this unique shop.

CHARLES P. ROGERS BRASS BED COMPANY
899 First Ave (bet 50th and 51st St)   212 594-8777
Mon-Fri: 11-7; Sat: 10-6; Sun: 12-5

Are you hunting for a real antique piece? Anyone who has been in the bed business for a century and a half should know almost everything about good looks and comfort when it comes to the sleeping department.

Rogers shows over 50 models in four-posters, contemporary, canopied, and hand-painted styles. There are replicas of original designs and old-time beds, and all sizes are available in stock or on order. These folks sell factory-direct, so prices are competitive.

DEUTSCH
31 E 32nd St   212 683-8746, 800 223-4550
Mon-Fri: 9–5; Sat: 10–4; closed Sat in summer

Wicker and rattan became popular in the mid-1970s, but Deutsch had been in the business for 20 years by that time. They originally sold mainly to interior designers, furniture stores, and large businesses, but now the public (as well as commercial customers) can benefit from this high-quality merchandise. All of it is imported, and there are no cheap weaves here. Roger Deutsch is rightfully proud of his position in the field, and you should seek him out for advice.

FOREMOST FURNITURE SHOWROOMS
8 W 30th St, 10th floor (at Fifth Ave)
212 242-3354, 212 889-6347
Mon-Wed, Fri, Sat: 9–4; Thurs: 9–7; Sun: 11–4

Decorators recommend Foremost to friends who want to avoid decorator commissions, because it's a good place to get quality furniture at a 20% to 50% discount. Foremost has five full floors of furniture, laid out by floor and room plans. The personnel are friendly, knowledgeable, and helpful, making this an excellent source. Comparison- and window-shopping are particularly difficult here, and though the values are indeed very good, it isn't obvious unless you've shopped around. So make this one of your last stops.

FRANK EASTERN COMPANY
599 Broadway (at Houston St)   212 219-0007
Mon-Fri: 9–5; Sat: 10–2; closed Sat in summer

For business supplies and furniture, Frank Eastern Company should be a first choice. They are capable of completely furnishing a business or home office with tables, desks, chairs, files, bookcases, partitions, and a full line of computer work stations for home or office. Frank Eastern Company specializes in advanced ergonomic chairs that prevent backache and premature fatigue. The company president has personally conducted 24 years of extensive research in this field and has actually tested over 2,000 different chairs from all over the world in an ongoing attempt to find the ultimate chair for the person who works at a desk or a computer. All of it is sold at a discount, and custom jobs are a specialty.

GRANGE
200 Lexington Ave (at 32nd St)   212 685-9057
Mon-Fri: 9–5 or by appointment

Superb French furniture and accessories dominate the selling floor of this very attractive boutique. The goods are all French-inspired, and the furniture is clean-lined, functional, and in great taste. What the Italians have contributed to the classy look in ready-to-wear, the French have achieved in home collections. Note, however, that this is not a place for bargain hunters.

HECHO A MANO
347 W Broadway (bet Broome and Grand St)   212 431-9346
Daily: 12–7; Sun: 12–6

Hecho a Mano has a great selection of Mexican furniture and accessories that are unique and colorful. Most of the products are designed by an American couple, then carved and painted south of the border. The quality is first-rate, and the prices are reasonable.

JENSEN-LEWIS
89 Seventh Ave (at 15th St)   212 929-4880
Mon-Wed, Fri, Sat: 10–7; Thurs: 10–8; Sun: 12–5

Jensen-Lewis had its origins in the late 19th-century sailmaking business of Charles Jensen and the canvas-awning business of Edward Lewis. In 1932, the two businesses united to become the premier canvas-awning dealer in the country. In 1964, they expanded to include canvas furniture. In very short order, the canvas furniture took off, and Jensen-Lewis now concentrates on canvas products and accessory pieces. There are bunk beds and bedroom sets, wardrobes in two heights and four sizes, home and office furniture, dining-room tables, lamps, and kitchen accessories. There's loads more, too—and we haven't even touched on such basic items as canvas chairs, bags, pillows, and futons. Not all of this is canvas, but it does fit the Jensen-Lewis "look." You'll recognize it when you see it. It's relaxed, practical, and very comfortable.

KENTSHIRE GALLERIES
37 E 12th St (bet University Pl and Broadway)   212 673-6644
Mon-Fri: 9–5; Sat: 10–3 (Oct-May)

Kentshire presents eight floors of English furniture and accessories, circa 1690-1870, with particular emphasis on the Georgian and Regency periods. This gallery has an excellent international reputation, and the displays are a delight to see, even if the price tags are a bit high. There is also a collection of 18th- and 19th-century English jewelry, and a Kentshire boutique at Bergdorf-Goodman features antiques, accessories, and old jewelry.

KLEINSLEEP/CLEARANCE
176 Sixth Ave (bet Spring and Prince St)   212 226-0900
Mon-Sat: 10–7; Sun: 11–6

Kleinsleep is a chain of stores in the New York area specializing in bedding needs. At each store, the byword is *discount,* and at this downtown location, prices are reduced even further. This is the final resting place for Klein's floor samples, close-outs, no-sells, mismatches, and mistakes. Since almost all of these pieces are going to be covered with linens, the mistakes don't matter in the least, and a trip down here is a must for anyone in need of a bed. They boast that all sizes and types of sleeping furniture are available, including brass headboards. In particular, they claim to have New York City's largest showing of innerspring and platform box springs. At the very least, this is a company that is experienced and knows what it's doing. The customer gets advice, expertise, and exceptional bargains. Shipping is additional, but considering the neighborhood, it is usually well worth it. It is against the New York City health code to sell a used bed. Therefore, the leftovers sold here have never been used.

NORTH CAROLINA FURNITURE SHOWROOM
12 W 21st (at Fifth Ave), 2nd floor   212 260-5850
Mon-Wed, Fri, Sat: 10–6; Thurs: 10–8; Sun: 12–5

Finding quality furniture at a decent price is not too easy these days. North Carolina Furniture Showroom is a unique establishment. Previously known as Apartment Living, they specialize in furnishings for apartments. It is the kind of merchandise New Yorkers need and love: lots of drawers, shelves, and storage space in functional form for those who have to live in somewhat cramped space where there are never enough closets. New lines have been added; they now offer over 400 famous name brands in furniture and bedding, all at substantial discounts. They will order items shown on the sales floor. It really pays to look over their living rooms, bedrooms, dining rooms, dinettes, den furniture, wall units, sofa beds, and recliners before making a final selection.

OAK-SMITH & JONES
1321 Second Ave (bet 69th and 70th St)   212 535-1451
Daily: 10–8

There is a distinct foreign accent in the furniture and accessories carried here. Unique original and reproduction antiques and accessories from all over the world are shown next to an outstanding collection of antique pine items and brass and iron beds. Upholstery and decorating services are available.

OSBORNE & OSBORNE
508 Canal St   212 431-7075
Sat-Sun: 1–6 or by appointment

Since 1975 Kipp and Margot Osborne have been building custom-made hardwood furniture for private and corporate clients. Each of their pieces is signed, dated, and numbered, marking both the continuing evolution of their work and the unique nature of each piece. They are shown in an 1827 landmark rowhouse in TriBeCa. Traditional, time-proven cabinet-making techniques and joinery provide the quality basis for Osborne furniture. Using these methods in conjunction with a careful process of wood selection and a sensibility that book-matches and balances wood grain, the Osbornes have created a body of work that to date numbers more than 1,200 pieces.

T&K FRENCH ANTIQUES
120 Wooster St   212 219-2472
Tues-Fri: 11–6:30; Sat: 12–6; Sun: 1–5

If you have a craving to accent your home with interesting French antiques, then T&K should be one of your first stops. They import directly from France and display an unusually interesting collection of antiques, including turn-of-the-century coffee dispensers, oak ice-cream boxes, bistro chairs, baskets, doctor's cabinets, and a fine collection of iron items. For unusual chairs and bird cages, look no further.

WICKERY
342 Third Ave (at 25th St)   212 889-3669
Mon-Fri: 10:30–6:30; Sat: 10:30–6

The Wickery handles wicker and rattan furniture, as well as accessories in tortoise shell, rolled bamboo, burned bamboo, and rattan core. Items range from basket to hamper size, and discounted prices range from pennies to hundreds of dollars.

WIM AND KAREN'S SCANDINAVIAN FURNITURE
319 E 53rd St   212 758-4207
Tues, Wed, Fri: 10–6; Thurs: 10–7:30; Sat: 11–6; Sun: 12–5

Wim Sanson's collection of Scandinavian furniture is light, airy, and functional. Unlike most Scandinavian and modern imports, they look and feel solid, which makes them a good investment. Wim and Karen import oak, cherry, ash, teak, and rosewood furniture for every room in the house. All of it is made in factories abroad. If you think that all Scandinavian furniture is blond Danish modern, Wim and Karen deserve your visit. Most noteworthy is the encouragement they have given native Scandinavian designers. Many of the styles sold here are unique and suited for life on both sides of the Atlantic. It is possible that the mobile New

York lifestyle finds its most sympathetic counterpart in Scandinavia. The convenient wall units in particular seem to bear this out, but there are also bedroom suites and super leather furniture for living-room seating.

Games — Adult

COMPLEAT STRATEGIST
11 E 33rd St (at Fifth Ave)   212 685-3880
Mon-Wed, Fri, Sat: 10:30–6; Thurs: 10:30–9

320 W 57th St (bet Eighth and Ninth Ave)   212 582-1272
Mon-Sat: 11–8; Sun: 12–5

630 Fifth Ave (Rockefeller Center)   212 265-7449
Mon-Fri: 10:30–5:30

The Compleat Strategist was established as a fortress for military games and equipment. As the only such place in the city — and possibly the country — it was an overwhelming success and was soon overrun with military strategists. As time went on, they branched into science fiction, fantasy, murder-mystery games, and adventure games and books. When this, too, seemed to capture the imagination of the public, the Compleat Strategist opened two more outposts. So today people who are fighting the Civil War all over again can browse alongside Dragon Masters at three locations in the city. The stock is more than ample for any military or Dungeons and Dragons addict, and the personnel are knowledgeable and friendly. For the less feisty, they have chess and backgammon sets, even good old Monopoly. These are adult games with no sneering or innuendo — unless, of course, you're playing the villain.

DOUBLING CUBE
80 E 2nd St   212 420-8557
Mail order only

Only in New York! This outfit is the only business in the country that supplies backgammon sets, monogrammed poker chips (ten kinds), chess equipment, and all kinds of gaming devices for home use. No need to go to Atlantic City; just call for their catalog.

GAME SHOW
474 Sixth Ave (bet 11th and 12th St)   212 633-6328
Mon-Sat: 12–7 (Thurs: 12–8); Sun: 12–5

1240 Lexington Ave (bet 83rd and 84th St)
212 472-8011, 212 472-6281
Mon-Sat: 11–6 (Thurs 11–7); Sun: 12–5

If you can't find the kid's or adult's game or puzzle you have heard about at the Game Show, it probably doesn't exist. This store is crammed with the best of the lot, and the folks here love to talk to customers about their stock.

MARION & COMPANY
147 W 26th St   212 727-8900
Mon-Fri: 8–5:30

When you think of casino and game equipment, think of Marion! This outfit has been in business for nearly a century, and it is still presided over by a family member, Ed Weinstein. Marion distributes a large selection of chess, backgammon, and dominoes items; all plastic cards; and casino equipment for home or professional use. They also make personalized poker chips and offer a wide range of gaming tables and roulette wheels. It is both a wholesale and retail operation.

VILLAGE CHESS SHOP
230 Thompson St (bet Bleecker and 3rd St)   212 475-9580
Daily: noon–midnight

People who enjoy chess can play at the Village Chess Shop for about $1.80 an hour. Those who are searching for really unique chess pieces would be wise to patronize this shop as well. Chess sets are available in pewter, brass, ebony, onyx, and more. Many boards can be flipped over for backgammon, and, in fact, Village Chess has outstanding sets for that game as well. In short, Village Chess should be a first stop when it comes to moving chess pieces – whether they are being moved from one square to another or from their store to your home.

Gifts, Accessories

BERTABRASIL BUTIK
151 W 46th St (bet Sixth and Seventh Ave), 7th floor
212 354-9616
Mon-Fri: 9–5:30; Sat: 9–2

This is a loft discount boutique featuring a number of well-known names in watches, sunglasses, electronics, cosmetics, and some clothing items. Don't expect to find depth in any classification, but you can find some good bargains if you don't mind disinterested salespeople and zero ambience. The folks here have promised me they are trying to improve their service! (Let me know.)

CABBAGES AND KINGS
813 Lexington Ave (bet 62nd and 63rd St)   212 355-5513
Mon-Sat: 10–6

In three separate areas full of all manner of gift items and home accessories, you will be able to do one-stop shopping for all of your thank-you's or expressions of holiday cheer. There are items for every member of the family, an especially good selection of merchandise with sports motifs, antiques, pictures, and more. Carol Ruderman and Linda Malamy treat them all as their own personal possessions, having shown tender loving care in picking them out.

CAROLE STUPELL
29 E 22nd St   212 260-3100
Mon-Sat: 10–6

Imagine the fun of being able to set a table with the most beautiful accessories available anywhere! The first place anyone with such a yen should visit is Carole Stupell. In my opinion, this is the finest home-accessory store in the country. The taste and thought that has gone into the selection of merchandise is simply unmatched. Keith Stupell, a second-generation chip-off-the-old-block, has assembled a fabulous array of china, glassware, silver, and gift treasures, and he displays them in spectacular settings. In addition, the store offers a large selection of china and glassware replacement patterns that date back over 30 years. The prices are not in the bargain range, but the quality is unequalled.

CERAMICA GIFT GALLERY
1009 Sixth Ave (bet 37th and 38th St)
212 354-9216, 800 666-9956
Mon-Fri: 9:30–6; Sun: 12–5

We've been looking a long time for a place that has good bridal-registry giftware at discount prices, as it's been one of the most frequent requests from readers. Finally, we've found just the place, and the convenient midtown location is an extra bonus. At Ceramica Gift Gallery, you'll find most, if not all, major brands of china, crystal, tableware, and collectibles, including Waterford, Royal Doulton, Gorham, Minton, Wedgwood, and Lenox. In addition, they ship anywhere in the country and will accept mail and phone orders. Discounts can go as high as 50%, and they will quote prices over the phone.

CONTEMPORARY PORCELAIN
105 Sullivan St (bet Spring and Prince St)   212 219-2172
Tues-Sun: 12–7

This is the only gallery in Manhattan exclusively showing ceramics from the United States and Europe. The pieces focus on functional and decorative design, and the majority are one-of-a-kind. Tea sets, plates, mugs, vases, and bowls are among the many attractive treasures.

CRYPTOGRAPHICS
40 E 32nd St   212 685-3377
Mon-Fri: 9–5

Whether it's a bowling trophy or the Man of the Year award, Cryptographics can design a piece that's exactly right. Their basic line is anything that has to do with awards. That includes plaques, nameplates, badges, signs, executive gifts, trophies, premiums, laminations, and signs. Any of these can be quickly personalized on the premises, but given ample time, Cryptographics can design outstanding pieces. The personalized gift items make really unique presents.

CURACAO
20 W 57th St, 4th floor   212 581-6970
Mon-Sat: 9–5:45; Sun: 9–2

This is a special find, but only for those with non-U.S. passports. There is a great selection of pens, electronics, perfumes, gifts, and some clothing at considerable savings. For visitors from overseas, Curacao is a bonanza. For New York residents, go with someone who has a foreign passport and share in the savings.

FLIGHTS OF FANCY
1502 First Ave (bet 78th and 79th St)   212 772-1302
Mon-Fri: 12–7 (Wed until 8); Sat: 10–6; Sun: 1–6

Flights of Fancy exudes charm, with soft music and an array of Americana treasures arranged in a Victorian parlor setting beckoning passers-by. Many of the gifts are handmade and exclusive to the shop, and the window display, which changes weekly, often showcases only one item in a line. That item is often so unusual and special that orders pour in from customers around the country. Prices range from $2 to $2,000, so there is something for every kind of gift-giving. July is the month to save 15% on holiday items. Some suggestions? It's hard to be specific since the stock is always changing. But there is a handmade American theme that runs through the selection, and the best sellers include pet-portrait dolls, jewelry, and home-accessory designs. (The pet-portrait dolls incorporate a photo of any pet on a doll resembling it, which is then dressed in a historical or literary costume.) There are other dolls, toys, soft sculptures, beautiful handcrafted eggs, and miniatures available on the premises or by customer order, plus the largest selection of one-of-a-kind gifts in the city.

JENNY B. GOODE
1194 Lexington Ave (bet 81st and 82nd St)   212 794-2492
Mon-Fri: 10–6:30; Sat: 10–6

Jenny B. Goode appears on everybody's list as *the* place for special household gifts. It is a super source for really unusual gift items; in fact, you may be tempted to buy something for yourself! Jenny keeps the store stocked with contemporary and antique jewelry and pottery, tapestry pillows, lace shams, majolica pottery, all kinds of scarfs, silver and silver-plated items, plush toys for the kids, handmade tapestry-and-lace photo albums, and imported frames. There's something for everyone. Jenny B Goode could charm Old Scrooge himself!

JOMPOLE COMPANY
330 Seventh Ave (at 29th St), 3rd floor   212 594-0440
Mon-Wed, Fri: 10–5; Thurs: 10–6

When the local bank offers an electric blanket to anyone depositing $500 or the academy gives every graduate a silver pin, odds are that it was bought here. Jompole is a dynamite company. They offer great service at super prices, and Irving Jompole and Shirley Smith are two of the friendliest, funniest people around. They bill themselves as suppliers of business gifts, sales incentives, premiums, and awards, and they claim to have supplied everything from lollipops and imprinted toothpicks to diamonds, color televisions, and Cadillacs. Their stock in trade is crystal, sterling silver, china, and top-name watches. There is no name they don't carry or can't get, and it is sold at a substantial discount of 30% to 50%. So you're not a bank, employer, or school? No problem, Jompole provides service to individuals at the same discount price. Jompole warns that everything is not always in stock (this is mostly a brokerage operation), but anything can be ordered. Customers are invited to call or come in to peruse the catalogs and place orders. Shipping is reasonable, and the prices may be the lowest in town.

LEONARD'S OF NEW YORK
New York Hilton (downstairs)
1335 Sixth Ave (at 54th St)   212 582-4184
Daily: 7:30 a.m.–11:15 p.m.

It's not often that you find a really good specialty shop in a hotel, but the New York Hilton has an exception. Leonard's of New York is one of the most complete gift, novelty, and food shops in the midtown area. Quality items for special occasions, snacks for the hotel room, and unusual souvenirs of the Big Apple are attractively displayed *and* attractively priced. Unlike most hotel gift shops, this one does not inflate price tags for the captive hotel customer.

LITTLE EXTRAS
550 Amsterdam Ave (bet 86th and 87th St)   212 721-6161
Mon-Wed: 10:30–6:30; Thurs: 10:30–7; Fri, Sat: 10:30–6;
Sun:11–5

Terry Siegel has put together a bright and cheerful shop that should appeal to both kids and parents. Much of the merchandise here is unique, with an emphasis on personalized gifts. There are hand-painted tables and chairs, upholstered furniture, toy chests, bookends, lamps, and much more for youngsters up to five years of age. Special extras: a gift registry, deliveries in Manhattan, and birth announcements accompanied by a red rose.

L S COLLECTION
765 Madison Ave (at 66th St)   212 472-3355
Mon-Wed, Fri, Sat: 10–6; Thurs: 10–7 (summer hours may vary)

Even if you have no intention of buying a thing, you'll get a thrill out of this superb collection. Seldom have I seen home and office accessory items done in such superb taste. Each piece is almost museum-quality. You'll find dishes, vases, glassware, tea and coffee sets, desk pieces, and leather goods that would be just the thing for your "dream pad." Prices are not low but for the quality represented are not out of line.

MABEL'S
849 Madison Ave (bet 70th and 71st St)   212 734-3263
Mon-Sat: 10–6

Mabel—owner Peaches Gilbert's black-and-white cat and business trademark—has gone to feline heaven, but her namesake store continues to delight hordes of Madison Avenue shoppers. The store is jam-packed with handmade accessories for decorating body and home, and virtually everything is made around an animal or fantasy theme. They have elegant to whimsical hand-painted furniture, hooked rugs, old-fashioned lamps, and chic wearables, and all are inspired by animals. Mabel must be looking down on this scene with glee!

NATURE COMPANY
Seaport Marketplace, South Street Seaport
8 Fulton St   212 422-8510
Mon-Sat: 10–7; Sun: 11–6 (Jan 2–March 31)
Mon-Sat: 10–9; Sun: 11–7 (rest of year)

One of the most fascinating of the newer trends in merchandising is the appeal to the naturalist, and no one does it better than the Nature Company. The store is a treasure chest for the browser or buyer; you don't have to be a nature lover to appreciate the unusual selection. There are beautiful marble desktop boxes, attractive jewelry, nature posters, books for the outdoors lover, inflatable toys, telescopes and watches, bird feeders and birdbaths, and all sorts of items that a stargazer would find irresistible. My favorite is a set of sound recordings on tape or CD that reproduce the music of the environment. Imagine being lulled to sleep by the rippling charm of a mountain stream!

NEW GLASS GALLERY
345 W Broadway (bet Broome and Grand St)   212 431-0050
Tues-Sat: 12–7; Sun: 12–6

This gallery is a sight for the eyes! Beautiful contemporary handblown colored glass from small studios all over the world is on display and for sale. The crafts here are in tune with modern design. This is one of the largest collections of glassworks in the country.

ONLY HEARTS
386 Columbus Ave (at 79th St)   212 724-5608
Mon-Sat: 11–8; Sun: 12–7

One of the most fun shops in New York! Helena Stuart offers the romantic in the family a fascinating array of intimate apparel and lingerie, heart-shaped or printed jewelry, balloons, boudoir pillows, soaps, tissues, and even plungers decorated with heart-shaped tops.

PRIVATE LIVES
22-A E 65th St (at Madison Ave)   212 472-6816
Mon-Sat: 11–6

Now here is a secret find! I have known Sally Safir for more years than either one of us wants to admit, and I know she has an excellent sense of style. Now she has opened (with a partner) a tiny boutique that is overflowing with those unusual little gifts that one is always looking for. You'll find accessories, toiletry items, knickknacks, and "just the right thing" to take along to your dinner hostess or for someone important in your life.

SEASHELL BOUTIQUE
208-A Columbus Ave (bet 69th and 70th St)   212 362-5943
Daily: 12–9

Seashell Boutique stocks its very precious space with shell objects, designer jewelry (semiprecious stones, porcelain, and sterling), small gifts, and other items. What they all have in common is their natural origins and their size.

WOLFMAN-GOLD & GOOD COMPANY
116 Greene St (bet Prince and Spring St)   212 431-1888
Mon-Sat: 11–6; Sun: 12–5

This SoHo shop is described as a "marriage of contemporary and antique table settings," and that probably says it best. There are linens (available by special order) that would look classy in a Park Avenue penthouse and a series of white-on-white tableware that would blend with the starkest loft in SoHo. Some of the tableware is imported from France, Italy, and England; the rest is domestic. But all of it is elegant. The store also stocks baskets, cutlery, glasses, linens, doilies, home accessories, furniture, and one of the best collections of cloth napkins in the city. The linens can be specially ordered, and Holophane light fixtures can be similarly ordered for the ultimate table setting. This is a first-choice source for an exquisite house gift.

YELLOW DOOR
1308 Avenue M
Brooklyn, NY   718 998-7382
Mon-Fri: 10–5:45; Sun: 11–5

Brooklyn is renowned for the number of famous people born there: Mary Tyler Moore, Sandy Koufax, Woody Allen, Barbra Streisand, and Larry King, to mention a few. Another famous thing about Brooklyn is a discount gift store on Avenue M in Flatbush, off the promenade of Ocean Parkway. It is run by a native-born entrepreneur by the name of Sallee Bijou. For over 30 years the Yellow Door has been providing "Madison Avenue style at Brooklyn prices." The store carries an unparalleled selection of the finest name brands (Lalique, Baccarat, Alessi,

Towle) in jewelry, gifts, china, table accessories, and bath items. All prices are at least 20% to 30% below suggested retail. Other services include free local delivery, a bridal registry, and phone orders.

Greeting Cards

GREETINGS
45 Christopher St (bet Sixth and Seventh Ave)   212 242-0424
Daily: 11–10

This store claims to have the largest collection of contemporary greeting cards and gifts in the country, and one would be hard-pressed to prove them wrong. The sheer number of cards is mind-boggling, and the types and titles cover topics Hallmark never thought of. "Congratulations on your divorce" is one wry example. Don't overlook the stationery department; it's really unique and well stocked with a collection of New York City memorabilia that makes the "I Love New York" campaign look malnourished.

UNTITLED
159 Prince St (at W Broadway)   212 982-2088
Mon-Sat: 10–9; Sun: 12–8

The Metropolitan Museum and the Louvre each have approximately 1,500 art cards. Untitled, whose reputation is not nearly as well known, has 4,000-plus cards in stock at any given moment. Those cards include modern-art postcards, greeting cards, and note cards, many of which are unused or old cards. The postcards are filed as either pre- or post-1945, and they're further ordered within those classifications by artist's name. There are also postcards of famous photos and depictions of every possible type of art. Some of these items are good for gags, and some are suitable for framing. Untitled also sells art magazines, books, and boxed cards.

Hearing Aids

EMPIRE STATE HEARING AID BUREAU
25 W 43rd St   212 921-1666
Mon-Wed, Fri: 9–5:30; Thurs: 9–6; Sat: 9–1;
closed Sat in summer

If President Reagan left no other legacy, he did set a shining example of not being ashamed to wear a hearing aid. The new aids are so small that most people are not even aware of their use. Empire State has been in the business for over 30 years and carries the top names in the field: Seimens, Starkey, Bosch, and Danabox. They have mature and skilled personnel who will do the proper testing and fitting in a quiet, unhurried atmosphere.

Hobbies

AMERICA'S HOBBY CENTER
146 W 22nd St   212 675-8922
Mon-Fri: 8:45–5:30; Sat: 8:30–3:30

Hobbies and models are a serious business here, but there's a light-hearted touch to remind everyone that hobbies are *fun*. It is evident everywhere in the shop, but nowhere more so than when Marshall Winston introduces himself as the "known authority on vehicular hobbies." Winston's vehicular hobbies include model airplanes, boats, ships, trains, cars, radio-controlled materials, model books, helicopters, model rocketry, tools, and everything for model builders. They also sell wholesale to dealers and by mail order to retail customers, as well as doing export business. In fact, they fill more orders by mail than at the store. Ask for a catalog to get a good indication of what they have in your specific field of interest.

JAN'S HOBBY SHOP
1557 York Ave (bet 82nd and 83rd St)   212 861-5075
Mon-Sat: 10–7; Sun: 12–5

When Fred Hutchins was young (he's now in his 30s), he was obsessed with building models and dioramas, particularly on historical themes. Eventually, it became economically viable for his parents to buy his favorite source of supply. Now he runs the shop. So while the front of the store is still a run-of-the-mill hobby shop, the star of the show is clearly the grown-up Fred, who keeps Jan's stocked with everything a serious model builder could possibly want. Jan's has a superb stock of plastic scale models, model war games, paints, books, brushes and other paraphernalia, toys, trains, planes, ships, and tank models. In the meantime, Fred himself has gone professional. He creates models and dioramas to order for television, advertising, and private customers. In addition to his craft skills, he is also noted for his accurate historical detail. And there is yet a third business: showcase building. Because any hobbyist likes to show his wares, Fred builds custom-made wood and plexiglass showcases for that purpose. Incredibly, he even offers two-day service. He also has remote-controlled cars, ships, and tanks. Did I mention that Jan's is one of my favorite examples of New York retailing?

Home Furnishings

ABC CARPET & HOME
881 and 888 Broadway (at 19th St)   212 473-3000
Mon, Thurs: 10–8; Tues, Wed, Fri: 10–7; Sat: 10–6; Sun: 11–6

What started in 1897 as a pushcart business has now expanded into one of the most complete home-furnishings centers in Manhattan. On ten crowded floors you will find carpets, design rugs, bed and bath items, linens, gifts and accessories, antiques and fine furniture, and handmade Oriental rugs. These folks have a huge inventory, especially in the floor-coverings departments, and are able to buy in large quantities, assuring very competitive prices. One of the very best!

BED, BATH & BEYOND
620 Sixth Ave (bet 18th and 19th St)   212 256-3550
Mon-Fri: 9:30–8; Sat: 9:30–7; Sun: 11–6

This place is an absolute must if you are in the market for anything for your apartment or home. In a huge, soon to be over 80,000-square-foot store in the midst of not very much else on lower Sixth Avenue, these home-furnishings experts show stocks like you have never seen before. As far as the eye can see, there are sheets, blankets, rugs, kitchen gadgets, hangers, towels, dinnerware, hampers, cookware, kiddie items, pillows, and much more. There are not just a dozen but hundreds of choices in each category. Best of all, prices are discounted all the time, the personnel are uniformly friendly and helpful, check-out is well organized, and carts are available so you can pile up purchases at will. I've been in the business for a long time, and I have to admit I have never seen one like this!

TO THE TRADE
212 877-3684, 800 786-1816

Tired of paying huge markups on merchandise from interior designers? If you know what you want, this outfit can save you big bucks. They will sell you goods normally sold just to the trade. Designer Suzy Taylor will get samples and photos, and place your order. The cost is designer's net cost plus 25% for orders up to $350; net cost plus 20% for orders of $350–$1,000; and net cost plus 15% for orders over $1,000. This is a great answer for those who drool over items in the "shelter" magazines and then wonder how they can afford to get them for their homes.

Housewares, Hardware

AMERICAN STEEL WINDOW SERVICE
108 W 17th St (bet Sixth and Seventh Ave)   212 242-8131
Mon-Fri: 7:30–4:30

Peter Weinberger has one of the most esoteric businesses in the city, one that his family has been in for over 75 years. What he does is sell window hardware. If you need a lock, latch, handle, or bracket, American undoubtedly has it. The "store" itself is a tiny office, but the warehouse is right next door. It resembles nothing so much as someone's garage crammed full of window hardware. How he stays in business is beyond comprehension.

APPLIANCES OVERSEAS
276 Fifth Ave (at 30th St), Suite 407   212 545-8001
Mon-Fri: 8:30–5

For nearly 40 years Appliances Overseas has been a valuable resource for folks traveling or living overseas. This firm offers a full range of appliances, large and small, for use in every country of the world. If purchased overseas, these same items are often considerably more expensive. Besides, all appliances sold here have full American features and usually are larger in capacity. Enzo Borges, formerly of Thor Export, now has joined Allen Sausen in providing superior service.

BARSON HARDWARE
35 W 44th St (bet Fifth and Sixth Ave)   212 944-8181
Mon-Fri: 8:30–6; Sat: 10–5

A hardware store in the middle of Manhattan that is well-organized and competitively priced? Impossible? No, sir. Founder Barney Rubin's daughter, Anita, and David Schneiderman operate a store that has everything from first-aid kits to drill bits, 29 sizes of scissors, hair curlers, and fire extinguishers. They specialize in travel needs, unique kitchen and housewares items, tools, and plumbing needs. The personnel know their stock and can come up with the right item to fix that "whatjamagig" in the bathroom. The staff is fluent in six languages, including Hebrew, Yiddish, Chinese, and Russian.

BLACK AND DECKER
50 W 23rd St (bet Fifth and Sixth Ave)   212 929-6450
Mon-Fri: 8:30–5:30; Sat: 9–4

Black and Decker is a name well known for power tools. At this location, the company sells, services, and reconditions Black and Decker tools and small appliances. If you already own such tools, this is the place to bring them when they don't work, since the company knows its products better than anyone else. If you wish to purchase tools, this is also a good source. New tools are sold at a discount, while reconditioned items go for even better prices. Everything is sold with a two-year guarantee. This is a real find. Imagine buying a power saw on your trip to ultra-urban New York!

BRIDGE KITCHENWARE
214 E 52nd St   212 688-4220
Mon-Fri: 9–5:30; Sat: 10–4:30

Bridge Kitchenware is a unique-to-New York store that supplies almost every restaurant and institution within 500 miles. Bridge carries bar equipment, cutlery, pastry equipment, molds, copperware, cast-iron ware, woodenware, stoneware, and kitchen gadgets. All goods are professional quality and excellent for the home gourmet. Be sure to see the line of imported copperware from France, as well as the professional knives and baking pans. After trying them, people use no other. By the way, Bridge takes its name from owner Fred Bridge, not from the nearby 59th Street Bridge.

BROADWAY PANHANDLER
520 Broadway (bet Spring and Broome St)   212 966-3434
Mon-Fri: 10:30–6; Sat: 11–6; Sun: 12–5;
closed Sun in July and Aug

Over 8,000 cutlery, bakeware, and cookware items are available at this SoHo store. Broadway Panhandler made its reputation supplying restaurants and hotels, and it sells everything at low prices.

CK&L SURPLUS
307 Canal St (at Broadway)   212 966-1745
Daily: 8:30–6

In New York, a shopping trip for hardware wouldn't mean a thing without a trip to Canal Street. And on Canal Street, CK&L is the oldest and best. Years ago, these very same Canal Street stores dealt in industrial and war surplus. With the passing demand for military supplies and an influx of electronics, the Canal Street surplus stores turned to areas best described as "hardware whatever." All of the stores do business the same way. Sawed-off cardboard boxes, containing an assortment of homogeneous but totally implausible merchandise, are "displayed" in front. The junk at the front is there to draw customers inside, where the real merchandise is sold. There are power tools, simple tools, plumbing and electrical goods, accessories, and supplies. Prices, even for the complete line of hardware, are much lower than retail stores uptown. When you see the place, you'll understand why the overhead is so low.

CLOSET KING
415 E 72nd St (bet First and York Ave)   212 717-6110
Mon-Sat: 10–6

Spend any time in New York, and you'll know that rarer than a parking space is a place to park yourself and your belongings. Living quarters in the city have always been notoriously tight, but with the current economy, people are staying put, and small apartments are being measured for every inch of usable space. Frequently, closets—if they exist at all—are the first things to go. They are reincarnated as nurseries, bars, bathrooms, eating areas, and even at-home offices. It was inevitable that there would be experts who would specialize in organizing closet space, and Don Constable and his Closet King staff do just that. The overall aim is to provide a maximum amount of storage space, tailored to a customer's needs. Since the store exists to sell components, they encourage "do-it-yourselfers." A customized system can be planned out and purchased here, then self-installed at a fraction of the cost a professional closet organizer would charge. Yes, such people exist. And they're not mothers!

CONRAN'S
2–8 Astor Pl (at Broadway)   212 505-1515
Mon-Sat: 10–9; Sun: 12–7

Citicorp Center, 160 E 53rd St (at Third Ave)   212 371-2225
Mon-Wed, Fri, Sat: 10–6:30; Thurs: 10–8; Sun: 12–6

2248 Broadway (at 81st St)   212 873-9250
Mon-Fri: 10–8; Sat: 10–7; Sun: 11–6

Now that former Bloomie's merchandising masters Marvin Traub and Les Gribetz have seized the reins of this home-furnishings outfit, expect the place to perk up in every way. They will still be carrying most of the old categories (office furniture, housewares, home furniture, linens, lighting, bath accessories, and the like), but the assortments will be deeper, the merchandise more stylish, and the prices more competitive. A good stock is at hand, so you don't have to wait for items to come from a stockroom or warehouse.

D.F. SANDERS
952 Madison Ave (at 75th St)   212 879-6161
Mon-Sat: 10–6:30; Sun: 12–5

There has been an almost complete change in direction in this upscale home-accessory store. The emphasis now is away from the commercial and industrial and onto the individual home. You'll find a classy selection of decorative gifts, vases, mirrors, silverware, china, clocks, frames, jewelry, lamps, bathroom accessories, and more. There are no bargains; be assured that everything here is of the latest design and best quality.

GARRETT WADE
161 Sixth Ave (at Spring St)   212 807-1155
Mon-Fri: 9–5:30; Sat: 10–3

The Garrett Wade customer is a person who uses and appreciates fine woodworking tools, for the store prides itself on offering only the best-made tools from all over the world. The main business is mail-order, and the catalog is all-encompassing. It lists every imaginable woodworking aid and makes a point of explaining each piece's function and advantage over its peers. It reads like a how-to guide! While some of the pieces are incomprehensible to a layman, Garrett Wade never accepts that supposition. They assume that anyone can put together a rocker or, at the very least, appreciate the function of their lightweight spokeshave. After a visit here, you may become a believer, too.

GEORGE TAYLOR SPECIALTIES
100 Hudson St (bet Franklin and Leonard St)   212 226-5369
Mon-Thurs: 7:30–6; Fri: 7:30–4

Taylor stocks plumbing replacement parts to fit all faucets, and custom
faucets can be fabricated via special order. There are also reproduction
faucets and custom designs of fittings for unique installations. Antique
towel bars, bath accessories, and pedestal sinks are a specialty. Founded
in 1869, Taylor remains a family-run operation. Ask for Chris, his
daughter Valerie, or son John.

GRACIOUS HOME
1217 and 1220 Third Ave (bet 70th and 71st St)
212 517-6300, 212 988-8990
Mon-Fri: 8–7; Sat: 9–7; Sun: 10:30–6

For over 30 years Gracious Home has been a local hardware store,
New York-style. It is run with a personal style, its products and services geared for New York life. They sell appliances, wall coverings,
security systems, sporting goods, china, casual furniture, bedding, shelv-
ing, pots and pans . . . you get the picture. Full-scale kitchen and
bathroom remodeling is a specialty. Services include cooking demonstrations, tool rental, and a repair department. They will try to order a special
item for you, and they will deliver in Manhattan.

LAMALLE
36 W 25th St, 6th floor   212 242-0750
Mon-Fri: 8–4

Since 1927 this has been the definitive place to find fine-quality French
cookware. Lamalle is both an importer and manufacturer of copperware,
sabatier, glassware, and china, and all is available at very reasonable
prices. Be sure to ask to go through their stockroom, as many treasures
are hidden in the stacks.

LEESAM KITCHEN AND BATH CENTER
124 Seventh Ave (at 17th St)   212 243-6482
Daily: 9:30–6 (Thurs: 9:30–8); Sat: 12–5

For over a half-century these folks have been fixing up kitchens and
bathrooms. Whether it is a medicine cabinet, kitchen cabinets, faucets,
shower enclosures, or counters, you will see one of the largest selections of top brands from both domestic and foreign suppliers. There's
no excuse now *not* to take care of that leaking faucet or the kitchen cabinet
that has outgrown its capacity!

LUDLOW HARDWARE AND VARIETY
246 Broome St (at Ludlow St)   212 673-1642
Mon-Thurs, Sun: 9:30–5

This is one of the last mom-and-pop hardware stores in the city, and the ambience and prices reflect its advantages. Ludlow has just about the lowest price tags around on hardware, housewares, paint, and tools. They also make keys and can speak Russian, Polish, Yiddish, and even a good bit of English.

M. WOLCHONOK & SON
155 E 52nd St (bet Lexington and Third Ave)
212 755-2168, 212 755-0895
Mon-Fri: 8:45–5:45; Sat: 9–4:30

Wolchonok has been a family wholesale-retail business in the midtown area for over six decades. In those years, the neighborhood has influenced their business and vice versa. So while they might have been a general hardware store elsewhere, in Manhattan Wolchonok is a prime source for furniture hardware, particularly legs and replacement pieces. Their business card says, "legs, legs, legs." (I wonder if they get calls from people expecting the Rockettes.) If a given limb, as the Victorians would call it, is not in stock, Wolchonok can make it to order. They do the same with towel bars, café curtain rods, brass switch plates, and decorator hardware. Speaking of the Victorians, the line of porcelain plumbing fixtures is authentically reproduced, while the other end of the bathroom spectrum features futuristic metal and Lucite fixtures. And while legs are the house specialty, Wolchonok can stand on an equally extensive line of casters, sockets, and glides.

NEW CATHAY HARDWARE CORPORATION
49 Mott St (at Canal St)   212 962-6648
Daily: 10–8

In the heart of Chinatown, this gem of a shop has been dispensing Chinese cooking items, utensils, hardware, small appliances, and restaurant equipment since 1928. There's no more authentic place to get your wok, chopsticks, steamer, or egg-roll roller, and prices and quality are geared for the professional. This is also a great place to find an unusual housewarming or shower gift.

P.E. GUERIN
23 Jane St (bet Greenwich St and Eighth Ave)   212 243-5270
Mon-Fri: 9:30–4:30 by appointment only;
closed first two weeks of July

Andrew F. Ward, P.E. Guerin's current president, is the fourth generation of the oldest decorative hardware firm in the country and the only foundry in the city. What's more, they've been on Jane Street for all 125 years plus of the firm's existence. In that time, though, the firm has grown into a worldwide operation. The main foundry is now in Valencia, Spain (although work is still done at the Village location), and there are branches and showrooms across the country and in Puerto Rico. The Jane Street location is still headquarters for manufacturing and importing decorative hardware and bath accessories. Much of it is done in brass or bronze, and Ward boasts that the foundry can make virtually anything in those materials, including copies and reproductions. The Gueridon table has garnered design and production awards and enjoys a worldwide reputation. Their fixtures have a similar reputation, yet no job is too small for this firm. It operates like the hometown industry it thinks it is. So they offer free estimates (for blueprints, etc.) and help with such hardware problems as locks that don't seem feasible. Their work is impressive.

PRO KITCHENWARE
204 Bowery   212 941-8118
Mon-Fri: 10–5

If you are a serious cook, then this is the place to shop. That goes for both home and restaurant chefs! Under one roof, you will find commercial kitchen supplies like glassware, china, pots, pans, bakeware, and just about every imaginable houseware utensil or gadget. They now sell heavy-duty restaurant equipment like ranges and refrigerators. Ask for Eva Taub; she is second-generation in the business.

SIMON'S HARDWARE
421 Third Ave (bet 29th and 30th St)   212 532-9220
Mon-Fri: 8–5:30; Sat: 10–5

This is really a hardware supermarket. Customers take numbers just as they would at a bakery counter. No one minds waiting, because Simon's offers one of the city's finest selections of quality hardware items, including custom-made decorative fixtures. The personnel are extremely patient, even if you just need something to fix a broken handle on a chest of drawers.

VAN WYCK DRAPERY HARDWARE SUPPLY
39 Eldridge St (near Canal St)   212 925-1300
Mon-Thurs: 8–5; Fri: 8–3; Sun: 9–4; closed Sun in summer

New York has four pages of listings in the Yellow Pages devoted solely to *retail* hardware stores, so to be singled out, a particular store has to be special. Van Wyck merits this distinction by virtue of its specialty in drapery hardware. Harold Lamm stocks all manner of drapery hardware, as well as supplies, urethane foam, and drapery trimmings. This is a particular boon to do-it-yourself drapery makers, since they can buy materials in the neighboring fabric shops, pick up the hardware here, and set it all up with one shopping trip. Should the draperies be ready-made (and these, too, can be purchased at a discount from stores close by on Grand Street), the same holds true. Even if your draperies were purchased elsewhere, the discount at Van Wyck makes a trip to the Lower East Side for hardware worthwhile.

W.G. LEMMON
755 Madison Ave (bet 65th and 66th St)   212 734-4400
Mon-Fri: 9–6; Sat: 9–5:30

W.G. Lemmon is a neighborhood housewares and hardware store that is totally aware of its location. Considering that the neighborhood is the Upper East Side in general and Madison Avenue in particular, it has to be a bit special, and it is. While they stock run-of-the-mill hardware and housewares, W.G. Lemmon manages to make this home-supply store look like a veritable boutique and gift center.

WILLIAMS-SONOMA
1175 Madison Ave (at 86th St)   212 289-6832
110 Seventh Ave (at 17th St)   212 633-2203
20 E 60th St (bet Madison and Park Ave)   212 980-5155
Mon-Fri: 10–7; Sat: 10–6; Sun: 12–5

1309 Second Ave (at 69th St)   212 288-8408
Mon-Fri: 10–8; Sat: 10–7; Sun: 12–6

From humble beginnings in the wine country of Sonoma, California, these stores have expanded over the nation and now are referred to as the "Tiffany of cookware stores." The serious lady or gentleman of the kitchen will find a vast display of quality cookware, bakeware, cutlery, kitchen linens, specialty foods, cookbooks, small appliances, kitchen furniture, glassware, and tableware. The stores also offer a gift and bridal-registry service, cooking demonstrations, free recipes, gift baskets, and shopping assistance for corporations or individuals. Ask for their very attractive catalog, which includes a number of excellent recipes.

Imports

Afghan

NUSRATY AFGHAN IMPORTS
215 W 10th St (at Bleecker St)   212 691-1012
Sun-Fri: 1–9; Sat: 1–11

Abdul Nusraty has transformed a corner of the Village into a corner of Afghanistan that is fascinating and free of politics. There are magnificently embroidered native dresses and shirts displayed alongside semiprecious stones mounted in jewelry or shown individually. One part of the store features carpets and rugs, while another displays antique silver and jewelry. Nusraty has an unerring eye; all of this is of the very best quality and often is unique as well. The business operates on both a wholesale and retail level. Nusraty is probably the best source for Afghan goods on this continent.

Arctic

ALASKA SHOP/GALLERY OF ESKIMO ART
31 E 74th St (nr Madison Ave)   212 879-1782
Tues-Sat: 11:30–6

This store and gallery is New York's most complete source for Eskimo art. Rare antiquities and artifacts of centuries-old Arctic cultures are displayed next to sculptures of Indians of the Northwest. Periodic shows highlight different aspects of Northern culture. A number of contemporary Eskimo artists whose works have been shown here have gained international acclaim.

Chinese

CHINESE PORCELAIN COMPANY
822 Madison Ave (bet 68th and 69th St)   212 628-4101
Mon-Fri: 10–5:30; Sat: 11–4; closed Sat in summer

Khalil Rizk and his partners began this company in 1985 as a source for Chinese decorative arts, with a particular emphasis on porcelain and furniture. Soon they had outgrown their quarters. Climbing half a flight of stairs sets the mood for one to become enthralled with the porcelain, period hardwood and lacquer furniture, cloisonné, woodcarvings, prints, and watercolors that make up the colorful stock. And that brief climb helps keep the overhead down!

WING-ON TRADING
145 Essex St   212 477-1450
Mon-Sat: 9–6

No need to go to Hong Kong to get your set of Chinese porcelain or earthenware. Wing-On, even though it is located on the disorganized Lower East Side, has a clean and complete stock of household goods. One of their specialties is Chinese tea, and they have just about any kind at prices considerably lower than your local grocery store.

General

BACK FROM GUATEMALA
306 E 6th St   212 260-7010
Mon-Sat: 12–11; Sun: 2–10

CHRYSALIS
340 E 6th St (bet First and Second Ave)   212 533-8252
Tues-Sun: 2:30–10:30

Even if these weren't two of New York's most intriguing import stores, I'd patronize them just for their names. Joe Grunberg and Susan Kaufman are the owners and buyers, and their devotion to Guatemalan artifacts is obvious. Their merchandise includes ethnic clothing, wall hangings, and jewelry from Central and South America, and from Asia as well. There are both exotic and classic styles of ethnic clothing. (Kaufman is a specialist in antique Tibetan jewelry.) Back from Guatemala also has the city's best collection of cloisonné earrings from mainland China. And there's more: preshrunk cotton clothing, masks, handmade sweaters, and artifacts from many different countries. Back from Guatemala has contacts with 35 countries and hundreds of world travelers, so it offers the best. Grunberg and Kaufman are among the most charming of New York's store owners. Their other store, Chrysalis, offers beautiful crystals, contemporary and ethnic jewelry, puppets, stationery, hand-made chiffon scarfs, body scents, and accessories.

JACQUES CARCANAGUES
106 Spring St (at Mercer St)   212 925-8110
Daily: 11:30–7

After a stint in the diplomatic service, Frenchman Jacques Carcanagues decided to assemble and sell the best of the world's artifacts that he had run across in his travels. So while the store has no particular ethnic or historical persuasion, it is, in his own words, "a complete ethnic depart-ment store, not a museum." Afghan textiles and Japanese *tansus* (dressers) are everywhere, as is more jewelry and lacquerware than can be counted. Despite protestations to the contrary, it is all of museum quality. It is also very appealing to SoHo shoppers, who may choose among Indian sculptures of many periods or kilims and rugs from places like Turkey, Afghanistan, and Tibet. The overall effect is like nothing so much as an Eastern marketplace; all that is lacking are the water pipes and music.

KATINKA
303 E 9th St (at Second Ave)   212 677-7897
Daily: 2–6 (call, as hours may vary)

This is an import paradise, with jewelry, natural-fiber clothing, shoes, scarfs, belts, hats, musical instruments, incense, and various artifacts from India, Thailand, Pakistan, Afghanistan, and South America. The most popular items are colorful shoes from India and embroidered silk skirts that look like they just came out of the Taj Mahal. The place is small, but so are the prices. Jane Williams and Billy Lyles will make you feel like you have just embarked on a worldwide shopping expedition!

PIER ONE IMPORTS
461 Fifth Ave (at 40th St)   212 447-1610
Mon-Fri: 8:30–8:30; Sat: 10–6; Sun: 11–6
71 Fifth Ave (at 15th St)   212 206-1911
Mon-Fri: 9–9; Sat: 10–7; Sun: 12–6
(New store at Third Ave and 87th St)

This is *the* import bazaar! No need to spend your time or money run-ning off to distant places; just come to Pier One. Here you will find dining-room sets, occasional furniture, bathroom accessories, picture frames, women's apparel, brassware, china and glassware, floor coverings, pillows, and much more. The goods come from exotic lands throughout Asia and the rest of the world. The selections are inviting, the prices right, and the place is fun to visit!

PUTUMAYO
857 Lexington Ave (bet 64th and 65th St)   212 734-3111
Mon-Sat: 11–7; Sun: 12–5
341 Columbus Ave (at 76th St)   212 595-3441
Mon-Sat: 11–7; Sun: 12–6
147 Spring St   212 966-4458
Mon-Sat: 11–7; Sun: 12–6

The merchandise is mostly designed by Putumayo and imported from Bali, Java, India, Sri Lanka, Portugal, Guatemala, China, and Uruguay. The emphasis is on fashions from around the world, and there is an extensive collection of folk art. In the fall, Putumayo displays a variety of hand-knit virgin-wool sweaters and jackets made from primitive fabrics. For summer, there are cotton sun dresses, skirts, and loose-fitting pants—all of them cool, comfortable, and practical.

Indian

HANDBLOCK
487 Columbus Ave (bet 83rd and 84th St)   212 799-4342
860 Lexington Ave (bet 64th and 65th St)   212 590-1816
Mon-Fri: 10–8; Sat: 10–7; Sun; 11–7

Handblocking, an ancient art of India, gives this store both its name and wares. The four partners divide their time overseeing production in India and merchandising at this store and other ones in Canada. There are linens, place mats, napkins, tablecloths, bedcovers, and dish towels, all created in India of cotton, tinted in brilliant colors and handblocked in designs that range from traditional to contemporary. One can also find rugs, dishes, jewelry, and pottery. The merchandise is distinctive and fashionable.

HIND INDIA COTTAGE EMPORIUM
1150 Broadway (at 27th St)   2l2 685-6943, 212 685-2460
Mon-Fri: 9:30–6:30; Sat: 11–5

Hind India Cottage Emporium features clothing, jewelry, handicrafts, and gifts imported directly from India. Moti R. Chani has a sharp eye for the finest details, and the saris and other Indian clothing he sells reflect that. The clothing is prized by both Indian nationals and neighborhood residents for its sheer beauty. The garments are made completely of cotton, feature many unique madras patterns, and come in small, medium, and large. Pay particular attention to the leather bags and jewelry.

Irish

THE GRAFTON SHOPPE
22 E 54th St (bet Madison and Fifth Ave)
212 826-6511, 800 643-7364
Mon-Sat: 11–9

The Grafton Shoppe is a delightful touch of Ireland in the middle of all the hustle and bustle of New York. You can stop by in the afternoon for a cup of tea with Bernadette Ryan. On the way out pick up some beautiful Irish imports, including sweaters, capes, blouses, hats, scarfs, jewelry, crystal, china, and even Irish food!

MATTIE HASKINS SHAMROCK IMPORTS
A&S Plaza, 901 Sixth Ave, (at 32nd St) 5th floor
212 564-7474
Mon, Thurs, Fri: 10–8:30; Tues, Wed, Sat: 10–6:45; Sun: 11–6

Several editions back, I commented about the housekeeping at the former address of this charming shop. To say the least, they were not happy! Now Cathy, Tom, and Kathleen have moved to sparkling new quarters, and their delightful bit of Old Ireland would pass any inspection. You can find anything and everything Irish, from tapes to candy, newspapers, tweed caps—and wonderful accents.

Italian

CAROSELLO MUSICALE COMPANY
119 Mulberry St (nr Canal St)   212 925-7253
Mon: 10 a.m.–11 p.m.; Tues: 10–10; Wed-Sun: 11–11

Every section of New York with a concentrated ethnic population has a group of stores that serve the specific needs of that nationality. Usually, the group will include a bakery and coffee shop, a bookstore, and an import shop featuring various items of the homeland. There is often one shop devoted to a distinctive characteristic of that nationality as well. What, therefore, could be more natural than a shop in Little Italy dedicated to recordings and music? Carosello is primarily a music shop specializing in Italian recordings and operas. But it is also a bookstore, import store, and gift shop. So you can find perfumes, Italian newspapers, magazines, and gifts, as well as Caruso recordings. The atmosphere is informal but proud, and frequently customers can be heard humming an aria while checking record labels. Even if you don't buy anything here, check out the espresso and breads at any of the neighboring cafés.

Japanese

THINGS JAPANESE
127 E 60th St, 2nd floor   212 371-4661
Mon-Sat: 11–5 (Tues: 11–6)

Things Japanese believes that the Japanese things that are most in demand are prints. So while there are all sorts of Japanese artworks and crafts, prints highlight the selection. They know the field well and believe that the market, while almost exhausted on the high-priced, established end, is only just beginning for newer and unknown artists. The store will help would-be collectors establish a grouping or assist decorators in finding the right pieces to round out the décor. There are also original 18th- to 20th-century Japanese woodblock prints, porcelains, baskets, chests, lacquers, and books. Prices range from ten to several thousand dollars, and everything is accompanied by a certificate of authenticity. Things Japanese claims that you need to appreciate both the subject matter and the artistry in the works it sells, and that's not a difficult task at all.

Korean

SEOUL HANDICRAFT TRADING
284 Fifth Ave (at 30th St)   212 564-5740
Mon-Fri: 9–6; Sat: 9–5; closed first week in July

If you want to really dress up your bedroom or dining room, the Korean hand-embroidered bedding, linens, tablecloths, and comforters from this house are unique and beautiful. Besides, the price is right!

Middle Eastern

PERSIAN SHOP
534 Madison Ave (bet 54th and 55th St)   212 355-4643
Mon-Sat: 10–7

This outfit has been in business since 1940, featuring unusual Middle Eastern items, including end tables, chairs, frames, mirrors, and brocades sold by the yard or made up in magnificent neckties for men. There are also Chinese vases, garden stools, and planters that will add a special air of interest to any setting. The jewelry selection is especially noteworthy: precious and semiprecious items, silver and gold cuff links, rings,

---

In 1664, the English king gave his brother, the Duke of York, all the territory in North America between the Delaware and Connecticut rivers. On August 28th, four British warships sailed into Nieuw Amsterdam harbor to claim the gift formally. On September 8th, 1664, Nieuw Amsterdam became known as New York.

earrings, bracelets, necklaces, belts, and heirloom pieces. And you won't have to go to Iran to pick up that caftan, Bedouin dress, water pipe, or Turkish coffee grinder you have always wanted!

Russian

VICTOR KAMKIN
925 Broadway (at 21st St)   212 673-0776
Mon-Fri: 9:30–5:30; Sat: 10–5

With the lessening of tension between the superpowers, more interest is being shown in all things Russian. Fluency in the Russian language is increasingly prized in business and government, and Victor Kamkin can be of great help in this area. His store features books in Russian, translations from Russian, guidebooks, art albums and reproductions, textbooks, and dictionaries. There is also an excellent stock of Russian music items (records and CDs), and souvenirs (like lacquer boxes and dolls). An added feature is a subscription service for Soviet magazines and newspapers.

Scandinavian

ALMUE STUEN
1061 Madison Ave (bet 80th and 81st St)   212 517-5744
Mon-Fri: 10–7; Sat: 10–6; Sun: 12–5

No need to take a trip to Scandinavia. Just come visit this delightful store that specializes in all sorts of items from this beautiful part of the world. Here you will find clothing, antique Scandinavian furniture, gifts, jewelry, glassware, toys, ironware, blankets and much more. Artists show off their talents in the gallery on the third floor. Almue Stuen is the center for Nordic art and craftsmanship in the New York area.

Ukrainian

SURMA "THE UKRAINIAN SHOP"
11 E 7th St (nr Third Ave)   212 477-0729
Mon-Sat: 11–6

Since 1918, Surma has conducted business as the "general store of the Slavic community in New York City." My only quarrel with the description is that it should not be limited to the city, since it seems capable of serving the entire hemisphere. More than a store, Surma is a bastion of Ukrainianism, and once inside, it is difficult to believe you're in New York. Fortunately, language is not much of a problem. The clothing here is ethnic opulence. There are dresses, vests, shirts, hand-tooled and soft-soled leather dancing shoes, hundreds of blouses, dresses, vests, and accessories. All are hand-embroidered with authentic detailing. For the home, there are accent pieces (including an entire section devoted to Ukrainian Easter-egg decorating), brocaded linens, and Surma's own Ukrainian-style honey (very different and very good). Above all, Surma is known for its records, stationery, and books; not surprisingly, the business is also known as the Surma Book and Music Company. Particularly note the collection of paintings and the stationery, which features modern-day depictions of ancient Ukrainian glass painting.

Jewelry

Pearls are very "in." Make sure you fully understand what you are buying. Practically all pearls on the market these days are cultured pearls, in which a mother-of-pearl bead is implanted in an oyster to start the pearl-coating process.

Akoya pearls: From Japan. The best ones are round and very white, with high luster and a slight rose tint.
South Sea pearls: Very large, from the South Pacific.
Black pearls: Grown in black-lipped oysters in Tahiti.
Baroque pearls: Less expensive, unusual shapes.
Mabe pearls: Grown as a blister on the inside of an oyster shell, these can be brittle and break easily. Prices have become inflated.
Dome pearl: Grown in Tennessee, these are more durable.
Freshwater pearls: Inexpensive and attractive, grown by a type of mollusk that produces many pearls simultaneously.

A correct description follows each misnomer. When it comes to buying any of the rocks listed below, be careful.

Japanese amethyst: synthetic amethyst
Alaskan black diamond: hematite
Herkimer diamond: colorless quartz
Matura diamond: colorless zircon
Mogok diamond: colorless topaz
Rangoon diamond: colorless zircon
Chatham emerald: synthetic
Gilson emerald: synthetic
Oriental emerald: green sapphire
Goldstone: glass with copper crystals
Australian jade: chrysoprase quartz
Indian jade: aventurine quartz
Korean jade: serpentine
Manchurian jade: soapstone
Mexican jade: dyed-green calcite
Soochow jade: serpentine, soapstone
German lapis: dyed-blue jasper
Swiss lapis: dyed-blue jasper
Atlas pearl: imitation
Red Sea pearl: coral

Adelaide ruby: garnet
Australian ruby: garnet
Balas ruby: spinel
Bohemian ruby: garnet
Brazilian ruby: tourmaline
Cape ruby: garnet
Lux sapphire: iolite
Water sapphire: iolite
Madeira topaz: quartz
Palmeira topaz: quartz
Rio topaz: quartz
Smoky topaz: smoky quartz

BILL SCHIFRIN
National Jewelers Exchange
4 W 47th St, Booth 86   212 221-1873, 212 944-1713
Mon-Fri: 10–5

From a booth in the National Jewelers Exchange—better known for its diamond engagement rings than its plain wedding bands—Bill Schifrin presides over a collection of 1,873 unusual wedding bands. Prices range from a few dollars to several thousand, depending upon the complexity of the work and the stones used. If you have the time, Bill Schifrin will tell you the story behind each ring: where it came from, how he got it, or about someone who bought a similar one recently. He's been doing this for over 40 years, and after all this time, you'd think he'd be cynical. But he's "just cautious," and his stories and prices draw customers from all over the world. The selection isn't bad, either.

DAVID SAITY/SAITY JEWELRY
48 E 57th St   212 223-8125

Trump Tower
725 Fifth Ave, (at 57th St) Level 5   212 308-6570
Both outlets: Mon-Sat: 10–6

David Saity's magnificent boutique creates a great showcase for his renowned collection of authentic Native American jewelry. In this collection are numerous rare and breathtaking turn-of-the-century collectors items, such as watchbands, belt buckles, bolo ties, squash-blossom necklaces, chokers, bracelets, rings, hair accessories, cuff links, earrings, and concha belts. Don't miss this one! The Trump Tower Saity gallery is a one-of-a-kind treasure trove, featuring the world's largest collection of authentic Native American jewelry. Over 8,000 original masterpieces, handcrafted by artisans of the Zuni, Navajo, Hopi, and Santa Domingo tribes, are shown here. The collection spans 50 years, featuring silver, turquoise, coral, jet, and mother-of-pearl gemstones.

FAR AND WIDE
175 E 86th St (at Third Ave)   212 369-0920
Mon-Sat: 10–8; Sun: 12–6

Subway arcades are neglected areas of commerce in New York (unlike in Vienna, for example), and with good reason. There is very little sold deep underground that could withstand scrutiny in the light of day. Furthermore, most shops whose sales depend upon bright, open displays that attract casual passers-by do not believe a potential clientele exists in a subway. There are two exceptions. The nut concessions are pretty universal and depend almost entirely upon impulse buying. Far and Wide is the other exception, and it's worth the trip to see why. They carry jewelry from 60 countries. Most is of a whimsical nature and is not made of valuable metals or precious stones, but all of it is very attractive and definitely not of the costume-jewelry class.

FORTUNOFF
681 Fifth Ave (at 54th St)   212 758-6660
Mon-Wed, Fri, Sat: 10–6; Thurs: 10–8

This is one of the best stores in Manhattan devoted to quality merchandise. Prices on all items are very competitive, and the store has a reputation for meeting or beating any legitimately quoted price in town. Although there are well-stocked housewares and gift departments, it is in the jewelry area—and especially antique silver—that the store really shines. There is a jeweler in residence at all times. Fortunoff shows one of the largest and finest collections of 14-, 18-, and 24-karat gold jewelry in the city, as well as a fine selection of precious and semiprecious stones and name-brand watches from the top watchmakers around the world.

GALERIA CANO
Trump Tower
725 Fifth Ave, (at 57th St) Level C-4   212 751-0946
Mon-Sat: 10–6

Galeria Cano is a third-generation jewelry and accessory business with items made from 24K gold-plated brass. If you want to attract some attention at the next big party, put on one of their dramatic, handcrafted reproductions of original pre-Columbian artifacts from the family collection. If you mention this book, they will smile upon you with some special prices for 18K jewelry!

JAN SKALA
1 W 47th St   212 246-2814
Mon-Sat: 9:30–5

Jan Skala is located in the diamond district, that mysterious one-block area of Manhattan that purportedly handles every diamond imported into this country. The retail customer's place here is nebulous at best. Jan

Skala, a reliable, non-"tourist trap" diamond dealer, is not averse to retail customers. Jan Skala is ostensibly wholesale-only, but its ground-floor storefront is the first spot off Fifth Avenue to welcome retail customers. In addition to diamonds, there is a large selection of pocket watches, antique watches, and jewelry. The latter includes a good selection of Russian enamels, Fabergé eggs, and the like. Quite a sight to see, even if you don't buy.

MAX NASS
118 E 28th St (bet Park Ave S and Lexington Ave)
212 679-8154
Mon-Fri: 9:30–6; Sat: 9:30–4

The Shah family members are jewelry artisans; Arati is the designer, and Parimal ("Perry") is the company president. Together, they make and sell handmade jewelry, and they also service, repair, and restore antique jewelry. At Max Nass, they deal in virtually any type of jewelry: antique (or merely old), silver, gold, and semiprecious. Two special sales each year bring their low prices down even lower. One occurs during the last three weeks in January (33% discount); the other runs for two weeks in July (25% discount). In between, Arati will design pieces on whim or commission. The necklaces are particularly impressive; his work is often one-of-a-kind. The store also restrings and redesigns necklaces.

MURREY'S
1395 Third Ave (bet 79th and 80th St)   212 879-3690
Daily: 9:30–6:30

Murrey's, family jewelers since 1936, sells fine jewelry and giftware. In the service area, they do fine-jewelry repair, European clock repair, machine engraving, stringing, and watch repair, and they have a talented goldsmith for custom-designed pieces.

MYRON TOBACK
25 W 47th St (bet Fifth and Sixth Ave)   212 398-8300
Mon-Fri: 8:30–4; closed first two weeks in July and Dec 25–Jan 1

You must meet Myron Toback. Ostensibly, he is a refiner of precious metals with a specialty in findings, plate, and wire. Not very exciting or helpful to the average customer, you might think. But you'd be wrong. Note the address. Toback is not only in the heart of the diamond district, he is a bona fide landlord of a new arcade that is crammed full of wholesale artisans of the jewelry trade. Taking their cue from Toback, they are open and friendly to individual retail customers. So note Toback as a source of gold, gold-filled, and silver chains sold by the foot at a wholesale price. And don't overlook the gold and silver earrings, beads, and other jewelry items that are sold at prices laughably less than those at establishments around the corner on Fifth Avenue. Even though most of the customers are professional jewelers or wholesale organizations, Toback is simply charming to do-it-yourselfers, schools, and hobbyists. They now carry the tools and other materials to string beads and pearls. Toback delights in showing people how to bypass jewelry middlemen in putting together their own custom-made items.

OCINO
66 John St (bet Nassau and William St)   212 269-3636
Mon-Fri: 8:30–6

Ocino is a fantastic find right in the middle of the financial district. At Ocino, there are diamonds, custom-made jewelry, handmade jewelry, resetting and redesigning, top brand-name watches, and gold chains sold by weight to those who want to make their own jewelry. For the latter, Ocino claims the lowest prices in the city. Ocino calls itself the "quality store downtown" and offers tableware by Lenox, Royal Copenhagen, Waterford, Kosja Boda—and more. Despite having a virtual monopoly on those brands in the area, everything is sold at a discount that ranks among the best in the city.

PEDRO BOREGAARD
48 W 48th St, #904   212 819-1060
Mon-Fri: 10–5:30 by appointment

Unusual rings, earrings, and bracelets—all one-of-a-kind and each a true work of art—are the hallmarks of this very talented designer. Boregaard's credentials are impressive: apprenticeship and professional work in Germany; a jewelry workshop in England; work with Tiffany for designers such as Angela Cummings, Elsa Peretto, and Paloma Picasso. His pieces can also be found at Bergdorf Goodman.

RENNIE ELLEN
15 W 47th St, Room 401   212 869-5525
Mon-Fri: 10–4:30 by appointment only

To visit New York without meeting Rennie Ellen is to miss what New York shopping is all about. For openers, she is a wholesaler offering the sort of discounts the city's wholesale businesses are famous for. Second, she deals in diamonds, which are certainly knockout souvenirs to bring back from the city. Third, not only was she the first woman diamond dealer in the male-dominated diamond district, but feminism has made her a world-renowned consumer advocate. Rennie Ellen personally spent so much time and effort to keep the diamond district straight and honest that she earned the title "Mayor of 47th Street." Finally, only a fool would negotiate a purchase in any wholesale area without knowing the merchant. This is particularly true when one is dealing with diamonds, since thousands of dollars depend upon quirks visible only to a jeweler's eye. In such a field, Rennie Ellen's reputation is impeccable. Her store deals exclusively in diamond jewelry. There are pendants, wedding bands, engagement rings, and diamonds to fit all sizes, shapes, and budgets. All sales are strictly confidential and are made under Rennie Ellen's personal supervision.

ROBERT LEE MORRIS
409 W Broadway (bet Spring and Prince St)   212 431-9405
Sun-Fri: 11–6; Sat: 12–7

ARTWEAR
456 W Broadway   212 673-2000
Sun-Fri: 11–6; Sat: 12–7

Robert Lee Morris often sets the pace in the jewelry world. Between periodic exhibitions of the latest in contemporary jewelry, Artwear sells the works of 25 different artists. If you want to be noticed, merchandise from either of these shops will make wonderful conversation pieces. The real emphasis here is on *art*.

SAVAGE UNIQUE JEWELRY
59 W 8th St (nr Sixth Ave)   212 473-8171
Mon-Sat: 11–7; Sun: 1–5

267 Columbus Ave (at 72nd St)   212 724-4662
Mon-Sat: 12–9:30; Sun: 1–6

1007 Madison Ave (at 78th St)   212 794-6463
Mon-Sat: 10–7; Sun: 1–6

Outrageous is the word here! Very unusual and unique watches, flamboyant accessories, and spectacular earrings will dazzle your eye. This is not a place for the conservative matron, but the fashion-conscious will be able to rub shoulders with many soap-opera actors and rock stars. Be sure to check out the large assortment of gold rings. As a special service, they will make appointments after hours for out-of-city visitors.

Ladders

PUTNAM ROLLING LADDER COMPANY
32 Howard St (bet Lafayette St and Broadway)   212 226-5147
Mon-Fri: 8–4:30

This is a great esoteric shop on an esoteric street. What, you might ask, would anyone in New York do with those magnificent rolling ladders used in traditional formal libraries? And could there possibly be enough business to keep a place like this running all those years? The answer is that Putnam has been in existence since 1905. Clever New Yorkers turn to Putnam for designing access to their lofts (especially sleeping lofts). Here's a partial list of ladders, which come in many different hardwoods: rolling ladders (custom-made, if you want), rolling work platforms, telephone ladders, portable automatic ladders, scaffold ladders, pulpit ladders, folding library ladders, library stools, aerial plat-forms, library carts with steps, steel warehouse ladders, safety ladders, electric stepladders for industrial use, and mechanics' stepladders. Then there are Alpine, Crosby, Peerless, Durable, twin, and dual-purpose stepladders; extension ladders; window cleaners' ladders; sectional lad-ders; shelf ladders; extension trestle ladders; custom ladders; and more.

Leather Goods, Luggage

ANANIAS
197 Bleecker St   212 254-9540
Daily: 11–10

901 Sixth Ave (A&S Plaza)   212 947-4814
Daily: 9:45–7

367 W Broadway   212 274-9229
Daily: 12–7

The owners of Ananias – one from Germany and the other from China – fell in love with each other and with the beautiful island of Crete, and decided to bring back a bit of that culture to our country. They have a large selection of handmade sandals, purses, knapsacks, school bags, belts, briefcases and wallets made from cowhide. The tanneries in Crete date back to the 16th century and produce some of the most durable goods around. I have been using cowhide suitcases that were purchased over 45 years ago. They have made dozens of trips around the world and are still very serviceable.

BETTINGER'S LUGGAGE SHOP
80 Rivington St   212 674-9411, 212 475-1690
Mon-Fri: 9–6; Sun: 9:30–6

This tiny shop can be located by keeping an eye peeled for a mound of luggage heaped all over the sidewalk in front of the store. Inside, it is even more crowded, but amazingly the people who run Bettinger's can put their hands on almost any piece of luggage in only a few minutes. Their merchandise includes Samsonite, American Tourister, Ventura, and Mark and Andiano luggage; camp trunks; briefcases; and leather envelopes – all in both first-quality and irregulars. The prices are among the best in New York, being at least 30% lower than you'd pay uptown.

JOBSON'S LUGGAGE
666 Lexington Ave (bet 55th and 56th St)
212 355-6846, 800 221-5238
Mon-Sat: 9–6

Apparently, the key to a successful luggage store in New York is to offer a vast selection at discount prices. With the exception of a store such as T. Anthony, which depends on quality and service to offset its high prices, most of the stores I've checked out offer good variety and a range of discounts. Naturally, the stores I've listed are the best of the genre. At Jobson's, they claim to have the largest selection of brand-name luggage, attaché cases, and small leather goods in the metropolitan area. (Their stock is enormous.) They also claim that their large sales volume enables them to sell at guaranteed low prices that are close to wholesale. Believe it or not, that is not enough to gain recognition in this book. There must be a dozen other stores with similar claims, but Jobson's sales staff and personal attention set it apart. They also offer free monogramming, a repair service, and free delivery in Manhattan.

ROBERTO VASCON HANDBAGS

194 Columbus Ave (bet 68th and 69th St)   212 721-0623
198 Spring St (bet Thompson and Sullivan St)   212 274-1213
Mon-Sat: 11–7; Sun: 11–6 (summer: Mon-Sat till 8)

If you are in the market for a really unusual handbag at a reasonable price, this is a good place to start. All of their items are made in New York. They feature a solid color trim, inlaid with exotic leathers. The limited editions look like they cost in the hundreds, but all are under $200. They also repair and refurbish their own merchandise. This talented young Brazilian started the hard way — on street corners — and has lately expanded his business to include belts and small leather goods.

T. ANTHONY

480 Park Ave (at 58th St)   212 750-9797, 800 722-2406
445 Park Ave (at 56th St) in early 1994
Mon-Fri: 9:30–6; Sat: 10–6

T. Anthony handles luxurious luggage of distinction. Anything purchased here will stand out in a crowd as being of really fine quality, and that is what T. Anthony customers expect and receive. Every person who comes into the store receives courteous attention. Luggage comes in sizes ranging from small overnight bags to massive pieces that just fall short of being steamer trunks. Gifts have a similar range. All are based on the leather-luggage theme, but the wallets, key cases, and bill-folds make terrific gifts, individually or in matched sets. Don't come looking for discount prices here, but the quality and service are well-established New York traditions. Exclusive T. Anthony products are also available through the store's catalog.

Lighting Fixtures and Accessories

JUST BULBS

938 Broadway (at E 22nd St)   212 228-7820
Mon-Fri: 9–6

From a practical point of view, this is probably the only shop in the world that can supply certain types of bulbs. In addition to the obvious ones, Just Bulbs has a collection for use in old fixtures. The staff boasts that the store stocks almost 25,000 types of bulbs. It's hard to imagine that many exist! The shop looks like an oversized stage dressing-room mirror, and everywhere you look there are bulbs connected to switches that customers are invited to flick on and off.

JUST SHADES
21 Spring St   212 966-2757
Thurs-Tues: 9:30–4

This store specializes in lampshades. They are experts on the proper shade for the proper lamp, and they share their expertise with retail customers. Their experience encompasses the entire subject, and they carry only the finest shades. They have lampshades of silk, string, parchment, and just about any other material imaginable. Interestingly, they say their biggest peeve is customers who "neglect" (a polite way of putting it) to take the protective cellophane off their shades, because the shade actually collects ruinous dust.

LIGHTING PLUS
676 Broadway (bet 2nd and 3rd St)   212 979-2000
Mon-Sat: 10–7; Sun: 11–7

Few things are more annoying than not having that special electrical gadget you need to fix a lamp, computer, hair dryer, or whatever. Running around from one store to another to find an elusive item is even more frustrating. Take heart. Go straight to Lighting Plus. In a thankfully well-organized store, you can find just about anything connected with electricity. And the personnel are eager to help amateur shoppers.

LOUIS MATTIA
980 Second Ave (bet 51st and 52nd St)   212 753-2176
Mon-Fri: 9–6

Few stores repair or stock parts for lamps, but Louis Mattia's crowded shop has enough spare parts to fix almost any lamp. Consequently, he is patronized by a wide variety of customers: socialites who need a priceless heirloom repaired; decorators, such as Denning-Fourcade; and other merchants who need quick repairs on slightly damaged merchandise for their customers. All of them receive prompt and courteous attention from one of the most knowledgeable staffs in New York.

NEW YORK GAS LIGHTING COMPANY
145 Bowery (bet Grand and Broome St)   212 226-2840
Mon-Fri: 9–5; Sat, Sun: 10:30–5

The definitive source for traditional and elegant quality lighting, New York Gas Lighting Company is mentioned repeatedly by decorators. Consumers will find a wide array of merchandise for all lighting applications at good prices. Be sure to go through all the rooms. There's lots to see!

ROSETTA ELECTRIC CO.
21 W 46th St (bet Fifth and Sixth Ave)   212 719-4381
Mon-Fri: 9–6; Sat: 9–5

Right in the middle of Manhattan, under one roof, you can buy top-name lighting fixtures like Lightolier, Stiffel, and Kovacs, and also find a great selection of electrical supplies. Rosetta started on Fulton Street in 1936, and it has been a reliable electrical-goods store for over half a century. Special orders are taken, delivery service is available, and best of all, prices are in the discount category. This is a personalized, boutique-style operation, with merchandise not usually found in a "home center" type of outlet.

TUDOR ELECTRICAL SUPPLY
222–26 E 46th St (bet Second and Third Ave)   212 867-7550
Mon-Thurs: 9–5; Fri: 9–4:30

Although you may feel like you need an engineering degree to enter Tudor Electrical, the staff is trained to explain everything in stock to even the proverbial novice who doesn't know how to replace a light bulb. Light bulbs are the store's forte. No one has ever counted the varieties available, but they are cataloged by wattage, color, and use by a staff who can almost immediately pull out the best bulb for your needs. Quartz, tungsten, and halogen bulbs don't distort light, while incandescent and fluorescent lamps offer the best lighting for desk work. Energy-efficient bulbs come with vital instructions, which is a boon to people who don't know wattage from lumens output. Better still, while discounting at least 20% off list price, Tudor Electrical Supply will guide a customer to the best bargains.

UPLIFT
506 Hudson St   212 929-3632
Daily: 1–8

The big question is, what does the name Uplift have to do with a store that mainly sells art-deco and Victorian lighting fixtures? In any event, Uplift has one of the largest collections of original American art-deco chandeliers in the country. They also have some less expensive reproductions and a full line of fantasy figures, like wizards and dragons made of pewter. They will rebuild old torchier lamps so that they are like new, but taller. Uplift also has accessories for lighting fixtures: lamps, wiring, bases, glass bowls, and shades, including glass ones for lamps suspended from the ceiling and replacement slip shades deco fixtures.

Magic

FLOSSO AND HORNMANN MAGIC
45 W 34th St, Room 607   212 279-6079
Mon-Fri: 10:30–5:30; Sat: 10:30–4

Harry Houdini got his tricks and kicks here. That is not surprising, since he is but one of a score of professional magicians who have owned this shop since its creation in 1856. Flosso and Hornmann is proof that magic is timeless, not only because its clientele spans all ages, but because the store seems unchanged since Houdini's day. In part, that's due to the dim light and dust, but mostly it's because the stock is so complete. It's hard to think of a trick that's *not* stocked here. The staff, if asked, will show you what's new. In addition to magic acts, the shop carries books, manuals, historical treatises, and photographs, and they'll even create stage sets. For their final act, ladies and gentlemen, they'll produce a professional magic catalog in which many of the tricks are explained in detail. Don't tell a living soul!

LOUIS TANNEN
6 W 32nd St, 4th floor   212 239-8383
Mon-Wed, Fri: 9–5:30; Thurs: 9–7; Sat: 9–3

This is a magical place! Tony Spina, or any of his very helpful associates, will spend time with both amateur and professional magicians. There is a fabulous catalog available for a modest price, and classes are offered each week. The quality here is first-rate, as they produce many pieces in their own machine and wood shops. There are over 8,000 individual items and 350 books in their inventory. Now, would they please tell me how the magician I saw got that caged tiger from one side of the stage to the other in a matter of an eyeblink?

Maps

HAGSTROM MAP AND TRAVEL CENTER
57 W 43rd St (at Sixth Ave)   212 398-1222
Mon-Fri: 9:30–5:30

Doug Rose and his crew are real experts when it comes to maps and travel information. They are just about the only complete map and chart dealer in the city; they highlight the maps of most every major manufacturer and five branches of the U.S. government, as well as their own. There are also nautical, hiking, global, and travel guides. A periodic newsletter is available, and maps can be shipped anywhere in the world.

MARTAYAN LAN
48 E 57th St (bet Park and Madison Ave)
212 308-0074, 800 423-3741
Mon-Fri: 10–6; Sat: by appointment

I am fascinated by maps, so this place — which features the world's leading stock of antique maps — is a real favorite of mine. There are also rare books, globes, decorative prints, and atlases. Outstanding pieces from the 16th and 17th centuries are a specialty. Even if you are not in the market for such items, you will enjoy chatting with the friendly and knowledgeable staff. An illustrated catalog is issued regularly.

Memorabilia

LOST CITY ARTS
275 Lafayette St (bet Prince and Houston St)   212 941-8025
Mon-Fri: 10–6; Sat, Sun: 12–6

Are you looking for a special old Coca-Cola advertising piece or a souvenir from the New York World's Fair? Lost City specializes in such items, with an emphasis on architectural antiques, old advertising fixtures, and a great collection of vintage New York souvenirs. They also carry furniture and lighting from the 1930s to 1960s.

MOTION PICTURE ARTS GALLERY
133 E 58th St, 10th floor   212 223-1009
Tues-Fri: 12–5

Ira Resnick runs the world's only gallery that treats movie posters as works of art. The Motion Picture Art Gallery is just that: a gallery that displays original posters and lobby cards from motion pictures as artwork and sells them. His customers include film buffs and vintage poster collectors and investors. A *Casablanca* poster that could be had for a couple of dollars in the early Sixties fetches upward of $4,500 today! There are over 15,000 items in stock here.

MOUSE 'N AROUND/CARTOON BUDDIES
A&S Plaza, 901 Sixth Ave, 7th floor (bet 32nd and 33rd St)
212 947-3954

7 W 42nd St (off Fifth Ave)   212 382-2051
Mon, Thurs, Fri: 9:45–8:30; Tues, Wed, Sat: 9:45–6:45;
Sun: 1–6

Mouse 'n Around has moved to the sparkling A&S Plaza, and Mickey seems happy in his new digs. In addition to all the Disney character merchandise, you will find Snoopy, Betty Boop, Looney Tunes, Aladdin, and Beauty and the Beast. The largest selection of cartoon watches in the city can be found here. The big stock is in clothing; there are sizes and styles for all members of the family, such as a reversible sweat shirt with Mickey's likeness on it.

MOVIE STAR NEWS
134 W 18th St (bet Sixth and Seventh Ave)   212 620-8160
Mon-Sat: 10–6

In what is becoming the movie memorabilia center of the city, Movie Star News claims to have the world's largest collection of movie photos. If you thought the heyday of movie stars was long gone, don't tell the folks here, because stars past and present still shine brightly in this shop. Movie Star News offers posters, press books, and other cinema publicity materials as well. The selection is arranged like a library; the Kramers, who run Movie Star News, actually do a lot of research for magazines, newspapers, and the media. This may be the closest thing to Hollywood on the East Coast.

ONE SHUBERT ALLEY
1 Shubert Alley (bet Broadway and Eighth Ave)
212 944-4133, 800 223-1320 (mail order only)
Mon-Sat: 9 a.m.–11:30 p.m.; Sun: 12–7:30

Shubert Alley is a narrow alleyway in the Broadway theater district that is often used as a shortcut between theaters. One Shubert Alley is the only retail establishment in the alley, and it's a fascinating place to browse. You will find T-shirts, posters, recordings, buttons, and other paraphernalia from current shows both on and off-Broadway. There is a mail-order catalog and a special number for telephone orders.

PERFORMING ARTS SHOP
Metropolitan Opera House at Lincoln Center
212 580-4356
Mon-Sat: 10–9; Sun: 12–6

This out-of-the-way shop on the lower level of the Metropolitan Opera House is an aria unto itself. Everything on sale has a tie to the performing arts, no matter how tenuous. All of it is high quality and in good taste. So there are top-notch gifts with a performing-arts motif (most with a music flavor) and an enviable collection of printed matter. CDs and tapes are balanced by beach towels and Beethoven T-shirts.

SILVER SCREEN
35 E 28th St (bet Park and Madison Ave)   212 679-8130
Mon-Fri: 12–7

If the 1950s were the silver years for you, this is your shop. Ken, Carol, and Irma sell posters, autographs, movie magazines, and other theatrical memorabilia. In addition, they rent out old photographs in either black-and-white or color. The place is jammed with memories of movie and stage personalities and events, evoking tears and thrills of glamorous yesteryears. Clients must write or phone in their wants. *No browsing!*

Mirrors

SUNDIAL-SCHWARTZ
159 E 118th St   212 289-4969
Mon-Fri: 8–4:30; Sat: 10–4

The people at Sundial claim they supply "decorative treatments of distinction," and anyone who has ever seen a cramped New York apartment suddenly appear to expand with the strategic placement of a few mirrors will understand how they can make that claim. Sundial deals with professional decorators as well as do-it-yourselfers, and both benefit from the staff's years of experience. There are mirrors for home, office, and showroom. In addition, Sundial will remodel, resilver, antique, and move mirrors. Sundial also custom-designs window treatments, blinds, shades, storm windows, draperies, and more. The primary service here, however, is the decorating advice.

Museum and Library Shops

As anybody who is on their mailing lists knows, many museums now produce catalogs that allow people who live thousands of miles away to browse through their gift shops. In New York, however, you can do it in person at more than two dozen different places. Whether you're looking for that one-of-a-kind gift, a poster for your college dorm room, or unusual books, I highly recommend shopping in the following places. They're short on Empire State Building salt-and-pepper shakers and long on well-made, classy items. In most cases, at least some of the wares in these shops directly relate to current and past exhibits or the museum's permanent collection. If you plan on going to do all your Christmas or birthday shopping at one of these stores, find out whether you would save money by becoming a member. Even at those museums that charge an admission fee, you need not pay if you're only there to shop.

AMERICAN BIBLE SOCIETY
1865 Broadway (at 61st Street)   212 408-1200

Located to the left of the entrance in the main lobby, this small store sells different versions of the Bible, study guides, and children's books with biblical themes. It's open on weekdays from 9 to 5.

AMERICAN CRAFT MUSEUM
40 W 53rd St (bet Fifth and Sixth Ave)   212 956-3535

Although quite small, this "sales desk" in the lobby of the American Craft Museum is worth a visit if you're interested in contemporary craft. Much of the selection changes with the exhibits, but you will always find exhibition catalogs and postcards, as well as interesting jewelry and other original work by contemporary artists. The shop and the museum share the same hours: Wednesday through Sunday from 10 to 5 and Tuesday from 10 to 8.

AMERICAN MUSEUM OF NATURAL HISTORY
Central Park W (bet 77th and 81st St)   212 769-5100

Because so many visiting children sometimes create a logjam in the exhibit areas, the designers had a great idea: separate gift shops for adults and children. Unfortunately, that's about the best thing about these gift shops. While the adult version does have lots of interesting jewelry, minerals, books on natural history, and knickknacks from around the world, the shop itself is very cramped and the displays are poorly presented. The children's shop—the Junior Shop on the lower level—is nothing special, although I've yet to meet a child who wouldn't be drawn in by all the dinosaur merchandise! The hours of these shops are a bit different than the hours of the museum itself. Both shops are open Sunday through Thursday from 10 to 4:45. The adult one is open Friday and Saturday from 10 to 7:45, while the Junior Shop is open only from 10 to 5:45 on those days.

ASIA SOCIETY
725 Park Ave (bet 70th and 71st St)   212 288-6400

Off the Asia Society's main lobby to the right is an exceptional book and gift shop that's a little-known treat for anyone interested in anything Asian. Its collection of books by American and Asian authors on Asian religions, philosophy, art, culture, history, and other topics is among the largest in the nation. The store also carries a wide range of children's books, language books, and coffee-table books. To your left, inside the bookstore, is a rather small but wonderful gift store full of games, dolls, prints and posters, jewelry, scarfs, wrapping paper, T-shirts, stationery, and other imports from all over Asia. They even carry an assortment of chopsticks! The store is open on weekdays from 10 to 6:30, on Saturday from 11 to 6, and on Sunday from noon to 5.

CATHEDRAL CHURCH OF ST. JOHN
THE DIVINE
Amsterdam Ave at 112th St   212 222-7200

Known as the Cathedral Shop, this eclectic gift shop and bookstore is tucked off the left side of the main sanctuary, about halfway between the main entrance and the altar. Because the cathedral is still under construction and a stoneworks operates on the site, the Cathedral Shop sells very reasonably priced gargoyles, grotesques, and other examples of the stonecutter's work. It also specializes in stained glass, antique and other kinds of crosses, Christian books, and things like creches and Christmas tree ornaments from all over the world. You can find a little bit of a lot of things here: Pressed flowers in glass, wrapping paper, wind chimes, mobiles, Ghanaian *kente* cloth, note cards and stationery, jams, spices, and children's books are just a sampling of the selection. The atmosphere is very pleasant, and browsing is encouraged. The shop is open every day from 9 to 5.

THE CLOISTERS
Fort Tryon Park   212 923-3700

The Cloisters gift shop is actually one of the Metropolitan Museum's satellite gift shops. It's smaller and less crowded than the ones inside the Metropolitan and stocked mostly with items related to the museum's medieval collection. Both the Cloisters and its gift shop are open Tuesday through Sunday. The doors open at 9:30 but the gift shop closes a half-hour earlier than the museum (about 4:45 in the warmer months and 4:15 in the winter). I can't imagine that anybody would come all the way up here just to shop, but check in at the front desk and let the attendant know if that's what you intend to do.

COOPER-HEWITT
2 E 91st St (bet Fifth and Madison Ave)   212 860-6868

After I complained in the last edition about the cramped quarters of the Cooper-Hewitt's gift shop and bookstore (it was stuck behind the main staircase), the curators informed me that they will move to roomier quarters in the mansion's music room. Hooray! This museum, dedicated to all aspects of design and run by the Smithsonian Institution, is exceptional, and its store is one-of-a-kind. Look for vases, tea sets, wallpaper, and an excellent collection of books on all aspects of design. As is the museum, the shop is open Tuesday from 10 until 9, Wednesday through Saturday from 10 to 5, and on Sunday from noon to 5. Check in at the front desk and let the attendant know if you're just here to shop.

THE FRICK COLLECTION
1 E 70th St (bet Fifth and Madison Ave)   212 288-0700

Rather than trying to be all things to all people, as some museum gift shops do, the Frick's gift shop makes the most of its small space by concentrating on exquisite cards and a few books. You can also find a small assortment of scarfs, maps, and other upscale tourist items here, but the cards and to some extent the books are what make a visit here worthwhile. The store is to the right of the main entrance, near the coat-check area. It's open Tuesday through Saturday from 10 to 6 and on Sunday from 1 to 6. Check in at the front desk and let the attendant know if you're just here to shop.

THE GUGGENHEIM MUSEUMS
1071 Fifth Ave (bet 88th and 89th St)
575 Broadway (at Prince St)   212 360-3500

Although many items for sale in these stores are ordinary — scarfs, T-shirts, prints and posters, tote bags, umbrellas, note cards and stationery, jewelry, and children's toys — the designs and craftsmanship are anything but. If you're after an unusual clock or the right pair of earrings to set you apart from the crowd, these are definitely places to look. Both shops also carry books on modern art as well as exhibition catalogs. The store at the Guggenheim on Fifth Avenue is located to the left of the main entrance and is open Friday through Wednesday from 10 to 8 and Thursday from 11 to 6. (The museum itself is closed on Thursday.) The store at the SoHo location is right inside the front door and is open Sunday, Monday, and Wednesday from 11 to 6 and Thursday through Saturday from 11 to 10.

INTERNATIONAL CENTER FOR PHOTOGRAPHY
1130 Fifth Ave (at 94th St)   212 860-1777
1133 Sixth Ave (at 43rd St)   212 768-4682

These two shops are definitely places to look if you're shopping for a photography buff. They are both relatively small but have excellent collections of books about the history and technology of photography. You can also find various coffee-table books of work by specific photographers, as well as prints, picture frames, and unusual postcards. Both are open Tuesday from 11 to 8 and Wednesday through Sunday from 11 to 6. Check in at the front desk and let the attendant know if you're just here to shop.

INTREPID SEA-AIR-SPACE MUSEUM
Pier 86 (at 46th St and the Hudson River)   212 245-0072

This museum's gift shop has all sorts of junk, but it's also a great source for books on military history, space exploration, and different aircraft and weapon systems. This is also a place to look for model airplanes and ships. The store is located to the right of the main museum entrance, and you need not pay admission to shop there. As is the museum, the gift shop is open every day from 10 to 5 between Memorial Day and Labor Day, and Wednesday through Sunday between 10 and 5 the rest of the year.

JULLIARD BOOKSTORE
W 65th St off Broadway, 2nd floor   212 799-5000, ext 237

The Julliard Bookstore is much like other college bookstores in that you can find pens, notebooks, sweat shirts, and stickers for your car. But the similarities stop there. If you are interested in music history and theory, there is no better bookstore in the city. You can also find lots of sheet music for the piano, guitar, violin, and other instruments. The store is open Monday, Wednesday, and Thursday from 9:30 to 7; Tuesday and Friday from 9:30 to 5:30; and Saturday from 10 to 4.

METROPOLITAN MUSEUM OF ART
Fifth Ave bet E 80th and 84th St   212 535-7710

Macy's Herald Square, W 34th St and Sixth Ave, mezzanine level
212 268-7266

New York Public Library, 40th St and Fifth Ave
212 332-1360

Rockefeller Center, 15 W 49th St (bet Fifth and Sixth Ave)
212 332-1360

The two-floor store inside the Metropolitan Museum of Art is the grandfather of all museum gift shops. They specialize in reproductions of paintings and other pieces from their incredible collection, as well as other museum collections around the world. That means you can find jewelry, statues, vases, scarfs, ties, porcelain, prints, rugs, napkins, silver serving dishes, and scores of other beautiful gift items. You can also find umbrellas, tote bags, and other things with the Metropolitan's name emblazoned on them, as well as books relating to special exhibits and the museum's extensive holdings. There's even a bridal registry department! The prices range from very reasonable to wildly expensive, and the salespeople are usually as patient as they are helpful. There are satellite gift shops inside the museum itself (a beautiful one specializing in jewelry is located directly across the main entrance hall to your right) and throughout Manhattan. Both the Metropolitan and the stores inside it are open Tuesday, Wednesday, Thursday, and Sunday from 9:30 to 5:15, and Friday and Saturday from 9:30 to 8:45. The hours of the satellite shops vary.

METROPOLITAN OPERA SHOP
Metropolitan Opera House, Lincoln Center   212 580-4090
835 Madison Ave (bet 69th and 70th St)   212 734-8406

Both the original shop and its new satellite on the East Side are slices of an opera lover's heaven. In addition to operas on video, compact disc, and other media, you'll find books, mugs, umbrellas, stationery, T-shirts, and even pillows for the opera buff. The store inside the Metropolitan Opera House opens at 10 on weekdays and Saturday and does not close until the second intermission of the evening's performance. It's also open Sunday from noon to 6. The East Side store is open Monday through Saturday from 10 to 6 and on Sunday from noon to 5. If you're at the Lincoln City store, be sure to check out the Performing Arts Shop on the lower concourse, too. And if you're looking for posters and prints from various seasons, go to the Gallery, on the lower concourse.

MUNICIPAL ART SOCIETY
457 Madison Ave (bet 50th and 51st St)   212 935-3960

The Municipal Art Society is a nonprofit organization dedicated to urban planning and historic preservation. Although it's best known for its excellent walking tours, you'll find both a gallery and a bookstore in its headquarters on the left side of the New York Palace. The bookstore, called Urban Center Books, is among the best sources for books and magazines on urban planning, architecture, and interior design in the country. In fact, students studying those subjects at Columbia University actually come here to buy their books. The store is open Monday through Thursday from 11 to 7 and Friday and Saturday from 10 to 6.

MUSEUM FOR AFRICAN ART
593 Broadway (bet Houston and Prince St)   212 966-1313

Anybody interested in African art—either books about the subject or the actual work of African artists and artisans—ought to make a stop at this relatively small but unusual gift shop. You can't miss it; the shop begins the moment you walk in the door and runs around the right side of the main desk. In addition to some beautiful coffee-table books, check out the wonderful collection of children's books. Both the museum and the shop are open Wednesday, Thursday, and Sunday from 11 to 6 and Friday and Saturday from 11 to 8.

MUSEUM OF AMERICAN FOLK ART
2 Lincoln Sq (Columbus Ave bet 65th and 66th St)
212 496-2966
62 W 50th St (bet Fifth and Sixth Ave)   212 247-5611

Like the small galleries at the museum's Lincoln Square location, these shops offer a range of Americana—innovative toys and books for children, quilts and the sort of knickknacks you would find in an upscale country cottage. The Lincoln Square location is adjacent to the museum and is open Monday, Tuesday, and Saturday from 11 to 6; Wednesday, Thursday, and Friday from 11 to 7:30; and Sunday from noon to 6. The midtown location is across the street from Radio City Music Hall. It's open Monday through Saturday from 10:30 to 5:30.

MUSEUM OF THE CITY OF NEW YORK
Fifth Avenue (bet 103rd and 104th St)
212 534-1672, ext 227

Although the relationship between the museum's collection and the items for sale in the gift shop is often tenuous at best, there is no better source in the city for books, posters, and other material relating to the city and its history (particularly since the New York Historical Society's gift shop closed its doors). The store is open Wednesday through Saturday from 10 to 5 and Sunday from 1 to 5.

MUSEUM OF MODERN ART
11 W 53rd St (bet Fifth and Sixth Ave)   212 708-9480

Most of the items in this two-story shop relate to the museum's incredible collection (as opposed to just its exhibits) of modern art. Its selection of books on the subject is second to none, but you'll also find such things as stationery, prints, wrapping paper, videos, and calendars. It is adjacent to the museum and open Friday through Wednesday from 11 to 5:45 and Thursday from 11 to 8:45.

MUSEUM OF MODERN ART DESIGN STORE
44 W 53rd St (bet Fifth and Sixth Ave)   212 767-1050

Across the street from the museum, this magnificent store is dedicated to what the curators consider to be the very best in modern design. Furniture, vases, ties, tablecloths, silverware, picture frames, lamps, and toys and books for children are just a few of the things you'll find here. You can even buy wall-to-wall carpeting for your home! These items are not cheap, but they are of the highest quality. The store is open Monday, Tuesday, Wednesday, Friday, and Saturday from 10 to 6; Thursday from 10 to 9; and Sunday from 11 to 6.

MUSEUM OF TELEVISION AND RADIO
25 W 52nd St (bet Fifth and Sixth Ave)   212 621-6800

This shop, across the main lobby from the information desk, is so small that I would almost describe it as a cubbyhole, but a stop here is a must for any fan of television or radio. Fans of such popular shows as *M*A*S*H, Star Trek,* and *Quantum Leap* will be particularly excited. Postcards, posters, books, T-shirts, videos, tapes of old radio shows, and relatively inexpensive knickknacks like key chains and magnets are among the things they've managed to squeeze into this tiny space. Some of the merchandise relates to the museum's constantly changing exhibits. The shop is open Tuesday, Wednesday, Friday, Saturday, and Sunday from noon to 6 and Thursday from noon to 8.

NEW YORK PUBLIC LIBRARY
Fifth Ave bet 41st and 42nd St, Room 116
212 869-8089

If ever there were a perfect gift shop for intellectuals (and those who fancy themselves as such), this is it. Located just off the main lobby and a bit to the right, this store features everything from magnets with sayings like "I think therefore I'm dangerous" and "Think for yourself, not for me" to books about the library's history. It rarely *seems* very busy, but I think this store is just terrific and have found its staff to be particularly pleasant and helpful. The library and the store share the same hours: Tuesday and Wednesday from 11 to 7:30, and Thursday, Friday, and Saturday from 10 to 6.

PERFORMING ARTS SHOP
Metropolitan Opera House, Lincoln Center, lower concourse
212 580-4356

Much like the Metropolitan Opera Shop one floor above it, but with a wide selection of things for children and an even wider selection of recordings, this store is lots of fun for anyone interested in opera, classical music, and the performing arts. It's open weekdays and Saturdays from 10 until the end of the second intermission of the evening's performance, and Sunday from noon to 6. If you're interested in prints and posters from past seasons, walk a little further down the hall and visit the Gallery.

PIERPONT MORGAN LIBRARY
29 E 36th St (at Madison Ave)   212 685-0008

Called Morgan House, this gift shop inside the prestigious Pierpont Morgan Library is located in an elegant room past the modern atrium in the middle of the complex. You'll find all sorts of books about Renaissance art, current and past exhibitions, and related subjects, as well as unusual china, clocks, painted trays, boxes, and other gifts. The shop also sells cards and postcards with pictures of paintings and other pieces from the library's remarkable collection. Morgan House is open Tuesday through Saturday from 10:30 to 4:45 and Sunday from 1 to 4:45. I can't imagine coming here without at least walking through J. P. Morgan's library and study, but check in at the front desk and let the attendant know you're headed for the shop, if that's all you plan to do.

SOUTH STREET SEAPORT
Fulton Street   212 669-9455

South Street Seaport is full of stores, and merchants in the surrounding area sell souvenirs, too, but the Seaport Museum itself runs three gift stores. The best one for adults is the Chandlery, at 209 Water Street, in the row of buildings to your left just inside the entrance to the complex. If you're a weekend sailor or are shopping for someone who is, this upscale store is a great find: you'll find everything from ties, umbrellas, and jewelry to prints, books, and maps with nautical themes. The store's collection of model boats is particularly impressive. The less expensive Museum Shop at 14 Fulton Street, next to the Visitors Center, is probably better for the sort of basic souvenirs that kids seem to eat up — ships in bottles, sweat shirts, magnets, and the like. Finally, if you're shopping for children or have some with you, make sure to look at the toys and accessories in the Container Store on Pier 16. The whole complex is open every day from 10 to 6 (10 to 5 during the winter).

THE UKRAINIAN MUSEUM
203 Second Ave, (bet 12th and 13th St) 5th floor
212 228-0110

This funny little place is hard to find and not exactly on the main tourist path, but it's a real treasure trove for anyone interested in Ukrainian eggs (already made and kits for decorating them yourself), embroidery, and other crafts. Like the small museum, the gift shop is open only Wednesday through Sunday from 1 to 5.

UNITED NATIONS
First Ave bet 45th and 46th St   212 963-4465

On the lower level of the main UN building you'll find a UN bookstore, a UN post office (a real treat for stamp collectors), a small UNICEF shop, and an even smaller shop run by the UN Women's Guild. That's in addition to the main UN gift shop, also on the lower level. The bookstore features calendars, postcards with the flags of all member nations, holiday cards in dozens of different languages, and a wide variety of books about the UN and related issues. The main gift shop features a wonderful array of carvings, jewelry, scarfs, dolls, and other items from all over the world. The nicest imports can get pretty pricey, but it's definitely going to a good cause! (Unfortunately, the gift shop also features some rather tacky New York tourist souvenirs.) Like the UN itself, the stores are open weekdays from 9 to 5 and weekends and holidays from 9:15 to 5. One final thought: if you are interested in UNICEF cards and gifts but find the selection at the UN itself rather thin, I encourage you to visit the store in the lobby of the nearby UNICEF House (E 44th St bet First and Second Ave).

THE WHITNEY MUSEUM'S STORE NEXT DOOR
943 Madison Ave (bet 74th and 75th St)   212 606-0200

Although there is a small and rather perfunctory gift shop in the lobby of the Whitney Museum itself, any fan of modern art looking for unusual gifts ought to stop by the Store Next Door. In addition to all sorts of creative toys and games for children, you'll find a changing collection of jewelry, T-shirts, scarfs, ties, and offbeat things like drawer handles made of silverware and lamps made from a boxing glove. Most things are pretty pricey and the staff is not always particularly helpful, but the store is a great hit with residents and visitors alike. The store is quite narrow, and its entrance—to the right of the Whitney itself—is easy to miss, so keep your eye out for it. The Store Next Door is open Tuesday, Wednesday, Friday, Saturday, and Sunday from 10 to 6, and Thursday from 10 to 8.

Music, Musical Instruments

BLEECKER BOB'S GOLDEN OLDIES RECORD SHOP
118 W 3rd St (bet MacDougal St and Sixth Ave)   212 475-9677
Sun–Thurs: noon–1 a.m.; Fri, Sat: noon–3 a.m.

Let us sing the praises of Bleecker Bob, who is nothing if not perverse. (Name another store open till 3 a.m. on Christmas Day!) For one thing, although there is a real Bob (Plotnik, the owner), the store isn't on

Bleecker Street. For another, Bleecker Bob is an institution to generations of New Yorkers who have sifted through the selection of virtually every rock record ever recorded. With a stock that includes all those old records (including rare jazz), autograph parties for rock stars, and a boast that they can fill any wish list from their stock, Bleecker Bob's is much more than a punk-rock store. It is also *the* gathering place in the wee hours of the morning in the Village. But above all, it's one great source for out-of-print, obscure, and imported discs.

DAYTON'S RECORD ARCHIVES
77 E 10th St (at Fourth Ave)   212 254-5084
Mon-Fri: 11–6:30; Sat: 11–6

Dayton's is to records what the Strand Book Store (their neighbor) is to books. They both have the same sources – reviewers' copies and promotional materials – and both pass on the savings to retail customers. Dayton's specializes in long-playing phonograph records, particularly those that are out-of-print.

DETRICH PIANOS
211 W 58th St (nr Broadway)   212 246-1766
Mon-Fri: 10–6; Sat: 10–4

Kalman Detrich fled Hungary for the United States many years ago, bringing his love and knowledge of pianos with him. His shop, within earshot of Carnegie Hall, ministers to any of the myriad needs the piano player might have. Detrich will tune, repair, polish, rent, buy, sell, and even buy back a piano with all the finesse of his Old World training. His specialty is antique pianos. He lovingly restores them, and the few he can't restore, he polishes to a gloss and sells as furniture rather than as musical pieces. The small shop is jammed with the cream of whatever is being revitalized at the moment, and passers-by cannot help but understand Detrich's pride when viewing the finished results.

DRUMMERS WORLD
147 W 46th St   212 840-3057
Mon-Fri: 10–6; Sat: 10–4

Rat-tat-tat! This is a great place, unless the patron is your teenager or an upstairs neighbor. In any case, Barry Greenspon and his staff take great pride in guiding students as well as professionals through one of the most well-rounded percussion stores in the country. Inside this drummer's paradise you'll find everything from commonplace equipment to one-of-a-kind antiques and imports. All of the instruments are high-quality symphonic percussion items, and customers receive the same attention whether they are members of an orchestra or kitchen-spoon rappers. For the latter, the store offers instructors and how-to books. There are esoteric and even ethnic instruments for virtuosos who want to experiment. Drummers World has a catalog and will ship anywhere in the country.

FOOTLIGHT RECORDS
113 E 12th St (bet Third and Fourth Ave)   212 533-1572
Mon-Fri: 11–7; Sat: 10–6; Sun: 12–5

At Footlight, the emphasis is on show tunes, film soundtracks, and jazz, in keeping with this outfit's passion for rare and odd records. For many albums, their prices are just about the best around—but many of their records just aren't around anyplace else. If an original cast album was made of a Broadway show, you can bet Footlight has it. What is really impressive is the organization that enables the store's personnel to know at a glance what is and is not available. They have one of the most comprehensive collections of film scores in the country, whole collections of artists from the 1920s through the 1960s, an impressive showing of European and Japanese imports in related fields, and a large selection of both big-band and early jazz.

FORD PIANO SUPPLY COMPANY
4898 Broadway (bet 204th and 207th St)   212 569-9200
Mon-Fri: 8:30–5:30

John Ford's father was in the piano-repair business. When John took over, he began collecting odds and ends whenever he found them, and he soon had more piano parts than pianos in his shop. Along with the best collection of supplies for piano repairs, Ford garnered a reputation as *the* place to go for piano tuners. So Ford all but abandoned buying and selling instruments and concentrated on rebuilding pianos (often from scratch) and supplying piano parts. The Ford family can refinish, tune, rebuild, and adjust any kind of acoustic piano. They will custom-make covers and benches, as well as pedals, and they sell an array of piano-tuning tools, lamps, chairs, and coasters. The Fords will happily conduct tours of their piano-rebuilding factory, which is a sight to see. But for the most part, Ford's customers never come to the shop. When you're the only store in town supplying everything for pianos, most customers order by mail or telephone. The Fords also rent and tune pianos.

GRYPHON RECORD SHOP
251 W 72nd St, 2nd floor   212 874-1588
Mon-Sat: 11–7; Sun: 12–6

Gryphon is one of a handful of stores specializing in rare and out-of-print LPs. They're world-famous for their collection. Raymond Donnell knows his business; he's able to help customers search out the most elusive LP, be it classical, jazz, Broadway, pop, or the spoken arts. But the emphasis is on classical recordings.

THE GUITAR SALON
45 Grove St (Seventh Ave and Bleecker St, at Sheridan Sq)
212 675-3236
By appointment

Beverly Maher's salon is a unique one-person operation located in a historic brownstone in Greenwich Village. Here you will find handmade classical and flamenco guitars for serious students and professionals, priced from $1,500. The shops buys and sells fine instruments, giving outstanding personal service from a talented guitarist. The salon specializes in 19th- and 20th-century vintage instruments. Appraisals are available, and lessons are given on all styles of guitars. Maher appraised Segovia's guitars, which he donated in 1987 to the Metropolitan Museum. Even the Rolling Stones shop here!

HMV U.S.A.
1280 Lexington Ave (at 86th St)   212 348-0800
Mon-Thur, Sun: 10–10; Fri, Sat: 10 a.m.–midnight

This is truly a musical supermarket! There are separate departments for rock and pop, classical, dance, jazz, and video. Listening booths are available, and a discount club is offered to regular patrons. This outfit is nearly a century old, with outlets all over the world. They know their business. If you are looking for CDs, cassettes, records, VHS tapes, laser discs, or accessories, HMV is a good place to visit.

JAZZ RECORD CENTER
236 W 26th St, Room 804   212 675-4480
Tues-Sat: 10–6; June 1-Labor Day: open Mon-Fri, closed Sat

This is the only jazz specialty store in the city. They deal primarily in out-of-print jazz records, but there are also CDs, videos, books, posters, photos, and periodicals on the topic. The center buys and sells collections, runs a search service, fills mail orders, offers appraisals, and holds an annual jazz rarities auction. All of this is run by Frederick Cohen, a world-famous specialist on jazz history. Cohen is a charming guy who really knows his business.

JOSEPH PATELSON MUSIC HOUSE
160 W 56th St   212 582-5840
Mon-Sat: 9–6; (closed Sat in summer)

Located behind Carnegie Hall, Joseph Patelson is a shop known to every student of music in the area. From little first-graders in need of theory books to artists from Carnegie Hall wanting an extra copy of sheet music, everyone stops here first because of the fabulous selection and excellent prices. The stock includes music scores, sheet music, music books, and orchestral and opera scores. All are neatly cataloged and

displayed in open cabinets. One can pore through the section of interest—
be it piano music, chamber music, orchestral scores, opera scores, old
popular songs, concerts, ethnic scores, or instrumental solos. Sheet
music, incidentally, is filed in bins the way records are elsewhere. There
are some musical accessories, like metronomes and pitch pipes, as well.
Patelson's is an unofficial meeting place for the city's young artists. Word
goes out that "we're looking for a violinist," and meetings are often arranged in the store. Mail and phone orders are accepted.

LAST WOUND-UP
1595 Second Ave (bet 82nd and 83rd St)   212 288-7585
Mon-Sat: 10–6; Sun: 11–6

If it winds up, it's probably here. Nathan Cohen has a vast selection
of intriguing windup toys, ranging in price from $1 to $800 (for antiques).
The Last Wound-Up is one of those fun places to shop, even when there
are no kids with you. But hold on to your wallet if Junior is tagging along!

LYRIC HIGH FIDELITY
1221 Lexington Ave (bet 82nd and 83rd St)
212 535-5710, 212 439-1900
Mon-Sat: 10–6

Lyric is the place for sound fanatics who know what they're doing.
As Michael Kay says, Lyric is not for beginners. But anyone who has
the knowledge and necessary cash can indulge his wildest audio fantasies
here. You can part with between $1,000 and $60,000 in a morning's
worth of shopping here. Lyric has been in business for over 30 years,
selling equipment to people who want the best. Kay sniffs at names like
Sony, which the average person considers top-of-the-line. Lyric carries
only the best lines of each component, and the names of its suppliers
are unknown to all but the most discriminating audiophile. If that's you,
this is your store.

MANNY'S
156 W 48th St (bet Sixth and Seventh Ave)   212 819-0576
Mon-Sat: 10–6

Manny's is a huge discount department store for musical instruments.
"Everything for the musician" is their motto, and it is borne out by a
collection of musical equipment so esoteric that different salesmen are
experts in different departments. There is an emphasis on modern music,
as evidenced by the hundreds of autographed pictures of contemporary
musicians and singers on the walls, and the huge collection of electronic
instruments. This does not, however, preclude classical instruments, and
there is a good collection of them as well. All of the musical instruments,
keyboards, accessories, electronic equipment, and supplies are sold at
very good discount prices.

MUSIC STORE AT CARL FISCHER

62 Cooper Sq (at 7th St and Fourth Ave)   212 677-0821
Mon-Sat: 10–5:45

Outside the Carnegie Hall area, the Music Store at Carl Fischer offers the best selection of sheet music from all publishers and categories, including pop, jazz, folk, rock, and classical. Everything is reasonably priced, with real bargains to be found in the older music. The store also has extended research facilities and background information for piano, vocal, instrumental, band, orchestral, and choral music. And that pretty much covers it all.

NOSTALGIA . . . AND ALL THAT JAZZ

217 Thompson St (bet Bleecker and 3rd St)   212 420-1940
Mon-Thurs: 1–8; Fri: 1–9; Sat: 1–10; Sun: 1–7:30

Guess what they sell here! The answer is recorded nostalgia, especially jazz LPs. Most of the recordings are of early radio programs, jazz programs, and soundtracks of old shows and movies. There are a few vocal LPs, too. All are very reasonably priced. The shop has set up a sideline in photography, and Kim Deul and Mort Alavi do a healthy business producing, cataloging, and reproducing photos. Nostalgia will reproduce any photograph, in any size or quantity, up to 30"x 40". They also have a good collection of posters, sports photos, movie and jazz stills, and large (16"x20") show-business photos in black-and-white and color. Prices are excellent.

RITA FORD

19 E 65th St (at Madison Ave)   212 535-6717
Mon-Sat: 9–5

Rita Ford collects antique music boxes, and in the process she has become an expert in all aspects of the business. Her stock consists of valuable old music boxes, not-so-valuable old pieces, and ones in various states of disrepair. (Rita Ford also does repairs.) The main stock in trade is expertise; Rita Ford knows all there is to know about the music-box business. She is an acknowledged expert on music-box scores, workings, and outer casings. Some of her pieces are rare, one-of-a-kind antiques, and they are priced accordingly. Somewhat more reasonable are the contemporary pieces, based upon original antiques.

TOWER RECORDS

See below for addresses and phone numbers
Daily: 9 a.m.–midnight

Tower Records provides a selection of music that can satisfy any New Yorker, young or old. Their stores are busy, crowded, noisy, and fun. There is almost as much amusement to be had watching the parade of shoppers as there is enjoying the music. The stores at 692 Broadway (at 4th St; 212 505-1500) and 1961 Broadway (at 66th St; 212 799-2500) carry records, tapes, and CDs. The annex at 4th St and Broadway (212 505-1500) features classical, Western, and used records. Tower Video Stores are located at 1977 Broadway (at 67th St; 212 496-2500), 215 East 86th St (bet Second and Third Ave; 212 369-2500), and Fourth Ave and Lafayette St (212 505-1166).

VENUS RECORDS
13 St. Mark's Place (bet Second and Third Ave)   212 598-4459
Mon-Thurs: 12–8; Fri: 12–12; Sat: 11 a.m.–midnight; Sun: 12–8

For the rock and roll enthusiast, Venus offers one of New York's finest selections of 1950s and 1960s reissues and original editions, hardcore, punk, and new and used rock records not usually found in the Top Forty. They also carry imported and independent releases, many out-of-print items, and a large selection of 45s. They are the only store in Manhattan with used cassettes. You can bring in used LPs, CDs, and cassettes at any time to sell for cash or trade. A wholesale service is available, and they will place special orders for individual customers.

VINYL MANIA RECORDS
60 and 43 Carmine St   212 924-7223
Mon-Fri: 11–9; Sat, Sun: 11–7

There are no other record stores quite like Vinyl Mania. If you can't find it at one of their outlets, it probably doesn't exist. The specialties are as follows: 60 Carmine (12" dance, R&B, funk, rap, hip-hop, and house); 43 Carmine (All techno 12", LPs, CDs, and cassettes). You can see why they call these places "adventures in recorded music" and why DJs call this place home base.

Newspapers, Magazines

A&S BOOK COMPANY
304 W 40th St (bet Eighth and Ninth Ave)
212 695-4897, 212 714-2712
Mon-Fri: 10:30–6:30; Sat: 11–5

For some reason, the sleazy Times Square area has always had backdated-periodical shops, even before the ubiquitous porno dives. A&S, one of the best, is a source of back issues of nearly every periodical. The more respectable the magazine, the better the possibility of finding it. Prices are reasonable, though they often surprise people who once threw out the very issue they now seek. A&S specializes in cinema, sports, and fashion magazines. You can avoid the neighborhood altogether and shop by mail or phone.

HOTALINGS NEWS AGENCY
142 W 42nd St   212 840-1868
Mon-Fri: 7:30 a.m.–9 p.m.; Sat, Sun: 7:30 a.m.–8 p.m.

As every homesick out-of-towner should know, hometown newspapers can be picked up at Hotalings for the regular price, plus the cost of transportation. Domestic and foreign newspapers are sold on the day of issue (or soon thereafter), and many non-natives keep in daily contact with their hometowns through these papers. However, as many a Hollywood movie will attest, Hotalings also carries back issues (thereby enabling the hero to learn that his adversary has ceased to exist months ago, so he can return home). Back issues are erratic at best, and the days of sending the secretary out for the papers from Peoria for the past six months probably never existed, but there is still an ample selection.

Occult

MAGICKAL CHILDE
35 W 19th St (bet Fifth and Sixth Ave)   212 242-7182
Mon-Sat: 11–8; Sun: 12–6

I asked the proprietor, Herman Slater, how one could describe this incredible place to readers of a book on New York. He answered that his shop was an "occult emporium," and I guess that is the best formal description. You have to see this place to believe it; there is nothing else quite like it in New York. There are shelves and bins of quartz crystals, gemstones, books, ritual accessories, videos, herbs and oils, powders and incense, curios and tarot cards, jewelry, and just about anything else that fits the occult image. The aisles are filled with readers and lookers, and they are just about as fascinating as the merchandise. Oh, yes, there are skulls, too.

Optical

THE EYE MAN
2266 Broadway (bet 81st and 82nd St)   212 873-4114
Mon, Wed: 10–7; Tues, Thurs: 10–7:30; Fri, Sat: 10–6;
Sun: 12–5 (closed Sun in summer)

There are dozens of places in Manhattan to find eyeglasses, but not too many take special time and care with children. The Eye Man carries a good selection of frames for young people, as well as specialty eyewear for grown-ups.

GRUEN OPTIKA
1225 Lexington Ave (bet 82nd and 83rd St)   212 628-2493
599 Lexington Ave (bet 52nd and 53rd St)   212 688-3580
1076 Third Ave (bet 63rd and 64th St)   212 751-6177
740 Madison Ave (at 64th St)   212 988-5832
2382 Broadway (at 88th St)   212 724-0850
Mon-Fri: 9:30–6:30; Sat: 10–5; open Sun at Madison Ave
and West Side: 12–5

Gruen Optika boasts the same faces and personal quality care year
after year. The firm enjoys a reputation for excellent service, be it
emergency fittings or one-day turnaround, and there's a super selection
of specialty eyewear. Their sunglasses, theater glasses, sport spectacles,
and party eyewear are particularly noteworthy.

JOEL NAME OPTIQUE DE PARIS
353 Bleecker St (nr 10th St)   212 929-5511
Mon, Tues, Thurs-Sat: 11–7; Wed: 12–8

When ordering glasses, I always feel more comfortable knowing that
the people who are helping me are true professionals. Service is the name
of the game here. Owner Joel Nommick and his crew will show you
some of the most fashionable specs in town.

MORGENTHAL-FREDERICS OPTICIANS
685 Madison Ave (bet 61st and 62nd St)
940 Madison Ave (bet 74th and 75th St)
212 838-3090
Mon-Fri: 9–6 (Thurs: 9–7); Sat: 10–5:30

If you are looking for state-of-the-art creative and elegant eyewear,
this is the place. Owner Richard Morgenthal, a very knowledgeable and
helpful gentleman, is on the job himself. He features his own designs,
manufactured in Europe and created in-house. As an added service, they
will make appointments with some of New York's best-known ophthal-
mologists. The fact that they have been in business in the city for eight
decades says something about the caliber of their products and service.

PILDES
111 Nassau St   212 227-9893, 800 427-4564
Mon-Fri: 8–6; Sat: 8:30–3:30

Pildes is the only "while you wait" eyeglasses chain in New York, and
it has an impeccable reputation. Nothing fancy here, just frames, styles,
and service, and all are first-class.

20/20 OPTICAL
210 E 86th St   212 517-4090
956 Third Ave (at 57th St)   212 754-0964
65 E 8th St (bet Broadway and Mercer St)   212 228-2192
Mon-Fri: 10–7:30; Sat: 10–6; Sun: 1–6

This is not just another optical store. All three branches of 20/20 carry highly styled eyewear that is sold only to a limited number of higher-grade outlets. Contact lenses are available, and special lenses can be ordered. Services include eye exams, one-hour glasses, and free delivery. A large selection of one-of-a-kind antique frames is also available.

WEINSTEIN OPTICS
1463 Second Ave (bet 76th and 77th St)   212 772-0404
Mon-Fri: 10:30–7:30; Sat: 10:30–5:30

Many children are faced with the need for professional advice on the proper kind of glasses. Weinstein, in addition to offering regular service for adults, has a dispensing room for children in order to make their experiences more pleasant and productive.

Photographic Equipment and Supplies

ADORAMA CAMERA
42 W 18th St (bet Fifth and Sixth Ave)   212 741-0052
Mon-Thurs: 9–6:45; Fri: 9–1:45; Sun: 9:30–6

These people operate one of the largest photographic mail order houses in the country. They carry a huge stock of photographic equipment and supplies, telescopes, and video paraphernalia, all at discount prices.

ALKIT CAMERA SHOP
866 Third Ave (bet 52nd and 53rd St)   212 832-2101
222 Park Ave S (at 18th St)   212 674-1555
Mon-Fri: 8:30–6:30; Sat: 9–5

If you're professional enough to want to go where the photographers of the Elite and Ford modeling agencies shop, Alkit is the place for you. But come here even if you haven't the faintest idea which end of a camera to look into. Most establishments that deal with the real pros have little time for amateurs. Not so here. Nothing gives Edward Buchbinder, the store's owner, more pleasure than introducing the world of photography to a neophyte. And few stores are better equipped to do so. Alkit maintains a full line of cameras, film, and equipment, as well as stereos, TVs, VCRs, and electronics, and they have a one-hour professional processing lab on-premises. The shop repairs and rents photographic equipment, and it also maintains a professional catalog full of praise and gripes about particular models. A recent addition is full-line electronic imaging. The attitude is always briskly professional.

47th STREET PHOTO
67 W 47th St (bet Fifth and Sixth Ave)   212 921-1287
Mon-Thurs: 9–6; Fri: 9–1:45; Sun: 10–4

115 W 45th St (bet Sixth Ave and Broadway)   212 921-1287
Mon-Thurs: 9:30–7; Fri: 9:30–3; Sun: 10–5

Before shopping here, be sure to check the Sunday *New York Times* ads. You will find some great prices on cameras and photographic equipment, FAX machines, phones, video items, CD and cassette players, and sunglasses. The 45th St store carries only computers.

KEN HANSEN PHOTOGRAPHIC
920 Broadway, 2nd floor (bet 20th and 21st St)   212 777-5900
Mon-Fri: 9:30–5:30; Sat: 9–5

This is *the* dream store for photographers, amateur or professional. It is all too common in many photo equipment outfits to be brushed off by distinterested, pushy salespeople. The exact opposite is true here. Hansen personnel are unfailingly polite and patient, and they will show customers a wide selection of products in every price category. There are major camera brands, lighting equipment, computer imaging products, binoculars, film, and accessories. Besides carrying new products, Hansen also has a good stock of quality used items. The folks here are very helpful for those who want hard-to-find merchandise not carried in regular stock. This place is a winner!

LAUMONT/NEWMAN PHOTOGRAPHICS
333 W 52nd St   212 245-2113
Mon-Fri: 9–5:30 (evenings and weekends by appointment)

Whether you are a professional or an amateur, Laumont/Newman can take care of your photographic needs. They do excellent work producing Cibachrome prints, all of them exhibition quality. They are also patient and understanding with those of us who need counseling and advice! They are not professional retouchers, but they can spot and make minor changes. Lamination and print-mounting are available on-premises.

WILLOUGHBY'S CAMERA STORE
110 W 32nd St (bet Sixth and Seventh Ave)   212 564-1600
Mon-Wed, Fri: 9–7; Thurs: 9–8; Sat: 9–7; Sun: 10–6

This is the largest camera shop in the world, boasting a huge stock, extensive clientele, and a good reputation. Willoughby's can handle almost any kind of camera order. For those in doubt, there is always the mail-order division. Ask for something really esoteric, and Willoughby's can probably fill it without a problem. In addition to selling all kinds of cameras, Willoughby's also services them, supplies photographic equipment, and recycles used cameras. A large computer division has been added, in addition to electronics and copiers.

Pictures, Posters, Prints

ARGOSY BOOK STORE
116 E 59th St   212 753-4455
Mon-Fri: 9–6; Sat: 10–5; closed Sat in summer

Ostensibly, the main stock in trade here is books (the older and rarer, the better), but knowledgeable browsers usually pass the books by in favor of the antique maps and prints. There is an excellent collection of Early American paintings and prints (Currier and Ives, among others) and a combination of maps and prints that would make a marvelous background. In fact, if a bookstore could be classified as a decorating accessory store, Argosy would qualify. The books are valued as much for their appearance and bindings as for their age and rarity, and maps and prints are similarly rated. Argosy handles first editions and Americana garnered from estate sales, and they will buy books from private sources. The specialties are antique prints, maps, autographs, and, surprisingly, medical books. The personnel seem rather too impressed with their own knowledge and position, so some customers feel intimidated. Too bad, because otherwise it is a great place to browse and shop.

JERRY OHLINGER'S MOVIE MATERIAL STORE
242 W 14th St   212 989-0869
Daily: 1–7:45 p.m.

How about a Bonnie and Clyde poster for the guest bedroom? Jerry Ohlinger has a huge selection of movie posters and movie and television photographs, and he will gladly provide a catalog to help with your selection. He also does research for these items.

OLD PRINT SHOP
150 Lexington Ave (bet 29th and 30th St)
212 686-2111, 212 683-3950
Mon-Sat: 9–4:30; closed Sat in summer

Glancing at the Old Print Shop while strolling down Lexington Avenue, one might think that time was suspended in the 19th century. Established in 1898, the shop exudes an old-fashioned charm that makes it appear timeless, and its stock only reinforces that impression. Kenneth M. Newman specializes in Americana. That includes original prints, paintings, town views, Currier and Ives prints, and original maps that reflect America as it used to be. Most of the nostalgic bicentennial pictures that adorned calendars and stationery were copies of prints found here. Amateur and professional historians have a field day in this shop. Kenneth Newman also does custom framing—"Correct period framing," he hastens to add—and prints in his frames are striking. Everything bought and sold here is original. Newman purchases estates and single items. A great place.

POSTER AMERICA
138 W 18th St (bet Sixth and Seventh Ave)   212 206-0499
Tues-Fri: 11–7; Sat, Sun: 12–5

You've never seen a poster gallery more interesting than this one! Jack Banning's store features original posters circa 1870–1950, nearly all of which are lithographs. But, ah, the setting! For ten years, he ran Poster America, the oldest gallery in the country devoted to vintage poster art. When that gallery on Ninth Avenue proved too small, he found and renovated a former stable and carriage house that used to serve the department stores on Ladies Mile in the 1880s. These quarters sport a magnificent mahogany-and-glass storefront; a huge, well-appointed gallery; and elegant living quarters for Banning. Poster America is known for brilliant graphics, rare posters, and the sheer magnitude of its pieces.

TRITON GALLERY
323 W 45th St (bet Eighth and Ninth Ave)   212 765-2472
Mon-Sat: 10–6

Theater posters are the show here, and Triton presents them like no one else. The complete list of current Broadway posters is but a small part of what's available, and it's balanced by an almost equally complete range of older show posters from here and abroad. Show cards are the standard 14"x22" size, and they seem to be the most readily available items. Posters range in size from 23"x46" to 42"x84" and are priced according to rarity, age, and demand. None of these criteria, incidentally, has much to do with the actual success of the show. Often, hundreds of posters were printed for shows that lasted less than a week and for which no one has any use. At the same time, a hit like *Annie* has produced more posters than anyone could use, so its show cards cost no more than some of the totally obscure ones. The collection is not limited to Broadway or even to American plays, and some of the more interesting pieces are of plays from other times. Triton also does custom-framing, and much of the business is conducted via mail and phone orders. Ask for Triton's catalog.

Plastics

PLASTIC PLACE
309 Canal St (bet Mercer St and Broadway)   212 226-2010
Mon-Fri: 9–5:30; Sat: 9–4:30

This large loft is dedicated to plastics—both the Lucite and soft plastic variety. Their line includes waterproofing material, Lucite cubes, and sheets of plastic. They are particularly accommodating to do-it-yourself customers.

PLEXI-CRAFT QUALITY PRODUCTS
514 W 24th St   212 924-3244
Mon-Fri: 9:30–5; Sat: 11–4

Plexi-Craft offers anything made of Lucite (and Plexiglas) at wholesale prices. If you can't find what you want among the pedestals, tables, chairs, shelves, and cubes, they will make it for you. The personnel are extremely helpful at pointing out the various styles in cocktail tables, shelves, magazine racks, and chairs. A catalog is available for $2.

Religious Arts

GRAND STERLING SILVER COMPANY
345 Grand St (bet Essex and Ludlow St)   212 674-6450
Sun-Thurs: 10:30–5:30

Ring the bell, and you will be admitted to a stunning collection of silver religious art. You'll also find almost anything from silver toothpick holders to baroque candelabra over six feet tall. Grand Sterling will repair and resilver any silver item, be it religious or secular. They are manufacturers and importers of fine sterling holloware, and silver is revered with a dedication unmatched elsewhere.

HOLY LAND ART COMPANY
160 Chambers St (bet W Broadway and Greenwich St)
212 962-2130
Mon-Thurs: 9–5:30; Fri: 9–4;
Sat: 9–2 (bet Thanksgiving and Christmas)

This store offers all kinds of religious articles to churches and the public. On hand is everything from Bibles to altars, although the latter — along with custom-made statues of wood, bronze, and marble — are usually special-ordered by churches rather than individuals. In December Holy Land is anything but pastoral, as customers snap up crèches, nativity scenes, and chalices. There's a tremendous selection, and prices are reasonable.

Rubber Goods

CANAL RUBBER SUPPLY COMPANY
329 Canal St (at Greene St)   212 226-7339
Mon-Fri: 9–5; Sat: 9–4:30

"If it's made of rubber, we have it" is this company's motto, and that sums up the supply at this wholesale-retail operation. There are foam mattresses, mats, bolsters, cushions, pads, pillow foam, pads cut to size, hydraulic hoses, rubber tubing, ventilation, vacuum hoses, sheet-rubber products of various kinds, and much more.

Safety Products

CONDOMANIA
351 Bleecker St   212 691-9442
Sun-Wed: 11–11; Thurs, Fri, Sat: 11 a.m.–midnight

Only in New York! Yes, Virginia, this is a store that specializes in condoms: all shapes, sizes, colors, and what-have-you. Mixed in are suggestive postcards and the like, and the place seems to be just as popular with the ladies as the gentlemen. I guess it was inevitable that someone would capitalize on the trend to make these items easily available, and your author is just keeping up with the times!

NEW YORK BABY PROOFING COMPANY
476 Columbus Ave (at 83rd St)   212 362-1262
Mon-Fri: 11–7; Sat: 11–6; Sun: 12–5

Safety first! This store started as a baby safety store but has expanded into a home safety emporium for the entire family. You can find personal protection and travel-safety merchandise and everything your home needs for fire safety. They will also come into your home and recommend, supply, and install safety products.

Security Devices

CCS COUNTER SPY SHOPPE
444 Madison Ave (at 49th St)   212 688-8500
Mon-Fri: 9–6; Sat: 11–4; Sun and evenings by appt

With security high on many people's minds these days, the CCS Counter Spy Shoppe provides mental and physical relief for worriers. These folks supply all manner of security items for business and private use. There is bulletproof clothing – everything from T-shirts to safari outfits. How about covert video systems, night-vision equipment, debugging devices, phone or FAX scramblers, voice-stress analyzers, lie detectors, and even bulletproof cars? It's all here. Confidential consultations can be arranged.

EMPIRE SAFE COMPANY
433 Canal St (at Varick St)   212 226-2255
Mon-Fri: 9–5; Sat: 10–3; closed Sat in July, Aug

Things have been safe around here since 1904! The same family has been in the business for three generations, and now they have the largest showroom of safes in the country. You can find vaults and safes for homes, offices, and restaurants. A great exhibit of antique and art-deco safes is well worth seeing. Empire also services all makes of safes. The newest: digital-look controls!

QÜARK SPY CENTRE
537 Third Ave (at 36th St)   212 889-1808, 800 343-6443
Mon-Fri: 9–6:30; Sat: 11–4 (by appointment)

This is where James Bond shops! Qüark is Manhattan's most exclusive and extensive countersurveillance showroom, with over 400 items on display. There is night-vision equipment, bug detection and telephone security items, audio devices, body armor, voice scramblers, long-play recording devices, alarm briefcases, and just about anything else you need to protect yourself these days.

Signs

CRYPTOGRAPHICS
40 E 32nd St   212 685-3377
Mon-Fri: 9–5

This is a handy service place to know about. They offer a complete service for signs, awards, advertising specialties, executive gifts, bulletin boards, and directories. Customized merchandise for businesses, organizations, and individuals is done quickly and accurately with computer-cut vinyl lettering, engraving, and silk-screening facilities on the premises.

LET THERE BE NEON CITY
38 White St   212 226-4883
Mon-Fri: 8:30–5:30; Sat by appointment

Though the image of neon is modern, it harks back to Georges Claudes' capturing of it (from oxygen) in 1915. And while the flashing neon sign is perhaps the ultimate urban cliché, Rudi Stern has turned the neon light into a modern art form. Let There Be Neon operates as a gallery; at any given moment, there is an assemblage of sizes, shapes, functions, and designs to entice the browser. Though they all have a neon base with a transformer, that is all they have in common. Almost all of Let There Be Neon's sales are custom-made, commissioned pieces. Stern claims that even a rough sketch is enough for them to create a literal or abstract sculpture within days.

Silver

EASTERN SILVER COMPANY
54 Canal St, 2nd floor   212 226-5708
Sun-Thurs: 9:30–5; Fri: 9:30–1 (showroom closed Fri)

Ascend to the second floor, ring the bell, and you enter a floor-to-ceiling wonderland of silver. Not all of it is clean or polished, but it has the potential of becoming as beautiful as only silver can be. The stock includes virtually any product made of silver or pewter, and Robert Gelbstein seems able to put his hand on any desired item almost immediately. Eastern has a large collection of Jewish ceremonial silver and secular silver items, such as candlesticks and wine decanters. However, most of the collection would be perfect gracing any home. Prices are extremely reasonable, and the quality is A-1. This place is a real find!

JEAN'S SILVERSMITHS
16 W 45th St (at Fifth Ave)   212 575-0723
Mon-Thurs: 9:15–4:45; Fri: 9:15–3:45

Having a problem replacing a fork that accidentally went down the garbage disposal? No worry. Proceed directly to Jean's, where you will find over a thousand discontinued, obsolete, and current flatware patterns. They specialize in antique and secondhand silver, gold and diamond jewelry, and watches.

ROGERS AND ROSENTHAL
22 W 48th St, Room 1102   212 827-0115
Mon-Fri: 10–3

Rogers and Rosenthal is one of the very best places in the city, if not *the* best, for silver, china, and crystal. Nearly all of their business is done by mail. ("Very slow delivery," they warn!) This shop features every major brand name, and a 25% or more discount on every piece by mail is an added bonus. They will send price lists upon request, and what isn't in stock will be ordered. They are very accommodating.

TIFFANY AND COMPANY
727 Fifth Ave (at 57th St)   212 755-8000
Mon-Sat: 10–5:30 (Thurs until 7)

What can you say about a store that's such an institution it has appeared in plays, movies, books, and even slogans? Almost nothing, except that the store really isn't *that* formidable or forbidding, and it can even be an exciting place to shop. Yes, there really is a Tiffany diamond, and it can be readily viewed on the first floor. That floor also houses the watch and jewelry departments, and while browsing is welcome, salespeople are quick to approach lingering customers. The second floor has clocks, silver jewelry, sterling silver, flatware, bar accessories, centerpieces, leather accessories, stationery, scarfs, and knickknack gifts. The third floor highlights china and crystal. The real surprise—and a fact not known to many New Yorkers—is that Tiffany has an excellent selection of reasonably priced items. Many come emblazoned with the Tiffany name and are wrapped in the famed Tiffany blue box—all at prices less than those of some neighborhood variety stores.

Sporting Goods

Bicycles and Accessories

THE BICYCLE & EXERCISE STORE
242 E 79th St (at Second Ave)   212 249-9344
Mon-Fri: 9:30–8; Sat, Sun: 9–7

This is *the* bike shop in New York. They feature children's bikes, racing bikes, tour bikes, fat-tire bikes, and BMX bikes—all made by leading manufacturers from around the world. Names like Raleigh and Peugeot are represented in quantity, and all kinds of accessories are available. The store will repair or rent any kind of bike, and now a big selection of exercise equipment is offered, including aerobic bikes, treadmills, and home gyms. They also guarantee to meet or beat any competitor's price. The service is good, the personnel knowledgeable, and the selection tremendous.

BICYCLE RENAISSANCE
491 Amsterdam Ave (at 84th St)   212 724-2350
Mon-Sat: 10–7; Sun: 10–5; summer: 10–7 daily

Biking is a way of life here, as are health foods to most of the staff. Services include custom-building bikes. Their mechanics aim for same-day service on all makes and models. They carry all manner of racing and mountain bikes. In stock are Trek, Giant, and Cannondale, and custom frames for Stronglight, Campagnolo, Ideale, and many others. I appreciate the fact that this was the only bike shop that did not pretend to have discount rates. And, in fact, its prices were exactly on par with the so-called discount stores.

STUYVESANT BIKE SHOP
349 W 14th St   212 254-5200
Mon-Fri: 9:30–6:30; Sat: 9:30–6; Sun: 12–5

When a customer comes into his shop, Salvatore Corso and his crew take time to find out what he or she really wants. Stuyvesant features a large selection of mountain bikes, models for off-road cycling, and all the new city bikes that are so hot and trendy. They cater not only to professionals but to family riders as well. A great deal of their business is in road-cycling and sport-touring. They have a large clothing and shoe department, with merchandise from Italy as well as top American manufacturers. Corso will store bikes over the winter months, and he will take care of most repairs within 24 hours from his large stock of spare parts.

Billiards Equipment

BLATT BILLIARD
809 Broadway (bet 11th and 12th St)   212 674-8855
Mon-Fri: 9–6; Sat: 10–4 (closed Sat in summer)

Blatt is outfitted from top to bottom with everything for billiards. You also get friendly pointers from a staff that seems, at first glance, to be all business.

Darts

DARTS UNLIMITED
30 E 20th St (bet Park Ave S and Broadway)   212 533-8684
Tues-Fri: 12–5:30; Sat: 11–4

Most towns have sporting goods shops, but few have even a department or a display for darts. In New York, things are different. There's Darts Unlimited, an emporium dedicated solely to darts and darting equipment. The collection of darts, dartboards, accessories, and English darting equipment (England's pubs are where it all started, you know) makes you wonder why they are not more prominent in other sports stores. Indeed, it seems that darts is a neglected game in America. That is a shame, since it's good for channeling aggression!

Diving

RICHARDS
233 W 42nd St (bet Seventh and Eighth Ave)   212 947-5018
Mon-Sat: 9–7:30

Aside from being near Times Square, there's nothing positive that can be said about the neighborhood, but much can be said about Richards' stock. The store calls itself an aqualung and skin-diving center, but there's also all kinds of sporting goods and clothing. The clothes are of the army/navy surplus variety. And in keeping with the low rent of the area, everything in the store is discounted. They claim to be the largest diving shop in the country.

Exercise Equipment

THE GYM SOURCE
45 E 51st St (bet Park and Madison Ave)   212 688-4222
Mon-Fri: 9–6; Sat: 10–5 (closed Sat in July and Aug)

This is the largest exercise-equipment dealer in the Northeast. They carry treadmills, bikes, stair and weight machines, rowers, and more. They will rent equipment or provide a visitor with an item to be used in a hotel room while in Manhattan.

Fishing Equipment

CAPITOL FISHING TACKLE COMPANY
Chelsea Hotel, 218 W 23rd St (nr Seventh Ave)
212 929-6132
Mon-Fri: 8–5:30; Sat: 9–4

Historical records show that over a hundred years ago the 42nd Street Library and the adjacent Bryant Park were once a cemetery and later a reservoir—an indication of just how distinct and countrified was their location in relationship to the rest of the city. In 1897, when Capitol Fishing Tackle Company was established, its present location would have justified a store dedicated to fishing. Today, in the hustle and bustle of Chelsea, the store is totally incongruous and yet it is typical of New York. Where else could one find a fishing store so totally landlocked that a subway roars beneath it, yet one that offers bargains unmatched at seaport stores? Capitol features a complete range of fishing tackle with such brand names as Penn, Shimano, Tycoon Finnor, Garcia, and Daiwa at the lowest possible prices. There is a constantly changing selection of fantastic specials and close-outs. Capitol buys up surplus inventories, bankrupt dealers, and liquidations. Almost nothing in the store was purchased at full wholesale, and those savings are passed on to the customer.

Game Equipment

V. LORIA AND SONS
178 Bowery (bet Kenmare and Spring St)   212 925-0300
Mon-Fri: 11–6; Sat: 11–4 (closed Sat in summer)

This family business, established in 1912, is a mecca for indoor sports enthusiasts. One can find a complete line of equipment. There are bowling and billiards items, pool tables, and such supplies as cues and chalk, plaques, and awards—not to mention ping-pong equipment and poker tables. When the family champion is triumphant, the winner's trophy can be ordered from Loria as well. It is impossible *not* to try out some of the equipment right on the premises, and Vernon and Roger Loria don't seem to mind.

General

EASTERN MOUNTAIN SPORTS (EMS)
20 W 61st St (bet Broadway and Columbus Ave)
212 397-4860

611 Broadway (at Houston St)   212 505-9860
Mon-Fri: 10–8; Sat: 10–6; Sun: 12–6

This is *the* place to go for authentic outdoor clothing and gear, although prices can be bettered elsewhere. Still, for one-stop shopping it's an excellent source, and the merchandise is of better quality and price than that of the department stores. Incidentally, EMS covers virtually all out-door sports, including mountain climbing, backpacking, skiing, hiking, tenting, kayaking, camping, and much more.

G&S SPORTING GOODS
43 Essex St (at Delancey St)   212 777-7590
Mon-Fri, Sun: 9:30–6

If you have a sports buff in the family and are looking for a place to buy him or her a birthday or Christmas gift, I'd recommend G&S. They have a large selection of brand-name sneakers, balls, gloves, toys and games, sports clothing, and accessory items. That isn't all the good news; the prices reflect a 20% to 25% discount.

HERMAN'S
135 W 42nd St   212 730-7400
Mon-Fri: 9:30–7; Sat: 9:30–6; Sun: 12–5

39 W 34th St   212 279-8900
Mon-Fri: 9–7; Sat: 9–6:30; Sun: 11–6

845 Third Ave (at 51st St)   212 688-4603
Mon-Fri: 9–8; Sat: 9:30–6; Sun: 11–6

1185 Ave of the Americas   212 944-6689
Mon-Fri: 9–7; Sat: 9:30–6; Sun: 12–5

Carrying only a moderate selection of women's and children's gear, Herman's is almost no *her* and all *man*. Long before the running and physical-fitness craze, this chain of sporting-goods shops was set up to equip men for sports, and the more macho, outdoorsy, and competitive the sport, the better. There are woodsmen's vests, plaid flannel shirts, and camping equipment, but the emphasis is more on clothing than equipment. As for price, you can generally do better. But there is a sale every week on something, and those prices can be good. Add the convenience of a vast selection of equipment for all types of sports, and you know why the Herman's chain is growing.

MODELL'S
280 Broadway   212 962-6200
200 Broadway   212 964-4007
243 W 42nd St   212 575-8111
109 E 42nd St   212 661-5966
A&S Plaza, Sixth Ave at 33rd St, lower level   212 594-1830
(call stores for hours, as they vary)

Founded in 1889, Modell's is America's oldest family-owned and -operated sporting-goods chain. The stores specialize in menswear, sporting goods, footwear, luggage, and sundries. Prices are right, especially on footwear. You can't beat this outfit for quality and value.

PARAGON SPORTING GOODS
871 Broadway (at 18th St)   212 255-8036
Mon-Fri: 10–8; Sat: 10–7; Sun: 11–6

This is truly a sporting-goods department store, with over 80,000 square feet of specialty shops devoted to all kinds of sports equipment and apparel. There are separate departments for skis, team equipment, athletic footwear, skateboards, ice skates, racquet sports, aerobics, swimming, golf, hiking, camping, diving, biking, sailing, and whatever else you want to do in the great outdoors. There are also gift items, and the stock is arranged for easy shopping. It is a pleasure to shop in this vast wonderland of fun!

SPIEGEL'S
105 Nassau St (at Ann St)   212 227-8400
Mon-Fri: 9–6:30; Sat: 10–5; closed Sat in summer

You wouldn't expect to find a good place to buy sporting goods in this neighborhood, but Spiegel's (established 1916) would be top-notch in any location. The most advantageous point is their discount prices, which are as good as those anywhere in the city. In addition, the selection is ample, the sales help excellent, and the supply amazing for a store of its size. Call and they will tell you if they have what you are looking for. They run advertisements in the *New York Times* for special items, and those prices can't be beat.

Golf

NEW YORK GOLF CENTER
131 W 35th St (nr Broadway)   212 564-2255
Mon-Fri: 10–7; Sat: 10–6

This shop is the ultimate hole-in-one for the golfer! In premises that provide the largest selection of quality brand-name golfing merchandise in the area, this outfit offers goods at an average of 20% off regular prices. There are clubs, bags, clothing and shoes, accessories, and novelties . . . everything except one's own hard-won expertise. In short, this is a great place to shop for gifts for the golfing enthusiast in your family.

Guns

JOHN JOVINO GUN SHOP
5 Centre Market Pl (at Grand St)   212 925-4881
Mon-Fri: 9–6; Sat: 8–3

These folks have been in business since 1911, and they are recognized leaders in the field. They carry all major brands of handguns, rifles, shotguns, and accessories, including ammunition, holsters, bulletproof vests, knives, and scopes. Major brands represented include Smith &

Wesson, Colt, Ruger, Beretta, Browning, Remington, Walther, Glock, Winchester, and Sig Sauer. Jovino is an authorized warranty repair station for all the gun manufacturers, and they have two licensed gunsmiths on the premises.

Horseback Riding Equipment

H. KAUFFMAN AND SONS
419 Park Ave S   212 684-6060
Mon-Sat: 9:30–6:30; Sun: 11–5

For the very best in riding equipment, Kauffman's is the place to go. They handle the field so well that no one even stops to think that one of the world's finest equestrian supply shops is located in the midst of one of the world's largest cities (not to mention miles from the borough's only bridal paths). This specialty store has literally everything for horse and rider. They even manage to sell a lot of hay! In addition to saddles, bridles, and riding equipment, there is a good line of gifts for horse lovers. Ladies' side saddles, Kauffman told me, are about the only thing he doesn't stock. A catalog is published for $3.

MILLER'S
117 E 24th St   212 673-1400
Mon-Sat: 10–6 (Thurs: 10–7)

The Miller's symbol (two boots) is displayed in hundreds of shops across North America. The exclusive Miller line is so distinctive it covers a rider and his horse from head to hoof. Sizes suit men, women, children, stallions, mares, and colts. The haberdashery offers proper riding gear and saddles. (The Hermes saddles are registry-numbered and go for $2,800 and up!) There are boots, helmets, riding shirts, plaques, and riding potpourri. This is a super place to find gifts for both horses and owners. The Sultan of Brunei was so impressed he bought 40 T-shirts, six pairs of breeches, and two pairs of cowboy boots.

Marine

GOLDBERG'S MARINE
12 W 37th St (at Fifth Ave)   212 594-6065
Mon-Fri: 9:30–5:45; Sat: 9:30–6; Sun: 9–4:45
(Sat closing hour is seasonal)

Goldbergs' sells marine supplies as if it were situated in the middle of a New England seaport rather than in the heart of Manhattan. The staff sometimes looks like a ship's crew on leave in the Big Apple, and they are as knowledgeable as if that were the case. They carry marine electronics, sailboat fittings, big-game fishing tackle, lifesaving gear, ropes, anchors, compasses, clothing, clocks, barometers, and books. Many items—the ropes and compasses, for example—are of professional quality, and Goldbergs' is an excellent source for purchasing such things for dry-land purposes. Foul-weather suits are a star attraction, but there is also a line of clothes suitable for yacht owners.

Outdoor Equipment

TENT AND TRAILS
21 Park Pl (bet Broadway and Church St)
212 227-1760, 800 237-1760
Mon-Wed, Fri, Sat: 9:30–6; Thurs: 9:30–7; Sun: 12–6

Whether you are buying for a weekend camp trip or an expedition to Mt. Everest, Tent and Trails is ready for the outfitting! In the urban canyons near City Hall you will find a store exclusively devoted to camping, with help that is both experienced and knowledgeable. There are boots from Merrell, Vasque, Hi Tec, and Nike, and camping gear from Lowe, Madden, Camp Trails, Moonstone, Jansport, Gregory Packs, Eureka Tent, Coleman, Moss Tent, and others. You'll find backpacks, sleeping bags, tents, down clothing, and much more. Tent and Trails rents camping equipment on a first-come, first-served basis.

Running

ATHLETIC STYLE
118 E 59th St (bet Park and Lexington Ave)   212 838-2564
Mon-Thurs: 10–6:30; Fri, Sat: 10–6

ATHLETIC STYLE AT BLOOMINGDALE'S
1000 Third Ave   212 355-5900
(same hours as Bloomingdale's)

Fitness buffs take note! Athletic Style was originally a running-shoe shop. They came by it naturally because the owners were and are avid joggers. But the store has grown and prospered, and it is now considered one of the top outlets in the city in terms of quality, value, and service. Owners Vic and Dave are always on the job. (Bloomingdale's was so impressed by this operation that they've opened a branch in their great store nearby.) Footwear includes many famous names, and both kids and their elders will also find a good stock of clothing items, including logo merchandise.

SUPER RUNNERS SHOP
1337 Lexington Ave (at 89th St)   212 369-6010
360 Amsterdam Ave (at 77th St)   212 787-7665
1170 Third Ave (at 68th St)   212 249-2133
416 Third Ave (at 29th St)   212 213-4560
Mon-Wed, Fri: 10–7; Thurs: 10–9; Sat: 10–6; Sun: 12–5

Gary and Jane Muhrcke are runners, as is every member of their staff. When they are *not* running, they are advising other runners at Super

Runners Shop. The original store was located in Huntington, Long Island. Gary or Jane would grab a handful of shoes whenever they ventured into Manhattan and peddle them on the street to whoever ran by. Their reputation grew so fast that the handful became a van full, the street a permanent spot and then a legitimate store, and ultimately they opened branches of that store. Although their prices have risen with the move, they are still probably the best athletic shoe store around. Unlike many such stores, they do not stock one brand exclusively. The staff really believes that each person has to be fitted individually, both in terms of sizing and need. Super Runners Shop stocks men's and women's sizes (a few children's, too) and a full range of paraphernalia for devotees. In fact, they consider themselves a running-equipment source.

Skating

BLADES WEST/EAST
105 W 72nd St (at Columbus Ave)   212 787-3911
160 E 86th St (bet Lexington and Third Ave)   212 996-1644
Summer: Mon-Fri: 10–9; Sat: 10–9; Sun: 10–6
Winter: Mon, Tues, Wed, Fri: 12–7:30; Thurs: 12–9;
Sat: 10–7:30; Sun: 10–6

When you jump out of the way for a rollerblade whiz, you can just about bet that the skates came from one of these stores. Here you will find all kinds of skates, skateboards, snowboards, surfboards, and bodyboards for rent and sale. You can look the part, too, as classy apparel and accessories are available. A repair shop is right on the premises, and party rentals are a specialty.

PECK AND GOODIE
917 Eighth Ave (bet 54th and 55th St)   212 246-6123
1414 Second Ave (bet 73rd and 74th St)   212 249-3178
Mon-Wed: 10–6; Thurs, Fri: 10–8; Sat: 10–6; Sun: 12–6

Skating is a popular means of summer transportation in Manhattan, so there are plenty of skate shops. But Peck and Goodie seems to have been in business forever, offering equipment and apparel to skaters who need the best with minimum fuss. Now they are doing the same for the hordes of neophytes who have suddenly discovered (or rediscovered) skating. The store offers a complete stock of roller and ice skates, rollerblades, skateboards, and accessories. With faddish skates costing a hundred dollars a pair or more, it's wise to go to an expert.

Skiing

SCANDINAVIAN SKI SHOP
40 W 57th St (bet Fifth and Sixth Ave) 212 757-8524
Mon-Wed, Fri, Sat: 9–6; Thurs: 9–7

Despite its name, this shop is really an all-around sporting-goods store with an emphasis on skiing and other winter sports. They stock a full range of goods, from skis and skiwear to a department that offers repairs and ski advice, as well as outfitting. The shop has also developed a good reputation for serving other, decidedly non-Scandinavian sports as well. It is capable of outfitting its customers with tennis and hiking gear, as well as skis and in-line skating gear. Its selection of competition swimwear rivals the store's namesake specialty.

Soccer

SOCCER SPORT SUPPLY COMPANY
1745 First Ave (bet 90th and 91st St)
212 427-6050, 800 223-1010
Mon-Fri: 10–6; Sat: 10–3

Max and Hermann Doss, the proprietors of this half-century-old soccer and rugby supply company, operate as if they were located in merry old England instead of New York. Indeed, they are international; half their business involves importing and exporting equipment around the world. Soccer Sport obtains the finest rugby and soccer equipment available and ships it to customers. Visitors to the store have the advantage of choosing from the entire selection, as well as receiving guidance from a staff that knows the field perfectly.

Tennis

MASON'S TENNIS MART
911 Seventh Ave (bet 57th and 58th St)   212 757-5374
Mon-Sat: 9–7; Sun: 10–4

Mason's is one of the last major tennis specialty stores in the country — and it is still a family shop! It was supplying tennis paraphernalia long before the tennis craze hit, and it will probably continue to do so long after it has peaked. As owner Mark Mason puts it: "We have everything but the courts, and if real estate weren't so high, we'd have that, too." They carry the clothing lines of tennis designers Ellesse, Fila, Fred Perry, Wimbledon, Maser, Nike, and Tacchini in a selection Mason claims is unrivaled anywhere. Once you're looking good on the court, Mason can supply rackets, ball machines, bags, and any other tennis paraphernalia you could possibly think of. They even offer a same-day stringing service. Watch for their sales events on clothing in mid-August and mid-January. Prices are 50% off!

You might want to visit **Designer Resale** (324 E 81 St, 212 734-3639), a consignment boutique where prices are reduced by 20% after 30 days and 50% after 60 days. They also operate a Gentlemen's Resale across the street at 303 E 81st St. Many of the items in both outlets have never been worn or used.

Stationery

HUDSON ENVELOPE
111 Third Ave (bet 13th and 14th St)   212 473-6666
621 Sixth Ave (at 19th St)   212 255-4593
125 Fifth Ave (bet 19th and 20th St)   212 388-9190
1111 Second Ave (at 59th St)   212 980-1999
Call individual stores for hours

These folks have become the largest single paper and envelope store in the city and perhaps the world! You can purchase as little as 100 sheets of paper and 25 envelopes. Their inventory of paper stocks includes about half recycled merchandise. Over 150 different kinds of paper, with matching card stock and envelopes, are available. They also have a vast selection of presentation folders. Close-outs and discounted items provide excellent bargains at all times.

JAMIE OSTROW
876 Madison Ave (bet 71st and 72nd St)   212 734-8890
Mon-Fri: 11–7; Sat: 11–6

For contemporary personalized stationery and invitations, you can't do better than Jamie Ostrow. They design and manufacture their own items to the specifications of the individual customer, and they also carry Crane stationery and wedding invitations. A good selection of boxed Christmas and holiday cards is shown, and personalized Christmas cards are a specialty.

KATE'S PAPERIE
8 W 13th St (at Fifth Ave)   212 633-0570
Mon-Fri: 10–7; Sat: 10–6

Here you will find one of the largest selections of decorative and exotic papers in the country. Kate has papers of all kinds and descriptions, including papyrus, hand-marbled French paper, Japanese lace papers, handmade paste papers, and just about anything else you can think of in the paper classification. But that isn't all that's available at this unique store. There are leather-bound albums and journals, classic and exotic stationery, and paper-related items like jewelry, crafts, boxes, and desk accessories. They will do custom printing and engraving, and personal or business embossing.

RITE STATIONERY
113 Ludlow St (at Delancey St)
212 477-0280, 212 477-1724
Mon-Fri: 9–5:30; Sun: 10–3

For stationery bargains, this is it! Bear in mind, however, that this is just about as far from Tiffany's and Fifth Avenue as you can get. When you don't need formal engraved calling cards, and paper and supplies is really what you're hunting for, Rite is just right. They also specialize in school supplies.

STATE OFFICE SUPPLY COMPANY
150 Fifth Ave (at 20th St)   212 243-8025
Mon-Fri: 9–5:30; Sat: 12–5 (closed Sat in summer)

This is indeed state of the art when it comes to office-supply shopping. Here you will find one of the area's largest selections of both commercial and socially upscale items. The vast stock includes international pens, leather goods, organizers, computer supplies, calculators, briefcases, picture frames, clocks, writing papers, photo albums, and rubber bands. The outstanding sales help are unusually well informed and very polite. After all, if they have been in the business for over half a century, they must be pretty good!

UNICEF CARD & GIFT SHOP
3 United Nations Plaza (44th St bet First and Second Ave)
212 326-7054
Mon-Fri: 10–6; Sat, Sun: 11–3

One way that UNICEF — the arm of the United Nations devoted to the health and welfare of the world's children — raises money for its life-saving projects and programs is through the sale of cards and gifts. If you've never seen UNICEF products before, you're in for a real treat at this well-planned and friendly store. In addition to selling holiday cards, stationery, educational games for children, and Nepalese paper products, this is the only UNICEF outlet in the country that stocks merchandise chosen by overseas committees for sale around the world. The store is located in the lobby of UNICEF House. You will find a smaller UNICEF store on the lower level of the UN itself, just downstairs from the visitor's entrance. (For information about other UNICEF outlets in the New York area, call 212 759-0760.)

Tiles

IDEAL TILE
405 E 51st St   212 759-2339
Broadway and 70th St   212 799-3600
Mon-Fri: 9–5:30; Sat: 10–5

Ideal Tile imports ceramics, porcelain, marble, granite, and terra cotta from Italy, Spain, Portugal, and Brazil. They have absolutely magnificent hand-painted Italian ceramic pottery as well! This outfit guarantees installation of their tiles by skilled craftsmen. They also offer marble and granite fabrication for fireplaces, countertops, saddles, window sills, and tables.

TILES - A REFINED SELECTION
42 W 15th St (bet Fifth and Sixth Ave)   212 255-4450
Mon-Fri: 9:30–6; Thurs: 9:30–8; Sat: 10–5

If you are in the market for quality tiles, come here first! There are American art tiles, slate, granite, molded tiles, marble and limestone mosaics, glass tiles, and a large assortment of handmade tiles. Design services are available, and the selection is tops.

Tobacco and Accessories

BARCLAY-REX
7 Maiden Lane (nr Broadway)   212 962-3355
Mon-Fri: 8–6

70 E 42nd St (bet Madison and Park Ave)   212 692-9680
Mon-Fri: 8–6:30; Sat: 10–5:30

This is a tobacco connoisseur's shop, and a specialty tobacco shop at that. The specialty is pipes (cigars are anathema and cigarettes more so), and third-generation owner Vincent Nastri knows the field inside out. His shop is prepared to create a pipe from scratch, fill it with any imaginable type of tobacco (including a good house brand), repair it if it should break, and offer advice on proper pipe care and the blending of pipe tobacco. Nastri has a good reputation for prompt quality repairs and reasonable prices. It might pay to buy a new "irregular" pipe, which can be had for a surprisingly low price. As with most specialties, esoteric models are available at astronomical prices. If you have $1,000 to send up in smoke, Nastri can come up with something extraordinary.

CONNOISSEUR PIPE SHOP
1285 Sixth Ave, concourse level   212 247-6054
Mon-Fri: 8:30–6; Sat: 10–5

Edward Burak is an artist. A pipe artist, that is. At his shop he has assembled a collection of hand-carved beauties that range in price from $27 to over $3,500. His store features natural unvarnished pipes, custom-made pipes, custom-blended tobacco, and expert repair of all kinds of pipes. Burak will also do appraisals for insurance purposes. Although you have to be careful about *where* you smoke a pipe these days, if it comes from Connoisseur you'll probably get admiring glances from those who really know quality.

INTERNATIONAL SMOKE SHOP
153 E 53rd St (Citicorp Center)   212 755-8339
Mon-Sat: 7–7

The Citicorp Center is one of the city's best tourist haunts, in part because its tri-level lobby is full of restaurants and other interesting shops that keep "tourist hours." Despite all this, the area can seem cold and impersonal. So even if it had no other virtues, Citicorp's International Smoke Shop would be noteworthy as a friendly oasis in a frigid zone. True to its name, the store stocks all kinds of tobacco and tobacco paraphernalia. But it also carries books, magazines (including foreign publications), gifts, Lotto tickets, New York souvenirs, and imported chocolates.

J. R. TOBACCO
11 E 45th St (at Madison Ave)   212 983-4160
Mon-Fri: 7:45–5:45; Sat: 9–3:45

219 Broadway (at Vesey St)   212 233-6620
Mon-Fri: 7:45–5

For years Lew Rothman has claimed to offer the world's largest selection of cigars and pipe tobaccos at the world's lowest prices. Now that cigar smoking isn't quite as popular as it used to be, he has diversified, offering discount prices on most major fragrance lines, Cross pens, Ray-Ban sunglasses, and Zippo lighters. The cigars come in over 3,000 different brands, and the fragrances include over 50 top names. Prices are 20% to 50% off regular retail.

PIPEWORKS & WILKE
16 W 55th St   212 956-4820
Mon-Fri: 10–6; Sat: 10–5

Elliott Nachwalter started creating briar pipes in Stowe, Vermont, more than a decade ago. He then moved to New York and established Pipeworks as the outlet for his exclusive handmade, custom-designed pipes. Nachwalter can create a pipe from a customer's design, as well as his own. Only Grecian Plateux briar is used for each pipe, and each goes through a 130-step process between design and the finished product. Once a pipe is in hand, customers can return to Pipeworks for custom tobacco blends, antique pipes, and repairs. Chances are that it won't be a Pipeworks' pipe that needs repair. Each is guaranteed for five years for most parts, and Nachwalter says they are created to last a lifetime. There is also a great assortment of antique pipes.

Toys, Trains

BIG CITY KITE COMPANY
1201 Lexington Ave (at 82nd St)   212 472-2623
Mon-Wed, Fri: 11–6:30; Thurs: 11–7:30; Sat: 10–6;
Sun (seasonally): 12–5

You would expect New York to have a store dedicated totally to kites, and of course it is a great one. David Klein sells kites for people's houses: i.e., mobiles and wall hangings. He sells custom-made specialty kites and brilliantly colored fighter kites made of tissue paper. He also has a kite-repair service. Prices begin at about $2 and go as high as $300. The staff's genuine devotion is most evident in the community programs Big City sponsors. There are kite festivals, kite exhibitions, even "kite-ins." They have now added a full line of darts, dartboards, and accessories for recreational and competitive throwers.

B. SHACKMAN AND COMPANY
85 Fifth Ave (at 16th St)   212 989-5162
Mon-Fri: 9–5; Sat: 10–4

In the midst of the wholesale toy district, B. Shackman has been playing house since 1898. But their play is a very serious business, devoted to manufacturing, importing, and selling toys, novelties, and miniatures. Though a large portion of their business is still on the wholesale level, it is run by people who obviously enjoy what they are doing. They are willing to take time to share their vocation with amateurs and single retail customers. Shackman carries a full line of aforementioned specialties. However, the items of interest to retail customers are their miniatures and a striking collection of Victoriana. Again, this is not at all in keeping with its neighbors, but Shackman excels in Victorian postcards, Christmas tree decorations, old-fashioned greeting cards, and children's books. There are also Steiff toys, lead hand-painted soldiers, dolls, contemporary stuffed toys, and paper dolls.

BURLINGTON ANTIQUE TOYS
1082 Madison Ave (at 82nd St)   212 861-9708
Tues-Sat: 12–6 and by appointment
(Sat in summer by appointment only)

Anyone who has been to the Forbes Gallery knows that toy soldiers are not just for children. Anyone who has been to Burlington Antique Toys has undoubtedly discovered that this is definitely not kid's stuff. The toy soldiers are antiques, as is virtually everything else in the store. That roll call includes toy cars, airplanes, boats, and other tin toys. There is a "used car" lot specializing in out-of-production, die-cast car models. Best of all, Burlington proves that not only fabulously rich men can play with toy soldiers or float their own armadas. This is a place for everyone, and the folks here couldn't be nicer.

CLASSIC TOYS
69 Thompson St (bet Spring and Broome St)   212 941-9129
Wed-Sun: noon–6:30

Classic carries both old and new toys that have proven to be popular with generations of youngsters. It is also a haven for collectors and those (like your author) who just like to browse in toy shops. Here you will find the largest selection of die-cast vehicles in New York, with pieces of old Matchbox, Dinky, and Corgi that go back to the 1930s. Over 100 years of miniature figures are on display, as well as soft toys, Christmas tree ornaments from Europe, and a great selection of antiques that will charm both parents and children. A nice extra service: they maintain a list of stores for shoppers who can't find just what they want here!

DINOSAUR HILL
302 E 9th St   212 473-5850
Daily: Noon–7

Here you can travel the world through toys! There are marbles from England, tin windups from China, papier-mâché masks from Mexico, wooden pull toys from Greece, and solid wooden blocks made right here in the USA. In addition, at Dinosaur Hill there is hand-made clothing in natural-fiber fabrics for infants through four years and a wonderful assortment of hats, plus music boxes, monkeys, moons, and mermaids!

DOLLHOUSE ANTICS
1343 Madison Ave (at 94th St)   212 876-2288
Mon-Fri: 11–5:30; Sat: 11–5

Dollhouse Antics is straight out of childhood dreams. They claim to be a shop dedicated to miniatures. Dollhouse-making is serious business here. Ever hear of custom-made dollhouses? Or mouse houses? The most popular orders are for replicas of ancestral homes, and you can bet your made-to-order miniature needlepoint rug that these dollhouses aren't made for eager little children. Dollhouses come in kit form, but if money is no object (or when the fun of assembling it yourself wanes), the store will put it together for you. But be wary: like real houses, these models need to be furnished. If you can afford the scaled-down Oriental rugs, custom upholstery, special wallpaper, electrical supplies, and made-to-order furniture, you'll eventually want to redecorate the whole house.

ENCHANTED FOREST
85 Mercer St (bet Spring and Broome St)   212 925-6677
Mon-Sat: 11–7; Sun: 12–6

The Enchanted Forest physically and philosophically matches its name. The husband-and-wife team of owners—David Wallace and Peggy Sloane—hired theatrical set designer Matthew Jacobs to create an enchanted-forest backdrop for a collection of toys, whimsies, and artwork. The announced intention of the shop was that it would be a "gallery of beasts, books, and handmade toys celebrating the spirit of the animals, the old stories, and the child within." The emphasis is on *gallery*. One can enter a crystal cave that transforms into an old wooden wardrobe, through which one passes into a small Victorian room. Other featured items include a fine selection of fairy tales, mythologies, children's stories, and various eclectic gems. This is truly an enchanted place.

F.A.O. SCHWARZ
767 Fifth Ave (bet 58th and 59th St)   212 644-9400
Mon-Wed, Fri, Sat: 10–6; Thurs: 10–8; Sun: 12–6

Schwarz is on the cutting edge of the toy business, because most manufacturers want to get their items in this store first. But it is more than just a retail establishment! Groups of youngsters grow wide-eyed at the enormous selection and exciting demonstrations. Moms and dads are just as wide-eyed—and that includes your author. The store has two levels, arranged into small shops that specialize in stuffed animals, bears, games, electronics, dolls, soldiers, and all the other things that you'd expect in a first-rate toy emporium. There is even a counter by the door where those in a hurry can pick up a last-minute gift to take home. I defy anyone to walk out of this place with a frown on their face! Oh yes, please don't expect bargains. We're talking top-of-the-line!

MANHATTAN DOLL HOUSE
176 Ninth Ave (at 21st St)   212 989-5220
Mon-Fri: 11–6; Sat: 10–5

Time marches on, and sadly some of New York's most talented folks are no longer with us. Jenny Grunewald, who handled the doll hospital part of this operation, has passed away, so now her son-in-law, Edwin Jacobowitz, operates the Manhattan Doll House. It boasts the city's largest collection of dolls (including Madame Alexander), dollhouses, dollhouse furniture, and doll paraphernalia. Jenny's husband, Herman, still comes in the shop from time to time, so you could have the pleasure of visiting with him. He can create a castle-like home for the new princess you might purchase for your grandchild!

RED CABOOSE
16 W 45th St, (bet Fifth and Sixth Ave) 4th floor
212 575-0155
Mon-Fri: 10–7; Sat: 10–5:30

At the Red Caboose, owner-operator Allan T. Spitz will tell you that 99% of his customers are not wide-eyed children but sharp-eyed adults who are dead serious about model railroads. Since these are the people Spitz serves, it is difficult for a Christmas-morning engineer to adequately describe his stock, but I'll try. The Red Caboose claims to have 100,000 items in stock. That includes a line of 300 hand-finished, imported brass locomotives *alone*. That doesn't begin to cover the tracks or track gauges available. (Spitz claims that the five basic sizes—1:22, 1:48, 1:87, 1:161, and 1:220, in a ratio of scale to life size—will allow a model railroader to build layouts sized to fit into a desk drawer or a basement.) The store also carries the city's largest model-ship selection. If New York has a model-train district, it is located on the upper floors of the buildings on this block. Spitz offers a 20% discount on most purchases over $10.

TOY BALLOON
204 E 38th St   212 682-3803
Mon-Fri: 9–5:30

I wandered in here by accident, but you'll want to wander in on purpose. This is a serious adult business, but how can one be serious when the product is balloons? The Toy Balloon tries. Balloons are sold individually or in multitudes of up to 50,000. Types are so varied that there are graduations in diameter, thickness, style, and type (including Mylar balloons). Sizes range from peewees to blimps, while shapes include dolls, rabbit heads, hearts, dachshunds (they're often used to advertise hot dogs), and extra-long shapes. Most of the business is done for advertising campaigns, and the Toy Balloon will make up and sell personalized logos, styles, or two-colored messages.

TOYS 'R' US
Herald Center, 1293 Broadway (at 34th St)   212 594-8697
Mon, Fri: 9–9; Tues, Wed, Sat: 9–8; Thurs: 9 a.m.–9:30 p.m.;
Sun: 10–7

This is the big one in the toy business! With over a million toys in stock and a location right in the heart of the city, this place is a zoo – as you might expect! If you're looking for ambience and a store that's easy to shop in, this is surely not it, as the aisles are crowded and there is not the excitement of an F.A.O. Schwarz. However, if selection and price are your main interests, you can't do better. The adjoining Kids 'R' Us does the same for clothing.

TRAIN SHOP
23 W 45th St, basement   212 730-0409
Mon-Fri: 10–6; Sat: 10–5

The second major resident of "model-train row," this shop differs from its fellow traveler only by its basement location and its insistence that it has *no* specialty. It merely stocks everything. The Train Shop's owner is Paul Schulhaus, who is about as knowledgeable as they come. He sums up the stock by saying, "Look around. If you need help, just give us a holler." Now isn't that just the way they'd do it at the local station? The shop claims to have at least 30,000 different model pieces in stock. What is not in stock can be ordered, and while they do not maintain their own catalog, they do accept phone and mail orders. The stock can in no way be described. It is simply incredible and an awful lot of fun! One favorite item is a train engine, complete with its own realistic sound system. Prices are competitive with the neighboring train store. Where else but Manhattan would you find two such shops within hollering distance of each other?

Travel Goods

THE CIVILIZED TRAVELLER

1072 Third Ave (bet 63rd and 64th St)   212 758-8305

2003 Broadway (bet 68th and 69th St)   212 875-0306

2 World Financial Center   212 786-3301
Mon-Sat: 10–7; Sun: 12–6

For the person on the go, these stores are the most helpful places around! Books, maps, and videos are the specialties of the house, but you can also find unique and handy travel items like personal grooming pieces, pocket tailors, shoe kits, water purifiers, packable rainwear, slippers, travel-size games, travel alarm clocks, world-time calculators and clocks, translators, doorknob burglar alarms, automobile tool kits, and even portable showers. How about some tasty prepackaged meals to take on a plane? Now there's an idea for someone!

Typewriters

EAST 33rd TYPEWRITERS AND ELECTRONICS

42 E 33rd St   212 686-0930
Mon-Fri: 9–7; Sat, Sun: 10–5

In this age of word processors and computers, some people still use the trusty old typewriter. At East 33rd they wholesale, retail, repair, rent, and sell all kinds of typewriters and business machines. Now they have added computers, cellular phones, car stereos, home audio, televisions, and video equipment to their stock. You will find excellent selections, a fine service record, and (best of all) reasonable prices.

TYTELL TYPEWRITER COMPANY

116 Fulton St, 2nd floor (bet William and Nassau St)
212 233-5333
Daily: 10:30–4 by appointment

Detective-story readers know that a typewriter's keys are as individual as fingerprints. In New York, Martin and Pearl Tytell have made a name for themselves by identifying typefaces. Today, the so-called "questioned document" service has become a major operation that requires the full-time expertise of Pearl and the Tytells' son, Peter. Martin devotes his time to running the typewriter sales and repair business, with rentals on the side. They have also become a center for old and antique typewriters. With a 62-year-old collection of typewriters and parts, they can restore virtually any machine. Tytell is also the United Nations, the Smithsonian, and the Elaine's of the typewriter business. They have in stock type changes required for 145 languages, as well as IBM Selectric elements for all the languages IBM had calls for during the years they were manufacturing the Selectric. If you're in a hurry, he's farsighted enough to have foreign-language typewriters made up for emergencies. In addition to typewriters for every language, he can make up keys for corporate logos, six-pitch double-case type (good for teleprompter reading), phonetic alphabets, stencil cutting, and jumbo type. There are over 2 million pieces of type in stock, as well as typewriters so old they're rented by movie studios.

Variety, Novelty

BARGAIN SPOT
64 Third Ave (at 11th St)   212 674-1188
Tues-Sat: 8:30–5

In one of Cynthia Freeman's books, the heroine makes her money by starting out in a pawnshop. The Bargain Spot also started as a pawnshop, but in this case, it's the consumer who makes the money. Established in 1909, the Bargain Spot is also known worldwide as the Unredeemed Pledge Sales Company, and that name says it all. If something has been pledged and left, the Bargain Spot will purchase and resell it. But the heyday of pawnshops in New York is long gone, so no one could rely on that angle alone for business. Today, the company uses its base of pawnshop spoils to buy, rent, sell, and exchange a tremendous variety of items. At this aptly named shop, it's possible to buy everything from diamonds to typewriters to antiques. If you call first, they will happily tell you what is in stock.

COME AGAIN
353 E 53rd St (at First Ave)   212 308-9394
Mon-Fri: 11–7:45; Sat: 11–6

Yes, you read right. Come Again is a one-stop shopping center for all your sexual needs. There are vibrators, bondage equipment, exotic lingerie for men and women, adult books, oils and lotions, gift baskets, party gifts, and favors. Now they boast the first of its kind: an X-rated shop-at-home adult-toy and lingerie video catalog. They claim it "combines an hour's hot entertainment with the convenience of shopping at home." If the entertainment gets too hot, you can always turn it off and return to reading this book. Bet it doesn't have quite the same sizzle!

EVE'S GARDEN
119 W 57th St, 4th floor   212 757-8651
Mon-Sat: 12–6:30

One of the real pleasures of the "New York Is Book Country" fair each September on Fifth Avenue is the opportunity to meet and exchange views with readers and business folk who are (or would like to be) featured in this book. During one of these fairs, Dell Williams, who runs Eve's Garden, suggested I visit her unusual emporium. The descriptive line in her literature is, "We grow pleasurable things for women." Well, you get the picture. It may not be a must-see place on your shopping list, but after all, this is a book designed for every type of reader, and women will find a unique selection of merchandise at this liberated garden. Dell claims her items are featured with "sex-positive experiences in mind." Gentlemen are welcome here only if they are accompanied by a woman.

JOB LOT TRADING COMPANY – THE PUSHCART
140 Church St   212 962-4142
Mon-Fri: 8:45–6:30; Sat: 9–5; Sun: 11–6

80 Nassau St   212 619-6868
Mon-Fri: 7:45–6:30

After only a day in New York, even the most casual visitor becomes aware of black-and-white paper bags (depicting jam-packed pushcarts) being carried around by all sorts of New Yorkers. Close examination would reveal that these bags all emanate from Job Lot Trading. Job Lot and the Pushcart were originally two separate stores dislocated by the World Trade Center. Of those original residents, only a few survived, and none survived as spectacularly as these two stores, which merged (on different floors of the same store) and took over a building. Week after week they offer some of the best bargains in the city. Job Lot carries an odd number of consignments that are unsalable through normal retail channels for one reason or another. Absolutely everything is sold below wholesale. The stock changes constantly, so some people make weekly shopping trips. There is no telling what will turn up.

JUNGLE FEVER
30 Rockefeller Plaza   212 265-6685
Mon-Fri: 10–6

The only thing missing here is Tarzan himself! This store features merchandise from and about the jungles of the world. Leopards, toucans, elephants, and lions leap out from T-shirts, and stuffed monkeys and gorillas hang overhead from bamboo rods. Tropical jewelry, straw bags, and hats are packed next to Rainforest Crunch, animal mugs, and posters. Many items sport a World Wildlife Fund sticker, which means that the organization receives a portion of the proceeds from the manufacturer.

ODD JOB TRADING
7 E 40th St (bet Fifth and Madison Ave)   212 686-6825
66 W 48th St (bet Fifth and Sixth Ave)   212 575-0477
149 W 32nd St (bet Sixth and Seventh Ave)   212 564-7370
10 Cortlandt St   212 571-0959
465 Lexington Ave (bet 45th and 46th St)   212 949-7401
Mon-Thurs: 8–6:30; Fri: 8–7:30; Sun: 10–5
(Cortlandt St store closed Sun)

Odd Job has been around for a while and seems to consistently come up with good buys on quality merchandise. What differentiates Odd Job from the other half-dozen stores of its type is that its quality merchandise is more *au courant*. You never know what is going to turn up here; it can be anything from book racks to perfume, but it's always interesting. It's also the perfect place for gifts for the folks back home; they'll never know how little it cost unless you tell. Odd Job is perhaps the most aggressive of the close-out stores. They are expanding rapidly and now have the reputation of being the best of their kind.

SOHO EMPORIUM
375 W Broadway (bet Spring and Broome St)   212 966-6091
Mon-Fri: 12–8; Sat, Sun: 11–8

Shopping here is a fun experience that can also be a serious venture. The SoHo Emporium is a consortium of individual shops selling an eclectic mixture of clothing, accessories, antique and contemporary jewelry, new and old artifacts, and gifts. A visit here will indeed brighten your spirits and offer further proof that innovation is still an important part of the American dream.

STAR MAGIC
743 Broadway (bet 8th St and Astor Pl)   212 228-7770
275 Amsterdam Ave (at 73rd St)   212 769-2020
1256 Lexington Ave (bet 84th and 85th St)   212 988-0300
500 Lexington Ave (bet 47th and 48th St)   212 888-1921
Mon-Sat: 10–10; Sun: 11–8

Step through Star Magic's door, and you step through a time warp into the future. From its midnight-black ceiling with suspended galactic spheres to its spacecraft-like walls, Star Magic is designed to make a visitor forget contemporary New York and enter a timeless universe. The setting is inducement enough to pay a visit. Star Magic's theme is "Yesterday's magic is today's science," and that perhaps is the only way to describe the eclectic selection that owners Shlomo Ayal and Justin Moreau call "space-age gifts." There are toys (literally for children of all ages) with a scientific bent, and scientific items strictly for fun. There are books specifically chosen for their ability to make a reader "ponder the cosmos." Star Magic offers minerals and prisms, scientific instruments to explore the universe, high-tech toys, and new-age music that is positively futuristic. Over and out.

THINK BIG
390 W Broadway (bet Spring and Broome St)   212 925-7300
Mon-Sat: 11–7; Sun: 12–6

If you are one of those *big* thinkers, then this is the ideal place for you to shop. In this unique store, you'll find larger-than-life toothbrushes (57"), erasers, desk calendars, paper clips, crayons, toy chests, baseball bats (66"), soccer balls, and even a 7"-diameter aspirin. If they don't have your own "big" idea in stock, tell them and they might have it made especially for you and other customers.

WARNER BROS. STUDIO STORE
Fifth Avenue and 57th St
(Opening is planned for fall 1993)

The guest list on Fifth Avenue is complete. Bugs Bunny, Tweety Bird, and Daffy Duck have come to town . . . and right in the middle of a very high-rent district. There are hand-carved bronze Looney Tune friezes and a glass elevator that takes Bugs and friends to selling spaces that show clothing, golf balls, movie posters, animation cells, an art gallery, and much more.

Videotapes

PALMER VIDEO STORE
470 Hudson St   212 463-9377
Mon-Thurs, Sun: 11 a.m.–midnight; Fri, Sat: 10 a.m.–midnight

The nice thing about this store is that the titles are all displayed in a neat and orderly way. Palmer carries popular titles, as well as unusual ones. There is a membership plan, reservation privileges, a deep stock of titles, and no deposit is required of members. And every Thursday is penny day: the 2nd, 4th, and 6th film (and so on) is a penny.

VIDEO ACCESS
2617 Broadway (at 99th St)   212 316-6666
2821 Broadway (at 109th St)   212 749-3900
Open seven days a week; hours vary by store

Video Access offers over 10,000 of the latest movies for sale or rent, and you can visit them every day of the year. They will transfer foreign tape formats to the standard used in this country, and will rent and repair camcorders, VCRs, and TVs.

Visually Impaired Help

LIGHTHOUSE SHOPPING &
INFORMATION CENTER
111 E 59th St (bet Park and Lexington Ave)   212 808-0077
Mon-Fri: 9–5

This is a wonderful place for the visually impaired! In this store, blind folks can browse, touch, and feel merchandise before they buy. Over 200 articles are carried, including reading and writing supplies, large print atlases, talking articles (talking clocks are a great item), and cassette players and recorders. An especially nice gift is the Old or New Testament on tape in a self-locking, dustproof cover.

Wall Coverings

PEARL PAINT COMPANY
308 Canal St (bet Church St and Broadway)   212 431-7932
Mon-Sat: 9–6; Thurs: 9–7; Sun: 10–5:30

With more than a hundred clerks on duty at all times, Pearl claims to be the world's largest art and graphics discount center. Who can disagree? Besides 11 selling areas of fine-arts discounts, Pearl has another building (42 Lispenard St; 212 226-3717) that is an art-furniture showroom. Pearl's is a jam-packed store divided into specialty sections of all kinds. It is the kind of place where house painters shop next to batik craftsmen, and moldings and castings are sold beside materials for etchings and silk screenings. Pearl's personnel are also very friendly, which is quite rare for a professional supply house.

PINTCHIK
278 Third Ave (at 22nd St)   212 982-6600, 212 777-3030
Mon-Fri: 8:30–7; Sat: 9–6; Sun: 11–6

Discount wallpaper shops are few and far between in Manhattan, despite its reputation as the discount center of the world. But Pintchik is one such source. They discount paint and wall coverings, as well as the supplies that go with them. Two of the better wall coverings they carry are Laura Ashley and Marimeko patterns—by coincidence, two manufacturers with large stores in Manhattan. Nonetheless, Pintchik can always beat even the manufacturer's prices, except during the rare clearance sales at the previously named stores. They are very good at coming up with solutions to problem walls (and there probably isn't an apartment in the city without a problem wall), as well as making accommodations to city living. Needless to say, white backgrounds don't go over very well with city soot.

SHEILA'S WALLSTYLES DECORATING CENTER
274 Grand St (bet Eldridge and Forsyth St)   212 966-1663
Sun-Thurs: 9:30–5; Fri: 9:30–4

Grand Street is a strange place for a wallpaper store, but Sheila opened her three-floor shop over a decade ago, and it proved so successful that she now has imitators. And why not? She took her cue from the retail motif of the Lower East Side, selling everything at a good discount. Then she located her store on a block that is quickly becoming a mecca for fashion and budget-conscious home decorators. The result is the very best in wall coverings, fabrics, drapes, bedspreads, vertical and horizontal blinds, shades, and coordinated accessories. Those who want a tissue box to match the boudoir can find it at Sheila's—and at a discount, to boot

Watches

Don't be taken by the watch peddlers who tackle you along Fifth Avenue, near Bloomie's, and on side streets in midtown. Most of the pieces they sell are fake, and you have no recourse if there are problems. For reliable watches and service, here are the best:

Aaron Faber Gallery (666 Fifth Ave, at 53rd St) – Vintage
Aaron M. Jewelers (526 Seventh Ave, at 38th St)
Cartier (653 Fifth Ave, at 52nd St)
Fortunoff (681 Fifth Ave, at 54th St)
Jerry Grant's (276 Columbus Ave, at 73rd St)
Stanley & Son (1006 Ave of the Americas, at 37th St)
Tourneau (500 Madison Ave, at 52nd St; and 635 Madison Ave, at 59th St)

VII. Where to "Extras"

Annual Events

In addition to all the stores, museums, restaurants, and other things that are open all year, some special events are held only during certain seasons or once a year. (Make sure to check the "Newspapers, Magazines, and Other Resources" section in this chapter for suggestions about where to look for what's happening at any given time.) You'll find a brief list of special events in the front section of the Manhattan Yellow Pages. In addition to shows, fairs, and festivals, I've included a couple of particularly big or worthwhile sales in the following list.

JANUARY – All the city's Christmas decorations come down in early January, but winter is far from over. Check out the ice skating at Rockefeller Center (212 757-5730) and in Central Park's two rinks or go see the Ice Capades at Madison Square Garden (212 465-6741) toward the end of the month. The Winter Festival (212 360-3456) is held in Central Park in early January, offering activities and demonstrations for young and old alike. The National Boat Show is held at the Jacob K. Javits Convention Center (212 216-2000) in the middle of the month, and the Winter Antiques Show at the Seventh Regiment Armory (Park Avenue and East 66th Street) begins at the end of the month. Depending on the lunar calendar, Chinese New Year falls anywhere between the middle of January and the middle of February, and Chinatown is definitely the place to be for the celebration. January is also winter sale time. One of the best is at Saks Fifth Avenue (212 753-4000).

FEBRUARY – February is Black History Month, and New York has all sorts of official and unofficial celebrations of it. Keep an eye out for announcements on public transportation, on the street and in newspapers. In early February, the Westminster Kennel Club's Dog Show moves into Madison Square Garden (212 465-6741) for two days; the National Antiques Show moves in later in the month. In mid-month, some of the city's more energetic people participate in the Empire State Building Run-Up (that's right – *up* means the stairs, from the lobby to the 86th floor!), an invitational event sponsored by the New York Road Runners Club (212 860-4455). President's Day, the third Monday in February, is a huge sales day at department stores, electronics stores, clothing stores, and just about everywhere else. The Art Dealers Association of America

(212 940-8590) holds an exhibition for its member galleries at the Seventh Regiment Armory (Park Avenue and East 66th Street) late in the month.

MARCH – The most famous New York event this month is the Saint Patrick's Day Parade, although this 200-year-old march up Fifth Avenue from 44th to 86th Street has been the center of great controversy lately. The International Cat Show is held at Madison Square Garden (212 465-6741) early in the month, as is the Spring Armory Antiques Show at the Seventh Regiment Armory (Park Avenue and East 66th Street). The circus comes to town in March, too – the Ringling Brothers and Barnum & Bailey Circus, that is – immediately preceded by a hush-hush march of the biggest animals up West 34th Street to Madison Square Garden in the middle of the night. The Golden Gloves boxing finals are also held at Madison Square Garden in March, as is the Big East college basketball tournament. The New York Flower Show (212 757-0915) is held at Pier 92 (West 51st Street at the Hudson River) in the middle of the month. And depending when Easter falls, you can also visit the Easter-egg exhibit at the Ukrainian Museum (212 228-0110) or the Easter lily displays in the Channel Gardens at Rockefeller Center (212 632-3975) and the Winter Garden at the World Financial Center. The Macy's Spring Flower Show is held at Macy's at Herald Square (212 560-4495) for several weeks, beginning around Palm Sunday. An Easter-egg roll for children is held at the East Meadow in Central Park (212 360-3456) on the Saturday before Easter. An informal Easter parade is held on Easter Day on Fifth Avenue around St. Patrick's Cathedral beginning at 11 a.m. You can catch the annual Easter Show at Radio City Music Hall (212 247-7777) throughout the Easter season.

APRIL – The month opens with the International Auto Show at the Jacob K. Javits Convention Center (212 216-2000). April also means the beginning of baseball season, so check out the home schedules for the Mets (718 507-8499) and the Yankees (718 293-6000). The year's first outdoor festival is held on the third Sunday in April at Stuyvesant Park, on both sides of Second Avenue from 15th Street to 17th Street. You can browse rare autographs, manuscripts, and first editions at the New York Antiquarian Book Fair at the Seventh Regiment Armory (Park Avenue and East 66th Street). Also check out the spring flower displays at Rockefeller Center (212 632-3975), at the World Trade Center, and in the Winter Garden at the World Financial Center. Finally, before Passover, go down to the Streits Matzoth Factory (212 475-7000) at 150 Rivington St. on the Lower East Side to watch matzos being made.

MAY – One of May's high points is the Ninth Avenue International Food Festival, held the third weekend in May along Ninth Avenue, from West 37th Street up to West 59th Street. The Ukrainian Festival on East 7th Street between Second Avenue and Bowery is usually held the same weekend. The American Ballet Theater begins its nine-week season this month at the Metropolitan Opera House in Lincoln Center

(212 362-6000). The Martin Luther King, Jr. Parade is held along Fifth Avenue this month, and the Spanish and Portuguese Synagogue (212 873-0300) on the Upper West Side holds a Sephardic Fair on a Sunday in the middle of the month. Over Memorial Day weekend and into early June, look for the Washington Square Outdoor Art Exhibit at the foot of Fifth Avenue in Greenwich Village. And keep an eye out for the Lower East Side Jewish Festival, held on a Sunday late in May.

JUNE – A number of cultural events that last all summer and are free to the public begin in June: Shakespeare in the Park (212 861-7277) at the Delacorte Theater in the southwest corner of Central Park's Great Lawn; Metropolitan Opera Company (212 362-6000) performances in Central Park; the Midsummer Night Swing concerts at Lincoln Center Plaza (212 875-5400); and Central Park Summer Stage performances (212 360-2777) are some of the highlights. Stargazers will want to check out the softball action at the summer-long Broadway Show League and the Soap Opera League at diamonds throughout Central Park. Although many museums along Fifth Avenue's Museum Mile offer free admission one night a week all year, ten of them offer free admission on the second Tuesday in June, and seemingly half the city turns out. An Italian street fair to commemorate the Feast of St. Anthony of Padua (212 777-2755) is held in Little Italy during two weeks in June. The annual Salute to Israel parade is held along Fifth Avenue above 59th Street in the middle of the month. And you can find real bargains this month at the United Jewish Appeal's upscale clothing sale to raise money for its humanitarian programs. Give the UJA a call at 212 836-1115 for details about where, when, and how much it will cost to get in.

JULY – The month kicks off with a bang at the Macy's Fireworks Display (212 560-4495), launched from barges on the East River. FDR Drive from East 14th Street to East 51st Street is closed to traffic so you can get really terrific views. Get ready for fireworks with the Fourth of July Festival, held all day on Water Street from Battery Park to John Street in lower Manhattan. Lincoln Center Plaza, on Columbus Avenue between 62nd and 65th streets, comes alive with the American Crafts Festival (212 877-2011) during the first two weekends of the month. The month offers free concerts galore: the New York Philharmonic (212 875-5700) plays on the Great Lawn in Central Park and in other parks throughout the city; there's live music in the Museum of Modern Art's Sculpture Garden (212 708-9480) every Friday night at six; concerts are given on Thursday and Friday evenings at South Street Seaport (212 669-9400); and you can listen to chamber music in Washington Square Park at the foot of Fifth Avenue in Greenwich Village every Tuesday night at eight. Also look for the Mostly Mozart concerts at Avery Fisher Hall (212 875-5030) in Lincoln Center.

AUGUST – August has never been New York's best month. It's usually hot and humid, and the piles of garbage on the city's streets make the whole island smell. You'll find that the city is relatively quiet, particularly on the weekend. That's because a lot of New Yorkers head out for summer homes on Long Island or other shores, or they pick this month for their vacation. That said, however, there's still lots to do this month. In early August, the Uptown Chamber of Commerce (212 427-7200) sponsors a week-long salute to Harlem's past, present, and future. There are outdoor performances throughout the month in the Lincoln Center Plaza (212 875-5400), on Columbus Avenue between 62nd and 65th streets. A big crafts fair is held there on weekends at the end of the month and the beginning of September. On the second Sunday of August, go down to Macy's at Herald Square (Broadway and 34th Street) and sign up for Tap-O-Mania, an annual attempt to assemble a group of tapping feet so large that it makes the Guinness Book of World Records. Look for the Festival Latino's concerts, films, and other events at the Public Theater (212 598-7100) and other locations. Of course, as any tennis fan knows, the U.S. Open (718 271-5100) begins in late August and runs through Labor Day weekend. It's lots of fun, but traffic is hell! The week-long warehouse sale at Barney's (212 929-9000) begins at eight in the morning on the last Monday in August, although the line starts forming in front of the store (at 107 Seventh Ave) much earlier than that.

SEPTEMBER – Labor Day weekend is the last breath of summer, and the roads in and out of the city are a nightmare on Monday evening. If you're in the city that weekend, check out the art fair in and around Washington Square, at the foot of Fifth Avenue in Greenwich Village (212 982-6255). My favorite event this month is the New York Is Book Country fair on the third Sunday of September – I haven't missed one yet, and we've made a tradition of releasing new editions of this book there. Fifth Avenue is closed to traffic between 48th and 57th streets, and there's something for just about everybody. The Third Avenue Festival, on Third Avenue between East 68th and 90th streets, is usually held the same day. Little Italy comes alive with the Feast of San Gennaro – for 11 days beginning in mid-September, there's food, fun and lots of family reunions. Alice Tully Hall at Lincoln Center is home to the New York Film Festival (212 875-5610), beginning the third week of the month. The New York Philharmonic begins its long season this month at Avery Fisher Hall (212 875-5030) in Lincoln Center. Look for lots of "Back to School" sales at the end of the month.

OCTOBER – The NBA's Knicks and the NHL's Rangers open their seasons this month at Madison Square Garden (212 465-6741), and there are three big parades: the Columbus Day Parade, the Polish Day Parade, and the Hispanic Day Parade. Keep an eye out for the Fall Antique Show at Pier 92 (52nd St and the Hudson River), arguably the most prestigious antique show in the country. Then there's the sporting event that draws more spectators (well over 2 million, at last count) than any other in the world: the New York Marathon, held on a Sunday in late October or early November. The 26-mile course runs through all five boroughs, starting on the Staten Island end of the Verrazano Narrows Bridge and ending at Tavern on the Green on West Drive in Central Park. Call the New York Road Runners Club (212 860-4455) for the exact date and viewing suggestions. Finally, there's a Halloween Parade geared for adults in Greenwich Village, but otherwise don't expect much. Kids wander through apartment buildings rather than neighborhoods on Halloween in Manhattan.

NOVEMBER — Christmas is still more than a month away, but you wouldn't know it from the way Manhattan gets decked out in November. The first sure sign is the annual Radio City Music Hall Christmas Show (212 247-4777), beginning in the middle of the month. The Christmas windows in major department stores start to go up the week before Thanksgiving — Lord & Taylor, at 424 Fifth Avenue, between 38th and 39th streets, is just one of the many displays worth seeing along Fifth Avenue. Santa Claus arrives at Macy's at Herald Square (212 560-4495) the day after Thanksgiving and stays through Christmas Eve. Of all the Santas to visit Manhattan, this is one of the best, year in and year out. If you're not yet in the holiday spirit or want to do a little shopping, check out the crafts and antiques at the Triple Pier Show at Piers 88, 90, and 92 (along the Hudson River, between 48th and 55th streets). You can catch the Virginia Slims Women's Tennis Tournament at Madison Square Garden (212 465-6741) in the middle of the month. Of course, November wouldn't be November without Thanksgiving and the Macy's Thanksgiving Day Parade (212 560-4495). The parade starts on Central Park West at about 79th Street and winds its way down to Columbus Circle; from there, it heads down Broadway to Macy's at Herald Square. (If you want a real treat, let the kids stay up to watch the giant balloons being inflated on Central Park West the night before!)

DECEMBER — December means Christmas in New York, and it's hard to turn around without seeing advertisements for performances of Handel's *Messiah* and *The Nutcracker* ballet. The best of the former is at the "Messiah Sing-In" at Avery Fisher Hall (212 875-5030), and the best of the latter is in the New York State Theater (212 870-5570) — they're both in Lincoln Center, on Columbus between 62nd and 65th streets. The famed Christmas tree at Rockefeller Center (212 632-3975), just off Fifth Avenue between 49th and 50th streets, is lit in the late afternoon of the first Monday in December, and Fifth Avenue in midtown is closed off between 11 and 3 on two Sunday afternoons this month for holiday shoppers. Check out the crafts fair in Ferris Booth Hall at Columbia University (212 297-0707), on Broadway at 115th Street. You can always do some shopping (window and otherwise) in midtown — assuming you can stand the crowds, which seem overwhelming even by New York standards on the weekends leading up to Christmas. The eight nights of Chanukah are commemorated with the lighting of candles on a giant menorah at sundown in Grand Army Plaza (Fifth Avenue and

59th Street), and Kwanzaa is celebrated at the end of the month with a variety of events throughout the city. Finally, two words about the annual New Year's celebration in Times Square: don't go. If you want to celebrate, try the Concert for Peace at the Cathedral Church of St. John the Divine, on Amsterdam Avenue at 112th Street (212 316-7400), or the fireworks, a midnight run, and other events in Central Park (212 360-3456).

Dancing and Other Clubs

Whether you want to go dancing, sit back and hear some stand-up comedy, or drop in on a set of live jazz, there are lots of good places to choose from in New York. For descriptions of various places and current information about who is playing where, I suggest looking under "Night Life" in the front of *The New Yorker* or under "Dance Clubs," "Comedy Clubs," "Jazz Clubs," and other such listings in the back of *New York* magazine. I've listed a couple of the most popular places in each category here to get you started. Most have a cover charge, many offer at least a light menu, and some require reservations and a jacket for men. As with so many other things, my advice is to call in advance.

Dancing

Laura Belle – Located at 120 West 43rd Street, this elegant movie theater-turned-supper club is a favorite of people who like big-band music. Call 212 819-1000 for more information.

Limelight – A converted (excuse the pun) church, this rock club at 47 West 20th Street used to be more trendy than it is now, but it remains popular. Call 212 807-7850 for more information.

The Rainbow Room – This expensive and expansive restaurant has dancing. Both the Rainbow Room and Rainbow & Stars, a more intimate supper club, are located on the 65th floor of 30 Rockefeller Plaza. Call 212 632-5000 for more information about both places.

The Ritz – Located in what used to be Studio 54 at 254 West 54th Street, this is a place for anybody who likes loud rock concerts. Call 212 541-8900 for more information.

Roma di Notte – Located at 137 East 55th Street, you can dance here every night except Sunday to a small live band. Call 212 832-1128 for more information.

Roseland – This enormous place is fading a bit but remains quite popular for both rock music and ballroom dancing (obviously not on the same nights). It's located at 239 West 52nd Street. Call 212 247-0200 for more information.

S.O.B. – The letters stand for "Sounds of Brazil and Beyond," and this enormous club at 204 Varick Street is a favorite eating and dancing club for those who favor Latino music. Call 212 243-4940 for more information.

Jazz and Other Music

The Bitter End — A longtime showcase for soon-to-be-discovered folk-rock musicians, this club is located at 149 Bleecker Street. Call 212 673-7030 for more information.

Blue Note — You'll find two and sometimes three sets a night of great jazz here. It's located at 131 West 3rd Street. Call 212 475-8592 for more information.

The Bottom Line — Bruce Springsteen played some of his definitive early shows here, but the club offers jazz, soul, and even country in addition to rock. It's located at 15 West 4th Street. Call 212 228-7880 for more information.

Cafe Carlyle — Home to jazz crooner and piano player Bobby Short part of the year and talents like Eartha Kitt at other times, this intimate and decidedly upscale club is in the Hotel Carlyle, at the corner of Madison Avenue and 76th Street. Call 212 744-1600 for more information.

Village Vanguard — A Greenwich Village institution for well over half a century, this jazz club is located at 178 Seventh Avenue. Call 212 255-4037 for more information.

Comedy Clubs

Catch a Rising Star — Not to mention ones who have already risen. Catch a Rising Star is located at 1487 First Avenue. Call 212 794-1906 for more information.

Dangerfield's — As in Rodney. It's located at 1118 First Avenue. Call 212 593-1650 for more information.

The Original Improvisation — Jay Leno, Lily Tomlin, and even Rodney Dangerfield started at this still popular club, located at 358 West 44th Street. Call 212 765-8268 for more information.

Holidays

1994		
	January 1	New Year's Day
	January 17	Martin Luther King Jr.'s Birthday
	February 12	Lincoln's Birthday
	February 14	Valentine's Day
	February 16	Ash Wednesday
	February 20	Presidents' Day
	February 22	Washington's Birthday
	March 17	Saint Patrick's Day
	March 27	Palm Sunday
	March 27	Passover begins (8 days)
	April 1	Good Friday
	April 3	Easter Sunday
	May 8	Mother's Day
	May 21	Armed Forces Day
	May 30	Memorial Day

1994

June 19	Father's Day
July 4	Independence Day
September 5	Labor Day
September 6	Rosh Hashana begins (2 days)
September 15	Yom Kippur
October 10	Columbus Day
October 31	Hallowe'en
November 8	Election Day
November 11	Veterans Day
November 24	Thanksgiving
November 28	Chanukah begins (8 days)
December 25	Christmas Day

1995

January 1	New Year's Day
January 16	Martin Luther King Jr.'s Birthday
February 12	Lincoln's Birthday
February 14	Valentine's Day
February 21	Presidents' Day
February 22	Washington's Birthday
March 1	Ash Wednesday
March 17	Saint Patrick's Day
April 9	Palm Sunday
April 14	Good Friday
April 15	Passover begins (8 days)
April 16	Easter Sunday
May 14	Mother's Day
May 20	Armed Forces Day
May 29	Memorial Day
June 18	Father's Day
July 4	Independence Day
September 4	Labor Day
September 26	Rosh Hashana begins (2 days)
October 4	Yom Kippur
October 9	Columbus Day
October 31	Hallowe'en
November 7	Election Day
November 11	Veterans Day
November 23	Thanksgiving
December 18	Chanukah begins (8 days)
December 25	Christmas Day

Japanese Visitor Hints

Accommodations: Hotel Kitano (66 Park Ave)
Books: N.Y. Kinokuniya (10 W 49th St)
Business meetings: The Nippon Club (115 E 57th St)
Designer clothes: Hanae Mori (27 E 79th St), Kenzo (824 Madison Ave), and Matsuda (156 Fifth Ave, at 20th St)

Furniture and accessory rental for home or office: AFR (711 Third Ave)

Gift items: Things Japanese (1109 Lexington Ave), Maki Fifth Avenue (575 Fifth Ave, 2nd floor, at 47th St), and Takashimaya (509 Fifth Ave, at 42nd St)

Hand tools: O-Zora (238 E 6th St)

Japanese screens, ceramics, and sculptures: Naga Antiques (145 E 61st St)

Japanese-style breakfast: Edwardian Room, Plaza Hotel (Central Park South and Fifth Ave), Grand Hyatt (42nd St and Grand Central Station), Hotel Pierre (2 E 61st St), and Drake Hotel (440 Park Ave)

Kobe beef: Old Homestead (56 Ninth Ave)

Specialty foods: Katagiri (224 E 59th St)

Sushi: Hatsuhana (237 Park Ave and 17 E 48th St)

Table pot cooking: Shinwa (Olympic Tower, 645 Fifth Ave, at 51st St)

Tasty Japanese cuisine: Nippon (155 E 52nd St)

Manhattan at Night

New York often bills itself as "the City That Never Sleeps," and a sizable number of the people who live here are night people. They include not only actors and artists but also the people who maintain and clean the huge office buildings; who work for answering services; who put together the morning newspapers and newscasts; who work the night shift at hospitals and other businesses that never close; and the secretaries, transcribers, and editors who must make sure that paperwork is ready overnight.

The following list includes an array of emergency services and other places that are open at night. In fact, **unless otherwise noted, they are open 24 hours a day, 7 days a week.** This list is not intended to be inclusive, but rather to give you some choices throughout Manhattan. In general, stores and restaurants in SoHo, TriBeCa, and Greenwich Village stay open later than ones in the rest of the city. Restaurants and mom-and-pop operations along Broadway on the Upper West Side and along both Lexington and Third avenues on the Upper East Side also tend to keep late hours. As with everything else, I suggest you call before setting out for any of these places to make sure they still exist and keep the same hours.

AUTO REPAIR AND TOWING — If you belong to an auto club, by all means call their 800 number and find out what garage or towing service they recommend. If you possibly can, try to get to a well-lit street before getting out of the car. Whatever else you do, put your own safety first and the car second! If you're in a jam, call **A Manhattan Towing**

(212 239-4953), **Express Towing** (212 242-5811), or **Gaseteria** (212 307-1099). These places all do repairs and towing 24 hours a day (as opposed to places that will tow you but do nothing to fix your car).

BANKS – Assuming you have a compatible card, thousands of automated teller machines (**ATMs**) are open all hours. For the location of the one nearest you, call 800 424-7787 if your bank is part of the **CIRRUS** system, 212 868-1100 if you have a **CITIBANK** card, 914 899-6777 if your bank is part of the **NYCE** system, and 800 843-7587 if your bank is part of the **PLUS** system. **Western Union** (212 354-9750), at 1440 Broadway near West 40th Street, is open to send or receive cash from 7 a.m. to midnight on weekdays, and from 8 a.m. to midnight on weekends.

BOOKSTORES – The following bookstores stay open until 11 p.m. (some close earlier on Sunday): **B. Dalton Bookstore,** at 396 Sixth Avenue, at 8th Street (212 674-8780); **Barnes and Noble,** at 1280 Lexington Avenue, between 86th and 87th streets (212 423-9900); **Rizzoli,** at 454 West Broadway (212 674-1616); **Shakespeare & Company,** on the corner of Broadway and 81st Street (212 580-7800); and **Tower Bookstore,** at 383 Lafayette Street (212 228-5100).

CAR RENTALS – All of the major car-rental companies have several offices in New York. Different offices of one company, however, often have different hours. The **Avis** office, at 217 East 43rd Street (800 831-2847), is open 24 hours; the **Hertz** office, at 222 East 40th Street (800 654-3131), is open until midnight; and the **National** offices, at 305 East 80th Street, 219 West 77th Street, and 21 East 19th Street (800 227-7368), are all open until 11 p.m.

CLEANERS – Although it's located in Long Island City, **Midnight Express Cleaners** (212 921-0111 or 718 392-9200) will pick up and deliver in Manhattan. They can turn things around in a day and cost a fraction of what hotels charge. Midnight Express is open from 9 a.m. until 11 p.m. on weekdays, and on Saturday from 9 a.m. until 3 p.m.

DELIVERY AND MESSENGER COMPANIES – If it "absolutely positively has to be there" at any time of day or night, call **Moonlight Courier** (212 473-2246). You can also try **Able Motorized Deliveries** (212 687-5515).

DENTIST – For 24-hour referrals, call **All City Emergency Services** (212 286-0716) or the **First District Dental Society** (212 679-4172 or 212 679-3966). The **Mount Sinai Hospital Emergency Room,** at Fifth Avenue and East 100th Street, also can handle dental emergencies.

DOCTORS – If you need to find a doctor who makes house calls at all hours of the night, call **Doctors on Call** (212 737-2333). Also see the listings under "Emergency Rooms."

ELECTRICIANS – If you need an electrician in the middle of the night, try **AC Green Electrical Contractors** (212 541-4100), **Marty Allen** (212 254-9600), or **Michael Altman** (718 681-2900 or 800 287-7774).

EMERGENCY ASSISTANCE – The citywide emergency number to call an ambulance, the police, or to report a fire is 911. The number for the city's **Victims Services Hotline** is 212 577-7777. To find out the location of the police precinct nearest you, call 212 374-5000. And if you smell gas, call Consolidated Edison's 24-hour emergency number at 212 683-8830.

EMERGENCY ROOMS – The citywide emergency number is 911. An ambulance called through 911 will take you to the nearest hospital – which may or may not be the one you want. If you want to be taken to a private hospital, if it's not a life-threatening emergency, and if you are willing to pay for the service, call **Keefe & Keefe** at 212 988-8800. If you are well enough to get to an emergency room under your own power, the following are some of the city's major hospitals that offer 24-hour services:

Bellevue Hospital: First Avenue at 27th Street (212 561-4347)
Beth Israel Medical Center: First Avenue at 16th Street
    (212 420-2840) and 170 East End Avenue, at 87th Street
    (212 870-9197)
Columbia Presbyterian Hospital: 622 West 168th Street, near Fort
    Washington Avenue (212 305-2500)
Lenox Hill Hospital: 100 East 77th Street, near Park Avenue (212
    439-2345)
Mount Sinai Hospital: Fifth Avenue and 100th Street
    (212 241-7171)
New York Hospital: 510 East 70th Street (212 746-5050)
New York University Medical Center: 500 First Avenue
    (212 263-5550)
St. Luke's-Roosevelt Hospital: 58th Street and Ninth Avenue
    (212 523-4000) and Amsterdam Avenue at 114th Street
    (212 523-3335)

ENTERTAINMENT – There is all sorts of entertainment open all night around West 42nd Street, but it's not the kind that I'm going to list here. For clubs that stay open all night or almost, look in the "Dancing and Other Clubs" section of this chapter. Otherwise, try:

Billiards: Tekk Billiards (212 463-9282), at 75 Christopher Street,
    between Seventh Avenue and Bleecker Street; and Chelsea
    Billiards (212 989-0096), at 54 West 21st Street, between Fifth
    and Sixth avenues, are open all night.
Bowling: Bowlmor Lanes (212 255-8188), at 110 University Place,
    near 12th Street, is open from 10 a.m. until 1 a.m. on Sunday
    through Thursday, and until 4 a.m. on Friday and Saturday.

Chess: The Chess Shop (212 475-9580), at 230 Thompson Street, near West 3rd Street, is open until midnight every night.

Racing: The Manhattan Raceway (212 673-4100), at 893 Broadway, is open until midnight Sunday through Thursday and until 2 a.m. on Friday and Saturday.

FLORISTS — If you want to send a bouquet in the middle of the night, try **Rialto** (212 688-3234), at 707 Lexington Avenue, between 57th and 58th streets. It never closes, and legends are made by its service. You can also try **Piccadilly Florist** (212 421-5176), at 110 East 59th Street, between Park and Lexington avenues. Piccadilly is not only open late but also delivers seven days a week, in the evenings, and on holidays. Many of the mom-and-pop operations on Broadway, Lexington Avenue, and Third Avenue also sell flowers and are open all night.

FOOD (DINE-IN) — With a few exceptions, you aren't exactly going to find an elegant dining experience at four in the morning. But you will find a surprising number of decent places open, including:

Around the Clock Café and Gallery: 8 Stuyvesant Street, near Third Avenue (212 598-0402)

Brasserie: 100 East 53rd Street (212 751-4840)

Chelsea Square Restaurant: 368 West 23rd Street (212 691-5400)

Cooper Square Restaurant: 87 Second Avenue, at 5th Street (212 420-8050)

Empire Diner: 210 Tenth Avenue, at 22nd Street (212 243-2736)

Kiev: 117 Second Avenue, at 64th Street (212 674-4040)

Lox Around the Clock: 676 Sixth Avenue, at 21st Street (212 691-3535)

McDonald's: 39th Street and Second Avenue, 56th Street and Eighth Avenue, 71st Street at Amsterdam Avenue and Broadway (weekends only), and Broadway between 95th and 96th streets (weekends only)

Morning Star Restaurant: 401 West 57th Street (212 246-1593)

New York Delicatessen: 104 West 57th Street (212 541-8320)

Silver Star: 1236 Second Avenue (212 249-4250)

Skyline Coffee Shop: 1055 Lexington Avenue, at 75th Street (212 861-2540)

Tramway Coffee House: 1143 Second Avenue, at 60th Street (212 758-7017)

FOOD (TAKEOUT): In addition to many all-night mom-and-pop operations along Broadway on the Upper West Side and Lexington and Third avenues on the East Side, you can try:

Bagels on the Square: 7 Carmine Street (212 691-3041)

The Best of New York Food: 150 Water Street, at Fletcher Street (212 952-1890)

Catalina Pizza and Deli: 684 Third Avenue, at 43rd Street
(212 687-5151)
Columbia Hot Bagels: 2836 Broadway, at 110th Street
(212 222-3200)
Crown Gourmet Deli: Broadway and 52nd Street (212 956-8410)
H&H Bagels: 2239 Broadway, at 80th Street (212 595-8000)
Jumbo Bagel and Bialys: 1070 Second Avenue (212 355-6185)

GAS — Gas stations in Manhattan tend to be in places where space is cheapest, and it follows that the neighborhoods are not always the most desirable. Between the price and the neighborhoods, I suggest you fill the tank somewhere else. If you have no alternative, however, try:

Amoco: Broadway at East Houston, and Tenth Avenue at
207th Street
Citgo: Bowery at 3rd Street
Getty: Eighth Avenue between Horatio and 13th streets
Gaseteria: West End Avenue at 59th Street and Broadway at 193rd
Street
Mobil: Eleventh Avenue at 51st Street and Eleventh Avenue at 57th
Street
Shell: Amsterdam Avenue at 181st Street

GROCERY STORES — Although Manhattan does have some chain supermarkets that vaguely resemble the kind in the suburbs, the shortage of space and the exorbitant rent means that Manhattan is full of mom-and-pop grocery stores. Sometimes you'll find three on one block—and chances are that at least one will be open all night or close to it.

Chain supermarkets in Manhattan include the Food Emporium, Sloan's, the Red Apple, and D'Agostino (or Dags, as New Yorkers call it). Most are open seven days a week, from early in the morning until at least 11 p.m. Some are open 24 hours. Many people in New York feel strongly that one chain is far superior to the others, but I've found that the quality of each depends more on the individual stores and their management than on the chain.

HAIR SALONS — If you need a late-night haircut, try **Heads and Tales Haircutting** (212 677-9125) at 22 St. Mark's Place, between Second and Third Avenue, or **Larry Matthews Beauty Salon** (212 355-1900), on the second floor of 536 Madison Avenue, between 54th and 55th streets.

LOCKSMITHS — Three things can be said of most locksmiths in Manhattan: They stay open all night; they put a lot of "A"s before their name, so they'll be near the top of the list in the Manhattan Yellow Pages; and they won't give you a good deal. If you're really desperate, try **AAAA Manhattan Locksmiths** (212 877-7787), **AAA Locksmiths** (212 732-0065), or **A Abbruzzi Lock & Key** (212 751-1380). Ask for an estimate when you call, and insist on one before the work begins.

NEWSSTANDS – Although there are some newspaper boxes in Manhattan, most people who don't get home delivery buy their newspapers and magazines at one of the newsstands all over the city. In addition to local newspapers, these newsstands sell a wide range of magazines and cigarettes. (Try not to be put off by the fact that many of these newsstands display pornographic magazines right alongside *The New Yorker* and *Newsweek*.) It's hard to miss these newsstands. Usually located on or near a corner, most are essentially big metal boxes with room for just one person inside. The vast majority are open seven days a week and late into the evening, but you can find ones open all night on:

- Second Avenue and St. Mark's Place
- Sixth Avenue and 8th Street
- 42nd Street and Park Avenue (Grand Hyatt)
- Broadway at 42nd Street (the first dropoff spot for the
  New York Times)
- Eighth Avenue at 42nd Street (Port Authority Bus Terminal)
- Broadway and 50th Street
- First Avenue and 63rd Street
- Broadway and 72nd Street
- Columbus Avenue and 81st Street
- Broadway and 116th Street

NOTARIES PUBLIC – If you know you're going to need to have something notarized in the middle of the night, call **West Side Stationers** (212 662-3151), 2620 Broadway, at 99th Street, to arrange an after-hours house call.

PHARMACIES – The only pharmacy in Manhattan that can fill prescriptions 24 hours a day, seven days a week is **Kaufman Pharmacy** (212 755-2266), off the lobby of the Beverly Hotel (at Lexington Avenue and 50th Street). Many Love pharmacies are open until the wee hours of the morning. **Columbia Love** (212 316-5113), on Broadway just south of Columbia University, between 111th and 112th streets, is open until 2 a.m. Monday through Thursday, and until 3 a.m. on weekends.

PHOTOCOPYING AND COMPUTER RENTALS – Part of a national chain, **Kinko's** stays open all night and offers photocopying services, Macintosh computer rentals (you use them there), and some basic office supplies. There are three Kinko's locations in Manhattan: 2872 Broadway, between 112th and 113th streets (316-3390); 191 Madison Avenue, between 34th and 35th streets (685-3449); and 24 East 12th Street, between Fifth Avenue and University Place (212 924-0802).

PHOTO DEVELOPING – Try **K&L Custom PhotoGraphics** (212 661-5600), at 222 East 44th Street, between Second and Third avenues.

PLUMBERS – Read what I said about locksmiths; the same is true here. You can try **A Aahron's Emergency Plumbing** (212 874-9066), **ABAC**

Contracting (212 473-2024), or **Roto-Rooter** (212 687-1661). All plumbers must be licensed by the city's Department of Buildings. Make sure anybody who shows up to fix your sink has a license, and call 212 312-8217 if you have any problems. (Unfortunately, you can't call the number in the middle of the night.) Make sure you get a written estimate before any work is done.

POST OFFICE — Although services are sometimes limited, windows at the main post office (212 330-2908), at Eighth Avenue between 33rd and 34th streets, are open all night, seven days a week.

RECORD AND TAPE STORES — The **Tower Records** stores at Broadway and 4th Street (212 505-1500) and Broadway and 66th Street (212 799-2500) are both open until midnight every night. You can also try **HMV,** at 1280 Lexington Avenue, at 86th Street (212 348-0800); and Broadway and 72nd Street (212 721-5900). Both locations are open Monday through Thursday until 10, Friday and Saturday to midnight, and Sunday to 8.

SECRETARIAL SERVICES — If you know in advance that you're going to need a secretary in the middle of the night, call **Dial-a-Secretary** at 212 348-9575 to make an appointment.

VETERINARIAN — Emergency services for pets are available at the **Animal Medical Center** (212 838-8100), at 510 East 62nd Street.

VIDEO STORES — More and more hotels are putting VCRs in their rooms. If you have one, check with the front desk to see if the hotel has a video library. Otherwise, you can become a member at a local video store with a credit card. **Blockbuster Video,** a huge national chain that is open nightly until midnight, has been opening a lot of stores in Manhattan lately. Look for Blockbuster on the corner of Lexington Avenue and 85th Street (212 439-0960), the corner of Amsterdam Avenue at 69th Street (212 787-0300), the corner of Third Avenue and 24th Street (212 686-0022), and the corner of Eighth Avenue and 17th Street (212 924-4771). The **Tower Video** chain is also open till midnight. You'll find them at Lafayette and 4th streets (212 505-1166), on the corner of Broadway and 67th Street (212 496-2500), and at 215 East 86th Street, between Madison and Park avenues (212 369-2500).

Manhattan for Children

When I first began writing this book, I did so from the perspective of a businessman who comes to New York without children. I quickly learned, however, that many people bring their kids to New York, whether they're coming for business or pleasure. New York can be a little overwhelming for kids at first (the same is true for adults), but it can also be a wonderland if you know where to go.

The Alliance for the Arts puts out a seasonal schedule of cultural events for children who live here. It can be a great source of events and special activities that you won't find in any of the guidebooks. Call the Alliance at 212 947-6340 for more information, or pick up a copy at the New York Convention and Visitors Bureau (at 2 Columbus Circle, near the southwest corner of Central Park). If you have a touch-tone phone, another source of information on events for children is *Listings Magazine*'s Arts and Festivals Hotline, which includes a special children's category and can be reached at 212 765-2787. Finally, the Friday *New York Times* Weekend section has a "For Children" column, listing events and activities for children planned for the coming weekend throughout the region. You'll also find a terrific "Activities for Children" page in the back of *New York* magazine.

Here I've listed some of the best museums, bookstores, restaurants, and sights for kids. When the specific place is described in another part of the book, I've simply included the address and phone number, along with instructions on where to look for more detailed information. When a place is not described elsewhere in the book, I've added a little more information. Of course, different children are interested in different things, so I've included some places that one child might love and another would find boring. I'll let you be the judge of that!

Abigail Adams Smith Museum: 421 East 61st Street, between First and York avenues (212 838-6878). For more information, see the "Museums" section of Chapter III.

American Museum of Natural History: Central Park West between 77th and 81st streets (212 769-5100). The hands-on Discovery Room is open on weekend afternoons, and tickets are handed out on a first come, first serve basis in late morning. For more information, see the "Museums" section of Chapter III.

Bank Street College Bookstore: In addition to being a terrific source of books for children, parents, and teachers, this bookstore has all sorts of special readings and other events for children. It's located at 2875 Broadway, on the corner of 112th Street, and is open from 10 to 9 on Monday through Thursday, from 10 to 6 on Friday and Saturday, and from noon to 5 on Sunday. Most special events are held on weekends. Call 212 679-1654 (800 724-1486 outside New York State) to find out what's scheduled.

Big Apple Circus: This very popular one-ring circus allows everyone to sit quite close to the performers. It is held in Damrosch Park at Lincoln Center from late October through early January (and at other locations throughout the country during the rest of the year). For recorded information about schedules and ticket prices, call 212 268-0055.

Central Park: Particularly during the spring and summer months, Central Park is full of events and activities for children. There is the Children's Zoo and Conservation Center, located inside the park just off Fifth Avenue at 65th Street (212 861-6030), and the Carousel further inside the park at the same cross street (212 879-0244). In addition, there are activities for children on Saturday and Sunday afternoons at Belvedere Castle, inside the park near West 79th Street (212 772-0210); a puppet theater on weekday mornings near the 62nd Street playground inside the park (call the Dairy at 212 794-6564 to make reservations); a marionette theater near West 81st Street (212 988-9093); and story-reading at the Hans Christian Anderson Statue by the Conservatory near 74th Street on Saturday mornings at 11. Make sure to call ahead, as some events require reservations and/or a small fee, and the hours and locations may vary. You can find out what is happening on any given day in Central Park and other parks throughout Manhattan by calling 212 360-3456.

Children's Museum of Manhattan: 212 West 83rd Street, between Broadway and Amsterdam Avenue (212 721-1234). For more information, see the "Museums" section in Chapter III.

Circle Line Sightseeing Yachts: Pier 83, at Twelfth Avenue and 43rd Street (212 563-3200). For more information, see the "Tours" section in Chapter III.

Classic Toys: 69 Thompson Street, between Spring and Broome streets (212 941-9129). For more information, see the "Toys, Trains" section in Chapter VI.

Dollhouse Antics: 1343 Madison Avenue, at 94th Street (212 876-2288). For more information, see the "Toys, Trains" section in Chapter VI.

Donnell Library Center: This branch of the New York Public Library houses a special room for children, with more than 100,000 books, magazines, and recordings. It's located at 20 West 53rd Street, between Fifth and Sixth avenues. Call 212 621-0636 for hours and other information.

Double Decker Bus Tours: Suite 825 of the Empire State Building, at 350 Fifth Avenue, between 33rd and 34th streets (212 967-6008). For more information, see the "Tours" section in Chapter III.

Eeyore's Books for Children: 2212 Broadway, at 79th Street (212 362-0634), and 25th East 83rd Street, near Madison Avenue (212 988-3404). For more information, see the listing of children's bookstores under "Books" section of Chapter VI.

Ellis Island: In New York Harbor, off Battery Park (212 363-7620). For more information, see the "Museums" section in Chapter III.

Empire State Building Observation Deck: Fifth Avenue between 33rd and 34th streets (212 736-3100). For more information, see the "Sights and Other Pleasant Places" section in Chapter III.

Enchanted Forest: 87 Mercer Street, between Spring and Broome streets (212 925-6677). For more information, see the "Toys, Trains" section in Chapter VI.

FAO Schwarz: 767 Fifth Avenue, between 58th and 59th streets (212 644-9400). For more information, see the "Toys, Trains" section in Chapter VI.

Fraunces Tavern Museum: 54 Pearl Street, at Broadway (212 425-1778). For more information, see the "Museums" section in Chapter III.

Guinness Book of World Records Exhibition Hall: This tacky and surprisingly expensive spot is next to the basement ticket office at the Empire State Building (Fifth Avenue between 33rd and 34th streets). It's open from 9 to 8. Admission is $7 for adults, $6 for senior citizens and children 12 and older, and $3.50 for children under 12. Call 212 947-2335 for more information.

Hard Rock Café: 221 West 57th Street (212 459-9320). For more information, see the restaurant review in Chapter II.

Hayden Planetarium: Inside the American Museum of Natural History on Central Park West, between 77th and 81st streets (212 769-5920). For more information, see the listing for the American Museum of Natural History in the "Museums" section of Chapter III.

Intrepid Sea-Air-Space Museum: Pier 86, at Twelfth Avenue and 46th Street (212 245-0072). For more information, see the "Museums" section in Chapter III.

Metropolitan Museum of Art: Fifth Avenue between 80th and 84th streets (212 879-5500). Although not everything here is for children, the Egyptian mummy exhibit and the gallery full of arms and armor will be big hits. For more information, see the "Museums" section in Chapter III.

Museum of the American Indian: In Audubon Terrace, just off Broadway between 155th and 156th streets (212 283-2420). For more information, see the "Museums" section in Chapter III.

Museum of the City of New York: 1220 Fifth Avenue, between 103rd and 104th streets (212 534-1672). For more information, see the "Museums" section in Chapter III.

Museum of Television and Radio: 25 West 52nd Street, between Fifth and Sixth avenues (212 621-6600). For more information, see the "Museums" section in Chapter III.

New York City Fire Museum: 278 Spring Street, between Hudson and Varick streets (212 691-1303). For more information, see the "Museums" section in Chapter III.

Peppermint Park Cafe: 1225 First Avenue, between 66th and 67th streets (212 288-5054). For more information, see the alphabetical listing of restaurant reviews at the end of Chapter II.

Police Academy Museum: 235 East 20th Street (212 477-9753). For more information, see the "Museums" section in Chapter III.

Red Caboose: The fourth floor of 16 West 45th Street, between Fifth and Sixth avenues (212 575-0155). For more information, see the "Toys, Trains" section in Chapter VI.

Roosevelt Island Tram: Leaves from a station on Second Avenue between 59th and 60th streets. For more information, see the "Sights and Other Pleasant Places" section in Chapter III.

Serendipity 3: 225 East 60th Street (212 838-3531). For more information, see the restaurant review in Chapter II.

South Street Seaport: At the eastern end of Fulton Street (212 669-9400). The Seaport produces a seasonal schedule of activities for children and families, and has a special center for children. For more information, see the "Museums" and "Sights and Other Pleasant Places" sections of Chapter III.

Statue of Liberty: On Liberty Island in New York Harbor, just off Battery Park. For more information, see the "Sights and Other Pleasant Places" section in Chapter III.

Storyland Bookstore: 1369 Third Avenue, at 78th Street (212 517-6951); and 379 Amsterdam Avenue, at 78th Street (212 769-2665). For more information, see the listing of children's bookstores under the "Books" section of Chapter VI.

Train Shop: In the basement of 23 West 45th Street, between Fifth and Sixth avenues (212 730-0409). For more information, see the "Toys, Trains" section in Chapter VI.

United Nations: The Visitors' Entrance is on First Avenue between 45th and 46th streets (212 963-7713). Be forewarned that strollers are not allowed on the grounds and children under five cannot go on the tour. For more information, see the "Sights and Other Pleasant Places" section in Chapter III.

World Trade Center Observation Deck: At the top of 1 World Trade Center (212 435-7377). For more information, see the "Sights and Other Pleasant Places" section in Chapter III.

If you have young children and want to let them play outside, Manhattan has lots of safe and clean public playgrounds. Look in Central Park along both Central Park West and Fifth Avenue, or call the Manhattan Department of Parks and Recreation at 212 360-8111 to find out the location of the playgrounds nearest you.

One final thought: There are definitely some things that you *shouldn't* do with kids. Museums like the Frick Collection and the Pierpont Morgan Library, for example, are not places to bring small children, and neither is Steinway Hall. If you're going shopping at a perpetually crowded place like Zabar's or Fairway, don't take the kids along or else make sure you keep a firm grip on their hand. The latter holds true just about everywhere—it's very easy to get lost in a crowd in New York! And remember that kids tire more quickly than adults. Chances are you'll be doing a lot of walking, and they're taking two or three steps for every one you take!

Manhattan for Free

There's no way to get around the fact that New York is expensive. Even the most frugal and resourceful people often feel like they're bleeding money ("Didn't we just get $100 out of the cash machine yesterday!?") after a couple of days here. But you can find some good deals and do a lot of sightseeing for free.

The first rule is to always be on the lookout for a good deal. (If it sounds too good to be true, however, it probably is!) You can subscribe to *Manhattan Cheapskate* for $15 a year; it's a monthly newsletter with hints about where and how to find the best deals here. Write Howard Seibel at 61 East 8th Street, Apt. 170, New York, NY 10003.

Concerts and Other Performances – In the summer, Central Park comes alive with free concerts by the New York Philharmonic (212 875-5700), operas by the Metropolitan Opera (212 362-6000), Shakespeare in the Park (212 861-7277), and all sorts of different performances on the SummerStage (212 360-2777). Call 212 360-3456 for recorded information about events in Central Park and other parks throughout the city. You'll also find the Midsummer Night Swing concerts at Lincoln Center Plaza (212 875-5400), live music in the Museum of Modern Art's Sculpture Garden (212 708-9480) every Friday night at 6, concerts on Thursday and Friday evenings at South Street Seaport (212 669-9400), and chamber music in Washington Square Park, at the foot of Fifth Avenue in Greenwich Village, every Tuesday night at 8.

Museums and Sights – In alphabetical order, the free museums and sights in Manhattan include the Alternative Museum, the American Bible Society's gallery, the Cathedral Church of St. John the Divine, the Commodities Exchange, Dyckman House, Federal Hall National Monument, the Forbes Magazine Galleries, the Ford Foundation Gardens, the Governor's Room at City Hall, Grant's Tomb, the Hispanic Society of America, the Japan Society's gallery, the Lower East Side Tenement Museum (on weekdays), the Municipal Art Society's gallery, the Museum of American Folk Art, the Museum of American Illustration, the New York Public Library, the New York Public Library for the Performing Arts, the New York Stock Exchange, the Nicholas Roerich Museum, the Police Academy Museum, the Schomburg Center for Research in Black Culture, the Trinity Church Museum, and the Whitney Gallery and Sculpture Garden at Philip Morris. Some of these places accept donations, but none of them pressures you for them.

Several other museums are technically free but make a point of telling you that they expect a "suggested contribution." These include the American Museum of Natural History, the China House Gallery, the Museum of the City of New York, the Museum of Television and Radio, and the New York City Fire Museum.

It used to be that the museums along Museum Mile offered free admission to everyone one night a week. Unfortunately, that tradition lives on only at several museums and on different nights. They include the Cooper-Hewitt (Tuesday between 5 and 9), the Museum of Modern Art (Thursday between 5 and 9), the National Academy of Design (Friday between 5 and 8), and the New Museum of Contemporary Art (Saturday from 6 to 8).

Finally, children under 12 are admitted a lot of places for free. Smithsonian Associates are admitted without charge to both the Cooper-Hewitt and the Museum of the American Indian. And although it isn't free, you can go to both the Cloisters and the Metropolitan Museum of Art on the same day and pay only one admission price. For more information about any of these places, see the "Museums" section in Chapter III.

Tours – Free tours are given of Grand Central Station (212 935-3960), the New York Police Academy (212 477-9753), the New York Public Library (212 930-0501), and Trinity Church (212 602-0800). The Urban Park Rangers (212 427-4040) also offer free walking tours and workshops in Central Park and other parks throughout the city on weekends. For more information, see the "Tours" section in Chapter III.

Views – The best bargain on a view of the New York skyline is a trip on the Staten Island Ferry (212 806-6940). A round-trip ticket costs 50 cents, and the ferry leaves almost continuously from the end of Whitehall Street, in Battery Park. A runner-up bargain view of the city is from the west side of Roosevelt Island. A trip on the tram (Second Avenue between 59th and 60th streets) costs $1.40 each way.

Walking – It doesn't cost a dime to just walk around. Some of the more pleasant walking areas include Fifth Avenue in midtown, SoHo (on Saturday afternoon and early evening), South Street Seaport and Central Park (particularly on weekends), Fifth Avenue and Madison Avenue on the Upper East Side, the Lower East Side (on Sunday), and the Lincoln Center area and Greenwich Village (particularly on weekends). Take a look at the "Flea Markets" section of Chapter III. Most of them are free (assuming you don't buy anything) and can be lots of fun!

Manhattan on the Water

Although it's easy to forget, Manhattan is an island surrounded on all four sides by water. Boat trips around the island (or even part of it) not only help convey a better sense of how the city is laid out but can also be lots of fun. Here are some of my favorite rides:

Circle Line: One of the most pleasant ways to see the city (and cool off on a hot summer afternoon), the Circle Line sightseeing cruises last three hours and circumnavigate the entire 35 miles around the island. See the listing under "Tours" in Chapter III, or call 212 563-3200 for more information.

Petrel: This is the 70-foot yawl that President John F. Kennedy sailed when he was in office. The 90-minute lunchtime cruises are particularly popular, but you can also take happy-hour, sunset, and moonlight cruises. The boat, which fits no more than three dozen people, sails every day between the middle of April and the middle of October from Battery Park. Call 212 825-1976 for more information.

Seaport Line: The *Andrew Fletcher,* a replica of a 19th-century paddlewheeler, and the *De Witt Clinton,* a replica of a 19th-century steamboat, sail several times a day (except in January, February, and early March) from Pier 16 at South Street Seaport. You can buy drinks and refreshments on board, and the tour of New York Harbor takes roughly an hour and a half. Tickets cost $12 for adults, $11 for senior citizens, $10 for students with identification, and $6 for children under 12. You can combine a sail on either boat with admission to the South Street Seaport Museum for slightly more. You can also take a one-hour twilight cocktail cruise or an evening music cruise. For information about sailing times, call 212 385-0791. In the summer, you can also take a ride on the *Pioneer,* a twin-masted schooner built in 1885. Call 212 669-9400 for more information.

Staten Island Ferry: There are two great bargain ferries left in the world, and this is one of them. (The other is the Star Ferry, in Hong Kong.) It runs 24 hours a day, seven days a week all year round – and costs 50 cents for a round-trip ticket! The loading terminals (in Battery Park at the foot of Whitehall Street in Manhattan, and at the end of Bay Street on Staten Island) aren't very nice, and they can get pretty smelly in the summer, but the views from the water are spectacular. Call 212 806-6940 for more information.

World Yacht: This is the upscale cousin of the Circle Line sightseeing trips. (They're owned by the same company.) You can have lunch, brunch, or dinner on board, and there is dancing at night. Some trips last longer than others, and prices vary accordingly. The World Yacht cruises leave every day (except Christmas) from their new home at Pier 81, at West 41st Street and the Hudson River. Call 212 630-8100 for more information.

Newspapers, Magazines, and Other Resources

If you like to plan in advance, there are a couple of things you can do before packing your bags and heading for New York. First, get in touch with the New York State Division of Tourism (call 800 342-3810, or write them at 97 Washington Street, Albany, NY 12245). Tell them you're planning a visit to New York. Then look through the "Tours" section of Chapter III and the "Tickets and Television Show Tapings" section to see if any of the things you want to do require advance reservations. You also may want to write the New York City Transit Authority (Customer Services, 370 John Jay Street, Brooklyn, NY 11201) for maps and brouchures about the public transportation system so you'll be ready to go the first morning you're in town.

Whether you're planning your trip in advance or sitting in your hotel room trying to figure out what to do tomorrow, get copies of *The New Yorker, New York* magazine, the *New York Times* and the *Village Voice.* All four are available throughout the country (although the national edition of the *New York Times* is smaller and less comprehensive than the metropolitan edition). Both *The New Yorker* (in the front) and *New York* magazine (in the back) have detailed information about current theater, movies, gallery and museum exhibitions, concerts, dance, and New York nightlife. The third section of the metropolitan edition of the *New York Times* always has a current calendar, as well as information on movies, new shows, theater, and even television and radio highlights (except on Sunday, when you should look in the Arts and Leisure section – *the* definitive guide for the week ahead). Friday's Weekend section is particularly useful. The *Village* (as in Greenwich, although it covers the whole city) *Voice* is published weekly on Wednesday, and it is a particularly good source for the younger set and for less conventional events and places.

If you don't have everything planned when you arrive, your first stop should be the New York Convention and Visitors Bureau. Located in the lobby of the unusually ugly building at 2 Columbus Circle (across from the southwest corner of Central Park, at West 59th Street), this is a gold mine of tourist information. You can pick up public transportation maps, "twofer" coupons for discount theater tickets, brochures and information about all sorts of upcoming events and tours, or one of the multilingual "counselors" can help give you ideas and answer your questions. The bureau is open from 9 to 6 on weekdays and from 10 to 6 on weekends and holidays (call 212 397-8222 for more information). A new and quite pleasant Visitor and Transit Information Center is located on the northwest corner of 42nd Street and Seventh Avenue in the heart of Times Square. There's also a tourist-information office on the main concourse of Grand Central Station, but I've found the staff to be exceedingly disinterested, and they don't have nearly as much material.

The front section of the Manhattan Yellow Pages is also a good place to look for information and ideas. In addition to lots of useful telephone numbers, it includes diagrams of major concert halls and sports stadiums. It also includes a relatively short calendar of major annual events and maps of both the subway and bus systems.

Finally, the one-stop phone number for information on current events is *Listing Magazine's* interactive (you need a touch-tone telephone) Big Apple Arts and Festivals Information Hotline (212 765-2787). You can also call a recording for upcoming events in Central Park and other parks throughout the city (212 360-3456) and the Visitors Center in Central Park (212 794-6564). Other potentially useful information numbers are listed at the end of this chapter.

New York is Always in a Hurry!

If you've got just an hour to get to a meeting, to catch a plane, to meet at a restaurant, here are some quick tips:

- To get clothing cleaned and pressed: One Hour Martinizing, 232 Ninth Ave, near 24th St; 212 255-7317
- To get glasses repaired: any of the Cohen Fashion Optical locations; call 516 358-4100 for the nearest one
- To get fed and out in one hour, guaranteed: The Hour Glass Tavern, 373 W 46th St; 212 265-2060
- To get photos developed in one hour: New York Film Works, 928 Broadway, at 21st St, 212 475-5700
- To get shoes repaired: Jim's Shoe Repair, 50 E 59th St, bet Madison and Park Ave; 212 355-8259

Party Places

If you're looking for the perfect spot to hold a wedding reception, bar mitzvah, or gala event for thousands, New York inevitably has the right place. The trick, of course, is finding it. What I've done below is give you some idea of the range of what's available rather than a comprehensive list. (If I did the latter, there would be no room in this book for anything else.)

You will not find museums, restaurants, or hotels on the following list. Many museums, including the Abigail Adams Smith Museum and the Roosevelt Rotunda of the American Museum of Natural History (complete with dinosaur display), do rent space for parties and other events. Many restaurants, including the Four Seasons and the Russian Tea Room, have spaces for private parties, as do most hotels. If you want to throw a party at your favorite museum, restaurant, or hotel, by all means ask.

No matter where you choose to throw a party, it's going to cost a great deal of money. Some places have their own catering service and will take care of every last detail for one set price, while others simply rent you the space. Don't be afraid to ask if the price is negotiable, but don't expect any great (or even particularly good) deals either.

Burden Mansion: Once given to a Vanderbilt as a wedding present, this mansion is good for an evening reception for up to 280 and half that for a sit-down dinner. It's located at 7 East 91st Street. Call 212 722-4745 for more information.

Central Park Zoo: Believe it or not, you can throw a party amid the animals! Call 212 988-0286 for more information.

Circle Line: This sightseeing operation will turn one of its boats over to you for a private charter. The boats are located at Pier 83, at West 43rd Street and the Hudson River. Call 212 563-3204 for more information.

Delegates' Dining Room at the United Nations: You can rent this room with wonderful views of the East River for up to 800 people. It's located inside the UN on First Avenue between 45th and 46th streets. Call 212 963-7098 for more information.

Dezerland: You'll find classic cars and an indoor drive-in theater in this funhouse. It's good for anywhere between 100 and 1,000 people and is located at 270 Eleventh Avenue. Ask about special parties for children. Call 212 564-4590 for more information.

Empire State Building Observation Deck: On a clear day, you really can see forever from this great space on the 86th floor of 350 Fifth Avenue. Call 212 736-3100 for more information.

Fisher & Levy: This pizza parlor on the concourse level of 875 Third Avenue will shut down for pizza-making parties for up to 15 children on weekday afternoons. Call 212 832-3880 for more information.

Glorious Food: A converted 1903 garage, complete with a terrace and open-air roof space, this place is run by very fashionable caterers and can accommodate up to 200 in warmer months. It's located at 522 East 74th Street. Call 212 628-2320 for more information.

The Grolier: If you're looking for Gothic elegance, try this 1890 mansion on 29 East 32nd Street. Call 212 679-2932 for more information.

Industria Superstudio: A 22,000-square foot photography studio by day, this space can accommodate just about any number of people. It's located at 775 Washington Street. Call 212 366-1114 for more information.

Lincoln Center: You have a lot of different spaces to choose from here, but they're all hard to get. For information about Alice Tully Hall, call 212 875-5009. For information about the Metropolitan Opera House, call 212 799-3100. And for information about the New York State Theater, call 212 870-5567.

Loeb Boathouse: In Central Park near Fifth Avenue at about 74th Street, this is an indoor-outdoor spot for up to 500 (half that for dinner). Call 212 988-0576 for more information.

Manhattan Room: A 10,000-square-foot loft, located at 24 Fifth Avenue. Call 212 255-8112.

Museum Club at Bridgewaters: This club in the Fulton Market Building at South Street Seaport can accommodate up to 2,000. Call 212 608-8823 for more information.

New York Public Library: The magnificent main branch of the New York Public Library on Fifth Avenue, between 40th and 42nd streets, has several different spaces available for up to 1,000 people (half that for dinner). Call 212 930-0730 for more information.

Octagon: A relatively small private club across the street from the Jacob K. Javits Convention Center at 55 West 33rd Street. Call 212 947-0400 for more information.

Pioneer: This 102-foot twin-masted schooner can be chartered for private excursions in the summer. It leaves from South Street Seaport. Call 212 233-5010 for more information.

Place des Antiquaires: This very upscale antique mall can be turned into a multilevel reception area for up to 1,200 people (no more than 125 for dinner). It's located at 125 East 57th Street. Call 212 758-2900 for more information.

Pockets: This upscale pool hall and café is a very trendy place for a cocktail party. It's located at 7 West 18th Street. Call 212 727-2701 for more information.

Pratt Mansion: You couldn't ask for a better location—across the street from the Metropolitan Museum of Art at 1026 Fifth Ave. This elegant home can accommodate up to 150 (half that for dinner). Call 212 744-4486 for more information.

Radio City Music Hall: It's hard to get, but the great hall of this magnificent place can accommodate up to 1,000 for cocktails. Radio City is located on the corner of 50th Street and Sixth Avenue. Call 212 632-4244 for more information.

Space II XI: This dramatic gallery space in TriBeCa can accommodate 175 for cocktails (half that for dinner). Located at 211 West Broadway, it is also available for press conferences and other daytime events. Call 212 966-1183 for more information.

Taste Caterers' River Room: Another place run by favorable caterers, this one offers great views of the Hudson River and New Jersey beyond. It can accommodate 150 for cocktails (half that for dinner) and is located at 113 Horatio Street, in the West Village. Call 212 255-8571 for more information.

Tiffany Hall: Receptions for up to 200 can be held in the landmark Tiffany Building (not to be confused with the Tiffany store on Fifth Avenue), at 2 East 37th Street. Call 212 685-8019 for more information.

TriBeCa Film Center: At 375 Greenwich Street, this is Robert DeNiro's film production center. Its theater and adjoining room can accommodate up to 200 people. Call 212 941-4000 for more information.

The Whitehall Club: A Victorian club founded by John D. Rockefeller, Jr. (among others), it's decorated with nautical memorabilia and art. It's located at 17 Battery Place in the financial district. Call 212 425-1960 for more information.

World Yachts: These upscale sightseeing and dining boats can be chartered for private parties. They leave from Pier 81, at West 42nd Street and the Hudson River. Call 212 630-8111 for more information.

Restrooms

Nothing can ruin your trek around New York (or anyplace else, for that matter) more quickly than having to go to the bathroom and not being able to find one. Assuming you don't live in New York, you probably can't just go to a friend's office or apartment. By law, public buildings are required to have public restrooms. They are, however, required to have clean and safe public restrooms. Leaving anything on the floor in a public restroom is a mistake: purses, packages, and everything else have a habit of disappearing while you're otherwise occupied. The same goes for hanging things on the back of the stall door. It's also probably a good idea to stay away from otherwise deserted bathrooms. No matter how badly you need to go, stay away from bathrooms in parks (except the ones listed below) and subway stations.

The following list ought to give you some ideas of specific bathrooms that I've found to meet at least a minimum standard of safety and cleanliness. (You may need to ask for directions or a key at some of them, but all are free to the public.) As a general rule, however, try major hotel lobbies, busy restaurants (if you act like a patron in a busy restaurant, you can probably get away with it), department stores, schools, theaters, churches, libraries, and hospitals. If you have small children in tow, managers of just about any store or restaurant are likely to take pity on you and let you use even their private facilities.

Below 14th Street

- Battery Park
- World Trade Center
- World Financial Center
- Federal Hall National Memorial (at the corner of Wall and Nassau streets)
- South Street Seaport
- Jacob K. Javits Federal Building
- Civil Court Building (75 Lafayette Street, between Franklin and White streets)
- New York Fire Museum (278 Spring Street, between Hudson and Varick streets)
- Strand Bookstore (828 Broadway, at 12th Street)
- Office of Family Services (11 West 13th Street, between Fifth and Sixth avenues)

Between 14th Street and 42nd Street

- Barney's (Seventh Avenue between 16th and 17th streets)
- Barnes and Noble Sales Annex (128 Fifth Avenue, near 18th Street)
- Gramercy Park Hotel (2 Lexington Avenue, betweem Gramercy Park North and 22nd Street)
- Supreme Court of the State of New York (25th Street between Madison and Park avenues)

- Macy's Herald Square (Broadway and 34th Street)
- Sheraton Park Avenue (Park Avenue and 37th Street)
- Grand Hyatt Hotel (42nd Street between Park and Lexington avenues)
- New York Public Library (Fifth Avenue between 40th and 42nd streets)
- Bryant Park (behind the New York Public Library)

Midtown

- United Nations (First Avenue between 45th and 46th streets)
- Crystal Pavilion (805 Third Avenue, between 49th and 50th streets)
- Rockefeller Center (between Fifth and Sixth avenues and 49th and 51st streets)
- Olympic Tower (between Fifth and Madison avenues and 51st and 52nd streets)
- Park Avenue Plaza (55 East 52nd Street, between Madison and Park avenues)
- Trump Tower (Fifth Avenue between 55th and 56th streets)
- Omni Park Central (870 Seventh Avenue, between 55th and 56th streets)
- Place des Antiquaires (125 East 57th Street, between Park and Lexington avenues)

Upper East Side

- McDonald's (Third Avenue between 57th and 58th streets)
- Bloomingdale's (between Lexington and Third avenues and 59th and 60th streets)
- Hunter College Student Center (Lexington Avenue at 68th Street)
- The Asia Society (725 Park Avenue, at 71st Street)
- 92nd Street YMHA (1395 Lexington Avenue, at 92nd Street)
- Museum of the City of New York (Fifth Avenue between 103rd and 104th streets)

Upper West Side

- New York Visitors Bureau (Columbus Circle across from the southwest corner of Central Park)
- Avery Fisher Hall at Lincoln Center (in Lincoln Center, near 64th Street)
- New York Public Library for the Performing Arts (in Lincoln Center, near 65th Street)
- Museum of American Folk Art (Columbus Avenue between 65th and 66th streets)
- Burger King (Broadway and 82nd Street)
- Cathedral Church of St. John the Divine (Amsterdam Avenue at 112th Street)
- Hispanic Society (Aududon Terrace, off Broadway between 155th and 156th streets)

Telephone Numbers

Emergency Services and Hotlines

AIDS hotline 212 447-8200
Alcoholics Anonymous 212 683-3900
Ambulance   911
Animal bites 212 566-2068
Better Business Bureau complaints 212 533-6200
Child abuse reports 800 342-3720
Domestic violence hotline 800 942-6906
Drug abuse information line 800 522-5353
Electricity outages and steam leaks 212 683-0862
Fire   911
Gamblers Anonymous 212 265-8600
Gas leaks 212 683-8830
Highway emergencies 212 566-3406
Immunization hotline 212 349-2664
Mayor's Action Center 212 566-5700
Narcotics Anonymous 718 601-5817
New York City Commission on Human Rights 212 417-5041
Planned Parenthood hotline 212 677-3320
Poison Control 212 764-7667
Police   911
Police precinct information 212 374-5000
Runaway hotline 212 619-6884
Sex crimes reports 212 267-7273
Suicide prevention hotline 212 532-2400
Traveller's Aid Services 212 944-0013
U.S. Customs emergencies 800 522-5270
Victims Services hotline 212 577-7777
Water and sewer emergencies 212 966-7500
Youth Crisis and Runaway hotline 800 448-4663

Entertainment and Information

Central Park Visitors Center 212 794-6564
Dow Jones information 212 976-4141*
Information (Manhattan)   411
Jacob K. Javits Convention Center event line 212 216-2000
Lincoln Center event line 212 875-5400
Listings Magazine hotline 212 765-2787
Macy's Herald Square event line 212 560-4495
Madison Square Garden box office 212 465-6741
Manhattan Department of Parks and Recreation 212 360-8111
Manhattan Department of Parks and Recreation
   event line 212 360-3456
Marriage Licenses 212 269-2900

Movie locator 212 777-3456
Music and Dance Booth (half-price tickets) 212 382-2323
New York Convention and Visitors Bureau 212 397-8222
New York Department of Cultural Affairs 212 956-2787
New York Public Library (branch information) 212 340-0849
Post Office (general information) 212 967-8585
Restaurant locator 212 888-3663
Rockefeller Center event line 212 632-3975
Sportsphone 212 976-1313*
Time 212 976-1616*
TKTS information (half-price theater tickets) 212 768-1818
Weather (daily) 212 976-1212*
Weather (hourly) 212 976-5555*

*Numbers that begin with the 976 prefix have a cost of 36 cents per
minute.

Transportation

Airports
Air-Ride (information about airport
    transportation options) 800 247-7433
Kennedy International Airport (general information) . . 718 656-4520
Kennedy International Airport (lost and found) 718 656-4120
La Guardia Airport (general information) 718 476-5000
La Guardia Airport (lost and found) 718 476-5115
Newark International Airport (general information) . . . 201 961-2000
Newark International Airport (lost and found) 201 961-2235

Bus and Subway
Greyhound/Trailways (information) 212 971-6363
New Jersey Transit (bus information) 201 762-5100
New Jersey Transit (lost and found) 212 630-7389
New York City Transit Authority (bus and subway
    route information) 718 330-1234
New York City Transit Authority (lost and found) . . . 718 625-6200
Port Authority Bus Terminal 212 564-8484
Port Authority Bus Terminal (lost and found) 212 435-2611

Trains
Amtrak (information) 800 872-7245
Amtrak Metroliner (information) 800 523-8720
Grand Central Station 212 340-3000
Grand Central Station (lost and found) 212 340-2555
Long Island Railroad (information) 718 217-5477
Long Island Railroad (lost and found) 718 990-8384
Metro North Railroad (information) 212 532-4900

New Jersey Transit train (information) 201 762-5100
New Jersey Transit (lost and found) 212 630-7389
PATH Train (information) 800 234-7284
PATH Train (lost and found) 212 435-2611
Pennsylvania Station (lost and found) 212 630-7389

Taxis
New York Taxi and Limousine Commission 212 221-8294
New York Taxi and Limousine Commission
  (lost and found) 212 869-4513

Roads Conditions and Parking
Municipal parking-lot information 718 786-6621
Parking information 212 566-4121
Parking violations 212 477-4430
Pothole and road condition complaints 212 768-4653
Road condition information 212 964-2110
Shadow Traffic area traffic reports 201 939-6688
Traffic light complaints 212 323-8503
Vehicle registration and licenses 212 645-5550

INDEX